Introduction to
Statistical Quality Control

Introduction to
Statistical Quality Control

Second Edition

Douglas C. Montgomery
Arizona State University

John Wiley & Sons

New York   *Chichester*   *Brisbane*   *Toronto*   *Singapore*

Copyright © 1985, 1991 by John Wiley & Sons, Inc.

Library of Congress Cataloging in Publication Data:

Montgomery, Douglas C.
    Introduction to statistical quality control / by Douglas C.
Montgomery.—2nd ed.
    p.   cm.
    Includes bibliographical references.
    ISBN 0-471-51988-X
    1. Quality control—Statistical methods. 2. Process control-
—Statistical methods.   I. Title.
TS156.M64   1990
658.5′62—dc20
                             90-31744
                                CIP

Printed in the United States of America

10 9 8 7 6 5 4 3 2 1

About the Author

Douglas C. Montgomery professor of industrial and management systems engineering at Arizona State University since 1988, received his B.S., M.S., and Ph.D. degrees from Virginia Polytechnic Institute, all in engineering. From 1969 to 1984 he was on the faculty of the School of Industrial & Systems Engineering at the Georgia Institute of Technology, and from 1984 to 1988 he was at the University of Washington, where he held the John M. Fluke Distinguished Chair of Manufacturing Engineering, was professor of mechanical engineering, and director of the program in industrial engineering.

In addition to his work in quality engineering, Dr. Montgomery has interests in experimental design, regression modeling and time series analysis, and the application of operations research methodology to problems in manufacturing systems. He has authored and coauthored many technical papers in these fields and is an author of six other books. Dr. Montgomery is a Fellow of the American Society for Quality Control, a Senior Member of the Institute of Industrial Engineers, a Senior Member of the Operations Research Society of America, a Senior Member of the Society of Manufacturing Engineers, and a Member of the American Statistical Association.

In addition to his academic activities, Dr. Montgomery is a partner in Statistical Productivity Consultants, a Seattle-based consulting organization specializing in quality and productivity improvement. Dr. Montgomery has served as a consultant in these areas to many major corporations in the electronics, aerospace, automotive, chemical, and process industries.

Preface

This book is about the modern practice of statistical quality control. It provides comprehensive coverage of the subject from basic principles to state-of-the-art concepts and applications. The objective is to give the reader a sound understanding of the principles and the basis for applying those principles in a wide variety of both product and nonproduct situations. While statistical techniques are used throughout, the book has a strong engineering and management orientation. Extensive knowledge of statistics is not a necessary prerequisite for using this book. Readers whose background includes a basic course in statistical methods will find the book easily accessible.

This book is an outgrowth of over 20 years of teaching, research, and consulting in the fields of quality engineering and quality improvement. It is designed as a textbook for students enrolled in colleges and universities, who are studying engineering, management, statistics, and related fields and are taking a first course in statistical quality control. Such courses are often taught at the junior or senior level. I have also used the text materials extensively in training programs for professional practitioners, including quality and reliability engineers, manufacturing and development engineers, managers, procurement specialists, marketing personnel, technicians and laboratory analysts, inspectors, and operators. Many professionals have also used the material for self-study.

Chapter 1 is an introduction to quality improvement in the modern business environment. It deals with the facts that quality has become a major business strategy and that organizations with successful quality-improvement programs can increase their productivity, enhance their market penetration, and achieve greater profitability and a strong competitive advantage.

Following the introductory chapter, the book is divided into four parts. Part I presents a description of statistical methods useful in quality improvement. Topics covered included sampling and descriptive statistics, the basic notions of probability and probability distributions, point and interval estimation of parameters, and statistical hypothesis testing. These topics are usually covered in a basic course in statistical methods; however, their presentation in this text is from the quality-engineering viewpoint. My experience has been that even readers with a strong statistical background will find the approach to this material useful and somewhat different from that used in a standard statistics textbook.

Part II contains seven chapters on statistical process control. While the entire range of statistical process-control tools are extensively discussed, the primary focus is on the control chart. The concept of control charts is certainly not new, but its use in modern-day business and industry is of tremendous value. Furthermore, as sensing and measurement technology develops, along with the widespread availability of powerful microcomputers, the implementation of statistical process control at the workplace is becoming a commonplace activity in many businesses. Statistical process control will play an even greater role in U.S. industry over the next 20 years than it has in the last 50.

Part III contains two chapters that show how statistical experiment-design methods can be used for process improvement. Chapter 11 presents the fundamental concepts of designed experiments and introduces the reader to some of the data analysis methods employed. While the treatment of the subject is not extensive and is no substitute for a formal course in experimental design, it will enable the reader to appreciate more sophisticated examples of experimental design. Chapter 12 illustrates factorial and fractional factorial designs, response surface designs, and gives an overview of Taguchi's contributions to quality engineering. I've tried to present my view that Taguchi has made many valuable contributions to quality improvement philosophy, but that his technical methods are often ineffective and inefficient, and can be improved. These points are discussed in Chapter 12. Throughout both Chapters 11 and 12, the important interrelationship between statistical process control and experimental design for process improvement is emphasized.

Part IV contains three chapters dealing with acceptance sampling. The focus is on lot-by-lot acceptance sampling, although there is some discussion of continuous sampling and MIL STD 1235B in Chapter 15. Other sampling topics presented include details of the design of acceptance-sampling plans; a discussion of MIL STD 105D, MIL STD 414, and their civilian counterparts, ANSI/ASQC Z1.4 and ANSI/ASQC Z1.9; and other important techniques useful in a near zero defects manufacturing environment, such as chain sampling and skip-lot sampling.

Throughout Parts II and IV guidelines are given for selecting the proper type of statistical process-control or sampling technique to use in a wide variety of product and nonproduct situations. There are also extensive references to journal articles and other technical literature that should assist the reader in applying the methods described.

CHANGES IN THE SECOND EDITION

I have made extensive changes in this edition of the book. A major change is a more detailed discussion of the basic SPC problem-solving tools including cause-and-effect analysis, Pareto analysis, defect concentration analysis, and check sheets for data collection. These topics are discussed in Chapter 4. This chapter also contains two case studies illustrating the implementation of SPC in a manufacturing and nonmanufacturing setting. Chapter 4 also contains a much broader and deeper coverage of the philosophy underlying SPC and the approach that must be taken to successfully implement these techniques in industry.

The material on variables control charts has also been greatly expanded. Chapter 6, which discusses the basic variables control charts, contains several new examples. Chapter 7 is now devoted exclusively to cumulative-sum control charts and exponentially weighted moving-average control charts. Chapter 8 discusses a variety of topics including how to implement control charts in the short production-run environment, along with expanded coverage of group control charts, acceptance control charts, control charts with modified limits, some new material on multivariate quality control, SPC with autocorrelated data, and several other topics. The coverage of process-capability analysis in Chapter 9 has been expanded to include more information on capability indices and techniques for assessing gage capability.

Part III on process improvement with designed experiments is new. I have added this material at the request of many users of the textbook, who wish to introduce students in their basic quality control courses to the fundamentals of experimental design, and show them several examples of using these techniques for quality and process improvement.

All of the examples in this book utilize data from real applications. In some cases, I have disguised the data or the application situation so that proprietary information will be protected.

ACKNOWLEDGMENTS

Many people have generously contributed their time and knowledge of quality improvement to this book. A complete list of colleagues with whom I have interacted in various academic or consulting projects over the years would be too extensive to include here. However, some of the major contributors and their professional affiliations are as follows: Dr. William W. Hines, Dr. Lynwood A. Johnson, Dr. Russell G. Heikes, Dr. David E. Fyffe, and Dr. H. M. Wadsworth, Jr., Georgia Institute of Technology; Dr. Richard L. Storch, University of Washington; Dr. J. Burt Keats, Dr. Dwayne A. Rollier, and Dr. Norma F. Hubele, Arizona State University; Dr. Joseph J. Moder, University of Miami; Dr. Erwin M. Saniga, University of Delaware; Dr. John S. Ramburg, University of Arizona; Dr. Frank B. Alt, University of Maryland; Dr. Kenneth E. Case, Oklahoma State University; Mr. John A. Butora, Mr. Leon V. Mason, Mr. Lloyd K. Collins, Mr. Dana D. Lesher, Mr. Roy E. Dent, Mr. Mark Fazey, Ms. Kathy Schuster, Mr. Dan Fritze,

Dr. J. S. Gardiner, Mr. Ariel Rosentrater, Mr. Lally Marwah, Mr. Ed Schleicher, Mr. Armin Weiner, and Ms. Elaine Baechtle, IBM; Mr. Thomas C. Bingham, Mr. K. Dick Vaughn, Mr. Robert LeDoux, Mr. John Black, Mr. Jack Wires, Dr. Julian Anderson, Mr. Richard Alkire, and Mr. Chase Neilsen, The Boeing Company; Ms. Karen Madison, Mr. Don Walton, and Mr. Mike Goza, Alcoa; Mr. Harry Peterson-Nedry and Dr. Russell A. Boyles, Precision Castparts Corp.; Dr. Sadre Khalessi and Mr. Frantz Wagner, Signetics Corporation; Mr. Larry Newton and Mr. C. T. Howlett, Georgia Pacific Corporation; Mr. Robert V. Baxley, Monsanto Chemicals; Dr. Craig Fox, Dr. Thomas L. Sadosky, Mr. James F. Walker, and Mr. John Belvins, The Coca-Cola Company; Mr. Bill Wagner and Mr. Al Pariseau, Litton Industries; Mr. John M. Fluke, Jr., John Fluke Manufacturing Company; and Dr. William DuMouchel, Dr. Cynthia Lowry, and Ms. Janet Olson, BBN Software Products Corporation. I would also like to acknowledge the contribution of my partners at Statistical Productivity Consultants, Mr. Sumner S. Averett, Dr. Luis E. Contreras, and Dr. Russell G. Heikes. All of these individuals, and many others, have contributed to my understanding of quality improvement. I am in their debt.

I would also like to thank Ms. Charity Robey, the editor at John Wiley that I worked with in preparing the second edition of this book. She has tolerated the peculiarities of authorship far better than did any other editor with whom I have worked. I would also like to thank the various professional societies and publishers who have given permission to reproduce their materials in my text. Credit for this permission is acknowledged at appropriate places in the book.

I am also indebted to two organizations, the Office of Naval Research and the IBM Corporation. These organizations have sponsored my research activities in quality improvement for a number of years. Both organizations have provided an open and stimulating environment for conducting research and have generated many opportunities to work with their personnel on actual quality engineering problems. It has been my particular pleasure to be associated with Mr. Seymour M. Selig of ONR and Dr. Paul A. Tobias of IBM. They have given me a great deal of insight regarding quality engineering and quality improvement in their business environments.

Finally, I would like to thank the many users of the first edition of this book including students, practicing professionals, and my academic colleagues. Many of the changes and (hopefully) improvements in this edition of the book are the direct result of feedback from you.

Douglas C. Montgomery

Contents

Appendix /A-1

Bibliography /B-1

Answers to Selected Exercises /ANS-1

Index /I-1

Chapter 1

Quality Improvement in The Modern Business Environment

This book is about the use of basic statistics and simple problem-solving methods to improve the quality of the products used by our society. These products consist of manufactured goods such as automobiles, computers, and clothing, as well as services such as electrical energy, public transportation, banking, and health care. Quality-improvement methods can be applied to any area within a company or organization, including manufacturing, process development, engineering design, finance and accounting, marketing, and field service. Our purpose is to present the technical tools that are needed to achieve quality improvement in these organizations.

1-1 THE MEANING OF QUALITY IMPROVEMENT

It is essential that products meet the requirements of those who use them. Therefore, we define quality as *fitness for use*. The term *consumer* applies to many different types of users. A purchaser of a product that is used as a raw material in its manufacturing operations is a consumer, and to the manufacturer fitness for use implies the ability to process this raw material with low cost and minimal scrap or rework. A retailer purchases finished goods with the expectation that they are properly packaged, labeled, and arranged for easy storage, handling, and display.

You and I may purchase automobiles that we expect to be free of initial manufacturing defects or *nonconformities*, and that should provide reliable and economical transportation over time.

There are two general aspects of quality: quality of design and quality of conformance. All goods and services are produced in various grades or levels of quality. These variations in grades or levels of quality are intentional, and, consequently, the appropriate technical term is *quality of design.* For example, all automobiles have as their basic objective providing safe transportation for the consumer. However, automobiles differ with respect to size, appointments, appearance, and performance. These differences are the result of intentional design differences between the types of automobiles. These design differences include the types of materials used in construction, tolerances in manufacturing, reliability obtained through engineering development of engines and drive trains, and other accessories or equipment.

The *quality of conformance* is how well the product conforms to the specifications and tolerances required by the design. Quality of conformance is influenced by a number of factors, including the choice of manufacturing processes, the training and supervision of the work force, the type of quality-assurance system (process controls, tests, inspection activities, etc.) used, the extent to which these quality-assurance procedures are followed, and the motivation of the work force to achieve quality.

There is considerable confusion in our society about quality. The term is often used without making clear whether we are speaking about quality of design or quality of conformance. To achieve quality of design requires conscious decisions during the product or process design stage to ensure that certain functional requirements will be satisfactorily met. For example, the designer of an office copier machine may design a circuit component with a redundant element, because he knows that this will enhance the reliability of the product in the field and will increase the mean time between failures. This in turn will result in fewer service calls to keep the copier running, and the consumer will be far more satisfied with the performance of the product. Designing quality into the product in this fashion often results in a higher product cost. However, such cost increases are actually *prevention costs*, as they are intended to prevent quality problems at later stages in the life cycle of the product. We discuss other aspects of quality costs in Section 1-3.

Every product possesses a number of elements that jointly describe its fitness for use. These parameters are often called *quality characteristics.* Quality characteristics may be of several types:

1. **Physical.** Length, weight, voltage, viscosity.
2. **Sensory.** Taste, appearance, color.
3. **Time Orientation.** Reliability, maintainability, serviceability.

Quality engineering is the set of operational, managerial, and engineering activities that a company uses to ensure that these quality characteristics are at the nominal or required levels.

Most organizations find it difficult (and expensive) to provide the customer with products that have flawless quality characteristics. A major reason for this difficulty is *variability*. There is a certain amount of variability in every product;

consequently, no two products are ever identical. For example, the thickness of the blades on a jet turbine engine impeller are not identical even on the same impeller. Blade thickness will also differ between impellers. If this variation in blade thickness is small, then it may have no impact on the customer. However, if the variation is large, then the customer may perceive the unit to be undesirable and unacceptable. Sources of this variability include differences in materials, differences in the performance and operation of the manufacturing equipment, and differences in the way the operators perform their tasks. Therefore, we may define *quality improvement* as the reduction of variability in processes and products. Since variation can only be described in statistical terms, *statistical methods* are of considerable use in quality-improvement efforts.

1-2 THE LINK BETWEEN QUALITY IMPROVEMENT AND PRODUCTIVITY

Quality is becoming the basic consumer decision factor in many products and services. This phenomenon is widespread, regardless of whether the consumer is an individual, an industrial corporation, a military defense program, or a retail store. Consequently, quality is a key factor leading to business success, growth, and enhanced competitive position. There is a substantial return on investment from an effective quality-improvement program that provides increased profitability to firms that effectively employ quality as a business strategy. Consumers feel that the products of certain companies are substantially better in quality than those of their competition, and make purchasing decisions accordingly. Effective quality-improvement programs can result in increased market penetration, higher productivity, and lower overall costs of manufacturing and service. Consequently, firms with such programs can enjoy significant competitive advantages.

Achieving quality in the modern business and manufacturing environment is not easy. A significant problem is the rapid evolution of technology. The last 20 years have seen an explosion of technology in such diverse fields as electronics, metallurgy, ceramics, composite materials, and the chemical and pharmaceutical sciences. This has resulted in many new products and services. For example, in the electronics field, the development of the integrated circuit has revolutionized the design and manufacture of computers and many electronic office products. Basic integrated circuit technology has been supplanted by large-scale integration (LSI) and very large-scale integration (VLSI) technology, with corresponding developments in semiconductor design and manufacturing. When technological advances occur rapidly, and when the new technologies are used quickly to exploit competitive advantages, the problems of manufacturing products with adequate levels of quality of design and quality of conformance are greatly complicated.

The basic problem in many industries is that of manufacturing a product in adequate volume. Often, too little attention is paid to achieving economy, efficiency, productivity, and quality in production. An effective quality-improvement program can be instrumental in increasing productivity and reducing cost. As an example, consider the manufacturer of a mechanical component used in a copier machine. The parts are manufactured in a machining process at a rate of approximately 100 parts per day. For various reasons, the process is operating at a first-pass yield of about 75%. (That is, about 75% of the process output conforms to specifications, and about 25% of the output is nonconforming.) About 60% of the fallout (the 25% nonconforming) can be reworked into an acceptable product, and the rest must be scrapped. The direct manufacturing cost through this stage of production per part is approximately $20. Parts that can be reworked incur an additional processing charge of $4. Therefore, the manufacturing cost per good part produced is:

$$\text{Cost/good part} = \frac{\$20(100) + \$4(15)}{90} = \$22.89$$

Note that the total yield from this process, after reworking, is 90 good parts per day.

An engineering study of this process reveals that the source of the extremely high fallout is inadequate process controls. A new statistical process-control procedure is implemented that reduces the fallout from 25% to 5%. Of the 5% fallout produced, about 60% can be reworked, and 40% are scrapped. After the process-control program is implemented, the manufacturing cost per good part produced is:

$$\text{Cost/good part} = \frac{\$20(100) + \$4(3)}{98} = \$20.53$$

Note that the installation of statistical process control results in a 10.3% reduction in manufacturing costs. Furthermore, productivity is up by almost 10%; 98 good parts are produced each day as opposed to 90 good parts previously. This amounts to an increase in production capacity of almost 10%, without any additional investment in equipment, work force, or overhead. What does this increase in productivity cost? In this particular situation, very little. The type of process-control procedure employed is the $\bar{x}$ and R control chart. (Control charts are discussed in Part II.) The control chart utilizes existing process data that are routinely collected, and presents this information in a format useful to management in defect prevention. Thus, the cost of achieving these improvements in quality and productivity is almost negligible.

Quality improvement has emerged as a major new business strategy. This has happened for a number of reasons, including:

1. Increasing consumer awareness of quality and strong consumer quality-performance orientation.
2. Product liability.
3. Increasing cost pressures on labor, energy, and raw materials.
4. More intensive competition.
5. Dramatic improvements in productivity through effective quality engineering programs.

Part of this business strategy is quality planning, analysis, and control to ensure that quality contributes positively to cash flow, return on investment, and overall business profitability. Quality improvement can provide business growth and enhanced competitive position for the company. At the same time, improvements in quality are often accompanied by reductions in cost. In the next section we will discuss quality costs and illustrate how an effective quality-improvement program reduces costs and increases profitability.

The office copier machine component example discussed previously illustrates an important aspect of quality improvement; namely, *quality improvement means elimination of waste.* Examples of waste include scrap and rework in manufacturing, unnecessary inspection and test, errors on documents (such as checks, purchase orders, and engineering drawings), and excessive engineering development time. Some people still think that quality improvement means gold-plating a product or spending more money on a product or process. This thinking is wrong, and the concept of quality costs is an effective way to see the benefits of eliminating waste.

1-3 QUALITY COSTS

All business organizations use financial controls. These financial controls involve a comparison of actual and budgeted costs, along with an associated analysis and action on the differences or *variances* between actual and budget. It is customary to apply these financial controls on a department or functional level. For many years, there was no direct effort to measure or account for the costs of the quality function. However, starting in the 1950s, many organizations began to formally evaluate the cost associated with quality. There are several reasons why the cost of quality should be explicitly considered in an organization. These include:

1. The increase in the cost of quality because of the increase in the complexity of manufactured products associated with advances in technology.
2. Increasing awareness of life cycle costs, including maintenance, labor, spare parts, and the cost of field failures.
3. The need for quality engineers and managers to effectively communicate the cost of quality in the language of general management—namely, money.

As a result, quality costs have emerged as a financial control tool for management and as an aid in identifying opportunities for reducing quality costs.

Generally speaking, quality costs are those categories of costs that are associated with producing, identifying, avoiding, or repairing products that do not meet requirements. Many manufacturing and service organizations use four categories of quality costs: prevention costs, appraisal costs, internal failure costs, and external failure costs. These cost categories are shown in Table 1-1. We now discuss these categories in more detail.

1-3.1 Prevention Costs

Prevention costs are those costs associated with efforts in design and manufacturing that are directed toward the prevention of nonconformance. Broadly speaking, prevention costs are all costs incurred in an effort to "make it right the first time." The important subcategories of prevention costs follow.

Table 1-1
Quality costs

PREVENTION COSTS

  Quality planning and engineering
  New products review
  Product/process design
  Process control
  Burn-in
  Training
  Quality data acquisition and analysis

APPRAISAL COSTS

  Inspection and test of incoming material
  Product inspection and test
  Materials and services consumed
  Maintaining accuracy of test equipment

INTERNAL FAILURE COSTS

  Scrap
  Rework
  Retest
  Failure analysis
  Downtime
  Yield losses
  Downgrading (off-specing)

EXTERNAL FAILURE COSTS

  Complaint adjustment
  Returned product/material
  Warranty charges
  Liability costs
  Indirect costs

Quality planning and engineering. Costs associated with the creation of the overall quality plan, the inspection plan, the reliability plan, the data system, and all specialized plans and activities of the quality-assurance function; the preparation of manuals and procedures used to communicate the quality plan; and the costs of auditing the system.

New products review. Costs of the preparation of bid proposals, the evaluation of new designs from a quality viewpoint, the preparation of tests and experimental programs to evaluate the performance of new products, and other quality activities during the development and preproduction stages of new products or designs.

Product/process design. Costs incurred during the design of the product or the selection of the production processes that are intended to improve the overall quality of the product. For example, an organization may decide to make a particular circuit component redundant because this will increase the reliability of the product by increasing the mean time between failures.

Alternatively, it may decide to manufacture a component using process A rather than process B, because process A is capable of producing the product at tighter tolerances, and this will result in fewer assembly and manufacturing problems. This may include a vendor's process, so the cost of dealing with other than the lowest bidder may also be a prevention cost.

Process control. The cost of process-control techniques, such as control charts, that monitor the manufacturing process in an effort to reduce variation and build quality into the product.

Burn-in. The cost of preshipment operation of the product to prevent early-life failures in the field.

Training. The cost of developing, preparing, implementing, operating, and maintaining formal training programs for quality.

Quality data acquisition and analysis. The cost of running the quality data system to acquire data on product and process performance. It also includes the cost of analyzing these data to identify problems. It includes the work of summarizing and publishing quality information for management.

1-3.2 Appraisal Costs

Appraisal costs are those costs associated with measuring, evaluating, or auditing products, components, and purchased materials to ensure conformance to the standards that have been imposed. These costs are incurred to determine the condition of the product from a quality viewpoint and ensure that it conforms to specifications. The major subcategories follow.

Inspection and test of incoming material. Costs associated with the inspection and testing of all vendor-supplied material. This subcategory includes receiving inspection and test, inspection, test, and evaluation at the vendor's facility, as well as a periodic audit of the vendor's quality-assurance system. This could also include intraplant vendors.

Product inspection and test. The cost of checking the conformance of the product throughout its various stages of manufacturing, including final acceptance testing, packing and shipping checks, and any test done at the customer's facilities prior to turning the product over to the customer. This also includes life testing, environmental testing, and reliability testing.

Materials and services consumed. The cost of material and products consumed in a destructive test, or devalued by reliability tests.

Maintaining accuracy of test equipment. The cost of operating a system that keeps the measuring instruments and equipment in calibration.

1-3.3 Internal Failure Costs

Internal failure costs are incurred when products, components, materials, and services fail to meet quality requirements, and this failure is discovered prior to delivery of the product to the customer. These costs would disappear if there were no defects in the product. The major subcategories of internal failure costs follow.

Scrap. The net loss of labor, material, and overhead resulting from defective product that cannot economically be repaired or used.

Rework. The cost of correcting nonconforming units so that they meet specifications. In some manufacturing operations rework costs include additional operations or steps in the manufacturing process that are created to solve either chronic defects or sporadic defects.

Retest. The cost of reinspection and retesting of products that have undergone rework or other modifications.

Failure analysis. The cost incurred to determine the causes of product failures.

Downtime. The cost of idle production facilities that result from nonconformance to requirements. The production line may be down because of nonconforming raw materials supplied by a vendor, which went undiscovered in receiving inspection.

Yield losses. The cost of process yields that are lower than might be attainable by improved controls (for example, soft drink containers that are overfilled because of excessive variability in the filling equipment).

Downgrading/off-specing. The price differential between the normal selling price and any selling price that might be obtained for a product that does not meet the customer's requirements. Downgrading is a common practice in the textile, apparel goods, and electronics industries. The problem with downgrading is that products sold do not recover the full contribution margin to profit and overhead as do products that conform to the usual specifications.

1-3.4 External Failure Costs

External failure costs occur when the product does not perform satisfactorily after it is supplied to the customer. These costs would also disappear if every unit of product conformed to requirements. Subcategories of external failure costs follow.

Complaint adjustment. All costs of investigation and adjustment of justified complaints attributable to the nonconforming product.

Returned product/material. All costs associated with receipt, handling, and replacement of the nonconforming product or material that is returned from the field.

Warranty charges. All costs involved in service to customers under warranty contracts.

Liability costs. Costs or awards incurred as a result of product liability litigation.

Indirect costs. In addition to direct operating costs of external failures, there are a significant number of indirect costs. These are incurred because of customer dissatisfaction with the level of quality of the delivered product. Indirect costs may reflect the customer's attitude toward the company. They include the costs of loss of business reputation, loss of future business, and loss of market share that inevitably results from delivering products and services that do not conform to the customer's expectations regarding fitness for use.

1-3.5 The Management of Quality Costs

How large are quality costs? The answer, of course, depends on the type of organization and the success of their quality-improvement effort. In some organizations quality costs are 4 or 5% of sales, while in others they can be as high as 35% or 40% of sales. Obviously, the cost of quality will be very different for a high-technology computer manufacturer than for a typical service industry, such as a department store or hotel chain. In most organizations, however, quality costs are higher than necessary, and management should make continuing efforts to appraise, analyze, and reduce these costs.

The usefulness of quality costs stems from the *leverage effect*; that is, dollars invested in prevention and appraisal have a payoff in reducing dollars incurred in internal and external failures that exceeds the original investment. For example, a dollar invested in prevention may return $10 or $100 (or more) in savings from reduced internal and external failures.

Quality-cost analyses have as their principal objective cost reduction through identification of improvement opportunities. This is often done with a *Pareto analysis*. The Pareto analysis consists of identifying quality costs by category, or by product, or by type of defect or nonconformity. For example, inspection of the quality-cost information in Table 1-2 concerning defects or nonconformities in the assembly of electronic components onto printed circuit boards reveals that insufficient solder is the highest quality cost incurred in this operation. Insufficient solder accounts for 42% of the total defects in this particular type of board, and for almost 52% of the total scrap and rework costs. If the wave solder process can be improved, then there will be dramatic reductions in the cost of quality.

How much reduction in quality costs is possible? While the cost of quality in many organizations can be significantly reduced, it is unrealistic to expect it can be reduced to zero. Before that level of performance is reached, the incremental costs of prevention and appraisal will rise more rapidly than the resulting cost reductions. However, a quality-cost program applied in conjunction with a good quality-improvement effort has the capability of reducing quality costs by 50% or 60% provided that no organized effort has previously existed. This cost reduction also follows the Pareto principle; that is, most of the cost reductions will come from attacking the few problems that are responsible for the majority of quality costs.

Table 1-2
Monthly quality-costs information for assembly of printed circuit boards

Type of Defect	Percent of Total Defects	Scrap and Rework Costs
Insufficient solder	42	$37,500.00 (52%)
Misaligned components	21	12,000.00
Defective components	15	8,000.00
Missing components	10	5,100.00
Cold solder joints	7	5,000.00
All other causes	5	4,600.00
Totals	100	$72,200.00

In analyzing quality costs and in formulating plans for reducing the cost of quality, it is important to note the role of prevention and appraisal. Many organizations spend far too much of their quality-management budget on appraisal, and not enough on prevention. This is an easy mistake for an organization to make, because appraisal costs are often budget line items in the quality-assurance or manufacturing areas. On the other hand, prevention costs may not be routinely budgeted items. It is not unusual to find in the early stages of a quality-cost program that appraisal costs are eight or ten times the magnitude of prevention costs. This is probably an unreasonable ratio, as dollars spent in prevention have a much greater payback than do dollars spent in appraisal.

Generating the quality-cost figures is not always easy, because most quality-cost categories are not directly reflected in the accounting records of the organization. Consequently, it may be difficult to obtain extremely accurate information on the costs incurred with respect to the various categories. The organization's accounting system can provide information on those quality-cost categories that coincide with the usual business accounts, such as, for example, product testing and evaluation. In addition, many companies will have detailed information on various categories of failure cost. The information for cost categories for which exact accounting information is not available should be generated by using estimates, or, in some cases, by creating special monitoring and surveillance procedures to accumulate those costs over the study period.

The reporting of quality costs is usually done on a basis that permits straightforward evaluation by management. Managers want quality costs expressed in an index that compares quality cost with the opportunity for quality cost. Consequently, the usual method of reporting quality costs is in the form of a ratio, where the numerator is quality-cost dollars and the denominator is some measure of activity, such as: (1) hours of direct production labor, (2) dollars of direct production labor, (3) dollars of processing costs, (4) dollars of manufacturing cost, (5) dollars of sales, or (6) units of product.

Upper management may want a standard against which to compare the current quality-cost figures. It is difficult to obtain absolute standards and almost as difficult to obtain quality-cost levels of other companies in the same industry. Therefore, the usual approach is to compare current performance with past performance so that, in effect, quality-cost programs report variances from past performance. These variance analyses are primarily a device for detecting departures from standard and for bringing them to the attention of the appropriate managers. They are not necessarily in and of themselves a device for ensuring quality improvements.

This brings us to an interesting observation: Some quality-cost programs fail. That is, a number of companies have started quality-cost programs, used them for some time, and then abandoned the programs as ineffective. There are several reasons why quality-cost programs sometimes fail. Chief among these is failure to use quality-cost information as a mechanism for generating improvement opportunities. If we use quality-cost information as a scorekeeping tool only, and do not make conscious efforts to identify problem areas and develop improved operating procedures and processes, then the programs will not be totally successful.

Another reason why quality-cost programs are unsuccessful is that managers become preoccupied with perfection in the cost figures. Overemphasis in treating quality costs as part of the accounting systems rather than as a management control tool is a serious mistake. This approach greatly increases the amount of time required to develop the cost data, analyze them, and identify opportunities for quality improvements. As the time required to generate and analyze the data increases, management becomes more impatient and less convinced of the effectiveness of the program. Any program that appears to management as going nowhere is likely to be abandoned.

A final reason for the failure of a quality-cost program is that management often underestimates the depth and extent of the commitment to prevention that must be made. As one of the senior partners in an engineering consulting firm that specializes in quality improvement, the author has had numerous opportunities to study quality costs in many companies. In companies without effective quality-improvement programs, the dollars allocated to prevention rarely exceed 1 to 2% of revenue. This must be increased to a threshold of about 5 to 6% of revenue, and these additional prevention dollars must be spent on the technical methods of quality improvement discussed in the next section. If management is persistent in this effort, then the cost of quality will decrease by 40 to 50% or more. These cost savings will typically begin to occur in one to two years, although it could be longer in some companies.

1-4 METHODS OF QUALITY IMPROVEMENT

As indicated earlier, this textbook concentrates on statistical and engineering technology useful in the quality-assurance function. Specifically, we focus on three major areas: statistical process control experimental design, and acceptance sampling. In addition to these techniques, a number of other statistical tools are useful in analyzing quality problems and improving the performance of production processes. The role of some of these tools is illustrated in Figure 1-1, which presents a production process as a system with a set of inputs and an output. The inputs $x_1, x_2, \ldots, x_p$ are controllable factors, such as temperatures, pressures, feed rates, and other process variables. The inputs $z_1, z_2, \ldots, z_q$ are uncontrollable inputs, such as environmental factors or the quality of raw materials submitted by the vendor. The manufacturing process transforms these inputs into a finished product that has several parameters describing its quality or fitness for use. The output variable y is a measure of process quality.

Designed experiments are extremely helpful in discovering the key variables influencing the quality characteristics of interest in the process. A designed experiment is an approach to systematically varying the controllable input factors and observing the effect these factors have on the output product parameters. Statistically designed experiments are invaluable in reducing the variability in the quality characteristics and in determining the levels of the controllable variables that optimize process performance. Designed experiments are a major off-line quality-control tool, because they are often used during development activities and the early stages of manufacturing, rather than as a routine *on-line* or *in-process* control procedure.

Once we have identified a list of important variables that affect the process output, it is usually necessary to model the relationship between the influential input variables and the output quality characteristics. Statistical techniques useful in constructing such models include regression analysis and time series analysis. Detailed discussions of design of experiments, regression analysis, and time series modeling are in Montgomery (1984), Montgomery and Peck (1982), and Box and

Questions:

1. Which inputs affect the output parameter y?

2. What is the relationship between the important inputs and the output parameter y?

3. How can y be improved?

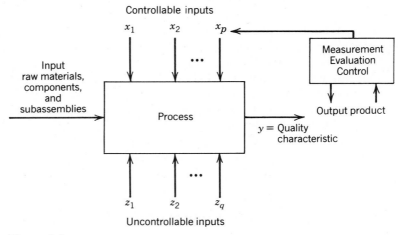

Figure 1-1
Production process inputs and outputs.

Jenkins (1976). When the important variables have been identified, and the nature of the relationship between the important variables and the process output model has been examined, then an on-line statistical process-control technique for monitoring and surveillance of the process can be employed with considerable effectiveness. Techniques such as control charts can be used to monitor the process output and detect when changes in the inputs are required to bring the process back to an in-control state. The models that relate the influential inputs to process outputs help determine the nature and magnitude of the adjustments required. Control charts also provide feedback to operators and engineers which is useful in reducing process variability.

Figure 1-2 shows the typical evolution in the use of these techniques in manufacturing organizations. At the lowest level of maturity, management is often completely unaware of quality problems, and there is likely to be no effective organized quality-assurance effort. There will frequently be some modest applications of acceptance-sampling methods, usually in receiving inspection. The first activity as maturity increases is to intensify the use of sampling inspection. The use of sampling will increase until we realize that quality cannot be inspected or tested into the product.

At that point, the organization usually begins to focus on process improvement. Statistical process control and experimental design potentially have major impact on manufacturing, product design activities, and process development. The systematic introduction of these methods usually marks the start of substantial quality, cost, and productivity improvements in the organization. At the highest levels of maturity, companies use designed experiments and statistical process control methods extensively, and make relatively modest use of acceptance sampling.

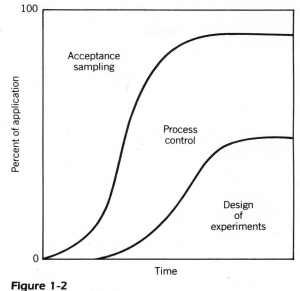

Figure 1-2

Phase diagram of the use of quality-engineering methods.

The primary objective of quality engineering is the *systematic reduction of variability* in the key quality characteristics of the product. Figure 1-3 shows how this happens over time. In the early stages, when acceptance sampling is the major technique in use, process "fallout," or units that do not conform to the specifications, constitute a high percentage of the process output. The introduction of statistical process controls will stabilize the process and reduce the variability. However, it is not satisfactory just to meet requirements—further reduction of variability usually leads to a lower cost of quality and an enhanced competitive position.

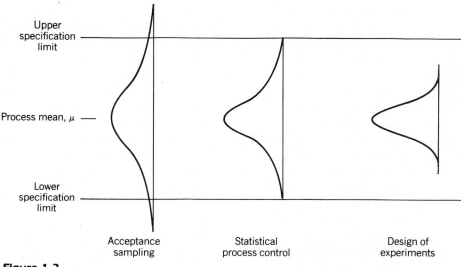

Figure 1-3

Application of quality-engineering techniques and the systematic reduction of process variability.

The design of experiments can be employed in conjunction with statistical process controls to minimize process variability, resulting in virtually defect-free manufacturing.

Statistical techniques in manufacturing and quality assurance have had a long history. In 1924 Walter A. Shewhart of the Bell Telephone Laboratories developed the statistical control-chart concept. This is generally considered as the beginning of statistical quality control. Toward the end of the 1920s, Harold F. Dodge and Harold G. Romig, both of Bell Telephone Laboratories, developed statistically based acceptance sampling as an alternative to 100% inspection. By the middle of the 1930s, statistical quality-control methods were in wide use at Western Electric, the manufacturing arm of the Bell System. However, the value of statistical quality control was not generally recognized by industry.

World War II saw the widespread use and acceptance of statistical quality-control concepts in manufacturing industries. Wartime experience made it apparent that statistical techniques were necessary to control product quality. The American Society for Quality Control was formed in 1946. This organization promotes the use of quality improvement techniques for all types of products and services. It offers a number of conferences, technical publications, and training programs in quality assurance. The 1950s and 1960s saw such developments in quality assurance as quality costs, reliability engineering, and the emergence of the viewpoint that quality is a way of managing the organization.

In the 1950s designed experiments for product and process improvement were first introduced in the United States. The initial applications were in the chemical industry. The spread of these methods was relatively slow until the late 1970s or early 1980s, when many Western companies discovered that their Japanese competitors had been systematically using designed experiments since the 1960s for process troubleshooting, new process development, evaluation of new product designs, improvement of reliability and field performance of products, and selection of component and system tolerances. This discovery sparked further interest in statistically designed experiments, and resulted in extensive efforts to introduce the methodology in engineering and development organizations in industry, as well as in academic engineering curricula.

There have been many important developments concerning work-force motivation and participative management. During the 1960s the defense and aerospace industries made wide use of zero-defects programs (ZD). Ideally, a zero-defects program has two aspects: a *motivation* aspect, aimed at stimulating employees to reduce their own errors, and a *prevention* aspect, aimed at encouraging employees to assist in reducing systematic controllable errors. The motivation programs make skillful use of product exhibits, slogans, contests, and other publicity vehicles in their design and execution. The prevention programs involve a deeper commitment. The basic philosophy of zero defects is that if a defect is identified, then engineers and managers will devote effort to isolating the source of the defect and take appropriate remedial action to ensure that that particular type of defect does not occur again. Industrial experience with zero-defects programs are mixed: Some report great success, others very little. Companies that embrace the prevention as well as the motivational philosophy are far more successful than those utilizing only the motivational program. However, the prevention aspect of zero defects implies a significant commitment by management to quality, along with developing and maintaining the necessary technical and engineering skills of the organization to carry out the program.

Another motivational program of widespread interest is the Japanese Quality Control (or QC) Circle. A QC circle is a team of about 10 workers and supervisors within a single company department. Its objective is to conduct studies that improve the effectiveness of work in that department. The studies are not necessarily restricted to quality and often involve productivity, costs, safety, or other aspects of the manufacturing environment. Participation in QC Circles is voluntary, although it is estimated that about half the workers in Japan are involved. The organization of the circle begins with a training program, which incorporates some aspects of data collection and analysis, a study of successful projects performed by other QC Circles, and the completion of an actual project, using such outside assistance as may be required.

In Japan, the QC Circle program has been extremely successful. It is estimated that about 10 million workers have undergone the training and participated in project studies. Several million projects have been performed, with an average return of about $5000 each. There have also been significant effects on product quality. The training and experience given these workers in preparing them to be better supervisors and managers have also been significant.

There has also been some adaptation of the QC Circle concept in Western industry, although the teams often have different names, such as "Productivity Improvement Team." It is not clear whether these teams have been as effective as their Japanese counterparts. There are both cultural and technological reasons why they may not have been as effective. In Western society the cultural resistance arises from engineers' and managers' reluctance to delegate to the work force certain functions and prerogatives that they have historically viewed as their own. Furthermore, the work force often does not consider that it has a responsibility to help management improve the performance of the company. However, workers frequently have some very good ideas about quality and process improvement. It is a major challenge to American management to change this attitude. Finally, many middle and senior managers in Western industry have a poor (or nonexistent) understanding of either the important role of quality in productivity improvement or the engineering and technical skills needed in the organization to achieve quality and productivity improvements. Technical knowledge of these skills is currently much more widespread in Japan than in the West.

One reason why Japanese manufacturing organizations have broad capabilities in statistical quality control is the work of Dr. W. Edwards Deming. During World War II, Dr. Deming worked for the War Department and the Census Bureau. Following the war, he became a consultant to Japanese industries and convinced their top management of the power of statistical quality control. This commitment to and use of these methods has been a key element in the expansion of Japan's industry and economy. In this country Deming and others are creating in industry an awareness of statistics in general and statistical quality control in particular.

1-5 TOTAL QUALITY MANAGEMENT

In the last three sections we have discussed the link between quality and productivity and the concept of quality costs. These are important aspects of the management of quality within an organization. In addition, certain other aspects of the total management of quality warrant some attention.

Quality is a multifaceted entity, having at least eight dimensions:

1. Performance
2. Reliability
3. Durability
4. Serviceability
5. Aesthetics
6. Features
7. Perceived quality
8. Conformance to standards

A critical part of the *strategic* management of quality within any business is the recognition of these dimensions by management and the selection of the dimensions along which the business will compete. It will be very difficult to compete against companies that can successfully accomplish this part of the strategy.

A good example is the Japanese dominance of the video cassette recorder (VCR) market. The Japanese did not invent the VCR; the first units for home use were produced in Europe by Phillips and Grundig. However, the early VCRs produced by these companies were very unreliable and frequently had high levels of manufacturing defects. When the Japanese entered the market, they elected to compete along the dimensions of reliability and conformance to standards (no defects). This strategy allowed them to quickly dominate the market. In subsequent years, they expanded the dimensions of quality to include added features, improved performance, easier serviceability, improved aesthetics, and so forth. They have used total quality as a competitive weapon to raise the entry barrier to this market so high that it is virtually impossible for a new competitor to enter.

Management must do this type of strategic thinking about quality. It is not necessary that the product be superior in all dimensions of quality, but management must *select and develop* the "niches" of quality along which the company can successfully compete. Typically, these dimensions will be those which the competition has forgotten or ignored. The American automobile industry has been severely impacted by foreign competitors who expertly practiced this strategy.

The critical role of suppliers in quality management must not be forgotten. In fact, vendor selection and vendor management may be the most critical aspects of successful quality management in industries such as automotive and electronics, where a very high percentage of the parts in the end item are manufactured by outside suppliers. Many companies are instituting formal supplier quality-improvement programs as part of their own *internal* quality-improvement efforts. Selection of suppliers based on *quality, schedule, and cost,* rather than on cost alone, is also a vital, strategic management decision that can have a long-term significant impact on overall competitiveness.

It is also critical that management recognize that quality improvement must be a total, company-wide activity, and that every organizational unit *must* actively participate. Obtaining this participation is the responsibility of (and a significant challenge to) senior management. What is the role of the quality-assurance organization in this effect? The responsibility of quality assurance is to assist general management and manufacturing management in providing quality assurance for the companies' products. Specifically, the quality-assurance function is a technology warehouse that contains the skills and resources necessary to generate products of acceptable quality in the marketplace. Quality management also has the responsibility for evaluating and using quality-cost information for identifying improvement opportunities in the system, and for making these opportunities known to higher management. It is important to note, however, that the quality function is not *responsible* for quality. After all, the quality organization does not design, manufacture, distribute, or service the product. This means that the responsibility for quality is spread throughout the entire organization. Some specific functional responsibilities are discussed below.

1. **Product planning, marketing, and sales.** These functions have responsibility for providing the market research activities that lead to a product description that best fulfills the customer's fitness-for-use objectives. They are also responsible for presenting product quality data to the consumer.

2. **Development engineering.** This function is responsible for the original product design, determining specifications, design for manufacturability, selection of materials, tolerances, and performance characteristics of the product.

3. **Manufacturing engineering.** This function is responsible for the selection of manufacturing processes, the design of appropriate production equipment, the selection of work methods, the design of workplaces, the provision of satisfactory working conditions, and the analysis of manufacturing-related problems that arise as a result of producing a product of the desired quality.

4. **Purchasing.** This function is responsible for selecting vendors and interacting with those vendors regarding the quality of the materials and components they supply.

5. **Manufacturing management.** These managers are responsible for operator education, proper maintenance of manufacturing facilities, correct interpretation of drawings and specifications, and control of the product as it is manufactured.

6. **Manufacturing employees.** All employees are responsible for exercising proper care in workmanship and for maintaining their technical skills.

7. **Inspection and test.** This function is responsible for measuring the quality of incoming parts and materials, and for appraising the performance of all manufactured products to the specifications.

8. **Packaging and shipping.** This function is responsible for the adequacy of the packaging and shipping materials in which the product is placed, and for the shipping and delivery of the product to the consumer.

9. **Customer service.** This function is responsible for maintenance of the product, including all repair activities and installation of replacement parts. The principal role of product service is to help the consumer realize the intended performance potential of the product over its useful life.

Obviously, the responsibility for quality spans the entire organization. However, there is a danger that if we adopt the philosophy that "quality is everybody's job," then quality will become nobody's job. This is why quality planning and analysis are important. Because assurance activities are so broad, successful quality-assurance programs require, as an initial step, top management commitment. This commitment involves emphasis on the importance of quality, identification of the respective quality responsibilities of the various organizational units, and explicit accountability of all managers and employees in the company.

Ideally, the quality-assurance function is staffed by engineers and managers with strong backgrounds in the appropriate product technology, modern systems engineering and management tools, training in statistical methods, including process controls, sampling inspection, reliability engineering, design of experiments, and process modeling techniques. Computers play an increasingly important role in quality assurance. Computers are useful in summarizing product quality and quality-cost data. Recent developments in microcomputer technology, robotics, and sensing and measurement technology will greatly increase the availability and use of automatic in-line test and inspection devices, and real-time, on-line statistical process controls. It is essential that modern quality engineers and managers understand the newest developments in these fields.

Finally, strategic management of quality in an organization will always be most effective when *all* the individuals in the organization have an understanding of the basic tools of quality improvement. Central among these tools are the elementary statistical concepts that form the basis of process control and that are used for the analysis of process data. It is increasingly important that everyone in an organization, from top management to operating personnel, have an awareness of basic statistical methods and of how these methods are useful in the production or manufacturing environment. Certain individuals must have higher levels of skills; for example, those engineers and managers in the quality-assurance function would generally be experts in one or more areas of process control, reliability engineering, inspection and testing procedures, or engineering data analysis. However, the key point is the philosophy that statistical methodology is a language of communication about problems that enables management to mobilize resources rapidly and to efficiently develop solutions to problems.

1-6 LEGAL ASPECTS

Consumerism and product liability are important reasons for the recent reemergence of quality assurance as an important business strategy. The rise of consumerism is in part due to the seemingly large number of failures in the field of consumer products. Highly visible field failures often prompt the questions of whether today's products are as good as their predecessors and whether manufacturers are really interested in quality. The answer to both of these questions is yes. Manufacturers are always vitally concerned about field failures because of heavy external failure costs and the related threat to their competitive position. Consequently, most producers have made product improvements directed toward reducing field failures. As examples, note that automobile tires now have over 10 times the life of many of their early predecessors and that solid-state and integrated-circuit technology has greatly reduced the failure of electronic equipment that once depended on the electron tube. Virtually every product line of today is superior to that of yesterday.

Consumer dissatisfaction, and the general feeling that today's products are inferior to their predecessors, arise from other phenomena. One of these is the explosion in the number of products. For example, a 1% field-failure rate for a consumer appliance with a production volume of 50,000 units per year means 500 field failures. However, if the production rate is 500,000 units per year, and the field-failure rate remains the same, then 5000 units will fail in the field. This is equivalent, in the total number of dissatisfied customers, to a 10% failure rate at the lower production level. Increasing production volume increases the *liability exposure* of the manufacturer. Even in situations where the failure rate declines, if the production volume increases more rapidly than the decrease in failure rate, the total number of customers who experience failures will still increase.

A second aspect of the problem is that consumer tolerance for minor defects and aesthetic problems has decreased considerably, so that blemishes, surface-finish defects, noises, and appearance problems that were once tolerated now attract attention and result in adverse consumer reaction. Finally, the competitiveness of the marketplace forces many manufacturers to introduce new designs before they are fully evaluated and tested in order to remain competitive. These "early releases" of unproved designs are a major reason for new product quality failures. Eventually, these design problems are corrected, but the high failure rate connected with new products often supports the belief that today's quality is inferior to that of yesterday's.

Product liability is a major social, market, and economic force. The legal obligation of manufacturers and sellers to compensate for injury or damage caused by defective products is not a recent phenomenon. The concept of product liability has been in existence for many years, but its emphasis has changed recently. The first major product liability case occurred in 1916 and was tried before the New York Court of Appeals. The court held that an automobile manufacturer had a product liability obligation to a car buyer, even though the sales contract was between the buyer and a third party, namely, a car dealer. The direction of the law has always been that manufacturers or sellers are likely to incur a liability when they have been unreasonably careless or negligent in what they have designed, or produced, or how they have produced it. In recent years, the courts have placed a more stringent rule in effect called *strict liability*. Two principles are characteristic of strict liability. The first of these is a strong responsibility for both manufacturer and merchandiser, requiring immediate responsiveness to unsatisfactory quality through product service, repair, or replacement of defective product. This extends into the period of actual use by the consumer. By producing a product, the manufacturer and seller must accept responsibility for the ultimate use of that product— not only for its performance, but also for its environmental effects, the safety aspects of its use, and so forth.

The second principle involves advertising and promotion of the product. Under strict product liability all advertising statements must be supportable by valid company quality or certification data, comparable to that now maintained for product identification under regulations for such products as automobiles.

These two strict product liability principles result in strong pressure on manufacturers, distributors, and merchants to develop and maintain a high degree of factually based evidence concerning the performance and safety of their products. This evidence must cover not only the quality of the product as it is delivered to the consumer, but also its durability or reliability, its protection from possible side effects or environmental hazards, and its safety aspects in actual use. A strong quality-assurance program can help management in ensuring that this information will be available, if needed.

1-7 SUMMARY

Modern manufacturing and service industries are faced with a considerable challenge. Customers have greatly increased their quality requirements, and this trend is likely to be intensified by competitive pressures in the future. New technology has made possible products that provide more functions and higher performance levels. As a result of increasing customer quality requirements and the development of new product technology, many existing quality-assurance practices and techniques need to be modified substantially. The need for statistical and analytical techniques in quality assurance is rapidly increasing. Finally, quality costs have become very high. In many businesses, quality costs are comparable in magnitude to direct labor costs, raw material costs, or distribution costs. There is a substantial danger that these costs may be too high for these companies to maintain and still improve their competitive position.

In summary, the quality challenge facing industry is to improve the quality of products and services, modernize modern quality practices, and simultaneously make substantial reductions in the cost of quality. These are difficult challenges; however, modern statistical quality-improvement methods, such as those discussed in Parts II, III and IV of this book, coupled with a strong, management-led quality-improvement effort, will provide a basis for successfully meeting this challenge.

PART I

Statistical Methods Useful in Quality Improvement

Statistics is the art of making decisions about a process or population based on an analysis of the information contained in a sample from that population. Statistical methods play a vital role in quality improvement. They provide the principal means by which a product is sampled, tested, and evaluated, and the information in those data is used to control and improve the manufacturing process. Furthermore, statistics is the language in which development engineers, manufacturing, procurement, management, and other functional components of the business communicate about quality.

This section contains two chapters. Chapter 2 gives a brief introduction to descriptive statistics, showing how simple graphical and numerical techniques can be used to summarize the information in sample data. The use of probability distributions to model the behavior of product parameters in a process or lot is then discussed. Chapter 3 presents techniques of statistical inference—that is, how the information contained in a sample can be used to draw conclusions about the population from which the sample was drawn.

Chapter 2

Modeling Process Quality

In this textbook we explore the use of statistical methodology in quality control and improvement. The purpose of this chapter is to introduce probability distributions and show how they provide a tool for modeling or describing the quality characteristics of a process.

2-1 DESCRIBING VARIATION

2-1.1 The Frequency Distribution and Histogram

No two units of product produced by a manufacturing process are identical. Some *variation* is inevitable. As examples, the net content of a can of soft drink varies slightly from can to can, and the output voltage of a power supply is not exactly the same from one unit to the next. Statistics is the science of analyzing data and drawing conclusions, taking variation in the data into account.

Table 2-1 presents 125 observations on the inside diameter of forged piston rings used in an automobile engine. The data were collected in 25 samples of five observations each. Notice that there is some variability in piston-ring diameter. However, it is very difficult to see any *pattern* in the variability or *structure* in the data, with the observations arranged as they are in Table 2-1. A *frequency distribution* is an arrangement of the data by magnitude. For example, a frequency

Table 2-1
Forged piston-ring inside diameter (mm)

Sample Number	Observations				
1	74.030	74.002	74.019	73.992	74.008
2	73.995	73.992	74.001	74.011	74.004
3	73.988	74.024	74.021	74.005	74.002
4	74.002	73.996	73.993	74.015	74.009
5	73.992	74.007	74.015	73.989	74.014
6	74.009	73.994	73.997	73.985	73.993
7	73.995	74.006	73.994	74.000	74.005
8	73.985	74.003	73.993	74.015	73.988
9	74.008	73.995	74.009	74.005	74.004
10	73.998	74.000	73.990	74.007	73.995
11	73.994	73.998	73.994	73.995	73.990
12	74.004	74.000	74.007	74.000	73.996
13	73.983	74.002	73.998	73.997	74.012
14	74.006	73.967	73.994	74.000	73.984
15	74.012	74.014	73.998	73.999	74.007
16	74.000	73.984	74.005	73.998	73.996
17	73.994	74.012	73.986	74.005	74.007
18	74.006	74.010	74.018	74.003	74.000
19	73.984	74.002	74.003	74.005	73.997
20	74.000	74.010	74.013	74.020	74.003
21	73.988	74.001	74.009	74.005	73.996
22	74.004	73.999	73.990	74.006	74.009
23	74.010	73.989	73.990	74.009	74.014
24	74.015	74.008	73.993	74.000	74.010
25	73.982	73.984	73.995	74.017	74.013

distribution of the piston-ring data is shown in Table 2-2. From this table we note that there was one ring that had a diameter between 73.965 mm and 73.970 mm, eight rings having diameters between 73.980 mm and 73.985 mm, and so forth.

A graph of the observed frequencies versus the ring diameter is shown in Figure 2-1. This display is called a *histogram*. The height of each bar in Figure 2-1 is equal to the frequency of occurrence of ring diameter. The histogram presents a visual display of the data in which one may more easily see three properties:

1. Shape
2. Location, or central tendency
3. Scatter, or spread

In the piston-ring diameter data, we see that the distribution of ring diameter is roughly symmetric and unimodal (mound shaped), with the central tendency very close to 74 mm. The variability in ring diameter is apparently relatively high, as some rings are as small as 73.967 mm, while others are as large as 74.030 mm. Thus, the histogram gives some insight into the process that inspection of the raw data above does not.

Table 2-2
Frequency distribution for piston-ring diameter

Ring Diameter, x (mm)	Tally	Frequency	Cumulative Frequency	Relative Frequency	Cumulative Relative Frequency
$73.965 \leq x < 73.970$	1	1	1	0.008	0.008
$73.970 \leq x < 73.975$		0	1	0.000	0.008
$73.975 \leq x < 73.980$		0	1	0.000	0.008
$73.980 \leq x < 73.985$	ЖЖ 111	8	9	0.064	0.072
$73.985 \leq x < 73.990$	ЖЖ ЖЖ	10	19	0.080	0.152
$73.990 \leq x < 73.995$	ЖЖ ЖЖ ЖЖ ЖЖ	19	38	0.152	0.304
$73.995 \leq x < 74.000$	ЖЖ ЖЖ ЖЖ ЖЖ 111	23	61	0.184	0.488
$74.000 \leq x < 74.005$	ЖЖ ЖЖ ЖЖ ЖЖ 11	22	83	0.176	0.664
$74.005 \leq x < 74.010$	ЖЖ ЖЖ ЖЖ ЖЖ 11	22	105	0.176	0.840
$74.010 \leq x < 74.015$	ЖЖ ЖЖ 111	13	118	0.104	0.944
$74.015 \leq x < 74.020$	ЖЖ	4	122	0.032	0.976
$74.020 \leq x < 74.025$	11	2	124	0.016	0.992
$74.025 \leq x < 74.030$	1	1	125	0.008	1.000
	Total	125		1.000	

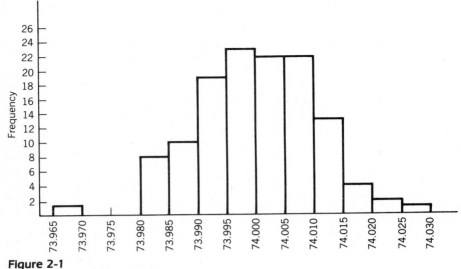

Figure 2-1
Histogram for piston-ring-diameter data.

Several guidelines are helpful in constructing histograms. When the data are numerous, grouping them into cells, as in the piston-ring example, is very useful. Generally:

1. Use between 4 and 20 cells—often choosing the number of cells approximately equal to the square root of the sample size works well.
2. Make the cells of uniform width.
3. Start the lower limit for the first cell just slightly below the smallest data value.

Grouping the data into cells condenses the original data, and as a result some detail is lost. Thus, when the number of observations is relatively small, or when the observations only take a few values, the histogram may be constructed from a frequency distribution of the ungrouped data.

2-1.2 Numerical Summary of Data

The histogram provides a visual display of three properties of sample data: the shape of the distribution of the data, the central tendency in the data, and the scatter or variability in the data. It is also helpful to use numerical measures of central tendency and scatter.

Suppose that $x_1, x_2, \ldots, x_n$ are the observations in a sample. The most important measure of central tendency in the sample is the *sample average*

$$\bar{x} = \frac{x_1 + x_2 + \cdots + x_n}{n}$$

$$= \frac{\sum_{i=1}^{n} x_i}{n} \tag{2-1}$$

Note that the sample average $\bar{x}$ is just the arithmetic mean of the n observations. The sample average for the piston-ring data is

$$\bar{x} = \frac{\sum\limits_{i=1}^{125} x_i}{125} = \frac{9250.125}{125} = 74.001 \text{ mm}$$

Refer to Figure 2-1 and note that the sample average is the point at which the histogram exactly "balances." Thus, the sample average represents the center of mass of the sample data.

The scatter or spread in the sample data is measured by the *sample* variance

$$S^2 = \frac{\sum\limits_{i=1}^{n} (x_i - \bar{x})^2}{n - 1} \tag{2-2}$$

Notice that the sample variance is just the sum of the squared deviations of each observation from the sample average $\bar{x}$, divided by the sample size minus one. If there is no variability in the sample, then each sample observation $x_i = \bar{x}$, and the sample variance $S^2 = 0$. Generally, the larger the sample variance S^2, the greater the scatter in the sample data.

The units of the sample variance S^2 are the square of the original units of the data. This is often inconvenient and difficult to interpret, and so we usually prefer to use the square root of S^2, called the *sample standard deviation S*, as a measure of scatter. Obviously,

$$S = \sqrt{\frac{\sum\limits_{i=1}^{n} (x_i - \bar{x})^2}{n - 1}} \tag{2-3}$$

The primary advantage of the sample standard deviation is that it is expressed in the original units of measurement. For the piston-ring data, we find that

$$S^2 = 0.000102 \text{ mm}^2$$

and

$$S = 0.010 \text{ mm}$$

To assist in understanding the standard deviation, consider the two samples shown below:

Sample 1	Sample 2
$x_1 = 1$	$x_1 = 1$
$x_2 = 3$	$x_2 = 5$
$x_3 = 5$	$x_3 = 9$
$\bar{x} = 3$	$\bar{x} = 5$

Obviously, Sample 2 has more scatter than Sample 1. This is reflected in the standard deviation, which for Sample 1 is

$$S = \sqrt{\frac{\sum_{i=1}^{3} (x_i - \bar{x})^2}{2}} = \sqrt{\frac{(1-3)^2 + (3-3)^2 + (5-3)^2}{2}} = \sqrt{4} = 2$$

and for Sample 2 is

$$S = \sqrt{\frac{\sum_{i=1}^{3} (x_i - \bar{x})^2}{2}} = \sqrt{\frac{(1-5)^2 + (5-5)^2 + (9-5)^2}{2}} = \sqrt{16} = 4$$

Thus, the larger variability in Sample 2 is reflected by its larger standard deviation. Now consider a third sample, say

Sample 3

$x_1 = 101$

$x_2 = 103$

$x_3 = 105$

$\bar{x} = 103$

The standard deviation for this third sample is $S = 2$, which is identical to the standard deviation of Sample 1. Comparing the two samples, we see that both samples have identical scatter about the average, and this is why they have identical standard deviation. This leads to an important point: *The standard deviation does not reflect the magnitude of the sample data, only the scatter about the average.*

Hand-held calculators, are frequently used for calculating the sample average and standard deviation. Note that Equations (2-2) or (2-3) are not very efficient computationally, because every number must be entered into the calculator twice. A more efficient formula is

$$S = \sqrt{\frac{\sum_{i=1}^{n} x_i^2 - \frac{\left(\sum_{i=1}^{n} x_i\right)^2}{n}}{n-1}} \tag{2-4}$$

In using (2-4), each number would only have to be entered once, provided that $\sum_{i=1}^{n} x_i$ and $\sum_{i=1}^{n} x_i^2$ could be simultaneously accumulated in the calculator. Many inexpensive hand-held calculators perform this function and have automatic calculation of $\bar{x}$ and S.

2-1.3 Other Useful Graphical Methods

The histogram is a very useful graphical display of sample data, giving the quality engineer a good understanding of the data and some basic information about *shape*, *location*, and *variability*. However, it does not allow individual observations to be identified, because all observations falling in a cell are indistinguishable. There are several graphical displays that are sometimes more informative than the histogram. Two of these, the stem and leaf plot and the box plot, are discussed in this section.

The Stem and Leaf Plot

Suppose that the data are represented by $x_1, x_2, \ldots, x_n$ and that each number x_i consists of at least two digits. To construct a stem and leaf plot, we divide each number x_i into two parts: a stem, consisting of one or more of the leading digits; and a leaf, consisting of the remaining digits. For example, if the data consist of percent defective information between 0 and 100 on lots of semiconductors wafers, then we can divide the value 76 into the stem 7 and the leaf 6. In general, we should choose relatively few stems in comparison with the number of observations. It is usually best to choose between 5 and 20 stems. Once a set of stems has been chosen, they are listed along the left-hand margin of the display, and beside each stem all leaves corresponding to the observed data values are listed in the order in which they are encountered in the data set.

Example 2-1

To illustrate the construction of a stem and leaf plot consider the data in Table 2-3, which represents weekly yield data from a semiconductor fabrication facility. To construct a stem and leaf plot, we select as stems the values 5, 6, 7, 8, and 9.

Table 2-3
Weekly yields from a semiconductor fabrication facility

Week	Yield	Week	Yield
1	58	21	64
2	63	22	68
3	69	23	67
4	72	24	60
5	51	25	59
6	79	26	63
7	83	27	64
8	86	28	52
9	85	29	70
10	78	30	92
11	87	31	75
12	83	32	76
13	64	33	81
14	73	34	74
15	81	35	82
16	68	36	76
17	72	37	75
18	65	38	62
19	91	39	63
20	88	40	92

Stem	Leaf	Frequency
5	8 1 9 2	4
6	3 9 4 8 5 4 8 7 0 3 4 2 3	13
7	2 9 8 3 2 0 5 6 4 6 5	11
8	3 6 5 7 3 1 8 1 2	9
9	1 2 2	3

Figure 2-2
Stem and leaf plot for the semiconductor yield data in
Table 2-3.

The resulting stem and leaf plot is shown in Figure 2-2. Inspection of the plot reveals that the yield distribution has an approximately symmetric shape, with a single peak or mode. The stem and leaf plot, like the histogram, allows us to quickly determine some important features of the data that are not obvious from the data table, but the original numbers are not lost, as they might have been in a histogram.

In order to help us find percentiles of the data distribution, we sometimes order the leaves by magnitude, producing an *ordered* stem and leaf plot, as in Figure 2-3. The *fiftieth percentile* of the data distribution is called the sample median $\tilde{x}$. The median can be thought of as the data value that exactly divides the sample in half, with half of the observations smaller than the median and half of them larger. Since $n = 40$ is an even number, the median is the average of the two observations with rank 20 and 21, or

$$\tilde{x} = \frac{72 + 73}{2} = 72.5$$

The *tenth percentile* is the observation with rank $(0.1)(40) + 0.5 = 4.5$ (halfway between the fourth and fifth observation), or $(59 + 60)/2 = 59.5$. The *first quartile* is the observation with rank $(0.25)(40) + 0.5 = 10.5$ (halfway between the tenth and eleventh observation) or $(64 + 64)/2 = 64$, and the *third quartile* is the ob-

Stem	Leaf	Frequency
5	1 2 8 9	4
6	0 2 3 3 3 4 4 4 5 7 8 8 9	13
7	0 2 2 3 4 5 5 6 6 8 9	11
8	1 1 2 3 3 5 6 7 8	9
9	1 2 2	3

Figure 2-3
Ordered stem and leaf plot for the semiconductor yield data.

servation with rank $(0.75)(40) + 0.5 = 30.5$ (halfway between the thirtieth and thirty-first observation), or $(81 + 82)/2 = 81.5$. The first and third quartiles are occasionally denoted by the symbols Q1 and Q3, respectively, and the *interquartile range* IQR $= Q_3 - Q1$ may be used as another measure of variability. For the semiconductor yield data the interquartile range is IQR $= Q3 - Q1 = 81.5 - 64 = 17.5$. The stem and leaf displays in Figures 2-2 and 2-3 are equivalent to a histogram with five class intervals. In some situations, it may be desirable to provide more classes or stems. One way to do so is to modify the original stems as follows: Divide the stem 5 (say) into two new stems, 5* and 5•. The stem 5* has leaves 0, 1, 2, 3, and 4, and the stem 5• has leaves 5, 6, 7, 8, and 9. This will double the number of original stems. We could increase the number of original stems by five by defining five new stems: 5* with leaves 0 and 1, 5t (for twos and threes) with leaves 2 and 3, 5f (for fours and fives) with leaves 4 and 5, 5s (for sixes and sevens) with leaves 6 and 7, and 5• with leaves 8 and 9.

The Box Plot

A box plot displays the three quartiles, the minimum, and the maximum of the data on a rectangular box, aligned either horizontally or vertically. The box encloses the interquartile range with the left (or lower) line at the first quartile Q1 and the right (or upper) line at the third quartile Q3. A line is drawn through the box at the second quartile (which is the fiftieth percentile or the median) Q2 $= \tilde{x}$. A line at either end extends to the extreme values. These lines, sometimes called whiskers, may only extend to the tenth and ninetieth percentiles or the fifth and ninety-fifth percentiles in large data sets. Some authors refer to the box plot as the box and whisker plot.

Example 2-2

The data in Table 2-4 are diameters (in mm) of holes in a group of 12 wing leading edge ribs for a commercial transport airplane. Note that the median of the sample is halfway between the sixth and seventh rank-ordered observation, or $(120.5 + 120.7)/2 = 120.6$, and that the quartiles are Q1 $= 120.45$ and Q3 $= 120.9$. The box plot is shown in Figure 2-4. This box plot indicates that the hole diameter distribution is not exactly symmetric around a central value, because the left and right whiskers and the left and right boxes around the median are not the same lengths.

Table 2-4
Hole diameters (in mm) in wing leading edge ribs

120.5	120.4	120.7
120.9	120.2	121.1
120.3	120.1	120.9
121.3	120.5	120.8

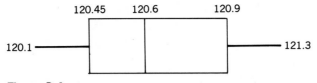

Figure 2-4
Box plot for the aircraft wing leading edge hole diameter data in Table 2-4.

2-1.4 Probability Distributions

The histogram (or stem and leaf plot, or box plot) is used to describe *sample* data. A sample is a collection of measurements selected from some larger source or *population*. For example, the 125 piston-ring diameters in Table 2-1 are a sample of piston-ring diameters selected from the manufacturing process. The population in this example is the collection of all piston rings produced by that process. By using statistical methods, we may be able to analyze the sample piston-ring-diameter data and draw certain conclusions about the process that manufactures the rings.

A *probability distribution* is a mathematical model that relates the value of the variable with the probability of occurrence of that value in the population. In other words, we might visualize piston-ring diameter as a *random variable*, because it takes on different values in the population according to some random mechanism, and then the probability distribution of ring diameter describes the probability of occurrence of any value of ring diameter in the population. There are two types of probability distributions:

1. **Continuous distributions.** When the variable being measured is expressed on a continuous scale, its probability distribution is called a *continuous distribution*. The probability distribution of piston-ring diameter is continuous.

2. **Discrete distributions.** When the parameter being measured can only take on certain values, such as the integers $0, 1, 2, \ldots$, the probability distribution is called a *discrete distribution*. For example, the distribution of the number of nonconformities or defects in printed circuit boards would be a discrete distribution.

Examples of discrete and continuous probability distributions are shown in Figure 2-5a and 2-5b, respectively. The appearance of a discrete distribution is that of a series of vertical "spikes," with the height of each spike proportional to the probability. We write the probability that the random variable x takes on the specific value x_i as

$$P\{x = x_i\} = p(x_i)$$

The appearance of a continuous distribution is that of a smooth curve, with the area under the curve equal to probability, so that the probability that x

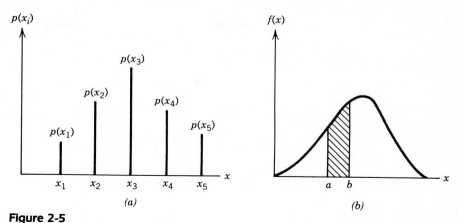

Figure 2-5
Probability distributions. (a) Discrete case. (b) Continuous case.

lies in the interval from a to b is written as

$$P\{a \leq x \leq b\} = \int_a^b f(x)\, dx$$

Example 2-3

A Discrete Distribution

A manufacturing process produces thousands of diodes per day. On the average, 1% of these diodes do not conform to specifications. Every hour, an inspector selects a random sample of 50 diodes and classifies each diode in the sample as conforming or nonconforming. If we let x be the random variable representing the number of nonconforming parts in the sample, then the probability distribution of x is

$$p(x) = \binom{50}{x}(0.01)^x(0.99)^{50-x} \qquad x = 0, 1, 2, \ldots, 50$$

where $\binom{50}{x} = [50!/x!(50-x)!]$. This is a *discrete* distribution, since the observed number of nonconformances is $x = 0, 1, 2, \ldots, 50$, and is called the *binomial distribution*. We may calculate the probability of finding one or less nonconforming parts in the sample as

$$\begin{aligned}
P(x \leq 1) &= P(x = 0) + P(x = 1) \\
&= p(0) + p(1) \\
&= \sum_{x=0}^{1} \binom{50}{x}(0.01)^x(0.99)^{50-x} \\
&= \frac{50!}{0!50!}(0.99)^{50}(0.01)^0 + \frac{50!}{1!49!}(0.99)^{49}(0.01)^1 \\
&= 0.6050 + 0.3056 = 0.9106
\end{aligned}$$

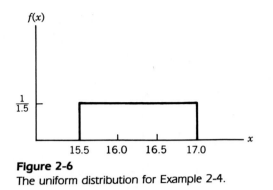

Figure 2-6
The uniform distribution for Example 2-4.

Example 2-4

A Continuous Distribution

Suppose that x is a random variable that represents the actual contents in ounces of a 1-lb can of coffee. The probability distribution of x is assumed to be

$$f(x) = \frac{1}{1.5} \qquad 15.5 \leq x \leq 17.0$$

This is a continuous distribution, since the range space of x is the interval $[15.5, 17.0]$. This distribution is called the uniform distribution, and it is shown graphically in Figure 2-6. Note that the area under the function $f(x)$ corresponds to probability, so that the probability of a can containing less than 16.0 oz is

$$P\{x \leq 16.0\} = \int_{15.5}^{16.0} f(x)\, dx$$

$$= \int_{15.5}^{16.0} \frac{1}{1.5}\, dx$$

$$= \frac{x}{1.5}\Big|_{15.5}^{16.0} = \frac{16.0 - 15.5}{1.5} = 0.3333$$

This follows intuitively from inspection of Figure 2-6.

In Sections 2-2 and 2-3 we present several useful discrete and continuous distributions.

The mean μ of a probability distribution is a measure of the *central tendency* in the distribution, or its *location*. If the population consists of N items, then the mean is defined as

$$\mu = \frac{\displaystyle\sum_{i=1}^{N} x_i}{N} \tag{2-5}$$

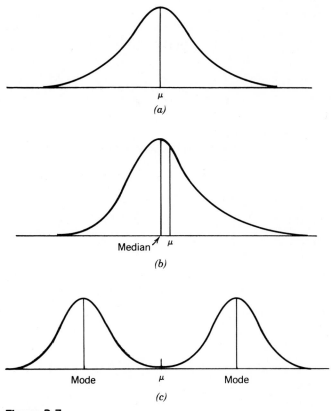

Figure 2-7
The mean of a distribution.

Note the similarity to the sample average $\bar{x}$ defined in Equation (2-1). The mean is the point at which the distribution exactly "balances" (see Figure 2-7). Thus, the mean is just the center of mass of the probability distribution. Note from Figure 2-7b that the mean is not necessarily the fiftieth percentile of the distribution (the *median*), and from Figure 2-7c it is not necessarily the most likely value of the variable (which is called the *mode*). The mean simply determines the *location* of the distribution, as shown in Figure 2-8.

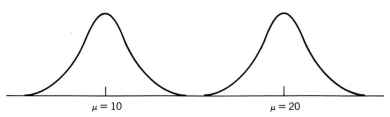

Figure 2-8
Two probability distributions with different means.

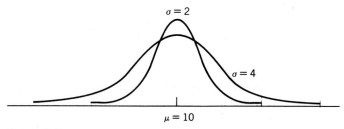

Figure 2-9
Two probability distributions with different standard deviations.

The scatter, spread, or variability in a distribution is expressed by the *variance* σ^2. If there are N items in the population, the variance is

$$\sigma^2 = \frac{\sum_{i=1}^{N} (x_i - \mu)^2}{N} \tag{2-6}$$

That is, the variance is just the average squared distance of each element of the population from the mean. Note the similarity to the sample variance S^2, defined in Equation (2-2). If $\sigma^2 = 0$, there is no variability in the population. As the variability increases, the variance σ^2 increases. The variance is expressed in the square of the units of the original variable. For example, if we are measuring voltages, the units of the variance are (volts)^2. Thus, it is customary to work with the square root of the variance, called the *standard deviation* σ. Obviously,

$$\sigma = \sqrt{\sigma^2} = \sqrt{\frac{\sum_{i=1}^{N} (x_i - \mu)^2}{N}} \tag{2-7}$$

The standard deviation is a measure of spread or scatter in the population expressed in the original units. Two distributions with the same mean but different standard deviations are shown in Figure 2-9.

2-2 IMPORTANT DISCRETE DISTRIBUTIONS

Several discrete probability distributions arise frequently in statistical quality control. In this section, we discuss the hypergeometric distribution, the binomial distribution, the Poisson distribution, and the Pascal or negative binomial distribution.

2-2.1 The Hypergeometric Distribution

Suppose that there is a finite population consisting of N items. Some number, say $D(D \leq N)$, of these items fall into a class of interest. A random sample of n items is selected from the population *without replacement*, and the number of items in the sample that fall into the class of interest, say x, is observed. Then x is a hypergeometric random variable with probability distribution

$$p(x) = \frac{\binom{D}{x}\binom{N-D}{n-x}}{\binom{N}{n}} \qquad x = 0, 1, 2, \ldots, \min(n, D) \qquad (2\text{-}8)$$

where

$$\binom{a}{b} = \frac{a!}{b!(a-b)!}$$

is the number of combinations of a items taken b at a time. The mean and variance of the hypergeometric distribution are

$$\mu = \frac{nD}{N} \qquad (2\text{-}9)$$

and

$$\sigma^2 = \frac{nD}{N}\left(1 - \frac{D}{N}\right)\left(\frac{N-n}{N-1}\right) \qquad (2\text{-}10)$$

The hypergeometric distribution is the appropriate probability model for selecting a random sample of n items without replacement from a lot of N items of which D are nonconforming or defective. In these applications, x usually represents the number of nonconforming items found in the sample. For example, suppose that a lot contains 100 items, 5 of which do not conform to requirements. If 10 items are selected at random without replacement, then the probability of finding one or less nonconforming item in the sample is

$$P\{x \leq 1\} = P\{x = 0\} + P\{x = 1\}$$

$$= \frac{\binom{5}{0}\binom{95}{10}}{\binom{100}{10}} + \frac{\binom{5}{1}\binom{95}{9}}{\binom{100}{10}}$$

$$= 0.923$$

In Chapter 13 we show how probability models such as this can be used to design acceptance-sampling procedures.

2-2.2 The Binomial Distribution

Consider a process that consists of a sequence of n independent trials, where the outcome of each trial is either a "success" or a "failure." Such trials are called *Bernoulli trials*. If the probability of "success" on any trial, say p, is constant, then the number of "successes" x in n Bernoulli trials has the binomial distribution

$$p(x) = \binom{n}{x} p^x (1 - p)^{n-x} \qquad x = 0, 1, \ldots, n \qquad (2\text{-}11)$$

The parameters of the binomial distribution are n and p, where n is a positive integer and $0 < p < 1$. The mean and variance of the binomial distribution are

$$\mu = np \qquad (2\text{-}12)$$

and

$$\sigma^2 = np(1 - p) \qquad (2\text{-}13)$$

The binomial distribution is used frequently in quality control. It is the appropriate probability model for sampling from an infinitely large population, where p represents the fraction of defective or nonconforming items in the population. In these applications, x usually represents the number of nonconforming items found in a random sample of n items. For example, if $p = 0.10$ and $n = 15$, then the probability of obtaining x nonconforming items is computed from (2-11) as

x	$p(x)$
0	0.2059
1	0.3432
2	0.2669
3	0.1285
4	0.0428
5	0.0105
6	0.0019
7	0.0003
8	0.0000
⋮	⋮
15	0.0000

The probability distribution is displayed graphically in Figure 2-10. The shape of the binomial distribution in Figure 2-10 is characteristic of *all* binomial distributions; the values $p(x)$ increase to a point and then decrease. Specifically, $p(x) > p(x - 1)$ for $x < (n + 1)p$ and $p(x) < p(x - 1)$ for $x > (n + 1)p$. If $(n + 1)p = m$ is an integer, then $p(m) = p(m - 1)$. There is only one integer m such that $(n + 1)p - 1 < m \leq (n + 1)p$.

A random variable that arises frequently in statistical quality control is

$$\hat{p} = \frac{x}{n} \qquad (2\text{-}14)$$

where x has a binomial distribution with parameters n and p. Often we think of $\hat{p}$ as the ratio of the number of defective or nonconforming items in the sample to

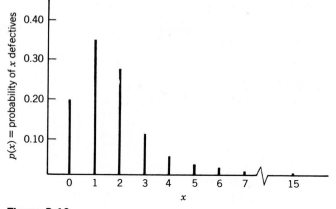

Figure 2-10
Binomial distribution with $p = 0.10$ and $n = 15$.

the sample size, and this is usually called the *sample fraction defective* or *sample fraction nonconforming*. The probability distribution of $\hat{p}$ is obtained from the binomial, since

$$P\{\hat{p} \le a\} = P\left\{\frac{x}{n} \le a\right\} = P\{x \le na\} = \sum_{x=0}^{[na]} \binom{n}{x} p^x (1-p)^{n-x}$$

where $[na]$ denotes the largest integer less than or equal to na. It is easy to show that the mean of $\hat{p}$ is p and that the variance of $\hat{p}$ is

$$\sigma_{\hat{p}}^2 = \frac{p(1-p)}{n}$$

2-2.3 The Poisson Distribution

A useful discrete distribution in statistical quality control is the Poisson distribution,

$$p(x) = \frac{e^{-\lambda}\lambda^x}{x!} \qquad x = 0, 1, \ldots \tag{2-15}$$

where the parameter $\lambda > 0$. The mean and variance of the Poisson distribution are

$$\mu = \lambda \tag{2-16}$$

and

$$\sigma^2 = \lambda \tag{2-17}$$

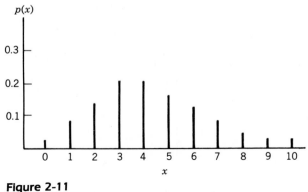

Figure 2-11
The Poisson distribution with $\lambda = 4$.

respectively. That is, the mean and variance of the Poisson distribution are *both* equal to the parameter λ.

A typical application of the Poisson distribution in quality control is as a model of the number of defects or nonconformities that occur in a unit of product. In fact, any random phenomenon that occurs on a per unit (or per unit area, per unit volume, per unit time, etc.) basis is often well approximated by the Poisson distribution. As an example, suppose that the number of wire-bonding defects per unit that occur in a semiconductor device is Poisson distributed with parameter $\lambda = 4$. Then the probability that a randomly selected semiconductor device will contain two or fewer wire-bonding defects is

$$P\{x \le 2\} = \sum_{x=0}^{2} \frac{e^{-4}4^x}{x!}$$
$$= 0.0183 + 0.0733 + 0.1464 = 0.2380$$

This Poisson distribution is illustrated in Figure 2-11. Note that the distribution is *skewed*; that is, it has a long tail to the right. As the parameter λ becomes larger, the Poisson distribution becomes symmetric in appearance.

Extensive tables for the Poisson distribution are available in Molina (1942). A brief table of Poisson probabilities is given in Appendix Table 1.

It is possible to derive the Poisson distribution as a limiting form of the binomial distribution. That is, in a binomial distribution with parameters n and p, if we let n approach infinity and p approach zero in such a way that $np = \lambda$ is a constant, then the Poisson distribution results. It is also possible to derive the Poisson distribution using a pure probability argument. For this approach, see Hines and Montgomery (1990, 165–166).

2-2.4 The Pascal and Related Distributions

The Pascal distribution, like the binomial distribution, has its basis in Bernoulli trials. Consider a sequence of independent trials, each with probability of success p, and let x denote the trial on which the rth success occurs. Then x is a Pascal random variable with probability distribution

$$p(x) = \binom{x-1}{r-1} p^r (1-p)^{x-r} \qquad x = r, r+1, r+2, \ldots \qquad (2\text{-}18)$$

where $r \geq 1$ is an integer. The mean and variance of the Pascal distribution are

$$\mu = \frac{r}{p} \qquad (2\text{-}19)$$

and

$$\sigma^2 = \frac{r(1-p)}{p^2} \qquad (2\text{-}20)$$

respectively.

Two special cases of the Pascal distribution are of interest. The first of these is if $r > 0$ and not necessarily an integer. The resulting distribution is called the *negative binomial distribution*. It is relatively standard to refer to (2-18) as the negative binomial distribution, even when r is an integer. The negative binomial distribution, like the Poisson distribution, is sometimes useful as the underlying statistical model for various types of "count" data, such as the occurrence of nonconformities in a unit of product (see Section 5-3.1). There is an important duality between the binomial and negative binomial distributions. In the binomial distribution, we fix the sample size (number of Bernoulli trials) and observe the number of successes; in the negative binomial distribution, we fix the number of successes and observe the sample size (number of Bernoulli trials) required to achieve them. This concept is particularly important in various kinds of sampling problems.

The other special case of the Pascal distribution is if $r = 1$, in which case we have the *geometric distribution*. It is the distribution of the number of Bernoulli trials until the *first* success.

2-3 IMPORTANT CONTINUOUS DISTRIBUTIONS

In this section we discuss several continuous distributions that are important in statistical quality control. These include the normal distribution, the exponential distribution, the gamma distribution, and the Weibull distribution.

2-3.1 The Normal Distribution

The normal distribution is probably the most important distribution in both the theory and application of statistics. If x is a normal random variable, then the probability distribution of x is

$$f(x) = \frac{1}{\sigma\sqrt{2\pi}} e^{-\frac{1}{2}\left(\frac{x-\mu}{\sigma}\right)^2} \qquad -\infty < x < \infty \qquad (2\text{-}21)$$

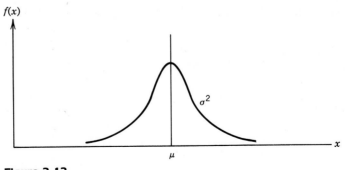

Figure 2-12
The normal distribution.

The parameters of the normal distribution are the mean $\mu(-\infty < \mu < \infty)$ and the variance $\sigma^2 > 0$. The distribution is used so extensively that we frequently employ a special notation, $x \sim N(\mu, \sigma^2)$, to imply that x is normally distributed with mean μ and variance σ^2. The visual appearance of the normal distribution is a symmetric, unimodal or *bell-shaped* curve, and is shown in Figure 2-12.

There is a simple interpretation of the standard deviation σ of a normal distribution, which is illustrated in Figure 2-13. Note that 68.26% of the population values fall between the limits defined by the mean plus and minus one standard deviation $(\mu \pm 1\sigma)$; 95.46% of the values fall between the limits defined by the mean plus and minus two standard deviations $(\mu \pm 2\sigma)$; and 99.73% of the population values fall within the limits defined by the mean plus and minus three standard deviations $(\mu \pm 3\sigma)$. Thus, the standard deviation measures the distance on the horizontal scale associated with the 68.26%, 95.46%, and 99.73% containment limits. It is common practice to round these percentages to 68%, 95%, and 99.7%.

The cumulative normal distribution is defined as the probability that the normal variable x is less than or equal to some value a, or

$$P\{x \le a\} = F(a) = \int_{-\infty}^{a} \frac{1}{\sigma\sqrt{2\pi}} e^{-\frac{1}{2}\left(\frac{x-\mu}{\sigma}\right)^2} dx \qquad (2\text{-}22)$$

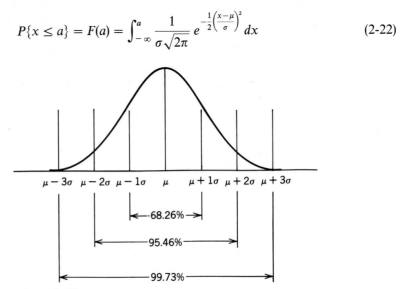

Figure 2-13
Areas under the normal distribution.

This integral cannot be evaluated in closed form. However, by using the change of variable

$$z = \frac{x - \mu}{\sigma} \tag{2-23}$$

the evaluation can be made independent of μ and σ^2. That is,

$$P\{x \le a\} = P\left\{z \le \frac{a - \mu}{\sigma}\right\} \equiv \Phi\left(\frac{a - \mu}{\sigma}\right)$$

where $\Phi(\cdot)$ is the cumulative distribution function of the *standard normal distribution* (mean $= 0$, standard deviation $= 1$). A table of the cumulative standard normal distribution is given in Appendix Table II. The transformation (2-23) is usually called *standardization*, because it converts a $N(\mu, \sigma^2)$ random variable into a $N(0, 1)$ random variable.

Example 2-5

The tensile strength of paper used to make grocery bags is an important quality characteristic. It is known that the strength, say x, is normally distributed with mean $\mu = 40$ lb/in^2 and standard deviation $\sigma = 2$ lb/in^2, denoted $x \sim N(40, 2^2)$. The purchaser of the bags requires them to have a strength of at least 35 lb/in^2. The probability that a bag produced from this paper will meet or exceed this specification is $P\{x \ge 35\}$. Note that

$$P\{x \ge 35\} = 1 - P\{x \le 35\}$$

To evaluate this probability from the standard normal tables, we standardize the point 35 and find

$$P\{x \le 35\} = P\left\{z \le \frac{35 - 40}{2}\right\}$$
$$= P\{z \le -2.5\}$$
$$= \Phi(-2.5)$$
$$= 0.0062$$

Consequently, the desired probability is

$$P\{x \ge 35\} = 1 - P\{x \le 35\} = 1 - 0.0062 = 0.9938$$

Figure 2-14 shows the tabulated probability for both the $N(40, 2^2)$ distribution and the standard normal distribution. Notice that the shaded area to the left of 35 lb/in^2 in Figure 2-14 represents the fraction nonconforming or "fallout" produced by the bag manufacturing process.

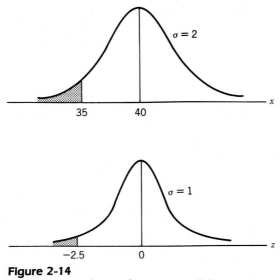

Figure 2-14
Calculation of $P\{x \le 35\}$ in Example 2-5.

Appendix Table II gives only probabilities to the left of positive values of z. We will need to utilize the symmetry property of the normal distribution to evaluate probabilities. Specifically, note that

$$P\{x \ge a\} = 1 - P\{x \le a\} \tag{2-24a}$$

$$P\{x \le -a\} = P\{x \ge a\} \tag{2-24b}$$

and

$$P\{x \ge -a\} = P\{x \le a\} \tag{2-24c}$$

It is helpful in problem solution to draw a graph of the distribution, as in Figure 2-14.

Example 2-6

The diameter of a metal shaft used in a disk-drive unit is normally distributed with mean 0.2508 in. and standard deviation 0.0005 in. The specifications on the shaft have been established as 0.2500 ± 0.0015 in. We wish to determine what fraction of the shafts produced conform to specifications. The appropriate normal distribution is shown in Figure 2-15. Note that

$$P\{0.2485 \le x \le 0.2515\} = P\{x \le 0.2515\} - P\{x \le 0.2485\}$$
$$= \Phi\left(\frac{0.2515 - 0.2508}{0.0005}\right) - \Phi\left(\frac{0.2485 - 0.2508}{0.0005}\right)$$
$$= \Phi(1.40) - \Phi(-4.60)$$
$$= 0.9265 - 0.0000$$
$$= 0.9265$$

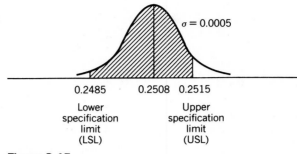

$\sigma = 0.0005$

0.2485	0.2508 0.2515
Lower specification limit (LSL)	Upper specification limit (USL)

Figure 2-15
Distribution of shaft diameters, Example 2-6.

Thus, we would expect the process yield to be approximately 92.65%; that is, about 92.65% of the shafts produced conform to specifications.

Note that almost all of the nonconforming shafts are too large, because the process mean is located very near to the upper specification limit. Suppose we can recenter the manufacturing process, perhaps by adjusting the machine, so that the process mean is exactly equal to the nominal value of 0.2500. Then we have

$$P\{0.2485 \le x \le 0.2515\} = P\{x \le 0.2515\} - P\{x \le 0.2485\}$$
$$= \Phi\left(\frac{0.2515 - 0.2500}{0.0005}\right) - \Phi\left(\frac{0.2485 - 0.2500}{0.0005}\right)$$
$$= \Phi(3.00) - \Phi(-3.00)$$
$$= 0.99865 - 0.00135$$
$$= 0.9973$$

By recentering the process we have increased the yield of the process to approximately 99.73%.

Example 2-7

Suppose that $x \sim N(10, 9)$. We wish to find the value of x, say a, such that $P\{x > a\} = 0.05$. Thus

$$P\{x > a\} = P\left\{z > \frac{a - 10}{3}\right\} = 0.05$$

or

$$P\left\{z \le \frac{a - 10}{3}\right\} = 0.95$$

From Appendix Table II, we have $P\{z \le 1.96\} = 0.95$, so

$$\frac{a - 10}{3} = 1.96$$

or

$$a = 10 + 3(1.96) = 15.88$$

The normal distribution has many useful properties. One of these is relative to linear combinations of normally and independently distributed random variables. If $x_1, x_2, \ldots, x_n$ are normally and independently distributed random variables with means $\mu_1, \mu_2, \ldots, \mu_n$ and variances $\sigma_1^2, \sigma_2^2, \ldots, \sigma_n^2$, respectively, then the distribution of

$$y = a_1 x_1 + a_2 x_2 + \cdots + a_n x_n$$

is normal with mean

$$\mu_y = a_1 \mu_1 + a_2 \mu_2 + \cdots + a_n \mu_n \qquad (2\text{-}25)$$

and variance

$$\sigma_y^2 = a_1^2 \sigma_1^2 + a_2^2 \sigma_2^2 + \cdots + a_n^2 \sigma_n^2 \qquad (2\text{-}26)$$

where $a_1, a_2, \ldots, a_n$ are constants.

The Central Limit Theorem
The normal distribution is often assumed as the appropriate probability model for a random variable. In many instances, it is difficult to check the validity of this assumption; however, the central limit theorem is often a justification of approximate normality.

The central limit theorem If $x_1, x_2, \ldots, x_n$ are independent random variables with mean μ_i and variance σ_i^2, and if $y = x_1 + x_2 + \cdots + x_n$, then the distribution of

$$\frac{y - \sum\limits_{i=1}^{n} \mu_i}{\sqrt{\sum\limits_{i=1}^{n} \sigma_i^2}}$$

approaches the $N(0, 1)$ distribution as n approaches infinity.

The central limit theorem implies that the sum of n independently distributed random variables is approximately normal, regardless of the distributions of the individual variables. The approximation improves as n increases. In some cases the approximation may be good for small n, say $n < 10$, while in other cases we may require very large n, say $n > 100$, for the approximation to be satisfactory. In general, if the x_i are identically distributed, and the distribution of each x_i does not depart radically from the normal, then the central limit theorem works quite well for $n \geq 4$. These conditions are met frequently in quality-control problems.

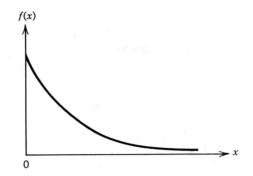

Figure 2-16
The exponential distribution.

2-3.2 The Exponential Distribution

The probability distribution of the exponential random variable is

$$f(x) = \lambda e^{-\lambda x} \qquad x \geq 0 \tag{2-27}$$

where $\lambda > 0$ is a constant. A graph of the exponential distribution is shown in Figure 2-16. The mean and variance of the exponential distribution are

$$\mu = \frac{1}{\lambda} \tag{2-28}$$

and

$$\sigma^2 = \frac{1}{\lambda^2} \tag{2-29}$$

respectively. The cumulative exponential distribution is

$$\begin{aligned}
F(a) &= P\{x \leq a\} \\
&= \int_0^a \lambda e^{-\lambda t}\, dt \\
&= 1 - e^{-\lambda a} \qquad a \geq 0
\end{aligned} \tag{2-30}$$

Figure 2-17 depicts the exponential cumulative distribution function.

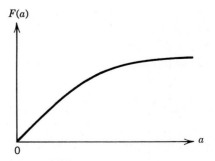

Figure 2-17
The exponential cumulative
distribution function.

The exponential distribution is widely used in the field of reliability engineering as a model of the time to failure of a component or system. In these applications, the parameter λ is called the *failure rate* of the system, and the mean of the distribution $1/\lambda$ is called the *mean time to failure*. For example, suppose that an electronic component in an airborne radar has a useful life described by an exponential distribution with failure rate 10^{-4} h, that is, $\lambda = 10^{-4}$. The mean time to failure for this component is $1/\lambda = 10^4 = 10{,}000$ h. If we wanted to determine the probability that this component would fail before its expected life, we would evaluate

$$P\left\{x \le \frac{1}{\lambda}\right\} = \int_0^{1/\lambda} \lambda e^{-\lambda t}\, dt = 1 - e^{-1} = 0.63212$$

This result holds regardless of the value of λ; that is, the probability that a value of an exponential random variable will be less than its mean is 0.63212. This happens, of course, because the distribution is not symmetric.

There is an important relationship between the exponential and Poisson distributions. If we consider the Poisson distribution as a model of the number of occurrences of some event in the interval $(0, t]$, then from (2-15) we have

$$p(x) = \frac{e^{-\lambda t}(\lambda t)^x}{x!}$$

Now $x = 0$ implies that there are no occurrences of the event in $(0, t]$, and $P\{x = 0\} = p(0) = e^{-\lambda t}$. We may think of $p(0)$ as the probability that the interval to the first occurrence is greater than t, or

$$P\{y > t\} = p(0) = e^{-\lambda t}$$

where y is the random variable denoting the interval to the first occurrence. Since

$$F(t) = P\{y \le t\} = 1 - e^{-\lambda t}$$

and using the fact that $f(y) = dF(y)/dy$, we have

$$f(y) = \lambda e^{-\lambda y} \tag{2-31}$$

as the distribution of the interval to the first occurrence. We recognize (2-31) as an exponential distribution with parameter λ. Therefore, we see that if the number of occurrences of an event has a Poisson distribution with parameter λ, then the distribution of the interval *between* occurrences is exponential with parameter λ.

2-3.3 The Gamma Distribution

The probability distribution of the gamma random variable is

$$f(x) = \frac{\lambda}{\Gamma(r)}(\lambda x)^{r-1}e^{-\lambda x} \qquad x \ge 0 \tag{2-32}$$

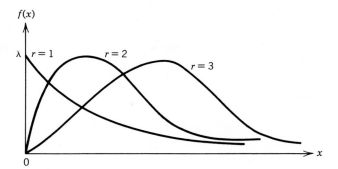

Figure 2-18
Gamma distributions for various *r* and λ constant.

where the parameters are $\lambda > 0$ and $r > 0$[1]. Usually, *r* is called the *shape* parameter and λ is called the *scale* parameter. The mean and variance of the gamma distribution are

$$\mu = \frac{r}{\lambda} \tag{2-33}$$

and

$$\sigma^2 = \frac{r}{\lambda^2} \tag{2-34}$$

respectively. Several gamma distributions are shown in Figure 2-18. Note that if $r = 1$, the gamma distribution reduces to the exponential distribution with parameter λ (Section 2-3.2). The gamma distribution can assume many different shapes, depending on the values chosen for *r* and λ. This makes it useful as a model for a wide variety of continuous random variables.

If the parameter *r* is an integer, then the gamma distribution is the sum of *r* independently and identically distributed exponential distributions, each with parameter λ. That is, if $x_1, x_2, \ldots, x_r$ are exponential with parameter λ and independent, then

$$y = x_1 + x_2 + \cdots + x_r$$

is distributed as gamma with parameters *r* and λ. There are a number of important applications of this result.

Example 2-8

Consider the system shown in Figure 2-19. This is called a *standby redundant system*, because while component 1 is on, component 2 is off, and when component 1 fails, the switch automatically turns component 2 on. If each component has a

---

[1] $\Gamma(r)$ in the denominator of (2-32) is the gamma function, defined as $\Gamma(r) = \int_0^\infty x^{r-1} e^{-x} \, dx$, $r > 0$. If *r* is a positive integer, then $\Gamma(r) = (r - 1)!$

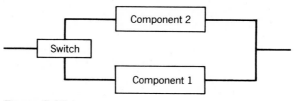

Figure 2-19
The standby redundant system for Example 2-8.

life described by an exponential distribution with $\lambda = 10^{-4}$ h, say, then the system life is gamma distributed with parameters $r = 2$ and $\lambda = 10^{-4}$. Thus, the mean time to failure is $\mu = r/\lambda = 2/10^{-4} = 2 \times 10^4$ h.

The cumulative gamma distribution is

$$F(a) = 1 - \int_a^\infty \frac{\lambda}{\Gamma(r)}(\lambda t)^{r-1}e^{-\lambda t}\, dt \tag{2-35}$$

If r is an integer, then (2-35) becomes

$$F(a) = 1 - \sum_{k=0}^{r-1} e^{-\lambda a}\frac{(\lambda a)^k}{k!} \tag{2-36}$$

Consequently, the cumulative gamma distribution can be evaluated as the sum of r Poisson terms with parameter λa. This result is not too surprising, if we consider the Poisson distribution as a model of the number of occurrences of some event in a fixed interval, and the gamma distribution as the model of the portion of the interval required to obtain a specific number of occurrences.

2-3.4 The Weibull Distribution

The Weibull distribution is defined as

$$f(x) = \frac{\beta}{\delta}\left(\frac{x-\gamma}{\delta}\right)^{\beta-1}\exp\left[-\left(\frac{x-\gamma}{\delta}\right)^{\beta}\right] \qquad x \geq \gamma \tag{2-37}$$

where $\gamma(-\infty < \gamma < \infty)$ is the *location* parameter, $\delta > 0$ is the *scale* parameter, and $\beta > 0$ is the *shape* parameter. The mean and variance of the Weibull distribution are

$$\mu = \gamma + \delta\Gamma\left(1 + \frac{1}{\beta}\right) \tag{2-38}$$

and

$$\sigma^2 = \delta^2\left[\Gamma\left(1 + \frac{2}{\beta}\right) - \Gamma\left(1 + \frac{1}{\beta}\right)^2\right] \tag{2-39}$$

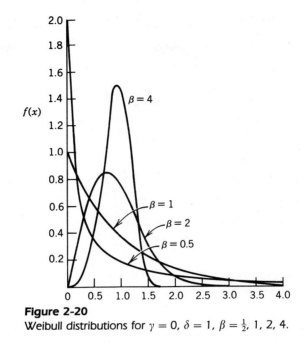

Figure 2-20
Weibull distributions for $\gamma = 0$, $\delta = 1$, $\beta = \frac{1}{2}$, 1, 2, 4.

The Weibull distribution is very flexible, and by appropriate selection of the parameters γ, δ, and β, the distribution can assume a wide variety of shapes. Several Weibull distributions are shown in Figure 2-20 for $\gamma = 0$, $\delta = 1$, and $\beta = \frac{1}{2}$, 1, 2, and 4. Notice that when $\gamma = 0$ and $\beta = 1$, the Weibull distribution reduces to the exponential distribution with mean $1/\delta$. The cumulative Weibull distribution is

$$F(a) = 1 - \exp\left[-\left(\frac{a - \gamma}{\delta}\right)^{\beta} \right] \qquad (2\text{-}40)$$

The Weibull distribution has been used extensively in reliability engineering as a model of time to failure in electrical and mechanical components and systems. Examples of situations where the Weibull has been used include electronic devices such as memory elements, mechanical components such as bearings, and structural elements in aircraft and automobiles.

Example 2-9

The time to failure for an electronic subassembly used in a word-processing work station is satisfactorily modeled by a Weibull distribution with $\gamma = 0$, $\beta = \frac{1}{2}$, and $\delta = 1000$. The mean time to failure is

$$\mu = \gamma + \delta\Gamma\left(1 + \frac{1}{\beta}\right)$$
$$= 0 + 1000\Gamma\left(1 + \frac{1}{(1/2)}\right)$$
$$= 1000\Gamma(3)$$
$$= 2000 \text{ h}$$

The fraction of subassemblies expected to survive $a = 4000$ h is

$$1 - F(a) = \exp\left[-\left(\frac{a}{\delta}\right)^{\beta} \right]$$

or

$$1 - F(4000) = \exp\left[-\left(\frac{4000}{1000}\right)^{1/2} \right]$$
$$= e^{-2}$$
$$= 0.1353$$

That is, all but about 13.53% of the subassemblies will fail by 4000 h.

2-4 SOME USEFUL APPROXIMATIONS

In certain quality-control problems, it is sometimes useful to approximate one probability distribution with another. This is particularly helpful in situations where the original distribution is difficult to manipulate analytically or is not well tabulated. In this section, we present three such approximations: (1) the binomial approximation to the hypergeometric, (2) the Poisson approximation to the binomial, and (3) the normal approximation to the binomial.

2-4.1 The Binomial Approximation to the Hypergeometric

Consider the hypergeometric distribution in Equation (2-8). If the ratio n/N (often called the *sampling fraction*) is small, say $n/N \leq 0.1$, then the binomial distribution with parameters $p = D/N$ and n is a good approximation to the hypergeometric. The approximation is better for small values of n/N.

This approximation is useful in the design of acceptance-sampling plans. Recall that the hypergeometric distribution is the appropriate model for the number of nonconforming items obtained in a random sample of n items from a lot of finite size N. Thus, if the sample size n is small relative to the lot size N, the binomial approximation may be employed, which usually simplifies the calculations considerably.

As an example, suppose that a production lot of 200 units contains five units that do not meet the specifications. The probability that a random sample of 10 units will contain no nonconforming items is, from Equation (2-8),

$$p(0) = \frac{\binom{5}{0}\binom{195}{10}}{\binom{200}{10}} = 0.7717$$

Note that since $n/N = 10/200 = 0.05$ is relatively small, we could use the binomial approximation with $p = D/N = 5/200 = 0.025$ and $n = 10$ to calculate

$$p(0) = \binom{5}{0}(0.025)^0(0.975)^{10} = 0.7763$$

2-4.2 The Poisson Approximation to the Binomial

It was noted in Section 2-2.3 that the Poisson distribution could be obtained as a limiting form of the binomial distribution for the case where p approaches zero and n approaches infinity with $\lambda = np$ constant. This implies that, for small p and large n, the Poisson distribution with $\lambda = np$ may be used to approximate the binomial distribution. The approximation is usually good for large n and if $p < 0.1$. The larger the value of n and the smaller the value of p, the better the approximation.

2-4.3 The Normal Approximation to the Binomial

In Section 2-2.2 we defined the binomial distribution as the sum of a sequence of n Bernoulli trials, each with probability of success p. If the number of trials n is large, then we may use the central limit theorem to justify the normal distribution with mean np and variance $np(1 - p)$ as an approximation to the binomial. That is,

$$P\{x = a\} = \binom{n}{a}p^a(1 - p)^{n-a}$$

$$= \frac{1}{\sqrt{2\pi np(1 - p)}} e^{-\frac{1}{2}[(a - np)^2/np(1 - p)]}$$

Since the binomial distribution is discrete and the normal distribution is continuous, it is common practice to use *continuity corrections* in the approximation, so that

$$P\{x = a\} \simeq \Phi\left(\frac{a + \frac{1}{2} - np}{\sqrt{np(1 - p)}}\right) - \Phi\left(\frac{a - \frac{1}{2} - np}{\sqrt{np(1 - p)}}\right)$$

where Φ denotes the standard normal cumulative distribution function. Other types of probability statements are evaluated similarly, such as

$$P\{a \leq x \leq b\} \simeq \Phi\left(\frac{b + \frac{1}{2} - np}{\sqrt{np(1 - p)}}\right) - \Phi\left(\frac{a - \frac{1}{2} - np}{\sqrt{np(1 - p)}}\right)$$

The normal approximation to the binomial is known to be satisfactory for p of approximately $\frac{1}{2}$ and $n > 10$. For other values of p, larger values of n are required. In general, the approximation is not adequate for $p < 1/(n + 1)$ or $p > n/(n + 1)$, or for values of the random variable outside an interval six standard deviations wide centered about the mean (i.e., the interval $np \pm 3\sqrt{np(1 - p)}$).

We may also use the normal approximation for the random variable $\hat{p} = x/n$, that is, the sample fraction defective of Section 2-2.2. The random variable $\hat{p}$ is

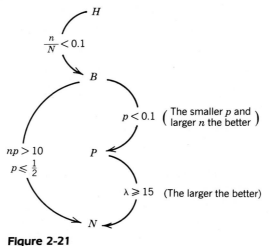

Figure 2-21
Approximations to probability distributions.

approximately normally distributed with mean p and variance $p(1 - p)/n$, so that

$$P\{u \le \hat{p} \le v\} = \Phi\left(\frac{v - p}{\sqrt{p(1 - p)/n}}\right) - \Phi\left(\frac{u - p}{\sqrt{p(1 - p)/n}}\right)$$

Since the normal will serve as an approximation to the binomial, and since the binomial and Poisson distributions are closely connected, it seems logical that the normal may serve to approximate the Poisson. This is indeed the case, and if the mean λ of the Poisson distribution exceeds 15 (or so), then the normal distribution with $\mu = \lambda$ and $\sigma^2 = \lambda$ is a satisfactory approximation.

2-4.4 Comments on Approximations

A summary of the approximations discussed above is presented in Figure 2-21. In this figure, H, B, P, and N represent the hypergeometric, binomial, Poisson, and normal distributions, respectively. The widespread availability of modern micro-computers and hand-held calculators has made reliance on these approximations unnecessary, but there are situations where they are useful, particularly in the application of the popular 3-sigma limit control charts.

2-5 Exercises

2-1 The fill volume of a soft drink beverage is being analyzed for variability. Ten bottles, randomly selected from the process, are measured, and the results are as follows (in fluid ounces): 10.05, 10.03, 10.02, 10.04, 10.05, 10.01, 10.02, 10.02, 10.03, 10.01.

a. Calculate the sample average.

b. Calculate the sample standard deviation.

2-2 The bore diameters of eight randomly selected bearings are shown below (in mm):

50.001	50.002
49.998	50.006
50.005	49.996
50.003	50.004

a. Calculate the sample average.

b. Calculate the sample standard deviation.

2-3 The time to failure in hours of an electronic component subjected to an accelerated life test is shown below. To accelerate the failure test, the units were tested at an elevated temperature.

127	124	121	118
125	123	136	131
131	120	140	125
124	119	137	133
129	128	125	141
121	133	124	125
142	137	128	140
151	124	129	132
160	142	130	129
125	123	122	126

a. Calculate the sample average and standard deviation.

b. Construct a histogram.

c. Construct a stem and leaf plot.

d. Find the sample median and the lower and upper quartiles.

2-4 The data shown below are chemical process yield readings on successive days (read across, then down). Construct a histogram for these data. Comment on the shape of the histogram. Does it resemble any of the distributions that we have discussed in this chapter?

94.1	87.3	94.1	92.4	84.6	85.4
93.2	84.1	92.1	90.6	83.6	86.6
90.6	90.1	96.4	89.1	85.4	91.7
91.4	95.2	88.2	88.8	89.7	87.5
88.2	86.1	86.4	86.4	87.6	84.2
86.1	94.3	85.0	85.1	85.1	85.1
95.1	93.2	84.9	84.0	89.6	90.5
90.0	86.7	87.3	93.7	90.0	95.6
92.4	83.0	89.6	87.7	90.1	88.3
87.3	95.3	90.3	90.6	94.3	84.1
86.6	94.1	93.1	89.4	97.3	83.7
91.2	97.8	94.6	88.6	96.8	82.9
86.1	93.1	96.3	84.1	94.4	87.3
90.4	86.4	94.7	82.6	96.1	86.4
89.1	87.6	91.1	83.1	98.0	84.5

2-5 Consider the chemical process yield data in Exercise 2-4. Calculate the sample average and standard deviation.

2-6 Consider the chemical process yield data in Exercise 2-4. Construct a stem and leaf plot for the data and compare it with the histogram from Exercise 2-4. Which display provides more information about the process?

2-7 Construct a box plot for the data in Exercise 2-1.

2-8 Construct a box plot for the data in Exercise 2-2.

2-9 Suppose that two fair dice are tossed and the random variable observed, say x, is the sum of the two up faces. Describe the sample space of this experiment, and determine the probability distribution of x.

2-10 Find the mean and variance of the random variable in Exercise 2-9.

2-11 Electronic calculators are given a final inspection following assembly. Three types of nonconformities may occur in the calculators, and they are classified as critical, major, and minor. Experience has indicated that the defects occur in the following manner:

Calculators with critical nonconformities	0.5%
Calculators with major nonconformities	1.0
Calculators with minor nonconformities	2.0
Calculators with both critical and major nonconformities	1.2
Calculators with both critical and minor nonconformities	0.8
Calculators with both major and minor nonconformities	0.5
Calculators with all three classes of nonconformities	0.1

a. Determine the percentage of production that conforms to requirements.

b. Calculators that have either critical nonconformities or critical and other types of nonconformities must be scrapped. What percentage of the production must be scrapped?

c. Calculators with either major or minor nonconformities (or both) may be reworked. What percentage of the production must be reworked?

2-12 The probability distribution of x is $f(x) = ke^{-x}$, $0 \leq x < \infty$. Find the appropriate value of k. Find the mean and variance of x.

2-13 The random variable x takes on the values 1, 2, or 3 with probabilities $(1 + 3k)/3$, $(1 + 2k)/3$, and $(0.5 + 5k)/3$, respectively.

a. Find the appropriate value of k.

b. Find the mean and variance of x.

c. Find the cumulative distribution function.

2-14 The probability distribution of the discrete random variable x is $p(x) = kr^x$, $0 < r < 1$. Find the appropriate value for k if x has range space 0, 1, ...

2-15 A manufacturer of electronic calculators offers a one-year warranty. If the calculator fails for any reason during this period, it is replaced. The time to failure is well modeled by the following probability distribution:

$$f(x) = 0.125e^{-0.125x} \qquad x > 0$$

a. What percentage of the calculators will fail within the warranty period?

b. The manufacturing cost of a calculator is $50, and the profit per sale is $25. What is the effect of warranty replacements on profit?

2-16 The net contents in ounces of a canned soft drink is a random variable with probability distribution

$$f(x) = \begin{cases} 4(x - 11.75) & 11.75 \le x \le 12.25 \\ 4(12.75 - x) & 12.25 \le x \le 12.75 \end{cases}$$

Find the probability that a can contains less than 12 oz of product.

2-17 A production process operates with 2% nonconforming output. Every hour a sample of 50 units of product is taken, and the number of nonconforming units counted. If one or more nonconforming units are found, the process is stopped and the quality-control technician must search for the cause of nonconforming production. Evaluate this decision rule.

2-18 A random sample of 100 units is drawn from a production process every half hour. The fraction of nonconforming product manufactured is 0.03. What is the probability that $\hat{p} \le 0.04$ if the fraction nonconforming really is 0.03?

2-19 A sample of 100 units is selected from a production process that is 2% nonconforming. What is the probability that $\hat{p}$ will exceed the true fraction nonconforming by k standard deviations, where $k = 1, 2$, and 3?

2-20 An electronic component for a laser range-finder is produced in lots of size $N = 25$. An acceptance testing procedure is used by the purchaser to protect against lots that contain too many nonconforming components. The procedure consists of selecting five components at random from the lot (without replacement) and testing them. If none of the components is nonconforming, the lot is accepted.

  a. If the lot contains three nonconforming components, what is the probability of lot acceptance?

  b. Calculate the desired probability in (a) using the binomial approximation. Is this approximation satisfactory? Why or why not?

  c. Suppose the lot size was $N = 150$. Would the binomial approximation be satisfactory in this case?

  d. Suppose that the purchaser will reject the lot with the decision rule of finding one or more nonconforming components in a sample of size n, and wants the lot to be rejected with probability at least 0.95 if the lot contains five or more nonconforming components. How large should the sample size n be?

2-21 A lot of size $N = 30$ contains five nonconforming units. What is the probability that a sample of five units selected at random contains exactly one nonconforming units? What is the probability that it contains one or more nonconformances?

2-22 A textbook has 500 pages on which typographical errors could occur. Suppose that there are exactly 10 such errors randomly located on those pages. Find the probability that a random selection of 50 pages will contain no errors. Find the probability that 50 randomly selected pages will contain at least two errors.

2-23 Surface-finish defects in a small electric appliance occur at random with a mean rate of 0.1 defects per unit. Find the probability that a randomly selected unit will contain at least one surface-finish defect.

2-24 Glass bottles are formed by pouring molten glass into a mold. The molten glass is prepared in a furnace lined with firebrick. As the firebrick wears, small pieces of brick are mixed into the molten glass and finally appear as defects (called "stones") in the bottle. If we can assume that stones occur randomly at the rate of 0.00001 per bottle, what is the probability that a bottle selected at random will contain at least one such defect?

2-25 The billing department of a major credit card company attempts to control errors (clerical, keypunch, etc.) on customers' bills. Suppose that errors occur according to a Poisson distribution with parameter $\lambda = 0.01$. What is the probability that a customer's bill selected at random will contain one error?

2-26 A production process operates in one of two states: the in-control state, in which most of the units produced conform to specifications, and an out-of-control state, in which most of the units produced are defective. The process will shift from the in-control to the out-of-control state at random. Every hour, a quality-control technician checks the process, and if it is in the out-of-control state, the technician detects this with probability p. Assume that when the process shifts out of control it does so immediately following a check by the inspector, and once a shift has occurred, the process cannot automatically correct itself. If t denotes the number of periods the process remains out of control following a shift before detection, find the probability distribution of t. Find the mean number of periods the process will remain in the out-of-control state.

2-27 An inspector is looking for nonconforming welds in a pipeline. The probability that any particular weld will be defective is 0.01. The inspector is determined to keep working until finding three defective welds. If the welds are located 100 ft apart, what is the probability that the inspector will have to walk 5000 ft? What is the probability that the inspector will have to walk more than 5000 ft?

2-28 The tensile strength of a metal part is normally distributed with mean 40 lb and standard deviation 8 lb. If 50,000 parts are produced, how many would fail to meet a minimum specification limit of 34-lb tensile strength? How many would have a tensile strength in excess of 48 lb?

2-29 The output voltage of a power supply is normally distributed with mean 12 V and standard deviation 0.05 V. If the upper and lower specifications for voltage are 11.90 V and 12.10 V, respectively, what is the probability that a power supply selected at random will conform to the specifications on voltage?

2-30 If x is normally distributed with mean μ and standard deviation four, and given that the probability that x is less than 32 is 0.0228, find the value of μ.

2-31 The life of an automotive battery is normally distributed with mean 900 days and standard deviation 35 days. What fraction of these batteries would be expected to survive beyond 1000 days?

2-32 A light bulb has a normally distributed light output with mean 5000 end foot-candles and standard deviation of 50 end foot-candles. Find a lower specification limit such that only 0.5% of the bulbs will not exceed this limit.

2-33 The specifications on an electronic component in a target-acquisition system are that its life must be between 5000 and 10,000 h. The life is normally distributed with mean 7500 h. The manufacturer realizes a price of $10 per unit produced; however, defective units must be replaced at a cost of $5 to the manufacturer. Two different manufacturing processes can be used, both of which have the same mean life. However, the standard deviation of life for process 1 is 1000 h, while for process 2 it is only 500 h. Production costs for process 2 are twice those for process 1. What value of production costs will determine the selection between processes 1 and 2?

2-34 A quality characteristic of a product is normally distributed with mean μ and standard deviation one. Specifications on the characteristic are $6 \le x \le 8$. A unit that falls within specifications on this quality characteristic results in a profit of C_0. However, if $x < 6$, the profit is $-C_1$, while if $x > 8$, the profit is $-C_2$. Find the value of μ that maximizes the expected profit.

Chapter 3

Inferences About
Process Quality

In the previous chapter we discussed the use of probability distributions in modeling or describing the output of a process. In all the examples presented we assumed that the parameters of the probability distribution, and hence, the parameters of the process, were known. This is usually a very unrealistic assumption. For example, in using the binomial distribution to model the number of nonconforming units found in sampling from a production process we assumed that the parameter p of the binomial distribution was known. The physical interpretation of p is that it is the true fraction of nonconforming units produced by the process. It is impossible to know this exactly in a real production process. Furthermore, if we did know the true value of p and it was relatively constant over time, we could argue that formal quality-control procedures were unnecessary, provided p was "acceptably" small.

In general, the parameters of a process are unknown; furthermore, they can usually change over time. Therefore, we need to develop procedures to estimate the parameters of probability distributions and solve other inference or decision-oriented problems relative to them. The standard statistical techniques of parameter estimation and hypothesis testing are useful in this respect. These techniques are the underlying basis for much of the methodology of statistical quality control. In this chapter we present some of the elementary results of statistical inference, indicating its usefulness in quality-improvement problems.

3-1 STATISTICS AND SAMPLING DISTRIBUTIONS

The objective of statistical inference is to draw conclusions or make decisions about a population based on a sample selected from the population. Frequently, we will assume that *random samples* are used in the analysis. The word "random" is often applied to any method of sample selection that lacks systematic direction. We will define a sample, say $x_1, x_2, \ldots, x_n$, as a *random sample* of size n if it is selected so that the observations $\{x_i\}$ are independently and identically distributed. This definition is suitable for random samples drawn from infinite populations or from finite populations where sampling is performed *with replacement*. In sampling *without replacement* from a finite population of N items we say that a sample of n items is a random sample if each of the $\binom{N}{n}$ possible samples has an equal probability of being chosen.

While most of the methods we will study assume that random sampling has been used, there are several other sampling strategies that are occasionally useful in quality control. Care must be exercised to use a method of analysis that is consistent with the sampling design; inference techniques intended for random samples can lead to serious errors when applied to data obtained from other sampling techniques.

Statistical inference uses quantities computed from the observations in the sample. A *statistic* is defined as any function of the sample data that does not contain unknown parameters. For example, let $x_1, x_2, \ldots, x_n$ represent the observations in a sample. Then the sample mean

$$\bar{x} = \frac{\sum_{i=1}^{n} x_i}{n} \tag{3-1}$$

the sample variance

$$S^2 = \frac{\sum_{i=1}^{n} (x_i - \bar{x})^2}{n - 1} \tag{3-2}$$

and the sample standard deviation

$$S = \sqrt{\frac{\sum_{i=1}^{n} (x_i - \bar{x})^2}{n - 1}} \tag{3-3}$$

are statistics. The statistics $\bar{x}$ and S (or S^2) measure the central tendency and dispersion, respectively, of the sample.

If we know the probability distribution of the population from which the sample was taken, we can often determine the probability distribution of various statistics computed from the sample data. The probability distribution of a statistic is called a *sampling distribution*. We now present the sampling distributions associated with three common sampling situations.

3-1.1 Sampling from a Normal Distribution

Suppose that x is a normally distributed random variable with mean μ and variance σ^2. If $x_1, x_2, \ldots, x_n$ is a random sample of size n from this process, then the distribution of the sample mean $\bar{x}$ is $N(\mu, \sigma^2/n)$. This follows directly from the results on the distribution of linear combinations of normal random variables in Section 2-3.1.

This property of the sample mean is not restricted exclusively to the case of sampling from normal populations. Note that we may write

$$\left(\frac{\bar{x} - \mu}{\sigma}\right)\sqrt{n} = \frac{\sum_{i=1}^{n} x_i - n\mu}{\sigma\sqrt{n}}$$

From the central limit theorem we know that, regardless of the distribution of the population, the distribution of $\sum_{i=1}^{n} x_i$ is approximately normal with mean $n\mu$ and variance $n\sigma^2$. Therefore, regardless of the distribution of the population, the sampling distribution of the sample mean is approximately

$$\bar{x} \sim N\left(\mu, \frac{\sigma^2}{n}\right)$$

An important sampling distribution defined in terms of the normal distribution is the chi-square or χ^2 distribution. If $x_1, x_2, \ldots, x_n$ are normally and independently distributed random variables with mean zero and variance one, then the random variable

$$\chi_n^2 = x_1^2 + x_2^2 + \cdots + x_n^2$$

is distributed as chi-square with n degrees of freedom. The probability distribution of χ^2 is

$$f(\chi^2) = \frac{1}{2^{n/2}\Gamma\left(\frac{n}{2}\right)} (\chi^2)^{(n/2) - 1} e^{-\chi^2/2} \qquad \chi^2 > 0 \qquad (3\text{-}4)$$

Several chi-square distributions are shown in Figure 3-1. The distribution is skewed with mean $\mu = n$ and variance $\sigma^2 = 2n$. A table of the percentage points of the chi-square distribution is given in Appendix Table III.

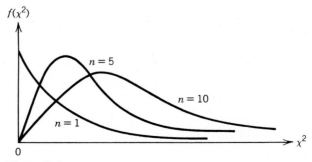

Figure 3-1
Several χ^2 distributions.

To illustrate the use of the chi-square distribution, suppose that $x_1, x_2, \ldots, x_n$ is a random sample from an $N(\mu, \sigma^2)$ distribution. Then the random variable

$$\frac{\sum_{i=1}^{n} (x_i - \bar{x})^2}{\sigma^2} \sim \chi_{n-1}^2 \tag{3-5}$$

However, using Equation (3-2), which defines the sample variance, we may rewrite (3-5) as

$$\frac{(n-1)S^2}{\sigma^2} \sim \chi_{n-1}^2$$

That is, the sampling distribution of $(n-1)S^2/\sigma^2$ is χ_{n-1}^2 when sampling from a normal distribution.

Another useful sampling distribution is the t distribution. If x and χ_k^2 are independent standard normal and chi-square random variables, respectively, then the random variable

$$t_k = \frac{x}{\sqrt{\chi_k^2/k}} \tag{3-6}$$

is distributed as t with k degrees of freedom, denoted t_k. The probability distribution of t is

$$f(t) = \frac{\Gamma[(k+1)/2]}{\sqrt{k\pi}\,\Gamma(k/2)} \left(\frac{t^2}{k} + 1\right)^{-(k+1)/2} \qquad -\infty < t < \infty \tag{3-7}$$

and the mean and variance of t are $\mu = 0$ and $\sigma^2 = k/(k-2)$ for $k > 2$, respectively. The degrees of freedom for t are the degrees of freedom associated with the chi-square random variable in the denominator of (3-6). Several t distributions are shown in Figure 3-2. Notice that if $k = \infty$, the t distribution reduces to the standard normal distribution. A table of percentage points of the t distribution is given in Appendix Table IV.

As an example of a random variable that is distributed as t, suppose that $x_1, x_2, \ldots, x_n$ is a random sample from the $N(\mu, \sigma^2)$ distribution. If $\bar{x}$ and S^2 are

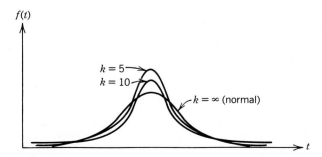

Figure 3-2
Several t distributions.

computed from this sample, then

$$\frac{\bar{x} - \mu}{S/\sqrt{n}} = \frac{\dfrac{\bar{x} - \mu}{\sigma/\sqrt{n}}}{S/\sigma} = \frac{N(0, 1)}{\sqrt{\chi_{n-1}^2/(n - 1)}}$$

using the fact that $(n - 1)S^2/\sigma^2 \sim \chi_{n-1}^2$. Consequently, the random variable

$$\frac{\bar{x} - \mu}{S/\sqrt{n}} \sim t_{n-1} \tag{3-8}$$

The last sampling distribution based on the normal process which we will consider is the F distribution. If χ_u^2 and χ_v^2 are two independent chi-square random variables with u and v degrees of freedom, respectively, then the ratio

$$F_{u,v} = \frac{\chi_u^2/u}{\chi_v^2/v} \tag{3-9}$$

is distributed as F with u numerator degrees of freedom and v denominator degrees of freedom. The density function of F is

$$g(f) = \frac{\Gamma\left(\dfrac{u + v}{2}\right)\left(\dfrac{u}{v}\right)^{u/2}}{\Gamma\left(\dfrac{u}{2}\right)\Gamma\left(\dfrac{v}{2}\right)} \frac{f^{(u/2) - 1}}{\left[\left(\dfrac{u}{2}\right)f + 1\right]^{(u+v)/2}} \qquad 0 < f < \infty \tag{3-10}$$

Several F distributions are shown in Figure 3-3. A table of percentage points of the F distribution is given in Appendix Table V.

As an example of a random variable that is distributed as F, suppose we have two independent normal processes, say $x_1 \sim N(\mu_1, \sigma_1^2)$, and $x_2 \sim N(\mu_2, \sigma_2^2)$. Let $x_{11}, x_{12}, \ldots, x_{1n_1}$ be a random sample of n_1 observations from the first normal process and $x_{21}, x_{22}, \ldots, x_{2n_2}$ be a random sample of size n_2 from the second. If S_1^2 and S_2^2 are the sample variances, then the ratio

$$\frac{S_1^2/\sigma_1^2}{S_2^2/\sigma_2^2} \sim F_{n_1 - 1, n_2 - 1}$$

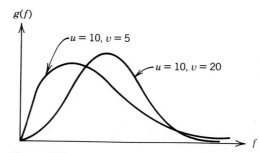

Figure 3-3
Several F distributions.

This follows directly from the sampling distribution of S^2 discussed previously. The F distribution will be used in making inferences about the variances of two normal distributions.

3-1.2 Sampling from a Bernoulli Distribution

In this section, we discuss the sampling distributions of statistics associated with the Bernoulli distribution. The random variable x with probability function

$$p(x) = \begin{cases} p & x = 1 \\ (1 - p) = q & x = 0 \end{cases}$$

is called a Bernoulli random variable. That is, x takes on the value 1 with probability p and the value 0 with probability $1 - p = q$. A realization of this random variable is often called a Bernoulli trial. The sequence of Bernoulli trials $x_1, x_2, \ldots,$ is a Bernoulli process. The outcome $x = 1$ is often called "success," and the outcome $x = 0$ is often called "failure."

Suppose that a random sample of n observations, say $x_1, x_2, \ldots, x_n$, is taken from a Bernoulli process with constant probability of success p. Then the sum of the sample observations

$$x = x_1 + x_2 + \cdots + x_n \tag{3-11}$$

has a binomial distribution with parameters n and p. Furthermore, since each x_i is either 0 or 1, the sample mean

$$\bar{x} = \frac{1}{n} \sum_{i=1}^{n} x_i \tag{3-12}$$

is a discrete random variable with range space $\{0, 1/n, 2/n, \ldots, (n - 1)/n, 1\}$. The distribution of $\bar{x}$ can be obtained from the binomial since

$$P\{\bar{x} \le a\} = P\{x \le an\} = \sum_{k=0}^{[an]} \binom{n}{k} p^k (1 - p)^{n-k}$$

where $[an]$ is the largest integer less than or equal to an. The mean and variance of $\bar{x}$ are

$$\mu_{\bar{x}} = p$$

and

$$\sigma_{\bar{x}}^2 = \frac{p(1 - p)}{n}$$

respectively. This same result was given previously in Section 2-2.2, where the random variable $\hat{p}$ (often called the sample fraction nonconforming) was introduced.

3-1.3 Sampling from a Poisson Distribution

The Poisson distribution was introduced in Section 2-2.3. Consider a random sample of size n from a Poisson distribution with parameter λ, say $x_1, x_2, \ldots, x_n$. The distribution of the sample sum

$$x = x_1 + x_2 + \cdots + x_n \tag{3-13}$$

is also Poisson with parameter $n\lambda$. More generally, the sum of n independent Poisson random variables is distributed Poisson with parameter equal to the sum of the individual Poissson parameters.

Now consider the distribution of the sample mean

$$\bar{x} = \frac{1}{n} \sum_{i=1}^{n} x_i \tag{3-14}$$

This is a discrete random variable that takes on the values $\{0, 1/n, 2/n, \ldots,\}$, and with probability distribution found from

$$P\{\bar{x} \le a\} = P\{x \le an\} = \sum_{k=0}^{[an]} \frac{e^{-n\lambda}(n\lambda)^k}{k!} \tag{3-15}$$

where $[an]$ is the largest integer less than or equal to an. The mean and variance of $\bar{x}$ are

$$\bar{x} = \lambda$$

and

$$\sigma_{\bar{x}}^2 = \frac{\lambda}{n}$$

respectively.

Sometimes more general linear combinations of Poisson random variables are used in quality-control work. For example, consider the linear combination

$$L = a_1 x_1 + a_2 x_2 + \cdots + a_m x_m$$
$$= \sum_{i=1}^{m} a_i x_i \tag{3-16}$$

where the $\{x_i\}$ are independent Poisson random variables each having parameter $\{\lambda_i\}$, respectively, and the $\{a_i\}$ are constants. This type of function occurs in situations where a unit of product can have m different types of defects or nonconformities (each modeled with a Poisson distribution with parameter λ_i) and the function used for quality management purposes is a linear combination of the number of observed nonconformities of each type. The constants $\{a_i\}$ in (3-16) might be chosen to weight some types of nonconformities more heavily than others. For example, functional defects on a unit would receive heavier weight than appearance flaws. These schemes are sometimes called *demerit* procedures (see Section 5-3.3). In general, the distribution of L is not Poisson unless all $a_i = 1$ in (3-16); that is, sums of independent Poisson random variables are Poisson distributed, but more general linear combinations are not.

3-2 ESTIMATION OF PROCESS PARAMETERS

A random variable is characterized or described by its probability distribution. This distribution is described by its *parameters*. For example, the mean μ and variance σ^2 of the normal distribution [Equation (2-21)] are its parameters, while λ is the parameter of the Poisson distribution [Equation (2-15)]. In statistical quality control, the probability distribution is used to describe or model some quality characteristic, such as a critical dimension of a product or the fraction defective of the manufacturing process. Therefore, we are interested in making inferences about the parameters of probability distributions. Since the parameters are generally unknown, we require procedures to estimate them from sample data.

We may define an estimator of an unknown parameter as a statistic that corresponds to the parameter. A particular numerical value of an estimator, computed from sample data, is called an *estimate*. A *point estimator* is a statistic that produces a single numerical value as the estimate of the unknown parameter. An *interval estimator* is a random interval in which the true value of the parameter falls with some level of probability. These random intervals are usually called *confidence intervals*.

3-2.1 Point Estimation

Consider the random variable x with probability distribution $f(x)$. Suppose that the mean μ and variance σ^2 of this distribution are both unknown. If a random sample of n observations is taken, then the *sample* mean $\bar{x}$ and *sample* variance S^2 are point estimators of the *population* mean μ and *population* variance σ^2, respectively. For example, suppose we wished to obtain point estimates of the mean and variance of the inside diameter of a bearing. We could measure the inside diameters of a random sample of $n = 20$ bearings (say). Then the sample mean and sample variance could be computed. If this yields $\bar{x} = 1.495$ and $S^2 = 0.001$, then the point estimate of μ is $\bar{x} = 1.495$ and the point estimate of σ^2 is $S^2 = 0.001$.

The mean and variance of a distribution are not necessarily the parameters of the distribution. For example, the parameter of the Poisson distribution is λ, while its mean and variance are $\mu = \lambda$ and $\sigma^2 = \lambda$ (*both* the mean *and* variance are λ), and the parameters of the binomial distribution are n and p, while its mean and variance are $\mu = np$ and $\sigma^2 = np(1 - p)$, respectively. We may show that a good point estimator of the parameter λ of a Poisson distribution is

$$\hat{\lambda} = \frac{1}{n} \sum_{i=1}^{n} x_i = \bar{x}$$

and that a good point estimator of the parameter p of a binomial distribution is

$$\hat{p} = \frac{1}{n} \sum_{i=1}^{n} x_i = \bar{x}$$

for fixed n. In the binomial distribution the observations in the random sample $\{x_i\}$ are either 1 or 0, corresponding to "success" and "failure," respectively.

A number of important properties are required of good point estimators. Two of the most important of these properties are the following:

1. The point estimator should be *unbiased*. That is, the expected value of the point estimator should be the parameter being estimated.

2. The point estimator should have *minimum variance*. Any point estimator is a random variable. Thus, a minimum variance point estimator should have a variance that is smaller than the variance of any other point estimator of that parameter.

The *sample* mean and variance $\bar{x}$ and S^2 are unbiased estimators of the *population* mean and variance μ and σ^2, respectively. One should note, however, that the sample standard deviation S is *not* an unbiased estimator of the population standard deviation σ.

In this section we have given only a brief overview of some of the more useful results on point estimation. More complete descriptions of point estimators and technical discussions of their properties are widely available. For example, see Hines and Montgomery (1990).

3-2.2 Interval Estimation

An interval estimate of a parameter is the interval between two statistics that includes the true value of the parameter with some probability. For example, to construct an interval estimator of the mean μ, we must find two statistics L and U such that

$$P\{L \le \mu \le U\} = 1 - \alpha \tag{3-17}$$

The resulting interval

$$L \le \mu \le U \tag{3-18}$$

is called a $100(1 - \alpha)\%$ confidence interval for the unknown mean μ. L and U are called the lower and upper confidence limits, respectively, and $1 - \alpha$ is called the confidence coefficient. Sometimes the half-interval width $U - \mu$ or $\mu - L$ is called the *accuracy* of the confidence interval. The interpretation of a confidence interval is that if a large number of such intervals are constructed, each resulting from a random sample, then $100(1 - \alpha)\%$ of these intervals will contain the true value of μ. Thus, confidence intervals have a frequency interpretation.

The confidence interval (3-18) might be more properly called a *two-sided* confidence interval, as it specifies both a lower and an upper limit on μ. Sometimes in quality-control applications, a *one-sided* confidence interval might be more appropriate. A one-sided lower $100(1 - \alpha)\%$ confidence interval on μ would be given by the interval

$$L \leq \mu \tag{3-19}$$

where L, the lower confidence limit, is chosen so that

$$P\{L \leq \mu\} = 1 - \alpha \tag{3-20}$$

A one-sided upper $100(1 - \alpha)\%$ confidence interval on μ would be the interval

$$\mu \leq U \tag{3-21}$$

where U, the upper confidence limit, is chosen so that

$$P\{\mu \leq U\} = 1 - \alpha \tag{3-22}$$

We will now summarize some of the more useful results on confidence intervals. For a more detailed development and discussion of these procedures, refer to Bowker and Lieberman (1972) or Hines and Montgomery (1990).

Confidence Interval on the Mean with Variance Known

Consider the random variable x, with unknown mean μ and known variance σ^2. Suppose a random sample of n observations is taken, say $x_1, x_2, \ldots, x_n$, and $\bar{x}$ is computed. Then the $100(1 - \alpha)\%$ two-sided confidence interval on μ is

$$\bar{x} - Z_{\alpha/2} \frac{\sigma}{\sqrt{n}} \leq \mu \leq \bar{x} + Z_{\alpha/2} \frac{\sigma}{\sqrt{n}} \tag{3-23}$$

where $Z_{\alpha/2}$ is the percentage point of the $N(0, 1)$ distribution such that $P\{z \geq Z_{\alpha/2}\} = \alpha/2$.

Note that $\bar{x}$ is distributed approximately $N(\mu, \sigma^2/n)$ regardless of the distribution of x, per the central limit theorem. Consequently, (3-23) is an approximate $100(1 - \alpha)\%$ confidence interval for μ regardless of the distribution of x. If x is distributed $N(\mu, \sigma^2)$, then (3-23) is an exact $100(1 - \alpha)\%$ confidence interval. Furthermore, a $100(1 - \alpha)\%$ upper confidence interval on μ is

$$\mu \leq \bar{x} + \frac{Z_\alpha \sigma}{\sqrt{n}} \tag{3-24}$$

while a $100(1 - \alpha)\%$ lower confidence interval on μ is

$$\bar{x} - \frac{Z_\alpha \sigma}{\sqrt{n}} \leq \mu \tag{3-25}$$

Confidence Interval on the Mean of a Normal Distribution with Variance Unknown

Suppose that x is a normal random variable with unknown mean μ and unknown variance σ^2. From a random sample of n observations the sample mean $\bar{x}$ and sample variance S^2 are computed. Then a $100(1 - \alpha)\%$ two-sided confidence interval on the true mean is

$$\bar{x} - t_{\alpha/2, n-1} \frac{S}{\sqrt{n}} \leq \mu \leq \bar{x} + t_{\alpha/2, n-1} \frac{S}{\sqrt{n}} \tag{3-26}$$

where $t_{\alpha/2, n-1}$ denotes the percentage point of the t distribution with $n - 1$ degrees of freedom such that $P\{t_{n-1} \geq t_{\alpha/2, n-1}\} = \alpha/2$. The corresponding upper and lower $100(1 - \alpha)\%$ confidence intervals are

$$\mu \leq \bar{x} + t_{\alpha, n-1} \frac{S}{\sqrt{n}} \tag{3-27}$$

and

$$\bar{x} - t_{\alpha, n-1} \frac{S}{\sqrt{n}} \leq \mu \tag{3-28}$$

respectively.

Example 3-1

The mean tensile strength of a synthetic fiber is an important quality characteristic that is of interest to the manufacturer, who would like to find a 95% confidence interval estimate of the mean. From past experience, the manufacturer is willing to assume that tensile strength is approximately normally distributed; however, both the mean tensile strength and standard deviation of tensile strength are unknown. A random sample of 16 fiber specimens is selected, and their tensile strengths are determined. The sample data are shown in Table 3-1.

Table 3-1
Tensile strength measurements on
synthetic fiber

Specimen	Strength (psi)
1	48.89
2	52.07
3	49.29
4	51.66
5	52.16
6	49.72
7	48.00
8	49.96
9	49.20
10	48.10
11	47.90
12	46.94
13	51.76
14	50.75
15	49.86
16	51.57

We may calculate the sample mean and sample standard deviation of the tensile strength data as

$$\bar{x} = \frac{1}{n} \sum_{i=1}^{n} x_i = \frac{1}{16} (797.83) = 49.86 \text{ psi}$$

and

$$S = \sqrt{\frac{\sum_{i=1}^{n} x_i^2 - \frac{\left(\sum_{i=1}^{n} x_i\right)^2}{n}}{n - 1}}$$

$$= \sqrt{\frac{39,824.69 - \frac{(797.83)^2}{16}}{15}}$$

$$= \sqrt{2.76} = 1.66 \text{ psi}$$

Since $t_{0.025,15} = 2.132$, we find the 95% two-sided confidence interval on μ from (3-26) as

$$49.86 - (2.132)1.66/\sqrt{16} \le \mu \le 49.86 + (2.132)1.66/\sqrt{16}$$

or

$$48.98 \le \mu \le 50.74.$$

Another way to express this result is that our estimate of the mean tensile strength is 49.86 ± 0.88 psi with 95% confidence.

The manufacturer may only be concerned about tensile strengths that are too low and may therefore feel that a one-sided confidence interval is more appropriate. The 95% lower confidence interval on mean strength is found from (3-28), using $t_{0.05,15} = 1.753$, as

$$49.86 - \frac{(1.753)1.66}{\sqrt{16}} \le \mu$$

or

$$49.13 \le \mu$$

Confidence Interval on the Variance of a Normal Distribution

Suppose that x is a normal random variable with unknown mean μ and unknown variance σ^2. Let the sample variance S^2 be computed from a random sample of n observations. Then a $100(1 - \alpha)\%$ two-sided confidence interval on the variance is

$$\frac{(n-1)S^2}{\chi^2_{\alpha/2, n-1}} \le \sigma^2 \le \frac{(n-1)S^2}{\chi^2_{1-\alpha/2, n-1}} \tag{3-29}$$

where $\chi^2_{\alpha/2, n-1}$ denotes the percentage point of the chi-square distribution such that $P\{\chi^2_{n-1} \geq \chi^2_{\alpha/2, n-1}\} = \alpha/2$. If one-sided confidence intervals are desired, they may be obtained from (3-29) by using only the upper (or lower) limit with the probability level increased from $\alpha/2$ to α. That is, the upper and lower $100(1 - \alpha)\%$ confidence intervals are

$$\sigma^2 \leq \frac{(n-1)S^2}{\chi^2_{1-\alpha, n-1}} \tag{3-30}$$

and

$$\frac{(n-1)S^2}{\chi^2_{\alpha, n-1}} \leq \sigma^2 \tag{3-31}$$

respectively.

We may use the data from Example 3-1 to demonstrate the computation of a 95% (say) confidence interval on σ^2. Note that for the data in Table 3-1, we have $S^2 = 2.76$. From Appendix Table III, we find that $\chi^2_{0.025, 15} = 27.49$ and $\chi^2_{0.975, 15} = 6.27$. Therefore, from (3-29) we find the 95% two-sided confidence interval on σ^2 as

$$\frac{(15)2.76}{27.49} \leq \sigma^2 \leq \frac{(15)2.76}{6.27}$$

which reduces to

$$1.51 \leq \sigma^2 \leq 6.60$$

Confidence Interval on the Difference in Two Means, Variances Known

Consider the two random variables x_1 with mean μ_1 and variance σ^2_1, and x_2 with mean μ_2 and variance σ^2_2. We assume that μ_1 and μ_2 are unknown, while σ^2_1 and σ^2_2 are known. A $100(1 - \alpha)\%$ confidence interval is desired on the true *difference* in these means, say $\mu_1 - \mu_2$. Let $x_{11}, x_{12}, \ldots, x_{1n_1}$ be a random sample of n_1 observations from the population denoted by x_1, and $x_{21}, x_{22}, \ldots, x_{2n_2}$ be a random sample of n_2 observations from the population denoted by x_2. If $\bar{x}_1$ and $\bar{x}_2$ denote the sample means, then the $100(1 - \alpha)\%$ two-sided confidence interval on the difference in means is

$$\bar{x}_1 - \bar{x}_2 - Z_{\alpha/2}\sqrt{\frac{\sigma^2_1}{n_1} + \frac{\sigma^2_2}{n_2}} \leq \mu_1 - \mu_2 \leq \bar{x}_1 - \bar{x}_2 + Z_{\alpha/2}\sqrt{\frac{\sigma^2_1}{n_1} + \frac{\sigma^2_2}{n_2}} \tag{3-32}$$

while the corresponding upper and lower one-sided confidence intervals are

$$\mu_1 - \mu_2 \leq \bar{x}_1 - \bar{x}_2 + Z_{\alpha}\sqrt{\frac{\sigma^2_1}{n_1} + \frac{\sigma^2_2}{n_2}} \tag{3-33}$$

and

$$\bar{x}_1 - \bar{x}_2 - Z_\alpha \sqrt{\frac{\sigma_1^2}{n_1} + \frac{\sigma_2^2}{n_2}} \leq \mu_1 - \mu_2 \tag{3-34}$$

respectively.

Confidence Interval on the Difference in Means of Two Normal Distributions, Variance Unknown

Suppose that there are two normal random variables, say $x_1 \sim N(\mu_1, \sigma_1^2)$ and $x_2 \sim N(\mu_2, \sigma_2^2)$. Both the means μ_1 and μ_2, and the variances σ_1^2 and σ_2^2 are unknown. However, it is reasonable to assume that the two variances are equal; that is, $\sigma_1^2 = \sigma_2^2 = \sigma^2$. We wish to find a $100(1 - \alpha)\%$ confidence interval on the difference in means $\mu_1 - \mu_2$.

Suppose that random samples of sizes n_1 and n_2 have been taken from populations 1 and 2, respectively and that the sample means $\bar{x}_1$ and $\bar{x}_2$ and sample variances S_1^2 and S_2^2 have been computed. A combined (or "pooled") estimate of the common variance is

$$S_p^2 = \frac{(n_1 - 1)S_1^2 + (n_2 - 1)S_2^2}{n_1 + n_2 - 2} \tag{3-35}$$

The $100(1 - \alpha)\%$ two-sided confidence interval on $\mu_1 - \mu_2$ is

$$\bar{x}_1 - \bar{x}_2 - t_{\alpha/2, n_1 + n_2 - 2} S_p \sqrt{\frac{1}{n_1} + \frac{1}{n_2}}$$
$$\leq \mu_1 - \mu_2 \leq \bar{x}_1 - \bar{x}_2 + t_{\alpha/2, n_1 + n_2 - 2} S_p \sqrt{\frac{1}{n_1} + \frac{1}{n_2}} \tag{3-36}$$

The corresponding upper and lower one-sided confidence intervals are

$$\mu_1 - \mu_2 \leq \bar{x}_1 - \bar{x}_2 + t_{\alpha, n_1 + n_2 - 2} S_p \sqrt{\frac{1}{n_1} + \frac{1}{n_2}} \tag{3-37}$$

and

$$\bar{x}_1 - \bar{x}_2 - t_{\alpha, n_1 + n_2 - 2} S_p \sqrt{\frac{1}{n_1} + \frac{1}{n_2}} \leq \mu_1 - \mu_2 \tag{3-38}$$

Example 3-2

A petroleum company will soon have to switch a large proportion of its production from a formulation containing tetra-ethyl lead to a lead-free formulation. An important quality characteristic of gasoline is the road octane number. If gasoline with a road octane number that is too low for the engine compression is used, excessive knocking will result. The company has formulated the lead-free product so that its road octane number should be identical to that of the older, lead-containing product. An experiment is performed in which 10 observations on road octane

Table 3-2
Road octance numbers for two gasoline
formulations

Formulation 1 (contains tetra-ethyl lead)	Formulation 2 (contains no lead)
89.5	89.5
90.0	91.5
91.0	91.0
91.5	89.0
92.5	91.5
91.0	92.0
89.0	92.0
89.5	90.5
91.0	90.0
92.0	91.0

number are obtained for each product formulation. These data are given in Table 3-2. We wish to construct a 99% confidence interval on the true mean difference in road octane number.

For formulation 1 (containing lead), we find $\bar{x}_1 = 90.70$ and $S_1^2 = 1.34$, and for formulation 2 (no lead), we find $\bar{x}_2 = 90.80$ and $S_2^2 = 1.07$. Assuming that the variances of the road octane numbers are equal, we may find an estimate of the common variance from (3-35) as

$$S_p^2 = \frac{(n_1 - 1)S_1^2 + (n_2 - 1)S_2^2}{n_1 + n_2 - 2}$$

$$= \frac{(9)1.34 + (9)1.07}{10 + 10 - 2}$$

$$= 1.21$$

The 99% two-sided confidence interval on $\mu_1 - \mu_2$ is computed using Equation (3-36) as follows:

$$\bar{x}_1 - \bar{x}_2 - t_{0.005,18}S_p\sqrt{\frac{1}{n_1} + \frac{1}{n_2}} \leq \mu_1 - \mu_2 \leq \bar{x}_1 - \bar{x}_2 + t_{0.005,18}S_p\sqrt{\frac{1}{n_1} + \frac{1}{n_2}}$$

$$90.70 - 90.80 - (2.878)1.10\sqrt{\frac{1}{10} + \frac{1}{10}} \leq \mu_1 - \mu_2$$

$$\leq 90.70 - 90.80 + (2.878)1.10\sqrt{\frac{1}{10} + \frac{1}{10}}$$

$$-1.51 \leq \mu_1 - \mu_2 \leq 1.31$$

Note that the confidence interval on the mean difference in road octane numbers includes zero. Thus, we have found no statistical evidence that the two gasoline formulations differ in their road octane numbers.

While we have concentrated on the case where $\sigma_1^2 = \sigma_2^2$, there are many practical problems in which we caannot reasonably make this assumption. If the assumption $\sigma_1^2 \neq \sigma_2^2$ is appropriate, then a confidence interval on $\mu_1 - \mu_2$ can be developed from the procedure given in Section 3-3.2.

Confidence Interval on the Ratio of the Variances of Two Normal Distributions

Suppose that $x_1 \sim N(\mu_1, \sigma_1^2)$ and $x_2 \sim N(\mu_2, \sigma_2^2)$, where μ_1, σ_1^2, μ_2, and σ_2^2 are unknown, and we wish to construct a $100(1 - \alpha)\%$ confidence interval on σ_1^2/σ_2^2. If S_1^2 and S_2^2 are the sample variances, computed from random samples of n_1 and n_2 observations, respectively, then the $100(1 - \alpha)\%$ two-sided confidence interval is

$$\frac{S_1^2}{S_2^2} F_{1-\alpha/2, n_2-1, n_1-1} \leq \frac{\sigma_1^2}{\sigma_2^2} \leq \frac{S_1^2}{S_2^2} F_{\alpha/2, n_2-1, n_1-1} \tag{3-39}$$

where $F_{\alpha/2, u, v}$ is the percentage point of the F distribution with u and v degrees of freedom such that $P\{F_{u,v} \geq F_{\alpha/2, u, v}\} = \alpha/2$. The corresponding upper and lower confidence intervals are

$$\frac{\sigma_1^2}{\sigma_2^2} \leq \frac{S_1^2}{S_2^2} F_{\alpha/2, n_2-1, n_1-1} \tag{3-40}$$

and

$$\frac{S_1^2}{S_2^2} F_{1-\alpha/2, n_2-1, n_1-1} \leq \frac{\sigma_1^2}{\sigma_2^2} \tag{3-41}$$

respectively.[1]

To illustrate the procedure, consider the data in Example 3-2. We wish to construct a 95% two-sided confidence interval on σ_1^2/σ_2^2. Using $S_1^2 = 1.34$ and $S_2^2 = 1.07$, $n_1 = n_2 = 10$, $F_{0.025,9,9} = 4.03$ from Appendix Table V, and $F_{0.975,9,9} = 0.248$ we find from (3-39) that

$$\frac{1.34}{1.07} 0.248 \leq \frac{\sigma_1^2}{\sigma_2^2} \leq \frac{1.34}{1.07} 4.03$$

or

$$0.31 \leq \frac{\sigma_1^2}{\sigma_2^2} \leq 5.05$$

Note that this confidence interval includes unity, implying that the data do not dispute the claim that $\sigma_1^2 = \sigma_2^2$. Thus, our assumption of equal variances in Example 3-2 is reasonable.

---

[1] Appendix Table V gives only upper tail points of F; that is, $F_{\alpha, u, v}$. Lower tail points $F_{1-\alpha, u, v}$ may be found using the relationship $F_{1-\alpha, u, v} = 1/F_{\alpha, v, u}$.

Confidence Intervals on Binomial Parameters

It is frequently necessary to construct $100(1 - \alpha)\%$ confidence intervals on the parameter p of a binomial distribution. This parameter frequently corresponds to a lot or process fraction nonconforming. It is usually assumed that the other binomial parameter n is known. If a random sample of n observations has been taken, and x "nonconforming" observations have been found in this sample, then the unbiased point estimator of p is $\hat{p} = x/n$.

There are several approaches to constructing the confidence interval on p. If n is large and $p \geq 0.1$ (say), then the normal approximation to the binomial can be used, resulting in the $100(1 - \alpha)\%$ confidence interval

$$\hat{p} - Z_{\alpha/2} \sqrt{\frac{\hat{p}(1 - \hat{p})}{n}} \leq p \leq \hat{p} + Z_{\alpha/2} \sqrt{\frac{\hat{p}(1 - \hat{p})}{n}} \tag{3-42}$$

If n is small, then tables of the binomial distribution should be used to establish the confidence interval on p. If n is large but p is small, then the Poisson approximation to the binomial is useful in constructing confidence intervals. Examples of these latter two procedures are given by Duncan (1974).

If there are two binomial parameters of interest, say p_1 and p_2, then it is possible to construct an approximate $100(1 - \alpha)\%$ confidence interval on their difference. The confidence interval is

$$\hat{p}_1 - \hat{p}_2 - Z_{\alpha/2} \sqrt{\frac{\hat{p}_1(1 - \hat{p}_1)}{n_1} + \frac{\hat{p}_2(1 - \hat{p}_2)}{n_2}}$$

$$\leq p_1 - p_2 \leq \hat{p}_1 - \hat{p}_2 + Z_{\alpha/2} \sqrt{\frac{\hat{p}_1(1 - \hat{p}_1)}{n_1} + \frac{\hat{p}_2(1 - \hat{p}_2)}{n_2}} \tag{3-43}$$

This result is based on the normal approximation to the binomial.

Example 3-3

In a random sample of 80 automotive crankshaft bearings, 15 of the bearings have a surface finish that is rougher than the specifications will allow. The point estimate of the fraction nonconforming in the process is

$$\hat{p} = \frac{15}{80} = 0.1875$$

Assuming that the normal approximation to the binomial is appropriate, a 95% confidence interval on the process fraction nonconforming is found from (3-42) as

$$0.1875 - 1.96 \sqrt{\frac{0.1875(0.8125)}{80}} \leq p \leq 0.1875 + 1.96 \sqrt{\frac{0.1875(0.8125)}{80}}$$

which reduces to

$$0.1020 \leq \hat{p} \leq 0.2730$$

3-3 HYPOTHESIS TESTING ON PROCESS PARAMETERS

A *statistical hypothesis* is a statement about the values of the parameters of a probability distribution. For example, suppose we think that the mean inside diameter of a bearing is 1.500 in. We may express this statement in a formal manner as

$$H_0: \quad \mu = 1.500$$
$$H_1: \quad \mu \neq 1.500 \tag{3.44}$$

The statement $H_0: \mu = 1.500$ in (3-44) is called the *null* hypothesis, and $H_1: \mu \neq 1.500$ is called the *alternative* hypothesis. In our example, H_1 specifies values of the mean diameter that are either greater than 1.500 or less than 1.500, and is called a *two-sided alternative* hypothesis. Depending on the problem, various one-sided alternative hypotheses may be appropriate.

Hypothesis-testing procedures are quite useful in many types of statistical quality-control problems. They also form the basis for most of the statistical process-control techniques to be described in Part II of this textbook. An important part of any hypothesis-testing problem is determining the parameter values specified in the null and alternative hypotheses. Generally, this is done in one of three ways. First, the values may result from past evidence or knowledge. This happens frequently in statistical quality control, where we use past information to specify values for a parameter corresponding to a state of control, and then periodically test the hypothesis that the parameter value has not changed. Second, the values may result from some theory or model of the process. Finally, the values chosen for the parameter may be the result of contractual or design specifications, a situation that occurs frequently. Statistical hypothesis-testing procedures may be used to check the conformity of the process parameters to their specified values, or to assist in modifying the process until the desired values are obtained.

To test a hypothesis, we take a random sample from the population under study, compute an appropriate test statistic, and then either reject or fail to reject the null hypothesis H_0. The set of values of the test statistic leading to rejection of H_0 is called the *critical region* or *rejection region* for the test.

Two kinds of errors may be committed when testing hypotheses. If the null hypothesis is rejected when it is true, then a type I error has occurred. If the null hypothesis is not rejected when it is false, then a type II error has been made. The probabilities of these two types of errors are denoted as

$$\alpha = P\{\text{type I error}\} = P\{\text{reject } H_0 | H_0 \text{ is true}\}$$
$$\beta = P\{\text{type II error}\} = P\{\text{fail to reject } H_0 | H_0 \text{ is false}\}$$

Sometimes it is more convenient to work with the *power* of the test, where

$$\text{Power} = 1 - \beta = P\{\text{reject } H_0 | H_0 \text{ is false}\}$$

Thus, the power is the probability of *correctly* rejecting H_0. In quality-control work, α is sometimes called the *producer's risk*, as it denotes the probability that a good lot will be rejected, or the probability that a process producing acceptable values of a particular quality characteristic will be rejected as performing unsatisfactorily. In addition, β is sometimes called the *consumer's risk*, as it denotes the probability of accepting a lot of poor quality, or allowing a process that is operating in an unsatisfactory manner relative to some quality characteristic to continue in operation.

The general procedure in hypothesis testing is to specify a value of the probability of type I error α, and then to design a test procedure so that a small value of the probability of type II error β is obtained. Thus, we speak of directly controlling or choosing the α risk. The β risk is generally a function of sample size and is controlled indirectly. The larger the sample size(s) used in the test, the smaller the β risk.

We now review several hypothesis-testing problems frequently encountered in quality-control applications. The following situations will be considered:

1. Comparison of means when the variance is known.

2. Comparison of means of normal distributions when the variance is unknown.

3. Comparison of variances of normal distributions.

4. Comparison of binomial parameters.

5. Comparison of Poisson parameters.

A more complete development of these and related hypothesis-testing procedures are given in Hines and Montgomery (1990) and Bowker and Lieberman (1972).

3-3.1 Tests on Means, Variance Known

Suppose that x is a random variable with unknown mean μ and known variance σ^2. We wish to test the hypothesis that the mean is equal to a standard value, say μ_0. The hypothesis may be formally stated as

$$
\begin{aligned}
H_0&: \quad \mu = \mu_0 \\
H_1&: \quad \mu \neq \mu_0
\end{aligned}
\tag{3-45}
$$

The procedure for testing this hypothesis is to take a random sample of n observations on the random variable x, compute the test statistic

$$
Z_0 = \frac{\bar{x} - \mu_0}{\sigma/\sqrt{n}}
\tag{3-46}
$$

and reject H_0 if $|Z_0| > Z_{\alpha/2}$, where $Z_{\alpha/2}$ is the upper $\alpha/2$ percentage point of the standard normal distribution.

We may give an intuitive justification of this test procedure. From the central limit theorem, we know that the sample mean $\bar{x}$ is distributed approximately $N(\mu, \sigma^2/n)$. Now if $H_0: \mu = \mu_0$ is true, then the test statistic Z_0 is distributed approximately $N(0, 1)$; consequently, we would expect $100(1 - \alpha)\%$ of the values of Z_0 to fall between $-Z_{\alpha/2}$ and $Z_{\alpha/2}$. A sample producing a value of Z_0 outside of these limits would be unusual if the null hypothesis were true, and is evidence that $H_0: \mu = \mu_0$ should be rejected. Note that α is the probability of type I error for the test, and the intervals $(Z_{\alpha/2}, \infty)$ and $(-\infty, -Z_{\alpha/2})$ form the critical region for the test.

In some situations we may wish to reject H_0 only if the true mean is larger than μ_0. Thus, the *one-sided* alternative hpothesis is $H_1: \mu > \mu_0$, and we would reject $H_0: \mu = \mu_0$ only if $Z_0 > Z_\alpha$. If rejection is desired only when $\mu < \mu_0$, then the alternative hypothesis is $H_1: \mu < \mu_0$, and we reject H_0 only if $Z_0 < -Z_\alpha$.

Suppose now that there are two populations with unknown means, say μ_1 and μ_2, and known variances σ_1^2 and σ_2^2. We wish to test the hypothesis that the two means are equal. The hypotheses are

$$H_0: \quad \mu_1 = \mu_2$$
$$H_1: \quad \mu_1 \neq \mu_2 \tag{3-47}$$

The test procedure is to take a random sample of n_1 observations from population 1 and n_2 observations from population 2, compute the test statistic

$$Z_0 = \frac{\bar{x}_1 - \bar{x}_2}{\sqrt{\dfrac{\sigma_1^2}{n_1} + \dfrac{\sigma_2^2}{n_2}}} \tag{3-48}$$

and reject H_0 if $|Z_0| > Z_{\alpha/2}$. If the one-sided alternative $H_1: \mu_1 > \mu_2$ is specified in (3-47), then H_0 will be rejected if $Z_0 > Z_\alpha$. If the other one-sided alternative $H_1: \mu_1 < \mu_2$ is specified, then H_0 will be rejected if $Z_0 < -Z_\alpha$.

A summary of these test procedures is given in Table 3-3.

Table 3-3

Tests on means with known variance

Hypothesis	Test Statistic	Criteria for Rejection
$H_0: \quad \mu = \mu_0$ $H_1: \quad \mu \neq \mu_0$		$\|Z_0\| > Z_{\alpha/2}$
$H_0: \quad \mu = \mu_0$ $H_1: \quad \mu < \mu_0$	$Z_0 = \dfrac{\bar{x} - \mu_0}{\sigma/\sqrt{n}}$	$Z_0 < -Z_\alpha$
$H_0: \quad \mu = \mu_0$ $H_1: \quad \mu > \mu_0$		$Z_0 > Z_\alpha$
$H_0: \quad \mu_1 = \mu_2$ $H_1: \quad \mu_1 \neq \mu_2$		$\|Z_0\| > Z_{\alpha/2}$
$H_0: \quad \mu_1 = \mu_2$ $H_1: \quad \mu_1 < \mu_2$	$Z_0 = \dfrac{\bar{x}_1 - \bar{x}_2}{\sqrt{\dfrac{\sigma_1^2}{n_1} + \dfrac{\sigma_2^2}{n_2}}}$	$Z_0 < -Z_\alpha$
$H_0: \quad \mu_1 = \mu_2$ $H_1: \quad \mu_1 > \mu_2$		$Z_0 > Z_\alpha$

Example 3-4

The internal pressure strength of glass bottles used to package a carbonated beverage is an important quality characteristic. The bottler wants to know whether the mean pressure strength exceeds 175 psi. From previous experience, he knows that the standard deviation of pressure strength is 10 psi. The glass manufacturer submits lots of these bottles to the bottler, who is interested in testing the hypothesis

$$H_0: \quad \mu = 175$$
$$H_1: \quad \mu > 175$$

Note that the lot will be accepted if the null hypothesis $H_0: \mu = 175$ is rejected. A random sample of 25 bottles is selected, and the bottles are placed on a hydrostatic pressure-testing machine that increases the pressure in the bottle until it fails. The sample average bursting strength is $\bar{x} = 182$ psi. The value of the test statistic is

$$Z_0 = \frac{\bar{x} - \mu_0}{\sigma/\sqrt{n}} = \frac{182 - 175}{10/\sqrt{25}} = 3.50$$

If we specify a type I error (or producer's risk) of $\alpha = 0.05$, then from Appendix Table I we find $Z_\alpha = Z_{0.05} = 1.645$. Therefore, we reject $H_0: \mu = 175$ and conclude that the lot mean pressure strength exceeds 175 psi.

3-3.2 Tests on Means of Normal Distributions, Variance Unknown

Suppose that x is a normal random variable with unknown mean μ and unknown variance σ^2. We wish to test the hypothesis that the mean equals a standard value μ_0, that is,

$$H_0: \quad \mu = \mu_0$$
$$H_1: \quad \mu \neq \mu_0 \tag{3-49}$$

Note that this problem is similar to that of Section 3-3.1, except that now the variance is unknown. Because the variance is unknown, we must make the additional assumption that the random variable is normally distributed. The normality assumption is needed to formally develop the statistical test, but moderate departures from normality will not seriously affect the results.

As σ^2 is unknown, it may be estimated by S^2. If we replace σ in (3-46) by S, we have the test statistic

$$t_0 = \frac{\bar{x} - \mu_0}{S/\sqrt{n}} \tag{3-50}$$

The null hypothesis $H_0: \mu = \mu_0$ will be rejected if $|t_0| > t_{\alpha/2, n-1}$, where $t_{\alpha/2, n-1}$ denotes the upper $\alpha/2$ percentage point of the t distribution with $n - 1$ degrees of freedom. The critical regions for the one-sided alternative hypotheses are shown in Table 3-4.

Table 3-4

Tests on means of normal distributions, variance unknown

Hypothesis	Test Statistic	Criteria for Rejection
H_0: $\mu = \mu_0$ H_1: $\mu \neq \mu_0$		$\lvert t_0 \rvert > t_{\alpha/2,\, n-1}$
H_0: $\mu = \mu_0$ H_1: $\mu < \mu_0$	$t_0 = \dfrac{\bar{x} - \mu_0}{S/\sqrt{n}}$	$t_0 < -t_{\alpha,\, n-1}$
H_0: $\mu = \mu_0$ H_1: $\mu > \mu_0$		$t_0 > t_{\alpha,\, n-1}$
H_0: $\mu_1 = \mu_2$ H_1: $\mu_1 \neq \mu_2$	$t_0 = \dfrac{\bar{x}_1 - \bar{x}_2}{S_p\sqrt{\dfrac{1}{n_1} + \dfrac{1}{n_2}}}$	$\lvert t_0 \rvert > t_{\alpha/2,\, v}$
	$v = n_1 + n_2 - 2$ or	
H_0: $\mu_1 = \mu_2$ H_1: $\mu_1 < \mu_2$	$t_0 = \dfrac{\bar{x}_1 - \bar{x}_2}{\sqrt{\dfrac{S_1^2}{n_1} + \dfrac{S_2^2}{n_2}}}$	$t_0 < -t_{\alpha,\, v}$
H_0: $\mu_1 = \mu_2$ H_1: $\mu_1 > \mu_2$	$v = \dfrac{\left(\dfrac{S_1^2}{n_1} + \dfrac{S_2^2}{n_2}\right)^2}{\dfrac{(S_1^2/n_1)^2}{n_1 + 1} + \dfrac{(S_2^2/n_2)^2}{n_2 + 1}} - 2$	$t_0 > t_{\alpha,\, v}$

Now suppose there are two normal populations with unknown means μ_1 and μ_2 and unknown variances σ_1^2 and σ_2^2. We wish to test the hypothesis that the two means are equal; that is,

$$H_0: \quad \mu_1 = \mu_2$$
$$H_1: \quad \mu_1 \neq \mu_2 \tag{3-51}$$

The test procedure for (3-51) depends on whether $\sigma_1^2 = \sigma_2^2$. First consider the case where this assumption is reasonable. Two random samples of sizes n_1 and n_2 are taken from populations 1 and 2, respectively, and a "pooled" or combined estimate of the common variance is obtained as

$$S_p^2 = \frac{(n_1 - 1)S_1^2 + (n_2 - 1)S_2^2}{n_1 + n_2 - 2} \tag{3-52}$$

where S_1^2 and S_2^2 are the individual sample variances. [Note that Equation (3-52) was used in Section 3-2.2, when constructing a confidence interval on the difference in two means, variances unknown but equal.] Then the test statistic

$$t_0 = \frac{\bar{x}_1 - \bar{x}_2}{S_p\sqrt{\dfrac{1}{n_1} + \dfrac{1}{n_2}}} \tag{3-53}$$

is computed, and H_0 is rejected if $|t_0| > t_{\alpha/2, n_1 + n_2 - 2}$. This procedure is often called the "pooled" t test, because the two samples are "pooled" or combined to estimate the common variance. The one-sided alternative hypotheses are summarized in Table 3-4.

If we cannot reasonably assume that $\sigma_1^2 = \sigma_2^2$, then the above procedure must be modified. The test statistic for (3-51) becomes

$$t_0 = \frac{\bar{x}_1 - \bar{x}_2}{\sqrt{\dfrac{S_1^2}{n_1} + \dfrac{S_2^2}{n_2}}} \tag{3-54}$$

and the number of degrees of freedom for t are

$$v = \frac{\left(\dfrac{S_1^2}{n_1} + \dfrac{S_2^2}{n_2}\right)^2}{\dfrac{(S_1^2/n_1)^2}{n_1 + 1} + \dfrac{(S_2^2/n_2)^2}{n_2 + 1}} - 2 \tag{3-55}$$

This is only an approximate test procedure.

Example 3-5

We will use the data in Example 3-2 pertaining to the observed road octane numbers of two formulations of gasoline to illustrate the above procedures. We wish to test the hypothesis that the mean road octane number of formulation 1 (which contains lead) equals the mean road octane number of formulation 2; that is,

$$H_0: \quad \mu_1 = \mu_2$$
$$H_1: \quad \mu_1 \neq \mu_2$$

Using the data in Table 3-2, we find $\bar{x}_1 = 90.70$, $S_1^2 = 1.34$, $\bar{x}_2 = 90.80$, $S_2^2 = 1.07$, $n_1 = n_2 = 10$, and, assuming that $\sigma_1^2 = \sigma_2^2$, from (3-52) we have $S_p^2 = 1.21$ or $S_p = 1.10$. Therefore, the test statistic (3-53) is

$$t_0 = \frac{\bar{x}_1 - \bar{x}_2}{S_p \sqrt{\dfrac{1}{n_1} + \dfrac{1}{n_2}}} = \frac{90.70 - 90.80}{1.10 \sqrt{\dfrac{1}{10} + \dfrac{1}{10}}} = -0.20$$

Using $\alpha = 0.01$, we find that $t_{0.005, 18} = 2.878$. Since $|t_0| = -0.20 < 2.878$, we cannot reject H_0, and we conclude that there is no strong statistical evidence to indicate that the two gasoline formulations differ in their mean road octane numbers. Note that the confidence interval on the difference in means, found in Example 3-2, includes zero; in other words, the two means do not differ. This points out an equivalence between confidence intervals and hypothesis testing. Finding that a $100(1 - \alpha)\%$ confidence interval on a parameter includes a particular value is identical to failing to reject the null hypothesis that the parameter is equal to that value with type I error probability α.

It should be emphasized that we have assumed that the two samples used in the above tests are independent. In some applications, *paired* data are encountered. Observations in an experiment are often paired to prevent extraneous factors from inflating the estimate of the variance; hence, this method can be used to improve the precision of comparisons between means. For a further discussion of paired data, see Montgomery (1984), Hines and Montgomery (1990), or Bowker and Lieberman (1972). The analysis of such a situation is illustrated in the following example.

Example 3-6

Two different types of machines are used to measure the tensile strength of synthetic fiber. We wish to determine whether or not the two machines yield the same average tensile strength values. Eight specimens of fiber are randomly selected, and one strength measure is made using each machine on each specimen. The coded data are shown in Table 3-5.

The data in this experiment have been paired to prevent the difference between fiber specimens (which could be substantial) from affecting the test on the difference between machines. The test procedure consists of obtaining the differences of the pair of observations on each of the n specimens, say $d_j = x_{1j} - x_{2j}$, $j = 1, 2, \ldots, n$, and then testing the hypothesis that the mean of the difference μ_d is zero. Note that testing H_0: $\mu_d = 0$ is equivalent to testing H_0: $\mu_1 = \mu_2$; furthermore, the test on μ_d is just the one-sample t test discussed at the beginning of this section. The test statistic is

$$t_0 = \frac{\bar{d}}{S_d/\sqrt{n}}$$

where

$$\bar{d} = \frac{1}{n} \sum_{j=1}^{n} d_j$$

Table 3-5
Paired tensile strength data for Example 3-6

Specimen	Machine 1	Machine 2	Difference
1	74	78	−4
2	76	79	−3
3	74	75	−1
4	69	66	3
5	58	63	−5
6	71	70	1
7	66	66	0
8	65	67	−2

and

$$S_d^2 = \frac{\sum\limits_{j=1}^{n} (d_j - \bar{d})^2}{n-1} = \frac{\sum\limits_{j=1}^{n} d_j^2 - \dfrac{\left(\sum\limits_{j=1}^{n} d_j\right)^2}{n}}{n-1}$$

and $H_0: \mu_d = 0$ is rejected if $|t_0| > t_{\alpha/2, n-1}$.

In our example we find that

$$\bar{d} = \frac{1}{n} \sum_{j=1}^{n} d_j = \frac{1}{8}(-11) = -1.38$$

$$S_d^2 = \frac{\sum\limits_{j=1}^{n} d_j^2 - \dfrac{\left(\sum\limits_{j=1}^{n} d_j\right)^2}{n}}{n-1} = \frac{65 - \dfrac{(-11)^2}{8}}{7} = 7.13$$

Therefore, the test statistic is

$$t_0 = \frac{\bar{d}}{S_d/\sqrt{n}} = \frac{-1.38}{2.67/\sqrt{8}} = -1.46$$

Choosing $\alpha = 0.05$, we find $t_{0.025,7} = 2.365$, and we conclude that there is no strong evidence to indicate that the two machines differ in their mean tensile strength measurements.

The procedure given in this section for testing the equality of the means of two normal populations with unknown but equal variances can be extended to the comparison of k population means. The test procedure is called the *analysis of variance*. For a systematic presentation of analysis of variance and some of its applications, see Montgomery (1984).

3-3.3 Tests on Variances of Normal Distributions

We now review hypothesis testing on the variance of a normal distribution. While tests on means are relatively insensitive to the normality assumption, test procedures for variances are not.

Suppose we wish to test the hypothesis that the variance of a normal distribution equals a constant, say σ_0^2. The hypotheses are

$$\begin{aligned} H_0: & \quad \sigma^2 = \sigma_0^2 \\ H_1: & \quad \sigma^2 \neq \sigma_0^2 \end{aligned}$$

$$(3\text{-}56)$$

Table 3-6

Tests on variances of normal distributions

Hypothesis	Test Statistic	Criteria for Rejection
H_0: $\sigma^2 = \sigma_0^2$ H_1: $\sigma^2 \neq \sigma_0^2$		$\chi_0^2 > \chi_{\alpha/2, n-1}^2$ or $\chi_0^2 < \chi_{1-\alpha/2, n-1}^2$
H_0: $\sigma^2 = \sigma_0^2$ H_1: $\sigma^2 < \sigma_0^2$	$\chi_0^2 = \dfrac{(n-1)S^2}{\sigma_0^2}$	$\chi_0^2 < \chi_{1-\alpha, n-1}^2$
H_0: $\sigma^2 = \sigma_0^2$ H_1: $\sigma^2 > \sigma_0^2$		$\chi_0^2 > \chi_{\alpha, n-1}^2$
H_0: $\sigma_1^2 = \sigma_2^2$ H_1: $\sigma_1^2 \neq \sigma_2^2$	$F_0 = \dfrac{S_1^2}{S_2^2}$	$F_0 > F_{\alpha/2, n_1-1, n_2-1}$ or $F_0 < F_{1-\alpha/2, n_1-1, n_2-1}$
H_0: $\sigma_1^2 = \sigma_2^2$ H_1: $\sigma_1^2 < \sigma_2^2$	$F_0 = \dfrac{S_2^2}{S_1^2}$	$F_0 > F_{\alpha, n_2-1, n_1-1}$
H_0: $\sigma_1^2 = \sigma_2^2$ H_1: $\sigma_1^2 > \sigma_2^2$	$F_0 = \dfrac{S_1^2}{S_2^2}$	$F_0 > F_{\alpha, n_1-1, n_2-1}$

The test statistic for this hypothesis is

$$\chi_0^2 = \frac{(n-1)S^2}{\sigma_0^2} \tag{3-57}$$

where S^2 is the sample variance computed from a random sample of n observations. The null hypothesis is rejected if $\chi_0^2 > \chi_{\alpha/2, n-1}^2$ or if $\chi_0^2 < \chi_{1-\alpha/2, n-1}^2$, where $\chi_{\alpha/2, n-1}^2$ and $\chi_{1-\alpha/2, n-1}^2$ are the upper $\alpha/2$ and lower $1-(\alpha/2)$ percentage points of the chi-square distribution with $n-1$ degrees of freedom. Table 3-6 gives the critical regions for the one-sided alternative hypotheses.

This test is very useful in many quality-control applications. For example, consider a normal random variable with mean μ and variance σ^2. If σ^2 is less than or equal to some value, say σ_0^2, then the natural inherent scatter of the process will be well within the design requirements, and consequently, almost all of the production will conform to specifications. However, if σ^2 exceeds σ_0^2, then the natural scatter in the process will exceed the specification limits, resulting in a high percentage of nonconforming production or "fallout." In other words, process *capability* is directly related to process *variability*. Equations (3-56) and (3-57) may be used to analyze various other similar situations, and as we will see subsequently, they form the basis for a control procedure for process variability.

Now consider testing the equality of the variances of two normal populations. If random samples of sizes n_1 and n_2 are taken from populations 1 and 2, respectively, then the test statistic for

$$H_0: \quad \sigma_1^2 = \sigma_2^2$$
$$H_1: \quad \sigma_1^2 \neq \sigma_2^2 \tag{3-58}$$

is the ratio of the two sample variances,

$$F_0 = \frac{S_1^2}{S_2^2} \qquad (3\text{-}59)$$

We would reject H_0 if $F_0 > F_{\alpha/2, n_1-1, n_2-1}$ or if $F_0 < F_{1-(\alpha/2), n_1-1, n_2-1}$, where $F_{\alpha/2, n_1-1, n_2-1}$ and $F_{1-(\alpha/2), n_1-1, n_2-1}$ denote the upper $\alpha/2$ and lower $1 - (\alpha/2)$ percentage points of the F distribution with $n_1 - 1$ and $n_2 - 1$ degrees of freedom, respectively. Table 3-6 summarizes the test procedures for the one-sided alternative hypotheses.

Example 3-7

We will test the hypothesis that the variances of the road octane numbers for the two gasoline formulations in Example 3-2 are the same; that is,

$$H_0: \quad \sigma_1^2 = \sigma_2^2$$
$$H_1: \quad \sigma_1^2 \neq \sigma_2^2$$

Since $S_1^2 = 1.34$ and $S_1^2 = 1.07$, the test statistic is

$$F_0 = \frac{S_1^2}{S_2^2} = \frac{1.34}{1.07} = 1.25$$

From Appendix Table V we find $F_{0.025,9,9} = 4.03$ and as in Example 3-2 we may compute the lower tail point $F_{0.975,9,9} = 0.248$, so since $0.248 < 1.25 < 4.03$ we conclude that there is no evidence to warrant rejection of H_0.

3-3.4 Tests on Binomial Parameters

Suppose we wish to test the hypothesis that the parameter p of a binomial distribution equals a standard value, say p_0. The test we will describe is based on the normal approximation to the binomial. If a random sample of n items is taken and x items in the sample belong to the class associated with p, then to test

$$H_0: \quad p = p_0$$
$$H_1: \quad p \neq p_0 \qquad (3.60)$$

we use the statistic

$$Z_0 = \begin{cases} \dfrac{(x + 0.5) - np_0}{\sqrt{np_0(1 - p_0)}} & \text{if } x < np_0 \\[3mm] \dfrac{(x - 0.5) - np_0}{\sqrt{np_0(1 - p_0)}} & \text{if } x > np_0 \end{cases} \qquad (3\text{-}61)$$

The null hypothesis H_0: $p = p_0$ is rejected if $|Z_0| > Z_{\alpha/2}$. The one-sided alternative hypotheses are treated similarly.

Example 3-8

A foundry produces steel castings used in the automotive industry. We wish to test the hypothesis that the fraction nonconforming or fallout from this process is 10%. In a random sample of 250 castings, 41 were found to be nonconforming. To test

$$H_0: \quad p = 0.1$$
$$H_1: \quad p \neq 0.1$$

we calculate the test statistic

$$Z_0 = \frac{(x - 0.5) - np_0}{\sqrt{np_0(1 - p_0)}} = \frac{(41 - 0.5) - (250)(0.1)}{\sqrt{250(0.1)(1 - 0.1)}} = 3.27$$

Using $\alpha = 0.05$ we find $Z_{0.025} = 1.96$, and therefore H_0: $p = 0.1$ is rejected. That is, the process fraction nonconforming or fallout is not equal to 10%.

We may also use the normal approximation to test the hypothesis that two binomial parameters are equal; that is,

$$H_0: \quad p_1 = p_2$$
$$H_1: \quad p_1 \neq p_2 \tag{3-62}$$

Let random samples of n_1 observations be taken from population 1 and n_2 observations be taken from population 2, and suppose that x_1 and x_2 items belong to the class associated with p in these two samples, respectively. Then $\hat{p}_1 = x_1/n_1$ and $\hat{p}_2 = x_2/n_2$ are the estimators of the binomial parameters from the two samples.

If the null hypothesis is true, then $p_1 = p_2 = p$, and the two sample statistics may be combined into a single estimator

$$\hat{p} = \frac{n_1 \hat{p}_1 + n_2 \hat{p}_2}{n_1 + n_2} \tag{3-63}$$

The statistic for testing H_0 is

$$Z_0 = \frac{\hat{p}_1 - \hat{p}_2}{\sqrt{\hat{p}(1 - \hat{p})\left(\dfrac{1}{n_1} + \dfrac{1}{n_2}\right)}} \tag{3-64}$$

We should reject H_0 when $|Z_0| > Z_{\alpha/2}$.

3-3.5 Tests on Poisson Parameters

The Poisson distribution

$$p(x) = \frac{e^{-\lambda}\lambda^x}{x!} \qquad x = 0, 1, \ldots$$

is frequently used in quality control to model the occurrence of nonconformities or defects in a product. In such applications, the parameter λ is called the mean rate of occurrence of nonconformities. In this section we investigate test procedures involving the parameter λ of the Poisson distribution.

Suppose we wish to test the hypothesis

$$\begin{aligned} H_0 &: \quad \lambda = \lambda_0 \\ H_1 &: \quad \lambda \neq \lambda_0 \end{aligned} \tag{3-65}$$

A random sample of n observations is taken, say $x_1, x_2, \ldots, x_n$. Each $\{x_i\}$ is Poisson distributed with parameter λ; furthermore, the sum $x = x_1 + x_2 + \cdots + x_n$ is Poisson distributed with parameter $n\lambda$. If n is large, we may use the fact that $\bar{x} = x/n$ is approximately normal with mean λ and variance λ/n to develop a test for H_0. The test statistic is

$$Z_0 = \frac{\bar{x} - \lambda_0}{\sqrt{\lambda_0/n}} \tag{3-66}$$

H_0: $\lambda = \lambda_0$ would be rejected if $|Z_0| > Z_{\alpha/2}$.

There are several other approaches to testing hypotheses about Poisson parameters. When n is small, the approach of the following example may be useful.

Example 3-9

A random sample of three office copiers yields $x_1 = 3$, $x_2 = 1$, and $x_3 = 6$ nonconformities per unit, respectively. We would like to test the hypothesis

$$\begin{aligned} H_0 &: \quad \lambda = 1 \\ H_1 &: \quad \lambda > 1 \end{aligned}$$

The test we use employs the property that $x = x_1 + x_2 + x_3$ is Poisson distributed with parameter 3λ. We evaluate

$$\theta = 1 - F(x - 1)$$

where $F(x - 1)$ is obtained from the cumulative Poisson distribution in Appendix Table II, assuming that H_0: $\lambda = \lambda_0$ is true. Note that θ is the probability of occurrence of the sample if H_0 is true. If $\theta \leq \alpha$, we would reject H_0: $\lambda = \lambda_0$.

For our data, we have $x = x_1 + x_2 + x_3 = 3 + 1 + 6 = 10$. Under H_0, x follows the Poisson distribution with parameter $3(\lambda_0) = 3(1) = 3$. From Appendix

Table II, we find for a Poisson distribution with parameter three that $F(x - 1) = F(9) = 0.998$. Thus, $\theta = 1 - F(x - 1) = 1 - 0.998 = 0.002$. Since $0.002 < \alpha = 0.05$ say, the null hypothesis H_0: $\lambda = 1$ would be rejected.

Another problem that occurs occasionally is the comparison of the parameters of several Poisson distributions. One method of analysis is demonstrated in the following example.

Example 3-10

Three different molds are used in a forming machine for glass bottles. The number of nonconformities or defects per 1000 bottles formed by each mold is of interest to the quality-assurance department as a measure of how well the process is performing. Five 1000-bottle lots are randomly selected from the output of each mold (this is relatively easy to do, since mold numbers are formed into the base of the bottle), and the data are shown in the second column of Table 3-7.

To test the hypothesis that the bottles produced by a particular mold have the same mean rate of occurrence of nonconformities, we may use a chi-square "goodness-of-fit" statistic of the general form

$$\chi^2 = \sum_{i=1}^{n} \frac{(O_i - E_i)^2}{E_i}$$

where O_i is the observed number of occurrences on the ith unit and E_i is the expected number of occurrences subject to the assumption that some model is true. The specific version of this statistic used in this problem is

$$\chi_i^2 = \frac{\sum_{j=1}^{n} (x_{ij} - \bar{x}_i)^2}{\bar{x}_i} \qquad i = 1, 2, \ldots, m$$

where x_{ij} represents the jth observation from the ith mold, and $\bar{x}_i$ is the average number of defects from the ith mold, $i = 1, 2, \ldots, m$, and $j = 1, 2, \ldots, n$. If the mean rate of occurrence of nonconformities for a particular mold is constant, then χ_i^2 is distributed approximately as chi-square with $n - 1$ degrees of freedom. We would reject this hypothesis if $\chi_i^2 > \chi_{\alpha, n-1}^2$. For our data, the values of χ_i^2 are shown in the last column of Table 3-7. Since $\chi_{0.05,4}^2 = 9.49$, we would conclude that bottles formed in the same mold are homogeneous.

We may also calculate a chi-square statistic that measures the homogeneity *between* molds, say

$$\chi_0^2 = \frac{\sum_{i=1}^{m} \left(\sum_{j=1}^{n} x_{ij} - \bar{x} \right)^2}{\bar{x}}$$

Table 3-7
Data and calculations for Example 3-10

Mold Number i	Number of Nonconformities per 1000 Bottles, x_{ij}	Mold Number Total $\sum_{j=1}^{5} x_{ij}$	Mold Number Average $\frac{1}{5}\sum_{j=1}^{5} x_{ij} = \bar{x}_i$	$\chi_i^2 = \dfrac{\sum_{j=1}^{5}(x_{ij} - \bar{x}_i)^2}{\bar{x}_i}$
1	8, 4, 3, 6, 4	25	5	3.20
2	5, 2, 3, 6, 4	20	4	2.50
3	12, 10, 8, 11, 9	50	10	1.00

where $\bar{x} = (1/m) \sum_{i=1}^{m} \left(\sum_{j=1}^{n} x_{ij} \right)$ is the average number of observed nonconformities. For our data, we have $\bar{x} = 95/3 = 31.67$, and

$$\chi_0^2 = \frac{(25 - 31.67)^2 + (20 - 31.67)^2 + (50 - 31.67)^2}{31.67} = 16.31$$

Comparing this to $\chi_{0.05,2}^2 = 5.99$, we would conclude that the molds are not homogeneous. Specifically, it seems that mold number 3 produces bottles with a higher mean rate of occurrence of nonconformities than the other two.

3-3.6 The Probability of Type II Error

In most hypothesis-testing situations, it is important to determine the probability of type II error associated with the test. Equivalently, we may elect to evaluate the power of the test. To illustrate how this may be done, we will find the probability of type II error associated with the test of

$$H_0: \quad \mu = \mu_0$$
$$H_1: \quad \mu \neq \mu_0$$

where the variance σ^2 is known. The test procedure was discussed in Section 3-3.1. The test statistic for this hypothesis is

$$Z_0 = \frac{\bar{x} - \mu_0}{\sigma/\sqrt{n}}$$

and under the null hypothesis the distribution of Z_0 is $N(0, 1)$. To find the probability of type II error, we must assume that the null hypothesis $H_0: \mu = \mu_0$ is false and then find the distribution of Z_0. Suppose that the mean of the distribution is really $\mu_1 = \mu + \delta$, where $\delta > 0$. Thus, the alternative hypothesis $H_1: \mu \neq \mu_0$ is true, and under this assumption the distribution of the test statistic Z_0 is

$$Z_0 \sim N\left(\frac{\delta\sqrt{n}}{\sigma}, 1\right) \tag{3-67}$$

The distribution of the test statistic Z_0 under both hypotheses H_0 and H_1 is shown in Figure 3-4. We note that the probability of type II error is the probability that Z_0 will fall between $-Z_{\alpha/2}$ and $Z_{\alpha/2}$ given that the alternative hypothesis H_1 is true. To evaluate this probability, we must find $F(Z_{\alpha/2}) - F(-Z_{\alpha/2})$, where F denotes the cumulative distribution function of the $N(\delta\sqrt{n}/\sigma, 1)$ distribution. In terms of the standard normal cumulative, we then have

$$\beta = \Phi\left(Z_{\alpha/2} - \frac{\delta\sqrt{n}}{\sigma}\right) - \Phi\left(-Z_{\alpha/2} - \frac{\delta\sqrt{n}}{\sigma}\right) \tag{3-68}$$

as the probability of type II error.

Example 3-11

The mean contents of coffee cans filled on a particular production line is being studied. Standards specify that the mean contents must be 16.0 oz, and from past experience it is known that the standard deviation of the can contents is 0.1 oz. The hypotheses are

$$H_0: \quad \mu = 16.0$$
$$H_1: \quad \mu \neq 16.0$$

A random sample of nine cans is to be used, and the type I error probability is specified as $\alpha = 0.05$. Therefore, the test statistic is

$$Z_0 = \frac{\bar{x} - 16.0}{0.1/\sqrt{9}}$$

and H_0 is rejected if $|Z_0| > Z_{0.025} = 1.96$. Suppose that we wish to find the probability of type II error if the true mean contents is $\mu_1 = 16.1$ oz. Since this implies that $\delta = \mu_1 - \mu_0 = 16.1 - 16.0 = 0.1$, we have

$$\beta = \Phi\left(Z_{\alpha/2} - \frac{\delta\sqrt{n}}{\sigma}\right) - \Phi\left(-Z_{\alpha/2} - \frac{\delta\sqrt{n}}{\sigma}\right)$$
$$= \Phi\left(1.96 - \frac{(0.1)(3)}{0.1}\right) - \Phi\left(-1.96 - \frac{(0.1)(3)}{0.1}\right)$$
$$= \Phi(-1.04) - \Phi(-4.96)$$
$$= 0.1492$$

That is, the probability that we will incorrectly fail to reject H_0 if the true mean contents is 16.1 oz is 0.1492. Equivalently, we can say that the power of the test is $1 - \beta = 1 - 0.1492 = 0.8508$.

We note from examining Equation (3-68) and Figure 3-4 that β is a function of n, δ, and α. It is customary to plot curves illustrating the relationship between

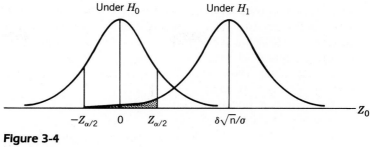

Figure 3-4
The distribution of Z_0 under H_0 and H_1.

these parameters. Such a set of curves is shown in Figure 3-5 for $\alpha = 0.05$. Graphs such as these are usually called *operating-characteristic* (OC) curves. The parameter on the vertical axis of these curves is β, and the parameter on the horizontal axis is $d = |\delta|/\sigma$. From examining the operating-characteristic curves, we see that:

1. The further the true mean μ_1 is from the hypothesized value μ_0 (i.e., the larger the value of δ), the smaller the probability of type II error for a given n and α. That is, for a specified sample size and α, the test will detect large differences more easily than small ones.

2. As the sample size n increases, the probability of type II error gets smaller for a specified δ and α. That is, to detect a specified difference we may make the test more powerful by increasing the sample size.

Operating-characteristic curves are useful in determining how large a sample is required to detect a specified difference with a particular probability. As an

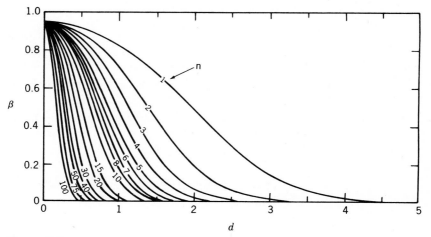

Figure 3-5
Operating-characteristic curves for the two-sided normal test with $\alpha = 0.05$.
(*Reproduced with permission from* C. L. Ferris, F. E. Grubbs, and C. L. Weaver, "Operating Characteristic Curves for the Common Statistical Tests of Significance," *Annals of Mathematical Statistics,* June 1946.)

illustration, suppose that in Example 3-11 we wish to determine how large a sample will be necessary to have a 0.90 probability of rejecting H_0: $\mu = 16.0$ if the true mean is $\mu = 16.05$. Since $\delta = 16.05 - 16.0 = 0.05$, we have $d = |\delta|/\sigma = |0.05|/0.1 = 0.5$. From Figure 3-5 with $\beta = 0.10$ and $d = 0.5$, we find $n = 45$, approximately. That is, 45 observations must be taken to ensure that the test has the desired probability of type II error.

Operating-characteristic curves are available for most of the standard statistical tests discussed in this chapter. For a detailed discussion of the use of operating-characteristic curves, refer to Hines and Montgomery (1990) or Bowker and Lieberman (1972).

3-4 Exercises

3-1 The inside diameters of bearings used in an aircraft landing gear assembly are known to have a standard deviation of $\sigma = 0.002$ cm. A random sample of 15 bearings has an average inside diameter of 8.2535 cm. Construct a 95% two-sided confidence interval on the mean bearing diameter.

3-2 The tensile strength of a fiber used in manufacturing cloth is of interest to the purchaser. Previous experience indicates that the standard deviation of tensile strength is 2 psi. A random sample of eight fiber specimens is selected, and the average tensile strength is found to be 127 psi. Construct a 95% lower confidence limit on the mean tensile strength.

3-3 The life of a battery used in a cardiac pacemaker is assumed to be normally distributed. A random sample of 10 batteries is subjected to an accelerated life test by running them continuously at an elevated temperature until failure, and the following lives are obtained.

25.5 h	26.1 h
26.8	23.2
24.2	28.4
25.0	27.8
27.3	25.7

Construct a 90% two-sided confidence interval on mean life in the accelerated test.

3-4 Using the data from Exercise 3-3, construct a 95% lower confidence limit on mean battery life.

3-5 A new process has been developed for applying photoresist to 125 mm silicon wafers used in manufacturing integrated circuits. Ten wafers were tested, and the results shown below were observed:

13.3946 ($\times$ 1000 Angstroms)	13.4002 ($\times$ 1000 Angstroms)
13.3987	13.3957
13.3902	13.4015
13.4001	13.3918
13.3965	13.3925

Find a 99% confidence interval on mean photoresist thickness.

3-6 A machine is used to fill containers with a liquid product. Fill volume can be assumed to be normally distributed. A random sample of 10 containers is selected, and the net contents are shown below. Construct a 95% two-sided confidence interval on the mean fill volume.

12.03 oz	12.01 oz
12.04	12.02
12.05	11.98
11.96	12.02
12.05	11.99

3-7 Ferric chloride is used as a flux in some types of extraction metallurgy processes. This material is shipped in containers, and the container weight will vary. It is important to obtain an accurate estimate of mean container weight. Suppose that from long experience a reliable value for the standard deviation of flux container weight is 4 lb. How large a sample would be required to construct a 95% two-sided confidence interval on the mean that has a total length of 1 lb?

3-8 The diameters of aluminum alloy rods produced on an extrusion machine are known to have a standard deviation of 0.0001 in. A random sample of 25 rods has an average diameter of 0.5046 in. Construct a 95% two-sided confidence interval on the mean rod diameter.

3-9 Consider the data in Exercise 3-3. Construct a 90% two-sided confidence interval on the variance of battery life. Convert this into a corresponding confidence interval on the standard deviation of battery life.

3-10 Consider the data in Exercise 3-6. Construct a 95% two-sided confidence interval on the variance of fill volume.

3-11 The output voltage of a power supply is assumed to be normally distributed. Sixteen observations taken at random on voltage are shown below.

10.35	9.30	10.00	9.96
11.65	12.00	11.25	9.58
11.54	9.95	10.28	8.37
10.44	9.25	9.38	10.85

a. Construct a 95% two-sided confidence interval on μ.
b. Construct a 95% two-sided confidence interval on σ.
c. Construct a 95% upper confidence interval on σ.

3-12 Two machines are used for filling glass bottles with a soft drink beverage. The filling processes have known standard deviations $\sigma_1 = 0.010$ liter and $\sigma_2 = 0.015$ liter, respectively. A random sample of $n_1 = 25$ bottles from machine 1 and $n_2 = 20$ bottles from machine 2 results in average net contents of $\bar{x}_1 = 2.04$ liters and $\bar{x}_2 = 2.07$ liters. Construct a 95% confidence interval on the difference in mean fill volume. Based on the results of this calculation, would you conclude that both machines fill to the same volume?

3-13 Use the data in Exercise 3-5 to construct a 95% one-sided lower confidence interval on the standard deviation of photoresist thickness.

3-14 Two quality-control technicians measured the surface finish of a metal part, obtaining the data shown below. Assume that the measurements are normally distributed.

Technician 1	Technician 2
1.45	1.54
1.37	1.41
1.21	1.56
1.54	1.37
1.48	1.20
1.29	1.31
1.34	1.27
	1.35

a. Assuming that the variances are equal, construct a 95% confidence interval on the mean difference in surface-finish measurements.

b. Construct a 95% confidence interval estimate of the ratio of the variances of technician measurement error.

c. Construct a 95% confidence interval on the variance of measurement error for Technician 2.

3-15 Twenty rounds of standard military rifle ammunition were fired from a test weapon, resulting in a mean muzzle velocity of $\bar{x}_1 = 595$ meters per second (m/s). Twenty rounds of test ammunition were also fired from the weapon, resulting in a mean muzzle velocity of $\bar{x}_2 = 600$ m/s. The sample variances were computed as $S_1^2 = 4.1$ and $S_2^2 = 5.0$, respectively. Assume that muzzle velocity is normally distributed.

a. Construct a 90% two-sided confidence interval on the difference in mean muzzle velocity, assuming that the variances are equal.

b. Construct a 95% two-sided confidence interval on the ratio σ_1^2/σ_2^2.

3-16 Suppose that $x_1 \sim N(\mu_1, \sigma_1^2)$ and $x_2 \sim N(\mu_2, \sigma_2^2)$, and that x_1 and x_2 are independent. Develop a procedure for constructing a $100(1 - \alpha)\%$ confidence interval on $\mu_1 - \mu_2$, assuming that σ_1^2 and σ_2^2 are unknown and cannot be assumed equal.

3-17 Two different hardening processes, saltwater quenching and oil quenching, are used on samples of a particular type of metal alloy. The results are shown below. Assume that hardness is normally distributed.

Saltwater Quench	Oil Quench
145	152
150	150
153	147
148	155
141	140
152	146
146	158
154	152
139	151
148	143

a. Assuming that the variances σ_1^2 and σ_2^2 are equal, construct a 95% confidence interval on the difference in hardness.

b. Construct a 95% confidence interval on the ratio σ_1^2/σ_2^2.

3-18 A random sample of 200 printed circuit boards contains 18 defective or nonconforming units. Estimate the process fraction nonconforming. Construct a 90% two-sided confidence interval on the true fraction nonconforming in the production process.

3-19 A random sample of 500 connecting rod pins contains 65 nonconforming units. Estimate the process fraction nonconforming. Construct a 95% upper confidence interval on the true process fraction nonconforming.

3-20 Two processes are used to produce forgings used in an aircraft wing assembly. Of 200 forgings selected from process 1, 10 do not conform to the strength specifications, while of 300 forgings selected from process 2, 20 are nonconforming. Estimate the fraction nonconforming for each process. Construct a 90% confidence interval on the difference in fraction nonconforming between the two processes.

3-21 Consider the data in Exercise 3-1. Test the hypothesis that the mean inside bearing diameter equals 8.25 cm.

3-22 Consider the data in Exercise 3-2. Test the hypothesis that the mean tensile strength equals 125 psi.

3-23 Consider the battery-life data in Exercise 3-3. The manufacturer wishes to be sure that the mean battery life exceeds 25 h. What conclusions can be drawn from these data?

3-24 Consider the filling process described in Exercise 3-6. The manufacturer wishes to be sure that the mean net contents exceeds 12.0 oz. What conclusions can be drawn from these data?

3-25 Using the data in Exercise 3-8, test the hypothesis that the mean rod diameter is 0.5025 in. What conclusions can be drawn?

3-26 Using the data in Exercise 3-11, test the hypothesis that $\sigma^2 = 1.0$.

3-27 Consider the surface-finish measurement data in Exercise 3-14.

    a. Test the hypothesis that the variances of the measurements made by the two technicians are equal.

    b. Using the results of part (a), conduct a test of the hypothesis that the mean surface-finish measurements made by the two technicians are equal. What conclusions can be drawn from the data?

3-28 Consider the muzzle velocity data in Exercise 3-15.

    a. Test the hypothesis that the variances of muzzle velocity for the two types of ammunition are equal.

    b. Using the results of part (a), test the hypothesis that both types of ammunition have the same mean muzzle velocity.

3-29 A new purification unit is installed in a chemical process. Before its installation, a random sample yielded the following data about the percentage of impurity: $\bar{x}_1 = 9.85$, $S_1^2 = 81.73$, and $n_1 = 10$. After installation, a random sample resulted in $\bar{x}_2 = 8.08$, $S_2^2 = 78.46$, and $n_2 = 8$.

    a. Can you conclude that the two variances are equal?

    b. Can you conclude that the new purification device has reduced the mean percentage of impurity?

3-30 Consider the hardness data in Exercise 3-17.

    a. Test the hypothesis that the variances of specimen hardness from the two quenching solutions are equal.

    b. Is there reason to conclude that the mean hardness resulting from oil quenching exceeds the mean hardness resulting from saltwater quenching?

3-31 Two different types of glass bottles are suitable for use by a soft drink beverage bottler. The internal pressure strength of the bottle is an important quality characteristic. It is known that $\sigma_1 = \sigma_2 = 3.0$ psi. From a random sample of $n_1 = n_2 = 16$ bottles, the mean pressure strengths are observed to be $\bar{x}_1 = 175.8$ psi and $\bar{x}_2 = 181.3$ psi. The company will not use bottle design 2 unless its pressure strength exceeds that of bottle design 1 by at least 5 psi. Based on the sample data, should they use bottle design 2?

3-32 The diameter of a metal rod is measured by 12 inspectors, each using both a micrometer caliper and a vernier caliper. The results are shown below. Is there a difference between the mean measurements produced by the two types of calipers?

Inspector	Micrometer Caliper	Vernier Caliper
1	0.150	0.151
2	0.151	0.150
3	0.151	0.151
4	0.152	0.150
5	0.151	0.151
6	0.150	0.151
7	0.151	0.153
8	0.153	0.155
9	0.152	0.154
10	0.151	0.151
11	0.151	0.150
12	0.151	0.152

3-33 Suppose we wish to test the hypothesis

$$H_0: \quad \mu = 15$$
$$H_1: \quad \mu \neq 15$$

where we know that $\sigma^2 = 9.0$. If the true mean is really 20, what sample size must be used to ensure that the probability of type II error is no greater than 0.10? Assume that $\alpha = 0.5$.

3-34 Consider the hypothesis

$$H_0: \quad \mu = \mu_0$$
$$H_1: \quad \mu \neq \mu_0$$

where σ^2 is known. Derive a general expression for determining the sample size for detecting a true mean of $\mu_1 \neq \mu_0$ with probability $1 - \beta$ if the type I error is α.

3-35 Sample size allocation. Suppose we are testing the hypothesis

$$H_0: \quad \mu_1 = \mu_2$$
$$H_1: \quad \mu_1 \neq \mu_2$$

where σ_1^2 and σ_2^2 are known. Resources are limited, and consequently the total sample size $n_1 + n_2 = N$. How should we allocate the N observations between the two populations to obtain the most powerful test?

3-36 Develop a test for the hypothesis

$$H_0: \quad \mu_1 = 2\mu_2$$
$$H_1: \quad \mu_1 \neq 2\mu_2$$

where σ_1^2 and σ_2^2 are known.

3-37 Consider the data in Exercise 3-18. Test the hypothesis that $p = 0.10$.

3-38 Consider the data in Exercise 3-19. Can you conclude that $p < 0.15$?

3-39 Consider the data in Exercise 3-20. Can you conclude that the fractions of noncon-forming forgings produced by the two processes are equal?

3-40 Nonconformities occur in glass bottles according to a Poisson distribution. A random sample of 100 bottles contains a total of 11 nonconformities. Test the hypothesis that the mean occurrence rate of nonconformities is $\lambda = 0.15$.

3-41 An inspector counts the surface-finish defects in dishwashers. A random sample of five dishwashers contains three such defects. Is there reason to conclude that the mean occurrence rate of surface-finish defects per dishwasher exceeds 0.5?

3-42 An in-line tester is used to evaluate the electrical function of printed circuit boards. This machine counts the number of defects observed on each board. A random sample of 1000 boards contains a total of 688 defects. Is it reasonable to conclude that the mean occurrence rate of defects is $\lambda = 1$?

PART II

Statistical Process Control

It is impossible to inspect or test quality into a product; the product must be built right the first time. This implies that the manufacturing processing must be stable and that all individuals involved with the process (including operators, engineers, quality-assurance personnel, and management) must continuously seek to improve process performance and reduce variability on key parameters. On-line statistical process controls are a primary tool for achieving this objective. Control charts are the simplest type of on-line statistical process-control procedure. Chapters 4 through 10 present statistical process-control techniques, concentrating primarily on the control chart.

Chapter 4 is an introduction to the general methodology of statistical process control (SPC). This chapter describes the basic SPC problem-solving tools, including an introduction to the control chart. A discussion of how to implement SPC is given, along with some comments on SPC in the nonmanufacturing environment. Chapter 5 presents control charts for attributes data, such as fraction defective or nonconforming, nonconformities (defects), or nonconformities per unit of product. Chapter 6 extends the control chart concept to measurement data. The $\bar{x}$ and R control charts, as well as several variations of these techniques, are discussed extensively. Chapter 7 discusses the cumulative sum and exponentially weighted moving average control charts. These procedures are very effective at detecting small process shifts, and have found extensive application in the chemical and process industries. Chapter 8 surveys other types of control charts and process-control techniques, including a brief introduction to evolutionary operation, a systematic method of applying designed experiments in an on-line manner for process improvement that is often useful in the chemical and process industries. Other important topics in this chapter include process control methods for multiple quality characteristics and methods for applying SPC in the chemical and process industries, where correlated observations often occur. Chapter 9 explores process-capability analysis, that is, how control charts and other statistical techniques can be used to estimate the natural capability of a process, and determine how it will perform relative to specifications on the product. Some aspects of setting specifications and tolerances, including the tolerance "stack-up" problem, are also presented. Chapter 10 presents a relatively new approach to the design of process-control procedures: the direct consideration of process economics. Throughout this section we stress the three fundamental uses of a control chart:

1. Reduction of process variability.
2. Monitoring and surveillance of a process.
3. Estimation of product or process parameters.

Chapter 4

Methods and Philosophy of Statistical Process Control

4-1 INTRODUCTION

If a product is to meet the customer's fitness for use criteria, generally it should be produced by a process that is stable or repeatable. That is, it must be capable of operating with little variability around the target or nominal dimensions of the product's quality characteristics. Statistical process control (SPC) is a powerful collection of problem-solving tools useful in achieving process stability and improving capability through the reduction of variability.

SPC can be applied to *any* process. Its seven major tools are:

1. Histogram
2. Check sheet
3. Pareto chart
4. Cause and effect diagram
5. Defect concentration diagram
6. Scatter diagram
7. Control chart

While these tools, often called "the magnificent seven," are an important part of SPC, they comprise only its technical aspects. SPC is an *attitude*—a desire of all individuals in an organization for continuous improvement in quality and productivity. This attitude is best developed when management becomes involved in an ongoing quality-improvement process. Once this attitude is established, routine application of the magnificent seven becomes part of the usual manner of doing business, and the organization is well on its way to achieving its quality-improvement objectives.

In this chapter we will present an overview of the magnificent seven. Of these tools, the control chart is probably the most technically sophisticated. It was developed in the 1920s by Dr. Walter A. Shewhart of the Bell Telephone Laboratories. In order to understand the statistical concepts that form the basis of SPC, we must first describe Shewhart's theory of variability.

4-2 CHANCE AND ASSIGNABLE CAUSES OF QUALITY VARIATION

In any production process, regardless of how well designed or carefully maintained it is, a certain amount of inherent or natural variability will always exist. This natural variability or "background noise" is the cumulative effect of many small, essentially unavoidable causes. When the background noise in a process is relatively small, we usually consider it an acceptable level of process performance. In the framework of statistical quality control, this natural variability is often called a "stable system of chance causes." A process that is operating with only chance causes of variation present is said to be in statistical control. In other words, the chance causes are an inherent part of the process.

Other kinds of variability may occasionally be present in the output of a process. This variability in key quality characteristics usually arises from three sources: improperly adjusted machines, operator errors, or defective raw materials. Such variability is generally large when compared to the background noise, and it usually represents an unacceptable level of process performance. We refer to these sources of variability that are not part of the chance cause pattern as "assignable causes." A process that is operating in the presence of assignable causes is said to be out of control.[1]

Often production processes will operate in the in-control state, producing acceptable product for relatively long periods of time. Occasionally, however, assignable causes will occur, seemingly at random, resulting in a "shift" to an out-of-control state where a larger proportion of the process output does not conform to requirements. A major objective of statistical process control is to quickly detect the occurrence of assignable causes or process shifts so that investigation of the process and corrective action may be undertaken before many nonconforming units are manufactured. The control chart is an on-line process-control technique widely used for this purpose. Control charts may also be used to estimate the parameters of a production process and, through this information, to determine process capability. The control chart may also provide information useful in improving the process. Finally, remember that the eventual goal of statistical process control is the *elimination of variability in the process*. It may not be

---

[1] The terminology *chance* and *assignable* causes was developed by Dr. Walter A. Shewhart. Today, some writers use *common* cause instead of *chance* cause and *special* cause instead of *assignable* cause.

possible to completely eliminate variability, but the control chart is an effective tool in reducing variability as much as possible.

We now present the statistical concepts that form the basis of control charts. Chapters 5 and 6 develop the details of construction and use of the standard types of control charts.

4-3 STATISTICAL BASIS OF THE CONTROL CHART

4-3.1 Basic Principles

A typical control chart is shown in Figure 4-1, which is a graphical display of a quality characteristic that has been measured or computed from a sample versus the sample number or time. The chart contains a center line that represents the average value of the quality characteristic corresponding to the in-control state. (That is, only chance causes are present.) Two other horizontal lines, called the upper control limit (UCL) and the lower control limit (LCL), are also shown on the chart. These control limits are chosen so that if the process is in control, nearly all of the sample points will fall between them. As long as the points plot within the control limits, the process is assumed to be in control, and no action is necessary. However, a point that plots outside of the control limits is interpreted as evidence that the process is out of control, and investigation and corrective action is required to find and eliminate the assignable cause or causes responsible for this behavior. It is customary to connect the sample points on the control chart with straight-line segments, so that it is easier to visualize how the sequence of points has evolved over time.

Even if all the points plot inside the control limits, if they behave in a systematic or nonrandom manner, then this is an indication that the process is out of

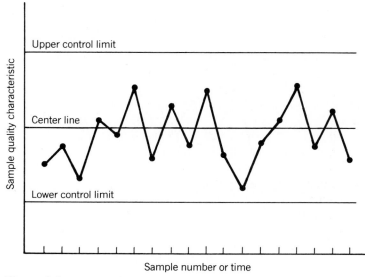

Figure 4-1
A typical control chart.

control. For example, if 18 of the last 20 points plotted above the center line but below the upper control limit and only two of these points plotted below the center line but above the lower control limit, we would be very suspicious that something was wrong. If the process is in control, all the plotted points should have an essentially random pattern. Methods for looking for sequences or nonrandom patterns can be applied to control charts as an aid in detecting out-of-control conditions. Usually, there is a reason why a particular nonrandom pattern appears on a control chart, and if it can be found and eliminated, process performance can be improved. This topic is discussed further in Sections 4-3.5 and 6-2.4.

There is a close connection between control charts and hypothesis testing. Essentially, the control chart is a test of the hypothesis that the process is in a state of statistical control. A point plotting within the control limits is equivalent to failing to reject the hypothesis of statistical control, and a point plotting outside the control limits is equivalent to rejecting the hypothesis of statistical control. Just as in hypothesis testing, we may think of the probability of type I error of the control chart (concluding the process is out of control when it is really in control) and the probability of type II error of the control chart (concluding the process is in control when it is really out of control). It is occasionally helpful to use the operating-characteristic curve of a control chart to display its probability of type II error. This would be an indication of the ability of the control chart to detect process shifts of different magnitudes.

To illustrate the preceding ideas, we give an example of a control chart. In the manufacture of automotive engine piston rings, a critical quality characteristic is the inside diameter of the ring. The process can be controlled at a mean inside ring diameter of 74 mm, and it is known that the standard deviation of ring diameter is 0.01 mm. A control chart for average ring diameter is shown in Figure 4-2. Every hour a random sample of five rings is taken, the average ring diameter of the sample (say $\bar{x}$) computed, and $\bar{x}$ plotted on the chart. Because this control chart utilizes the sample average $\bar{x}$ to monitor the process mean, it is usually called

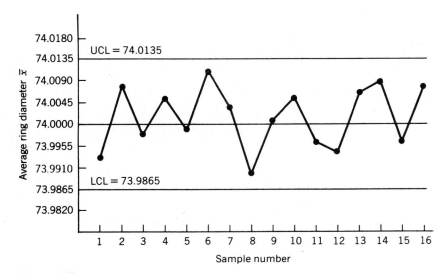

Figure 4-2
$\bar{x}$ control chart for piston-ring diameter.

an $\bar{x}$ control chart. Note that all the points fall within the control limits, so that the chart indicates that the process is in statistical control.

To assist in understanding the statistical basis of this control chart, consider how the control limits were determined. The process average is 74 mm, and the process standard deviation is $\sigma = 0.01$ mm. Now if samples of size $n = 5$ are taken, the standard deviation of the sample average $\bar{x}$ is

$$\sigma_{\bar{x}} = \frac{\sigma}{\sqrt{n}} = \frac{0.01}{\sqrt{5}} = 0.0045$$

Therefore, if the process is in control with a mean diameter of 74 mm, then by using the central limit theorem to assume that $\bar{x}$ is approximately normally distributed, we would expect $100(1 - \alpha)\%$ of the sample mean diameters $\bar{x}$ to fall between $74 + Z_{\alpha/2}(0.0045)$ and $74 - Z_{\alpha/2}(0.0045)$. We will arbitrarily choose the constant $Z_{\alpha/2}$ to be 3, so that the upper and lower control limits become

$$UCL = 74 + 3(0.0045) = 74.0135$$

and

$$LCL = 74 - 3(0.0045) = 73.9865$$

as shown on the control chart. These are typically called "3-sigma"[2] control limits. The width of the control limits is inversely proportional to the sample size n for a given multiple of sigma. Note that choosing the control limits is equivalent to setting up the critical region for testing the hypothesis

$$H_0: \quad \mu = 74$$
$$H_1: \quad \mu \neq 74$$

where $\sigma = 0.01$ is known. Essentially, the control chart just tests this hypothesis repeatedly at different points in time. The situation is illustrated graphically in Figure 4-3.

We may give a general *model* for a control chart. Let w be a sample statistic that measures some quality characteristic of interest, and suppose that the mean of w is μ_w and the standard deviation of w is σ_w. Then the center line, the upper control limit, and the lower control limit become

$$UCL = \mu_w + k\sigma_w$$
$$\text{Center line} = \mu_w \tag{4-1}$$
$$LCL = \mu_w - k\sigma_w$$

where k is the "distance" of the control limits from the center line, expressed in standard deviation units. This general theory of control charts was first proposed by Dr. Walter A. Shewhart, and control charts developed according to these principles are often called *Shewhart control charts*.

---

[2] Note that "sigma" refers to the standard deviation of the statistic plotted on the chart (i.e., $\sigma_{\bar{x}}$), *not* the standard deviation of the quality characteristic.

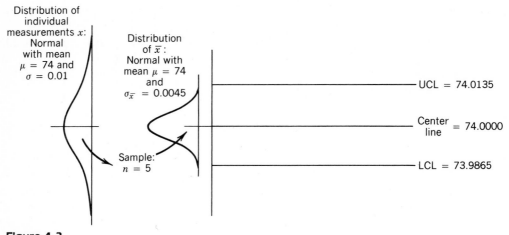

Figure 4-3
How the control chart works.

The control chart is a device for describing in a precise manner exactly what is meant by statistical control; as such, it may be used in a variety of ways. In many applications, it is used for on-line process surveillance. That is, sample data are collected and used to construct the control chart, and if the sample values of $\bar{x}$ (say) fall within the control limits and do not exhibit any systematic pattern, we say the process is in control at the level indicated by the chart. Note that we may be interested here in determining *both* whether the past data came from a process that was in control and whether future samples from this process indicate statistical control.

The most important use of a control chart is to *improve* the process. We have found that, generally:

1. Most processes do not operate in a state of statistical control.

2. Consequently, the routine and attentive use of control charts will identify assignable causes. If these causes can be eliminated from the process, variability will be reduced and the process will be improved.

This process improvement activity using the control chart is illustrated in Figure 4-4. Notice that:

3. The control chart will only *detect* assignable causes. Management, operator, and engineering *action* will usually be necessary to eliminate the assignable cause.

In identifying and eliminating assignable causes, it is important to find the underlying *root cause* of the problem and to attack it. A cosmetic solution will not result in any real, long-term process improvement. Developing an effective system for corrective action is an essential component of an effective SPC implementation.

We may also use the control chart as an *estimating device*. That is, from a control chart that exhibits statistical control, we may estimate certain process pa-

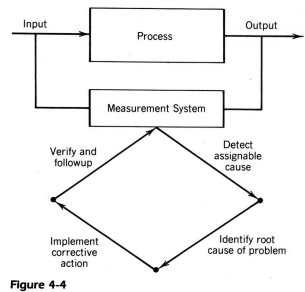

Figure 4-4
Process improvement using the control chart.

rameters, such as the mean, standard deviation, fraction nonconforming or fallout, and so forth. These estimates may then be used to determine the *capability* of the process to produce acceptable products. Such *process-capability studies* have considerable impact on many management decision problems that occur over the product cycle, including make or buy decisions, plant and process improvements that reduce process variability, and contractual agreements with customers or vendors regarding product quality.

Control charts may be classified into two general types. If the quality characteristic can be measured and expressed as a number on some continuous scale of measurement, it is usually called a *variable*. In such cases, it is convenient to describe the quality characteristic with a measure of central tendency and a measure of variability. Control charts for central tendency and variability are collectively called *variables control charts*. The $\bar{x}$ chart is the most widely used chart for controlling central tendency, while charts based on either the sample range or the sample standard deviation are used to control process variability. Control charts for variables are discussed in Chapter 6. Many quality characteristics are not measured on a continuous scale or even a quantitative scale. In these cases, we may judge each unit of product as either conforming or nonconforming on the basis of whether or not it possesses certain attributes, or we may count the number of nonconformities (defects) appearing on a unit of product. Control charts for such quality characteristics are called *attributes* control charts and are discussed in Chapter 5.

An important factor in control chart usage is the *design* of the control chart. By this we mean the selection of the sample size, control limits, and frequency of sampling. For example, in the $\bar{x}$ chart of Figure 4-2, we specified a sample size of 5 measurements, 3-sigma control limits, and the sampling frequency to be every hour. In most quality-control problems, it is customary to design the control chart using primarily statistical considerations. For example, we know that increasing the sample size will decrease the probability of type II error, thus enhancing the chart's ability to detect an out-of-control state, and so forth. The use of statistical criteria such as these along with industrial experience has led to general guidelines and procedures for designing control charts. These procedures usually consider cost factors only in an implicit manner. Recently, however, we have begun to examine control chart design from an *economic* point of view, considering explicitly the cost of sampling, losses from allowing excessive amounts of defective product to be produced, and the costs of investigating out-of-control signals that are really "false alarms."

Chapters 5, 6, and 10 investigate these concepts in more detail. In the next two sections we give a brief general discussion of factors to consider when choosing the control limits, sample size, and sampling frequency for a control chart.

Control charts have had a long history of use in U.S. industries and in many offshore industries as well. There are at least five reasons for their popularity.

1. **Control charts are a proven technique for improving productivity.** A successful control chart program will reduce scrap and rework, which are the primary productivity-killers in *any* operation. If you reduce scrap and rework, then productivity increases, cost decreases, and production capacity (measured in the number of *good* parts per hour) increases.

2. **Control charts are effective in defect prevention.** The control chart helps keep the process in control, which is consistent with the "do it right the first time" philosophy. It is never cheaper to sort out "good" units from "bad" units later on than it is to build it right initially. If you do not have effective process control, you are paying someone to make a nonconforming product.

3. **Control charts prevent unnecessary process adjustments.** A control chart can distinguish between background noise and abnormal variation; no other device including a human operator is as effective in making this distinction. If process operators adjust the process based on periodic tests unrelated to a control chart program, they will often overreact to the background noise and make unneeded adjustments. These unnecessary adjustments can actually result in a deterioration of process performance. In other words, the control chart is consistent with the "if it isn't broken, don't fix it" philosophy.

4. **Control charts provide diagnostic information.** Frequently, the pattern of points on the control chart will contain information of diagnostic value to an experienced operator or engineer. This information allows the implementation of a change in the process that improves its performance.

5. **Control charts provide information about process capability.** The control chart provides information about the value of important process parameters and their stability over time. This allows an estimate of process capability to be made. This information is of tremendous use to product and process designers.

Control charts are among the most important management control tools; they are as important as cost controls and material controls. Modern computer technology has made it easy to implement control charts in *any* type of process, as data collection and analysis can be performed on a microcomputer or a local area network terminal in real-time, on-line at the work center. Some additional guidelines for implementing a control chart program are given in Chapter 6.

4-3.2 Choice of Control Limits

Specifying the control limits is one of the critical decisions that must be made in designing a control chart. By moving the control limits further from the center line, we decrease the risk of a type I error—that is, the risk of a point falling beyond the control limits, indicating an out-of-control condition when no assignable cause is present. However, widening the control limits will also increase the risk of a type II error—that is, the risk of a point falling between the control limits when the process is really out of control. If we move the control limits closer to the center line, the opposite effect is obtained: The risk of type I error is increased, while the risk of type II error is decreased.

For the $\bar{x}$ chart shown in Figure 4-2, where 3-sigma control limits were used, if we assume that the piston-ring diameter is normally distributed, we find from the standard normal table that the probability of type I error is 0.0027. That is, an incorrect out-of-control signal or false alarm will be generated in only 27 out of 10,000 points. Furthermore, the probability that a point taken when the process is in control will exceed the 3-sigma limits in one direction only is 0.00135. Instead of specifying the control limit as a multiple of the standard deviation of $\bar{x}$, we could have directly chosen the type I error probability and calculated the corresponding control limit. For example, if we specified a 0.001 type I error probability in one direction, then the appropriate multiple of the standard deviation would be 3.09. The control limits for the $\bar{x}$ chart would then be

$$UCL = 74 + 3.09(0.0045) = 74.0139$$
$$LCL = 74 - 3.09(0.0045) = 73.9861$$

These control limits are called 0.001 *probability limits*. The $\bar{x}$ chart with both 3-sigma limits and 0.001 limits is shown in Figure 4-5. There is only a slight difference between the two limits.

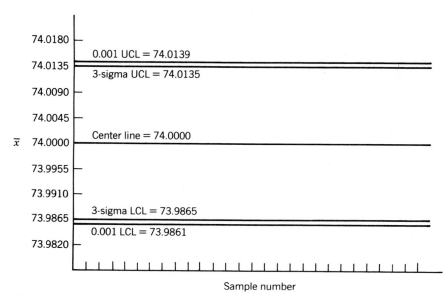

Figure 4-5
Comparison of 3-sigma and 0.001 probability limits for the $\bar{x}$ chart.

Regardless of the distribution of the quality characteristic, it is standard practice in the United States to determine the control limits as a multiple of the standard deviation of the statistic plotted on the chart. The multiple usually chosen is 3; hence, 3-sigma limits are customarily employed on control charts, regardless of the type of chart employed. In the United Kingdom and parts of Western Europe, probability limits are used, with the standard probability level being 0.001.

We typically justify the use of 3-sigma control limits on the basis that they give good results in practice. Moreover, in many cases, the true distribution of the quality characteristic is not known well enough to compute exact probability limits. If the distribution of the quality characteristic is reasonably approximated by the normal distribution, then there will be little difference between 3-sigma and 0.001 probability limits. While 3-sigma limits are widely used in practice, the choice of the multiple of sigma used should be dictated by economic considerations. For example, if the losses associated with allowing the process to operate in the out-of-control state are large relative to the cost of investigating and possibly correcting assignable causes, then a smaller multiple of sigma, such as 2 or 2.5, may be appropriate. A more complete discussion of this subject is given in Chapter 10.

Warning Limits on Control Charts

Some analysts suggest using two sets of limits on control charts, such as those shown in Figure 4-6. The outer limits, say at 3-sigma, are the usual action limits; that is, when a point plots outside of this limit, a search for an assignable cause is made and corrective action is taken if necessary. The inner limits, usually at 2-sigma, are called warning limits. In Figure 4-6, we have shown the 3-sigma upper and lower control limits for the $\bar{x}$ chart for the piston-ring diameter. The upper and lower warning limits are located at

$$\text{UWL} = 74 + 2(0.0045) = 74.0090$$
$$\text{LWL} = 74 - 2(0.0045) = 73.9910$$

When probability limits are used, the action limits are generally 0.001 limits and the warning limits are 0.025 limits.

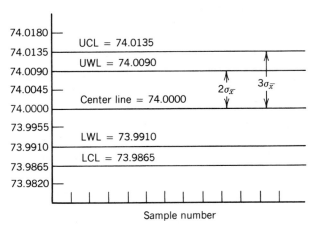

Figure 4-6
An $\bar{x}$ chart with 2-sigma warning limits.

If one or more points fall between the warning limits and the action limits, or very close to the warning limit, we should be suspicious that the process may not be operating properly. One possible action to take when this occurs is to increase the sampling frequency and to use these additional data in conjunction with the suspicious points to investigate the state of control of the process.

Warning limits increase the sensitivity of the control chart. Their disadvantage is that they do not have a precise interpretation and may be confusing to operating personnel. This is not usually a serious objection, however.

4-3.3 Sample Size and Sampling Frequency

In designing a control chart, we must specify both the sample size to use and the frequency of sampling. In general, larger samples will make it easier to detect small shifts in the process. This is demonstrated in Figure 4-7, where we have plotted the operating-characteristic curve for the $\bar{x}$ chart in Figure 4-1 for various sample sizes. Note that the probability of detecting a shift from 74.0000 mm to 74.0100 mm (for example) increases as the sample size n increases. When choosing the sample size, we must keep in mind the size of the shift that we are trying to detect. If the process shift is relatively large, then we use smaller sample sizes than those that would be employed if the shift of interest were relatively small.

We must also determine the frequency of sampling. The most desirable situation from the point of view of detecting shifts would be to take large samples very frequently; however, this is usually not economically feasible. The general problem is one of *allocating sampling effort*. That is, either we take small samples at short intervals or larger samples at longer intervals. Current industry practice tends to favor smaller, more frequent samples, particularly in high-volume manufacturing processes, or where a great many types of assignable causes can occur. Furthermore, as automatic sensing and measurement technology develops, it is becoming possible to greatly reduce sampling frequencies. Ultimately, every unit can be tested as it is manufactured. Automatic sensing and powerful microcomputers with

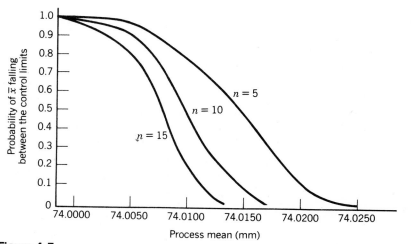

Figure 4-7
Operating-characteristic curves for an $\bar{x}$ chart.

statistical process-control software applied at the work center for on-line process control in real time is an important new dimension in statistical process control.

Another way to approach the decisions regarding sample size and sampling frequency is through the *average run length* (ARL) of the control chart. Essentially, the ARL is the average number of points that must be plotted before a point indicates an out-of-control condition. For any Shewhart control chart, the ARL can be calculated easily from

$$ARL = \frac{1}{p} \tag{4-2}$$

where p is the probability that any point exceeds the control limits. Thus, for an $\bar{x}$ chart with 3-sigma limits, $p = 0.0027$ is the probability that a single point falls outside the limits when the process is in control, so

$$ARL = \frac{1}{p} = \frac{1}{0.0027} = 370$$

is the average run length of the $\bar{x}$ chart when the process is in control. That is, even if the process remains in control, an out-of-control signal will be generated every 370 samples, on the average.

Consider the piston-ring process discussed earlier, and suppose we are sampling every hour. Thus, we will have a *false alarm* about every 370 hours on the average. Suppose we are using a sample size of $n = 5$ and that when the process goes out of control the mean shifts to 74.015 mm. From the operating characteristic curve in Figure 4-7 we find that if the process mean is 74.015 mm the probability of $\bar{x}$ falling between the control limits is approximately 0.50. Therefore, p in Equation (4-2) is 0.50, and the out-of-control ARL is

$$ARL = \frac{1}{p} = \frac{1}{0.5} = 2$$

That is, the control chart will require two samples to detect the process shift, on the average, so two hours will elapse between the shift and its detection (*again on the average*). Suppose this is unacceptable, because production of piston rings with a mean diameter of 74.015 mm results in excessive scrap costs and delays final engine assembly. How can we reduce the time needed to detect the out-of-control condition? One method is to sample more frequently. For example, if we sample every half hour, then only one hour will elapse (on the average) between the shift and its detection. The second possibility is to increase the sample size. For example, if we use $n = 10$, then Figure 4-7 shows that the probability of $\bar{x}$ falling between the control limits when the process mean is 74.015 mm is approximately 0.1, so that $p = 0.9$, and from (4-2) the out-of-control ARL is

$$ARL = \frac{1}{p} = \frac{1}{0.9} = 1.11$$

Thus, the larger sample size would allow the shift to be detected about twice as quickly as the old one. If it became important to detect the shift in the first hour after it occurred, two control chart designs would work:

Design 1	**Design 2**
Sample Size: $n = 5$	Sample Size: $n = 10$
Sampling Frequency: every half hour	Sampling Frequency: every hour

In order to answer the question of sampling frequency more precisely, we must take several factors into account, including the cost of sampling, the losses associated with allowing the process to operate out of control, the rate of production, and the probabilities with which various types of process shifts occur. We discuss various methods for selecting an appropriate sample size and sampling frequency for a control chart in the next four chapters, including both economic and statistical approaches. Some of the current results on the economic design of control charts are summarized in Chapter 10.

4-3.4 Rational Subgroups

A fundamental idea in the use of control charts is the collection of sample data according to what Shewhart called the *rational subgroup* concept. Generally, this means that subgroups or samples should be selected so that if assignable causes are present, the chance for differences *between* subgroups will be maximized, while the chance for differences due to these assignable causes *within* a subgroup will be minimized.

When control charts are applied to production processes, the time order of production is a logical basis for rational subgrouping. Even though time order is preserved, it is still possible to form subgroups erroneously. If some of the observations in the sample are taken at the end of one shift and the remaining observations are taken at the start of the next shift, then any differences between shifts might not be detected. Time order is frequently a good basis for forming subgroups because it allows us to detect assignable causes that occur over time.

Two general approaches to constructing rational subgroups are used. In the first approach, each sample consists of units that were produced at the same time (or as closely together as possible). This approach is used when the primary purpose of the control chart is to detect process shifts. It minimizes the chance of variability due to assignable causes *within* a sample, and it maximizes the chance of variability *between* samples if assignable causes are present. It also provides better estimates of the standard deviation of the process in the case of variables control charts. This approach to rational subgrouping essentially gives a "snapshot" of the process at each point in time where a sample is collected.

In the second approach, each sample consists of units of product that are representative of *all* units that have been produced since the last sample was taken. Essentially, each subgroup is a *random sample* of *all* process output over the sampling interval. This method of rational subgrouping is often used when the control chart is employed to make decisions about the acceptance of all units of product that have been produced since the last sample. In fact, if the process shifts to an out-of-control state and then back in control again *between* samples, it is sometimes argued that the first method of rational subgrouping defined above will be ineffective against these types of shifts, and so the second method must be used.

When the rational subgroup is a random sample of all units produced over the sampling interval, considerable care must be taken in interpreting the control charts. If the process mean drifts between several levels during the interval between samples, this may cause the range of the observations within the sample to be relatively large, resulting in wider limits on the $\bar{x}$ chart. In fact, we can often make *any* process appear to be in statistical control just by stretching out the interval between observations in the sample. It is also possible for shifts in the process average to cause points on a dispersion control chart (such as a control chart for the range or standard deviation) to plot out of control, even though there has been no shift in process variability.

There are other bases for forming rational subgroups. For example, suppose a process consists of several machines that pool their output into a common stream. If we sample from this common stream of output, it will be very difficult to detect whether or not some of the machines are out of control. A logical approach to rational subgrouping here is to apply control chart techniques to the output for each individual machine. Sometimes this concept needs to be applied to different heads on the same machine, different work stations, different operators, and so forth.

The rational subgroup concept is very important. The proper selection of samples requires careful consideration of the process, with the objective of obtaining as much useful information as possible from the control chart analysis.

4-3.5 Analysis of Patterns on Control Charts

A control chart may indicate an out-of-control condition either when one or more points fall beyond the control limits, or when the plotted points exhibit some nonrandom pattern of behavior. For example, consider the $\bar{x}$ chart shown in Figure 4-8. Although all 25 points fall within the control limits, the points do not

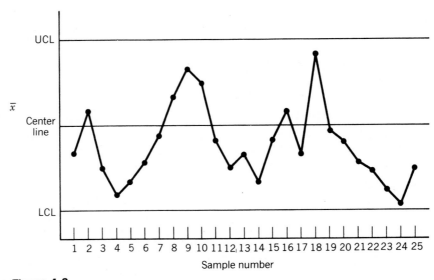

Figure 4-8
An $\bar{x}$ control chart.

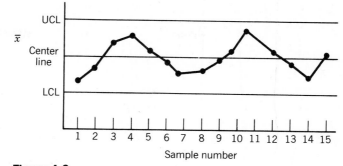

Figure 4-9
An $\bar{x}$ chart with a cyclic pattern.

indicate statistical control because their pattern is very nonrandom in appearance. Specifically, we note that 19 of the 25 points plot below the center line, while only 6 of them plot above. If the points are truly random, we should expect a more even distribution of them above and below the center line. We also observe that following the fourth point, five points in a row increase in magnitude. This arrangement of points is called a *run*. Since the observations are increasing, we could call this a run up. Similarly, a sequence of decreasing points is called a run down. This control chart has an unusually long run up (beginning with the fourth point) and an unusually long run down (beginning with the eighteenth point.)

In general, we define a run as a sequence of observations of the same type. In addition to runs up and runs down, we could define the types of observations as those above and below the center line, respectively, so that two points in a row above the center line would be a run of length 2.

A run of length 8 or more points has a very low probability of occurrence in a random sample of points. Consequently, any type of run of length 8 or more is often taken as a signal of an out-of-control condition. For example, eight consecutive points on one side of the center line will indicate that the process is out of control.

While runs are an important measure of nonrandom behavior on a control chart, other types of patterns may also indicate an out-of-control condition. For example, consider the $\bar{x}$ chart in Figure 4-9. Note that the plotted sample averages exhibit a cyclic behavior, yet they all fall within the control limits. Such a pattern may indicate a problem with the process, such as operator fatigue, raw material deliveries, heat or stress buildup, and so forth. While the process is not really out of control, the yield may be improved by elimination or reduction of the sources of variability causing this cyclic behavior (see Figure 4-10).

The problem is one of *pattern recognition*, that is, recognizing systematic or nonrandom patterns on the control chart and identifying the reason for this behavior. The ability to interpret a particular pattern in terms of assignable causes requires experience and knowledge of the process. That is, we must not only know the statistical principles of control charts, but we must also have a good understanding of the process. We discuss the interpretation of patterns on control charts in more detail in Chapter 6.

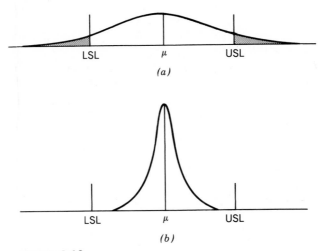

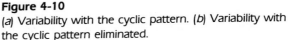

Figure 4-10
(*a*) Variability with the cyclic pattern. (*b*) Variability with
the cyclic pattern eliminated.

The Western Electric Handbook (1956) suggests a set of decision rules for detecting nonrandom patterns on control charts. Specifically, it suggests concluding that the process is out of control if either

1. One point plots outside the 3-sigma control limits.
2. Two out of three consecutive points plot beyond the 2-sigma warning limits.
3. Four out of five consecutive points plot at a distance of 1-sigma or beyond from the center line.
4. Eight consecutive points plot on one side of the center line.

Those rules apply to one side of the center line at a time. A point above the *upper* warning limit followed immediately by a point below the *lower* warning

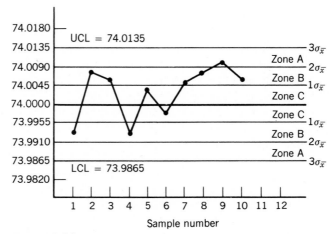

Figure 4-11
The Western Electric zone rules.

limit would not signal an out-of-control alarm. We have found these rules very effective in practice for enhancing the sensitivity of control charts.

Figure 4-11 shows an $\bar{x}$ control chart for the piston-ring process with the 1-sigma, 2-sigma, and 3-sigma limits used in the Western Electric procedure. Notice that these limits partition the control chart into three zones A, B, and C on each side of the center line. Consequently, the Western Electric rules are sometimes called the *zone rules* for control charts. Notice that the last four points fall in zone B or beyond. Thus, since four of five consecutive points exceed the 1-sigma limit, the Western Electric procedure will conclude that the pattern is nonrandom and the process is out of control.

4-3.6 Summary of Sensitizing Rules for Control Charts

As may be gathered from earlier sections, several criteria may be applied simultaneously to a control chart to determine whether the process is out of control. The basic criterion is one or more points outside of the control limits. The supplementary criteria are generally used to increase the *sensitivity* of the control charts to small process shifts so that we may respond more quickly to the assignable cause. Some of the *sensitizing rules* that are widely used in practice are listed below. Frequently we will inspect the control chart and conclude that the process is out of control if any *one* or more of the criteria is met.

1. One or more points outside of the control limits.
2. A run of at least eight points, where the type of run could be either a run up or down, a run above or below the center line, or a run above or below the median.
3. Two of three consecutive points outside the 2-sigma warning limits but still inside the control limits.
4. Four of five consecutive points beyond the 1-sigma limits.
5. An unusual or nonrandom pattern in the data.
6. One or more points near a warning or control limit.

When several of these sensitizing rules are applied simultaneously, we often use a *graduated response* to out-of-control signals. For example, if a point exceeded a control limit, we would immediately begin to search for the assignable cause, but if two out of three consecutive points exceeded only the 2-sigma warning limit, we might increase the frequency of sampling from every hour, say, to every 15 minutes. This response might not be as severe as a complete search for an assignable cause, but if the process was really out of control it would give us a high probability of detecting this situation more quickly than we would by maintaining the longer sampling interval.

In general, care should be exercised when using several of these sensitizing rules simultaneously. Suppose that the analyst uses k such criteria and that criterion i has type I error probability α_i. Then the overall type I error or false-alarm probability for the decision based on all k tests is

$$\alpha = 1 - \prod_{i=1}^{k} (1 - \alpha_i) \tag{4-3}$$

Thus, while using several out-of-control criteria simultaneously increases the sensitivity of the control chart, it also increases the overall false-alarm rate. In effect, if enough out-of-control criteria were applied, almost every sample would indicate an out-of-control condition. Note that Equation (4-3) assumes that the k criteria are independent. The out-of-control criteria listed above are probably *not* independent, and consequently, (4-3) should be regarded as only an approximation. Finally, as more out-of-control criteria are applied to the chart, the decision process becomes more complicated, and the inherent simplicity of the Shewhart control chart is lost. The decision rules could be easily implemented in a computer program, however.

4-4 THE REST OF THE "MAGNIFICENT SEVEN"

Although the control chart is a very powerful problem-solving and process improvement tool, it is most effective when its use is fully integrated into a comprehensive SPC program. The seven major SPC problem-solving tools should be widely taught throughout the organization and used routinely to identify improvement opportunities and to assist in reducing variability and eliminating waste. These "magnificent seven," introduced in Section 4-1, are listed again here for convenience:

1. Histogram
2. Check sheet
3. Pareto chart
4. Cause and effect diagram
5. Defect concentration diagram
6. Scatter diagram
7. Control chart

We have already introduced the histogram (Chapter 2) and control chart. In this section we will briefly illustrate the rest of the tools.

Check Sheet
In the early stages of an SPC implementation, it will often become necessary to collect either historical or current operating data about the process under investigation. A check sheet can be very useful in this data collection activity. The check sheet shown in Figure 4-12 was developed by an engineer at an aerospace firm who was investigating the various types of defects that occurred on a tank used in one of their products with a view toward improving the process. The engineer designed this check sheet to facilitate summarizing all the historical defect data available concerning the tanks. As only a few tanks were manufactured each month, it seemed appropriate to summarize the data monthly and to identify as many different types of defects as possible. The *time-oriented* summary is particularly valuable in looking for *trends* or other meaningful patterns. For example, if many defects occur during the summer, one possible cause that should be investigated is the use of temporary workers during a heavy vacation period.

When designing a check sheet, it is important to clearly specify the type of data to be collected, the part or operation number, the date, the analyst, and any

CHECK SHEET
DEFECT DATA FOR 1988–1989 YTD

Part No.: TAX-41
Location: Bellevue
Study Date: 6/5/89
Analyst: TCB

Defect	1988												1989					Total
	1	2	3	4	5	6	7	8	9	10	11	12	1	2	3	4	5	
Parts damaged		1		3	1	2		1		10	3		2	2	7	2		34
Machining problems			3	3				1	8		3		8	3				29
Supplied parts rusted			1	1		2	9											13
Masking insufficient		3	6	4	3	1												17
Misaligned weld	2																	2
Processing out of order	2															2		4
Wrong part issued		1				2												3
Unfinished fairing			3															3
Adhesive failure				1						1			2			1	1	6
Powdery alodine					1													1
Paint out of limits						1								1				2
Paint damaged by etching			1															1
Film on parts								3	1	1								5
Primer cans damaged						1												1
Voids in casting								1	1									2
Delaminated composite										2								2
Incorrect dimensions											13	7	13	1		1	1	36
Improper test procedure											1							1
Salt-spray failure													4					4
TOTAL	4	5	14	12	5	9	9	6	10	14	20	7	29	7	7	6	2	166

Figure 4-12
A check sheet to record defects on a tank used in an aerospace application.

other information useful in diagnosing the cause of poor performance. If the check sheet is the basis for performing further calculations or is used as a worksheet for data entry into a computer, then it is important to be sure that the check sheet will be adequate for this purpose before considerable effort is expended in actually collecting data. In some cases, a "trial run" to validate the check sheet layout and design may be helpful.

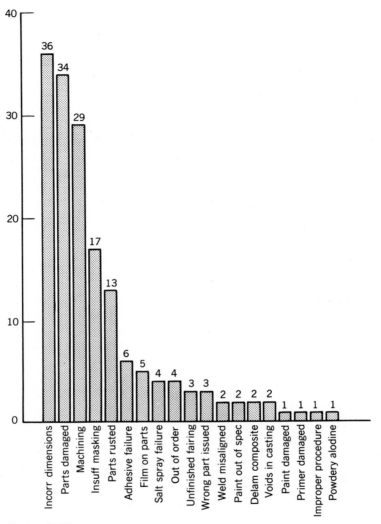

Figure 4-13
Pareto chart of the tank defect data.

Pareto Chart

The Pareto chart is simply a frequency distribution (or histogram) of attribute data arranged by category. To illustrate a Pareto chart, consider the tank defect data presented in Figure 4-12. Plot the total frequency of occurrence of each defect type (the last column of the table in Figure 4-12) against the various defect types to produce Figure 4-13, which is called a Pareto chart.[3] Through this chart the user can quickly and visually identify the most frequently occurring types of defects.

---

[3] The name Pareto chart is derived from Italian economist Vilfredo Pareto (1848–1923), who theorized that in certain economies the majority of the wealth was held by a disproportionately small segment of the population. Quality engineers have observed that defects usually follow a similar Pareto distribution.

For example, Figure 4-13 indicates that incorrect dimensions, parts damaged, and machining are the most commonly encountered defects. Thus, the causes of these defect types should probably be identified and attacked first.

Notice that the Pareto chart does not automatically identify the most *important* defects, but rather only those that occur most frequently. For example, in Figure 4-13, casting voids occur very infrequently (2 of 166 defects, or 1.2%). However, voids could result in scrapping the tank, a potentially large cost exposure— perhaps so large that casting voids should be elevated to a major defect category. When the list of defects contains a mixture of those that might have extremely serious consequences and others of much less importance, one of two methods can be used:

1. Use a weighting scheme to modify the frequency counts. Weighting schemes for defects are discussed in Chapter 5.
2. Accompany the *frequency* Pareto chart analysis with a *cost* or *exposure* Pareto chart.

There are many variations of the basic Pareto chart. Figure 4-14*a* shows a Pareto chart applied to an electronics assembly process using surface-mount components. The vertical axis is the percent of components incorrectly located, and the horizontal axis is the component number, a code that locates the device on the printed circuit board. Notice that locations 27 and 39 account for 70% of the errors. This may be the result of the *type* or *size* of components at these locations, or of *where* these locations are on the board layout. Figure 4-14*b* presents another Pareto chart from the electronics industry. The vertical axis is the number of defective components, and the horizontal axis is the component number. Notice that each vertical bar has been broken down by supplier to produce a *stacked Pareto chart*. This analysis clearly indicates that supplier A provides a disproportionally large share of the defective components.

Pareto charts are widely used in *nonmanufacturing applications* of quality-improvement methods. A Pareto chart used by a quality-improvement team in a procurement organization is shown in Figure 4-14*c*. The team was investigating errors on purchase orders in an effort to reduce the number of purchase order changes issued by the organization. (Each change typically costs between $100 and $500, and this organization issued several hundred purchase order changes each month.) This Pareto chart has two scales—one for the actual error frequency and another for the percentage of errors.

In general, the Pareto chart is one of the most useful of the "magnificent seven." Its applications to quality improvement are limited only by the ingenuity of the analyst.

Cause and Effect Diagram

Once a defect, error, or problem has been identified and isolated for further study, we must begin to analyze potential *causes* of this undesirable *effect*. In situations where causes are not obvious (sometimes they are) the cause and effect diagram is a formal tool frequently useful in unlayering potential causes. The cause and effect diagram constructed by a quality-improvement team assigned to identify potential problem areas in the tank manufacturing process mentioned earlier is shown in Figure 4-15. The steps in constructing the cause and effect diagram

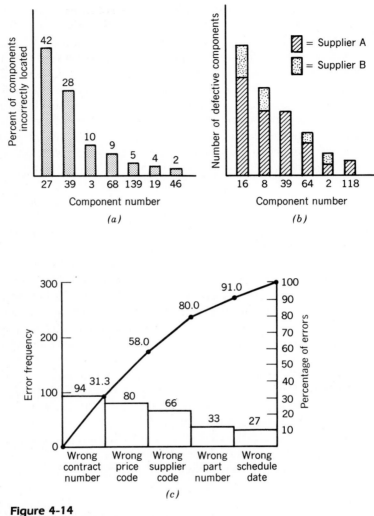

Figure 4-14
Various examples of Pareto charts.

are as follows:

1. Define the problem or effect to be analyzed.
2. Form the team to perform the analysis. Often the team will uncover potential causes through brainstorming.
3. Draw the effect box and the center line.
4. Specify the major potential cause categories and join them as boxes connected to the center line.
5. Identify the possible causes and classify them into the categories in steps 4. Create new categories, it necessary.
6. Rank order the causes to identify those that seem most likely to impact the problem.
7. Take corrective action.

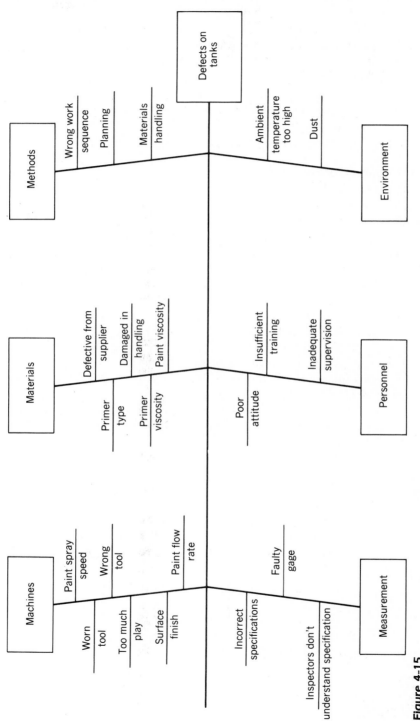

Figure 4-15
Cause and effect diagram for the tank defect problem.

In this example, the team elected to lay out the major categories of tank defects as machines, materials, methods, personnel, measurement, and environment. A brainstorming session ensued to identify the various subcauses in each of these major categories and to prepare the diagram in Figure 4-15. Then through discussion and the process of elimination, the group decided that material and methods contained the most likely cause categories.

Cause and effect analysis is an extremely powerful tool. A highly detailed cause and effect diagram can serve as an effective trouble-shooting aid. Furthermore, the construction of a cause and effect diagram as a *team* experience tends to get people involved in attacking a problem rather than in affixing blame.

Defect Concentration Diagram

A defect concentration diagram is a picture of the unit, showing all relevant views. Then the various types of defect are drawn on the picture, and the diagram is analyzed to determine whether the *location* of the defects on the unit conveys any useful information about the potential causes of the defects.

Figure 4-16 presents a defect concentration diagram for the final assembly stage of a refrigerator manufacturing process. Surface-finish defects are identified by the dark shaded areas on the refrigerator. From inspection of the diagram it seems clear that materials handling is responsible for the majority of these defects. The unit is being moved by securing a belt around the middle, and this belt is either too loose (tight), worn out, made of abrasive material, or too narrow. Furthermore, when the unit is moved the corners are being damaged. It is possible that worker fatigue is a factor in this process. In any event, proper work methods and improved materials handling will likely improve this process dramatically.

Figure 4-17 shows the defect concentration diagram for the tank problem mentioned earlier. Notice that this diagram shows several different broad categories of defects, each identified with a specific code. Often different colors are used to indicate different types of defects.

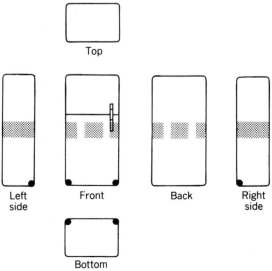

Figure 4-16
Surface-finish defects on a refrigerator.

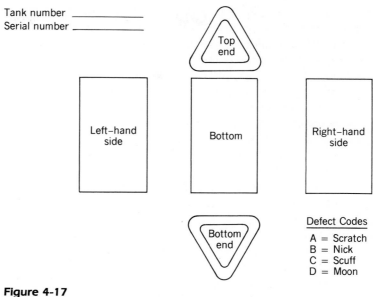

Figure 4-17
Defect concentration diagram for the tank.

When defect data are portrayed on a defect concentration diagram over a sufficient number of units, patterns frequently emerge, and the location of these patterns often contains much information about the causes of the defects. We have found defect concentration diagrams to be important problem-solving tools in many industries, including plating, painting and coating, casting and foundry operations, machining, and electronics assembly.

Scatter Diagram

The scatter diagram is a useful plot for identifying a potential relationship between two variables. Data are collected in pairs on the two variables, say (y_i, x_i), for $i = 1, 2, \ldots, n$. This y_i is plotted against the corresponding x_i. The shape of the scatter diagram often indicates what type of relationship may be occurring between the two variables.

Figure 4-18 shows a scatter diagram relating metal recovery (in percent) from a magnathermic smelting process for magnesium against corresponding values of

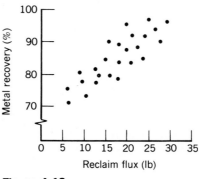

Figure 4-18
A scatter diagram.

the amount of reclaim flux added to the crucible. The scatter diagram indicates a strong *positive correlation* between metal recovery and flux amount; that is, as the amount of flux added is increased, the metal recovery also increases. It is tempting to conclude that the relationship is one based on cause and effect: By increasing the amount of reclaim flux used, we can always insure high metal recovery. This thinking is potentially dangerous, because *correlation* does not necessarily imply *causality*. This apparent relationship could be caused by something quite different. For example, both variables could be related to a third one, such as the temperature of the metal prior to the reclaim pouring operation, and this relationship could be responsible for what we see in Figure 4-18. If higher temperatures lead to higher metal recovery, and the practice is to add reclaim flux in proportion to temperature, adding more flux when the process is running at low temperature will do nothing to enhance yield. The scatter diagram is useful for identifying *potential relationships. Designed experiments* [see Montgomery (1984)] must be used to verify causality.

4-5 IMPLEMENTING SPC

The methods of statistical process control can provide significant payback to those companies that can successfully implement them. While SPC seems to be a collection of statistically based problem-solving tools, there is more to the successful use of SPC than learning and using these tools. Management involvement and commitment to the quality-improvement process is the most vital component of SPC's potential success. Management is a role model, and others in the organization will look to management for guidance and for example. A team approach is also important, as it is usually difficult for one person alone to introduce process improvements. Many of the "magnificent seven" are helpful in building an improvement team, including cause and effect diagrams, Pareto charts, and defect concentration diagrams. The basis SPC problem-solving tools must become widely known and widely used throughout the organization. Continuous training in SPC and quality improvement is necessary to achieve this widespread knowledge of the tools.

The objective of an SPC-based quality-improvement program is continuous improvement on a weekly, quarterly, and annual basis. SPC is not a one-time program to be applied when the business is in trouble and later abandoned. Quality improvement must become part of the culture of the organization.

The control chart is an important tool for process improvement. Processes do not naturally operate in an in-control state, and the use of control charts is an important step that must be taken early in an SPC program to eliminate assignable causes, reduce process variability, and stabilize process performance. In order to improve quality and productivity, we must begin to manage with facts and data, and not just rely on judgment. Control charts are an important part of this change in management approach.

In implementing a company-wide SPC program, we have found that the following elements are usually present in all successful efforts:

1. Management leadership.
2. A team approach.

3. Education of employees at all levels.

4. Emphasis on continuous improvement.

5. A mechanism of recognizing success.

We cannot overemphasize the importance of management leadership and the team approach. Successful quality improvement is a "top-down" management-driven activity. It is also important to measure progress and success, and to spread knowledge of this success throughout the organization. When successful improvements are communicated throughout the company, this can provide motivation and incentive to improve other processes and to make continuous improvement a normal part of the way of doing business.

The philosophy of W. Edwards Deming is an important framework for implementing quality and productivity improvement. Deming's philosophy is summarized in his 14 points for management. The adherence to these management principles has been an important factor in Japan's industrial success and continues to be the catalyst in that nation's quality- and productivity-improvement efforts. This philosophy is also now spreading rapidly in the west. We now give a brief statement and discussion of Deming's 14 points.

1. Create a constancy of purpose focused on the improvement of products and services. Constantly try to improve product design and performance. Investment in research, development, and innovation will have a long-term payback to the organization.

2. Adopt a new philosophy of rejecting poor workmanship, defective products, or bad service. It costs as much to produce a defective unit as it does to produce a good one (and sometimes more). The cost of dealing with scrap, rework, and other losses created by defectives is an enormous drain on company resources.

3. Do not rely on mass inspection to "control" quality. All inspection can do is to sort out defectives, and at this point it is too late because we have already paid to produce these defectives. Inspection occurs too late in the process, it is expensive, and it is often ineffective. Quality results from prevention of defectives through process improvement, not inspection.

4. Do not award business to suppliers on the basis of price alone, but also consider quality. Price is a meaningful measure of a supplier's product only if it is considered in relation to a measure of quality. In other words, the total cost of the item must be considered, not just the purchase price. When quality is considered, the lowest bidder is frequently not the low-cost supplier. Preference should be given to suppliers who use modern methods of quality improvement in their business and who can demonstrate process control and capability.

5. Focus on continuous improvement. Constantly try to improve the production and service system. Involve the work force in these activities and make use of statistical methods, particularily the SPC problem-solving tools discussed in the previous section.

6. Practice modern training methods and invest in training for all employees. Everyone should be trained in the technical aspects of their job, and in modern quality- and productivity-improvement methods as well. The training should encourage all employees to practice these methods every day.

7. Practice modern supervision methods. Supervision should not consist merely of passive surveillance of workers, but should be focussed on helping the employees improve the system in which they work. The number one goal of supervision should be to improve the work system and the product.

8. Drive out fear. Many workers are afraid to ask questions, report problems, or point out conditions that are barriers to quality and effective production. In many organizations the economic loss associated with fear is large; only management can eliminate fear.

9. Break down the barriers between functional areas of the business. Teamwork among different organizational units is essential for effective quality and productivity improvement to take place.

10. Eliminate targets, slogans, and numerical goals for the work force. A target such as "zero defects" is useless without a plan as to how to achieve this objective. In fact, these slogans and "programs" are usually counterproductive. Work to improve the system and provide information on that.

11. Eliminate numerical quotas and work standards. These standards have historically been set without regard to quality. Work standards are symptoms of management's inability to understand the work process and to provide an effective management system focused on improving this process.

12. Remove the barriers that discourage employees from doing their jobs. Management must listen to employee suggestions, comments, and complaints. The person who is doing the job is the one who knows the most about it, and usually has valuable ideas about how to make the process work more effectively. The work force is an important participant in the business, and not just an opponent in collective bargaining.

13. Institute an ongoing program of training and education for all employees. Education in simple, powerful statistical techniques should be mandatory for all employees. Use of the basic SPC problem-solving tools, particularly the control chart, should become widespread in the business. As these charts become widespread, and as employees understand their uses, they will be more likely to look for the causes of poor quality and to identify process improvements. Education is a way of making everyone partners in the quality-improvement process.

14. Create a structure in top management that will vigorously advocate the first 13 points.

As we read Deming's 14 points we notice two things. First, there is a strong emphasis on change. Second, the role of management in guiding this change process is of dominating importance. But what should be changed, and how should this change process be started? For example, if we want to improve the yield of a semiconductor manufacturing process, what should we do? It is in this area that SPC methods come into play most frequently. To improve the semiconductor process, we must determine which controllable factors in the process influence the number of defective units produced. To answer this question, we must collect data on the process and see how the system reacts to changes in the process variables. Statistical methods, including the SPC techniques in this book, can contribute to these activities. In the next two sections, we present two brief case studies that illustrate the use of SPC methods in process change and improvement.

4-6 AN APPLICATION OF SPC

In this section, we give an account of applying SPC methods to improve quality and productivity in a copper plating operation at a printed circuit board fabrication facility. This process was characterized by high levels of defects such as brittle copper and copper voids and by long flow time. The long flow time was particularly troublesome, as it had led to an extensive work backlog and was a major contributor to poor conformance to the factory production schedule.

Management chose this process area for an initial implementation of SPC. An improvement team was formed, consisting of the plating tank operator, the manufacturing engineer responsible for the process, and a quality engineer. All members of the team had been exposed to the "magnificent seven" in a company-sponsored SPC seminar. During the first team meeting, it was decided to concentrate on reducing the flow time through the process, as the missed delivery targets were considered to be the most serious obstacle to improving productivity. The team quickly determined (based on operator experience) that excessive downtime on the controller that regulated the copper concentration in the plating tank was a major factor in the excessive flow time, as controller downtime translated directly into lost production.

The team decided to use a cause and effect analysis to begin to isolate the potential causes of controller downtime. Figure 4-19 shows the cause and effect diagram that was produced during a brainstorming session focused on controller downtime. The team was able to quickly identify 11 major potential causes of controller downtime. However, when they examined the equipment logbook to make a more definitive diagnosis of the causes of downtime based on actual process performance, the results were disappointing. The logbook contained little useful information about causes of downtime; instead, it contained only a chronological record of when the machine was up and when it was down.

The team then decided that it would be necessary to collect valid data about the causes of controller downtime. They designed the check sheet shown in Figure 4-20 as a supplemental page for the logbook. The team agreed that whenever the equipment was down one team member would assume responsibility for filling out the check sheet. Notice that the major causes of controller downtime identified on the cause and effect diagram have been used to structure the headings and subheadings on the check sheet. The team agreed that data would be collected over a four- to six-week period.

As more reliable data concerning the causes of controller downtime became available, the team was able to analyze it using other SPC techniques. Figure 4-21 presents the Pareto analysis of the controller failure data produced during the six-week study of the process. Notice that concentration variation is a major cause of downtime. Actually, the situation is probably more complex than it appears. The third largest category of downtime causes is reagent replenishment. Frequently, the reagent in the colorimeter on the controller is replenished because concentration has varied so far outside the process specifications that reagent replenishment and colorimeter recalibration is the only step that can be used to bring the process back on line. Therefore, it is possible that up to 50% of the downtime associated with controller failures can be attributed to concentration variation. Figure 4-22 presents a Pareto analysis of only the concentration variation data. From this diagram we know that colorimeter drift and problems with reagents are major causes of concentration variation. This information led the manufacturing engineer

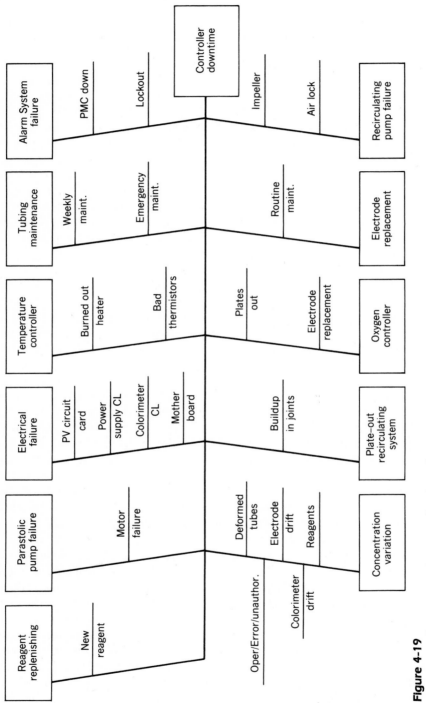

Figure 4-19
Cause and effect diagram for controller downtime.

WEEKLY TALLY	OPERATOR _____		
WEEK ENDING _____	ERRORS	DESCRIPTION	ACTION
1. CONCENTRATION VARIATION			
a. Colorimeter drift	_____		
b. Electrode failure	_____		
c. Reagents	_____		
d. Deformed tubes	_____		
e. Oper/error/unauthorized	_____		
2. ALARM SYSTEM FAILURE			
a. PMC down	_____		
b. Lockout	_____		
3. RECIRCULATING PUMP FAILURE			
a. Air lock	_____		
b. Impeller	_____		
4. REAGENT REPLENISHING			
a. New reagent	_____		
5. TUBING MAINTENANCE			
a. Weekly maintenance	_____		
b. Emergency maintenance	_____		
6. ELECTRODE REPLACEMENT			
a. Routine maintenance	_____		
7. TEMPERATURE CONTROLLER			
a. Burned out heater	_____		
b. Bad thermistors	_____		
8. OXYGEN CONTROLLER			
a. Plates out	_____		
b. Electrode replacement	_____		
9. PARASTOLIC PUMP FAILURE			
a. Motor failure	_____		
10. ELECTRICAL FAILURE			
a. PV circuit card	_____		
b. Power supply CL	_____		
c. Colorimeter CL	_____		
d. Mother board	_____		
11. PLATE-OUT RECIRCULATING			
a. Buildup at joints	_____		
TOTAL COUNT			

Figure 4-20
Check sheet for logbook.

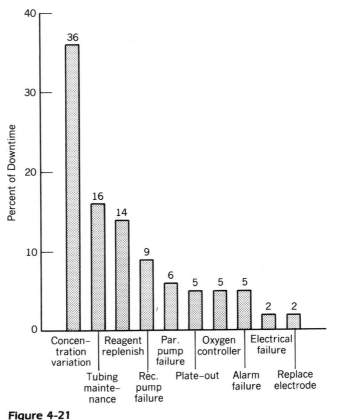

Figure 4-21
Pareto analysis of controller failures.

on the team to conclude that rebuilding the colorimeter would be an important step in improving the process.

During the time that these process data were collected, the team decided to run statistical control charts on the process. Copper concentration is measured in this process manually three times per day. Figure 4-23 presents the $\bar{x}$ control chart for average daily copper concentration. That is, each point plotted in Figure 4-23 is a daily average. The chart shows the center line and 3-sigma statistical control limits. (We will discuss the construction of these limits in more detail in the next few chapters.) Notice that there are a number of points outside the control limits, indicating that assignable causes are present in the process. Figure 4-24 presents an R chart for daily copper concentration. The symbol R represents the range, that is, the difference between the maximum and minimum copper concentration readings in a day. Notice that the R chart also exhibits lack of statistical control. In particular, the second half of the R chart appears much more unstable than the first half. Examining the dates along the horizontal axis, the team noticed that severe variation in average daily copper concentration only appeared after January 3. The last observations on copper concentration had been taken on November 22. From November 23 until January 3 the process had been in a shutdown mode because of holidays. Apparently, when the process was restarted, substantial deterioration in controller/colorimeter performance had occurred. This hastened engineering's decision to rebuild the colorimeter.

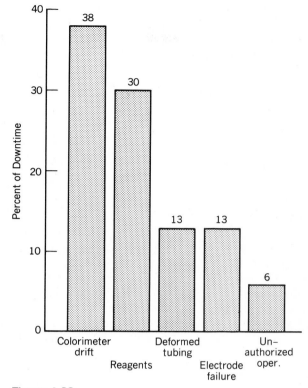

Figure 4-22
Pareto analysis of concentration variation.

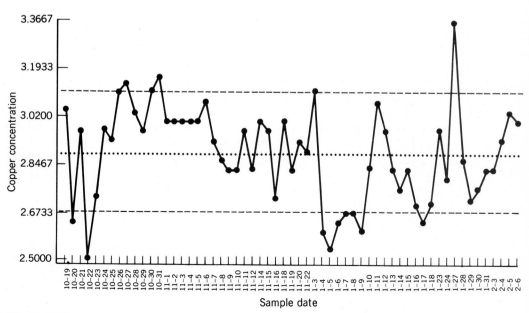

Figure 4-23
$\bar{X}$ chart for average daily copper concentration.

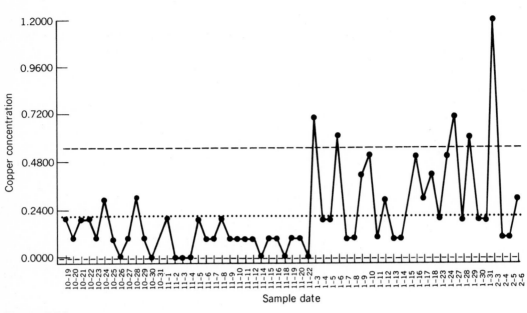

Figure 4-24
R chart for daily copper concentration.

Figure 4-25 presents a tolerance diagram of daily copper concentration readings. In this figure, each day's copper concentration readings are plotted, and the extremes connect with a vertical line. In some cases more than one observation plotted at a single position, so a numeral is used to indicate the number of obser-

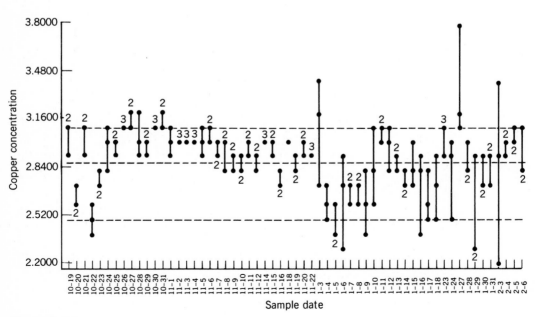

Figure 4-25
Tolerance diagram of daily copper concentration.

vations plotted at each particular point. The center line on this chart is the process average over the time period studied, and the upper and lower limits are the specification limits on copper concentration. Every instance in which a point is outside the specification limits would correspond to nonscheduled downtime on the process. Several things are evident from examining the tolerance diagram. First, the process average is significantly different from the nominal specification on copper concentration (the midpoint of the upper and lower tolerance band). This implies that the calibration of the colorimeter may be inadequate. That is, we are literally aiming at the wrong target. Second, we notice that there is considerably more variation in the daily copper concentration readings after January 3 than there was prior to shutdown. Finally, if we could reduce variation in the process to a level roughly consistent with that observed prior to shutdown and correct the process centering, many of the points outside specifications would not have occurred, and downtime on the process should be reduced.

In early February, the colorimeter and controller were rebuilt by manufacturing engineering. The result of this maintenance activity was to restore the variability in daily copper concentration readings to the pre-shutdown level. The rebuilt colorimeter was recalibrated and was subsequently able to hold the correct target. This recentering and recalibration of the process reduced the downtime on the controller from approximately 60% to less than 20%. At this point the process was capable of meeting the required production rate.

Once this aspect of process performance was improved, the team directed its efforts to reducing the number of defective units produced by the process. Generally, as noted earlier, defects fell into two major categories: brittle copper and copper voids. The team decided that, while control charts and statistical process techniques could be applied to this problem, the use of experimental design methods might lead to a more rapid solution. Statistically designed experiments can be used in any fabrication process for which we can identify controllable input variables to the process. The objective of a designed experiment is to generate information that will allow us to understand and model the relationship between these process variables and measures of the process performance. A designed experiment is simply a test, or a series of tests, in which the factors or process variables are varied according to a particular pattern.

The designed experiment for the plating process is shown in Table 4-1. The objective of this experiment was to minimize the plating defects. The process variables considered in the experiment were copper concentration, sodium hydroxide concentration, formaldehyde concentration, temperature, and oxygen. A low and high level, represented symbolically by the minus and plus signs in Table 4-1, were chosen for each process variable. The team initially considered a factoral experiment, that is, an experiment design in which all possible combinations of these factor levels would be run. This design would have required 32 runs, however, so a fractional factorial design that used only 16 runs was ultimately selected. This fractional factorial design is shown in the bottom half of Table 4-1. In this experiment design, each row of the table is a run on the process. The combination of minus and plus signs in each column of that row determines the low and high levels of the five process variables to be used during that run. For example, in Run 1 copper concentration, sodium hydroxide concentration, formaldehyde concentration, and temperature are run at the low level and oxygen is run at the high level. The process would be run at each of the 16 sets of conditions described by the design (for reasons to be discussed later, the runs would not be made in the order

Table 4-1
A designed experiment for the plating process

OBJECTIVE: MINIMIZE PLATING DEFECTS.

Process Variables	Low Level	High Level
A = Copper concentration	−	+
B = Sodium hydroxide concentration	−	+
C = Formaldehyde concentration	−	+
D = Temperature	−	+
E = Oxygen	−	+

EXPERIMENT DESIGN

Run	A	B	C	D	E	Response (Defects)
1	−	−	−	−	−	
2	+	−	−	−	−	
3	−	+	−	−	−	
4	+	+	−	−	+	
5	−	−	+	−	−	
6	+	−	+	−	+	
7	−	+	+	−	+	
8	+	+	+	−	−	
9	−	−	−	+	−	
10	+	−	−	+	+	
11	−	+	−	+	+	
12	+	+	−	+	−	
13	−	−	+	+	+	
14	+	−	+	+	−	
15	−	+	+	+	−	
16	+	+	+	+	+	

shown in Table 4-1), and a response variable (an observed number of plating defects) would be recorded for each run. Then these data could be analyzed using simple statistical techniques to determine which factors have a significant influence on plating defects, whether or not any of the factors jointly influence the occurrence of defects, and whether it is possible to adjust these variables to new levels that will reduce plating defects below their current level. While a complete discussion of design of experiments is beyond the scope of this text, we will present examples of designed experiments for improving process performance in Part III.

After the team had conducted the experiment shown in Table 4-1 and analyzed the resulting process data, they determined that several of the process variables that they had identified for the study were important and had significant impact on the occurrence of plating defects. They were able to adjust these factors to new levels, as a result of which plating defects were reduced by approximately a factor of 10. Therefore, at the conclusion of the team's initial effort at applying SPC to the plating process, it had made substantial improvements in product flow time through the process and had taken a major step in driving the process toward a near-zero-defect capability.

4-7 NONMANUFACTURING APPLICATION OF STATISTICAL PROCESS CONTROL

This book presents the underlying principles of statistical process control. Most of the examples used to reinforce these principles are in an industrial, product-oriented framework. There have been many successful applications of statistical process-control methods in the manufacturing environment. However, the principles themselves are general; consequently, there are many nonindustrial or service industry applications of statistical process-control and quality-improvement methodology.

These nonmanufacturing applications do not differ substantially from the more usual industrial applications. As an example, the control chart for fraction nonconforming (which is discussed in the next chapter) could be applied to reducing billing errors in a bank credit card operation as easily as it could be used to reduce the fraction of nonconforming printed circuit boards produced in an electronics plant. The $\bar{x}$ and R charts discussed in this chapter and applied to the piston-ring manufacturing process could be used to monitor and control the flow time of accounts payable through a finance function. Nonmanufacturing or non-product applications of statistical process-control and quality-improvement methodology sometimes require ingenuity beyond that normally required for the more typical manufacturing applications. There seems to be two primary reasons for this difference:

1. Most nonmanufacturing operations do not have a natural measurement system that allows the analyst easily to define quality.
2. The system that is to be improved is usually fairly obvious in a manufacturing setting, while the observability of the process in a nonmanufacturing setting may be fairly low.

For example, if we are trying to improve the performance of a personal computer assembly line, then it is likely that the line will be contained within one facility and the activities of the system will be readily observable. However, if we are trying to improve the operation of a finance organization, then the observability of the process may be low. The actual activities of the process may be performed by a group of people who work in different locations, and the operation steps or workflow sequence may be difficult to observe. Furthermore, the lack of a quantitative and objective measurement system in most nonmanufacturing processes complicates the problem.

The key to applying statistical process-control and other quality-improvement methods in a nonmanufacturing environment is to focus initial efforts on resolving these two issues. We have found that once the system is adequately defined and a valid measurement system has been developed, most of the SPC tools discussed in this chapter can be easily applied to a wide variety of nonmanufacturing operations including finance, marketing, materiel and procurement, customer support, field service, engineering development and design, and software development and programming.

Flow charts and operation process charts are particularly useful in developing process definition and process understanding. A flow chart is just a chronological sequence of process steps or workflow. Flow charts must be constructed in sufficient detail to identify value-added versus nonvalue-added work activity in the process.

Most nonmanufacturing operations have scrap, rework, and other nonvalue-add operations, such as unnecessary work steps and choke-points or bottlenecks that can be eliminated by

1. Rearranging the sequence of worksteps.
2. Rearranging the physical location of the operators in the system.
3. Changing work methods.
4. Changing the type of equipment used in the process.
5. Redesigning forms and documents for more efficient use.
6. Improving operator training.
7. Improving supervision.
8. Identifying more clearly the function of the process to all employees.
9. Trying to eliminate unnecessary steps.
10. Trying to consolidate process steps.

As an illustration of some of these ideas, we present a brief example of applying quality-improvement methods in a planning organization. This planning organization, part of a large aerospace manufacturing concern, produces the plans and documents that accompany each job to the factory floor. These plans are quite extensive, often several hundred pages long. Errors in the planning process can have major impact on the factory floor, contributing to scrap and rework, lost production time, overtime, missed delivery schedules, and many other problems.

Figure 4-26 presents a high-level flow chart of this planning process. After plans are produced, they are sent to a checker who tries to identify obvious errors and defects in the plans. The plans are also reviewed by a quality-assurance organization to insure that process specifications are being met and that the final product will conform to engineering standards. Then the plans are sent to the shop, where a liaison engineering organization deals with any errors in the plan encountered

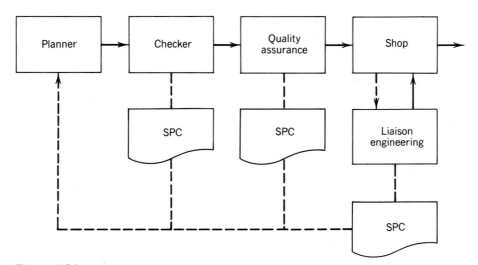

Figure 4-26
A high-level flow chart of the planning process.

Data Sheet P/N _____	ERROR	DESCRIPTION	ACTION TAKEN
1. HEADER SECT.			
a. PART NO.			
b. ITEM			
c. MODEL			
2. DWG/DOC SECT.			
3. COMPONENT PART SECT.			
a. PROCUREMENT CODES			
b. STAGING			
c. MOA (# SIGNS)			
4. MOTE SECT.			
5. MATERIAL SECT.			
a. MCC CODE (NON MP&R)			
6. OPERATION SECT.			
a. ISSUE STORE(S)			
b. EQUIPMENT USAGE			
c. OPC FWC MNEMONICS			
d. SEQUENCING			
e. OPER'S OMITTED			
f. PROCESS SPEC'S			
g. END ROUTE STORE			
h. WELD GRID			
7. TOOL/SHOP AIDS ORDERS			
8. CAR/SHOP STOCK PREP.			

REMARKS:

CHECKER _____

NO. OF OPERATIONS _____   DATE _____

Figure 4-27
The check sheet for the planning example.

Monthly Data Summary					
1. HEADER SECT.					
a. PART NO.					
b. ITEM					
c. MODEL					
2. DWG/DOC SECT.					
3. COMPONENT PART SECT.					
a. PROCUREMENT CODES					
b. STAGING					
c. MOA (# SIGNS)					
4. MOTE SECT.					
5. MATERIAL SECT.					
a. MCC CODE (NON MP&R)					
6. OPERATION SECT.					
a. ISSUE STORE(S)					
b. EQUIPMENT USAGE					
c. OPC FWC MNEMONICS					
d. SEQUENCING					
e. OPER'S OMITTED					
f. PROCESS SPEC'S					
g. END ROUTE STORE					
h. WELD GRID					
7. TOOL/SHOP AIDS ORDERS					
8. CAR/SHOP STOCK PREP.					
TOTAL NUMBER ERRORS					
TOTAL OPERATIONS CHECKED					
WEEK ENDING					

Figure 4-28
The summary check sheet.

by manufacturing. This flow chart is useful in presenting an overall picture of the planning system. It is not particularly helpful in uncovering nonvalue-add activities as there is insufficient detail in each of the major blocks. However, each block, such as the planner, checker, and quality-assurance block, could be broken down into a more detailed sequence of work activities and steps. The step-down approach is frequently helpful in constructing flow charts for complex processes. However, even at the relatively high level shown, it is possible to identify at least three areas where SPC methods could be usefully applied in the planning process.

The management of the planning organization decided to use the reduction of planning errors as a quality-improvement project for their organization. A team of managers, planners, and checkers was chosen to begin this implementation. The team decided that each week three plans would be selected at random from the week's output of plans and that these plans would be analyzed extensively to record all planning errors that could be found. The check sheet shown in Figure 4-27 was used to record the errors found in each plan. These weekly data were summarized monthly, using the summary check sheet presented in Figure 4-28. After several weeks, the team was able to summarize the planning error data obtained using the Pareto analysis in Figure 4-29. This Pareto chart implies that errors in

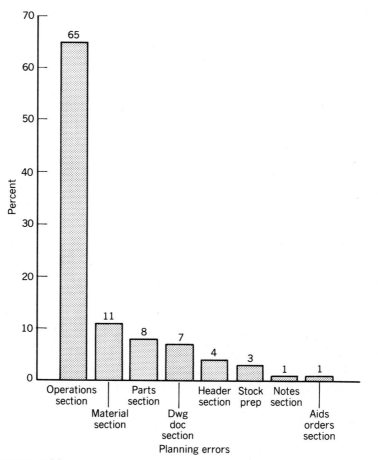

Figure 4-29
Pareto analysis of planning errors.

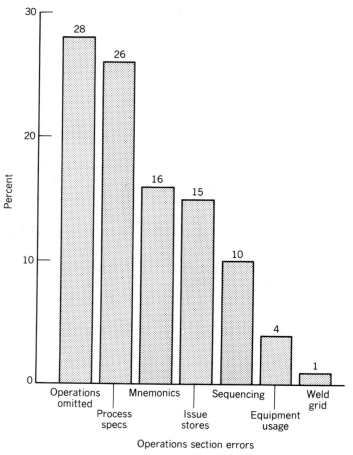

Figure 4-30
Pareto analysis of operations section errors.

the operations section of the plan are predominant. In fact, 65% of the planning errors are in the operations section. Figure 4-30 presents a further Pareto analysis of the operations section errors. We see that omitted operations and process specifications are the major contributors to the problem.

The team decided that many of the operations errors were occurring because planners were not sufficiently familiar with the manufacturing operations and the process specifications that were currently in place. Consequently, a program was undertaken to refamiliarize planners with the details of factory floor operations and to provide more feedback on the type of planning errors actually experienced. Figure 4-31 presents a run chart of the planning errors per operation for 25 consecutive weeks. Notice that there is a general tendency for the planning errors per operation to decline over the first half of the study period. This decline may be partly due to the increased training and supervision activities for the planners and partly to the additional feedback they were given regarding the types of planning errors that were occurring. The team also recommended that substantial changes be made in the work methods used to prepare plans. Rather than an individual

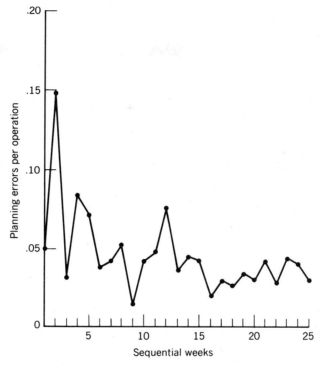

Figure 4-31
A run chart of planning errors.

planner with overall responsibility for the operations section, it recommended that this task become a team activity so that knowledge and experience regarding the interface between factory and planning operations could be shared in an effort to further improve the process.

This planning organization began to use other statistical process-control tools as part as their quality-improvement effort. For example, note that the run chart in Figure 4-31 could be converted to a statistical control chart with the addition of a center line and appropriate control limits. Once the planners were exposed to the concepts of SPC, these control charts came into use in the organization. The control charts proved effective in identifying assignable causes: that is, periods of time in which the error rates produced by the system were higher than those that could be justified by chance cause alone. It is its ability to differentiate between assignable and chance causes that makes the control chart so indispensable. Management must react differently to an assignable cause than it does to a chance or random cause. Assignable causes are due to phenomena external to the system, and they must be tracked down and their underlying root causes eliminated. Chance or random causes are part of the system itself. They can only be reduced or eliminated by making changes in how the system operates. This may mean changes in work methods and procedures, improved levels of operator training, different types of equipment and facilities, or improved input materials, all of which are the responsibility of management. In the planning process, many of the common causes identified were related to the experience, training, and supervision of the individual planners, as well as poor input information from design and development engineering. These common causes were systematically removed from the process, and the long-term impact of the SPC implementation in this organization was to reduce planning errors to a level of less one planning error per 1000 operations.

4-8 Exercises

4-1   Discuss the concepts of chance and assignable causes of variability and the part they play in statistical quality control.

4-2   Is the control chart equivalent to a statistical test of a hypothesis?

4-3   Discuss type I and type II errors relative to the control chart. What practical implication in terms of process operation do these two types of errors have?

4-4   What is meant by the statement that a process is in a state of statistical control?

4-5   Discuss the logic behind the general use of 3-sigma limits on Shewhart control charts.

4-6   What are warning limits on a control chart? How are they used?

4-7   Discuss the rational subgroup concept. What part does it play in control chart analysis?

4-8   What information is provided by the operating-characteristic curve of a control chart?

4-9   How do the costs of sampling, the costs of producing an excessive number of defective units, and the costs of searching for assignable causes impact on the choice of the parameters of a control chart?

4-10   Consider the control chart shown below. Does the pattern appear random?

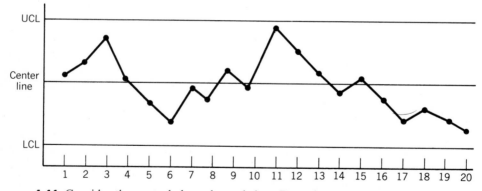

4-11   Consider the control chart shown below. Does the pattern appear random?

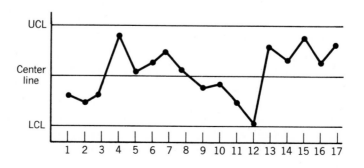

4-12 Consider the control chart shown below. Does the pattern appear random?

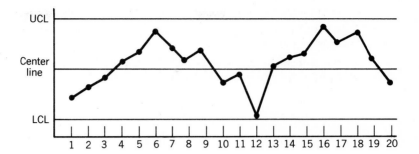

4-13 Consider the control chart shown in Exercise 4-10. Would the use of warning limits reveal any out-of-control conditions?

4-14 Apply the Western Electric rules to the control chart in Exercise 4-10. Are any of the criteria for declaring the process out of control satisfied?

4-15 Sketch warning limits on the control chart in Exercise 4-12. Do these limits indicate any out-of-control conditions?

4-16 Apply the Western Electric rules to the control chart presented in Exercise 4-12. Would these rules result in any out-of-control signals?

4-17 Suppose that an $\bar{x}$-chart with 2-sigma limits is used to control a process. If the process remains in control, find the average run length until a false out-of-control signal is observed. Compare this with the in-control ARL for 3-sigma limits and discuss.

4-18 Two decision rules are given below. Assume they apply to a normally distributed quality characteristic. Further assume that the control chart has 3-sigma control limits.

> **Rule 1:** If *one or more* of the next seven samples yield values of the test statistic that fall outside the control limits, conclude that the process is out of control.
>
> **Rule 2:** If *all* of the next seven points fall on the same side of the center line, conclude that the process is out of control.

What is the overall α-risk for each of these rules?

4-19 **Continuation of Exercise 4-18.** Consider the situation in Exercise 4-18. If the mean of the quality characteristic shifts one standard deviation, that is, goes out of control by 1-sigma, and remains there during the collection of the next seven samples, what is the β-risk associated with both decision rules?

4-20 A normally distributed quality characteristic is monitored by a control chart with 3-sigma control limits. Develop a general expression for the probability that a point will plot outside the control limits when the process is really in control.

4-21 A quality characteristic is monitored by a control chart designed so that the probability that a certain out-of-control condition will be detected on the first sample following the shift to that state is $1 - \beta$. Find the following:

a. The probability that the out-of-control condition will be detected on the second sample following the shift.

b. The probability that the out-of-control condition will be detected on the kth sample following the shift.

c. The expected number of subgroups analyzed before the shift is detected.

d. The probability that the first sample following the shift produces a statistic that plots inside the control limits.

e. The probability that the shift is not detected on the kth subsequent sample.

f. The probability that two consecutive samples produce statistics that plot outside of the control limits.

g. The probability that at least one of the next k samples yields values of the test statistic that plot outside the control limits.

Chapter 5

Control Charts
for Attributes

5-1 INTRODUCTION

Many quality characteristics cannot be conveniently represented numerically. In such cases, we usually classify each item inspected as either conforming or nonconforming to the specifications on that quality characteristic. The terminology "defective" or "nondefective" is often used to identify these two classifications of product. More recently, the terminology "conforming" and "nonconforming" has become popular. Quality characteristics of this type are called *attributes*. Some examples of quality characteristics that are attributes include the occurrence of warped automobile engine connecting rods in a day's production, the proportion of nonfunctional semiconductor chips in a production run, and so forth.

In this chapter, we present three widely used attributes control charts. The first of these relates to the fraction of nonconforming or defective product produced by a manufacturing process, and is called the control chart for fraction nonconforming, or *p* chart. In some situations it is more convenient to deal with the number of *defects* or *nonconformities* observed rather than the fraction nonconforming. The second type of control chart that we study, called the control chart for nonconformities, or the *c* chart, is designed to deal with this case. Finally, we present a control chart for nonconformities per unit, or the *u* chart, which is useful in situations where the average number of nonconformities per unit is a more convenient basis for process control.

5-2 THE CONTROL CHART FOR FRACTION NONCONFORMING

The fraction nonconforming is defined as the ratio of the number of nonconforming items in a population to the total number of items in that population. The items may have *several* quality characteristics that are examined simultaneously by the inspector. If the item does not conform to standard on one or more of these characteristics, the item is classified as nonconforming. We usually express the fraction nonconforming as a decimal, although occasionally the percent nonconforming (which is just 100% times the fraction nonconforming) is used. When demonstrating or displaying the control chart to production personnel or presenting results to management, the percent nonconforming is often used, as it has more intuitive appeal. While it is customary to work with fraction nonconforming, we could also analyze the fraction conforming just as easily, resulting in a control chart on *process yield*. For example, many manufacturing organizations operate a yield-management system at each stage of their manufacturing process, with the first-pass yield tracked on a control chart.

The statistical principles underlying the control chart for fraction nonconforming are based on the binomial distribution. Suppose the production process is operating in a stable manner, such that the probability that any unit will not conform to specifications is p, and that successive units produced are independent. Then each unit produced is a realization of a Bernoulli random variable with parameter p. If a random sample of n units of product is selected, and if D is the number of units of product that are nonconforming, then D has a binomial distribution with parameters n and p, that is,

$$P\{D = x\} = \binom{n}{x} p^x (1 - p)^{n - x} \qquad x = 0, 1, \ldots, n \qquad (5\text{-}1)$$

From Section 2-2.2 we know that the mean and variance of the random variable D are np and $np(1 - p)$, respectively.

The *sample* fraction nonconforming is defined as the ratio of the number of nonconforming units in the sample D to the sample size n; that is,

$$\hat{p} = \frac{D}{n} \qquad (5\text{-}2)$$

As noted in Section 2-2.2, the distribution of the random variable $\hat{p}$ can be obtained from the binomial. Furthermore, the mean and variance of $\hat{p}$ are

$$\mu = p \qquad (5\text{-}3)$$

and

$$\sigma_{\hat{p}}^2 = \frac{p(1 - p)}{n} \qquad (5\text{-}4)$$

respectively. We will now see how this theory can be applied to the development of a control chart for fraction nonconforming. Because the chart controls the process fraction nonconforming p, it is also called the p chart.

5-2.1 Development and Operation of the Control Chart

In Chapter 4, we discussed the general statistical principles on which the Shewhart control chart is based. If w is a statistic that measures a quality characteristic, and if the mean of w is μ_w and if the variance of w is σ_w^2, then the general model for the Shewhart control chart is as follows:

$$
\begin{aligned}
\text{UCL} &= \mu_w + k\sigma_w \\
\text{Center line} &= \mu_w \\
\text{LCL} &= \mu_w - k\sigma_w
\end{aligned}
\tag{5-5}
$$

where k is the distance of the control limits from the center line, in multiples of the standard deviation of w. It is customary to choose $k = 3$.

Suppose that the true fraction nonconforming p in the production process is known or is a *standard value* specified by management. Then from (5-5), the center line and control limits of the fraction nonconforming control chart would be

$$
\begin{aligned}
\text{UCL} &= p + 3\sqrt{\frac{p(1-p)}{n}} \\
\text{Center line} &= p \\
\text{LCL} &= p - 3\sqrt{\frac{p(1-p)}{n}}
\end{aligned}
\tag{5-6}
$$

The actual operation of this chart would consist of taking subsequent samples of n units, computing the sample fraction nonconforming $\hat{p}$, and plotting the statistic $\hat{p}$ on the chart. As long as $\hat{p}$ remains within the control limits and the sequence of plotted points does not exhibit any systematic nonrandom pattern, we can conclude that the process is in control at the level p. If a point plots outside of the control limits, or if a nonrandom pattern in the plotted points is observed, we can conclude that the process fraction nonconforming has shifted to a new level and the process is out of control.

When the process fraction nonconforming p is not known, then it must be estimated from observed data. The usual procedure is to select m preliminary samples, each of size n. As a general rule, m should be 20 or 25. Then if there are D_i nonconforming units in sample i, we compute the fraction nonconforming in the ith sample as

$$
\hat{p}_i = \frac{D_i}{n} \qquad i = 1, 2, \ldots, m
$$

and the average of these individual sample fractions nonconforming is

$$
\bar{p} = \frac{\displaystyle\sum_{i=1}^{m} D_i}{mn} = \frac{\displaystyle\sum_{i=1}^{m} \hat{p}_i}{m}
\tag{5-7}
$$

The statistic $\bar{p}$ estimates the unknown fraction nonconforming p. The center line and control limits of the control chart for fraction nonconforming are computed as

$$\text{UCL} = \bar{p} + 3\sqrt{\frac{\bar{p}(1 - \bar{p})}{n}}$$

$$\text{Center line} = \bar{p} \tag{5-8}$$

$$\text{LCL} = \bar{p} - 3\sqrt{\frac{\bar{p}(1 - \bar{p})}{n}}$$

We regard the control limits obtained in (5-8) as *trial control limits*. They allow us to determine whether the process was in control when the m initial samples were selected. To test the hypothesis of past control, plot the sample fraction nonconforming from each sample on the chart and analyze the resulting display. If all points plot inside the control limits and no systematic behavior is evident, then we conclude that the process was in control in the past, and the trial control limits are suitable for controlling current or future production.

Suppose that one or more of the statistics $\hat{p}_i$ plot out of control when compared to the trial control limits. Clearly, if control limits for current or future production are to be meaningful, they must be based on data from a process that is in control. Therefore, when the hypothesis of past control is rejected, it is necessary to *revise* the trial control limits. This is done by examining each of the out-of-control points, looking for an assignable cause. If an assignable cause is found, the point is discarded and the trial control limits are recalculated, using only the remaining points. Then these remaining points are reexamined for control. (Note that points that were in control initially may now be out of control, because the new trial control limits will generally be tighter than the old ones.) This process is continued until all points plot in control, at which point the trial control limits are adopted for current use.

In some cases, it may not be possible to find an assignable cause for a point that plots out of control. There are two courses of action open to us. The first of these is to eliminate the point, just as if an assignable cause had been found. There is no analytical justification for choosing this action, other than that points that are outside of the control limits are likely to have been drawn from a probability distribution characteristic of an out-of-control state. The alternative is to retain the point (or points) considering the trial control limits as appropriate for current control. Of course, if the point really does represent an out-of-control condition, the resulting control limits will be too wide. However, if there are only one or two such points, this will not distort the control chart significantly. If future samples still indicate control, then the unexplained points can probably be safely dropped.

Occasionally, when the initial sample values of $\hat{p}_i$ are plotted against the trial control limits, many points will plot out of control. Clearly, if we arbitrarily drop the out-of-control points, we will have an unsatisfactory situation, as few data will remain with which we can recompute reliable control limits. We also suspect that this approach would ignore much useful information in the data. On the other hand, searching for an assignable cause for *each* out-of-control point is unlikely to be successful. We have found that when many of the initial samples plot out of control against the trial limits, it is better to concentrate on the *pattern* formed by these points. Such a pattern will almost always exist. Usually, the assignable causes associated with the pattern of out-of-control points are fairly easy to identify. Removal of this process problem generally results in a major process improvement.

If the control chart is based on a known or standard value for the fraction nonconforming p, then the calculation of trial control limits is generally unnecessary. However, one should be cautious when working with a standard value for p. Since in practice the true value of p would rarely be known with certainty, we would usually be given a standard value of p that represents a desired or target value for the process fraction nonconforming. If this is the case, and future samples indicate an out-of-control condition, we must determine whether the process is out of control at the *target* p but in control at some *other* value of p. For example, suppose management specifies a target value of $p = 0.01$, but the process is really in control at a larger value of fraction nonconforming, say $p = 0.05$. Using the control chart based on $p = 0.01$, we see that many of the points will plot above the upper control limit, indicating an out-of-control condition. However, the process is really out of control only with respect to the target $p = 0.01$. Sometimes it may be possible to "improve" the level of quality by using target values, or to bring a process into control at a particular level of quality performance. In processes where the fraction nonconforming can be controlled by relatively simple process adjustments, target values of p may be useful.

Example 5-1

Frozen orange juice concentrate is packed in 6-oz cardboard cans. These cans are formed on a machine by spinning them from cardboard stock and attaching a metal bottom panel. By inspection of a can, we may determine whether, when filled, it could possibly leak either on the side seam or around the bottom joint. Such a nonconforming can has an improper seal on either the side seam or the bottom panel. We wish to set up a control chart to improve the fraction of nonconforming cans produced by this machine.

To establish the control chart, 30 samples of $n = 50$ cans each were selected at half-hour intervals over a three-shift period in which the machine was in continuous operation. The data are shown in Table 5-1.

We construct a preliminary control chart to see whether the process was in control when these data were collected. Since the 30 samples contain $\sum_{i=1}^{30} D_i = 347$ nonconforming cans, we find from Equation (5-7),

$$\bar{p} = \frac{\sum_{i=1}^{m} D_i}{mn} = \frac{347}{(30)(50)} = 0.2313$$

Using $\bar{p}$ as an estimate of the true process fraction nonconforming, we can now calculate the upper and lower control limits as

$$\bar{p} \pm 3 \sqrt{\frac{\bar{p}(1 - \bar{p})}{n}} = 0.2313 \pm 3 \sqrt{\frac{0.2313(0.7687)}{50}}$$
$$= 0.2313 \pm 3(0.0596)$$
$$= 0.2313 \pm 0.1789$$

Table 5-1

Data for trial control limits, Example 5-1 sample size $n = 50$

Sample Number	Number of Nonconforming Cans, D_i	Sample Fraction Nonconforming, $\hat{p}_i$
1	12	0.24
2	15	0.30
3	8	0.16
4	10	0.20
5	4	0.08
6	7	0.14
7	16	0.32
8	9	0.18
9	14	0.28
10	10	0.20
11	5	0.10
12	6	0.12
13	17	0.34
14	12	0.24
15	22	0.44
16	8	0.16
17	10	0.20
18	5	0.10
19	13	0.26
20	11	0.22
21	20	0.40
22	18	0.36
23	24	0.48
24	15	0.30
25	9	0.18
26	12	0.24
27	7	0.14
28	13	0.26
29	9	0.18
30	6	0.12
	347	$\bar{p} = 0.2313$

Therefore,

$$\text{UCL} = \bar{p} + 3\sqrt{\frac{\bar{p}(1 - \bar{p})}{n}} = 0.2313 + 0.1789 = 0.4102$$

and

$$\text{LCL} = \bar{p} - 3\sqrt{\frac{\bar{p}(1 - \bar{p})}{n}} = 0.2313 - 0.1789 = 0.0524$$

The control chart with center line at $\bar{p} = 0.2313$ and the above upper and lower control limits is shown in Figure 5-1. The sample fraction nonconforming from each preliminary sample is plotted on this chart. We note that two points, those from samples 15 and 23, plot above the upper control limit, so the process is not

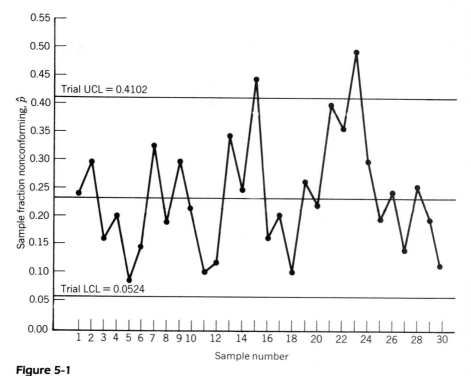

Figure 5-1
Initial fraction nonconforming control chart for the data in Table 5-1.

in control. These points must be investigated to see whether an assignable cause can be determined.

Analysis of the data from sample 15 indicates that a new batch of cardboard stock was put into production during that half-hour period. The introduction of new batches of raw material sometimes causes irregular production performance, and it is reasonable to believe that this has occurred here. Furthermore, during the half-hour period in which sample 23 was obtained, a relatively inexperienced operator had been temporarily assigned to the machine, and this could account for the high fraction nonconforming obtained from that sample. Consequently, samples 15 and 23 are eliminated, and the new center line and revised control limits are calculated as

$$\bar{p} = \frac{301}{(28)(50)} = 0.2150$$

$$\text{UCL} = \bar{p} + 3\sqrt{\frac{\bar{p}(1-\bar{p})}{n}} = 0.2150 + 3\sqrt{\frac{0.2150(0.7850)}{50}} = 0.3893$$

$$\text{LCL} = \bar{p} - 3\sqrt{\frac{\bar{p}(1-\bar{p})}{n}} = 0.2150 - 3\sqrt{\frac{0.2150(0.7850)}{50}} = 0.0407$$

The revised center line and control limits are shown on the control chart shown in Figure 5-2. Note that we have not dropped samples 15 and 23 from the chart, but they have been excluded from the control limit calculations, and we have noted this directly on the control chart. This annotation of the control chart to

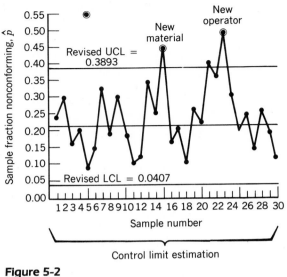

Figure 5-2
Revised control limits for the data in Table 5-1.

indicate unusual points, process adjustments, or the type of investigation made at a particular point in time forms a useful record for future process analysis and should become a standard practice in control chart usage.

Note also that the fraction nonconforming from sample 21 now exceeds the upper control limit. However, analysis of the data does not produce any reasonable or logical assignable cause for this, and we decide to retain the point. Therefore, we conclude that the new control limits in Figure 5-2 can be used for future samples. Thus, we have concluded the control limit estimation phase of control chart usage.

Sometimes examination of control chart data reveals information that affects other points that are not necessarily outside the control limits. For example, if we had found that the temporary operator working when sample 23 was obtained was actually working during the entire two-hour period in which samples 21–24 were obtained, then we should discard all four samples, even if only sample 21 exceeded the control limits, on the grounds that this inexperienced operator probably had some adverse influence on the fraction nonconforming during the entire period.

Before we conclude that the process is in control at this level, we should examine the remaining 28 samples for runs and other nonrandom patterns. The largest run is one of length 5 above the center line, and there are no obvious patterns present in the data. There is no strong evidence of anything other than a random pattern of variation about the center line.

We conclude that the process is in control at the level $p = 0.2150$ and that the revised control limits should be adopted for monitoring current production. However, we note that although the process is in control, the fraction nonconforming is much too high. That is, the process is operating in a stable manner, and no unusual *operator-controllable* problems are present. It is unlikely that the process quality can be improved by action at the work-force level. The nonconforming cans produced are *management controllable* because an intervention by management in the process will be required to improve performance. Plant management agrees with this observation and directs that, in addition to implementing the control chart program, the engineering staff should analyze the process in an effort to improve the process yield. This study indicates that several adjustments can be made on the machine that should improve its performance.

During the next three shifts following the machine adjustments and the introduction of the control chart, an additional 24 samples of $n = 50$ observations each are collected. These data are shown in Table 5-2, and the sample fractions nonconforming are plotted on the control chart in Figure 5-3.

From an examination of Figure 5-3, our immediate impression is that the process is now operating at a new quality level that is substantially less than the center line $\bar{p} = 0.2150$. One point, that from sample 41, is below the lower control limit. No assignable cause for this out-of-control signal can be determined. The only logical reasons for this ostensible change in process performance are the machine adjustments made by the engineering staff and possibly, the operators themselves. It is not unusual to find that process performance improves following the introduction of formal statistical process-control procedures, often because the operators are more aware of process quality and because the control chart provides a continuing visual display of process performance.

We may test the hypothesis that the process fraction nonconforming in this current three-shift period differs from the process fraction nonconforming in the

Table 5-2
Orange juice concentrate can data in samples of size $n = 50$

Sample Number	Number of Nonconforming Cans, D_i	Sample Fraction Nonconforming, $\hat{p}_i$
31	9	0.18
32	6	0.12
33	12	0.24
34	5	0.10
35	6	0.12
36	4	0.08
37	6	0.12
38	3	0.06
39	7	0.14
40	6	0.12
41	2	0.04
42	4	0.08
43	3	0.06
44	6	0.12
45	5	0.10
46	4	0.08
47	8	0.16
48	5	0.10
49	6	0.12
50	7	0.14
51	5	0.10
52	6	0.12
53	3	0.10
54	5	0.10
	133	$\bar{p} = 0.1108$

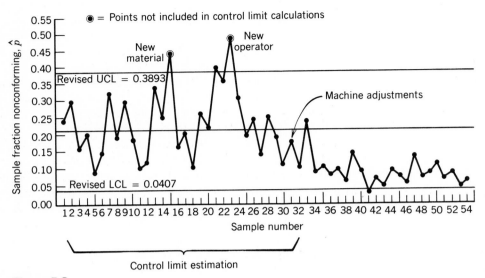

Figure 5-3
Continuation of the fraction nonconforming control chart, Example 5-1.

preliminary data, using the procedure given in Section 3-3.4. The hypotheses are

$$H_0: \quad p_1 = p_2$$
$$H_1: \quad p_1 > p_2$$

where p_1 is the process fraction nonconforming from the preliminary data and p_2 is the process fraction nonconforming in the current period. We may estimate p_1 by $\hat{p}_1 = \bar{p} = 0.2150$, and p_2 by

$$\hat{p}_2 = \frac{\sum\limits_{i=31}^{54} D_i}{(50)(24)} = \frac{133}{1200} = 0.1108$$

The test statistic for the above hypothesis is, from Equations (3-62) and (3-63),

$$Z_0 = \frac{\hat{p}_1 - \hat{p}_2}{\sqrt{\hat{p}(1 - \hat{p})\left(\dfrac{1}{n_1} + \dfrac{1}{n_2}\right)}}$$

where

$$\hat{p} = \frac{n_1 \hat{p}_1 + n_2 \hat{p}_2}{n_1 + n_2}$$

In our example, we have

$$\hat{p} = \frac{(1400)(0.2150) + (1200)(0.1108)}{1400 + 1200} = 0.1669$$

and

$$Z_0 = \frac{0.2150 - 0.1108}{\sqrt{(0.1669)(0.8331)\left(\dfrac{1}{1400} + \dfrac{1}{1200}\right)}} = 7.10$$

Comparing this to the upper 0.05 point of the standard normal distribution, we find that $Z_0 = 7.10 > Z_{0.05} = 1.645$. Consequently, we reject H_0 and conclude that there has been a significant decrease in the process fallout.

Based on the apparently successful process adjustments, it seems logical to revise the control limits again, using only the most recent samples (numbers 31–54). This results in the new control chart parameters:

$$\text{Center line} = \bar{p} = 0.1108$$

$$\text{UCL} = \bar{p} + 3\sqrt{\frac{\bar{p}(1 - \bar{p})}{n}} = 0.1108 + 3\sqrt{\frac{(0.1108)(0.8892)}{50}} = 0.2440$$

$$\text{LCL} = \bar{p} - 3\sqrt{\frac{\bar{p}(1 - \bar{p})}{n}} = 0.1108 - 3\sqrt{\frac{(0.1108)(0.8892)}{50}} = -0.0224 = 0$$

Figure 5-4 shows the control chart with these new parameters. Notice that since the calculated lower control limit is less than zero, we have set LCL = 0. Therefore, the new control chart will have only an upper control limit. From inspection of Figure 5-4, we note that all the points would fall inside the revised upper control limit; therefore, we conclude that the process is in control at this new level.

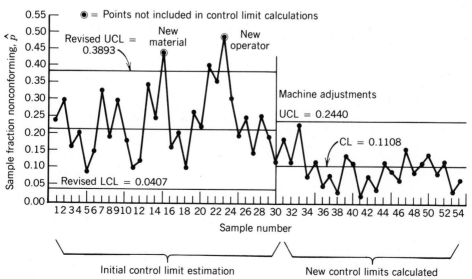

Figure 5-4
New control limits on the fraction nonconforming control chart, Example 5-1.

The continued operation of this control chart for the next five shifts is shown in Figure 5-5. Data for the process during this period are shown in Table 5-3. The control chart does not indicate lack of control. Despite the improvement in yield following the engineering changes in the process and the introduction of the control chart, the process fallout of $\bar{p} = 0.1108$ is still too high. Further management

Table 5-3
New data for the fraction nonconforming control chart in Figure 5-5, $n = 50$

Sample Number	Number of Nonconforming Cans, D_i	Sample Fraction Nonconforming Cans, $\hat{p}_i$
55	8	0.16
56	7	0.14
57	5	0.10
58	6	0.12
59	4	0.08
60	5	0.10
61	2	0.04
62	3	0.06
63	4	0.08
64	7	0.14
65	6	0.12
66	5	0.10
67	5	0.10
68	3	0.06
69	7	0.14
70	9	0.18
71	6	0.12
72	10	0.20
73	4	0.08
74	3	0.06
75	5	0.10
76	8	0.16
77	11	0.22
78	9	0.18
79	7	0.14
80	3	0.06
81	5	0.10
82	2	0.04
83	1	0.02
84	4	0.08
85	5	0.10
86	3	0.06
87	7	0.14
88	6	0.12
89	4	0.08
90	4	0.08
91	6	0.12
92	8	0.16
93	5	0.10
94	6	0.12

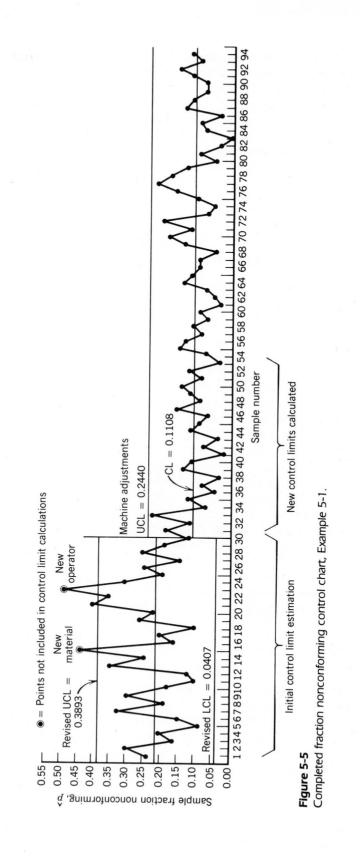

Figure 5-5

Completed fraction nonconforming control chart, Example 5-1.

action will be required to improve the yield. These management interventions may be further adjustments to the machine. Statistically designed experiments (see Part III) are an appropriate way to determine which machine adjustments are critical to defect-free manufacturing, and the appropriate magnitude and direction of these adjustments. The control chart should be continued during the period in which the adjustments are made. By marking the time scale of the control chart *when* a process change is made, the control chart becomes a *logbook* in which the timing of process interventions and their subsequent effect on process performance are easily seen. This logbook aspect of control chart usage is extremely important.

Design of the Fraction Nonconforming Control Chart

The fraction nonconforming control chart has three parameters that must be specified: the sample size, the frequency of sampling, and the width of the control limits. Ideally, we should select these parameters according to some economic criterion, and in Chapter 10 we will present some economic models for control chart design. However, it is also useful to have some general guidelines for selecting those parameters.

It is relatively common to base a control chart for fraction nonconforming on 100% inspection of *all* process output over some convenient period of time, such as a shift or a day. In this case, both sample size and sampling frequency are interrelated. We would generally select a sampling frequency appropriate for the production rate, and this fixes the sample size. Rational subgrouping may also play a role in determining the sampling frequency. For example, if there are three shifts, and we suspect that shifts differ in their general quality level, then we should use the output of each shift as a subgroup rather than pooling the output of all three shifts together to obtain a daily fraction defective.

If we are to select a sample of process output, then we must choose the sample size n. Various rules have been suggested for the choice of n. If p is very small, we should choose n sufficiently large so that we have a high probability of finding at least one nonconforming unit in the sample. Otherwise, we might find that the control limits are such that the presence of only one nonconforming unit in the sample would indicate an out-of-control condition. For example, if $p = 0.01$ and $n = 8$, we find that the upper control limit is

$$\text{UCL} = p + 3 \sqrt{\frac{p(1 - p)}{n}} = 0.01 + 3 \sqrt{\frac{(0.01)(0.99)}{8}} = 0.1155$$

If there is one nonconforming unit in the sample, then $\hat{p} = \frac{1}{8} = 0.1250$, and we can conclude that the process is out of control. Since for any $p > 0$ there is a positive probability of producing *some* defectives, it is unreasonable in many cases to conclude that the process is out of control upon observing a single nonconforming item.

To avoid this pitfall, we can choose the sample size n so that the probability of finding at least one nonconforming unit per sample is at least γ. For example, suppose that $p = 0.01$, and we want the probability of at least one nonconforming unit in the sample to be at least 0.95. If D denotes the number of nonconforming units, then we want to find n such that $P\{D \geq 1\} \geq 0.95$. Using the Poisson approximation to the binomial, we find from the cumulative Poisson table that $\lambda = np$ must exceed 3.00. Consequently, since $p = 0.01$, this implies that the sample size should be 300.

Duncan (1974) has suggested that the sample size should be large enough that we have approximately a 50% chance of detecting a process shift of some specified amount. For example, suppose that $p = 0.01$, and we want the probability of detecting a shift to $p = 0.05$ to be 0.50. Assuming that the normal approximation to the binomial applies, we should choose n so that the upper control limit exactly coincides with the fraction nonconforming in the out-of-control state.[1] If δ is the magnitude of the process shift, then n must satisfy

$$\delta = k \sqrt{\frac{p(1 - p)}{n}} \tag{5-9}$$

Therefore,

$$n = \left(\frac{k}{\delta}\right)^2 p(1 - p) \tag{5-10}$$

In our example, $p = 0.01$, $\delta = 0.05 - 0.01 = 0.04$, and if 3-sigma limits are used, then from (5-10),

$$n = \left(\frac{3}{0.04}\right)^2 (0.01)(0.99) = 56$$

If the in-control value of the fraction nonconforming is small, another useful criterion is to choose n large enough so that the control chart will have a positive lower control limit. This ensures that we will have a mechanism to force us to investigate one or more samples that contain an unusually small number of nonconforming items. Since we wish to have

$$\text{LCL} = p - k \sqrt{\frac{p(1 - p)}{n}} > 0 \tag{5-11}$$

this implies that

$$n > \frac{(1 - p)}{p} k^2 \tag{5-12}$$

For example, if $p = 0.05$ and 3-sigma limits are used, the sample size must be

$$n > \frac{0.95}{0.05} (3)^2 = 171$$

Thus, if $n \geq 172$ units, the control chart will have a positive lower control limit.

---

[1] If $\hat{p}$ is approximately normal, then the probability that $\hat{p}$ exceeds the UCL is 0.50 if the UCL equals the out-of-control fraction nonconforming p, due to the symmetry of the normal distribution. See Section 2-4.3 for a discussion of the normal approximation to the binomial.

Three-sigma control limits are usually employed on the control chart for fraction nonconforming on the grounds that they have worked well in practice. As discussed in Section 4-3.2, narrower control limits would make the control chart more sensitive to small shifts in p but at the expense of more frequent "false alarms." Occasionally, we have seen narrower limits used in an effort to *force* improvement in process quality. Care must be exercised in this, however, as too many false alarms will destroy the operating personnel's confidence in the control chart program.

We should note that the fraction nonconforming control chart is not a universal model for *all* data on fraction nonconforming. It is based on the binomial probability model; that is, the probability of occurrence of a nonconforming unit is *constant*, and successive units of production are *independent*. In processes where nonconforming units are clustered together, or where the probability of a unit being nonconforming depends on whether or not previous units were nonconforming, the fraction nonconforming control chart is often of little use.

Interpretation of Points on the Control Chart
for Fraction Nonconforming

Example 5-1 illustrated how points that plot beyond the control limits are treated, both in establishing the control chart and during its routine operation. Care must be exercised in interpreting points that plot *below* the lower control limit. These points often do not represent a real improvement in process quality. Frequently, they are caused by errors in the inspection process, resulting from inadequately trained or inexperienced inspectors, or from improperly calibrated test and inspection equipment. We have also seen cases in which inspectors deliberately passed nonconforming units or reported fictitious data. The analyst must keep these warnings in mind when looking for assignable causes if points plot below the lower control limits. Not all "downward shifts" in p are attributable to improved quality.

The *np* Control Chart

It is also possible to base a control chart on the number nonconforming, rather than the fraction nonconforming. This is often called an *np* control chart. The parameters of this chart are

$$\text{UCL} = np + 3\sqrt{np(1 - p)}$$
$$\text{Center line} = np \qquad\qquad (5\text{-}13)$$
$$\text{LCL} = np - 3\sqrt{np(1 - p)}$$

If a standard value for p is unavailable, then $\bar{p}$ can be used to estimate p. Many nonstatistically trained personnel find the *np* chart easier to interpret than the usual fraction nonconforming control chart.

Example 5-2

To illustrate the construction of an *np* control chart, consider the data in Example 5-1 for the fraction nonconforming orange juice concentrate cans. Using the data in Table 5-1, we found that

$$\bar{p} = 0.2313, \qquad n = 50$$

Therefore, the parameters of the np control chart would be

$$\text{UCL} = n\bar{p} + 3\sqrt{n\bar{p}(1 - \bar{p})}$$
$$= 50(0.2313) + 3\sqrt{(50)(0.2313)(0.7687)}$$
$$= 20.510$$
$$\text{Center line} = n\bar{p} = 50(0.2313) = 11.565$$
$$\text{LCL} = n\bar{p} - 3\sqrt{n\bar{p}(1 - \bar{p})}$$
$$= 50(0.2313) - 3\sqrt{(50)(0.2313)(0.7687)}$$
$$= 2.620$$

Now in practice, the number of nonconforming units in each sample is plotted on the np control chart, and the number of nonconforming units is an integer. Thus, if 20 units are nonconforming the process is in control, but if 21 occur the process is out of control. Similarly, if there are three nonconforming units in the sample, the process is in control, but two nonconforming units would imply an out-of-control process. Some practitioners prefer to use integer values for control limits on the np chart instead of their decimal fraction counterparts. In this example we could choose 2 and 21 as the LCL and UCL, respectively, and the process would be considered out of control if a sample value of np plotted at or beyond the control limits.

5-2.2 Variable Sample Size

In some applications of the control chart for fraction nonconforming, the sample is a 100% inspection of process output over some period of time. Since different numbers of units could be produced in each period, the control chart would then have a variable sample size. There are several approaches to constructing and operating a control chart with a variable sample size.

The first and perhaps the most simple approach is to determine control limits for each individual sample that are based on the specific sample size. That is, if the ith sample is of size n_i, then the upper and lower control limits are $p \pm 3\sqrt{p(1 - p)/n_i}$. Note that the width of the control limits is inversely proportional to the square root of the sample size. To illustrate this approach, consider the data in Table 5-4. For the 25 samples, we calculate

$$\bar{p} = \frac{\sum\limits_{i=1}^{25} D_i}{\sum\limits_{i=1}^{25} n_i} = \frac{234}{2450} = 0.096$$

Consequently, the center line is at 0.096, and the control limits are

$$\text{UCL} = \bar{p} + 3\hat{\sigma}_{\hat{p}} = 0.096 + 3\sqrt{\frac{(0.096)(0.904)}{n_i}}$$

Table 5-4
Data for a control chart for fraction nonconforming with variable sample size

Sample Number, i	Sample Size, n_i	Number of Nonconforming Units, D_i	Sample Fraction Nonconforming, $\hat{p}_i = D_i/n_i$	Standard Deviation $\hat{\sigma}_{\hat{p}} = \sqrt{\dfrac{(0.096)(0.904)}{n_i}}$	Control Limits LCL	UCL
1	100	12	0.120	0.029	0.009	0.183
2	80	8	0.100	0.033	0	0.195
3	80	6	0.075	0.033	0	0.195
4	100	9	0.090	0.029	0.009	0.183
5	110	10	0.091	0.028	0.012	0.180
6	110	12	0.109	0.028	0.012	0.180
7	100	11	0.110	0.029	0.009	0.183
8	100	16	0.160	0.029	0.009	0.183
9	90	10	0.110	0.031	0.003	0.189
10	90	6	0.067	0.031	0.003	0.189
11	110	20	0.182	0.028	0.012	0.180
12	120	15	0.125	0.027	0.015	0.177
13	120	9	0.075	0.027	0.015	0.177
14	120	8	0.067	0.027	0.015	0.177
15	110	6	0.055	0.028	0.012	0.180
16	80	8	0.100	0.033	0	0.195
17	80	10	0.125	0.033	0	0.195
18	80	7	0.088	0.033	0	0.195
19	90	5	0.056	0.031	0.003	0.189
20	100	8	0.080	0.029	0.009	0.183
21	100	5	0.050	0.029	0.009	0.183
22	100	8	0.080	0.029	0.009	0.183
23	100	10	0.100	0.029	0.009	0.183
24	90	6	0.067	0.031	0.003	0.189
25	90	9	0.100	0.031	0.003	0.189
	2450	234	0.096			

and

$$\text{LCL} = \bar{p} - 3\hat{\sigma}_{\hat{p}} = 0.096 - 3\sqrt{\frac{(0.096)(0.904)}{n_i}}$$

where $\hat{\sigma}_{\hat{p}}$ is the estimate of the standard deviation of the sample fraction noncon-forming $\hat{p}$. The calculations to determine the control limits are displayed in the last three columns of Table 5-4. The control chart is plotted in Figure 5-6.

The second approach is to base the control chart on an *average* sample size, resulting in an approximate set of control limits. This assumes that future sample sizes will not differ greatly from those previously observed. If this approach is used, the control limits will be *constant,* and the resulting control chart will not look as formidable to operating personnel as the control chart with variable limits. However, if there is an unusually large variation in the size of a particular sample or if a point plots near the approximate control limits, then the *exact* control limits for that point should be determined and the point examined relative to that value. For the data in Table 5-4, we find that the average sample size is

$$\bar{n} = \frac{\sum_{i=1}^{25} n_i}{25} = \frac{2450}{25} = 98$$

Therefore, the approximate control limits are

$$\text{UCL} = \bar{p} + 3\sqrt{\frac{\bar{p}(1-\bar{p})}{\bar{n}}} = 0.096 + 3\sqrt{\frac{(0.096)(0.904)}{98}} = 0.185$$

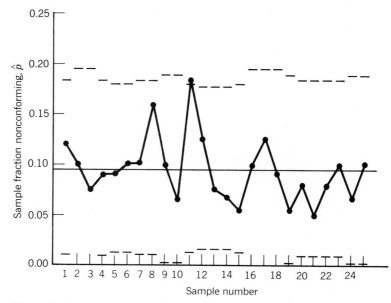

Figure 5-6
Control chart for fraction nonconforming with variable sample size.

and

$$\text{LCL} = \bar{p} - 3\sqrt{\frac{\bar{p}(1-\bar{p})}{\bar{n}}} = 0.096 - 3\sqrt{\frac{(0.096)(0.904)}{98}} = 0.007$$

The resulting control chart is shown in Figure 5-7. Notice that $\hat{p}$ for sample 11 plots close to the approximate upper control limit, yet it appears to be in control. However, when compared to its exact upper control limit (0.180, from Table 5-4), the point indicates an out-of-control condition. Similarly, points that are outside the approximate control limits may be inside their exact control limits. In general, care must be taken in the interpretation of points near the approximate control limits.

We must also be careful in analyzing runs or other apparently abnormal patterns on control charts with variable sample sizes. The problem is that a change in the sample fraction nonconforming $\hat{p}$ must be interpreted relative to the sample size. For example, suppose that $p = 0.20$ and that two successive sample fractions nonconforming are $\hat{p}_i = 0.28$ and $\hat{p}_{i+1} = 0.24$. The first observation seems to indicate poorer quality than the second, since $\hat{p}_i > \hat{p}_{i+1}$. However, suppose that the sample sizes are $n_i = 50$ and $n_{i+1} = 250$. In *standard deviation units*, the first point is 1.89 units above average, while the second point is 2.11 units above average. That is, the second point actually represents a *greater* deviation from the standard of $p = 0.20$ than does the first, even though the second point is the smaller of the two. Clearly, looking for runs or other nonrandom patterns is virtually meaningless here.

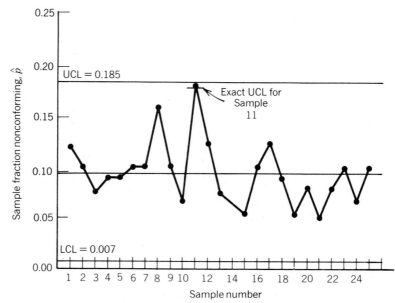

Figure 5-7
Control chart for fraction nonconforming based on average sample size.

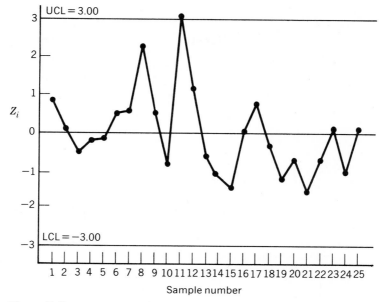

Figure 5-8
Standardized control chart for fraction nonconforming.

One solution to this problem is to use a "standardized" control chart, where the points are plotted in standard deviation units. Such a control chart has the center line at zero, and upper and lower control limits of $+3$ and -3, respectively. The variable plotted on the chart is

$$Z_i = \frac{\hat{p}_i - p}{\sqrt{\dfrac{p(1-p)}{n_i}}}$$

where p (or $\bar{p}$ if no standard is given) is the process fraction nonconforming in the in-control state. The standardized control chart for the data in Table 5-4 is shown in Figure 5-8. The calculations associated with this control chart are shown in Table 5-5. Tests for runs and pattern-recognition methods could safely be applied to this chart, as the relative changes from one point to another are all expressed in terms of the same units of measurement.

The standardized control chart is no more difficult to construct or maintain than either of the other two procedures discussed in the section. Conceptually, however, it may be more difficult for operating personnel to understand and interpret, as reference to the actual process fraction defective has been "lost." However, if there is large variation in sample size, then runs and pattern-recognition methods can only be safely applied to the standardized control chart. In such a case, it might be advisable to maintain a control chart with individual control limits for each sample (as in Figure 5-6) for the operating personnel, while simultaneously maintaining a standardized control chart for the quality engineer's use.

The standardized control chart is also recommended when the length of the production run is short, as in many job–shop settings. Control charts for short production runs are discussed in Chapter 8.

Table 5-5

Calculations for the standardized control chart in Figure 5-8, $\bar{p} = 0.096$

Sample Number, i	Sample Size n_i	Number of Nonconforming Units, D_i	Sample Fraction Nonconforming, $\hat{p}_i = D_i/n_i$	Standard Deviation $\hat{\sigma}_{\hat{p}} = \sqrt{\dfrac{(0.096)(0.904)}{n_i}}$	$Z_i = \dfrac{\hat{p} - \bar{p}}{\sqrt{\dfrac{(0.096)(0.904)}{n_i}}}$
1	100	12	0.120	0.029	0.83
2	80	8	0.100	0.033	0.12
3	80	6	0.075	0.033	−0.64
4	100	9	0.090	0.029	−0.21
5	110	10	0.091	0.028	−0.18
6	110	12	0.109	0.028	0.46
7	100	11	0.110	0.029	0.48
8	100	16	0.160	0.029	2.21
9	90	10	0.110	0.031	0.45
10	90	6	0.067	0.031	−0.94
11	110	20	0.182	0.028	3.07
12	120	15	0.125	0.027	1.07
13	120	9	0.075	0.027	−0.78
14	120	8	0.067	0.027	−1.07
15	110	6	0.055	0.028	−1.46
16	80	8	0.100	0.033	0.12
17	80	10	0.125	0.033	0.88
18	80	7	0.088	0.033	−0.24
19	90	5	0.056	0.031	−1.29
20	100	8	0.080	0.029	−0.55
21	100	5	0.050	0.029	−1.59
22	100	8	0.080	0.029	−0.55
23	100	10	0.100	0.029	0.14
24	90	6	0.067	0.031	−0.94
25	90	9	0.100	0.031	0.13

5-2.3 Nonmanufacturing Applications

The control chart for fraction nonconforming is widely used in nonmanufacturing applications of statistical process control. In the nonmanufacturing environment, many quality characteristics can be observed on a conforming or nonconforming basis. Some examples would include the number of employee paychecks that are in error or distributed late during a pay period, the number of check requests that are not paid within the standard accounting cycle, and the number of deliveries made by a supplier that are not on-time.

Many nonmanufacturing applications of the fraction nonconforming control chart will involve the variable sample size case. For example, the total number of check requests during an accounting cycle is most likely not constant, and since information about the timeliness of processing for all check requests is generally available, we would calculate $\hat{p}$ as the ratio of all late checks to the total number of checks processed during the period.

As an illustration consider the data in Table 5-4. These data originally came from the purchasing group of a large aerospace company. This group issues purchase orders weekly to the company's suppliers. The sample sizes in Table 5-4 are the actual number of purchase orders issued each week. Note that not all purchase orders are correct. Among the most common errors are specifying incorrect part numbers, incorrect delivery dates, incorrect prices or terms, and wrong supplier number. Any of these errors can result in a purchase order change, which is costly and may delay delivery of material. The purchasing group's quality-improvement team decided to investigate how many purchase orders issued each week resulted in a corresponding purchase order change document owing to errors in the original work. This quantity is the number nonconforming in Table 5-4, and the fraction conforming in this example can be viewed as the fraction of purchase orders in error for the week. The use of this control chart was a key initial step in identifying the underlying root cause of the errors on purchase orders and in developing the corrective actions necessary to improve the process.

5-2.4. The Operating-Characteristic Function and Average Run Length Calculations

The operating-characteristic (or OC) function of the fraction nonconforming control chart is a graphical display of the probability of incorrectly accepting the hypothesis of statistical control (i.e., a type II or β error) against the process fraction nonconforming. The OC curve provides a measure of the *sensitivity* of the control chart that is, its ability to detect a shift in the process fraction nonconforming from the nominal value $\bar{p}$ to some other value p. The probability of type II error for the fraction nonconforming control chart may be computed from

$$
\begin{aligned}
\beta &= P\{\hat{p} < \text{UCL}|p\} - P\{\hat{p} \leq \text{LCL}|p\} \\
&= P\{D < n\text{UCL}|p\} - P\{D \leq n\text{LCL}|p\}
\end{aligned}
\tag{5-14}
$$

Since D is a binomial random variable with parameters n and p, the β error defined in (5-14) can be obtained from the cumulative binomial distribution.

Table 5-6[a]

Calculations for constructing the OC curve for a control chart for fraction nonconforming with $n = 50$, LCL $= 0.0303$, and UCL $= 0.3697$

p	$P\{D \leq 18\|p\}$	$P\{D \leq 1\|p\}$	$\beta = P\{D \leq 18\|p\} - P\{D \leq 1\|p\}$
0.01	1.0000	0.9106	0.0894
0.03	1.0000	0.5553	0.4447
0.05	1.0000	0.2794	0.7206
0.10	1.0000	0.0338	0.9662
0.15	0.9999	0.0291	0.9708
0.20	0.9975	0.0002	0.9973
0.25	0.9713	0.0001	0.9712
0.30	0.8594	0.0000	0.8594
0.35	0.6216	0.0000	0.6216
0.40	0.3356	0.0000	0.3356
0.45	0.1273	0.0000	0.1273
0.50	0.0325	0.0000	0.0325
0.55	0.0053	0.0000	0.0053

[a] The probabilities in this table were found by evaluating the cumulative binomial distribution. For small $p(p < 0.1$, say) the Poisson approximation could be used, and for larger values of p the normal approximation could be used.

Table 5-6 illustrates the calculations required to generate the OC curve for a control chart for fraction nonconforming with parameters $n = 50$, LCL $= 0.0303$, and UCL $= 0.3697$. Using these parameters, Equation (5-14) becomes

$$\beta = P\{D < (50)(0.3697)|p\} - P\{D \leq (50)(0.0303)|p\}$$
$$= P\{D < 18.49|p\} - P\{D \leq 1.52|p\}$$

However, since D must be an integer, we find that

$$\beta = P\{D \leq 18|p\} - P\{D \leq 1|p\}$$

The OC curve is plotted in Figure 5-9.

We may also calculate average run lengths (ARLs) for the fraction nonconforming control chart. Recall from Chapter 4 that the ARL for any Shewhart control chart can be written as

$$\text{ARL} = \frac{1}{P(\text{sample points plots out of control})}$$

Thus, if the process is in control, the ARL is

$$\text{ARL} = \frac{1}{\alpha}$$

and if it is out of control, then

$$\text{ARL} = \frac{1}{1 - \beta}$$

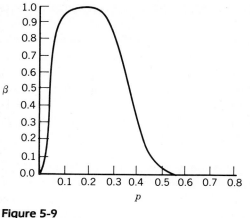

Figure 5-9
Operating-characteristic curve for the fraction
nonconforming control chart with $\bar{p} = 0.20$,
LCL = 0.0303, and UCL = 0.3697.

These probabilities (α, β) can be calculated directly from the binomial distribution or read from an OC curve.

To illustrate, consider the control chart for fraction nonconforming used in the OC curve calculations in Table 5-6. This chart has parameters $n = 50$, UCL = 0.3697, LCL = 0.0303, and the center line is $\bar{p} = 0.20$. From Table 5-6 (or the OC curve in Figure 5-9) we find that if the process is in control with $p = \bar{p}$, the probability of a point plotting in control is $= 0.9973$. Thus, in this case $\alpha = 1 - \beta = 0.0027$, and the ARL is

$$\text{ARL} = \frac{1}{\alpha} = \frac{1}{0.0027} = 370$$

Therefore, if the process is really in control, we will experience a "false-alarm" out-of-control signal about every 370 samples. (This will be approximately true, in general, for any Shewhart control chart with 3-sigma limits.) This in-control ARL is generally considered to be satisfactorily large. Now suppose that the process shifts out of control to $p = 0.3$. Table 5-6 indicates that if $p = 0.3$, then $\beta = 0.8594$. Therefore, the ARL is

$$\text{ARL} = \frac{1}{1 - \beta} = \frac{1}{1 - 0.8594} = 7$$

and it will take about seven samples, on the average, to detect this shift with a point outside of the control limits. If this is unsatisfactory, then action must be taken to reduce the out-of-control ARL. Increasing the sample size would result in a smaller value of β and a shorter out-of-control ARL. Another approach would be to reduce the interval *between* samples. That is, if we are currently sampling every hour, it will take about seven hours, on the average, to detect the shift. If we take the sample every half hour, it will require only 3.5 hours, on the average, to detect the shift.

5-3 CONTROL CHARTS FOR NONCONFORMITIES (DEFECTS)

A nonconforming item is a unit of product that does not satisfy one or more of the specifications for that product. Each specific point at which a specification is not satisfied results in a *defect* or *nonconformity*. Consequently, a nonconforming item will contain at least one nonconformity. However, depending on their nature and severity, it is quite possible for a unit to contain several nonconformities and *not* be classified as nonconforming. As an example, suppose we are manufacturing personal computers. Each unit could have one or more very minor flaws in the cabinet finish, and since these flaws do not seriously affect the unit's functional operation, it could be classified as conforming. However, if there are too many of these flaws, the personal computer should be classified as nonconforming, since the flaws would be very noticeable to the customer and might affect the sale of the unit. There are many practical situations in which we prefer to work directly with the number of defects or nonconformities, rather than the fraction nonconforming. These include the number of defective welds in 100 m of oil pipeline, the number of broken rivets in an aircraft wing, the number of functional defects in an electronic logic device, and so forth.

It is possible to develop control charts for either the total number of nonconformities in a unit or the average number of nonconformities per unit. These control charts usually assume that the occurrence of nonconformities in samples of constant size is well modeled by the Poisson distribution. Essentially, this requires that the number of opportunities or potential locations for nonconformities be infinitely large and that the probability of occurrence of a nonconformity at any location be small and constant. Furthermore, the *inspection unit* must be the same for each sample. That is, each inspection unit must always represent an identical "area of opportunity" for the occurrence of nonconformities. In addition, we can count nonconformities of several different types on one unit, as long as the above conditions are satisfied for each class of nonconformity.

In most practical situations, these conditions will not be satisfied exactly. The number of opportunities for the occurrence of nonconformities may be finite, or the probability of occurrence of nonconformities may not be constant. As long as these departures from the assumptions are not severe, the Poisson model will usually work reasonably well. There are cases, however, in which the Poisson model is completely inappropriate. These situations are discussed in more detail at the end of Section 5-3.1.

5-3.1 Procedures with Constant Sample Size

Consider the occurrence of nonconformities in an inspection unit of product. In most cases, the inspection unit will be a single unit of product, although this is not necessarily always so. The inspection unit is simply an entity for which it is convenient to keep records. It could be a group of 5 units of product, 10 units of product, and so on. Suppose that defects or nonconformities occur in this inspection unit according to the Poisson distribution; that is,

$$p(x) = \frac{e^{-c}c^x}{x!} \qquad x = 0, 1, 2, \ldots$$

where x is the number of nonconformities and $c > 0$ is the parameter of the Poisson distribution. From Section 2-2.3 we recall that both the mean and variance of the Poisson distribution are the parameter c. Therefore, a control chart for nonconformities with 3-sigma limits[2] would be given by

$$UCL = c + 3\sqrt{c}$$
$$\text{Center line} = c \tag{5-15}$$
$$LCL = c - 3\sqrt{c}$$

assuming that a standard value for c is available. Should these calculations yield a negative value for the LCL, set LCL = 0.

If no standard is given, then c may be estimated as the observed average number of nonconformities in a preliminary sample of inspection units, say $\bar{c}$. In this case, the control chart has parameters

$$UCL = \bar{c} + 3\sqrt{\bar{c}}$$
$$\text{Center line} = \bar{c} \tag{5-16}$$
$$LCL = \bar{c} - 3\sqrt{\bar{c}}$$

When no standard is given, the control limits in (5-16) should be regarded as *trial* control limits, and the preliminary samples examined for lack of control. The control chart for nonconformities is also sometimes called the c chart.

Example 5-3

Table 5-7 presents the number of nonconformities observed in 26 successive samples of 100 printed circuit boards. Note that, for reasons of convenience, the inspection unit is defined as 100 boards. Since the 26 samples contain 516 total nonconformities, we estimate c by

$$\bar{c} = \frac{516}{26} = 19.85$$

Therefore, the trial control limits are given by

$$UCL = \bar{c} + 3\sqrt{\bar{c}} = 19.85 + 3\sqrt{19.85} = 33.22$$
$$\text{Center line} = \bar{c} = 19.85$$
$$LCL = \bar{c} - 3\sqrt{\bar{c}} = 19.85 - 3\sqrt{19.85} = 6.48$$

The control chart is shown in Figure 5-10. The number of observed nonconformities from the preliminary samples is plotted on this chart. Two points plot outside the control limits, samples 6 and 20. Investigation of sample 6 revealed that a new inspector had examined the boards in this sample and that he did not

---

[2] The α risk for 3-sigma limits is not equally allocated above the UCL and below the LCL, because the Poisson distribution is asymmetric. Some authors recommend the use of probability limits for this chart, particularly when c is small.

Table 5-7
Data on the number of nonconformities in samples of 100 printed circuit boards

Sample Number	Number of Nonconformities	Sample Number	Number of Nonconformities
1	21	14	19
2	24	15	10
3	16	16	17
4	12	17	13
5	15	18	22
6	5	19	18
7	28	20	39
8	20	21	30
9	31	22	24
10	25	23	16
11	20	24	19
12	24	25	17
13	16	26	15

recognize several of the types of nonconformities that could have been present. Furthermore, the unusually large number of nonconformities in sample 20 resulted from a temperature control problem in the wave soldering machine, which was subsequently repaired. Therefore, it seems reasonable to exclude these two samples and revise the trial control limits. The estimate of c is now computed as

$$\bar{c} = \frac{472}{24} = 19.67$$

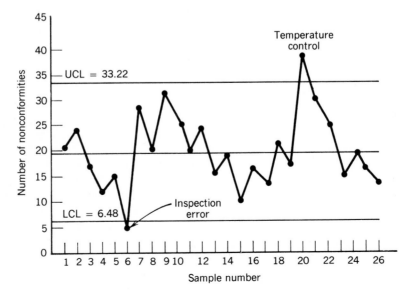

Figure 5-10
Control chart for nonconformities for Example 5-3.

Table 5-8
Additional data for the control chart for nonconformities,
Example 5-3

Sample Number	Number of Nonconformities	Sample Number	Number of Nonconformities
27	16	37	18
28	18	38	21
29	12	39	16
30	15	40	22
31	24	41	19
32	21	42	12
33	28	43	14
34	20	44	9
35	25	45	16
36	19	46	21

and the revised control limits are

$$\text{UCL} = \bar{c} + 3\sqrt{\bar{c}} = 19.67 + 3\sqrt{19.67} = 32.97$$
$$\text{Center line} = \bar{c} = 19.67$$
$$\text{LCL} = \bar{c} - 3\sqrt{\bar{c}} = 19.67 - 3\sqrt{19.67} = 6.37$$

These become the standard values against which production in the next period can be compared.

Twenty new samples, each consisting of one inspection unit (i.e., 100 boards), are subsequently collected. The number of nonconformities in each sample is noted and recorded in Table 5-8. These points are plotted on the control chart in Figure 5-11. No lack of control is indicated; however, the number of nonconformities per

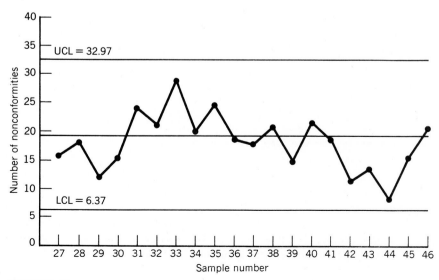

Figure 5-11
Continuation of the control chart for nonconformities, Example 5-3.

board is still unacceptably high. Management action is necessary to improve the process.

Further Analysis of Nonconformities

Defect or nonconformity data are always more informative than fraction nonconforming, because there will usually be several different *types* of nonconformities. By analyzing the nonconformities by type, we can often gain considerable insight into their cause. For example, in the printed circuit board process, there are 16 different types of defects. Defect data for 500 boards are plotted on a Pareto chart in Figure 5-12. Note that over 60% of the total number of defects is due to *two defect types*: solder insufficiency and solder cold joints. This points to further problems with the wave soldering process. If these problems can be isolated and eliminated, there will be a dramatic increase in process yield. Notice that the nonconformities follow the Pareto distribution; that is, most of the defects are attributable to a few (in this case, two) defect types.

This process manufactures several different types of printed circuit boards. Therefore, it may be helpful to examine the occurrence of defect type by type of printed circuit board (part number). Table 5-9 presents this information. Notice that all 40 solder insufficiencies and all 20 solder cold joints occurred on the same part number, 0001285. This implies that this particular type of board is very susceptible to problems in wave soldering, and special attention must be directed toward improving this step of the process for this part number.

Another useful technique for further analysis of nonconformities is the *cause and effect diagram* discussed in Chapter 4. The cause and effect diagram is used to illustrate the various sources of nonconformities in products and their interrelationships. It is useful in focusing the attention of operators, manufacturing engineers, and managers on quality problems. Developing a good cause and effect diagram usually advances the level of technological understanding of the process.

A cause and effect diagram for the printed circuit board assembly process is shown in Figure 5-13. Since most of the defects in this example were solder-related, tthe cause and effect diagram could be used here to help choose the variables for a designed experiment to optimize the wave soldering process. There are several ways to draw the diagram. This one focuses on the three main generic sources of nonconformities: materials, operators, and equipment. Another useful approach is to organize the diagram according to the flow of material through the process.

Choice of Sample Size: The *u* Chart

Example 5-3 illustrates a control chart for nonconformities with the sample size exactly equal to one inspection unit. The inspection unit is chosen for operational or data-collection simplicity. However, there is no reason why the sample size must be restricted to one inspection unit. In fact, we would often prefer to use *several* inspection units in the sample, thereby increasing the area of opportunity for the occurrence of nonconformities. The sample size should be chosen according to statistical considerations, such as specifying a sample size large enough to ensure a positive lower control limit or to obtain a particular probability of detecting a process shift. Alternatively, economic factors could enter into sample-size determination.

DEFECT CODE		FREQ	CUM. FREQ	PERCENT	CUM. PERCENT
SOLD. INSUFFICIE	*************************************	40	40	40.82	40.82
SOLD. COLD JOINT	******************	20	60	20.41	61.23
SOLD. OPENS/DEWE	*******	7	67	7.14	68.37
COMP. IMPROPER 1	******	6	73	6.12	74.49
SOLD. SPLATTER/W	*****	5	78	5.10	79.59
TST. MARK EC MARK	***	3	81	3.06	82.65
TST. MARK WHITE M	***	3	84	3.06	85.71
RAW CD SHROUD RE	***	3	87	3.06	88.78
COMP. EXTRA PART	**	2	89	2.04	90.82
COMP. DAMAGED	**	2	91	2.04	92.86
COMP. MISSING	**	2	93	2.04	94.90
WIRE INCORRECT S	*	1	94	1.02	95.92
STAMPING OPER ID	*	1	95	1.02	96.94
STAMPING MISSING	*	1	96	1.02	97.96
SOLD. SHORT	*	1	97	1.02	98.98
RAW CD DAMAGED	*	1	98	1.02	100.00

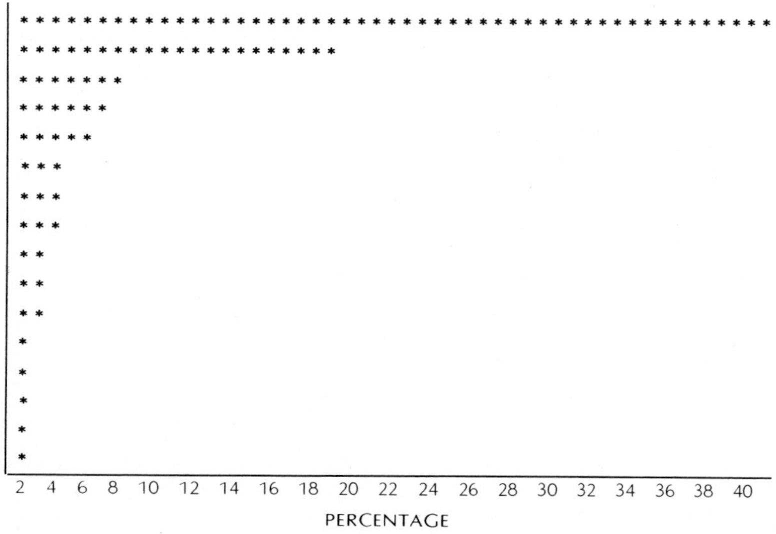

2 4 6 8 10 12 14 16 18 20 22 24 26 28 30 32 34 36 38 40

PERCENTAGE

Figure 5-12

Pareto analysis of nonconformities for the printed circuit board process.

Table 5-9
Table of defects classified by part number and defect code

Part Number
Frequency
Percent
Row Percent
Column Percent

	Component Missing	Component Damaged (NO)	Component Extra Part	Defect Code Component Improper I	Raw Card Shroud RE	Raw Card Damaged	Solder Short	Solder Opens/DEWE	Solder Cold Joint
0001285	1	0	0	0	0	1	0	5	20
	1.02	0.00	0.00	0.00	0.00	1.02	0.00	5.10	20.41
	1.41	0.00	0.00	0.00	0.00	1.41	0.00	7.04	28.17
	50.00	0.00	0.00	0.00	0.00	100.00	0.00	71.43	100.00
0001481	1	2	2	6	3	0	1	2	0
	1.02	2.04	6.12	3.06	0.00	0.00	1.02	2.04	0.00
	3.70	7.41	22.22	11.11	0.00	0.00	3.70	7.41	0.00
	50.00	100.00	100.00	100.00	100.00	0.00	100.00	28.57	0.00
0006429	0	0	0	0	0	0	0	0	0
	0.00	0.00	0.00	0.00	0.00	0.00	0.00	0.00	0.00
	0.00	0.00	0.00	0.00	0.00	0.00	0.00	0.00	0.00
	0.00	0.00	0.00	0.00	0.00	0.00	0.00	0.00	0.00
Total	2	2	2	6	3	1	1	7	20
	2.04	2.04	2.04	6.12	3.06	1.02	1.02	7.14	20.41

Table 5-9 (continued)

Part Number Frequency Percent Row Percent Column Percent	Solder Insufficiencies	Solder Splatter	Stamping Missing	Defect Code Stamping Operator ID	Test Mark White M	Test Mark EC Mark	Wire Incorrect 5	Good Unit(s)	Total
0001285	40 40.82 56.32 100.00	0 0.00 0.00 0.00	0 0.00 0.00 0.00	0 0.00 0.00 0.00	2 2.04 2.82 66.67	1 1.02 1.41 33.33	1 1.02 1.41 100.00	0 0.00 0.00 0.00	71 72.45
0001481	0 0.00 0.00 0.00	5 5.10 18.52 100.00	1 1.02 3.70 100.00	1 1.02 3.70 100.00	1 1.02 3.70 33.33	2 2.04 7.41 66.67	0 0.00 0.00 0.00	0 0.00 0.00 0.00	27 27.55
0006429	0 0.00 0.00 0.00	0 0.00 0.00 0.00	0 0.00 0.00 0.00	0 0.00 0.00 0.00	0 0.00 0.00 0.00	0 0.00 0.00 0.00	0 0.00 0.00 0.00	0 0.00 0.00 0.00	0 0.00
Total	40 40.82	5 5.10	1 1.02	1 1.02	3 3.06	3 3.06	1 1.02	0 0.00	98 100.00

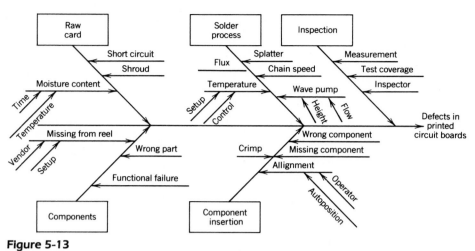

Figure 5-13
Cause and effect diagram.

Suppose we decide to base the control chart on a sample size of n inspection units. Note that n does not have to be an integer. To illustrate this, suppose that in Example 5-3 we were to specify a subgroup size of $n = 2.5$ inspection units. Then the sample size becomes $(2.5)(100) = 250$ boards. There are two general approaches to constructing the revised chart once a new sample size has been selected. One approach is simply to redefine a new inspection unit that is equal to n times the old inspection unit. In this case, the center line on the new control chart is $n\bar{c}$ and the control limits are located at $n\bar{c} \pm 3\sqrt{n\bar{c}}$, where $\bar{c}$ is the observed mean number of nonconformities in the *original* inspection unit. Suppose that in Example 5-2, after revising the trial control limits, we decided to use a sample size of $n = 2.5$ inspection units. Then the center line would have been located at $n\bar{c} = (2.5)(19.67) = 49.18$ and the control limits would have been $49.18 \pm 3\sqrt{49.18}$, or LCL = 28.14 and UCL = 70.22.

The second approach involves setting up a control chart based on the average number of nonconformities per inspection unit. If we find c *total* nonconformities in a sample of n inspection units, then the *average* number of nonconformities per inspection unit is

$$u = \frac{c}{n} \tag{5-17}$$

Note that c is a Poisson random variable; consequently, the parameters of the control chart are

$$UCL = \bar{u} + 3\sqrt{\frac{\bar{u}}{n}}$$
$$\text{Center line} = \bar{u} \tag{5-18}$$
$$LCL = \bar{u} - 3\sqrt{\frac{\bar{u}}{n}}$$

where $\bar{u}$ represents the observed average number of nonconformities per unit in a preliminary set of data. Control limits found from (5-18) would be regarded as trial control limits. This chart is called the control chart for *nonconformities per unit*, or the *u* chart.

Example 5-4

A personal computer manufacturer wishes to establish a control chart for nonconformities per unit on the final assembly line. The sample size is selected as five computers. Data on the number of nonconformities in 20 samples of 5 computers each are shown in Table 5-10. From these data, we would estimate the average number of nonconformities per unit to be

$$\bar{u} = \frac{\sum_{i=1}^{20} u_i}{20} = \frac{38.60}{20} = 1.93$$

Therefore, the parameters of the control chart are

$$\text{UCL} = \bar{u} + 3\sqrt{\frac{\bar{u}}{n}} = 1.93 + 3\sqrt{\frac{1.93}{5}} = 3.79$$

$$\text{Center line} = \bar{u} = 1.93$$

$$\text{LCL} = \bar{u} - 3\sqrt{\frac{\bar{u}}{n}} = 1.93 - 3\sqrt{\frac{1.93}{5}} = 0.07$$

Table 5-10
Data on number of nonconformities in personal computers

Sample Number	Sample Size n	Total Number of Nonconformities, c	Average Number of Nonconformities per Unit, $u = c/n$
1	5	10	2.0
2	5	12	2.4
3	5	8	1.6
4	5	14	2.8
5	5	10	2.0
6	5	16	3.2
7	5	11	2.2
8	5	7	1.4
9	5	10	2.0
10	5	15	3.0
11	5	9	1.8
12	5	5	1.0
13	5	7	1.4
14	5	11	2.2
15	5	12	2.4
16	5	6	1.2
17	5	8	1.6
18	5	10	2.0
19	5	7	1.4
20	5	5	1.0
		$\overline{193}$	$\overline{38.6}$

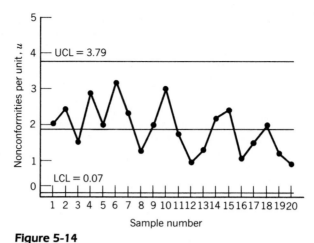

Figure 5-14
A control chart for nonconformities per unit.

The control chart is shown in Figure 5-14. The preliminary data do not exhibit lack of statistical control; therefore, the trial control limits above would be adopted for current control purposes. Once again, note that, although the process is in control, the average number of nonconformities per unit is unacceptably high. Even if these are nonfunctional or appearance nonconformities, there are too many of them. Management must take action to improve the process.

Alternative Probability Models for Count Data

Most applications of the c chart assume that the Poisson distribution is the correct probability model underlying the process. However, it is not the only distribution that could be utilized as a model of "count" or nonconformities per unit-type data. Various types of phenomena can produce distributions of defects that are not well modeled by the Poisson distribution. For example, suppose that nonconformities tend to occur in *clusters*; that is, if there is one nonconformity in some part of a product, then it is likely that there will be others. Note that there are at least two random processes at work here: one generating the number and location of clusters, and the second generating the number of nonconformities within each cluster. If the number of clusters has a Poisson distribution and the number of nonconformities within each cluster has a common distribution (say f), then the total number of nonconformities has a *compound Poisson distribution*. Many types of compound or generalized distributions could be used as a model for count-type data. As an illustration, if the number of clusters has a Poisson distribution and the number of nonconformities within each cluster is also Poisson, then Neyman's type-A distribution models the total number of nonconformities. Alternatively, if the cluster distribution is gamma and the number of nonconformities within each cluster is Poisson, the negative binomial distribution results. Johnson and Kotz (1969) give a good summary of these and other discrete distributions that could be useful in modeling count-type data.

Mixtures of various types of nonconformities can lead to situations in which the total number of nonconformities is not adequately modeled by the Poisson distribution. Similar situations occur when the count data have either too many or too few zeros. A good discussion of this general problem is the paper by Jackson (1972). The use of the negative binomial distribution to model count data in inspection units of varying size has been studied by Sheaffer and Leavenworth (1976). The dissertation by Gardiner (1987) describes the use of various discrete distributions to model the occurrence of defects in integrated circuits.

5-3.2 Procedures with Variable Sample Size

Control charts for nonconformities are occasionally formed using 100% inspection of the product. When this method of sampling is used, the number of inspection units in a sample will usually not be constant. For example, the inspection of rolls of cloth or paper often leads to a situation in which the size of the sample varies, because not all rolls are exactly the same length or width. If a control chart for nonconformities (c chart) is used in this situation, both the center line and the control limits will vary with the sample size. Such a control chart would be very difficult to interpret. The correct procedure is to use a control chart for nonconformities per unit (u chart). This chart will have a constant center line; however, the control limits will vary inversely with the square root of the sample size n.

Example 5-5

In a textile finishing plant, dyed cloth is inspected for the occurrence of defects per 50 square meters. The data on ten rolls of cloth are shown in Table 5-11. We will use these data to set up a control chart for nonconformities per unit.

The center line of the chart should be the average number of nonconformities per inspection unit—that is, the average number of nonconformities per 50 square

Table 5-11
Occurrence of nonconformities in dyed cloth

Roll Number	Number of Square Meters	Total Number of Nonconformities	Number of Inspection Units in Roll, n	Number of Nonconformities per Inspection Unit
1	500	14	10.0	1.40
2	400	12	8.0	1.50
3	650	20	13.0	1.54
4	500	11	10.0	1.10
5	475	7	9.5	0.74
6	500	10	10.0	1.00
7	600	21	12.0	1.75
8	525	16	10.5	1.52
9	600	19	12.0	1.58
10	625	23	12.5	1.84
		153	107.50	

Table 5-12
Calculation of control limits, Example 5-5

Roll Number, i	n_i	UCL $= \bar{u} + 3\sqrt{\bar{u}/n_i}$	LCL $= \bar{u} - 3\sqrt{\bar{u}/n_i}$
1	10.0	2.55	0.29
2	8.0	2.68	0.16
3	13.0	2.41	0.43
4	10.0	2.55	0.29
5	9.5	2.58	0.26
6	10.0	2.55	0.29
7	12.0	2.45	0.39
8	10.5	2.52	0.32
9	12.0	2.45	0.39
10	12.5	2.43	0.41

meters. This is computed as

$$\bar{u} = \frac{153}{107.5} = 1.42$$

Note that $\bar{u}$ is the ratio of the total number of observed nonconformities to the total number of inspection units.

The control limits on this chart are computed from Equation (5-18) with n replaced by n_i. The width of the control limits will vary inversely with n_i, the number of inspection units in the roll. The calculations for the control limits are displayed in Table 5-12. Figure 5-15 plots the control chart.

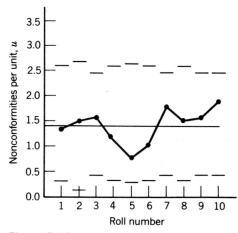

Figure 5-15
Nonconformities per unit control chart with variable sample size, Example 5-5.

As noted previously, the u chart should always be used when the sample size is variable. The most common implementation involves variable control limits, as illustrated in Example 5-5. There are, however, two other possible approaches:

1. Use control limits based on an average sample size

$$\bar{n} = \sum_{i=1}^{m} n_i/m$$

2. Use a standardized control chart.

This second alternative would involve plotting a standardized statistic

$$Z_i = \frac{u_i - \bar{u}}{\sqrt{\dfrac{\bar{u}}{n_i}}} \tag{5-19}$$

on a control chart with LCL $= -3$ and UCL $= +3$ and the center line at zero. This chart is appropriate if tests for runs and other pattern-recognition methods are to be used in conjunction with the chart. This standardized control chart could also be useful in the short production run situation (see Chapter 8).

5-3.3 Demerit Systems

With complex products such as automobiles, computers, or major appliances, we usually find that many different types of nonconformities or defects can occur. Not all of these types of defects are equally important. A unit of product having one very serious defect would probably be classified as nonconforming to requirements, but a unit having several minor defects might not necessarily be nonconforming. In such situations as, we need a method to classify nonconformities or defects according to severity and to weight the various types of defects in a reasonable manner.

One possible demerit scheme is the following:

Class A Defects—Very Serious. The unit is either completely unfit for service, or will fail in service in such a manner that cannot be easily corrected in the field, or will cause personal injury or property damage.

Class B Defects—Serious. The unit will possibly suffer a Class A operating failure, or will certainly cause somewhat less serious operating problems, or will certainly have reduced life or increased maintenance cost.

Class C Defects—Moderately Serious. The unit will possibly fail in service, or cause trouble that is less serious than operating failure, or possibly have reduced life or increased maintenance costs, or have a major defect in finish, appearance, or quality of work.

Class D Defects—Minor. The unit will not fail in service but has minor defects in finish, appearance, or quality of work.

Let c_A, c_B, c_C, and c_D represent the number of Class A, Class B, Class C, and Class D defects, respectively, in an inspection unit. We assume that each class of defect is independent, and the occurrence of defects in each class is well modeled by a Poisson distribution. Then we define the number of *demerits* in the inspection unit as

$$D = 100c_A + 50c_B + 10c_C + c_D \tag{5-20}$$

The demerit weights of Class A-100, Class B-50, Class C-10, and Class D-1 are used fairly widely in practice. However, any reasonable set of weights appropriate for a specific problem may also be used.

Suppose that a sample of n inspection units is used. Then the number of demerits per unit is

$$u = \frac{D}{n} \tag{5-21}$$

where D is the total number of demerits in all n inspection units. Since u is a linear combination of independent Poisson random variables, statistics u could be plotted on a control chart with the following parameters:

$$UCL = \bar{u} + 3\hat{\sigma}_u$$
$$\text{Center line} = \bar{u} \tag{5-22}$$
$$LCL = \bar{u} - 3\hat{\sigma}_u,$$

where

$$\bar{u} = 100\bar{u}_A + 50\bar{u}_B + 10\bar{u}_C + \bar{u}_D \tag{5-23}$$

and

$$\hat{\sigma}_u = \left[\frac{(100)^2\bar{u}_A + (50)^2\bar{u}_B + (10)^2\bar{u}_C + \bar{u}_D}{n} \right]^{1/2} \tag{5-24}$$

$\bar{u}_A, \bar{u}_B, \bar{u}_C$, and $\bar{u}_D$ represent the average number of Class A, Class B, Class C, and Class D defects per unit. The values of $\bar{u}_A, \bar{u}_B, \bar{u}_C$, and $\bar{u}_D$ are obtained from the analysis of preliminary data, taken when the process is supposedly operating in control. Standard values for u_A, u_B, u_C, and u_D may also be used, if they are available.

Many variations of this idea are possible. For example, we can classify non-conformities as either *functional defects* or *appearance* defects, if a two-class system is preferred. It is also fairly common practice to maintain separate control charts on each defect class rather than combining them into one chart.

5-3.4 The Operating-Characteristic Function

The operating-characteristic (OC) curves for both the c chart and the u chart can be obtained from the Poisson distribution. For the c chart, the OC curve plots the probability of type II error β against the true mean number of defects c. The expression for β is

$$\beta = P\{x < UCL|c\} - P\{x \le LCL|c\} \tag{5-25}$$

where x is a Poisson random variable with parameter c.

Table 5-13
Calculation of the OC curve for a c chart with UCL = 33.22 and
LCL = 6.48

c	$P\{x \le 33|c\}$	$P\{x \le 6|c\}$	$\beta = P\{x \le 33|c\} - P\{x \le 6|c\}$
1	1.000	0.999	0.001
3	1.000	0.967	0.033
5	1.000	0.762	0.238
7	1.000	0.450	0.550
10	1.000	0.130	0.870
15	0.999	0.007	0.992
20	0.997	0.000	0.997
25	0.950	0.000	0.950
30	0.709	0.000	0.709
33	0.500	0.000	0.500
35	0.367	0.000	0.367
40	0.131	0.000	0.131
45	0.037	0.000	0.037

We will generate the OC curve for the c chart in Example 5-3. For this example, since the LCL = 6.48 and the UCL = 33.22, Equation (5-25) becomes

$$\beta = P\{x < 33.22|c\} - P\{x \le 6.48|c\}$$

Since the number of nonconformities must be integer, this is equivalent to

$$\beta = P\{x \le 33|c\} - P\{x \le 6|c\}$$

These probabilities are evaluated in Table 5-13. The OC curve is shown in Figure 5-16.

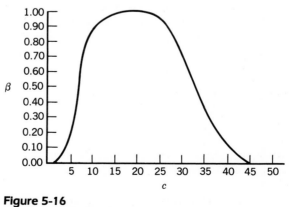

Figure 5-16
OC curve of a c chart with LCL = 6.48 and
UCL = 33.22.

For the u chart, we may generate the OC curve from

$$
\begin{aligned}
\beta &= P\{x < \text{UCL}\,|\,u\} - P\{x \le \text{LCL}\,|\,u\} \\
&= P\{c < n\text{UCL}\,|\,u\} - P\{c \le n\text{LCL}\,|\,u\} \\
&= P\{n\text{LCL} < c \le n\text{UCL}\,|\,u\} \\
&= \sum_{c = \langle n\text{LCL} \rangle}^{[n\text{UCL}]} \frac{e^{-nu}(nu)^c}{c!}
\end{aligned}
\tag{5-26}
$$

where $\langle n\text{LCL} \rangle$ denotes the smallest integer greater than or equal to $n\text{LCL}$ and $[n\text{UCL}]$ denotes the largest integer less than or equal to $n\text{UCL}$. The limits on the summation in (5-26) follow from the fact that the total number of nonconformities observed in a sample of n inspection units must be an integer. Note that n need not be integer.

5-3.5 Dealing With Low-Defect Levels

When defect levels in a process become very low, say under 1000 occurrences per million, there will be very long periods of time between the occurrence of a nonconforming unit. In these situations many samples will have zero defects, and a control chart with the statistic consistently plotting at zero will be relatively uninformative. Thus, conventional c and u charts become ineffective as defect levels are driven into the low parts per million (PPM) range.

One way to deal with this problem is to control chart a new variable, the time *between* successive occurrences of defects. The time between events control chart has been very effective as a process-control procedure for processes with low-defect levels. The best way to implement these procedures is with either *cumulative sum* control charts or *exponentially weighted moving average* control charts. These charts are discussed in Chapter 7.

5-3.6 Nonmanufacturing Applications

The c chart and u chart are widely used in nonmanufacturing applications of statistical process control. In effect, we can treat *errors* in the nonmanufacturing environment just as we treat defects or nonconformities in the manufacturing world. To give just a few examples, we can plot errors on engineering drawings, errors on plans and documents, and errors in computer software as c or u charts. An example using u charts to control errors in computer software during product development is given in Gardiner and Montgomery (1987).

5-4 EXERCISES

5-1 The data below give the number of nonconforming bearing and seal assemblies in samples of size 100. Construct a fraction nonconforming control chart for these data. If any points plot out of control, assume that assignable causes can be found and determine the revised control limits.

Sample Number	Number of Nonconforming Assemblies	Sample Number	Number of Nonconforming Assemblies
1	7	11	6
2	4	12	15
3	1	13	0
4	3	14	9
5	6	15	5
6	8	16	1
7	10	17	4
8	5	18	5
9	2	19	7
10	7	20	12

5-2 The number of nonconforming switches in samples of size 150 are shown below. Construct a fraction nonconforming control chart for these data. Does the process appear to be in control? If not, assume that assignable causes can be found for all points outside the control limits and calculate the revised control limits.

Sample Number	Number of Nonconforming Switches	Sample Number	Number of Nonconforming Switches
1	8	11	6
2	1	12	0
3	3	13	4
4	0	14	0
5	2	15	3
6	4	16	1
7	0	17	15
8	1	18	2
9	10	19	3
10	6	20	0

5-3 The data below represent the results of inspecting all units of a personal computer produced for the last 10 days. Does the process appear to be in control?

Day	Units Inspected	Nonconforming Units	Fraction Nonconforming
1	80	4	0.050
2	110	7	0.064
3	90	5	0.056
4	75	8	0.107
5	130	6	0.038
6	120	6	0.050
7	70	4	0.057
8	125	5	0.040
9	105	8	0.076
10	95	7	0.074

5-4 A process that produces titanium forgings for automobile turbocharger wheels is to be controlled through use of a fraction nonconforming chart. Initially, one sample of size 150 is taken each day for 20 days, and the results shown below are observed.

Day	Nonconforming Units	Day	Nonconforming Units
1	3	11	2
2	2	12	4
3	4	13	1
4	2	14	3
5	5	15	6
6	2	16	0
7	1	17	1
8	2	18	2
9	0	19	3
10	5	20	2

a. Establish a control chart to control future production.

b. What is the smallest sample size that could be used for this process and still give a positive lower control limit on the chart?

5-5 A process produces rubber belts in lots of size 2500. Inspection records on the last 20 lots reveal the following data:

Lot Number	Number of Nonconforming Belts	Lot Number	Number of Nonconforming Belts
1	230	11	456
2	435	12	394
3	221	13	285
4	346	14	331
5	230	15	198
6	327	16	414
7	285	17	131
8	311	18	269
9	342	19	221
10	308	20	407

a. Compute trial control limits for a fraction nonconforming control chart.

b. If you wanted to set up a control chart for controlling future production, how would you use the above data to obtain the center line and control limits for the chart?

5-6 Based on these data, if an np chart is to be established, what would you recommend as the center line and control limits? Assume that $n = 500$.

Day	Number of Nonconforming Units
1	3
2	4
3	3
4	2
5	6
6	12
7	5
8	1
9	2
10	2

5-7 A control chart indicates that the current process fraction nonconforming is 0.02. If 50 items are inspected each day, what is the probability of detecting a shift in the fraction nonconforming to 0.04 on the first day after the shift? By the end of the third day following the shift?

5-8 A company purchases a small metal bracket in containers of 5000 each. Ten containers have arrived at the unloading facility, and 250 brackets are selected at random from each container. The fraction nonconforming in each sample are: 0, 0, 0.004, 0.008, 0.020, 0.004, 0, 0, and 0.008. Do the data from this shipment indicate statistical control?

5-9 Diodes used on printed circuit boards are produced in lots of size 1000. We wish to control the process producing these diodes by taking samples of size 64 from each lot. If the nominal value of the fraction nonconforming is $p = 0.10$, determine the parameters of the appropriate control chart. To what level must the fraction nonconforming increase to make the β risk equal to 0.50? What is the minimum sample size that would give a positive lower control limit for this chart?

5-10 A control chart for the number of nonconforming piston rings is maintained on a forging process with $np = 16.0$. A sample of size 100 is taken each day and analyzed.

a. What is the probability that a shift in the process average to $np = 20.0$ will be detected on the first day following the shift? What is the probability that the shift will be detected by at least the end of the third day?

b. Find the smallest sample size that will give a positive lower control limit.

5-11 A control chart for the fraction nonconforming is to be established using a center line of $p = 0.10$. What sample size is required if we wish to detect a shift in the process fraction nonconforming to 0.20 with probability 0.50?

5-12 A process is controlled with a fraction nonconforming control chart with 3-sigma limits, $n = 100$, UCL = 0.161, center line = 0.080, and LCL = 0.

a. Find the equivalent control chart for the number nonconforming.

b. Use the Poisson approximation to the binomial to find the probability of a type I error.

c. Use the correct approximation to find the probability of a type II error if the process fraction nonconforming shifts to 0.2.

d. What is the probability of detecting the shift in part (c) by at most the fourth sample after the shift?

5-13 A process is being controlled with a fraction nonconforming control chart. The process average has been shown to be 0.07. Three-sigma control limits are used, and the procedure calls for taking daily samples of 400 items.

a. Calculate the upper and lower control limits.

b. If the process average should suddenly shift to 0.10, what is the probability that the shift would be detected on the first subsequent sample?

c. What is the probability that the shift in part (b) would be detected on the first or second sample taken after the shift?

5-14 In designing a fraction nonconforming chart with center line at $p = 0.20$ and 3-sigma control limits, what is the sample size required to yield a positive lower control limit? What is the value of n necessary to give a probability of 0.50 of detecting a shift in the process to 0.26?

5-15 A control chart is used to control the fraction nonconforming for a plastic part manufactured in an injection molding process. Ten subgroups yield the following data:

Sample Number	Sample Size	Number Nonconforming
1	100	10
2	100	15
3	100	31
4	100	18
5	100	26
6	100	12
7	100	25
8	100	15
9	100	8
10	100	8

a. Set up a control chart for the number nonconforming in samples of $n = 100$.

b. For the chart established in part (a), what is the probability of detecting a shift in the process fraction nonconforming to 0.30 on the first sample after the shift has occurred?

5-16 A control chart for fraction nonconforming indicates that the current process average is 0.03. The sample size is constant at 200 units.

a. Find the 3-sigma control limits for the control chart.

b. What is the probability that a shift in the process average to 0.08 will be detected on the first subsequent sample? What is the probability that this shift will be detected at least by the fourth sample following the shift?

5-17 a. A control chart for the number nonconforming is to be established, based on samples of size 400. To start the control chart, 30 samples were selected and the number nonconforming in each sample determined, yielding $\sum_{i=1}^{30} D_i = 1200$. What are the parameters of the np chart?

b. Suppose the process average fraction nonconforming shifted to 0.15. What is the probability that the shift would be detected on the first subsequent sample?

5-18 A fraction nonconforming control chart with center line 0.10, UCL = 0.19, and LCL = 0.01 is used to control a process.

a. If 3-sigma limits are used, find the sample size for the control chart.

b. Use the Poisson approximation to the binomial to find the probability of type I error.

c. Use the Poisson approximation to the binomial to find the probability of type II error if the process fraction defective is actually $p = 0.20$.

5-19 Consider the control chart designed in Exercise 5-17. Find the average run length to detect a shift to a fraction nonconforming of 0.15.

5-20 Consider the control chart in Exercise 5-18. Find the average run length if the process fraction nonconforming shifts to 0.20.

5-21 A maintenance group improves the effectiveness of its repair work by monitoring the number of maintenance requests that require a second call to complete the repair. There are 20 weeks of data available.

Week	Total Requests	Second Visit Required	Week	Total Requests	Second Visit Required
1	200	6	11	100	1
2	250	8	12	100	0
3	250	9	13	100	1
4	250	7	14	200	4
5	200	3	15	200	5
6	200	4	16	200	3
7	150	2	17	200	10
8	150	1	18	200	4
9	150	0	19	250	7
10	150	2	20	250	6

a. Find trial control limits for this process.

b. Design a control chart for controlling future production.

5-22 Analyze the data in Exercise 5-21 using an average sample size.

5-23 Construct a standardized control chart for the data in Exercise 5-21.

5-24 **Continuation of Exercise 5-21.** Notice that in Exercise 5-21 there are only four different sample sizes; $n = 100$, 150, 200, and 250. Prepare a control chart that has a set of limits for each possible sample size and show how it could be used as an alternative to the variable-width control limit method used in Exercise 5-21. How easy would this method be to use in practice?

5-25 A fraction nonconforming control chart has center line 0.01, UCL = 0.0399, LCL = 0, and $n = 100$. If 3-sigma limits are used, find the smallest sample size that would yield a positive lower control limit.

5-26 Why is the np chart not appropriate with variable sample size?

5-27 A fraction nonconforming control chart with $n = 400$ has the following parameters:

$$\text{UCL} = 0.0809$$
$$\text{Center line} = 0.0500$$
$$\text{LCL} = 0.0191$$

a. Find the width of the control limits in standard deviation units.

b. What would be the corresponding parameters for an equivalent control chart based on the number nonconforming?

c. What is the probability that a shift in the process fraction nonconforming to 0.0300 will be detected on the first sample following the shift?

5-28 A fraction nonconforming control chart with $n = 400$ has the following parameters:

$$\text{UCL} = 0.0962$$
$$\text{Center line} = 0.0500$$
$$\text{LCL} = 0.0038$$

a. Find the width of the control limits in standard deviation units.

b. Suppose the process fraction nonconforming shifts to 0.15. What is the probability of detecting the shift on the first subsequent sample?

5-29 A fraction nonconforming control chart is to be established with a center line of 0.01 and 2-sigma control limits.

a. How large should the sample size be if the lower control limit is to be nonzero?

b. How large should the sample size be if we wish the probability of detecting a shift to 0.04 to be 0.50?

5-30 The following fraction nonconforming control chart with $n = 100$ is used to control a process:

$$\text{UCL} = 0.0750$$
$$\text{Center line} = 0.0400$$
$$\text{LCL} = 0.0050$$

a. Use the Poisson approximation to the binomial to find the probability of a type I error.

b. Use the Poisson approximation to the binomial to find the probability of a type II error, if the true process fraction nonconforming is 0.0600.

c. Draw the OC curve for this control chart.

d. Find the ARL when the process is in control and the ARL when the process fraction nonconforming is 0.0600.

5-31 A process that produces bearing housings is controlled with a fraction nonconforming control chart, using sample size $n = 100$ and a center line $\bar{p} = 0.02$.

a. Find the 3-sigma limits for this chart.

b. Analyze the ten new samples ($n = 100$) shown below for statistical control. What conclusions can you draw about the process now?

Sample Number	Number Nonconforming
1	5
2	2
3	3
4	8
5	4
6	1
7	2
8	6
9	3
10	4

5-32 Consider an *np* chart with *k*-sigma control limits. Derive a general formula for determining the minimum sample size to ensure that the chart has a positive lower control limit.

5-33 Consider the fraction nonconforming control chart in Exercise 5-4. Find the equivalent *np* chart.

5-34 Consider the fraction nonconforming control chart in Exercise 5-5. Find the equivalent *np* chart.

5-35 Construct a standardized control chart for the data in Exercise 5-3.

5-36 Surface defects have been counted on 25 rectangular steel plates, and the data are shown below. Set up a control chart for nonconformities using these data. Does the process producing the plates appear to be in statistical control?

Plate Number	Number of Nonconformities	Plate Number	Number of Nonconformities
1	1	14	0
2	0	15	2
3	4	16	1
4	3	17	3
5	1	18	5
6	2	19	4
7	5	20	6
8	0	21	3
9	2	22	1
10	1	23	0
11	1	24	2
12	0	25	4
13	8		

5-37 A paper mill uses a control chart to monitor the imperfection in finished rolls of paper. Production output is inspected for 20 days, and the resulting data are shown below. Use these data to set up a control chart for nonconformities per roll of paper. Does the process appear to be in statistical control? What center line and control limits would you recommend for controlling current production?

Day	Number of Rolls Produced	Total Number of Imperfections	Day	Number of Rolls Produced	Total Number of Imperfections
1	18	12	11	18	18
2	18	14	12	18	14
3	24	20	13	18	9
4	22	18	14	20	10
5	22	15	15	20	14
6	22	12	16	20	13
7	20	11	17	24	16
8	20	15	18	24	18
9	20	12	19	22	20
10	20	10	20	21	17

5-38 Continuation of Exercise 5-37. Consider the papermaking process in Exercise 5-37. Set up a u chart based on an average sample size to control this process.

5-39 Continuation of Exercise 5-37. Consider the papermaking process in Exercise 5-37. Set up a standardized u chart for this process.

5-40 The number of nonconformities found on final inspection of a cassette deck is shown below. Can you conclude that the process is in statistical control? What center line and control limits would you recommend for controlling future production?

Deck Number	Number of Nonconformities	Deck Number	Number of Nonconformities
2412	0	2421	1
2413	1	2422	0
2414	1	2423	3
2415	0	2424	2
2416	2	2425	5
2417	1	2425	1
2418	1	2426	2
2419	3	2427	1
2420	2	2428	1

5-41 The data below represent the number of nonconformities per 1000 meters in telephone cable. From analysis of these data, would you conclude that the process is in statistical control? What control procedure would you recommend for future production?

Sample Number	Number of Nonconformities	Sample Number	Number of Nonconformities
1	1	12	6
2	1	13	9
3	3	14	11
4	7	15	15
5	8	16	8
6	10	17	3
7	5	18	6
8	13	19	7
9	0	20	4
10	19	21	9
11	24	22	20

5-42 Consider the data in Exercise 5-40. Suppose we wish to define a new inspection unit of four cassette decks.

a. What are the center line and control limits for a control chart for monitoring future production based on the total number of defects in the new inspection unit?

b. What are the center line and control limits for a control chart for nonconformities per unit used to monitor future production?

5-43 Consider the data in Exercise 5-41. Suppose a new inspection unit is defined as 2500 m of wire.

a. What are the center line and control limits for a control chart for monitoring future production based on the total number of nonconformities in the new inspection unit?

b. What are the center line and control limits for a control chart for nonconformities per unit used to monitor future production?

5-44 An automobile manufacturer wishes to control the number of nonconformities in a subassembly area producing manual transmissions. The inspection unit is defined as four transmissions, and data from 16 samples (each of size 4) are shown on page 197.

Sample Number	Number of Nonconformities	Sample Number	Number of Nonconformities
1	1	9	2
2	3	10	1
3	2	11	0
4	1	12	2
5	0	13	1
6	2	14	1
7	1	15	2
8	5	16	3

a. Set up a control chart for nonconformities per unit.

b. Do these data come from a controlled process? If not, assume that assignable causes can be found for all out-of-control points and calculate the revised control chart parameters.

c. Suppose the inspection unit is redefined as eight transmissions. Design an appropriate control chart for monitoring future production.

5-45 Find the 3-sigma control limits for:

a. A c chart with process average equal to four nonconformities.

b. A u chart with $c = 4$ and $n = 4$.

5-46 Find 0.900 and 0.100 probability limits for a c chart when the process average is equal to 16 nonconformities.

5-47 Find the 3-sigma control limits for

a. A c chart with process average equal to nine nonconformities.

b. A u chart with $c = 16$ and $n = 4$.

5-48 Find 0.980 and 0.020 probability limits for a control chart for nonconformities per unit when $u = 6.0$ and $n = 3$.

5-49 Find 0.975 and 0.025 probability limits for a control chart for nonconformities when $c = 7.6$.

5-50 A control chart for nonconformities per unit uses 0.95 and 0.05 probability limits. The center line is at $u = 1.4$. Determine the control limits if the sample size is $n = 10$.

5-51 The number of workmanship nonconformities observed in the final inspection of disk-drive assemblies has been tabulated as shown below. Does the process appear to be in control?

Day	Number of Assemblies Inspected	Total Number of Nonconformities
1	2	10
2	4	30
3	2	18
4	1	10
5	3	20
6	4	24
7	2	15
8	4	26
9	3	21
10	1	8

5-52 A control chart for nonconformities is to be constructed with $c = 2.0$, LCL $= 0$, and UCL such that the probability of a point plotting outside control limits when $c = 2.0$ is only 0.005.

   a. Find the UCL.

   b. What is the type I error probability if the process is assumed to be out of control only when two consecutive points fall outside the control limits?

5-53 A textile mill wishes to establish a control procedure on flaws in towels it manufactures. Using an inspection unit of 50 units, past inspection data show that 100 previous inspection units had 850 total flaws. What type of control chart is appropriate? Design the control chart such that it has two-sided probability control limits of $\alpha = 0.06$, approximately. Give the center line and control limits.

5-54 The manufacturer wishes to set up a control chart at the final inspection station for a gas water heater. Defects in workmanship and visual quality features are checked in this inspection. For the last 22 working days, 176 water heaters were inspected and a total of 924 nonconformities reported.

   a. What type of control chart would you recommend here and how would you use it?

   b. Using two water heaters as the inspection unit, calculate the center line and control limits that are consistent with the past 22 days of inspection data.

   c. What is the probability of type I error for the control chart in part (b)?

5-55 Assembled portable television sets are subjected to a final inspection for surface defects. A control procedure is established based on the requirement that if the average number of nonconformities per unit is 4.0, the probability of concluding that the process is in control will be 0.99. There is to be no lower control limit. What is the appropriate type of control chart and what is the required upper control limit?

5-56 A control chart is to be established on a process producing refrigerators. The inspection unit is one refrigerator, and a control chart for nonconformities is to be used. As preliminary data, 16 nonconformities were counted in inspecting 30 refrigerators.

   a. What are the 3-sigma control limits?

   b. What is the α-risk for this control chart?

   c. What is the β-risk if the average number of defects is actually 2 (i.e., if $c = 2.0$)?

   d. Find the average run length if the average number of defects is actually 2.

5-57 Consider the situation described in Exercise 5-56.

   a. Find 2-sigma control limits and compare these with the control limits found in part (a) of Exercise 5-56.

   b. Find the α-risk for the control chart with 2-sigma control limits and compare with the results of part (b) of Exercise 5-56.

   c. Find the β-risk for $c = 2.0$ for the chart with 2-sigma control limits and compare with the results of part (c) of Exercise 5-56.

   d. Find the ARL if $c = 2.0$ and compare with the ARL found in part (d) of Exercise 5-56.

5-58 A control chart for nonconformities is to be established in conjunction with final inspection of a radio. The inspection unit is to be a group of ten radios. The average number of nonconformities per radio has, in the past, been 0.5. Find 3-sigma control limits for a c chart based on this size inspection unit.

5-59 A control chart for nonconformities is maintained on a process producing desk calculators. The inspection unit is defined as two calculators. The average number of nonconformities per machine when the process is in control is estimated to be two.

   a. Find the appropriate 3-sigma control limits for this size inspection unit.

b. What is the probability of type I error for this control chart?

5-60 A production line assembles electric clocks. The average number of nonconformities per clock is estimated to be 0.75. The quality engineer wishes to establish a *c* chart for this operation, using an inspection unit of six clocks. Find the 3-sigma limits for this chart.

5-61 Suppose that we wish to design a control chart for nonconformities per unit with *k*-sigma limits. Find the minimum sample size that would result in a positive lower control limit for this chart.

Chapter 6

Control Charts for Variables

6-1 INTRODUCTION

Many quality characteristics can be expressed in terms of a numerical measurement. For example, the diameter of a bearing could be measured with a micrometer and expressed in millimeters. A single measurable quality characteristic, such as a dimension, weight, or volume, is called a *variable*. Control charts for variables are used extensively. They usually lead to more efficient control procedures and provide more information about process performance than attributes control charts.

When dealing with a quality characteristic that is a variable, it is a standard practice to control both the mean value of the quality characteristic and its variability. Control of the process average or mean quality level is usually with the control chart for means, or the $\bar{x}$ chart. Process variability or dispersion can be controlled with either a control chart for the standard deviation, called the S chart, or a control chart for the range, called an R chart. The R chart is more widely used. Usually, separate $\bar{x}$ and R charts are maintained for each quality characteristic of interest. (However, if the quality characteristics are closely related, this can sometimes cause misleading results; refer to Section 8-5.) The $\bar{x}$ and R (or S) charts are among the most important and useful on-line statistical process-control techniques.

Notice that it is important to maintain control over both the process mean and process variability. Figure 6-1 illustrates the output of a production process.

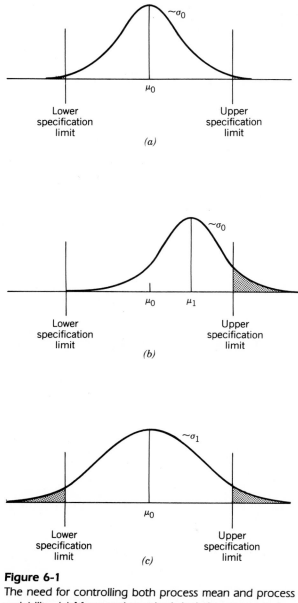

Figure 6-1
The need for controlling both process mean and process
variability. (a) Mean and standard deviation at nominal
levels. (b) Process mean $\mu_1 > \mu_0$. (c) Process standard
deviation $\sigma_1 > \sigma_0$.

In Figure 6-1a both the mean μ and standard deviation σ are in control at their
nominal values (say μ_0 and σ_0); consequently, most of the process output falls
within the specification limits. However, in Figure 6-1b the mean has shifted to a
value $\mu_1 > \mu_0$, resulting in a higher fraction of nonconforming product. In Figure
6-1c the process standard deviation has shifted to a value $\sigma_1 > \sigma_0$. This also results
in higher process fallout, even though the process mean is still at the nominal
value.

6-2 CONTROL CHARTS FOR $\bar{x}$ AND R

6-2.1 Statistical Basis of the Charts

Suppose that a quality characteristic is normally distributed with mean μ and standard deviation σ, where both μ and σ are known. If $x_1, x_2, \ldots, x_n$ is a sample of size n, then the average of this sample is

$$\bar{x} = \frac{x_1 + x_2 + \cdots + x_n}{n}$$

and we know that $\bar{x}$ is normally distributed with mean μ and standard deviation $\sigma_{\bar{x}} = \sigma/\sqrt{n}$. Furthermore, the probability is $1 - \alpha$ that any sample mean will fall between

$$\mu + Z_{\alpha/2}\sigma_{\bar{x}} = \mu + Z_{\alpha/2}\frac{\sigma}{\sqrt{n}} \qquad (6\text{-}1a)$$

and

$$\mu - Z_{\alpha/2}\sigma_{\bar{x}} = \mu - Z_{\alpha/2}\frac{\sigma}{\sqrt{n}} \qquad (6\text{-}1b)$$

Therefore, if μ and σ are known, Equations (6-1a) and (6-1b) could be used as upper and lower control limits on a control chart for sample means. As noted previously, it is customary to replace $Z_{\alpha/2}$ by 3, so that 3-sigma limits are employed. If a sample mean falls outside of these limits, it is an indication that the process mean is no longer equal to μ.

We have assumed that the distribution of the quality characteristic is normal. However, the above results are still approximately correct even if the underlying distribution is nonnormal, because of the central limit theorem. We discuss the effect of the normality assumption on variables control charts in Section 6-2.5.

In practice, we usually will not know μ and σ. Therefore, they must be estimated from preliminary samples taken when the process is thought to be in control. These estimates should usually be based on at least 20 to 25 samples. Suppose that m samples are available, each containing n observations on the quality characteristic. Typically, n will be small, often either 4, 5, or 6. These small sample sizes usually result from the construction of rational subgroups, and from the fact that the sampling and inspection costs associated with variables measurements are usually relatively large. Let $\bar{x}_1, \bar{x}_2, \ldots, \bar{x}_m$ be the average of each sample. Then the best estimator of μ, the process average, is the grand average, say

$$\bar{\bar{x}} = \frac{\bar{x}_1 + \bar{x}_2 + \cdots + \bar{x}_m}{m} \qquad (6\text{-}2)$$

Thus, $\bar{\bar{x}}$ would be used as the center line on the $\bar{x}$ chart.

To construct the control limits, we need an estimator of the standard deviation σ. We may estimate σ from either the standard deviations or the ranges of the m samples. For the present, we will concentrate on the range method. If $x_1, x_2, \ldots,$

x_n is a sample of size n, then the range of the sample is the difference between the largest and smallest observations; that is,

$$R = x_{max} - x_{min}$$

There is a well-known relationship between the range of a sample from a normal distribution and the standard deviation of that distribution. The random variable $W = R/\sigma$ is called the *relative range*. The parameters of the distribution of W are a function of the sample size n. The mean of W is d_2. Consequently, an estimator of σ is $\hat{\sigma} = R/d_2$. Values of d_2 for various sample sizes are given in Appendix Table VI.

Let $R_1, R_2, \ldots, R_m$ be the ranges of the m samples. The average range is

$$\bar{R} = \frac{R_1 + R_2 + \cdots + R_m}{m} \tag{6-3}$$

Then an estimate of σ would be computed as

$$\hat{\sigma} = \frac{\bar{R}}{d_2} \tag{6-4}$$

If the sample size is relatively small, the range method yields almost as good an estimator of the variance as does the usual quadratic estimator (the sample variance S^2). The relative efficiency of the range method to S^2 is shown below for various sample sizes:

n	*Relative Efficiency*
2	1.000
3	0.992
4	0.975
5	0.955
6	0.930
10	0.850

For moderate values of n, say $n \geq 10$, the range loses efficiency rapidly, as it ignores all the information in the sample between x_{max} and x_{min}. However, for the small sample sizes often employed on variables control charts ($n = 4, 5,$ or 6), it is entirely satisfactory.

If we use $\bar{\bar{x}}$ as an estimator of μ and $\bar{R}/d_2$ as an estimator of σ, then the parameters of the $\bar{x}$ chart are

$$\text{UCL} = \bar{\bar{x}} + \frac{3}{d_2\sqrt{n}}\bar{R}$$

$$\text{Center line} = \bar{\bar{x}} \tag{6-5}$$

$$\text{LCL} = \bar{\bar{x}} - \frac{3}{d_2\sqrt{n}}\bar{R}$$

We note that the quantity

$$A_2 = \frac{3}{d_2 \sqrt{n}} \tag{6-6}$$

is a constant that depends only on the sample size, so it is possible to rewrite (6-5) as

$$\begin{aligned}
\text{UCL} &= \bar{\bar{x}} + A_2 \bar{R} \\
\text{Center line} &= \bar{\bar{x}} \\
\text{LCL} &= \bar{\bar{x}} - A_2 \bar{R}
\end{aligned} \tag{6-7}$$

The constant A_2 is tabulated for various sample sizes in Appendix Table VI.

We have seen that the sample range is related to the process standard deviation. Therefore, processs variability may be controlled by plotting values of R from successive samples on a control chart. This control chart would be called an R chart. The parameters of the R chart may be easily determined. The center line will be $\bar{R}$. To determine the control limits, we need an estimate of σ_R. Assuming that the quality characteristic is normally distributed, $\hat{\sigma}_R$ can be found from the distribution of the relative range $W = R/\sigma$. The standard deviation of W, say d_3, is a known function of n. Thus, since

$$R = W\sigma$$

the standard deviation of R is

$$\sigma_R = d_3 \sigma$$

Since σ is unknown, we may estimate σ_R by

$$\hat{\sigma}_R = d_3 \frac{\bar{R}}{d_2} \tag{6-8}$$

Consequently, the parameters of the R chart with the usual 3-sigma control limits are

$$\begin{aligned}
\text{UCL} &= \bar{R} + 3\hat{\sigma}_R = \bar{R} + 3d_3 \frac{\bar{R}}{d_2} \\
\text{Center line} &= \bar{R} \\
\text{LCL} &= \bar{R} - 3\hat{\sigma}_R = \bar{R} - 3d_3 \frac{\bar{R}}{d_2}
\end{aligned} \tag{6-9}$$

If we let

$$D_3 = 1 - 3\frac{d_3}{d_2}$$

and

$$D_4 = 1 + 3\frac{d_3}{d_2}$$

we may redefine the R chart parameters as

$$\text{UCL} = \bar{R}D_4$$
$$\text{Center line} = \bar{R} \qquad (6\text{-}10)$$
$$\text{LCL} = \bar{R}D_3$$

The constants D_3 and D_4 are tabulated for various values of n in Appendix Table VI.

When preliminary samples are used to construct $\bar{x}$ and R control charts, it is customary to treat the control limits as trial values. Then the m sample means and ranges should be plotted on the charts and any points that exceed the control limits should be investigated. If assignable causes for these points are discovered, they should be discarded and new trial control limits determined.

6-2.2 Development and Use of $\bar{x}$ and R Charts

In the previous section we presented the statistical background for $\bar{x}$ and R control charts. We now illustrate the construction and application of these charts. We also discuss some guidelines for using these charts in practice.

Example 6-1

Piston rings for an automotive engine are produced by a forging process. We wish to establish statistical control of the inside diameter of the rings manufactured by this process using $\bar{x}$ and R charts. Twenty-five samples, each of size five, have been taken when we think the process is in control. The inside diameter measurement data from these samples are shown in Table 6-1.

When setting up $\bar{x}$ and R control charts, it is best to begin with the R chart. Because the control limits on the $\bar{x}$ chart depend on the process variability, unless process variability is in control, these limits will not have much meaning. Using the data in Table 6-1, we find that the center line for the R chart is

$$\bar{R} = \frac{\sum\limits_{i=1}^{25} R_i}{25} = \frac{0.581}{25} = 0.023$$

For samples of $n = 5$, we find from Appendix Table VI that $D_3 = 0$ and $D_4 = 2.115$. Therefore, the control limits for the R chart are, using (6-10),

$$\text{LCL} = \bar{R}D_3 = 0.023(0) = 0$$
$$\text{UCL} = \bar{R}D_4 = 0.023(2.115) = 0.049$$

Table 6-1
Inside diameter measurements (mm) on forged piston rings, Example 6-1

Sample Number	Observations					$\bar{x}_i$	R_i
1	74.030	74.002	74.019	73.992	74.008	74.010	0.038
2	73.995	73.992	74.001	74.011	74.004	74.001	0.019
3	73.988	74.024	74.021	74.005	74.002	74.008	0.036
4	74.002	73.996	73.993	74.015	74.009	74.003	0.022
5	73.992	74.007	74.015	73.989	74.014	74.003	0.026
6	74.009	73.994	73.997	73.985	73.993	73.996	0.024
7	73.995	74.006	73.994	74.000	74.005	74.000	0.012
8	73.985	74.003	73.993	74.015	73.988	73.997	0.030
9	74.008	73.995	74.009	74.005	74.004	74.004	0.014
10	73.998	74.000	73.990	74.007	73.995	73.998	0.017
11	73.994	73.998	73.994	73.995	73.990	73.994	0.008
12	74.004	74.000	74.007	74.000	73.996	74.001	0.011
13	73.983	74.002	73.998	73.997	74.012	73.998	0.029
14	74.006	73.967	73.994	74.000	73.984	73.990	0.039
15	74.012	74.014	73.998	73.999	74.007	74.006	0.016
16	74.000	73.984	74.005	73.998	73.996	73.997	0.021
17	73.994	74.012	73.986	74.005	74.007	74.001	0.026
18	74.006	74.010	74.018	74.003	74.000	74.007	0.018
19	73.984	74.002	74.003	74.005	73.997	73.998	0.021
20	74.000	74.010	74.013	74.020	74.003	74.009	0.020
21	73.988	74.001	74.009	74.005	73.996	74.000	0.033
22	74.004	73.999	73.990	74.006	74.009	74.002	0.019
23	74.010	73.989	73.990	74.009	74.014	74.002	0.025
24	74.015	74.008	73.993	74.000	74.010	74.005	0.022
25	73.982	73.984	73.995	74.017	74.013	73.998	0.035
						$\sum = 1850.028$	0.581
						$\bar{\bar{x}} = 74.001$	$\bar{R} = 0.023$

The R chart is shown in Figure 6-2. When the 25 sample ranges are plotted on this chart, there is no indication of an out-of-control condition.

Since the R chart indicates that process variability is in control, we may now construct the $\bar{x}$ chart. The center line is

$$\bar{\bar{x}} = \frac{\sum_{i=1}^{25} \bar{x}}{25} = \frac{1850.028}{25} = 74.001$$

To find the control limits on the $\bar{x}$ chart, we use $A_2 = 0.577$ from Appendix Table VI for samples of size $n = 5$ and Equation (6-7) to find

$$\text{UCL} = \bar{\bar{x}} + A_2\bar{R} = 74.001 + (0.577)(0.023) = 74.014$$

and

$$\text{LCL} = \bar{\bar{x}} - A_2\bar{R} = 74.001 - (0.577)(0.023) = 73.988$$

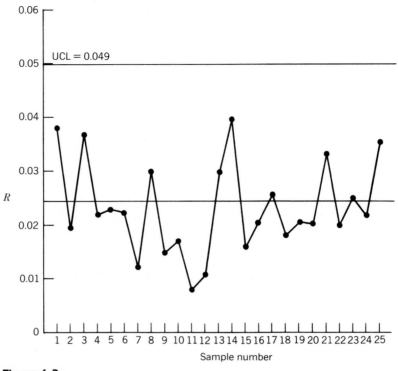

Figure 6-2
R chart for Example 6-1.

The $\bar{x}$ chart is shown in Figure 6-3. When the preliminary sample means are plotted on this chart, no indication of an out-of-control condition is observed. Therefore, since both the $\bar{x}$ and R charts exhibit control, we would conclude that the process is in control at the stated levels and adopt the trial control limits for use in on-line statistical process control.

Estimating Process Capability

The $\bar{x}$ and R charts provide information about the performance or *capability* of the process. From the $\bar{x}$ chart, we may estimate the mean diameter of the piston rings as $\bar{\bar{x}} = 74.001$ mm. The process standard deviation may be estimated using Equation (6-4); that is,

$$\hat{\sigma} = \frac{\bar{R}}{d_2} = \frac{0.023}{2.326} = 0.0099$$

where the value of d_2 for samples of size five is found in Appendix Table VI. The specification limits on this piston ring are 74.000 ± 0.05 mm. The control chart data may be used to describe the capability of the process to produce piston rings relative to these specifications. Assuming that piston-ring diameter is a normally

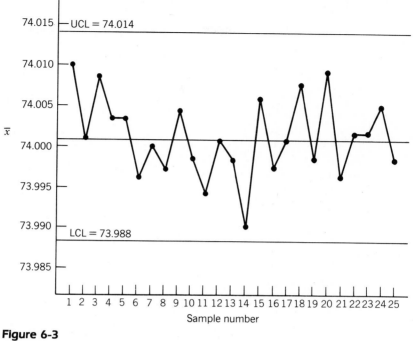

Figure 6-3
$\bar{x}$ chart for Example 6-1.

distributed random variable, with mean 74.001 and standard deviation 0.0099, we may estimate the fraction of nonconforming piston rings produced as

$$\hat{p} = P\{x < 73.950\} + P\{x > 74.050\}$$

$$= \Phi\left(\frac{73.950 - 74.001}{0.0099}\right) + 1 - \Phi\left(\frac{74.050 - 74.001}{0.0099}\right)$$

$$= \Phi(-5.15) + 1 - \Phi(4.04)$$

$$\simeq 0 + 1 - 0.99998$$

$$\simeq 0.00002$$

That is, about 0.002% [20 parts per million (PPM)] of the piston rings produced will be outside of the specifications.

Another way to express process capability is in terms of the process-capability ratio (PCR), which for a quality characteristic with both upper and lower specification limits (USL and LSL, respectively) is

$$\text{PCR} = \frac{\text{USL} - \text{LSL}}{6\sigma} \tag{6-11}$$

Notice that the 6σ spread of the process is the basic definition of process capability. Since σ is usually unknown, we must replace it with an estimate. We frequently use $\hat{\sigma} = \bar{R}/d_2$ as an estimate of σ, resulting in an estimate $\widehat{\text{PCR}}$ of PCR.

For the piston-ring process, since $\bar{R}/d_2 = \hat{\sigma} = 0.0099$, we find that

$$\widehat{\text{PCR}} = \frac{74.05 - 73.95}{6(0.0099)}$$

$$= \frac{0.10}{0.0594}$$

$$= 1.68$$

This implies that the "natural" tolerance limits in the process (3-sigma above and below the mean) are well inside the lower and upper specification limits. Consequently, a relatively low number of nonconforming piston rings will be produced. The PCR may be interpreted another way. The quantity

$$P = \left(\frac{1}{\text{PCR}}\right) 100\%$$

is just the percentage of the specification band that the process uses up. For the piston-ring process an estimate of P is

$$\hat{P} = \left(\frac{1}{\widehat{\text{PCR}}}\right) 100\%$$

$$= \left(\frac{1}{1.68}\right) 100\%$$

$$= 59.5\%$$

That is, the process uses up about 60% of the specification band.

Figure 6-4 illustrates three cases of interest relative to the PCR and process specifications. In Figure 6-4a the PCR is greater than unity. This means that the process uses up much less than 100% of the tolerance band. Consequently, relatively few nonconforming units will be produced by this process. Figure 6-4b shows a process for which PCR = 1; that is, the process uses up all the tolerance band. For a normal distribution this would imply about 0.27% (or 2700 PPM) nonconforming units. Finally, Figure 6-4c presents a process for which the PCR < 1; that is, the process uses up more than 100% of the tolerance band. In this case the process is very yield-sensitive, and a large number of nonconforming units will be produced.

Notice that all the cases in Figure 6-4 assume that the process is centered at the midpoint of the specification band. In many situations this will not be the case, and as we will see in Chapter 9 (which is devoted to a more extensive treatment of process-capability analysis), some modification of the PCR is necessary to describe this situation adequately.

Revision of Control Limits and Center Lines

We have discussed revision of control limits in Chapter 5 relative to attributes control charts (see Example 5-1). We should always treat the initial set of control limits as *trial* limits, subject to subsequent revision. Generally, the effective use of any control chart will require periodic revision of the control limits and center lines. Some practitioners establish regular periods for review and revision of control chart limits, such as every week, every month, or every 25, 50, or 100 samples.

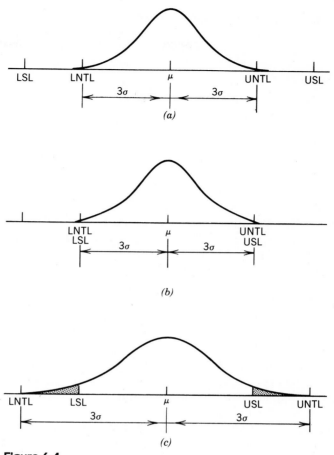

Figure 6-4
Process fallout and the process-capability ratio (PCR).

Sometimes the user will replace the center line of the $\bar{x}$ chart with a target value, say $\bar{\bar{x}}_0$. If the R chart exhibits control, this can be helpful in shifting the process average to the desired value, particularly in processes where the mean may be changed by a fairly simple adjustment of a process variable. If the mean is not easily influenced by a simple process adjustment, then it is likely to be a complex and unknown function of several process variables and a target value $\bar{\bar{x}}_0$ may not be helpful, as use of that value could result in many points outside the control limits. In such cases we would not necessarily know if the point was really associated with an assignable cause or if it plotted outside the limits because of a poor choice for the center line.

When the R chart is out of control, we often eliminate the out-of-control points and recompute a revised value of $\bar{R}$. This value is then used to determine new limits and center line on the R chart and new limits on the $\bar{x}$ chart. This will tighten the limits on both charts, making them consistent with a process standard deviation σ consistent with use of the *revised* $\bar{R}$ in the relationship $\bar{R}/d_2$. This estimate of σ could be used as the basis of a preliminary analysis of process capability.

Continuation of the $\bar{x}$ and R Charts

Fifteen additional samples from the piston-ring manufacturing process were collected after the control charts were established. The data from these new samples are shown in Table 6-2, and the continuations of the $\bar{x}$ and R charts are shown in Figure 6-5. The control charts indicate that the process is in control, until the $\bar{x}$ value from the thirty-seventh sample is plotted. Since this point and the three subsequent ones plot above the upper control limit, we would suspect that an assignable cause has occurred around that time. The general pattern of points on the $\bar{x}$ chart from about subgroup 34 or 35 onward is indicative of a shift in the process mean. In on-line control, the shift would probably have been detected by sample 35, particularly if warning limits or any of the other decision rules for sensitizing and interpreting the control chart discussed in Chapter 4 are in use.

In examining control chart data, it is sometimes helpful to construct a run chart of the individual observations in each sample. This chart is sometimes called a *tolerance chart* or *tier diagram*. This may reveal some pattern in the data, or it may show that a particular value of $\bar{x}$ or R was produced by one or two unusual observations in the sample. When the sample size is larger than 7 or 8, the box plot will usually be a good alternative to the tier diagram. A tier chart of the individual observations in the last 15 samples is shown in Figure 6-6. This chart does not indicate that the out-of-control signals were generated by unusual individual observations, but instead, they probably resulted from a shift in the mean around the time that sample 34 or 35 was taken. The average of the means of samples 34 through 40 is 74.015 mm. The specification limits of 74.000 ± 0.05 mm are plotted on Figure 6-6, along with a sketch of the normal distribution that represents process output when the process mean equals the in-control value 74.001 mm. A sketch of the normal distribution representing process output at the new apparent mean diameter of 74.015 mm is also shown in Figure 6-6. It is obvious that a much higher percentage of nonconforming piston rings will be produced at this new mean diameter; in fact, about 0.021% (or 210 ppm) of the process output is

Table 6-2
Additional samples for Example 6-1

Sample Number, i	Observations					$\bar{x}_i$	R_i
26	74.012	74.015	74.030	73.986	74.000	74.009	0.044
27	73.995	74.010	73.990	74.015	74.001	74.002	0.025
28	73.987	73.999	73.985	74.000	73.990	73.992	0.015
29	74.008	74.010	74.003	73.991	74.006	74.004	0.019
30	74.003	74.000	74.001	73.986	73.997	73.997	0.017
31	73.994	74.003	74.015	74.020	74.004	74.007	0.026
32	74.008	74.002	74.018	73.995	74.005	74.006	0.023
33	74.001	74.004	73.990	73.996	73.998	73.998	0.014
34	74.015	74.000	74.016	74.025	74.000	74.011	0.025
35	74.030	74.005	74.000	74.016	74.012	74.013	0.030
36	74.001	73.990	73.995	74.010	74.024	74.004	0.034
37	74.015	74.020	74.024	74.005	74.019	74.017	0.019
38	74.035	74.010	74.012	74.015	74.026	74.020	0.025
39	74.017	74.013	74.036	74.025	74.026	74.023	0.023
40	74.010	74.005	74.029	74.000	74.020	74.015	0.029

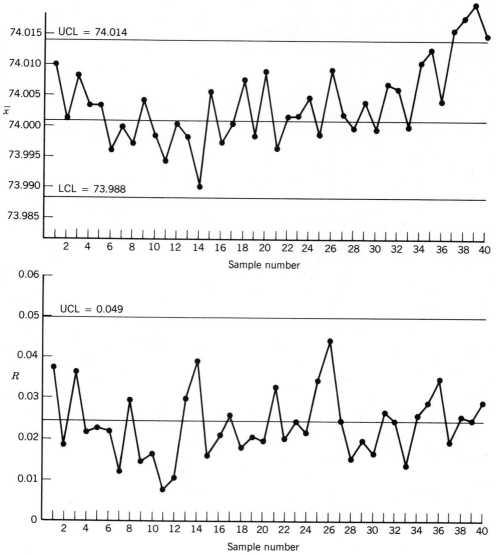

Figure 6-5
Continuation of the $\bar{x}$ and R charts, Example 6-1.

now nonconforming. A search for the cause of this shift in the mean must be conducted. Often input from operators, manufacturing engineers, management, and the quality engineering staff is necessary to find and eliminate assignable causes.

Control Limits, Specification Limits, and Natural Tolerance Limits

A point that should be emphasized is that there is no connection or relationship between the *control limits* on the $\bar{x}$ and R charts and the *specification limits* on the process. The control limits are driven by the natural variability of the process (measured by the process standard deviation σ), that is, by the *natural tolerance limits* of the process. It is customary to define the upper and lower natural tolerance limits, say UNTL and LNTL, as 3σ above and below the process mean. The

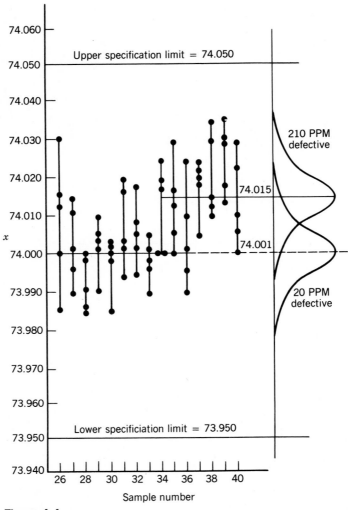

Figure 6-6
Plot of individual observations, Example 6-1.

specification limits, on the other hand, are determined externally. They may be set by management, the manufacturing engineers, the customer, or by product developers/designers. One should have knowledge of inherent process variability when setting specifications, but *remember that there is no mathematical or statistical relationship between the control limits and specification limits*. The situation is summarized in Figure 6-7. We have encountered practitioners who have plotted specification limits on the $\bar{x}$ control chart. This practice is completely incorrect and should not be done. When dealing with plots of *individual* observations (not averages), as in Figure 6-6, it is helpful to plot the specification limits on that chart.

Rational Subgroups
The rational subgroup concept plays an important role in the use of $\bar{x}$ and R control charts. Defining a rational subgroup in practice may be easier if we have a clear understanding of the functions of the two types of control charts. The $\bar{x}$ chart

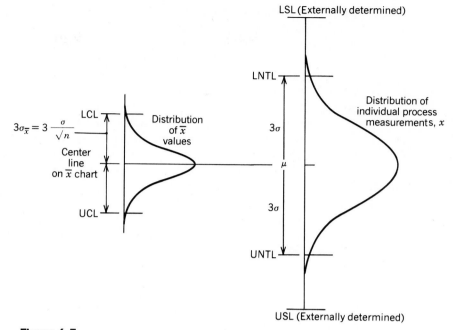

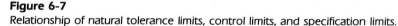

Figure 6-7
Relationship of natural tolerance limits, control limits, and specification limits.

monitors the average quality level in the process. Therefore, samples should be selected in such a way that maximizes the chances for shifts in the process average to occur between samples, and thus to show up as out-of-control points on the $\bar{x}$ chart. The R chart, on the other hand, measures the variability *within* a sample. Therefore, samples should be selected so that variability within samples measures only chance or random causes. Another way of saying this is that the $\bar{x}$ chart monitors *between*-sample variability (variability in the process over time), and the R chart measures *within*-sample variability (the instantaneous process variability at a given time).

An important aspect of this is evident from carefully examining how the control limits for the $\bar{x}$ and R charts are determined from past data. The estimate of the process standard deviation σ used in constructing the control limits is calculated from the variability *within* each sample (i.e., from the individual sample ranges). Consequently, the estimate of σ reflects *within*-sample variability only. It is not correct to estimate σ based on the usual quadratic estimator, say

$$S = \sqrt{\frac{\sum_{i=1}^{m} \sum_{j=1}^{n} (x_{ij} - \bar{\bar{x}})^2}{mn - 1}}$$

where x_{ij} is the jth observation in the ith sample, because if the sample *means* differ, then this will cause S to be too large. Consequently, σ will be overestimated. Pooling all of the preliminary data in this manner to estimate σ is dangerous, because it potentially combines *both between*-sample and *within*-sample variability. The control limits must be based on *within*-sample variability only.

Guidelines for the Design of the Control Chart

To design the $\bar{x}$ and R chart, we must specify the sample size, control limit width, and frequency of sampling to be used. It is not possible to give an exact solution to the problem of control chart design, unless the analyst has detailed information both about the statistical characteristics of the control chart tests and the economic factors that affect the problem. A complete solution of the problem would require knowledge of the cost of sampling, the costs of investigating and possibly correcting the process in response to out-of-control signals, and the costs associated with producing a product that does not meet specifications. Given this kind of information, an economic decision model could be constructed to allow economically optimum control chart design. In Chapter 10 we discuss this approach to the problem. However, it is possible to give some general guidelines now that will aid in control chart design.

If the $\bar{x}$ chart is being used primarily to detect moderate-to-large process shifts, say on the order of 2σ or larger, then relatively small samples of size $n = 4$, 5, or 6 are reasonably effective. On the other hand, if we are trying to detect small shifts, then larger sample sizes of possibly $n = 15$ to $n = 25$ are needed. When smaller samples are used, there is less risk of a process shift occurring while a sample is taken. If a shift does occur while a sample is taken, the sample average can obscure this effect. Consequently, this is an argument for using as small a sample size as is consistent with the magnitude of the process shift that one is trying to detect. An alternative to increasing the sample size is to use warning limits and other sensitizing procedures to enhance the ability of the control chart to detect small process shifts.

The R chart is relatively insensitive to shifts in the process standard deviation for small samples. For example, samples of size $n = 5$ have only about a 40% chance of detecting on the first sample a shift in the process standard deviation from σ to 2σ. Larger samples would seem to be more effective, but we also know that the range method for estimating the standard deviation drops dramatically in efficiency as n increases. Consequently, for large n, say $n > 10$ or 12, it is probably best to use a control chart for S or S^2 instead of the R chart. Details of the construction of these charts are shown in Sections 6-3.1 and 6-3.2.

From a statistical point of view, the operating-characteristic curves of the $\bar{x}$ and R charts can be helpful in choosing the sample size. They will provide the analyst with a feel for the magnitude of process shift that will be detected with a stated probability for any sample size n. These operating characteristics curves are discussed in Section 6-2.6.

The problem of choosing the sample size and the frequency of sampling is one of *allocating sampling effort*. Generally, the decision maker will have only a limited number of resources to allocate to the inspection process. The available strategies will usually be either to take small, frequent samples or to take larger samples less frequently. For example, the choice may be between samples of size five every half hour or samples of size 20 every 2 hours. It is impossible to say which strategy is best in all cases, but current industry practice favors small, frequent samples. The general feeling is that if the interval between samples is too great, too much defective product will be produced before another opportunity to detect the process shift occurs. From economic considerations, if the cost associated with producing defective items is high, smaller, more frequent samples are better than larger, less frequent ones.

The rate of production also influences the choice of sample size and sampling frequency. If the rate of production is high, say 50,000 units per hour, then more frequent sampling is called for than if the production rate is extremely slow. At high rates of production, many nonconforming units of product will be produced in a very short time when process shifts occur. Furthermore, at high production rates, it is sometimes possible to obtain fairly large samples economically. For example, if we produce 50,000 units per hour, it does not take an appreciable difference in time to collect a sample of size twenty compared to a sample of size five. If per unit inspection and testing costs are not excessive, high-speed production processes are often monitored with moderately large sample sizes.

The use of 3-sigma control limits on the $\bar{x}$ and R control charts is a widespread practice. There are situations, however, when departures from this customary choice of control limits are helpful. For example, if false alarms or type I errors (an out-of-control signal is generated when the process is really in control) are very expensive to investigate, then it may be best to use wider control limits than 3-sigma—perhaps as wide as 3.5-sigma. However, if the process is such that out-of-control signals are quickly and easily investigated with a minimum of lost time and cost, then narrower control limits, perhaps at 2.5-sigma, are appropriate. Warning limits on the $\bar{x}$ and R chart and procedures such as the Western Electric rules may also be useful to improve sensitivity to small process shifts.

Changing Sample Size on the $\bar{x}$ and R chart

We have presented the development of $\bar{x}$ and R charts assuming that the sample size n is constant from sample to sample. However, there are situations in which the sample size n is not constant. One situation is that of *variable* sample size; that is, each sample may consist of a different number of observations. The $\bar{x}$ and R charts are generally not used in this case because they lead to a changing center line on the R chart which is difficult to interpret for many users. The $\bar{x}$ and S charts in Section 6-3.1 would be preferable in this case.

Another situation is that of making a permanent (or semipermanent) change in the sample size because of cost, or because the process has exhibited good stability and fewer resources are being allocated for sampling. In this case it is easy to recompute the new control limits directly from the old ones without collecting additional samples based on the new sample size. The procedure is as follows: Let

$\bar{R}_{\text{old}}$ = average range for the old sample size

$\bar{R}_{\text{new}}$ = average range for the new sample size

n_{old} = old sample size

n_{new} = new sample size

$d_2(\text{old})$ = factor d_2 for the old sample size

$d_2(\text{new})$ = factor d_2 for the new sample size

For the $\bar{x}$ chart the new control limits are

$$\text{UCL} = \bar{\bar{x}} + A_2 \left[\frac{d_2(\text{new})}{d_2(\text{old})} \right] \bar{R}_{\text{old}}$$

$$\text{LCL} = \bar{\bar{x}} - A_2 \left[\frac{d_2(\text{new})}{d_2(\text{old})} \right] \bar{R}_{\text{old}}$$

$$(6\text{-}12)$$

where the center line $\bar{\bar{x}}$ is unchanged and the factor A_2 is selected for the *new* sample size. For the R chart, the new parameters are

$$\text{UCL} = D_4 \left[\frac{d_2(\text{new})}{d_2(\text{old})} \right] \bar{R}_{\text{old}}$$

$$\text{CL} = \bar{R}_{\text{new}} = \left[\frac{d_2(\text{new})}{d_2(\text{old})} \right] \bar{R}_{\text{old}} \qquad (6\text{-}13)$$

$$\text{LCL} = \max \left\{ 0, D_3 \left[\frac{d_2(\text{new})}{d_2(\text{old})} \right] \bar{R}_{\text{old}} \right\},$$

where D_3 and D_4 are selected for the *new* sample size.

Example 6-2

To illustrate the above procedure, consider the $\bar{x}$ and R charts developed for the piston-ring data in Example 6-1. These charts were based on a sample size of five rings. Suppose that since the process exhibits good control, manufacturing engineering personnel want to reduce the sample size to three rings. From Example 6-1, we know that

$$n_{\text{old}} = 5, \qquad \bar{R}_{\text{old}} = 0.023$$

and from Appendix Table VI we have

$$d_2(\text{old}) = 2.326, \qquad d_2(\text{new}) = 1.693$$

Therefore, the new control limits on the $\bar{x}$ chart are found from Equation (6-12) as

$$\text{UCL} = \bar{\bar{x}} + A_2 \left[\frac{d_2(\text{new})}{d_2(\text{old})} \right] \bar{R}_{\text{old}}$$

$$= 74.001 + (1.023) \left[\frac{1.693}{2.326} \right] (0.023)$$

$$= 74.018$$

and

$$\text{LCL} = \bar{\bar{x}} - A_2 \left[\frac{d_2(\text{new})}{d_2(\text{old})} \right] \bar{R}_{\text{old}}$$

$$= 74.001 - (1.023) \left[\frac{1.693}{2.326} \right] (0.023)$$

$$= 73.984$$

For the R chart, the new parameters are given by Equation (6-13):

$$\text{UCL} = D_4 \left[\frac{d_2(\text{new})}{d_2(\text{old})} \right] \bar{R}_{\text{old}}$$

$$= (2.578) \left[\frac{1.693}{2.326} \right] (0.023)$$

$$= 0.043$$

$$\text{CL} = \bar{R}_{\text{new}} = \left[\frac{d_2(\text{new})}{d_2(\text{old})} \right] \bar{R}_{\text{old}}$$

$$= \left[\frac{1.693}{2.326} \right] (0.023)$$

$$= 0.017$$

$$\text{LCL} = \max \left\{ 0, D_3 \left[\frac{d_2(\text{new})}{d_2(\text{old})} \right] \bar{R}_{\text{old}} \right\}$$

$$= 0$$

Figure 6-8 shows the new control limits. Notice that the effect of reducing the sample size is to *increase* the width of the limits on the $\bar{x}$ chart (because $\sigma/\sqrt{n}$ is smaller when $n = 5$ than when $n = 3$) and to *lower* the center line and the upper control limit on the R chart (because the expected range from a sample of $n = 3$ is smaller than the expected range from a sample of $n = 5$).

Probability Limits on the $\bar{x}$ and R Chart

It is customary to express the control limits on the $\bar{x}$ and R charts as a multiple of the standard deviation of the statistic plotted on the charts. If the multiple chosen is k, then the limits are referred to as k-sigma limits, the usual choice being $k = 3$. As mentioned in Chapter 4, however, it is also possible to define the control limits by specifying the type I error level for the test. Such control limits are called probability limits, and are used extensively in the United Kingdom and some parts of Western Europe.

It is easy to choose probability limits for the $\bar{x}$ chart. Since $\bar{x}$ is approximately normally distributed, we may obtain a desired type I error of α by choosing the multiple of sigma for the control limit as $k = Z_{\alpha/2}$, where $Z_{\alpha/2}$ is the upper $\alpha/2$ percentage point of the standard normal distribution. Note that the usual 3-sigma limits imply that the type I error probability is $\alpha = 0.0027$. If we choose $\alpha = 0.002$, for example, as most writers who recommend probability limits do, then $Z_{\alpha/2} = Z_{0.001} = 3.09$. Consequently, there is very little difference between such control limits and 3-sigma control limits.

We may also construct R charts using probability limits. If $\alpha = 0.002$, the 0.001 and 0.999 percentage points of the distribution of the relative range $W = R/\sigma$ are required. These points obviously depend on the subgroup size n. Denoting these points by $W_{0.001}(n)$ and $W_{0.999}(n)$, and estimating σ by $\bar{R}/d_2$, we would have the 0.001 and 0.999 limits for R as $W_{0.001}(n)(\bar{R}/d_2)$ and $W_{0.999}(n)(\bar{R}/d_2)$. If we let

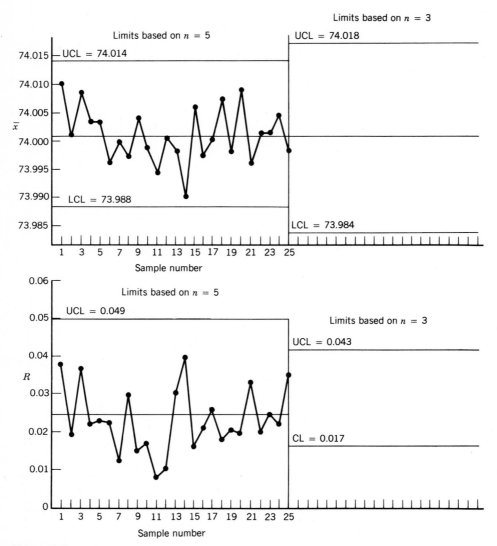

Figure 6-8
Recalculated control limits for the piston-ring data to reflect changing the sample size
from $n = 5$ to $n = 3$.

$D_{0.001} = W_{0.001}(n)/d_2$ and $D_{0.999} = W_{0.999}(n)/d_2$, then the probability limits for the R chart are

$$\text{UCL} = D_{0.999}\bar{R}$$
$$\text{LCL} = D_{0.001}\bar{R}$$

Tables of pairs of values $(D_{0.001}, D_{0.999})$, $(D_{0.005}, D_{0.995})$, and $(D_{0.025}, D_{0.975})$ for $2 \le n \le 10$ are in Grant and Leavenworth (1980, 292). These control limits will not differ substantially from the customary 3-sigma limits. However, for sample sizes $3 \leq n \leq 6$, they will produce a positive lower control limit for the R chart while the conventional 3-sigma limits do not.

6-2.3 Charts Based on Standard Values

When it is possible to specify standard values for the process mean and standard deviation, we may use these standards to establish the control charts for $\bar{x}$ and R without analysis of past data. Suppose that the standards given are μ and σ. Then the parameters of the $\bar{x}$ chart are

$$\text{UCL} = \mu + 3 \frac{\sigma}{\sqrt{n}}$$

$$\text{Center line} = \mu \tag{6-14}$$

$$\text{LCL} = \mu - 3 \frac{\sigma}{\sqrt{n}}$$

The quantity $3/\sqrt{n} = A$, say, is a constant that depends on n, which has been tabulated in Appendix Table VI. Consequently, we could write the parameters of the $\bar{x}$ chart as

$$\text{UCL} = \mu + A\sigma$$

$$\text{Center line} = \mu \tag{6-15}$$

$$\text{LCL} = \mu - A\sigma$$

To construct the R chart with a standard value of σ, recall that $\sigma = R/d_2$, where d_2 is the mean of the distribution of the relative range. Furthermore, the standard deviation of R is $\sigma_R = d_3\sigma$, where d_3 is the standard deviation of the distribution of the relative range. Therefore, the parameters of the control chart are

$$\text{UCL} = d_2\sigma + 3d_3\sigma$$

$$\text{Center line} = d_2\sigma \tag{6-16}$$

$$\text{LCL} = d_2\sigma - 3d_3\sigma$$

It is customary to define the constants

$$D_1 = d_2 - 3d_3$$
$$D_2 = d_2 + 3d_3$$

These constants are tabulated in Appendix Table VI. Thus, the parameters of the R chart with standard σ given are

$$\text{UCL} = D_2\sigma$$

$$\text{Center line} = d_2\sigma \tag{6-17}$$

$$\text{LCL} = D_1\sigma$$

One must exercise care when standard values of μ and σ are given. It may be that these standards are not really applicable to the process, and as a result, the

$\bar{x}$ and R charts will produce many out-of-control signals relative to the specified standards. If the process is really in control at some *other* mean and standard deviation, then the analyst may spend considerable effort looking for assignable causes that do not exist. Standard values of σ seem to give more trouble than standard values of μ. In processes where the mean of the quality characteristic is controlled by adjustments to the machine, standard or target values of μ are sometimes helpful in achieving management goals with respect to process performance.

6-2.4 Interpretation of $\bar{x}$ and R Charts

We have noted previously that a control chart can indicate an out-of-control condition even though no single point plots outside the control limits, if the pattern of the plotted points exhibits nonrandom or systematic behavior. In many cases, the pattern of the plotted points will provide useful diagnostic information on the process, and this information can be used to make process modifications that reduce variability (the goal of statistical process controls). In this section, we briefly discuss some of the more common patterns that appear on $\bar{x}$ and R charts, and indicate some of the process characteristics that may produce these patterns. To effectively interpret $\bar{x}$ and R charts, the analyst must be familiar with both the statistical principles underlying the control chart and the process itself. Additional information on the interpretation of patterns on control charts is in the Western Electric *Statistical Quality Control Handbook* (1956, 149–183).

In interpreting patterns on the $\bar{x}$ chart, we must first determine whether or not the R chart is in control. Some assignable causes show up on *both* the $\bar{x}$ and R charts. If both the $\bar{x}$ and R charts exhibit a nonrandom pattern, the best strategy is to eliminate the R chart assignable causes first. In many cases, this will automatically eliminate the nonrandom pattern on the $\bar{x}$ chart. Never attempt to interpret the $\bar{x}$ chart when the R chart indicates an out-of-control condition.

Cyclic patterns occasionally appear on the control chart. A typical example is shown in Figure 6-9. Such a pattern on the $\bar{x}$ chart may result from systematic environmental changes such as temperature, operator fatigue, regular rotation of operators and/or machines, or fluctuation in voltage or pressure or some other variable in the production equipment. R charts will sometimes reveal cycles because

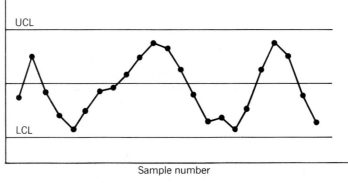

Figure 6-9
Cycles on a control chart.

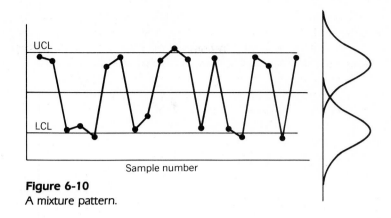

Figure 6-10
A mixture pattern.

of maintenance schedules, operator fatigue, or tool wear resulting in excessive variability. In one study in which this author was involved, systematic variability in the fill volume of a metal container was caused by the on–off cycle of a compressor in the filling machine.

A *mixture* is indicated when the plotted points tend to fall near or slightly outside the control limits, with relatively few points near the center line, as shown in Figure 6-10. A mixture pattern is generated by two (or more) overlapping distributions generating the process output. The probability distributions that could be associated with the mixture pattern in Figure 6-10 are shown on the right-hand side of that figure. The severity of the mixture pattern depends on the extent to which the distributions overlap. Sometimes mixtures result from "overcontrol," where the operators make process adjustments too often, responding to random variation in the output rather than systematic causes.

A *shift in process level* is illustrated in Figure 6-11. These shifts may result from the introduction of new workers, methods, raw materials, or machines, a change in the inspection method or standards, or a change in either the skill, attentiveness, or motivation of the operators. Sometimes an improvement in process performance is noted following introduction of a control chart program, simply because of motivational factors influencing the workers.

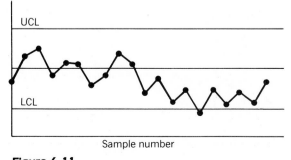

Figure 6-11
A shift in process level.

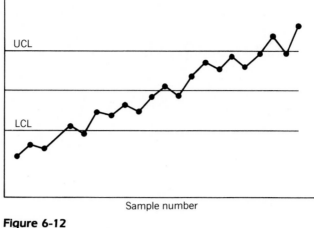

Figure 6-12
Trend.

A *trend*, or continuous movement in one direction, is shown on the control chart in Figure 6-12. Trends are usually due to a gradual wearing out or deterioration of a tool or some other critical process component. In chemical processes they often occur because of settling or separation of the components of a mixture. They can also result from human causes, such as operator fatigue or the presence of supervision. Finally, trends can result from seasonal influences, such as temperature. When trends are due to tool wear or other systematic causes of deterioration, this may be directly incorporated into the control chart model. A device useful for monitoring and analyzing processes with trends is the *regression control chart* [see Mandel (1969)]. The modified control chart, discussed in Chapter 8, is also used when the process exhibits tool wear.

Stratification, or a tendency for the points to cluster artificially around the center line, is illustrated in Figure 6-13. We note that there is a marked lack of natural variability in the observed pattern. One potential cause of stratification is

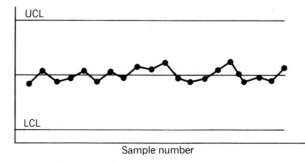

Figure 6-13
Stratification.

incorrect calculation of control limits. This pattern may also result when the sampling process collects one or more units from several different underlying distributions within each subgroup. If the largest and smallest units in each sample are relatively far apart because they come from two different distributions, then $\bar{R}$ will be incorrectly inflated, causing the limits on the $\bar{x}$ chart to be too wide. In this case $\bar{R}$ incorrectly measures the variability *between* the different underlying distributions, in addition to the chance cause variation that it is intended to measure.

In interpreting patterns on the $\bar{x}$ and R charts, one should consider the two charts jointly. If the underlying distribution is normal, then the random variables $\bar{x}$ and R computed from the same sample are statistically independent. Therefore, $\bar{x}$ and R should behave independently on the control chart. If there is correlation between the $\bar{x}$ and R values, that is, if the points on the two charts "follow" each other, then this indicates that the underlying distribution is skewed. If specifications have been determined assuming normality, then those analyses may be in error.

6-2.5 The Effect of Nonnormality on $\bar{x}$ and R Charts

A fundamental assumption in the development of $\bar{x}$ and R control charts is that the underlying distribution of the quality characteristic is normal. In many situations we may have reason to doubt the validity of this assumption. For example, we may know that the underlying distribution is not normal, because we have collected extensive data that indicate the normality assumption is inappropriate. Now if we know the form of the underlying distribution, it is possible to derive the sampling distributions of $\bar{x}$ and R (or some other measure of process variability) and to obtain exact probability limits for the control charts. This approach could be difficult in some cases, and most analysts would probably prefer to use the standard approach based on the normality assumption if they felt that the effect of departure from this assumption was not serious. However, we may know nothing about the form of the underlying distribution, and then our only choice may be to use the normal theory results. Obviously, in either case, we would be interested in knowing the effect of departures from normality on the usual control charts for $\bar{x}$ and R.

Several authors have investigated the effect of departures from normality on control charts. Burr (1967) notes that the usual normal theory control limit constants are very robust to the normality assumption and can be employed unless the population is extremely nonnormal. Schilling and Nelson (1976) have also studied the effect of nonnormality on the control limits of the $\bar{x}$ chart. They investigated the uniform, right triangular, gamma (with $\lambda = 1$ and $r = \frac{1}{2}$, 1, 2, 3, and 4) and two bimodal distributions formed as mixtures of two normal distributions. Their study indicates that, in most cases, samples of size four or five are sufficient to ensure reasonable robustness to the normality assumption. The worst cases observed were for small values of r in the gamma distribution [$r = \frac{1}{2}$ and $r = 1$ (the exponential distribution)]. For example, they report the actual α-risk to be 0.014 or less if $n \geq 4$ for the gamma distribution with $r = \frac{1}{2}$, as opposed to a theoretical value of 0.0027 for the normal distribution.

While the use of 3-sigma control limits on the $\bar{x}$ chart will produce an α-risk of 0.0027 if the underlying distribution is normal, the same is not true for the R chart. The sampling distribution of R is not symmetric, even when sampling from the normal distribution, and the long tail of the distribution is on the high or positive side. Thus, symmetric 3-sigma limits are only an approximation, and the α-risk on such an R chart is *not* 0.0027. (In fact, for $n = 4$, it is $\alpha = 0.00461$.) Furthermore, the R chart is more sensitive to departures from normality than the $\bar{x}$ chart.

6-2.6 The Operating-Characteristic Function

The ability of the $\bar{x}$ and R charts to detect shifts in process quality is described by their operating-characteristic (OC) curves. In this section, we present these OC curves for charts used for on-line control of a process.

Consider the OC curve for an $\bar{x}$ chart with the standard deviation σ known and constant. If the mean shifts from the in-control value, say μ_0, to another value $\mu_1 = \mu_0 + k\sigma$, the probability of *not* detecting this shift on the first subsequent sample or the β-risk is

$$\beta = P\{\text{LCL} \le \bar{x} \le \text{UCL}|\mu = \mu_1 = \mu_0 + k\sigma\} \tag{6-18}$$

Since $\bar{x} \sim N(\mu, \sigma^2/n)$, and the upper and lower control limits are $\text{UCL} = \mu_0 + 3\sigma/\sqrt{n}$ and $\text{LCL} = \mu_0 - 3\sigma/\sqrt{n}$, we may write (6-18) as

$$
\begin{aligned}
\beta &= \Phi\left[\frac{\text{UCL} - (\mu_0 + k\sigma)}{\sigma/\sqrt{n}}\right] - \Phi\left[\frac{\text{LCL} - (\mu_0 + k\sigma)}{\sigma/\sqrt{n}}\right] \\
&= \Phi\left[\frac{\mu_0 + 3\sigma/\sqrt{n} - (\mu_0 + k\sigma)}{\sigma/\sqrt{n}}\right] - \Phi\left[\frac{\mu_0 - 3\sigma/\sqrt{n} - (\mu_0 + k\sigma)}{\sigma/\sqrt{n}}\right] \\
&= \Phi(3 - k\sqrt{n}) - \Phi(-3 - k\sqrt{n}) \tag{6-19}
\end{aligned}
$$

where Φ denotes the standard normal cumulative distribution function. For example, suppose that $n = 5$, and we wish to determine the probability of detecting a shift to $\mu_1 = \mu_0 + 2\sigma$ on the first sample following the shift. Then, since $k = 2$ and $n = 5$, we have

$$
\begin{aligned}
\beta &= \Phi[3 - 2\sqrt{5}] - \Phi[-3 - 2\sqrt{5}] \\
&= \Phi(-1.47) - \Phi(-7.37) \\
&\simeq 0.0708
\end{aligned}
$$

This is the β-risk, or the probability of not detecting such a shift. The probability that such a shift *will* be detected on the first subsequent sample is $1 - \beta = 1 - 0.0708 = 0.9292$.

To construct the OC curve for the $\bar{x}$ chart, plot the β-risk against the magnitude of the shift we wish to detect expressed in standard deviation units for various sample sizes n. These probabilities may be evaluated directly from Equation (6-19). This OC curve is shown in Figure 6-14.

Figure 6-14 indicates that for the typical sample sizes of four, five, and six, the $\bar{x}$ chart is not particularly effective in detecting a small shift, say those on the order of 1.5σ or less, on the first sample following the shift. For example, if the shift is 1.0σ and $n = 5$, then from Figure 6-14, we have $\beta = 0.75$, approximately.

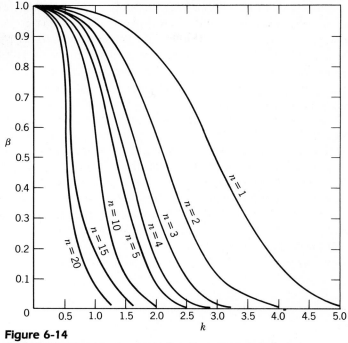

Figure 6-14
Operating-characteristic curves for the $\bar{x}$ chart with 3-sigma limits. $\beta = P$ (not detecting a shift of $k\sigma$ in the mean on the first sample following the shift).

Thus, the probability that the shift will be detected on the first sample is only $1 - \beta = 0.25$. However, the probability that the shift is detected on the second sample is $\beta(1 - \beta) = 0.75(0.25) = 0.19$, while the probability that it is detected on the third sample is $\beta^2(1 - \beta) = (0.75^2)0.25 = 0.14$. Thus, the probability that the shift will be detected on the kth subsequent sample is simply $1 - \beta$ times the probability of not detecting the shift on each of the initial $k - 1$ samples, or

$$\beta^{k-1}(1 - \beta)$$

In general, the expected number of samples taken before the shift is detected is just the average run length, or

$$\text{ARL} = \sum_{k=1}^{\infty} k\beta^{k-1}(1 - \beta) = \frac{1}{1 - \beta}$$

Therefore, in our example, we have

$$\text{ARL} = \frac{1}{1 - \beta} = \frac{1}{0.25} = 4$$

In other words, the expected number of samples taken to detect a shift of 1.0σ with $n = 5$ is 4.

The above discussion provides a supportive argument for the use of small sample sizes on the $\bar{x}$ chart. Even though small sample sizes often result in a relatively large β-risk, because samples are collected and tested periodically, there is a very good chance that the shift will be detected reasonably quickly, although perhaps not on the first sample following the shift. In addition, remember that the use of warning limits and sensitizing procedures such as the Western Electric rules will further improve the ability of the control chart to detect process shifts.

To construct the OC curve for the R chart, the distribution of the relative range $W = R/\sigma$ is employed. Suppose that the in-control value of the standard deviation is σ_0. Then the OC curve plots the probability of not detecting a shift to a new value of σ, say $\sigma_1 > \sigma_0$, on the first sample following the shift. Figure 6-15 presents the OC curve, in which β is plotted against $\lambda = \sigma_1/\sigma_0$ (the ratio of new to old process standard deviation) for various values of n.

From examining Figure 6-15, we observe that the R chart is not very effective in detecting process shifts for small sample sizes. For example, if the process standard deviation doubles (i.e., $\lambda = \sigma_1/\sigma_0 = 2$), which is a fairly large shift, then samples of size five have only about a 40% chance of detecting this shift on each

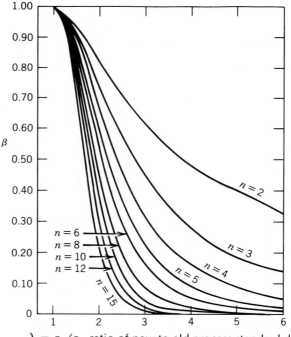

$\lambda = \sigma_1/\sigma_0$, ratio of new to old process standard deviation

Figure 6-15
Operating-characteristic curves for the R chart with 3-sigma limits. (Adapted from A. J. Duncan, "Operating Characteristics of R Charts," *Industrial Quality Control*, vol. 7, no. 5, pp. 40–41, 1951, with permission of the American Society for Quality Control.)

subsequent sample. Most quality-control engineers feel that the R chart is insensitive to small or moderate shifts for the usual subgroup sizes of $n = 4$, 5, or 6. However, the sensitizing procedures discussed above can also be applied to the R chart to improve its performance. If $n > 10$ or 12, the S chart discussed in Section 6-3.1 should generally be used instead of the R chart.

The OC curves in Figures 6-14 and 6-15 assume that the $\bar{x}$ and R charts are used for on-line process control. It is occasionally useful to study the OC curve for the chart used to analyze past data. This can give some indication of how the number of preliminary subgroups used to establish the control chart affects the ability of the chart to detect out-of-control conditions that existed when the data were collected. It is from such analytical studies, as well as practical experience, that the recommendation to use about 20 to 25 preliminary subgroups in establishing $\bar{x}$ and R charts has evolved.

6-2.7 The Average Run Length for the $\bar{x}$ Chart

For any Shewhart control chart, we have noted previously that the ARL can be expressed as

$$\text{ARL} = \frac{1}{P(\text{one point plots out of control})}$$

or

$$\text{ARL} = \frac{1}{\alpha}$$

for the in-control ARL and

$$\text{ARL} = \frac{1}{1 - \beta}$$

for the out-of-control ARL. Since it is relatively easy to develop a general expression for β for the $\bar{x}$ control chart to detect a shift in the mean of $k\sigma$ [see Equation (6-19)], then it is not difficult to construct a set of ARL curves for the $\bar{x}$ chart. Figure 6-16 presents these ARL curves for sample sizes of $n = 1$, 2, 3, 4, 5, 7, 9, and 16 for the $\bar{x}$ control chart, where the ARL is in terms of the expected number of *samples* taken in order to detect the shift. To illustrate the use of Figure 6-16, note that if we wish to detect a shift of 1.5σ using a sample size of $n = 3$, then the average number of samples required will be 3. Note also that we could reduce the ARL to approximately 1 if we increased the sample size to $n = 16$.

Sometimes it is useful to express the ARL in terms of the expected number of individual *units* sampled, say I, rather than the number of samples taken to detect a shift. If the sample size is n, the relationship between I and ARL is

$$I = n\text{ARL} \tag{6-20}$$

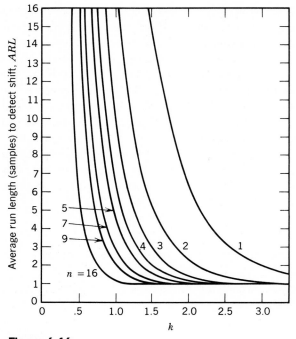

Figure 6-16
Average run length (samples) for the $\bar{x}$ chart with
3-sigma limits, where the process mean shifts by $k\sigma$.
(Adapted from *Modern Methods for Quality Control
and Improvement*, by H. M. Wadsworth, K. S. Stephens,
and A. B. Godfrey, John Wiley & Sons, 1986.)

Figure 6-17 presents a set of curves that plot the expected number of individual units I that must be sampled in order for the $\bar{x}$ chart to detect a shift of $k\sigma$. To illustrate the use of the curve, note that in order to detect a shift of 1.5σ, an $\bar{x}$ chart with $n = 16$ will require that approximately 16 units be sampled, while if the sample size is $n = 3$ only about 9 units will be required, on the average.

6-3 CONTROL CHARTS FOR $\bar{x}$ AND S

While $\bar{x}$ and R charts are widely used, it is occasionally desirable to estimate the process standard deviation directly instead of indirectly through the use of the range R. This leads to control charts for $\bar{x}$ and S, where S is the sample standard deviation.[1] Generally, $\bar{x}$ and S charts are preferable to their more familiar counterparts, $\bar{x}$ and R charts, when either

1. The sample size n is moderately large, say $n > 10$ or 12. (Recall that the range method for estimating σ loses statistical efficiency for moderate to large samples.)
2. The sample size n is variable.

---
[1] Some authors refer to the S chart as the σ chart.

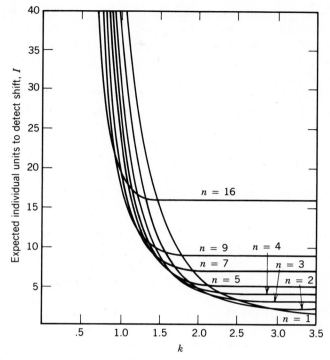

Figure 6-17

Average run length (individual units) for the $\bar{x}$ chart with 3-sigma limits, where the process mean shifts by $k\sigma$. (Adapted from *Modern Methods for Quality Control and Improvement*, by H. M. Wadsworth, K. S. Stephens, and A. B. Godfrey, John Wiley & Sons, 1986.)

In this section, we illustrate the construction and operation of $\bar{x}$ and S control charts. We also show how to deal with variable sample size and discuss an alternative to the S chart.

6-3.1 Construction and Operation of $\bar{x}$ and S Charts

Setting up and operating control charts for $\bar{x}$ and S requires about the same sequence of steps as those for $\bar{x}$ and R charts, except that for each sample we must calculate the sample average $\bar{x}$ and the sample standard deviation S. For example, Table 6-3 presents the inside diameter measurements on the piston rings used in Example 6-1. Notice that we have calculated the sample average and sample standard deviation for each of the 25 samples. We will use these data to illustrate the construction and operation of $\bar{x}$ and S charts.

If σ^2 is the unknown variance of a probability distribution, then an unbiased estimator of σ^2 is the sample variance

$$S^2 = \frac{\sum_{i=1}^{n} (x_i - \bar{x})^2}{n - 1}$$

However, the sample standard deviation S is *not* an unbiased estimator of σ. If the underlying distribution is normal, then S actually estimates $c_4\sigma$, where c_4 is a constant[2] that depends on the sample size n. Furthermore, the standard deviation of S is $\sigma\sqrt{1 - c_4^2}$. This information can be used to establish control charts on $\bar{x}$ and S.

Consider the case where a standard value is given for σ. Since $E(S) = c_4\sigma$, the center line for the chart is $c_4\sigma$. The 3-sigma control limits for S are then

$$\text{UCL} = c_4\sigma + 3\sigma\sqrt{1 - c_4^2}$$
$$\text{LCL} = c_4\sigma - 3\sigma\sqrt{1 - c_4^2} \tag{6-21}$$

It is customary to define the two constants

$$B_5 = c_4 - 3\sqrt{1 - c_4^2} \tag{6-22a}$$

and

$$B_6 = c_4 + 3\sqrt{1 - c_4^2} \tag{6-22b}$$

Consequently, the parameters of the S chart with a standard value for σ given become

$$\text{UCL} = B_6\sigma$$
$$\text{Center line} = c_4\sigma \tag{6-23}$$
$$\text{LCL} = B_5\sigma$$

Values of B_5 and B_6 are tabulated for various sample sizes in Appendix Table VI. The parameters of the corresponding $\bar{x}$ chart are given in Equation (6-15), Section 6-2.3.

If no standard is given for σ, then it must be estimated by analyzing past data. Suppose that m preliminary samples are available, each of size n, and let S_i be the standard deviation of the ith sample. The average of the m standard deviations is

$$\bar{S} = \frac{1}{m}\sum_{i=1}^{m} S_i$$

The statistic $\bar{S}/c_4$ is an unbiased estimator of σ. Therefore, the parameters of the S chart would be

$$\text{UCL} = \bar{S} + 3\frac{\bar{S}}{c_4}\sqrt{1 - c_4^2}$$
$$\text{Center line} = \bar{S} \tag{6-24}$$
$$\text{LCL} = \bar{S} - 3\frac{\bar{S}}{c_4}\sqrt{1 - c_4^2}$$

---

[2] It can be shown that

$$c_4 = \left(\frac{2}{n - 1}\right)^{1/2}\frac{\Gamma(n/2)}{\Gamma[(n - 1)/2]}$$

We usually define the constants

$$B_3 = 1 - \frac{3}{c_4}\sqrt{1 - c_4^2} \qquad (6\text{-}25a)$$

and

$$B_4 = 1 + \frac{3}{c_4}\sqrt{1 - c_4^2} \qquad (6\text{-}25b)$$

Consequently, we may write the parameters of the S chart as

$$\begin{aligned} \text{UCL} &= B_4\bar{S} \\ \text{Center line} &= \bar{S} \\ \text{LCL} &= B_3\bar{S} \end{aligned} \qquad (6\text{-}26)$$

Note that $B_4 = B_6/c_4$ and $B_3 = B_5/c_4$.

When $\bar{S}/c_4$ is used to estimate σ, we may define the control limits on the corresponding $\bar{x}$ chart as

$$\begin{aligned} \text{UCL} &= \bar{\bar{x}} + \frac{3\bar{S}}{c_4\sqrt{n}} \\ \text{Center line} &= \bar{\bar{x}} \\ \text{LCL} &= \bar{\bar{x}} - \frac{3\bar{S}}{c_4\sqrt{n}} \end{aligned} \qquad (6\text{-}27)$$

Let the constant $A_3 = 3/(c_4\sqrt{n})$. Then the $\bar{x}$ chart parameters become

$$\begin{aligned} \text{UCL} &= \bar{\bar{x}} + A_3\bar{S} \\ \text{Center line} &= \bar{\bar{x}} \\ \text{LCL} &= \bar{\bar{x}} - A_3\bar{S} \end{aligned} \qquad (6\text{-}28)$$

The constants B_3, B_4, and A_3 for construction of $\bar{x}$ and S charts from past data are listed in Appendix Table VI for various sample sizes.

Note that we have assumed that the sample standard deviation is defined as

$$S = \sqrt{\frac{\sum_{i=1}^{n}(x_i - \bar{x})^2}{n - 1}} \qquad (6\text{-}29)$$

Some authors define S with n in the denominator of Equation (6-29) instead of $n - 1$. When this is the case, the definitions of the constants c_4, B_3, B_4, and A_3 are altered. The corresponding constants based on the use of n in calculating S are called c_2, B_1, B_2, and A_1, respectively. See Bowker and Lieberman (1972) for their definitions.

Traditionally, quality-control engineers have preferred the R chart to the S chart because of the simplicity of calculating R from each sample. The current availability of hand-held calculators with automatic calculation of S and the increased availability of microcomputers for on-line implementation of control charts directly at the work station have eliminated any computational difficulty. Furthermore, we know from study of the OC curve in Section 6-2.6 that the R chart is relatively insensitive to small or moderate shifts for small sample sizes. Thus, in many practical situations where reasonably tight control of process variability is needed, moderately large sample sizes will be required, and the S chart should be used.

Example 6-3

We will illustrate the construction of $\bar{x}$ and S charts using the piston-ring inside diameter measurements in Table 6-3. The grand average and the average standard deviation are

$$\bar{\bar{x}} = \frac{1}{25} \sum_{i=1}^{25} \bar{x}_i = \frac{1}{25} (1850.028) = 74.001$$

Table 6-3
Inside diameter measurements (mm) for automobile engine piston rings

Sample Number	Observations					$\bar{x}_i$	S_i
1	74.030	74.002	74.019	73.992	74.008	74.010	0.0148
2	73.995	73.992	74.001	74.011	74.004	74.001	0.0072
3	73.988	74.024	74.021	74.005	74.002	74.008	0.0106
4	74.002	73.996	73.993	74.015	74.009	74.003	0.0091
5	73.992	74.007	74.015	73.989	74.014	74.003	0.0122
6	74.009	73.994	73.997	73.985	73.993	73.996	0.0087
7	73.995	74.006	73.994	74.000	74.005	74.000	0.0055
8	73.985	74.003	73.993	74.015	73.988	73.997	0.0123
9	74.008	73.995	74.009	74.005	74.004	74.004	0.0055
10	73.998	74.000	73.990	74.007	73.995	73.998	0.0063
11	73.994	73.998	73.994	73.995	73.990	73.994	0.0029
12	74.004	74.000	74.007	74.000	73.996	74.001	0.0042
13	73.983	74.002	73.998	73.997	74.012	73.998	0.0105
14	74.006	73.967	73.994	74.000	73.984	73.990	0.0153
15	74.012	74.014	73.998	73.999	74.007	74.006	0.0073
16	74.000	73.984	74.005	73.998	73.996	73.997	0.0078
17	73.994	74.012	73.986	74.005	74.007	74.001	0.0106
18	74.006	74.010	74.018	74.003	74.000	74.007	0.0070
19	73.984	74.002	74.003	74.005	73.997	73.998	0.0085
20	74.000	74.010	74.013	74.020	74.003	74.009	0.0080
21	73.988	74.001	74.009	74.005	73.996	74.000	0.0053
22	74.004	73.999	73.990	74.006	74.009	74.002	0.0074
23	74.010	73.989	73.990	74.009	74.014	74.002	0.0119
24	74.015	74.008	73.993	74.000	74.010	74.005	0.0087
25	73.982	73.984	73.995	74.017	74.013	73.998	0.0162

$$\sum = 1850.028 \qquad 0.2238$$
$$\bar{\bar{x}} = 74.001 \qquad \bar{S} = 0.0090$$

and

$$\bar{S} = \frac{1}{25} \sum_{i=1}^{25} S_i = \frac{1}{25} (0.2238) = 0.0090$$

Consequently, the parameters for the $\bar{x}$ chart are

$$\text{UCL} = \bar{\bar{x}} + A_3\bar{S} = 74.001 + (1.427)(0.0090) = 74.014$$
$$\text{CL} = \bar{\bar{x}} = 74.001$$
$$\text{LCL} = \bar{\bar{x}} + A_3\bar{S} = 74.001 - (1.427)(0.0090) = 73.988$$

and for the S chart

$$\text{UCL} = B_4\bar{S} = (2.089)(0.0090) = 0.019$$
$$\text{CL} = \bar{S} = 0.0090$$
$$\text{LCL} = B_3\bar{S} = (0)(0.0090) = 0$$

The control charts are shown in Figure 6-18.

Notice that the control limits for the $\bar{x}$ chart based on $\bar{S}$ are identical to the $\bar{x}$ chart control limits in Example 6-1 where the limits were based on $\bar{R}$. They will not always be the same, and in general, the $\bar{x}$ chart control limits based on $\bar{S}$ will be slightly different than limits based on $\bar{R}$.

Estimation of σ

We can estimate the process standard deviation using the fact that S/c_4 is an unbiased estimate of σ. Therefore, since $c_4 = 0.9400$ for samples of size five, our estimate of the process standard deviation is

$$\hat{\sigma} = \frac{\bar{S}}{c_4} = \frac{0.0090}{0.9400} = 0.0096$$

This estimate is very similar to that of σ obtained via the range method in Example 6-1.

6-3.2 The $\bar{x}$ and S Control Charts with Variable Sample Size

The $\bar{x}$ and S control charts are relatively easy to apply in cases where the sample sizes are variable. In this case, we should use a weighted average approach in calculating $\bar{\bar{x}}$ and $\bar{S}$. If n_i is the number of observations in the ith sample, then use

$$\bar{\bar{x}} = \frac{\sum_{i=1}^{m} n_i \bar{x}_i}{\sum_{i=1}^{m} n_i} \tag{6-30}$$

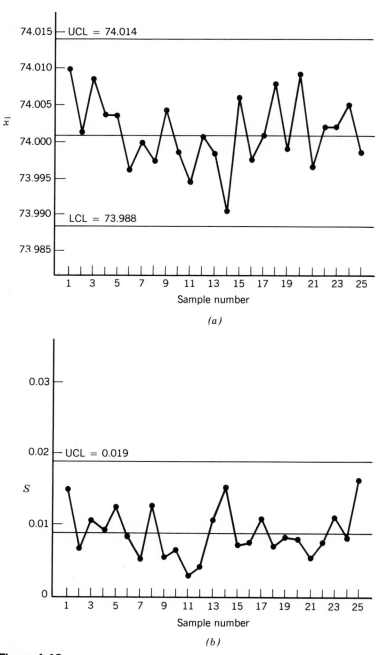

Figure 6-18
The $\bar{x}$ and S control charts for Example 6-3. (a) The $\bar{x}$ chart with control limits based on $\bar{S}$. (b) The S control chart.

and

$$\bar{S} = \left[\frac{\displaystyle\sum_{i=1}^{m} (n_i - 1)S_i^2}{\displaystyle\sum_{i=1}^{m} n_i - m} \right]^{1/2} \tag{6-31}$$

as the center lines on the $\bar{x}$ and S control charts, respectively. The control limits would be calculated from Equations (6-26) and (6-28), respectively, but the constants A_3, B_3, and B_4 will depend on the sample size used in each individual subgroup.

Example 6-4

Consider the data in Table 6-4, which is a modification of the piston-ring data used previously. Notice that the sample sizes vary from $n = 3$ to $n = 5$. We may use the procedure described above to set up the $\bar{x}$ and S control charts. The weighted grand mean and weighted average standard deviation are computed from (6-30) and (6-31) as follows:

$$\bar{\bar{x}} = \frac{\sum\limits_{i=1}^{25} n_i \bar{x}_i}{\sum\limits_{i=1}^{25} n_i} = \frac{5(74.010) + 3(73.996) + \cdots + 5(73.998)}{5 + 3 + \cdots + 5}$$

$$= \frac{8362.075}{113}$$

$$= 74.001$$

Table 6-4
Inside diameter measurements (mm) on automobile engine piston rings

Sample Number	Observations					$\bar{x}_i$	S_i
1	74.030	74.002	74.019	73.992	74.008	74.010	0.0148
2	73.995	73.992	74.001			73.996	0.0046
3	73.988	74.024	74.021	74.005	74.002	74.008	0.0106
4	74.002	73.996	73.993	74.015	74.009	74.003	0.0091
5	73.992	74.007	74.015	73.989	74.014	74.003	0.0122
6	74.009	73.994	73.997	73.985		73.996	0.0099
7	73.995	74.006	73.994	74.000		73.999	0.0055
8	73.985	74.003	73.993	74.015	73.988	73.997	0.0123
9	74.008	73.995	74.009	74.005		74.004	0.0064
10	73.998	74.000	73.990	74.007	73.995	73.998	0.0063
11	73.994	73.998	73.994	73.995	73.990	73.994	0.0029
12	74.004	74.000	74.007	74.000	73.996	74.001	0.0042
13	73.983	74.002	73.998			73.994	0.0100
14	74.006	73.967	73.994	74.000	73.984	73.990	0.0153
15	74.012	74.014	73.998			74.008	0.0087
16	74.000	73.984	74.005	73.998	73.996	73.997	0.0078
17	73.994	74.012	73.986	74.005		73.999	0.0115
18	74.006	74.010	74.018	74.003	74.000	74.007	0.0070
19	73.984	74.002	74.003	74.005	73.997	73.998	0.0085
20	74.000	74.010	74.013			74.008	0.0068
21	73.988	74.001	74.009	74.005	73.996	74.000	0.0053
22	74.004	73.999	73.990	74.006	74.009	74.002	0.0074
23	74.010	73.989	73.990	74.009	74.014	74.002	0.0119
24	74.015	74.008	73.993	74.000	74.010	74.005	0.0087
25	73.982	73.984	73.995	74.017	74.013	73.998	0.0162

and

$$\bar{S} = \left[\frac{\sum_{i=1}^{25} (n_i - 1)S_i^2}{\sum_{i=1}^{25} n_i - 25} \right]^{1/2} = \left[\frac{4(0.0148)^2 + 2(0.0046)^2 + \cdots + 4(0.0162)^2}{5 + 3 + \cdots + 5 - 25} \right]^{1/2}$$

$$= \left[\frac{0.008426}{88} \right]^{1/2}$$

$$= 0.0098$$

Therefore, the center line of the $\bar{x}$ chart is $\bar{\bar{x}} = 74.001$, and the center line of the S chart is $\bar{S} = 0.0098$. The control limits may now be easily calculated. To illustrate, consider the first sample. The limits for the $\bar{x}$ chart are

$$\text{UCL} = 74.001 + (1.427)(0.0098) = 74.015$$
$$\text{CL} = 74.001$$
$$\text{LCL} = 74.001 - (1.427)(0.0098) = 73.987$$

The control limits for the S chart are

$$\text{UCL} = (2.089)(0.0098) = 0.020$$
$$\text{CL} = 0.0098$$
$$\text{LCL} = 0(0.0098) = 0$$

Notice that we have used the values of A_3, B_3, and B_4 for $n_1 = 5$. The limits for the second sample would use the values of these constants for $n_2 = 3$. The control limit calculations for all 25 samples are summarized in Table 6-5. The control charts are plotted in Figure 6-19.

An alternative to using variable width control limits on the $\bar{x}$ and S control charts is to base the control limit calculations on an average sample size $\bar{n}$. If the n_i are not very different, this approach may work well in practice; it is particularly helpful if the charts are to be used in a presentation to management. Since the average sample size n_i may not be an integer, a useful alternative is to base these approximate control limits on a modal (most common) sample size.

Estimation of σ

We may estimate the process standard deviation, σ, from the individual sample values S_i. First, average all the values of S_i for which $n_i = 5$ (the most frequently occurring value of n_i). This gives

$$\bar{S} = \frac{0.1605}{17}$$

$$= 0.0094$$

Table 6-5
Computation of control limits for $\bar{x}$ and S charts with variable sample size

Sample	n	$\bar{x}$	S	A_3	$\bar{x}$ Chart LCL	$\bar{x}$ Chart UCL	B_3	B_4	S Chart LCL	S Chart UCL
1	5	74.010	0.0148	1.427	73.987	74.015	0	2.089	0	0.020
2	3	73.996	0.0046	1.954	73.982	74.020	0	2.568	0	0.025
3	5	74.008	0.0106	1.427	73.987	74.015	0	2.089	0	0.020
4	5	74.003	0.0091	1.427	73.987	74.015	0	2.089	0	0.020
5	5	74.003	0.0122	1.427	73.987	74.015	0	2.089	0	0.020
6	4	73.996	0.0099	1.628	73.985	74.017	0	2.266	0	0.022
7	4	73.999	0.0055	1.628	73.985	74.017	0	2.266	0	0.022
8	5	73.997	0.0123	1.427	73.987	74.015	0	2.089	0	0.020
9	4	74.004	0.0064	1.628	73.985	74.017	0	2.266	0	0.022
10	5	73.998	0.0063	1.427	73.987	74.015	0	2.089	0	0.020
11	5	73.994	0.0029	1.427	73.987	74.015	0	2.089	0	0.020
12	5	74.001	0.0042	1.427	73.987	74.015	0	2.089	0	0.020
13	3	73.994	0.0100	1.954	73.982	74.020	0	2.568	0	0.025
14	5	73.990	0.0153	1.427	73.987	74.015	0	2.089	0	0.020
15	3	74.008	0.0087	1.954	73.982	74.020	0	2.568	0	0.025
16	5	73.997	0.0078	1.427	73.987	74.015	0	2.089	0	0.020
17	4	73.999	0.0115	1.628	73.985	74.017	0	2.226	0	0.022
18	5	74.007	0.0070	1.427	73.987	74.015	0	2.089	0	0.020
19	5	73.998	0.0085	1.427	73.987	74.015	0	2.089	0	0.020
20	3	74.008	0.0068	1.954	73.982	74.020	0	2.568	0	0.025
21	5	74.000	0.0053	1.427	73.987	74.015	0	2.089	0	0.020
22	5	74.002	0.0074	1.427	73.987	74.015	0	2.089	0	0.020
23	5	74.002	0.0119	1.427	73.987	74.015	0	2.089	0	0.020
24	5	74.005	0.0087	1.427	73.987	74.015	0	2.089	0	0.020
25	5	73.998	0.0162	1.427	73.987	74.015	0	2.089	0	0.020

The estimate of the process σ is then

$$\hat{\sigma} = \frac{\bar{S}}{c_4} = \frac{0.0094}{0.9400} = 0.01$$

where the value of c_4 used is for samples of size $n = 5$.

6-3.3 The S^2 Control Chart

Most quality engineers use either the R chart or the S chart to control process dispersion, with S preferable to R for moderate-to-large sample sizes. Some practitioners recommend a control chart based directly on the sample variance S^2.

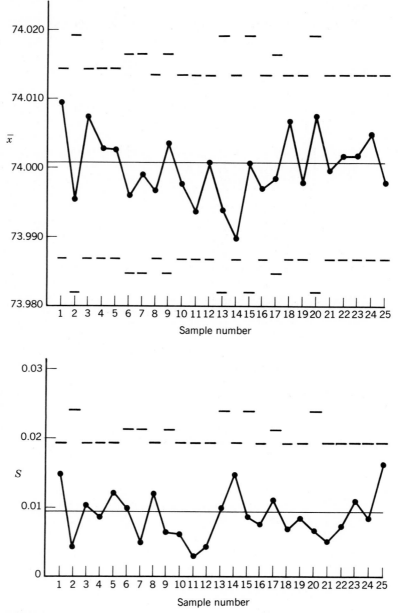

Figure 6-19
The $\bar{x}$ and S control charts for the piston-ring data with variable sample size, Example 6-4.

The parameters for the S^2 control chart are

$$\text{UCL} = \frac{\bar{S}^2}{n-1} \chi^2_{\alpha/2, n-1}$$

$$\text{Center line} = \bar{S}^2 \qquad\qquad (6\text{-}32)$$

$$\text{LCL} = \frac{\bar{S}^2}{n-1} \chi^2_{1-(\alpha/2), n-1}$$

where $\chi^2_{\alpha/2, n-1}$ and $\chi^2_{1-(\alpha/2), n-1}$ denote the upper and lower $\alpha/2$ percentage points of the chi-square distribution with $n - 1$ degrees of freedom, and $\bar{S}^2$ is an average sample variance obtained from the analysis of preliminary data. A standard value σ^2 could be used in Equation (6-32) instead of $\bar{S}^2$ if one were available. Note that this control chart is defined with probability limits.

6-3.4 Control Limits Based on a Small Number of Samples (Short Production Runs)

When control charts are established with no standards given, it is necessary to estimate the process parameters (say $\bar{x}$ and R) from the analysis of past data. The usual approach is to select m preliminary samples when we think the process is in control and use these samples to establish trial control limits. If any of the preliminary samples plot out of control against the trial control limits, these samples are discarded and revised control limits obtained. This process is continued until an acceptable set of control limits is produced. Generally, we would prefer to have 20 to 25 preliminary samples to establish trial control limits.

This requirement for a relatively large number of preliminary samples sometimes prevents the statistically correct use of control charts during the start-up phases of a process, or for processes whose total output is too small to allow collection of appropriate preliminary data. Conventional control limits based on m preliminary samples can be shown to produce an actual type I error that is larger than the nominal values of $\alpha = 0.0027$. (For $m = 5$ samples, the true type I error probability for the $\bar{x}$ chart is $\alpha = 0.012$, for $m = 10$ samples, it is $\alpha = 0.0067$, and for $m = 25$ samples, it is $\alpha = 0.0040$.) Hillier (1969) has described a two-stage approach to setting control limits for the $\bar{x}$ and R charts that will produce statistically correct results regardless of how many samples are used to establish the charts. Since these charts provide the advertised levels of the type I error exactly, they may be used as soon as necessary after process start-up, regardless of how much preliminary data are available.

Since this method will produce statistically valid control limits for any number of preliminary samples, it can be used in job-shop or short production run environments. Such applications frequently occur in electronics and aerospace manufacturing organizations. Other approaches to SPC for short production runs are discussed in Chapter 8.

6-4 CONTROL CHARTS FOR INDIVIDUAL MEASUREMENTS

There are many situations where the sample size used for process control is $n = 1$; that is, the sample consists of an individual unit. Some examples of these situations are as follows:

1. Automated inspection and measurement technology is used, and every unit manufactured is analyzed.

2. The production rate is very slow, and it is inconvenient to allow samples sizes of $n > 1$ to accumulate before analysis.

3. Repeat measurements on the process differ only because of laboratory or analysis error, as in many chemical processes.

4. In process plants, such as papermaking, measurements on some parameter such as coating thickness *across* the roll will differ very little and produce a standard deviation that is much too small if the objective is to control coating thickness *along* the roll.

In such situations, the control chart for individual units is useful. (The cumulative sum and exponentially weighted moving-average control charts discussed in Chapter 7 may be a better alternative when the magnitude of the shift in process mean that is of interest is small.) The control procedure uses the moving range of two successive observations to estimate the process variability. The moving range is defined as $MR_i = |x_i - x_{i-1}|$. It is also possible to establish a control chart on the moving range. The procedure is illustrated in the following example.

Example 6-5

The viscosity of an aircraft primer paint is an important quality characteristic. The product is produced in batches, and as each batch takes several hours to produce, the production rate is too slow to allow sample sizes greater than one. The viscosity of the previous 15 batches is shown in Table 6-6.

To set up the control chart for individual observations, note that the sample average of the 15 viscosity readings is $\bar{x} = 33.52$ and that the average of the moving ranges of two observations is $\overline{MR} = 0.48$. To set up the moving-range chart, we note that $D_3 = 0$ and $D_4 = 3.267$ for $n = 2$. Therefore, the moving-range chart has center line $\overline{MR} = 0.48$, $LCL = 0$, and $UCL = D_4\overline{MR} = (3.267)0.48 = 1.57$. The control chart is shown in Figure 6-20a. As no points exceed the upper control limit, we may now set up the control chart for individual viscosity measurements.

Table 6-6
Viscosity of aircraft primer paint

Batch Number	Viscosity x	Moving Range MR
1	33.75	
2	33.05	0.70
3	34.00	0.95
4	33.81	0.19
5	33.46	0.35
6	34.02	0.56
7	33.68	0.34
8	33.27	0.41
9	33.49	0.22
10	33.20	0.29
11	33.62	0.42
12	33.00	0.62
13	33.54	0.54
14	33.12	0.42
15	33.84	0.72
	$\bar{x} = 33.52$	$\overline{MR} = 0.48$

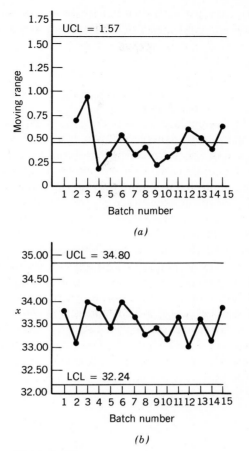

Figure 6-20
Control charts for (*a*) the moving range and for
(*b*) individual observations on viscosity.

For the control chart for individual measurements, the parameters are

$$\text{UCL} = \bar{x} + 3\,\frac{\overline{\text{MR}}}{d_2}$$

$$\text{Center line} = \bar{x} \tag{6-33}$$

$$\text{LCL} = \bar{x} - 3\,\frac{\overline{\text{MR}}}{d_2}$$

If a moving range of $n = 2$ observations is used, then $d_2 = 1.128$. For the data in Table 6-6, we have

$$\text{UCL} = \bar{x} + 3\,\frac{\overline{\text{MR}}}{d_2} = 33.52 + 3\,\frac{0.48}{1.128} = 34.80$$

$$\text{Center line} = \bar{x} = 33.52$$

$$\text{LCL} = \bar{x} - 3\,\frac{\overline{\text{MR}}}{d_2} = 33.52 - 3\,\frac{0.48}{1.128} = 32.24$$

The control chart for individual batch viscosity measurements is shown in Figure 6-20b. There is no indication of an out-of-control condition.

Interpretation of the Charts

The chart for individuals can be interpreted much like an ordinary $\bar{x}$ control chart. A shift in the process average will result in either a point (or points) outside the control limits, or a pattern consisting of a run on one side of the center line.

Table 6-7 contains data on aircraft primer paint viscosity for batches 16-30. These data are plotted in Figure 6-21 on the continuation of the control chart for individuals and the moving-range control chart developed in Example 6-5. As this figure makes clear, an upward shift in mean viscosity has occurred around batch 20 or 21, since there is an obvious "shift in process level" pattern on the chart for individuals. Note that the moving-range chart also reacts to this level shift with a single large spike at sample 20. This spike on the moving-range chart is sometimes helpful in identifying exactly where a process shift in the mean has occurred.

Some care should be exercised in interpreting patterns on the moving-range chart. The moving ranges are correlated, and this correlation may often induce a pattern of runs or cycles on the chart. Such a pattern is evident on the moving-range chart in Figure 6-21. The individual measurements on the x chart are assumed to be uncorrelated, however, and any apparent pattern on this chart should be carefully investigated.

Table 6-7
Viscosity for aircraft primer paint, batches 16–30

Batch Number	Viscosity x	Moving Range MR
16[a]	33.50	0.34
17	33.25	0.25
18	33.40	0.15
19	33.27	0.13
20	34.65	1.38
21	34.80	0.15
22	34.55	0.25
23	35.00	0.45
24	34.75	0.25
25	34.50	0.25
26	34.70	0.20
27	34.29	0.41
28	34.61	0.32
29	34.49	0.12
30	35.03	0.54

[a] The moving range for batch 16 was computed as the difference in viscosity readings between batches 16 and 15; that is, $MR_{16} = |x_{16} - x_{15}| = |33.50 - 33.84| = 0.34$.

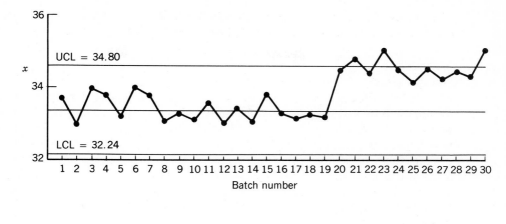

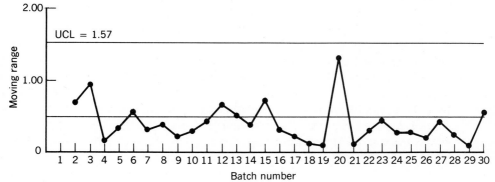

Figure 6-21
Continuation of the control chart for individuals and the moving range using the additional data in Table 6-7.

Average Run Lengths

Crowder (1987b) has studied the average run length of the combined control chart for individuals and moving-range chart. He produces ARLs for various settings of the control limits and shifts in the process mean and standard deviation. In general, his work shows that the ARL of the combined procedure will generally be much less than the ARL of a standard Shewhart control chart when the process is in control (recall that this ARL is 370 samples), if we use the conventional 3-sigma limits on the charts. In general, results closer to the Shewhart in-control ARL are obtained if we use 3-sigma limits on the chart for individuals and compute the upper control limit on the moving-range chart from

$$UCL = D\overline{MR}$$

where the constant D should be chosen such that $4 \leq D \leq 5$.

Some individuals have suggested that limits narrower than 3-sigma be used on the chart for individuals in order to enhance its ability to detect small process shifts. This is a dangerous suggestion, as narrower limits will dramatically reduce the in-control ARL and increase the occurrence of false alarms to the point where the charts are ignored and hence become useless. If we are interested in detecting small shifts, then the correct approach is to use either the cumulative-sum control chart or the exponentially weighted moving-average control chart (see Chapter 7).

Normality

Our discussion in this section has made an assumption that the observations follow a normal distribution. If the process shows evidence of a marked departure from normality, however, then the control limits given here may be entirely inappropriate. In such cases, it will usually be best to determine the control limits for the individuals control chart based on the percentiles of the correct underlying distribution. These percentiles could be obtained from a histogram if a large sample (at least 100 but preferably 200 observations) were available, or from a probability distribution fit to the data. Another approach would be to transform the original variable to a new variable that is approximately normally distributed, and then apply control charts to the new variable.

6-5 CHOICE BETWEEN ATTRIBUTES AND VARIABLES CONTROL CHARTS

In many applications, the analyst will have to choose between using a variables control chart, such as the $\bar{x}$ and R charts, and an attributes control chart, such as the p chart. In some cases, the choice will be clear-cut. For example, if the quality characteristic is the color of the item, such as might be the case in carpet or cloth production, then attributes inspection would often be preferred over an attempt to quantify the quality characteristic "color." In other cases, the choice will not be obvious, and the analyst must take several factors into account in choosing between attributes and variables control charts.

Attributes control charts have the advantage that several quality characteristics can be considered jointly and the unit classified as nonconforming if it fails to meet the specification on any one characteristic. On the other hand, if the several quality characteristics are treated as variables, then each one must be measured, and either a separate $\bar{x}$ and R chart must be maintained on each or some multivariate control technique that considers all the characteristics must simultaneously be employed. There is an obvious simplicity associated with the attributes chart in this case. Furthermore, expensive and time-consuming measurements may be avoided by attributes inspection.

Variables control charts, in contrast, provide much more useful information about process performance than does an attributes control chart. Specific information about the process mean and variability is obtained directly. In addition, when points plot out of control on variables control charts, usually much more information is provided relative to the potential *cause* of that out-of-control signal. For a process-capability study, variables control charts are almost always preferable to attributes control charts. The exceptions to this are studies relative to nonconformities produced by machines or operators in which there are a very limited number of sources of nonconformities, or studies directly concerned with process yields and fallouts.

Perhaps the most important advantage of the $\bar{x}$ and R control chart is that they often provide an indication of impending trouble and allow operating personnel to take corrective action *before* any defectives are actually produced. Thus,

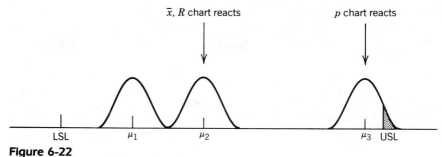

Figure 6-22
Why the $\bar{x}$ and R charts can warn of impending trouble.

$\bar{x}$ and R charts are *leading indicators* of trouble, whereas p charts (or c and u charts) will not react unless the process has already changed so that *more* nonconforming units are being produced. To illustrate, consider the production process depicted in Figure 6-22. When the process mean is at μ_1, few nonconforming units are produced. Suppose the process mean begins to shift upward. By the time it has reached μ_2, the $\bar{x}$ and R charts will have reacted to the change in the mean by generating a strong nonrandom pattern and possibly several out-of-control points. However, a p chart would not react until the mean had shifted all the way to μ_3, or until the actual number of nonconforming units produced had increased. Thus, the $\bar{x}$ and R charts are more powerful control tools than the p chart.

For a specified level of protection against process shifts, variables control charts usually require a much smaller sample size than does the corresponding attributes control chart. Thus, while variables-type inspection is usually more expensive and time consuming on a per unit basis than is attributes inspection, many fewer units must be examined. This is an important consideration, particularly in cases where inspection is destructive (such as opening a can to measure the volume of product within or to test chemical properties of the product). The following example demonstrates the economic advantage of variables control charts.

Example 6-6

The nominal value of the mean of a quality characteristic is 50, and the standard deviation is 2. The process is controlled by an $\bar{x}$ chart. Specification limits on the process are established at ± 3-sigma, such that the lower specification limit is 44 and the upper specification limit is 56. When the process is in control at the nominal level of 50, the fraction of nonconforming product produced, assuming that the quality characteristic is normally distributed, is 0.0027. Suppose that the process mean were to shift to 52. The fraction of nonconforming product produced following the shift is approximately 0.0202. If we want the probability of detecting this shift on the first subsequent sample to be 0.50 (say), then the sample size on the $\bar{x}$ chart must be large enough for the upper 3-sigma control limit to be 52. This implies that

$$50 + \frac{3(2)}{\sqrt{n}} = 52$$

or $n = 9$. If a p chart is used, then we may find the required sample size to give the same probability of detecting the shift from Equation (5-10), that is

$$n = \left(\frac{k}{\delta}\right)^2 p(1 - p)$$

where $k = 3$ is the width of the control limits, $p = 0.0027$ is the in-control fraction nonconforming, and $\delta = 0.0202 - 0.0027 = 0.0175$ is the magnitude of the shift. Consequently, we find

$$n = (3/0.0175)^2(0.0027)(0.9963) = 79.23$$

or $n \simeq 80$ would be required for the p chart. Unless the cost of measurements inspection is more than nine times as costly as attributes inspection, the $\bar{x}$ chart is less expensive to operate.

6-6 SUMMARY OF PROCEDURES FOR $\bar{x}$, R, AND S CHARTS

It is convenient to summarize in one place the various computational formulas for the major types of variables control charts discussed in this chapter. Table 6-8 summarizes the formulas for $\bar{x}$, R, and S charts when standard values for μ and σ are given. Table 6-9 provides the corresponding summary when no standard values are given and trial control limits must be established from analysis of past data. The constants given for the S chart assume that $n - 1$ is used in the denominator of S. All constants are tabulated for various sample sizes in Appendix Table VI.

6-7 GUIDELINES FOR IMPLEMENTING CONTROL CHARTS

Almost any process will benefit from statistical process-control methods, including the use of control charts. In this section, we present some general guidelines helpful in implementing control charts. Specifically, we deal with the following:

1. Choosing the proper *type* of control charts.
2. Determining *which* process characteristics to control.
3. Determining *where* the charts should be implemented in the process.
4. Taking actions to improve processes as the result of SPC/control chart analysis.
5. Selecting data-collection systems and computer software.

Table 6-8
Formulas for control charts, standards given

Chart	Center Line	Control Limits
$\bar{x}$ (μ and σ given)	μ	$\mu \pm A\sigma$
R (σ given)	$d_2\sigma$	UCL $= D_2\sigma$, LCL $= D_1\sigma$
S (σ given)	$c_4\sigma$	UCL $= B_6\sigma$, LCL $= B_5\sigma$

Table 6-9
Formulas for control charts, control limits based on
past data (no standards given)

Chart	Center Line	Control Limits
$\bar{x}$ (using R)	$\bar{\bar{x}}$	$\bar{\bar{x}} \pm A_2\bar{R}$
$\bar{x}$ (using S)	$\bar{\bar{x}}$	$\bar{\bar{x}} \pm A_3\bar{S}$
R	$\bar{R}$	$\text{UCL} = D_4\bar{R}, \text{LCL} = D_3\bar{R}$
S	$\bar{S}$	$\text{UCL} = B_4\bar{S}, \text{LCL} = B_3\bar{S}$

The guidelines are applicable to both measurements and attributes control charts. Remember, control charts are not just for process surveillance; they should be used as an active, on-line method for reduction of process variability.

Choosing the Proper Type of Control Chart

A. **$\bar{x}$ and R (or $\bar{x}$ and S) charts.** Consider using measurements control charts in these situations:

1. A new process is coming on stream, or a new product is being manufactured by an existing process.

2. The process has been in operation for some time, but it is chronically in trouble or unable to hold the specified tolerances.

3. The process is in trouble, and the control chart can be useful for diagnostic purposes (troubleshooting).

4. Destructive testing (or other expensive testing procedures) is required.

5. It is desirable to reduce acceptance-sampling or other downstream testing to a mininum when the process can be operated in control.

6. Attributes control charts have been used, but the process is either out of control, or is in control but the yield is unacceptable.

7. There are very tight specifications, overlapping assembly tolerances, or other difficult manufacturing problems.

8. The operator must decide whether or not to adjust the process, or where a set-up must be evaluated.

9. A change in product specifications is desired.

10. Process stability and capability must be continually demonstrated, such as in regulated industries.

B. **Attributes Charts (p charts, c charts, and u charts).** Consider using attributes control charts in these situations:

1. Operators control the assignable causes, and it is necessary to reduce process fallout.

2. The process is a complex assembly operation and product quality is measured in terms of the occurrence of nonconformities, successful or unsuccessful product function, and so forth. (Examples include computers, office automation equipment, automobiles, and the major subsystems of these products.)

3. Process control is necessary, but measurement data cannot be obtained.

4. A historical summary of process performance is necessary. Attributes control charts, such as p charts, c charts, and u charts, are very effective for summarizing information about the process for management review.

C. **Control Charts for Individuals.** Consider using the control chart for individuals in conjunction with a moving-range chart in these situations:

1. It is inconvenient or impossible to obtain more than one measurement per sample, or repeat measurements will only differ by laboratory or analysis error. Examples often occur in chemical processes.

2. Automated testing and inspection technology allow measurement of every unit produced. In these cases, also consider the cumulative-sum control chart and the exponentially weighted moving-average control chart discussed in Chapter 7.

3. The data become available very slowly, and waiting for a larger sample will be impratical or make the control procedure too slow to react to problems. This often happens in nonproduct situations; for example, accounting data may become available only monthly.

Determining Which Characteristics to Control and Where to Put the Control Charts

At the start of a control chart program, it is usually difficult to determine which product or process characteristics should be controlled and at which points in the process to apply control charts. Some useful guidelines follow.

1. At the beginning of a control chart program, control charts should be applied to any product characteristics or manufacturing operations believed to be important. The charts will provide immediate feedback as to whether they are actually needed.

2. The control charts found to be unnecessary should be removed, and others that engineering and operator judgement indicates may be required should be added. More control charts will usually be employed at the beginning than after the process has stabilized.

3. Information on the number and types of control charts on the process should be kept current. It is best to keep separate records on the variables and attributes charts. In general, after the control charts are first installed, we often find that the number of control charts tends to increase rather steadily. After that, it will usually decrease. When the process stabilizes, we typically find that it has the same number of charts from one year to the next. However, they are not necessarily the same charts.

4. If control charts are being used effectively and if new knowledge is being gained about the key process variables, we should find that the number of $\bar{x}$ and R charts increases and the number of attributes control charts decreases.

5. At the beginning of a control chart program there will usually be more attributes control charts, applied to semifinished or finished units near the *end* of the manufacturing process. As we learn more about the process, these charts will be replaced with $\bar{x}$ and R charts applied *earlier* in the process to the critical parameters and operations that result in nonconformities in the finished product. Generally, *the earlier in the process control can be established, the*

better. In a complex assembly process, this may imply that process controls need to be implemented at the vendor or supplier level.

6. Control charts are an on-line process-control procedure. They should be implemented and maintained as close to the work center as possible, so that feedback will be rapid. Furthermore, the process operators and manufacturing engineering should have direct responsibility for collecting the process data, maintaining the charts, and interpreting the results. The operators and engineers have the detailed knowledge of the process required to correct process upsets and use the control chart as a device to improve process performance. Microcomputers can speed up the feedback and should be an integral part of any modern on-line process-control procedure.

Actions Taken to Improve the Process

Process improvement is the primary objective of statistical process control. The application of control charts will give information on two key aspects of the process: (1) statistical control and (2) capability. Figure 6-23 shows the possible states in which the process may exist with respect to these two issues. Technically speaking, the capability of a process cannot be adequately assessed until statistical control has been established, but we will use a less precise definition of capability that is just a qualitative assessment of whether or not the level of nonconforming units produced is low enough to warrant no immediate *additional* effort to further improve the process.

Figure 6-23 gives the answers to two questions: "Is the process in control?", and "Is the process capable (in the sense of the previous paragraph)?" Each of the four cells in the figure contains some recommended courses of action that depend on the answers to these two questions. The box in the northwest corner is the "ideal state"; the process is in statistical control and exhibits adequate capability for present business objectives. In this case, SPC methods are valuable for process monitoring and for warning against the occurrence of any new assignable causes that could cause slippage in performance. The northeast corner implies that the process exhibits statistical control but has poor capability. Perhaps the PCR is lower than the value required by the customer, or there is sufficient variability remaining to result in excessive scrap or rework. In this case SPC methods may be useful for process diagnosis and improvement, primarily through the recognition of *patterns* on the control chart, but the control charts will not produce very

IS THE PROCESS CAPABLE?

		Yes	No
Is the process in control?	Yes	SPC	SPC Experimental design Investigate specifications Change process
	No	SPC	SPC Experimental design Investigate specifications Change process

Figure 6-23
Actions taken to improve a process.

many out-of-control signals. It will usually be necessary to intervene actively in the process to improve it. Experimental design methods are helpful in this regard [see Montgomery (1984)]. Usually, it is also helpful to reconsider the specifications: They may have been set at levels tighter than necessary to achieve function or performance from the part. As a last resort we may have to consider changing the process—that is, investigating or developing new technology that has less variability with respect to this quality characteristic than the existing process.

The lower two boxes in Figure 6-23 deal with the case of an out-of-control process. The southeast corner presents the case of a process that is out of control and not capable. (Remember our nontechnical use of the term *capability*.) The actions recommended here are identical to those for the box in the northeast corner, except that SPC would be expected to yield fairly rapid results now, because the control charts should be identifying the presence of assignable causes. The other methods of attack will warrant consideration and use in many cases, however. Finally, the southwest corner treats the case of a process that exhibits lack of statistical control but does not produce a meaningful number of defectives because the specifications are very wide. SPC methods should still be used to establish control and reduce variability in this case, for the following reasons:

1. Specifications can change without notice.

2. The customer may require both *control* and capability.

3. The fact that the process experiences assignable causes implies that unknown forces are at work; these unknown forces could result in poor capability in the near future.

Selection of Data-Collection Systems and Computer Software

The last few years have witnessed an explosion of quality-control software and electronic data-collection devices. For example, the March 1988 issue of *Quality Progress* contains a directory of 415 software packages available from over 60 suppliers, arranged in 16 applications categories. (Some software packages appear in more than one category.) The wide range of software and data-collection equipment available is somewhat surprising, since most applications of SPC in Japan have emphasized the *manual* use of control charts. If the Japanese have been successful using manual control charting methods, then does the computer truly have a useful role in SPC?

The answer to this question is yes, for several reasons:

1. While it is usually helpful to begin with manual methods of control charting at the start of an SPC implementation, it is necessary to move successful applications to the computer very soon. The computer is a great productivity-improvement device and one in which the United States has an enormous lead over our foreign competitors. Using the computer to its fullest extent will enable the United States to move forward rather than merely duplicate the Japanese experience. It will enable us to leap ahead.

2. The computer will enable the SPC data to become part of the company-wide manufacturing data base, and in that form, the data will be useful (and hence more likely to be used) to everyone—management, engineering, marketing, and so on, *not* just manufacturing and quality.

3. A computer-based SPC system can provide more information than any manual system. It permits the user to monitor many quality characteristics and to provide automatic signaling of assignable causes.

What type of software should be used? This is a difficult question to answer, because all applications have unique requirements and the capability of the software is constantly changing. However, several features are necessary for successful results:

1. The software should be capable of stand-alone operation on a personal computer, on a multiterminal local area network, or on a multiterminal minicomputer-host system. SPC packages that are exclusively tied to a large mainframe system are frequently not very useful because they usually cannot produce control charts and other routine reports in a timely manner.

2. The system must be "user friendly." If operating personnel are to use the system, it must have limited options, be easy to use, provide adequate error-correction opportunities, and contain many on-line help features. It should ideally be possible to tailor or customize the system for each application, although this installation activity may have to be carried out by engineering/technical personnel.

3. The system should provide video display of control charts for at least the last 25 samples. Ideally, the length of record displayed should be controlled by the user. Printed output should be immediately available on either a line printer or a plotter.

4. File storage should be sufficient to accomodate at least 300 samples of typical size. Editing and updating files should be straightforward. Provision to download files to other storage media or to transfer the data to a master manufacturing data base as working files become full is critical.

5. The system should be able to handle multiple files simultaneously. Only rarely does a process have only one quality characteristic that needs to be examined.

6. The user should be able to calculate control limits from any subset of the data on the file. The user should have the capability to input center lines and control limits directly.

7. The system should be able to accept a variety of inputs, including manual data entry, RS-232 input from an electronic gage, or input from another computer or instrument controller.

8. Other statistical applications, including as a minimum histograms and computation of process-capability indices, should be supported.

9. Service and support from the software supplier after purchase is always an important factor in deciding which software package to use.

The purchase price of commercially available software ranges from $50 to over $150,000. Obviously, the total cost of software is very different from the purchase price. In many cases a $500 SPC package is really a $10,000 package when we take into account the total costs of making the package work correctly in the intended application.

There are several sources of free software. In addition to the packages available on various personal computer bulletin boards, the *Journal of Quality Technology* has published computer programs in either BASIC or FORTRAN since 1969. Table 6-10 presents a selected list of these programs through 1989.

Table 6-10
Software available in the *Journal of Quality Technology*

Subject Area	Program Capability	Volume and Year	Page Reference
Control Charts	Plotting $\bar{x}$ and R charts	1/1969	149
	Plotting p and np charts	1/1969	217
	Plotting c and u charts	1/1969	285
	Economic design of $\bar{x}$ charts	2/1970	40
	Plotting cumulative-sum control charts	2/1970	54
	Plotting exponentially weighted moving average control charts	5/1973	84
	ARL for cumulative-sum control charts for controlling normal means	18/1986	189
	ARL for combined individual measurement and moving-range charts	19/1987	103
	ARL for exponentially weighted moving-average control charts	19/1987	161
	New limits for $\bar{x}$ and R charts when sample size is changed	20/1988	149
	Optimal design parameters of joint $\bar{x}$ and R charts	21/1989	65
Sampling Plans	Single sampling plans given an AQL, LTPD, producer and consumer risks	4/1972	168
	OC curves for double sampling plans	4/1972	205
	Determination of multiple sampling plans	5/1973	39
	Dodge's continuous sampling plans	7/1975	43
	MIL-STD 414	9/1977	82
	General routine for attribute sampling plan evaluation	10/1978	125
	Selecting efficient binomial double sampling plans	18/1980	67
	Minimum sample size single sampling plans	12/1980	230
	Algorithm for determining double attribute sampling plans	14/1982	166

Table 6-10 (*Continued*)

Subject Area	Program Capability	Volume and Year	Page Reference
	Determination of rectifying inspection plans for single sampling by attributes	16/1984	56
	Wald sequential sampling for attribute inspection	16/1984	172
	ASN of curtailed attributes sampling plans	17/1985	108
	AOQ after multiple inspections	19/1987	52
Testing Hypotheses and Parameter Estimation	Student's t-test	2/1970	243
	Computation of a two-tailed Fisher's test	11/1979	44
	Small sample test for nonnormality	11/1979	95
	Randomization tests for K sample binomial data	14/1982	220
	Testing for normality	15/1983	141
Design of Experiments, Analysis of Variance, and Analysis of Means	Variance components for unbalanced multilevel hierarchic designs	7/1973	144
	Analysis of variance of an $n \times n$ Latin square, with a subroutine for Duncan's multiple range test	7/1975	90
	Runs test for sample nonrandomness	7/1975	196
	Analysis of randomized complete block designs	10/1978	40
	Analysis of replicated randomized complete block design	10/1978	84
	Comparison of K sample means involving variables or attributes data	12/1980	47
	Analysis of variance and analysis of means	12/1980	106
	Simultaneous pairwise comparison tests among treatment means	13/1981	65
	Two-sample Kolmogorov-Smirnov test	13/1982	139
	Analysis of two-level factorial experiments	14/1982	95

Table 6-10 (*Continued*)

Subject Area	Program Capability	Volume and Year	Page Reference
	Analysis of means for balanced experimental designs	15/1983	43
	Variance estimation using staggered, nested design	15/1983	195
	Allocating observations in the random effects balanced one way ANOVA	19/1987	221
	Generating fractional factorial experiments	20/1988	63
	Generating experimental designs for mixtures	20/1988	125
	Probability plotting of effects from two-level factorial experiments	20/1989	140
Regression and Correlation	Scatter diagrams	3/1971	38
	Coefficient of correlation	3/1971	95
	Simple linear regression	3/1971	138
	Multiple linear regression	3/1971	184
	Constructing orthogonal polynomials when the independent variable is unequally spaced	6/1974	113
	Doolittle technique	6/1974	160
	Orthogonal polynomial regression for unequal spacing and frequencies	10/1978	170
	Interior analysis of the observations in multiple linear regression	12/1980	165
Sample Frequency Distribution Analysis and Probability Distributions	Analysis of frequency distribution	1/1969	68
	Probability plotting	5/1973	135
	Cumulative probabilities for the standard normal, χ^2, F and t distributions	16/1984	232
	Computation of some common discrete distributions	17/1985	160
	Interactive probability plotting	20/1988	196

6-8 APPLICATIONS OF VARIABLES CONTROL CHARTS

There are many interesting applications of variables control charts. In this section, a few of them will be described in order to give the reader additional insights into how the control chart works, as well as ideas for further applications.

Example 6-7

Using Control Charts to Improve Suppliers' Processes

A large aerospace manufacturer purchased an aircraft component from two suppliers. These components frequently exhibited excessive variability on a key dimension which made it impossible to assemble them into the final product. This problem always resulted in expensive rework costs and occasionally caused delay in finishing the assembly of an airplane.

   The materials-receiving group performed 100% of the inspection of these parts in an effort to improve the situation. They maintained $\bar{x}$ and R charts on the dimension of interest for both suppliers. They found that the fraction of nonconforming units was about the same for both suppliers, but for very different reasons. Supplier A could produce parts with mean dimension equal to the required value, but the process was out of statistical control. Supplier B could maintain good statistical control and, in general, produced a part that exhibited considerably less variability than parts from supplier A, but his process was centered so far off the nominal required dimension that many parts were out of specification.

   This situation convinced the procurement organization to work with both suppliers, persuading supplier A to install an SPC activity and to begin working at continuous improvement, and assisting supplier B to find out why his process was consistently centered incorrectly. Supplier B's problem was ultimately tracked to some incorrect code in an NC (numerical-controlled) machine, and the use of SPC at supplier A resulted in considerable reduction in variability over a six-month period. As a result of these actions, the problem with these parts was essentially eliminated.

Example 6-8

Using SPC to Purchase a Machine Pool

An article in *Manufacturing Engineering* ("Picking a Marvel at Deere," January 1989, pp. 74–77) describes how the John Deere Company uses SPC methods to help choose production equipment. When a machine tool is purchased, it must go through the company capability demonstration prior to shipment to demonstrate that the tool has the ability to meet or exceed the established performance criteria. The procedure was applied to a programmable controlled bandsaw. The bandsaw supplier cut 45 pieces which were analyzed using $\bar{x}$ and R charts to demonstrate statistical control and to provide the basis for process-capability analysis. The saw proved capable, and the supplier learned many useful things about the performance of his equipment. Control and capability tests such as this one are becoming a basic part of the equipment selection and aquisition process in many companies.

Example 6-9

SPC Implementation in a Short-run Job-shop

One of the more interesting aspects of SPC is the successful implementation of control charts in a job-shop manufacturing environment. Most job-shops are characterized by short production runs, and many of these shops produce parts on production runs of less than 50 units. This situation can make the routine use of control charts appear to be somewhat of a challenge, as not enough units are produced in any one batch to establish the control limits.

This problem can usually be easily solved. Since statistical process-control methods are most frequently applied to a characteristic of a product, we can extend SPC to the job-shop environment by focusing on the *process characteristic* in each unit of product. To illustrate, consider a drilling operation in a job-shop. The operator drills holes of various sizes in each part passing through the machine center. Some parts require one hole, and others several holes of different sizes. It is almost impossible to construct an $\bar{x}$ and R chart on hole diameter, since each part is potentially different. The correct approach is to focus on the characteristic of interest in the *process*. In this case, the manufacturer is interested in drilling holes that have the correct diameter, and therefore wants to reduce the variability in hole diameter as much as possible. This may be accomplished by control charting the *deviation* of the actual hole diameter from the nominal diameter. Depending on the process production rate and the mix of parts produced, either a control chart for individuals with a moving-range control chart or a conventional $\bar{x}$ and R chart can be used. In these applications it is usually very important to mark the start of each lot or to batch carefully on the control chart, so that if changing the size, position, or number of holes drilled on each part affects the process the resulting pattern on the control charts will be easy to interpret.

Example 6-10

Use of $\bar{x}$ and R Charts in a Nonmanufacturing Environment

Variables control charts have found frequent application in both manufacturing and nonmanufacturing settings. A fairly widespread but erroneous notion about these charts is that they do not apply to the nonmanufacturing environment because the "product is different." Actually, if we can make measurements on the product that are reflective of quality, function, or performance, then the *nature* of the product has no bearing on the general applicability of control charts. There are, however, two commonly encountered differences between manufacturing and nonmanufacturing situations: (1) In the nonmanufacturing environment specification limits rarely apply to the product, so the notion of process capability is often undefined, and (2) more imagination may be required to select the proper variable or variables for measurement.

One application of $\bar{x}$ and R control charts in a nonmanufacturing environment involved the efforts of a finance group to reduce the time required to process its accounts payable. The division of the company in which the problem occurred had recently experienced a considerable increase in business volume, and along with this expansion came a gradual lengthening of the time the finance department needed to process check requests. As a result, many suppliers were being paid beyond the normal 30-day period, and the company was failing to capture the discounts available from its suppliers for prompt payment. The quality-improvement team assigned to this project used the flow time through the finance department as the variable for control chart analysis. Five completed check requests were selected each day, and the average and range of flow time were plotted on $\bar{x}$ and R charts. While management and operating personnel had addressed this problem before, the use of $\bar{x}$ and R charts was responsible for substantial improvements. Within nine months, the finance department had reduced the percentage of invoices paid late from over 90% to under 3%, resulting in an annual savings of several hundred thousand dollars in realized discounts to the company.

Example 6-11

A Misapplication of $\bar{x}$ and R Charts

This example illustrates a misapplication of $\bar{x}$ and R charts which the author encountered in the electronics industry. A company manufacturing a box-level product inspected a sample of the production units several times each shift using attributes inspection. The output of each sample inspection was an estimate of the process fraction nonconforming $\hat{p}_i$. The company personnel were well aware that attributes data did not contain as much information about the process as variables data, and were exploring ways to get more useful information about their process. A consultant to the company (*not* the author) had suggested that they could achieve this objective by converting their fraction nonconforming data into $\bar{x}$ and R charts. To do so, each group of five successive values of $\hat{p}_i$ was treated as if it were a sample of five *variables* measurements; then the average and range were computed as

$$\bar{x} = \frac{1}{5} \sum_{i=1}^{5} \hat{p}_i$$

and

$$R = \max(\hat{p}_i) - \min(\hat{p}_i),$$

and these values were plotted on $\bar{x}$ and R charts. The consultant claimed that this procedure would provide more information than the fraction nonconforming control chart.

This suggestion was incorrect. If the inspection process actually produces attributes data governed by the binomial distribution with fixed n, then the sample fraction nonconforming contains *all* the information in the sample (this is an application of the concept of minimal sufficient statistics) and forming two new functions of $\hat{p}_i$ will not provide any additional information.

To illustrate this idea, consider the control chart for fraction nonconforming in Figure 6-24. This chart was produced by drawing 100 samples (each of size 200) from a process for which $p = 0.05$ and by using these data to compute the control limits. Then the sample draws were continued until sample 150, where the population fraction nonconforming was increased to $p = 0.06$. At each subsequent 50-sample interval, the value of p was increased by 0.01. Notice that the control chart reacts to the shift in p at sample number 196. Figures 6-25 and 6-26 present the

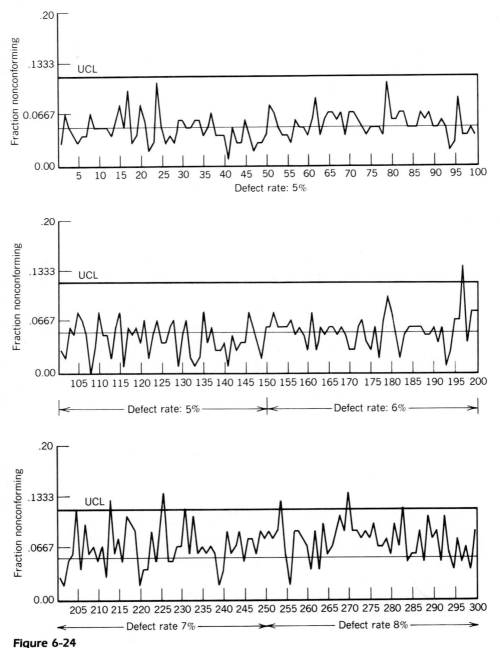

Figure 6-24
Fraction nonconforming control chart for Example 6-11.

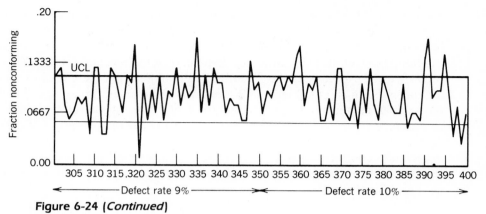

Figure 6-24 (*Continued*)
Fraction nonconforming control chart for Example 6-11.

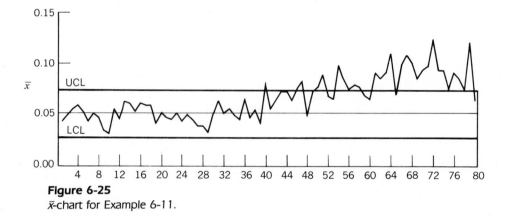

Figure 6-25
$\bar{x}$-chart for Example 6-11.

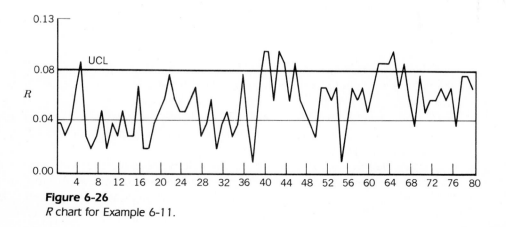

Figure 6-26
R chart for Example 6-11.

$\bar{x}$ and R charts obtained by subgrouping the sample values of $\hat{p}_i$ as suggested above. The first 20 of those subgroups were used to compute the center line and control limits on the $\bar{x}$ and R charts. Notice that the $\bar{x}$ chart reacts to the shift in $\hat{p}$ at about subgroup number 40. (This would correspond to *original* samples 196–200.) This result is to be expected, as the $\bar{x}$ chart is really monitoring the fraction nonconforming p. The R chart in Figure 6-26 is misleading, however. One subgroup within the original set used to construct the control limits is out of control. (This is a false alarm, since $p = 0.05$ for all 100 original samples.) Furthermore, the out-of-control points beginning at about subgroup 40 do not contribute any additional useful information about the process because when $\hat{p}$ shifts from 0.05 to 0.06 (say), the standard deviation of p will *automatically* increase. Therefore, in this case there is no added benefit to the user from $\bar{x}$ and R charts.

This is not to say that the conventional fraction nonconforming control chart based on the binomial probability distribution is the right control chart for all fraction nonconforming data, just as the c chart (based on the Poisson distribution) is not always the right control chart for defect data. If the variability in $\hat{p}_i$ from sample to sample is greater than that which could plausibly be explained by the binomial model, then the analyst should determine the *correct* underlying probability model and base the control chart on that distribution.

Example 6-12

The Need for Care in Selecting Rational Subgroups

Figure 6-27a shows a casting used in a gas turbine jet aircraft engine. This part is typical of those produced by both casting and machining processes for use in gas turbine engines and auxiliary power units in the aerospace industry—cylindrical parts created by rotating the cross-section around a central axis. The vane height on this part is a critical quality characteristic.

Data on vane heights are collected by randomly selecting five vanes on each casting produced. Initially, the company constructed $\bar{x}$ and S control charts on these data to control and improve the process. This usually produced many out-of-control points on the $\bar{x}$ chart, with an occasional out-of-control point on the S chart. A more careful analysis of the problem revealed that the chief problem was the use of the five measurements on a single part as a rational subgroup, and that the out-of-control conditions on the $\bar{x}$ chart did not provide a valid basis for corrective action.

Remember that the control chart for $\bar{x}$ deals with the issue of whether or not the between-sample variability is consistent with the within-sample variability. In this case it is not: The vanes on a single casting are formed together in a common wax mold assembly. It is likely that the vane heights on a specific casting will be very similar, and it is reasonable to believe that there will be more variation in average vane height between the castings.

This situation was handled by using the S chart in the ordinary way to measure variation in vane height. However, as this standard deviation is clearly too small to provide a valid basis for control of $\bar{x}$, the quality engineer at the company decided to treat the average vane height on each casting as an *individual measurement*

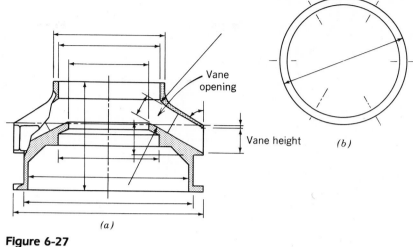

Figure 6-27
An aerospace casting.

and to control average vane height by using a control chart for individuals with a moving-range chart. This solution worked extremely well in practice, and the group of three control charts provided an excellent basis for process improvement.

Figure 6-28a shows a typical control chart for S for the vane height data. Notice that one point plots out of control. The tolerance diagram in Figure 6-28b reveals that this out-of-control point is most likely the result of a local deformation in a single vane due to a weld repair. Generally, the within-part variation is very consistent; company personnel also found the tolerance chart a useful supplement to the control charts.

Another quality characteristic of interest on the same casting is the opening diameter (see Figure 6-27b). Typically, diameters are measured on a coordinate measuring machine at 24 equal angular increments around the part. Once again, the conventional $\bar{x}$ chart is not appropriate for controlling average diameter because between-part variability always tends to be much greater than within-part variability. The correct approach is to treat the average of 24 diameter measurements as an individual measurement and to control the process diameter with a control chart for individuals and a moving-range chart. The S chart for the 24 diameter measurements on each part is essentially a control chart for *roundness*. Points that are out of control on this chart would lead to investigation of roundness of the tool that produced the wax mold. A typical S chart for this diameter measurement is shown in Figure 6-29a, and a box plot of the diameter measurements is shown in Figure 6-29b. The out-of-control points on the S chart are due in most cases to a general increase (or decrease) in the within-part variability of diameters, and *not* due to just one or two aberrant points. This problem was traced to the wax patterns, and one corrective action that was highly successful was to use wooden cooling fixtures to keep the patterns from deforming. The box plot does indicate that the out-of-control point for casting number 12 was caused by two aberrant hits, however. When the sample size is large, say $n > 10$ or 12, the box plot is often a more useful display than the conventional tolerance diagram.

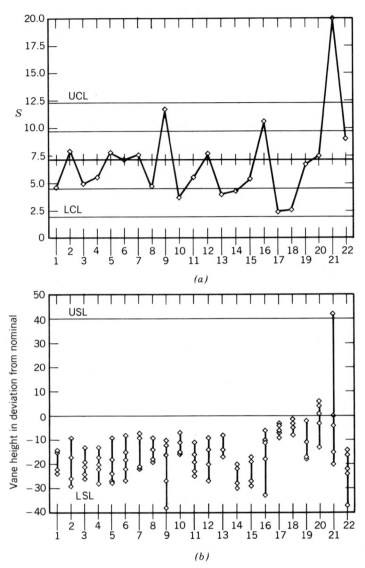

Figure 6-28
(a) Control chart for S and (b) tolerance chart for vane height data,
Example 6-12.

Situations such as those described in Example 6-12 occur frequently in the application of control charts. For example, the author has encountered many similar problems in the semiconductor industry. In such cases, it is important to study carefully the behavior of the variables being measured and to have a clear understanding of the purpose of the control charts. For instance, if the variation in vane height on a specific casting were completely unrelated, using the average height as an individual measurement could be very inappropriate. It would be necessary to (1) use a control chart on each individual vane included in the sample, (2) investigate the use of a control chart technique for multistream processes, or (3) use some multivariate control chart technique. Some of these possibilities are discussed in Chapter 8.

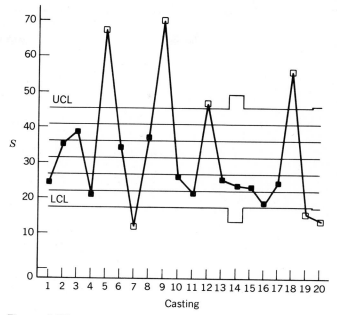

Figure 6-29a
S chart for diameter, Example 6-12. This is essentially a control chart for roundness.

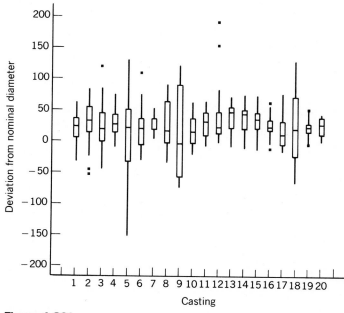

Figure 6-29b
Box plot for diameters (deviation from nominal), Example 6-12.

6-9 Exercises

6-1 The data below are $\bar{x}$ and R values for 24 samples of size $n = 5$ taken from a process producing bearings. The measurements are made on the inside diameter of the bearing, with only the last three decimals recorded (i.e., 34.5 should be 0.50345).

Sample Number	$\bar{x}$	R	Sample Number	$\bar{x}$	R
1	34.5	3	13	35.4	8
2	34.2	4	14	34.0	6
3	31.6	4	15	37.1	5
4	31.5	4	16	34.9	7
5	35.0	5	17	33.5	4
6	34.1	6	18	31.7	3
7	32.6	4	19	34.0	8
8	33.8	3	20	35.1	4
9	34.8	7	21	33.7	2
10	33.6	8	22	32.8	1
11	31.9	3	23	33.5	3
12	38.6	9	24	34.2	2

a. Set up $\bar{x}$ and R charts on this process. Does the process seem to be in statistical control? If necessary, revise the trial control limits.

b. If specifications on this diameter are 0.5030 ± 0.0010, find the percentage of non-conformities produced by this process.

6-2 A high-voltage power supply should have a nominal output voltage of 350 V. A sample of four units are selected each day and tested for process-control purposes. The data shown below give the difference between the observed reading on each unit and the nominal voltage times ten; that is,

$$x_i = (\text{observed voltage on unit } i - 350)10.$$

Sample Number	x_1	x_2	x_3	x_4	Sample Number	x_1	x_2	x_3	x_4
1	6	9	10	15	11	8	12	14	16
2	10	4	6	11	12	6	13	9	11
3	7	8	10	5	13	16	9	13	15
4	8	9	6	13	14	7	13	10	12
5	9	10	7	13	15	11	7	10	16
6	12	11	10	10	16	15	10	11	14
7	16	10	8	9	17	9	8	12	10
8	7	5	10	4	18	15	7	10	11
9	9	7	8	12	19	8	6	9	12
10	15	16	10	13	20	14	15	12	16

a. Set up $\bar{x}$ and R charts on this process. Is the process in statistical control?

b. If specifications are at 350 V + 5 V, what can you say about process capability?

6-3 The data shown below are the deviations from nominal diameter for holes drilled in a carbon-fiber composite material used in aerospace manufacturing. The values reported are deviations in ten thousands of an inch.

Sample Number	x_1	x_2	x_3	x_4	x_5
1	− 30	+ 50	− 20	+ 10	+ 30
2	0	+ 50	− 60	− 20	+ 30
3	− 50	+ 10	+ 20	+ 30	+ 20
4	− 10	− 10	+ 30	− 20	+ 50
5	+ 20	− 40	+ 50	+ 20	+ 10
6	0	0	+ 40	− 40	+ 20
7	0	0	+ 20	− 20	− 10
8	+ 70	− 30	+ 30	− 10	0
9	0	0	+ 20	− 20	10
10	+ 10	+ 20	+ 30	+ 10	+ 50
11	+ 40	0	+ 20	0	+ 20
12	+ 30	+ 20	+ 30	+ 10	+ 40
13	+ 30	− 30	0	+ 10	+ 10
14	+ 30	− 10	+ 50	− 10	− 30
15	+ 10	− 10	+ 50	+ 40	0
16	0	0	+ 30	− 10	0
17	+ 20	+ 20	+ 30	+ 30	− 20
18	+ 10	− 20	+ 50	+ 30	+ 10
19	+ 50	− 10	+ 40	+ 20	0
20	+ 50	0	0	+ 30	+ 10

a. Set up $\bar{x}$ and R charts on the process. Is the process in statistical control?

b. Estimate the process standard deviation using the range method.

c. If specifications are at nominal ± 100, what can you say about the capability of this process? Calculate the PCR.

6-4 The thickness of a printed circuit board is an important quality parameter. Data on board thickness (in inches) are given below, for 25 samples of three boards each.

Sample Number	x_1	x_2	x_3	Sample Number	x_1	x_2	x_3
1	0.0629	0.0636	0.0640	13	0.0635	0.0631	0.0630
2	0.0630	0.0631	0.0622	14	0.0645	0.0640	0.0631
3	0.0628	0.0631	0.0633	15	0.0619	0.0644	0.0632
4	0.0634	0.0630	0.0631	16	0.0631	0.0627	0.0630
5	0.0619	0.0628	0.0630	17	0.0616	0.0623	0.0631
6	0.0613	0.0629	0.0634	18	0.0630	0.0630	0.0626
7	0.0630	0.0639	0.0625	19	0.0636	0.0631	0.0629
8	0.0628	0.0627	0.0622	20	0.0640	0.0635	0.0629
9	0.0623	0.0626	0.0633	21	0.0628	0.0625	0.0616
10	0.0631	0.0631	0.0633	22	0.0615	0.0625	0.0619
11	0.0635	0.0630	0.0638	23	0.0630	0.0632	0.0630
12	0.0623	0.0630	0.0630	24	0.0635	0.0629	0.0635
				25	0.0623	0.0629	0.0630

    a. Set up $\bar{x}$ and R control charts. Is the process in statistical control?

    b. Estimate the process standard deviation.

    c. What are the limits that you would expect to contain nearly all the process measurements?

    d. If the specifications are at 0.0630 in. $\pm$ 0.0015 in. what is the PCR?

6-5   Rework Exercise 6-2 using the S chart.

6-6   Rework Exercise 6-3 using the S chart.

6-7   Control charts on $\bar{x}$ and S are to be maintained on the torque readings of a bearing used in a wingflap actuator assembly. Samples of size $n = 10$ are to be used, and we know from past experience that when the process is in control, bearing torque has a normal distribution with mean $\mu = 80$ inch-pounds and standard deviation $\sigma = 10$ inch-pounds. Find the center line and control limits for these control charts.

6-8   Samples of $n = 8$ items each are taken from a manufacturing process at regular intervals. A quality characteristic is measured, and $\bar{x}$ and R values are calculated for each sample. After 50 samples, we have

$$\sum_{i=1}^{50} \bar{x}_i = 2000 \quad \text{and} \quad \sum_{i=1}^{50} R_i = 250$$

Assume that the quality characteristic is normally distributed.

    a. Compute control limits for the $\bar{x}$ and R control charts.

    b. All points on both control charts fall between the control limits computed in part (a). What are the natural tolerance limits of the process?

    c. If the specifications limits are 41 ± 5.0, what are your conclusions regarding the ability of the process to produce items within these specifications?

    d. Assuming that if an item exceeds the upper specification limit it can be reworked, and if it is below the lower specification limit it must be scrapped, what percent scrap and rework is the process producing?

    e. Make suggestions as to how the process performance could be improved.

6-9   Samples of $n = 6$ items are taken from a manufacturing process at regular intervals. A normally distributed quality characteristic is measured and $\bar{x}$ and S values are calculated for each sample. After 50 subgroups have been analyzed, we have

$$\sum_{i=1}^{50} \bar{x}_i = 1000 \quad \text{and} \quad \sum_{i=1}^{50} S_i = 75$$

    a. Compute the control limit for the $\bar{x}$ and S control charts.

    b. Assume that all points on both charts plot within the control limits. What are the natural tolerance limits of the process?

    c. If the specification limits are 19 ± 4.0, what are your conclusions regarding the ability of the process to produce items conforming to specifications?

    d. Assuming that if an item exceeds the upper specification limit it can be reworked, while if it is below the lower specification limit it must be scrapped, what percent scrap and rework is the process now producing?

    e. If the process were centered at $\mu = 19.0$, what would be the effect on percent scrap and rework?

6-10 The fill volume of soft drink beverage bottles is an important quality characteristic. The volume is measured (approximately) by placing a gauge over the crown and comparing the height of the liquid in the neck of the bottle against a coded scale. On this scale, a reading of zero corresponds to the correct fill height. Fifteen samples of size $n = 10$ have been analyzed, and the fill heights are shown below.

Sample Number	x_1	x_2	x_3	x_4	x_5	x_6	x_7	x_8	x_9	x_{10}
1	2.5	0.5	2.0	-1.0	1.0	-1.0	0.5	1.5	0.5	-1.5
2	0.0	0.0	0.5	1.0	1.5	1.0	-1.0	1.0	1.5	-1.0
3	1.5	1.0	1.0	-1.0	0.0	-1.5	-1.0	-1.0	1.0	-1.0
4	0.0	0.5	-2.0	0.0	-1.0	1.5	-1.2	0.0	-2.0	-1.5
5	0.0	0.0	0.0	-0.5	0.5	1.0	-0.5	-0.5	0.0	0.0
6	1.0	-0.5	0.0	0.0	0.0	0.5	-1.0	1.0	-2.0	1.0
7	1.0	-1.0	-1.0	-1.0	0.0	1.5	0.0	1.0	0.0	0.0
8	0.0	-1.5	-0.5	1.5	0.0	0.0	0.0	-1.0	0.5	-0.5
9	-2.0	-1.5	1.5	1.5	0.0	0.0	0.5	1.0	0.0	1.0
10	-0.5	3.5	0.0	-1.0	-1.5	-1.5	-1.0	-1.0	1.0	0.5
11	0.0	1.5	0.0	0.0	2.0	-1.5	0.5	-0.5	2.0	-1.0
12	0.0	-2.0	-0.5	0.0	-0.5	2.0	1.5	0.0	0.5	-1.0
13	-1.0	-0.5	-0.5	-1.0	0.0	0.5	0.5	-1.5	-1.0	-1.0
14	0.5	1.0	-1.0	-0.5	-2.0	-1.0	-1.5	0.0	1.5	1.5
15	1.0	0.0	1.5	1.5	1.0	-1.0	0.0	1.0	-2.0	-1.5

a. Set up $\bar{x}$ and S control charts on this process. Does the process exhibit statistical control? If necessary, construct revised control limits.

b. Set up an R chart, and compare with the S chart in part (a).

c. Set up an S^2 chart, and compare with the S chart in part (a).

6-11 Control charts for $\bar{x}$ and R are maintained for an important quality characteristic. The sample size is $n = 7 \cdot \bar{x}$ and R are computed for each sample. After 35 samples, we have found that

$$\sum_{i=1}^{35} \bar{x}_i = 7805 \quad \text{and} \quad \sum_{i=1}^{35} R_i = 1200$$

a. Set up $\bar{x}$ and R charts using these data.

b. Assuming that both charts exhibit control, estimate the process mean and standard deviation.

c. If the quality characteristic is normally distributed and if the specifications are 220 ± 35, can the process meet the specifications? Estimate the fraction nonconforming.

d. Assuming the variance to remain constant, state where the process mean should be located to minimize the fraction nonconforming. What would be the value of the fraction nonconforming under these conditions?

6-12 Samples of size $n = 5$ are taken from a manufacturing process every hour. A quality characteristic is measured, and $\bar{x}$ and R are computed for each sample. After 25 samples have been analyzed, we have

$$\sum_{i=1}^{25} \bar{x}_i = 662.50 \quad \text{and} \quad \sum_{i=1}^{25} R_i = 9.00$$

a. Find the control limits for the $\bar{x}$ and R charts.

b. Assume that both charts exhibit control. If specifications are 26.40 ± 0.50, estimate the fraction nonconforming.

c. If the mean of the process were 26.40, what fraction nonconforming would result?

6-13 Samples of size $n = 5$ are collected from a process every half hour. After 50 samples have been collected, we calculate $\bar{\bar{x}} = 20.0$ and $\bar{S} = 1.5$. Assume that both charts exhibit control and that the quality characteristic is normally distributed.

a. Estimate the process standard deviation.

b. Find the control limits on the $\bar{x}$ and S charts.

c. If the process mean shifts to 22, what is the probability of concluding that the process is still in control?

6-14 An $\bar{x}$ chart is used to control the mean of a quality characteristic. It is known that $\sigma = 6.0$ and $n = 4$. The center line $= 200$, UCL $= 209$, and LCL $= 191$. If the process mean shifts to 188, find the probability that this shift is detected on the first subsequent sample.

6-15 A parameter of a part being produced on a lathe has specifications 100 ± 10. Control chart analysis indicates that the process is in control with $\bar{x} = 104$ and $\bar{R} = 9.30$. The control charts use samples of size $n = 5$. If we assume that the characteristic is normally distributed, can the mean be located (by adjusting the tool position) so that all output meets specifications? What is the present capability of the process?

6-16 A process is to be controlled with standard values $\mu = 10$ and $\sigma = 2.5$. The sample size is ten.

a. Find the center line and control limits for the $\bar{x}$ chart.

b. Find the center line and control limits for the R chart.

c. Find the center line and the control limits for the S chart.

6-17 Samples of $n = 5$ units are taken from a process every hour. The $\bar{x}$ and R values for a particular quality characteristic are determined. After 25 samples have been collected, we calculate $\bar{\bar{x}} = 20$ and $\bar{R} = 4.56$.

a. What are the 3-sigma control limits for $\bar{x}$ and R?

b. Both charts exhibit control. Estimate the process standard deviation.

c. Assume that the process output is normally distributed. If the specifications are 19 ± 5, what are your conclusions regarding the process capability?

d. If the process mean shifts to 24, what is the probability of not detecting this shift on the first subsequent sample?

6-18 Control charts for $\bar{x}$ and R are to be established to control the tensile strength of a metal part. Assume that tensile strength is normally distributed. Thirty samples of size $n = 6$ parts are collected over a period of time with the following results:

$$\sum_{i=1}^{36} \bar{x}_i = 6000 \quad \sum_{i=1}^{36} R_i = 150$$

a. Calculate control limits for $\bar{x}$ and R.

b. Both charts exhibit control. The specifications on tensile strength are 200 ± 5. What are your conclusions regarding process capability?

c. For the above $\bar{x}$ chart, find the β-risk when the true process mean is 199.

6-19 An $\bar{x}$ chart has a center line of 100, uses 3-sigma control limits, and is based on a sample size of nine. The process standard deviation is known to be six. If the process mean shifts from 100 to 92, what is the probability of detecting this shift on the first sample following the shift?

6-20 The following data were collected from a process manufacturing power supplies. The variable of interest is output voltage, and $n = 5$.

Sample Number	$\bar{x}$	R	Sample Number	$\bar{x}$	R
1	103	4	11	105	4
2	102	5	12	103	2
3	104	2	13	102	3
4	105	11	14	105	4
5	104	4	15	104	5
6	106	3	16	105	3
7	102	7	17	106	5
8	105	2	18	102	2
9	106	4	19	105	4
10	104	3	20	103	2

a. Compute center lines and control limits suitable for controlling future production.

b. Assume that the quality characteristic is normally distributed. Estimate the process standard deviation.

c. What are the apparent 3-sigma natural tolerance limits of the process?

d. What would be your estimate of the process fraction nonconforming if the specifications on the characteristic were 103 ± 4?

e. What approaches to reduction of the fraction nonconforming can you suggest?

6-21 Control charts on $\bar{x}$ and R for samples of size $n = 5$ are to be maintained on the tensile strength in pounds of a yarn. To start the charts, 30 samples were selected, and the mean and range of each computed. This yields

$$\sum_{i=1}^{30} \bar{x}_i = 607.8 \quad \text{and} \quad \sum_{i=1}^{30} R_i = 144$$

a. Compute the center line and control limits for the $\bar{x}$ and R control charts.

b. Suppose both charts exhibit control. There is a single lower specification limit of 16 lb. If strength is normally distributed, what fraction of yarn would fail to meet specifications?

6-22 Specifications on a cigar lighter detent are 0.3220 and 0.3200 in. Samples of size five are taken every 45 min with the following results (measured as deviations from 0.3210 in 0.0001 in.).

Sample Number	x_1	x_2	x_3	x_4	x_5
1	1	9	6	9	6
2	9	4	3	0	3
3	0	9	0	3	2
4	1	1	0	2	1
5	−3	0	−1	0	−4
6	−7	2	0	0	2
7	−3	−1	−1	0	−2
8	0	−2	−3	−3	−2
9	2	0	−1	−3	−1
10	0	2	−1	−1	2
11	−3	−2	−1	−1	2
12	−16	2	0	−4	−1
13	−6	−3	0	0	−8
14	−3	−5	5	0	5
15	−1	−1	−1	−2	−1

a. Set up an R chart and examine the process for statistical control.

b. What parameters would you recommend for an R for on-line control?

c. Estimate the standard deviation of the process.

d. What is the process capability?

6-23 Two parts are assembled as shown below. Assume that the dimensions x and y are normally distributed with means μ_x and μ_y and standard deviations σ_x and σ_y, respectively. The parts are produced on different machines and are assembled at random. Control charts are maintained on each dimension for the range of each sample ($n = 5$). Both range charts are in control.

a. Given that for 20 samples on the range chart controlling x and 10 samples on the range chart controlling y, we have

$$\sum_{i=1}^{20} R_{x_i} = 18.608 \quad \text{and} \quad \sum_{i=1}^{10} R_{y_i} = 6.978$$

Estimate σ_x and σ_y.

b. If it is desired that the probability of a smaller clearance (i.e., $x - y$) than 0.09 should be 0.006, what distance between the average dimensions (i.e., $\mu_x - \mu_y$) should be specified?

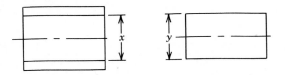

6-24 Control charts for $\bar{x}$ and R are maintained on the tensile strength of a metal fastener. After 30 samples of size $n = 6$ are analyzed, we find that

$$\sum_{i=1}^{30} \bar{x}_i = 12,870 \quad \text{and} \quad \sum_{i=1}^{30} R_i = 1350$$

a. Compute control limits on the R chart.

b. Assuming that the R chart exhibits control, estimate the parameters μ and σ.

c. If the process output is normally distributed, and if the specifications are 440 ± 40, can the process meet the specifications? Estimate the fraction nonconforming.

d. If the variance remains constant, where should the mean be located to minimize the fraction nonconforming?

6-25 Control charts for $\bar{x}$ and S are maintained on a quality characteristic. The sample size is $n = 4$. After 30 samples, we obtain

$$\sum_{i=1}^{30} \bar{x}_i = 12{,}870 \quad \text{and} \quad \sum_{i=1}^{30} S_i = 410$$

a. Find the 3-sigma limits for the S chart.

b. Assuming that both charts exhibit control, estimate the parameters μ and σ.

6-26 An $\bar{x}$ chart is to be established with the standard values $\mu = 100$, $\sigma = 8$, and $n = 4$. Find the following:

a. The 2-sigma control limits.

b. The 0.005 probability limits.

6-27 An $\bar{x}$ chart has parameters as follows:

$$\text{UCL} = 104$$
$$\text{Center line} = 100$$
$$\text{LCL} = 96$$
$$n = 5$$

Suppose the process quality characteristic being controlled has a true mean of 98 and a standard deviation of 8. What is the probability that the control chart would exhibit lack of control by at least the third point plotted?

6-28 Consider the $\bar{x}$ chart defined in Exercise 6-27. Find the average run length for the chart.

6-29 Control charts for $\bar{x}$ and S with $n = 4$ are maintained on a quality characteristic. The parameters of these charts are as follows:

$\bar{x}$ **chart**	S **chart**
UCL = 201.88	UCL = 2.266
Center line = 200.00	Center line = 1.000
LCL = 198.12	LCL = 0

Both charts exhibit control. Specifications on the quality characteristic are 197.50 and 202.50. What can be said about the ability of the process to produce product that conforms to specifications?

6-30 A control procedure for a quality characteristic uses both an $\bar{x}$ and an S chart. The charts are to be based on the standard values $\mu = 200$ and $\sigma = 10$, with $n = 4$.

a. Find 3-sigma control limits for the S chart.

b. Find a center line and control limits for the $\bar{x}$ chart such that the probability of a type I error is 0.05.

6-31 Specifications on a part are 600 ± 20. $\bar{x}$ and R charts are maintained on this part and have been in control over a long period of time. The parameters of these control charts are as follows ($n = 9$):

$\bar{x}$ chart	R chart
UCL = 616	UCL = 32.36
Center line = 610	Center line = 17.82
LCL = 604	LCL = 3.28

   a. What are your conclusions regarding the capability of the process to produce items within specifications?

   b. Construct an OC curve for the $\bar{x}$ curve assuming that σ is constant.

6-32 Thirty samples each of size seven have been collected in order to establish control over a process. The following data were collected:

$$\sum_{i=1}^{30} \bar{x}_i = 2700 \qquad \sum_{i=1}^{30} R_i = 120$$

   a. Calculate trial control limits for the two charts.

   b. On the assumption that the R chart is in control, estimate the process standard deviation.

   c. Suppose an S chart were desired. What would be the appropriate control limits and center line?

6-33 An $\bar{x}$ chart is to be established based on the standard values $\mu = 600$ and $\sigma = 12$, with $n = 9$. The control limits are to be based on an α-risk of 0.01. What are the appropriate control limits?

6-34 $\bar{x}$ and R charts with $n = 4$ are used to monitor a quality characteristic. The control chart parameters are

$\bar{x}$ chart	R chart
UCL = 815	UCL = 46.98
Center line = 800	Center line = 20.59
LCL = 785	LCL = 0

Both charts exhibit control. What is the probability that a shift in the process mean to 790 will be detected on the first sample following the shift?

6-35 Consider the $\bar{x}$ chart in Exercise 6-34. Find the average run length for the chart.

6-36 Control charts for $\bar{x}$ and R are in use with the following parameters:

$\bar{x}$ chart	R chart
UCL = 363.0	UCL = 16.18
Center line = 360.0	Center line = 8.91
LCL = 357.0	LCL = 1.64

The sample size is $n = 9$. Both charts exhibit control.

   a. What is the α-risk associated with the $\bar{x}$ chart?

   b. Specifications on this quality characteristic are 358 ± 6. What are your conclusions regarding the ability of the process to produce items within specifications?

c. Suppose the mean shifts to 357. What is the probability that the shift will not be detected on the first sample following the shift?

d. What would be the appropriate control limits for the $\bar{x}$ chart if the type I error probability were to be 0.01?

6-37 A normally distributed quality characteristic is controlled through use of an $\bar{x}$ and an R chart. These charts have the following parameters ($n = 4$):

$\bar{x}$ chart	R chart
UCL = 626.0	UCL = 18.795
Center line = 620.0	Center line = 8.236
LCL = 614.0	LCL = 0

Both charts exhibit control.

a. What is the estimated standard deviation of the process?

b. Suppose an S chart were to be substituted for the R chart. What would be the appropriate parameters of the S chart?

c. If specifications on the product were 610 ± 15, what would be your estimate of the process fraction nonconforming?

d. What could be done to reduce this fraction nonconforming?

e. What is the probability of detecting a shift in the process mean to 610 or the first sample following the shift (σ remains constant)?

f. What is the probability of detecting the shift in part (e) by at least the third sample after the shift occurs?

6-38 Control charts for $\bar{x}$ and S have been maintained on a process and have exhibited statistical control. The sample size is $n = 6$. The control chart parameters are as follows:

$\bar{x}$ chart	S chart
UCL = 708.20	UCL = 3.420
Center line = 706.00	Center line = 1.738
LCL = 703.80	LCL = 0.052

a. Estimate the mean and standard deviation of the process.

b. Estimate the natural tolerance limits for the process.

c. Assume that the process output is well modeled by a normal distribution. If specifications are 703 and 709, estimate the fraction nonconforming.

d. Suppose the process mean shifts to 702.00 while the standard deviation remains constant. What is the probability of an out-of-control signal occurring on the first sample following the shift?

e. For the shift in part (d), what is the probability of detecting the shift by at least the third subsequent sample?

6-39 The following $\bar{x}$ and S charts based on $n = 4$ have shown statistical control:

$\bar{x}$ chart	S chart
UCL = 710	UCL = 18.08
Center line = 700	Center line = 7.979
LCL = 690	LCL = 0

a. Estimate the process parameters μ and σ.

b. If the specifications are at 705 ± 15, and the process output is normally distributed, estimate the fraction nonconforming.

c. For the $\bar{x}$ chart, find the probability of a type I error, assuming σ is constant.

d. Suppose the process mean shifts to 693 and the standard deviation simultaneously shifts to 12. Find the probability of detecting this shift on the $\bar{x}$ chart on the first subsequent sample.

e. For the shift of part (d), find the average run length.

6-40 One-pound coffee cans are filled by a machine, sealed, and then weighed automatically After adjusting for the weight of the can, any package that weighs less than 16 oz is cut out of the conveyor. The weights of 25 successive cans are shown below. Set up a moving-range control chart and a control chart for individuals. Estimate the mean and standard deviation of the amount of coffee packed in each can. If the process remains in control at this level, what percentage of cans will be underfilled?

Can Number	Weight	Can Number	Weight
1	16.11	14	16.12
2	16.08	15	16.10
3	16.12	16	16.08
4	16.10	17	16.13
5	16.10	18	16.15
6	16.11	19	16.12
7	16.12	20	16.10
8	16.09	21	16.08
9	16.12	22	16.07
10	16.10	23	16.11
11	16.09	24	16.13
12	16.07	25	16.10
13	16.13		

6-41 Fifteen successive heats of a steel alloy are tested for hardness. The resulting data are shown below. Set up a control chart for the moving range and a control chart for individual hardness measurements.

Heat	Hardness (coded)	Heat	Hardness (coded)
1	52	9	58
2	51	10	51
3	54	11	54
4	55	12	59
5	50	13	53
6	52	14	54
7	50	15	55
8	51		

6-42 The purity of a chemical product is measured on each batch. Purity determinations for 20 successive batches are shown below. Is the process in statistical control?

Batch	Purity	Batch	Purity
1	0.81	11	0.81
2	0.82	12	0.83
3	0.81	13	0.81
4	0.82	14	0.82
5	0.82	15	0.81
6	0.83	16	0.85
7	0.81	17	0.83
8	0.80	18	0.87
9	0.81	19	0.86
10	0.82	20	0.84

6-43 In the semiconductor industry, the production of microcircuits involves many steps. The wafer fabrication process typically builds these microcircuits on silicon wafers, and there are many microcircuits per wafer. Each production lot consists of between 16 and 48 wafers. Some processing steps treat each wafer separately, so that the batch size for that step is one wafer. It is usually necessary to estimate several components of variation: within-wafer, between-wafer, between-lot; and the total variation.

a. Suppose that one wafer is randomly selected from each lot and that a single measurement on a critical dimension of interest is taken. Which components of variation could be estimated with these data? What type of control charts would you recommend?

b. Suppose that each wafer is tested at five fixed locations (say, the center and four points at the circumference). The average and range of these within-wafer measurements are $\bar{x}_{ww}$ and R_{ww}, respectively. What components of variability are estimated using control charts based on these data?

c. Suppose that one measurement point on each wafer is selected and that this measurement is recorded for five consecutive wafers. The average and range of these between-wafer measurements are $\bar{x}_{BW}$ and R_{BW}, respectively. What components of variability are estimated using control charts based on these data? Would it be necessary to run separate $\bar{x}$ and R charts for all five locations on the wafer?

d. Consider the question in part (c). How would your answer change if the test sites on each wafer were randomly selected and varied from wafer to wafer?

e. What type of control charts and rational subgroup scheme would you recommend to control the batch-to-batch variability?

6-44 Consider the situation described in Exercise 6-43. A critical dimension (measured in μm) is of interest to the process engineer. Suppose that five fixed positions are used on each wafer (position 1 is the center) and that two consecutive wafers are selected from each batch. The data that result from several batches are shown below.

a. What can you say about overall process capability?

b. Can you construct control charts that allow within-wafer variability to be evaluated?

c. What control charts would you establish to evaluate variability between wafers? Set up these charts and use them to draw conclusions about the process.

d. What control charts would you use to evaluate lot-to-lot variability? Set up these charts and use them to draw conclusions about lot-to-lot variability.

Lot Number	Wafer Number	Position 1	2	3	4	5
1	1	2.15	2.13	2.08	2.12	2.10
	2	2.13	2.10	2.04	2.08	2.05
2	1	2.02	2.01	2.06	2.05	2.08
	2	2.03	2.09	2.07	2.06	2.04
3	1	2.13	2.12	2.10	2.11	2.08
	2	2.03	2.08	2.03	2.09	2.07
4	1	2.04	2.01	2.10	2.11	2.09
	2	2.07	2.14	2.12	2.08	2.09
5	1	2.16	2.17	2.13	2.18	2.10
	2	2.17	2.13	2.10	2.09	2.13
6	1	2.04	2.06	2.00	2.10	2.08
	2	2.03	2.10	2.05	2.07	2.04
7	1	2.04	2.02	2.01	2.00	2.05
	2	2.06	2.04	2.03	2.08	2.10
8	1	2.13	2.10	2.10	2.15	2.13
	2	2.10	2.09	2.13	2.14	2.11
9	1	2.00	2.03	2.08	2.07	2.08
	2	2.01	2.03	2.06	2.05	2.04
10	1	2.04	2.08	2.09	2.10	2.01
	2	2.06	2.04	2.07	2.04	2.01
11	1	2.15	2.13	2.14	2.09	2.08
	2	2.11	2.13	2.10	2.14	2.10
12	1	2.03	2.06	2.05	2.01	2.00
	2	2.04	2.08	2.03	2.10	2.07
13	1	2.05	2.03	2.05	2.09	2.08
	2	2.08	2.01	2.03	2.04	2.10
14	1	2.08	2.04	2.05	2.01	2.08
	2	2.09	2.11	2.06	2.04	2.05
15	1	2.14	2.13	2.10	2.10	2.08
	2	2.13	2.10	2.09	2.13	2.15
16	1	2.06	2.08	2.05	2.03	2.09
	2	2.03	2.01	2.00	2.06	2.05
17	1	2.05	2.03	2.08	2.01	2.04
	2	2.06	2.05	2.03	2.05	2.00
18	1	2.03	2.08	2.04	2.00	2.03
	2	2.04	2.03	2.05	2.01	2.04
19	1	2.16	2.13	2.10	2.13	2.12
	2	2.13	2.15	2.18	2.19	2.13
20	1	2.06	2.03	2.04	2.09	2.10
	2	2.01	2.00	2.05	2.08	2.06

Chapter 7

Cumulative-Sum and Exponentially Weighted Moving-Average Control Charts

Chapters 4, 5, and 6 have concentrated on the basic methods of SPC. The control charts discussed in these chapters are usually called Shewhart control charts, as they are based on the principles of control charts developed by Dr. Walter A. Shewhart. A major disadvantage of any Shewhart control chart is that it only uses the information about the process contained in the last plotted point, and it ignores any information given by the entire sequence of points. This feature makes the Shewhart control chart relatively insensitive to small shifts in the process, say on the order of about 1.5σ, or less. Of course, other criteria can be applied to Shewhart charts, such as tests for runs and the use of warning limits, which attempt to incorporate information from the entire set of points into the decision procedure. However, the use of these supplemental sensitizing rules reduces the simplicity and ease of interpretation of the Shewhart control chart.

Two very effective alternatives to the Shewhart control chart may be used when small shifts are of interest: the cumulative-sum (or cusum) control chart, and the exponentially weighted moving-average (EWMA) control chart. These control charts will be presented in this chapter.

7-1 THE CUMULATIVE-SUM CONTROL CHART

7-1.1 Basic Principles: The Cusum Control Chart for Sample Averages

Consider the data in Table 7-1, column (a). The first 20 of these observations were drawn at random from a normal distribution with mean $\mu = 10$ and standard deviation $\sigma = 1$. These observations have been plotted on a Shewhart control chart in Figure 7-1. The center line and 3-sigma control limits on this chart are at

$$UCL = 13$$
$$CL = 10$$
$$LCL = 7$$

Notice that all 20 observations plot in control.

The last 10 observations in column (a) of Table 7-1 were drawn from a normal distribution with mean $\mu = 10.5$ and standard deviation $\sigma = 1$. Consequently, we can think of these last 10 observations as having been drawn from the process when it is out of control, that is, after the process has experienced a shift in the mean of 0.5σ. These last 10 observations are also plotted on the control chart in Figure 7-1. None of these points plots outside the control limits, so we have no strong evidence that the process is out of control. Notice that there is a slight indication of a shift in process level for the last 10 points, as all but two of the points plot above the center line. However, if we rely on the traditional signal of an out-of-control process, one or more points beyond a 3-sigma control limit, then the Shewhart control chart has failed to detect the shift.

The reason for this failure, of course, is the relatively small magnitude of the shift. The Shewhart $\bar{x}$ chart for averages is very effective if the magnitude of the shift is 1.5σ to 2σ or larger. For smaller shifts, it may not be very effective. The cumulative-sum (or cusum) control chart is a good alternative when small shifts are important.

The cusum chart directly incorporates all the information in the sequence of sample values by plotting the cumulative sums of the deviations of the sample values from a target value. For example, suppose that samples of size $n \geq 1$ are collected, and $\bar{x}_j$ is the average of the jth sample. Then if μ_0 is the target for the process mean, the cumulative-sum control chart is formed by plotting the quantity

$$S_i = \sum_{j=1}^{i} (\bar{x}_j - \mu_0) \tag{7-1}$$

against the sample number i. S_i is called the cumulative sum up to and including the ith sample. Because they combine information from *several* samples, cumulative-sum charts are more effective than Shewhart charts for detecting small process shifts. Furthermore, they are particularly effective with samples of $n = 1$. This makes the cumulative-sum control chart a good candidate for use in the chemical and process industries where rational subgroups are frequently of size one, and in discrete parts manufacturing with automatic measurement of each part and on-line control using a microcomputer directly at the work center.

Cumulative-sum control charts were first proposed by Page (1954) and have been studied by many authors; in particular, see Ewan (1963), Page (1961), Johnson (1961), Johnson and Leone (1962a, 1962b, 1962c), and Lucas (1976). In this section, we concentrate on the cumulative-sum chart for the process mean. It is possible

Table 7-1
Data for the cusum example

Sample, i	(a) x_i	(b) $x_i - 10$	(c) $S_i = (x_i - 10) + S_{i-1}$
1	9.45	−0.55	−0.55
2	7.99	−2.01	−2.56
3	9.29	−0.71	−3.27
4	11.66	1.66	−1.61
5	12.16	2.16	0.55
6	10.18	0.18	0.73
7	8.04	−1.96	−1.23
8	11.46	1.46	0.23
9	9.20	−0.80	−0.57
10	10.34	0.34	−0.23
11	9.03	−0.97	−1.20
12	11.47	1.47	0.27
13	10.51	0.51	0.78
14	9.40	−0.60	0.18
15	10.08	0.08	0.26
16	9.37	−0.63	−0.37
17	10.62	0.62	0.25
18	10.31	0.31	0.56
19	8.52	−1.48	−0.92
20	10.84	0.84	−0.08
21	10.40	0.40	0.32
22	8.83	−1.17	−0.85
23	11.79	1.79	0.94
24	11.00	1.00	1.94
25	10.10	0.10	2.04
26	10.58	0.58	2.62
27	9.88	−0.12	2.50
28	11.12	1.12	3.62
29	10.81	0.81	4.43
30	10.02	0.02	4.45

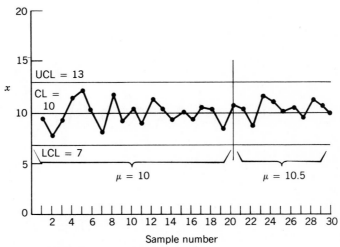

Figure 7-1
A Shewhart control chart for the data in Table 7-1.

to devise cumulative-sum procedures for other variables, such as Poisson and binomial variables for modeling nonconformities and process fallout, or sample standard deviations and ranges. See Johnson and Leone (1962a, 1962b, 1962c) and Page (1963).

We note that if the process remains in control at the target value μ_0, the cumulative sum defined in Equation (7-1) should fluctuate stochastically around zero. (In fact, the cusum is a random walk with mean zero.) However, if the mean shifts upward to some value $\mu_1 > \mu_0$, say, then an upward or positive drift will develop in the cumulative sum S_i. Conversely, if the mean shifts downward to some $\mu_1 < \mu_0$, then a downward or negative drift in S_i will develop. Therefore, if a trend develops in the plotted points either upward or downward, we should consider this as evidence that the process mean has shifted, and a search for some assignable cause should be performed.

This theory can be easily demonstrated by using the data in column (a) of Table 7-1 again. To apply the cusum in Equation (7-1) to these observations, we would take $\bar{x}_i = x_i$ (since our sample size is $n = 1$) and let the target value $\mu_0 = 10$. Therefore, the cusum becomes

$$S_i = \sum_{j=1}^{i} (x_j - 10)$$
$$= (x_i - 10) + \sum_{j=1}^{i-1} (x_j - 10)$$
$$= (x_i - 10) + S_{i-1}$$

Column (b) of Table 7-1 contains the differences $x_i - 10$, and the cumulative sums are computed in column (c). The starting value for the cusum, S_0, is taken to be zero. Figure 7-2 plots the cusum from column (c) of Table 7-1. Notice that for the first 20 observations where $\mu = 10$, the cusum tends to vary randomly around zero. However, in the last 10 observations, where the mean has shifted to $\mu = 10.5$, an upward trend develops.

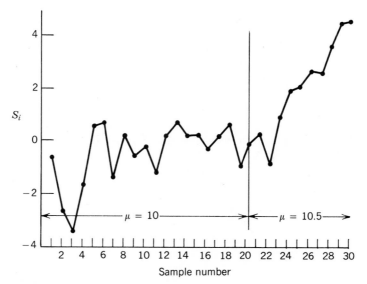

Figure 7-2
Plot of the cumulative sum from column (c) of Table 7-1.

It would be helpful to have a formal procedure for determining whether the process is out of control. One way to do so is by using the V-mask procedure proposed by Barnhard (1959). A typical V mask is shown in Figure 7-3a. The decision procedure consists of placing the V mask on the cumulative-sum control chart with the point O on the last value of S_i and the line OP parallel to the horizontal axis. If all the previous cumulative sums, $S_1, S_2, \ldots, S_i$ lie within the two arms of the V mask, the process is in control. However, if any S_j lies outside the arms of the mask, the process is considered to be out of control. In actual use, the V mask would be applied to each new point on the cusum chart as soon as it was plotted. In the example shown in Figure 7-3b, an upward shift in the mean

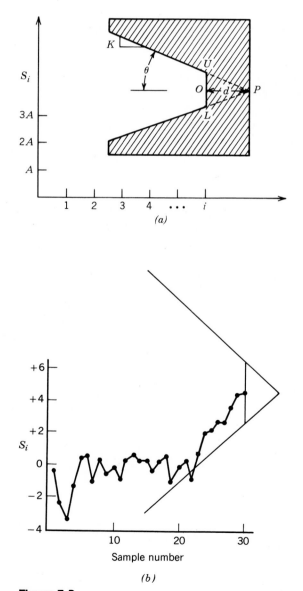

(a)

(b)

Figure 7-3
The cumulative-sum control chart. (a) The V mask and scaling. (b) The cumulative-sum control chart in operation.

is indicated, since the point corresponding to sample 22 now lies below the lower arm of the mask, when the V mask is centered on the thirtieth observation. If the point lies above the upper arm, a downward shift in the mean is indicated. Thus, the V mask forms a visual frame of reference similar to the control limits on an ordinary Shewhart control chart.

Once an out-of-control point has been detected, we can directly estimate the new process level from the cusum. On a cusum chart, the mean process level is determined by the slope of the plotted points. If the process is operating with the mean equal to the target value μ_0, the slope is zero. For a sustained pattern with constant slope running from observation j to observation i, the estimate of the mean over this segment is

$$\hat{\mu} = \mu_0 + \frac{S_i - S_j}{i - j} \tag{7-2}$$

We can apply this to the cusum chart in Figure 7-3b. Since sample number 22 was out of control, we will compute the new estimate of the mean over the interval from $j = 21$ to $i = 30$. (Notice that we will make j equal to the period just before the shift was detected.) Since $S_{21} = 0.32$ and $S_{30} = 4.45$ (refer to Table 7-1), Equation (7-2) becomes

$$\hat{\mu} = \mu_0 + \frac{S_i - S_j}{i - j}$$
$$= 10 + \frac{4.45 - 0.32}{30 - 21}$$
$$= 10.46$$

Recall that the true mean over the interval from the twenty-first to the thirtieth observation was 10.5.

The performance of the cumulative-sum control chart is determined by the parameters of the V mask. One may use the *lead distance d* and the angle θ to define the V mask. If $\sigma_{\bar{x}}$ is the standard deviation of $\bar{x}$, α is the advertized probability of incorrectly concluding that a shift has occurred (a false alarm), β is the advertized probability of failing to detect a shift in the mean, and Δ is the shift in the process mean that it is desired to detect, then a widely used design procedure for the cumulative-sum control chart is to choose

$$d = \left(\frac{2}{\delta^2}\right) \ln\left(\frac{1-\beta}{\alpha}\right) \tag{7-3}$$

and

$$\theta = \tan^{-1}\left(\frac{\Delta}{2A}\right) \tag{7-4}$$

where

$$\delta = \frac{\Delta}{\sigma_{\bar{x}}} \tag{7-5}$$

is the magnitude of the shift that we wish to detect in standard deviation of $\bar{x}$ units and A is a scale factor relating the vertical scale unit to the horizontal scale unit. It is usually recommended that A lie between $\sigma_{\bar{x}}$ and $2\sigma_{\bar{x}}$, with $A = 2\sigma_{\bar{x}}$ being the preferred value. If β is small, then (7-3) simplifies to

$$d = -2\frac{\ln \alpha}{\delta^2} \tag{7-6}$$

Note that if the sample consists of a single observation ($n = 1$), then use the process σ instead of $\sigma_{\bar{x}}$ in the calculations in Equations (7-3) through (7-6).

In constructing a V mask, it is helpful to define the following additional quantities:

H = The decision interval of the procedure, or the half-height of the V mask at point O. This is the distance OU (or OL) in Figure 7-3a.

h = The decision interval in multiples of the standard deviation of the sample statistic; i.e., $H = h\sigma_{\bar{x}}$.

K = The slope of the arms of the V mask. It is also called the reference value in tabular cusum schemes; see Sections 7-1.3 and 7-1.4.

k = The slope of the arms of the V mask in multiples of the standard deviation of the sample statistic; i.e., $K = k\sigma_{\bar{x}}$.

It can be readily shown that

$$\tan(\theta) = \frac{\Delta}{2A} = \frac{\delta\sigma_{\bar{x}}}{2(2\sigma_{\bar{x}})} = \frac{\delta}{2(2)}, \tag{7-7}$$

and since $K = k\sigma_{\bar{x}}$ is the slope of the V-mask arms per sample interval, and one sample interval equals $A = 2\sigma_{\bar{x}}$ units on the cusum scale,

$$\tan(\theta) = \frac{K}{A} = \frac{k\sigma_{\bar{x}}}{2\sigma_{\bar{x}}} = \frac{k}{2}. \tag{7-8}$$

From (7-7) and (7-8) we obtain

$$k = \frac{\delta}{2} \tag{7-9a}$$

or

$$K = \frac{\Delta}{2} = \frac{\delta\sigma_{\bar{x}}}{2} \tag{7-9b}$$

Also,

$$\tan(\theta) = \frac{H}{Ad} = \frac{h\sigma_{\bar{x}}}{(2\sigma_{\bar{x}})d} = \frac{h}{2d} \tag{7-10}$$

so that

$$h = 2d \tan(\theta) \qquad \text{(7-11a)}$$

or

$$H = 2d\sigma_{\bar{x}} \tan(\theta). \qquad \text{(7-11b)}$$

Example 7-1

Designing a V Mask—I

To illustrate how the above relationships are actually used to design a V mask, consider the data in Table 7-1. We know that $\sigma = 1$ (usually in practice σ is unknown and must be estimated either from an R chart or from a previous capability study), $n = 1$ so that in each period we will observe an individual measurement x_j, and we wish to design a V mask that would be effective in detecting a shift of 1.5σ. We choose $\alpha = 0.005$, and from (7-5) we find that

$$\delta = \frac{\Delta}{\sigma_{\bar{x}}} = \frac{\Delta}{\sigma} = \frac{1.5\sigma}{\sigma} = 1.5$$

The lead distance d is found from (7-6):

$$d = -2 \frac{\ln \alpha}{\delta^2} = -2 \frac{\ln(0.005)}{(1.5)^2} = 4.71$$

The angle θ is found from (7-4) using $A = 2\sigma_{\bar{x}} = 2\sigma = 2(1) = 2$ and $\Delta = 1.5\sigma = 1.5(1) = 1.5$

$$\theta = \tan^{-1}\left(\frac{\Delta}{2A}\right) = \tan^{-1}\left[\frac{1.5}{2(2)}\right] = 20.55°$$

We will round these values to $d = 5$ and $\theta = 21°$. To construct the V mask, it is easier to parameterize the mask in terms of H and K. To find H, use Equation (7-11b):

$$\begin{aligned} H &= 2d\sigma_{\bar{x}} \tan(\theta) \\ &= 2(5)(1) \tan(21°) \\ &= 3.8 \end{aligned}$$

and to find K use Equation (7-9b):

$$K = \frac{\Delta}{2} = \frac{1.5}{2} = 0.75$$

The V mask is shown in Figure 7-4. We drew this mask by first scaling the cusum axis using $A = 2\sigma_{\bar{x}} = 2(1) = 2$ (so that one unit on the sample number scale

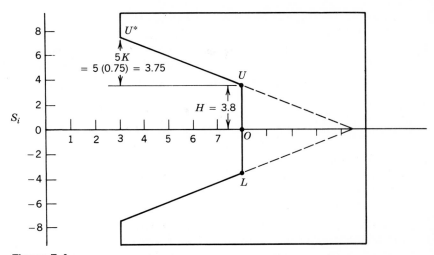

Figure 7-4
Design of the V mask in Example 7-1.

corresponds to 2 units on the cusum scale). Then we drew the line OU (the length of this line is $H = 3.8$) and located the point U^* by moving a distance 5 units on the sample number scale and plotting U^* on the cusum scale at $H + 5K$. The line connecting U and U^* is the upper arm of the V mask. The lower arm can be drawn similarly.

Because the advertized α and β risks for the cusum in the above design procedure do not closely match the actual risks, most authors have adopted average run length or ARL as a method of summarizing cusum performance. Recall that the ARL is the average number of sample points that must be plotted before a point indicates an out-of-control condition. For any Shewhart control chart, the ARL is

$$\text{ARL} = \frac{1}{p} \tag{7-12}$$

where p is the probability that a single point exceeds the control limits. Thus, for the $\bar{x}$ chart with the usual 3-sigma limits, $p = 0.0027$ is the probability that a single point falls outside the control limits when the process is in control, so the ARL of the $\bar{x}$ chart is

$$\text{ARL} = \frac{1}{p} = \frac{1}{0.0027} = 370$$

when the process is in control. That is, even if the process remains in control, an out-of-control signal will be generated every 370 samples, on the average. For the cumulative-sum control chart parameters in Example 7-1 obtained from

Equations (7-4) and (7-6), the ARL when the process is in control is approximately 500. In the next section we discuss how to design a cumulative-sum control chart to obtain a particular ARL curve.

Cumulative-sum control charts have several advantages relative to Shewhart control charts. First, they are more effective in detecting relatively small shifts in the process mean, say on the order of $0.5\sigma_{\bar{x}}$ to about $2\sigma_{\bar{x}}$. Over this region the cumulative-sum control chart will detect shifts approximately twice as quickly (or with a smaller sample size) as the corresponding Shewhart chart. Second, the process shift is often easy to detect visually by the change in slope of the plotted points. Finally, it is often relatively easy to detect the point at which the shift occurs simply by visual examination of the plotted data, noting where the change in slope occured.

Two disadvantages of the cumulative-sum control chart should be noted. First, and perhaps most important, the cumulative-sum control chart can be very slow to detect large process shifts. Lucas (1973) has proposed a modification of the V mask to improve cumulative-sum control chart performance relative to large shifts. His procedure is briefly discussed in Section 7-1.5, along with other suggestions to improve cusum performance. Second, the cumulative-sum control chart is not a very effective procedure for analyzing past data to detect control in a process or to bring a process into control. Diagnosis of patterns on the cumulative-sum control chart is very difficult because the usual assumption in pattern recognition is that the sequence of points is uncorrelated. The cumulative sums are not uncorrelated because successive values of S_{i-1} and S_i differ by only one observation. Consequently, the cumulative-sum control chart will often exhibit runs or other patterns that are an artifact of this correlation.

7-1.2 Designing a Cumulative-Sum Control Chart to obtain a Particular ARL

The standard design given in Equations (7-3) and (7-4) for the parameters of the V mask may be thought of as analogous to the use of 3-sigma control limits on Shewhart control charts; that is, they will work satisfactorily in many situations. However, in some cases, the analyst may wish to design a cumulative-sum control chart that has certain properties. The usual basis for the design of a cumulative-sum control chart is the ARL. In general, we would like the ARL of the chart to be long when the process is in control and very short when the process is out of control. Let $L(\delta)$ be the ARL of the control chart when the process mean differs from the in-control or target value μ_0 by $\delta\sigma_{\bar{x}}$. We call $L(\delta)$ the ARL curve of the cumulative-sum control chart.

Goel and Wu (1971) have published a nomogram that is useful in the design of cumulative-sum control charts. Duncan (1974) shows how to use this nomogram to design a cumulative-sum control chart with an ARL curve that passes through two specified points, one at $[L(0), 0]$, and the other at $[L(\delta), \delta]$. Note that this is analogous to finding an acceptance-sampling plan or a Shewhart control chart whose OC curve passes through two specified points.

Bowker and Lieberman (1972) provide a table for choosing d and θ to minimize $L(\delta)$ when the analyst is able to specify $L(0)$ and δ. This is reproduced as Table 7-2. This table gives the values of $(A/\sigma_{\bar{x}}) \tan \theta$, d and the minimum value of $L(\delta)$ for various values of δ and $L(0)$.

Table 7-2
Cumulative-sum control chart parameters

		$L(0) =$ Average run length when process is in control.					
		50	100	200	300	400	500
	$(A/\sigma_{\bar{x}}) \tan \theta$	0.125			0.195		0.248
0.25	d	47.6			46.2		37.4
	$L(0.25)$	28.3			74.0		94.0
	$(A/\sigma_{\bar{x}}) \tan \theta$	0.25	0.28	0.29	0.28	0.28	0.27
0.50	d	17.5	18.2	21.4	24.7	27.3	29.6
	$L(0.5)$	15.8	19.0	24.0	26.7	29.0	30.0
	$(A/\sigma_{\bar{x}}) \tan \theta$	0.375	0.375	0.375	0.375	0.375	0.375
0.75	d	9.2	11.3	13.8	15.0	16.2	16.8
	$L(0.75)$	8.9	11.0	13.4	14.5	15.7	16.5
	$(A/\sigma_{\bar{x}}) \tan \theta$	0.50	0.50	0.50	0.50	0.50	0.50
1.0	d	5.7	6.9	8.2	9.0	9.6	10.0
	$L(1.0)$	6.1	7.4	8.7	9.4	10.0	10.5
	$(A/\sigma_{\bar{x}}) \tan \theta$	0.75	0.75	0.75	0.75	0.75	0.75
1.5	d	2.7	3.3	3.9	4.3	4.5	4.7
	$L(1.5)$	3.4	4.0	4.6	5.0	5.2	5.4
	$(A/\sigma_{\bar{x}}) \tan \theta$	1.0	1.0	1.0	1.0	1.0	1.0
2.0	d	1.5	1.9	2.2	2.4	2.5	2.7
	$L(2.0)$	2.26	2.63	2.96	3.15	3.3	3.4

(Left axis label: δ = Deviation from Target Value (in standard deviations))

Source: Adapted from A. H. Bowker and G. J. Lieberman, *Engineering Statistics*, 2nd ed., Prentice-Hall, Englewood Cliffs, N.J., 1972, with permission of the publisher.

Example 7-2

Designing a V mask—II

To illustrate the use of Table 7-2, suppose we wish to detect a shift of $\pm 1.5\sigma_{\bar{x}}$ from the target value of μ_0, and we want the in-control ARL $L(0) = 500$. From Table 7-2, we find that $d = 4.7$ and $(A/\sigma_{\bar{x}}) \tan \theta = 0.75$. If $A = 2\sigma_{\bar{x}}$, which is the usual choice, then

$$(A/\sigma_{\bar{x}}) \tan \theta = 0.75$$
$$2 \tan(\theta) = 0.75$$

or

$$\theta = 20.55°$$

Notice that this is identical to the cusum design from Example 7-1. The out-of-control ARL is found from Table 7-2 as $L(1.5) = 5.4$ periods.

Example 7-3

Designing a V mask—III

To illustrate the design of a cusum procedure for detecting a smaller shift, suppose that we want to detect a shift of $\pm 1.0\sigma_{\bar{x}}$ from the target value of μ_0 with an in-control ARL $L(0) = 500$. Table 7-2 shows that a V mask with $d = 10$ and $(A/\sigma_{\bar{x}}) \tan \theta = 0.50$ will give the desired performance. If $A = 2\sigma_{\bar{x}}$, then the angle θ is found from $(A/\sigma_{\bar{x}}) \tan \theta = 0.50$, or $\theta = 14°$. Notice that, in order to detect the smaller shift, the lead distance d is increased and the angle θ is smaller. The out-of -control ARL for this chart is $L(1.0) = 10.5$ samples.

Now suppose that the analyst decides that he or she wishes to detect this shift more rapidly than 10.5 time periods and would like to specifically require that $L(1.0) < 10$. From Table 7-2, we note that for $\delta = 1$, the largest value of $L(1.0)$ that is less than 10 is $L(1.0) = 9.4$, for which the corresponding cumulative-sum chart parameters are $(A/\sigma_{\bar{x}}) \tan \theta = 0.50$, $d = 9.0$, and $L(0) = 300$. By increasing the sensitivity of the chart to detect the specified shift, we have reduced the ARL, when the process is in control, from 500 samples to 300 samples.

In this last example, another alternative can be used to detect the shift more rapidly: sample more frequently. For example, if $d = 10$ and $(A/\sigma_{\bar{x}}) \tan \theta = 0.5$, the out-of-control ARL is $L(1.0) = 10.5$, and if we are sampling every hour this means that 10.5 hours go by, on the average, until the shift is detected. If we wish to reduce the time the process runs out of control before detection via the cusum by one-half, we will achieve that by sampling every half hour.

7-1.3 The One-Sided Cusum

The cumulative-sum charts described in the previous two sections assume that a process shift could occur in either direction from the target value of μ_0. Consequently, the procedures devised are usually called two-sided tests. However, the cumulative-sum control chart was originally designed to detect shifts in one direction only. Such a procedure is called a one-side test. In a one-sided cumulative-sum chart, it is customary to plot the quantity

$$S_i = \sum_{j=1}^{i} [\bar{x}_j - (\mu_0 + K)] \tag{7-13}$$

where K is the reference value, usually chosen about halfway between the target or goal μ_0, and the value $\mu_1 = \mu_0 + \Delta$, corresponding to rejectable quality, or $K \simeq \Delta/2$. If S_i falls below zero, it is automatically reset to zero (assuming $\mu_1 > \mu_0$; that is, the process shifts upward). Should S_i exceed the decision interval $H = 2d\sigma_{\bar{x}} \tan\theta$, the process mean is assumed to have shifted to some value $\mu_1 > \mu_0$. The nomogram given by Goel and Wu (1971) can be used to design one-sided cumulative-sum charts that have specified ARL characteristics.

A two-sided procedure can be devised by simultaneously running two one-sided procedures with upper and lower reference values K_1 and K_2. However, this is equivalent to the usual V-mask scheme used for two-sided procedures. Furthermore, the ARLs of the one-sided schemes, say $L_1(\delta)$, $L_2(\delta)$, are related to the ARL of the two-sided procedure $L(\delta)$ by

$$L^{-1}(\delta) = L_1^{-1}(\delta) + L_2^{-1}(\delta) \tag{7-14}$$

7-1.4 A Tabular Form of the Cusum

While the V-mask method described previously is relatively easy to implement, most practitioners prefer a tabular version of the cusum. The tabular procedure is particularly useful when the cusum is implemented on a computer. Let $S_H(i)$ be an upper one-sided tabular cusum for period i and let $S_L(i)$ be a lower one-sided tabular cusum for period i. The quantities $S_H(i)$ and $S_L(i)$ are calculated from

$$S_H(i) = \max[0, \bar{x}_i - (\mu_0 + K) + S_H(i-1)] \tag{7-15}$$

and

$$S_L(i) = \max[0, (\mu_0 - K) - \bar{x}_i + S_L(i-1)] \tag{7-16}$$

respectively, where the starting values $S_H(0) = S_L(0) = 0$. In Equation (7-15) and (7-16) K is called the reference value, which is usually chosen about halfway between the target μ_0 and the value of the mean corresponding to the out-of-control state, $\mu_1 = \mu_0 + \Delta$. That is, K is about one-half the magnitude of the shift we are interested in, or

$$K = \frac{\Delta}{2}$$

[see Equation (7-9b)]. Notice that $S_H(i)$ and $S_L(i)$ accumulate deviations from the target value that are greater than K, with both quantities reset to zero upon becoming negative. If either $S_H(i)$ or $S_L(i)$ exceeds the decision interval H, the process is out of control.

Example 7-4

A Tabular Cusum

We will demonstrate the calculation for the tabular cusum by using the data from Table 7-1. Recall that the target value is $\mu_0 = 10$, $n = 1$ so that $\bar{x}_i = x_i$, the process standard deviation is $\sigma = 1$, and suppose that the magnitude of the shift we are interested in is $\Delta = 1$. We will use a tabular cusum with $K = \Delta/2 = \frac{1}{2}$, and $H = 5$. This value of H was found using Equation (7-11b) after choosing the optimum d and θ to detect a shift of 1σ from Table 7-2. That is, Table 7-2 indicates that $d = 10$ and $\theta = 14°$ would be optimum for detecting a shift of 1σ, so from (7-11b),

$$H = 2d\sigma_{\bar{x}} \tan(\theta)$$
$$= 2(10)(1) \tan(14°) \simeq 5$$

Table 7-3 presents the tabular cusum scheme. To illustrate the calculations, consider period 1. The equations for $S_H(1)$ and $S_L(1)$ are

$$S_H(1) = \max[0, x_i - 10.5 + S_H(0)]$$

and

$$S_L(1) = \max[0, 9.5 - x_i + S_L(0)]$$

Table 7-3
A tabular cusum

Period		a			b		
i	x_i	$x_i - 10.5$	$S_H(i)$	N_H	$9.5 - x_i$	$S_L(i)$	N_L
1	9.45	−1.05	0	0	0.05	0.05	1
2	7.99	−2.51	0	0	1.51	1.56	2
3	9.29	−1.21	0	0	0.21	1.77	3
4	11.66	1.16	1.16	1	−2.16	0	0
5	12.16	1.66	2.82	2	−2.16	0	0
6	10.18	−0.32	2.50	3	−0.68	0	0
7	8.04	−2.46	0.04	4	1.46	1.46	1
8	11.46	0.96	1.00	5	−1.96	0	0
9	9.20	−1.30	0	0	0.03	0.03	1
10	10.34	−0.16	0	0	−0.84	0	0
11	9.03	−1.47	0	0	0.47	0.47	1
12	11.47	0.97	0.97	1	−1.97	0	0
13	10.51	0.01	0.98	2	−1.01	0	0
14	9.40	−1.10	0	0	0.10	0.10	1
15	10.08	−0.42	0	0	−0.58	0	0
16	9.37	−1.13	0	0	0.13	0.13	1
17	10.62	0.12	0.12	1	−1.12	0	0
18	10.31	−0.19	0	0	−0.81	0	0
19	8.52	−1.98	0	0	0.98	0.98	1
20	10.84	0.34	0.34	1	−1.34	0	0
21	10.40	−0.10	0.24	2	−0.90	0	0
22	8.83	−1.67	0	0	0.67	0.67	1
23	11.79	1.29	1.29	1	−2.29	0	0
24	11.00	0.50	1.70	2	−1.50	0	0
25	10.10	−0.40	1.39	3	−0.60	0	0
26	10.58	0.08	1.47	4	−1.08	0	0
27	9.88	−0.62	0.85	5	−0.38	0	0
28	11.12	0.62	1.47	6	−1.62	0	0
29	10.81	−0.31	1.88	7	−1.31	0	0
30	10.02	−0.48	1.40	8	−0.52	0	0

since $K = 0.5$ and $\mu_0 = 10$. Now $x_1 = 9.45$, so

$$S_H(1) = \max[0, 9.45 - 10.5 + 0] = 0$$

and

$$S_L(1) = \max[0, 9.5 - 9.45 + 0] = 0.05.$$

For period 2, we would use

$$S_H(2) = \max[0, x_i - 10.5 + S_H(1)]$$
$$= \max[0, x_i - 10.5 + 0]$$

and

$$S_L(2) = \max[0, 9.5 - x_i + S_L(1)]$$
$$= \max[0, 9.5 - x_i + 0.05]$$

Since $x_2 = 7.99$, we obtain

$$S_H(2) = \max[0, 7.99 - 10.5 + 0] = 0$$

and

$$S_L(2) = \max[0, 9.5 - 7.99 + 0.05] = 1.56$$

Panels (a) and (b) of Table 7-3 summarize the remaining calculations. The quantities N_H and N_L in Table 7-3 indicate the number of periods that the cusum $S_H(i)$ or $S_L(i)$ have been nonzero.

The cusum for Example 7-4 in Table 7-3 indicates that the process is in control at period 30. Suppose that the observation for periods 31 and 32 are $x_{31} = 12.50$ and $x_{32} = 12.25$, respectively. Then

$$S_H(31) = \max[0, 12.50 - 10.5 + 1.40]$$
$$= 3.40$$
$$N_H = 9$$

and

$$S_H(32) = \max[0, 12.25 - 10.5 + 3.40]$$
$$= 5.15$$
$$N_H = 10$$

and since $S_H(32) \geq 5$, we conclude that the process is out of control.

When the process goes out of control, we should search for the assignable cause, take any corrective actions indicated, and restart the cusums at zero. It may be helpful to have an estimate of the new process mean following the shift. This can be computed from

$$\hat{\mu} = \begin{cases} \mu_0 + K + \dfrac{S_H(i)}{N_H}, & \text{if } S_H(i) > H \\[2ex] \mu_0 - K - \dfrac{S_L(i)}{N_L}, & \text{if } S_L(i) > H \end{cases} \tag{7-17}$$

To illustrate the use of Equation (7-17), consider the cusum in period 32 with $S_H(32) = 5.15$. From (7-17), we would estimate the new process average as

$$\hat{\mu} = \mu_0 + K + \frac{S_H(32)}{N_H}$$

$$= 10.0 + 0.5 + \frac{5.15}{10}$$

$$= 11.015$$

It is also useful to present a graphical display for the tabular cusum. These charts are sometimes called *cusum status charts*. They are constructed by plotting $S_H(i)$ and $S_L(i)$ versus the sample number. Figure 7-5 shows the cusum status chart for the data in Example 7-4. Each vertical bar represents the value of $S_H(i)$ and $S_L(i)$ in period i. With the decision interval plotted on the chart, the cusum status chart resembles a Shewhart control chart. We have also plotted the sample statistics x_i for each period on the cusum status chart as the solid dots. This frequently

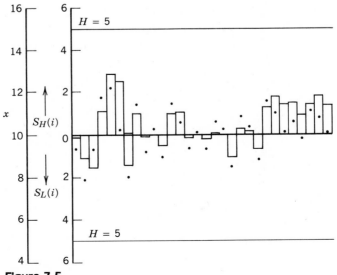

Figure 7-5
A cusum status chart for Example 7-4.

helps the user of the control chart to visualize the actual process performance that has led to a particular value of the cusum.

Finally, we should note that runs tests, and other sensitizing rules such as the zone rules cannot be safely applied to the cusum, as successive values of $S_H(i)$ and $S_L(i)$ are not independent. In fact, the cusum can be thought of as a weighted average, where the weights are stochastic or random. For example, consider the cusum shown in Table 7-3. The cusum at period 30 is $S_H(30) = 1.4$. This can be thought of as a weighted average in which we give equal weight to the last $N_H = 8$ observations and weight zero to all other observations.

General Recommendations for Cusum Design

The tabular cusum is designed by choosing values for the reference value K and the decision interval H. It is usually recommended that these parameters be selected to provide good average run length values. There have been many analytical studies of cusum ARL performance. Based on these studies, we may give some general recommendations for selecting H and K. Recall that $H = h\sigma_{\bar{x}}$ and $K = k\sigma_{\bar{x}}$, where $\sigma_{\bar{x}}$ is the standard deviation of the sample variable used in forming the cusum (if $n = 1$, $\sigma_{\bar{x}} = \sigma_x$). Using $h = 4$ or $h = 5$ and $k = \frac{1}{2}$ will generally provide a cusum that has good ARL properties, against a shift of about $1\sigma_{\bar{x}}$ (or $1\sigma_x$) in the process mean. If much larger or smaller shifts are of interest, set $k = \delta/2$ (see Equation 7-9a). Some practitioners prefer to use a standardized variable $\bar{y}_i = (\bar{x}_i - \mu_0)/S_{\bar{x}}$ as the basis of the cusum. In that case, Equations (7-15) and (7-16) become

$$S_H(i) = \max[0, \bar{y}_i - K + S_H(i - 1)]$$

and

$$S_L(i) = \max[0, K - \bar{y}_i + S_L(i - 1)]$$

For this scheme, we would usually select $K = \frac{1}{2}$ and $H = 4$ or $H = 5$.

To illustrate how well the recommendations of $H = 4$ or $H = 5$ with $K = \frac{1}{2}$ work, consider the average run lengths shown below:

Shift in Mean (multiple of $\sigma_{\bar{x}}$)	$H = 4$	$H = 5$
0	168	465
0.25	74.2	139
0.50	26.6	38.0
0.75	13.3	17.0
1.00	8.38	10.4
1.50	4.75	5.75
2.00	3.34	4.01
2.50	2.62	3.11
3.00	2.19	2.57
4.00	1.71	2.01

Notice that a $1\sigma_{\bar{x}}$ shift would be detected in either 8.38 samples (with $K = \frac{1}{2}$ and $H = 4$) or 10.4 samples (with $K = \frac{1}{2}$ and $H = 5$). By comparison, an $\bar{x}$ chart would require 43.96 samples, on the average, to detect this shift.

7-1.5 Some Other Cusum Procedures

There are many interesting and useful variations of the cusum. In this section we briefly discuss some of these procedures.

Improving Responsiveness to Large Shifts
We have observed that the cumulative-sum control chart is not very effective in detecting large process shifts. A modification in the shape of the mask can improve its performance relative to large process shifts. The modification consists of adding a parabolic section to the mask, as shown in Figure 7-6. Lucas (1973) describes the construction of these modified V masks in detail and has obtained (using simulation) ARL curves for the procedure. He also presents a brief comparison of the modified V mask, the conventional V mask, and the Shewhart chart, and gives a tabular algorithm that can be substituted for the V mask.

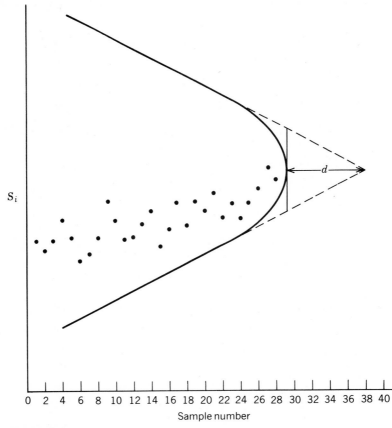

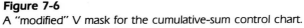

Figure 7-6
A "modified" V mask for the cumulative-sum control chart.

Another approach to improving the ability of the cumulative-sum control chart to detect large process shifts is to use a *combined* cusum-Shewhart procedure for on-line control. Adding the Shewhart control chart is the simplest possible modification of the cumulative-sum control procedure. The Shewhart control limits should be approximately 3.5 standard deviations of $\bar{x}$ away from the center line or target value μ_0. An out-of-control signal on either (or both) charts constitutes an action signal. Lucas (1982) gives a good discussion of this technique. He notes that the combined cusum-Shewhart procedure is almost as responsive to large shifts as the parabolic V mask and easier to implement. This scheme will give excellent protection against both large and small shifts.

Fast Initial Response or Headstart

This procedure was devised by Lucas and Crosier (1982) to improve the sensitivity of a cusum at process start-up. Increased sensitivity at process start-up would be desirable if the corrective action did not reset the mean to the target value. The fast initial response (FIR) or *headstart* essentially just sets the starting values $S_H(0)$ and $S_L(0)$ equal to some nonzero value, typically $H/2$.

To illustrate the headstart procedure, consider the data in Table 7-4. These data have a target value of 100, $K = 3$, and $H = 12$. We will use a headstart value of $S_H(0) = S_L(0) = H/2 = 6$. The first 10 samples are in control with mean equal to the target value of 100. Since $x_1 = 102$, the cusums for the first period will be

$$S_H(1) = \max[0, x_i - 103 + S_H(0)]$$
$$= \max[0, 102 - 103 + 6] = 5$$
$$S_L(1) = \max[0, 97 - x_i + S_L(0)]$$
$$= \max[0, 97 - 102 + 6] = 1$$

Notice that the starting cusum value is the headstart $H/2 = 6$. In addition, we see from panels (a) and (b) of Table 7-4 that both cusums decline rapidly to zero from the starting value. In fact, from period 2 onward $S_H(i)$ is unaffected by the headstart, while from period 3 onward $S_L(i)$ is unaffected by the headstart. This has occurred because the process is in control at the target value of 100, and several consecutive observations near the target value were observed.

Table 7-4
A cusum with a headstart, process mean equal to 100

Period		a			b		
i	x_i	$x_i - 103$	$S_H(i)$	N_H	$97 - x_i$	$S_L(i)$	N_L
1	102	−1	5	1	−5	1	1
2	97	−6	0	0	0	1	2
3	104	1	1	1	−7	0	0
4	93	−6	0	0	4	4	1
5	100	−3	0	0	−3	1	2
6	105	2	2	1	−8	0	0
7	96	−7	0	0	1	1	1
8	98	−5	0	0	−1	0	0
9	105	2	2	1	−8	0	0
10	99	−4	0	0	−2	0	0

Table 7-5
A cusum with a headstart, process mean equal to 105

Period		a			b		
i	x_i	$x_i - 103$	$S_H(i)$	N_H	$97 - x_i$	$S_L(i)$	N_L
1	107	4	10	1	−10	0	0
2	102	−1	9	2	−5	0	0
3	109	6	15	3	−12	0	0
4	98	−5	10	4	−1	0	0
5	105	2	12	5	−8	0	0
6	110	7	19	6	−13	0	0
7	101	−2	17	7	−4	0	0
8	103	0	17	8	−6	0	0
9	110	7	24	9	−13	0	0
10	104	1	25	10	−7	0	0

Now suppose the process had been out of control at process start-up, with mean 105. Table 7-5 presents the data that would have been produced by this process and the resulting cusums. Notice that the third sample causes $S_H(3)$ to exceed the limit $H = 12$. If no headstart had been used, we would have started with $S_H(0) = 0$, and the cusum would not exceed H until sample number 6.

This example demonstrates the benefits of a headstart. If the process starts in control at the target value, the cusums will quickly drop to zero and the headstart will have little effect on the performance of the cusum procedure. However, if the process starts at some level different from the target value, the headstart will allow the cusum to detect it more quickly, resulting in shorter out-of-control ARL values.

Some ARL Values
To illustrate how the combined cusum-Shewhart procedure and the headstart (or FIR) modification work, we provide a list of some ARL values. All of the cusums below use $K = \frac{1}{2}$ and $H = 5$:

Shift in Mean (multiple of $\sigma_{\bar{x}}$)	Basic Cusum	Cusum-Shewhart (Shewhart limits at 3.5 $\sigma_{\bar{x}}$)	Cusum with FIR	FIR Cusum-Shewhart (Shewhart limits at 3.5 $\sigma_{\bar{x}}$)
0	465	391	430	360
0.25	139	130.9	122	113.9
0.50	38.0	37.20	28.7	28.1
0.75	17.0	16.80	11.2	11.2
1.00	10.4	10.20	6.35	6.32
1.50	5.75	5.58	3.37	3.37
2.00	4.01	3.77	2.36	2.36
2.50	3.11	2.77	1.86	1.86
3.00	2.57	2.10	1.54	1.54
4.00	2.01	1.34	1.16	1.16

Note that the ARL values for the FIR cusum are valid when the shift occurs at the time the cusums are reset. When the process is in control, the headstart value quickly drops to zero. Thus, if the process is in control when the cusum is reset but shifts out of control later the appropriate ARL for such a case should be read from the cusum without the FIR feature.

Cusums for Other Sample Statistics

We have concentrated on cusums for sample averages. However, it is possible to develop cusums for other sample statistics such as ranges, standard deviations, fractions nonconforming, and defects. Some of these cusums are discussed in the papers by Johnson and Leone (1962a, 1962b, 1962c). The paper by Lucas (1985) on cusums for count data is also of interest.

One variation of the cusum is extremely useful when working with count data and the count rate is very low. In this case, it is frequently more effective to form a cusum using the time between events. The most common situation encountered in practice is to use the time-between-events cusum to detect an *increase* in the count rate. This is equivalent to detecting a *decrease* in the time between events. An appropriate cusum scheme is

$$S_L(i) = \max[0, K - Y_i + S_L(i - 1)] \tag{7-18}$$

where K is the reference value and Y_i is the time that has elapsed since that last observed count. Lucas (1985) discusses the choice of K and H for this procedure.

7-2 THE EXPONENTIALLY WEIGHTED MOVING-AVERAGE CONTROL CHART

The exponentially weighted moving-average (or EWMA) control chart is also a good alternative to the Shewhart control chart when we are interested in detecting small shifts. The performance of the EWMA control chart is approximately equivalent to that of the cumulative-sum control chart, and in some ways, it is easier to set up and operate.

7-2.1 The Exponentially Weighted Moving-Average Control Chart for Sample Averages

The EWMA control chart was introduced by Roberts (1959). See also Hunter (1986) for a good discussion of the EWMA. The exponentially weighted moving average is defined as

$$z_t = \lambda \bar{x}_t + (1 - \lambda)z_{t-1} \tag{7-19}$$

where $0 < \lambda \leq 1$ is a constant and the starting value (required with the first sample at $t = 1$) is

$$z_0 = \bar{\bar{x}}$$

To demonstrate that the EWMA z_t is a weighted average of all previous sample means, we may substitute for z_{t-1} on the right-hand side of (7-19) to obtain

$$z_t = \lambda \bar{x}_t + (1 - \lambda)[\lambda \bar{x}_{t-1} + (1 - \lambda)z_{t-2}]$$
$$= \lambda \bar{x}_t + \lambda(1 - \lambda)\bar{x}_{t-1} + (1 - \lambda)^2 z_{t-2}$$

Continuing to substitute recursively for $z_{t-j}, j = 2, 3, \ldots, t$, we obtain

$$z_t = \lambda \sum_{j=0}^{t-1} (1 - \lambda)^j \bar{x}_{t-j} + (1 - \lambda)^t z_0 \qquad (7\text{-}20)$$

The weights $\lambda(1 - \lambda)^j$ decrease geometrically with the age of the sample mean. Furthermore, the weights sum to unity, since

$$\lambda \sum_{j=0}^{t-1} (1 - \lambda)^j = \lambda \left[\frac{1 - (1 - \lambda)^t}{1 - (1 - \lambda)} \right] = 1 - (1 - \lambda)^t.$$

If $\lambda = 0.2$, then the weight assigned to the current sample mean is 0.2 and the weights given to the preceding means are 0.16, 0.128, 0.1024, and so forth. A comparison of these weights with those of a five-period moving average is shown in Figure 7-7. Because these weights decline geometrically when connected by a smooth curve, the EWMA is sometimes called a geometric moving average (GMA). The EWMA is used extensively in time series modeling and in forecasting [see Box and Jenkins (1976) and Montgomery and Johnson (1976)]. Since the EWMA can be viewed as a weighted average of all past and current observations, it is very insensitive to the normality assumption. It is therefore an ideal control chart to use with individual observations.

If the $\bar{x}_i$ are independent random variables with variance σ^2/n, then the variance of z_t is

$$\sigma_{z_t}^2 = \frac{\sigma^2}{n} \left(\frac{\lambda}{2 - \lambda} \right) [1 - (1 - \lambda)^{2t}] \qquad (7\text{-}21)$$

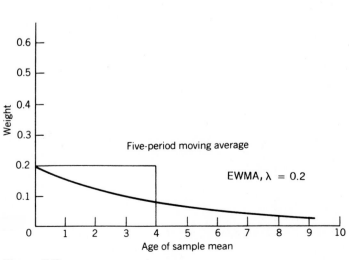

Figure 7-7
Weights of past sample means.

As t increases, $\sigma_{z_t}^2$ increases to a limiting value

$$\sigma_z^2 = \frac{\sigma^2}{n}\left(\frac{\lambda}{2-\lambda}\right) \tag{7-22}$$

Consequently, the upper and lower control limits are

$$\text{UCL} = \bar{\bar{x}} + 3\sigma\sqrt{\frac{\lambda}{(2-\lambda)n}} \tag{7-23a}$$

and

$$\text{LCL} = \bar{\bar{x}} - 3\sigma\sqrt{\frac{\lambda}{(2-\lambda)n}} \tag{7-23b}$$

respectively, if the sample number t is moderately large. For small t, control limits could be based on (7-21).

Example 7-5

An $\bar{x}$ control chart with center line $\bar{\bar{x}} = 10$ and upper and lower 3-sigma control limits at $\text{UCL}_{\bar{x}} = 16.0$ and $\text{LCL}_{\bar{x}} = 4.0$ is shown in Figure 7-8a. Values of the sample statistic $\bar{x}$ are plotted on the chart and listed in Table 7-6 for periods $1 \leq t \leq 38$. Suppose that we wish to construct an EWMA chart for these data using $\lambda = 0.2$. Since $\bar{\bar{x}} = 10$, the center line of the EWMA chart will be 10 and the starting value $z_0 = \bar{\bar{x}} = 10$.

The upper and lower control limits on the EWMA chart would be found from Equation (7-23) as

$$\begin{aligned}
\text{UCL} &= \bar{\bar{x}} + 3\sigma\sqrt{\frac{\lambda}{(2-\lambda)n}} \\
&= \bar{\bar{x}} + 3\frac{\sigma}{\sqrt{n}}\sqrt{\frac{\lambda}{(2-\lambda)}} \\
&= 10.0 + 6.0\sqrt{\frac{0.2}{1.8}} \\
&= 12.0
\end{aligned}$$

and

$$\begin{aligned}
\text{LCL} &= \bar{\bar{x}} - 3\sigma\sqrt{\frac{\lambda}{(2-\lambda)n}} \\
&= \bar{\bar{x}} - 3\frac{\sigma}{\sqrt{n}}\sqrt{\frac{\lambda}{(2-\lambda)}} \\
&= 10.0 - 6.0\sqrt{\frac{0.2}{1.8}} \\
&= 8.0
\end{aligned}$$

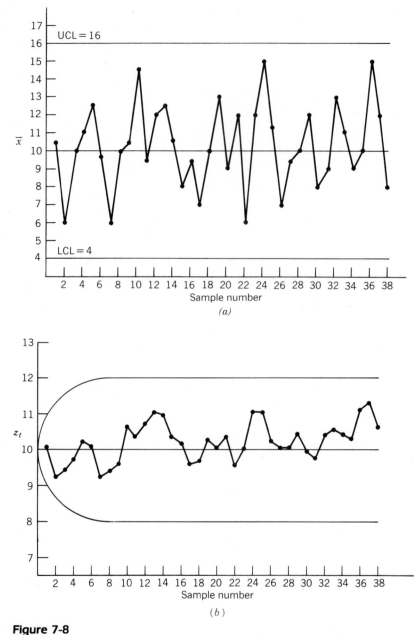

Figure 7-8
Control charts for Example 7-5. (a) The $\bar{x}$-chart. (b) The EWMA chart with $\lambda = 0.2$.

for large t. For the first few samples the control limits could be calculated from

$$\bar{\bar{x}} \pm 3\,\frac{\sigma}{\sqrt{n}}\,\sqrt{\left(\frac{\lambda}{2-\lambda}\right)[1 - (1-\lambda)^{2t}]}$$

These control limits will increase rapidly to their limiting value, as shown in Figure 7-8b.

Table 7-6

Data and calculations for the EWMA control chart in Figure 7-8*b*

Sample, t	$\bar{x}_t$	z_t	Control Limits for z_t LCL	UCL
1	10.5	10.10	8.80	11.20
2	6.0	9.28	8.46	11.54
3	10.0	9.42	8.26	11.72
4	11.0	9.74	8.18	11.82
5	12.5	10.29	8.11	11.89
6	9.5	10.13	8.07	11.93
7	6.0	9.31	8.04	11.96
8	10.0	9.45	8.03	11.97
9	10.5	9.66	8.00	12.00
10	14.5	10.62	⋮	⋮
11	9.5	10.40		
12	12.0	10.72		
13	12.5	11.07		
14	10.5	10.96		
15	8.0	10.37		
16	9.5	10.19		
17	7.0	9.56		
18	10.0	9.64		
19	13.0	10.32		
20	9.0	10.05		
21	12.0	10.44		
22	6.0	9.55		
23	12.0	10.04		
24	15.0	11.03		
25	11.0	11.03		
26	7.0	10.22		
27	9.5	10.08		
28	10.0	10.06		
29	12.0	10.45		
30	8.0	9.96		
31	9.0	9.77		
32	13.0	10.41		
33	11.0	10.53		
34	9.0	10.23		
35	10.0	10.18		
36	15.0	11.14		
37	12.0	11.32		
38	8.0	10.65		

Since the first sample mean $\bar{x}_1 = 10.5$, we calculate the first value of the exponentially weighted moving average from (7-19) as

$$z_1 = \lambda \bar{x}_1 + (1 - \lambda)z_0$$
$$= (0.2)10.5 + (0.8)10.0$$
$$= 10.10$$

Thus $z_1 = 10.10$ is the first point plotted on the control chart. The second sample mean is $\bar{x}_2 = 6.0$, resulting in

$$z_2 = \lambda\bar{x}_2 + (1 - \lambda)z_1$$
$$= (0.2)6.0 + (0.8)10.10$$
$$= 9.28$$

The remaining values of the EWMA z_t may be calculated similarly. The calculations are summarized in Table 7-6. The complete EWMA chart is shown in Figure 7-8b.

We have illustrated the EWMA chart for the σ-known case. Usually, σ must be estimated from an R chart. If this is the case, then the control limits for the EWMA chart become:

$$\text{UCL} = \bar{\bar{x}} + A_2\bar{R}\sqrt{\frac{\lambda}{(2 - \lambda)}} \tag{7-24a}$$

$$\text{LCL} = \bar{\bar{x}} - A_2\bar{R}\sqrt{\frac{\lambda}{(2 - \lambda)}} \tag{7-24b}$$

Although we have discussed the EWMA primarily as a statistical process-control tool, it actually has a much broader interpretation. From an SPC viewpoint, the EWMA is roughly equivalent to the cusum in its ability to *monitor* a process and detect the presence of assignable causes that result in a process shift. However, the EWMA provides a *forecast* of where the process mean will be at the next time period. That is, z_t is actually a forecast of the value of the process mean μ at time $t + 1$. Thus, the EWMA could be used as the basis for a dynamic process-control algorithm.

In computer-integrated manufacturing where sensors are used to measure every unit manufactured, a forecast of the process mean based on previous behavior would be very useful. If the forecast of the mean is different from target by a critical amount, then either the operator or some electro-mechanical control system can make the necessary process adjustment. If the operator makes the adjustment, then he or she must exercise caution and not make adjustments too frequently as this will actually cause process variability to increase. The control limits on the EWMA chart can be used to signal *when* an adjustment is necessary, and the difference between the target and the forecast of the mean μ_{t+1} can be used to determine *how much* adjustment is necessary.

The EWMA can be modified to enhance its ability to forecast the mean. Suppose that the process mean trends or drifts steadily away from the target. The forecasting performance of the EWMA can be improved in this case. First, note that the usual EWMA can be written as

$$z_t = \lambda\bar{x}_t + (1 - \lambda)z_{t-1}$$
$$= z_{t-1} + \lambda(\bar{x}_t - z_{t-1})$$

and if we view z_{t-1} as a forecast of the process mean in period t we can think of $\bar{x}_t - z_{t-1}$ as the forecast error e_t for period t. Therefore,

$$z_t = z_{t-1} + \lambda e_t.$$

Thus, the EWMA for period t is equal to the EWMA for period $t - 1$ plus a fraction λ of the forecast error for the mean in period t. Now add a second term to this last equation to give

$$z_t = z_{t-1} + \lambda_1 e_t + \lambda_2 \sum_{j=1}^{t} e_j$$

where λ_1 and λ_2 are constants that weight the error at time t and the *sum* of the errors accumulated to time t. If we let $\nabla e_t = e_t - e_{t-1}$ be the first difference of the errors, then we can arrive at a final modification of the EWMA:

$$z_t = z_{t-1} + \lambda_1 e_t + \lambda_2 \sum_{j=1}^{t} e_j + \lambda_3 \nabla e_t$$

Notice that in this empirical control equation the EWMA in period t (which is the forecast of the process mean in period $t + 1$) equals the current estimate of the mean (z_{t-1} estimates μ_t), plus a term proportional to the error, plus a term related to the sum of the errors, plus a term related to the first difference of the errors. These three terms are sometimes called the *proportional*, *integral*, and *differential* components of the classical control theory engineer's PID (proportional, integral, differential) control equation. The parameters λ_1, λ_2, and λ_3 would be chosen to give the best forecasting performance. An extensive literature exists on this type of discrete process-control methodology.

Because the EWMA statistic z_t can be viewed as a *forecast* of the mean of the process at time $t + 1$, we often plot the EWMA statistic one time period ahead. That is, we actually plot z_t at time period $t + 1$ on the control chart. This allows the analyst to visually see how much difference there is between the current observation and the estimate of the current mean of the process. In statistical process-control applications where the mean may "wander" over time, this approach has considerable appeal. Situations where the process mean may drift over time are discussed in Section 8-8.

7-2.2 Design of an EWMA Control Chart

The EWMA control chart is very effective against small process shifts. The design parameters of the chart are the multiple of sigma used in the control limits (k) and the value of λ. It is possible to choose these parameters to give ARL performance from the EWMA control chart that closely approximates cusum ARL performance for detecting small shifts.

There have been several theoretical studies of the average run length properties of the EWMA control chart. For example, see the papers by Crowder (1987a, 1989) and Lucas and Saccucci (1990). These studies provide average run length tables for a range of values of λ and k. The optimal design procedure would consist of specifying the desired in-control and out-of-control average run lengths and the magnitude of the process shift that is anticipated, and then to select the combination of λ and k that provide the desired ARL performance.

In general, we have found that values of λ in the interval $0.05 \le \lambda \le 0.25$ work well in practice, with $\lambda = 0.08$, $\lambda = 0.10$, and $\lambda = 0.15$ being popular choices. A good rule of thumb is to use smaller values of λ to detect smaller shifts. We have also found that $k = 3$ (the usual 3-sigma limits) works well, although when $\lambda \le 0.10$ there is some advantage to reducing k to 2.75.

Like the cusum, the EWMA performs well against small shifts but does not react to large shifts as quickly as the Shewhart $\bar{x}$ chart. However, the EWMA is often superior to the cusum for large shifts, particularly if $\lambda > 0.10$. A good way to further improve the sensitivity of the control procedure to large shifts without sacrificing the ability to detect small shifts quickly is to combine a Shewhart $\bar{x}$ chart with the EWMA. These combined Shewhart–EWMA control procedures are effective against both large and small shifts. When using such schemes, we have found it helpful to use slightly wider than usual limits on the $\bar{x}$ chart (say 3.25 sigma, or even 3.5 sigma). It is also possible to plot *both* $\bar{x}_t$ and the EWMA statistic z_t on the same control chart along with both the Shewhart and EWMA limits. This produces one chart for the combined control procedure which operators quickly become adept at interpreting. When the plots are computer-generated, different colors or plotting symbols can be used for the two sets of control limits and statistics.

7-2.3 EWMA Charts for Other Sample Statistics

The EWMA control chart can be easily extended to other sample statistics. For example, if the count of the number of nonconformances (c) is of interest, then the EWMA statistic would be

$$z_t = \lambda c_t + (1 - \lambda)z_{t-1}.$$

This statistic would be plotted on a control chart with center line $\bar{c}$ and control limits at

$$\text{UCL} = \bar{c} + 3\sqrt{\frac{\lambda\bar{c}}{2 - \lambda}}$$

$$\text{LCL} = \bar{c} - 3\sqrt{\frac{\lambda\bar{c}}{2 - \lambda}}$$

The EWMA chart can also be used when the time between events is the variable of interest. Such control charts are often used in low defect-level manufacturing environments. If Y_i is the time between occurrence of the $(i - 1)st$ and the ith event, then the EWMA statistic is

$$z_i = \lambda Y_i + (1 - \lambda)z_{i-1}$$

This statistic would be plotted on a control chart with center line $\bar{Y}$, and assuming Poisson events, the control limits are:

$$\text{UCL} = \bar{Y} + 3\bar{Y}\sqrt{\frac{\lambda}{2 - \lambda}}$$

$$\text{LCL} = \max\left[\bar{Y} - 3\bar{Y}\sqrt{\frac{\lambda}{2 - \lambda}}, 0\right]$$

7-2.4 The Moving-Average Control Chart

The EWMA chart uses a weighted average as the chart statistic. Occasionally, a control chart based on a simple, unweighted moving average may be of interest.

Suppose that samples of size n have been collected, and let $\bar{x}_1, \bar{x}_2, \ldots, \bar{x}_t, \ldots$ denote the corresponding sample means. The moving average of span w at time t is defined as

$$M_t = \frac{\bar{x}_t + \bar{x}_{t-1} + \cdots + \bar{x}_{t-w+1}}{w} \tag{7-25}$$

That is, at time period t, the oldest sample mean is dropped and the newest one added to the set. The variance of the moving average M_t is

$$V(M_t) = \frac{1}{w^2} \sum_{i=t-w+1}^{t} V(\bar{x}_i) = \frac{1}{w^2} \sum_{i=t-w+1}^{t} \frac{\sigma^2}{n} = \frac{\sigma^2}{nw} \tag{7-26}$$

Therefore, if $\bar{\bar{x}}$ denotes the center line of the control chart, then the 3-sigma control limits for M_t are

$$\text{UCL} = \bar{\bar{x}} + \frac{3\sigma}{\sqrt{nw}} \tag{7-27a}$$

and

$$\text{LCL} = \bar{\bar{x}} - \frac{3\sigma}{\sqrt{nw}} \tag{7-27b}$$

The control procedure would consist of calculating the new moving average M_t as each sample mean $\bar{x}_t$ becomes available, plotting M_t on a control chart with upper and lower control limits given by (7-27), and concluding that the process is out of control if M_t exceeds the control limits. In general, the magnitude of the shift of interest and w are inversely related; smaller shifts would be guarded against more effectively by longer moving averages.

Example 7-6

We will set up a moving-average control chart for the data used in Example 7-5 using $w = 8$. Values of the statistic $\bar{x}_t$ for periods $1 \leq t \leq 38$ are shown in Table 7-7. The statistic plotted on the moving-average control chart will be

$$M_t = \frac{\bar{x}_t + \bar{x}_{t-1} + \cdots + \bar{x}_{t-7}}{8}$$

for period $t \geq 8$. For time periods $t \leq 8$ the average of the observations for periods $1, 2, \ldots, t$ is plotted. The values of these moving averages are shown in Table 7-7.

The control limits for the moving-average control chart may be easily obtained from (7-27). Since for the $\bar{x}$ chart in Example 7-5 we have $3\sigma_{\bar{x}} = 6.0$, then

Table 7-7
Data and calculations for the moving-average control chart in Figure 79 ($w = 8$)

Sample, t	$\bar{x}_t$	M_t	Control Limits for M_t LCL	Control Limits for M_t UCL
1	10.5	10.50	4.00	16.00
2	6.0	8.25	5.76	14.24
3	10.0	8.83	6.54	13.46
4	11.0	9.38	7.00	13.00
5	12.5	10.00	7.32	12.68
6	9.5	9.92	7.55	12.45
7	6.0	9.36	7.73	12.27
8	10.0	9.44	7.88	12.12
9	10.5	9.44	7.88	12.12
10	14.5	10.50	⋮	⋮
11	9.5	10.44		
12	12.0	10.57		
13	12.5	10.57		
14	10.5	10.69		
15	8.0	10.94		
16	9.5	10.88		
17	7.0	10.44		
18	10.0	9.88		
19	13.0	10.31		
20	9.0	9.94		
21	12.0	9.88		
22	6.0	9.31		
23	12.0	9.81		
24	15.0	10.50		
25	11.0	11.00		
26	7.0	10.63		
27	9.5	10.19		
28	10.0	10.31		
29	12.0	10.31		
30	8.0	10.56		
31	9.0	10.19		
32	13.0	9.94		
33	11.0	9.94		
34	9.0	10.18		
35	10.0	10.25		
36	15.0	10.88		
37	12.0	10.88		
38	8.0	10.88		

$\sigma_{\bar{x}} = \sigma/\sqrt{n} = 2.0$. Consequently, we find the upper and lower control limits for the moving-average control chart as

$$\text{UCL} = \bar{\bar{x}} + \frac{3\sigma}{\sqrt{nw}} = \bar{\bar{x}} + \frac{3\sigma_{\bar{x}}}{\sqrt{w}} = 10.0 + \frac{(3)(2.0)}{\sqrt{8}} = 12.12$$

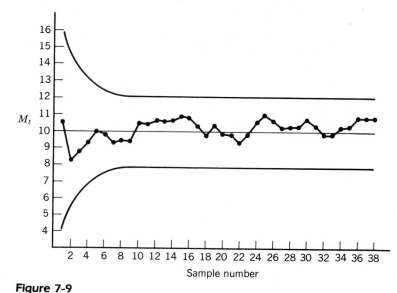

Figure 7-9
Moving-average control chart with $w = 8$, Example 7-6.

and

$$\text{LCL} = \bar{\bar{x}} - \frac{3\sigma}{\sqrt{nw}} = \bar{\bar{x}} - \frac{3\sigma_{\bar{x}}}{\sqrt{w}} = 10.0 - \frac{(3)(2.0)}{\sqrt{8}} = 7.88$$

The control limits for M_t apply for periods $t \geq 8$. For periods $0 < t < 8$, the control limits are given by $\bar{\bar{x}} \pm 3\sigma/\sqrt{nt}$. These control limits are shown in Table 7-7. An alternative procedure that avoids using special control limits for periods $t < w$ is to use an ordinary $\bar{x}$ chart until at least w sample means have been obtained.

The moving-average control chart is shown in Figure 7-9. No points exceed the control limits. Note that for the initial periods $t < w$ the control limits are wider than their final steady-state value. Moving averages that are less than w periods apart are highly correlated, which often complicates interpreting patterns on the control chart. This is easily seen by examining Figure 7-9.

The moving-average control chart is more effective than the usual $\bar{x}$ chart in detecting small process shifts. However, it is generally not as effective against small shifts as either the cusum or the EWMA. The moving average control chart is considered by some to be simpler to implement than the cusum. This author prefers the EWMA to the moving average control chart.

Moving-average control charts can also be used in cases where each sample consists of a single observation. This situation occurs frequently when production of a single unit of product requires a very long time, and where automatic measurement and test procedures are used. It is also possible to construct a moving-range control chart. An example of the moving-range control chart for $w = 2$ and $n = 1$ was given in Chapter 6.

7-3 Exercises

7-1 The data below represent averages of samples of size five selected hourly from a manufacturing process with $\sigma = 2.0$. Set up a cumulative-sum control chart and V mask for this process. Analyze the data.

Sample Number	$\bar{x}$	Sample Number	$\bar{x}$
1	10.45	11	11.39
2	10.55	12	11.69
3	10.37	13	11.51
4	10.64	14	11.28
5	10.95	15	11.38
6	10.08	16	11.25
7	10.50	17	11.63
8	10.87	18	11.88
9	11.25	19	11.46
10	11.46	20	11.67

7-2 Set up a tabular cusum scheme for the data in Exercise 7-1.

7-3 Set up a tabular cusum scheme for the piston-ring data used in Example 6-1 (see Tables 6-1 and 6-2). When the procedure is applied to all 40 samples, does the cusum react more quickly than the $\bar{x}$ chart to the shift in the process mean? Use $\sigma = 0.01$ in setting up the cusum, and design the procedure to detect a shift of about 1σ.

7-4 A machine is used to fill cans with motor oil additive. A sample of four cans is selected every half hour and the average weight of the cans is obtained. Since the filling process is automated, it has very stable variability, and long experience indicates that $\sigma = 0.10$ oz. Construct a cumulative-sum control chart and V mask for the sample data shown below.

Sample Number	$\bar{x}$	Sample Number	$\bar{x}$
1	8.00	9	8.05
2	8.01	10	8.04
3	8.02	11	8.03
4	8.01	12	8.05
5	8.00	13	8.06
6	8.01	14	8.04
7	8.06	15	8.05
8	8.07	16	8.06

7-5 Rework Exercise 7-4 using a tabular cusum.

7-6 Consider the data in Exercise 7-1. Suppose it is necessary to design the cumulative-sum control chart to detect a shift in the process mean of 1.3 units and that $L(0) = 500$. Use Table 7-2 to design the cumulative-sum control chart.

7-7 Suppose that in Exercise 7-6, the analyst wishes to find a cumulative-sum control chart that has $L(\Delta) \leq 4.0$. Does the chart designed in Exercise 7-6 have this property? If not, use Table 7-2 to redesign a new chart. What is $L(0)$ for this cumulative-sum control chart?

7-8   Design a cumulative-sum control chart to detect a shift of $\Delta = 0.75$ that has $L(0) = 400$. Is it possible to find a cumulative-sum control chart for detecting this shift that has $L(0.75) \leq 12$? What is $L(0)$ for this chart?

7-9   Design a cusum procedure with $\alpha = 0.002$, $\beta = 0.10$, $\Delta = 0.5$, $\sigma = 1.0$, and $n = 4$. Set up both the V mask and the parameters K and H for the tabular scheme. Assume that the target value is $\mu_0 = 100$.

7-10   Design a cusum procedure with $\alpha = 0.005$, $\beta = 0.20$, $\Delta = 1$, $\sigma = 3$, and $n = 5$. Set up both the V mask and the parameters K and H for the tabular scheme. Assume that the target value $\mu_0 = 50$.

7-11   Analyze the data in Exercise 7-1 using an exponentially weighted moving-average control chart with $\lambda = 0.2$. Compare the results obtained with the cumulative-sum control chart in Exercise 7-1.

7-12   Rework Exercise 7-11 using $\lambda = 0.1$. How does this affect the control limits on the EWMA chart? Would control limits at ± 2.5 sigma be a good idea?

7-13   Analyze the piston-ring data in Example 6-1 with an EWMA control chart using $\lambda = 0.15$. Compare the performance with the ordinary $\bar{x}$ chart.

7-14   Analyze the data in Exercise 7-4 with an EWMA chart with $\lambda = 0.10$. Compare the results with the cusum from Exercise 7-4.

7-15   Show how the EWMA control chart could be used with fraction nonconforming data. What are the control limits for the chart?

7-16   Analyze the data in Exercise 7-1 using a moving-average control chart with $w = 6$. Compare the results obtained with the cumulative-sum control chart in Exercise 7-1.

7-17   Analyze the data in Exercise 7-4 using a moving-average control chart with $w = 5$. Compare the results obtained with the cumulative-sum control chart in Exercise 7-4.

7-18   Show that if the process is in control at the level μ, the exponentially weighted moving average is an unbiased estimator of the process mean.

7-19   Derive the variance of the exponentially weighted moving-average z_t.

7-20   **Equivalence of moving-average and exponentially weighted moving-average control charts.** Show that if $\lambda = 2/(w + 1)$ for the EWMA control chart, then this chart is equivalent to a w-period moving-average control chart in the sense that the control limits are identical for large t.

7-21   **Continuation of Exercise 7-20.** Show that if $\lambda = 2/(w + 1)$, then the average "age" of the data used in computing the statistics z_t and M_t is identical.

7-22   The data below are temperature readings from a chemical process in degrees centigrade, taken every two minutes. Analyze these data using cumulative-sum control charts. What can you say about overall process variability and process capability? (Read the observations down, from left.)

953	985	949	937	959	948	958	952
945	973	941	946	939	937	955	931
972	955	966	954	948	955	947	928
945	950	966	935	958	927	941	937
975	948	934	941	963	940	938	950
970	957	937	933	973	962	945	970
959	940	946	960	949	963	963	933
973	933	952	968	942	943	967	960
940	965	935	959	965	950	969	934
936	973	941	956	062	938	981	927

7-23 Repeat Exercise 7-22 using an EWMA control chart. What can you say about overall process variability and process capability?

7-24 Bath concentrations are measured hourly in a chemical process. Analyze the concentration data shown below using the cumulative-sum control chart. What can you say about process variability and process capability. (Data in PPM; read down from left.)

160	186	190	206
158	195	189	210
150	179	185	216
151	184	182	212
153	175	181	211
154	192	180	202
158	186	183	205
162	197	186	197
169	205	185	188
173	203	187	183
162	209	192	175
154	208	199	174
139	211	197	171
145	214	193	180
160	215	190	179
172	209	183	175
175	203	197	174
159	192	194	176
184	195	201	170
187	193	204	173

7-25 Repeat Exercise 7-24 using the EWMA control chart. What can you say about process variability and process capability?

Chapter 8

Other Statistical
Process-Control Techniques

In addition to the standard control charts presented in Chapters 5, 6, and 7, a number of other statistical process-control techniques are useful in certain situations. Some of these procedures are described in this chapter.

8-1 STATISTICAL PROCESS CONTROL FOR SHORT PRODUCTION RUNS

Statistical process-control methods have found wide application in almost every type of business. Some of the most interesting applications occur in job-shop manufacturing systems, or, generally in any type of system characterized by short production runs. SPC methods for these situations are straightforward adaptations of the standard concepts and require no new methodology. In fact, Example 6-9 illustrated one of the basic techniques of control charting used in the short-run environment—using deviation from the nominal dimension as the variable on the control chart. In this section, we present a summary of several techniques that have proven successful in the short production run situation.

8-1.1 $\bar{x}$ and R Charts for Short Production Runs

The simplest technique for using $\bar{x}$ and R charts in the short production run situation was introduced previously in Example 6-9: namely, use deviation from nominal instead of the measured variable on the control chart. To illustrate the procedure, consider the data in Table 8-1. The first four samples represent hole diameters in a particular part (say part A). Panel (a) of this table shows the actual diameters in millimeters. For this part, the nominal diameter is $N_A = 50$ mm. Thus, if M_i represents the ith actual sample measurement in millimeters, then

$$x_i = M_i - N_A$$

would be the deviation from nominal. Panel (b) of Table 8-1 shows the deviations from nominal x_i, as well as the $\bar{x}$ and R values for each sample. Now consider the last six samples in Table 8-1. These hole diameters are from a different part number, B, for which the nominal dimension is $N_B = 25$ mm. Panel (b) of Table 8-1 presents the deviations from nominal and the averages and ranges of the deviations from nominal for the part B data.

The control charts for $\bar{x}$ and R using deviation from nominal are shown in Figure 8-1. Notice that control limits have been calculated using the data from all 10 samples. In practice, we would recommend waiting until approximately 20 samples are available before calculating control limits. However, for purposes of illustration we have calculated the limits based on 10 samples to show that, when using deviation from nominal as the variable on the chart, it is not necessary to have a long production run for each part number. It is also customary to use a dashed vertical line to separate different products or part numbers and to identify clearly which section of the chart pertains to each part number, as shown in Figure 8-1.

Three important points should be made relative to this technique:

1. An assumption is that the process standard deviation is approximately the same for all parts. If this assumption is invalid, use a *standardized* $\bar{x}$ and R chart (see the next subsection).

2. This procedure works best when the sample size is constant for all part numbers.

3. Deviation from nominal control charts have intuitive appeal when the nominal specification is the desired target value for the process.

This last point deserves some additional discussion. In some situations the process should not (or cannot) be centered at the nominal dimension. For example, when the part has one-sided specifications, frequently a nominal dimension will not be specified. (For an example, see the data on bottle-bursting strength in the next chapter.) In cases where either no nominal is given or a nominal is not the desired process target, then in constructing the control chart, use the historical process average ($\bar{\bar{x}}$) instead of the nominal dimension. In some cases it will be necessary to compare the historical average to a desired process target to determine whether the true process mean is different from the target. Standard hypothesis-testing procedures can be used to perform this task.

Standardized $\bar{x}$ and R Charts

If the process standard deviations are different for different part numbers, the deviation from nominal (or the deviation from process target) control charts described above will not work effectively. However, *standardized* $\bar{x}$ and R charts will

Table 8-1
Data for short-run $\bar{x}$ and R charts

Sample Number	Part Number	(a) Measurements			(b) Deviation from Nominal				
		M_1	M_2	M_3	x_1	x_2	x_3	$\bar{x}$	R
1	A	50	51	52	0	1	2	1.00	2
2	A	49	50	51	−1	0	1	0.00	2
3	A	48	49	52	−2	−1	2	−0.33	4
4	A	49	53	51	−1	3	1	1.00	4
5	B	24	27	26	−1	2	1	0.67	2
6	B	25	27	24	0	2	−1	0.33	2
7	B	27	26	23	2	1	−2	0.33	4
8	B	25	24	23	0	−1	−2	−1.00	2
9	B	24	25	25	−1	0	0	−0.33	1
10	B	26	24	25	1	−1	0	0.00	2

$$\bar{\bar{x}} = 0.17 \qquad \bar{R} = 2.5$$

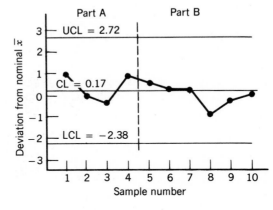

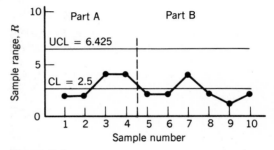

Figure 8-1
Deviation from nominal $\bar{x}$ and R charts.

handle this situation easily. Consider the ith part number. Let $\bar{R}_i$ and N_i be the average range and nominal value of x for this part number. Then for all the samples from this part number, plot

$$R^s = \frac{R}{\bar{R}_i} \tag{8-1}$$

on a standardized R chart with control limits at $LCL = D_3$ and $UCL = D_4$, and plot

$$\bar{x}^s = \frac{\bar{x} - N_i}{\bar{R}_i}$$

on a standardized $\bar{x}$ chart with control limits at $LCL = -A_2$ and $UCL = +A_2$. Notice that the center line of the standardized R chart is unity and that the center line of the standardized $\bar{x}$ chart is zero.

The target values $\bar{R}_i$ and N_i for each part number can be determined by using specifications for N_i and taking $\bar{R}_i$ from prior history (often in the form of a control chart, or by converting an estimate of σ into $\bar{R}_i$ by the relationship $\bar{R}_i = (Sd_2)/c_4$). For new parts, it is a common practice to utilize prior experience on similar parts to set the targets.

8-1.2 Attribute Control Charts for Short Production Runs

Dealing with attribute data in the short production run environment is extremely simple; the proper method is to use a standardized control chart for the attribute of interest. This method will allow different part numbers to be plotted on the same chart, and will automatically compensate for variable sample size.

Standardized control charts for attributes have been discussed previously in Chapter 5. For convenience, the relevant formulas are presented in Table 8-2. All standardized attribute control charts have the center line at zero, and the upper and lower control limits are at $+3$ and -3, respectively.

Table 8-2
Standardized attribute control charts suitable for short production runs

Attribute	Target Value	Standard Deviation	Statistic to Plot on the Control Chart
$\hat{p}_i$	$\bar{p}$	$\sqrt{\dfrac{\bar{p}(1 - \bar{p})}{n}}$	$Z_i = \dfrac{\hat{p}_i - \bar{p}}{\sqrt{\bar{p}(1 - \bar{p})/n}}$
$n\hat{p}_i$	$n\bar{p}$	$\sqrt{n\bar{p}(1 - \bar{p})}$	$Z_i = \dfrac{n\hat{p}_i - n\bar{p}}{\sqrt{n\bar{p}(1 - \bar{p})}}$
c_i	$\bar{c}$	$\sqrt{\bar{c}}$	$Z_i = \dfrac{c_i - \bar{c}}{\sqrt{\bar{c}}}$
u_i	$\bar{u}$	$\sqrt{\bar{u}/n}$	$Z_i = \dfrac{u_i - \bar{u}}{\sqrt{\bar{u}/n}}$

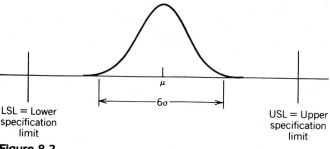

Figure 8-2
A process with the spread of the natural tolerance limits less than the spread of the specification limits, or $6\sigma <$ USL $-$ LSL.

8-2 MODIFIED AND ACCEPTANCE CONTROL CHARTS

In most situations in which control charts are used, the focus is on statistical control of the process, reduction of variability, and continuous process improvement. When an $\bar{x}$ chart is used to control the fraction of conforming units produced by the process rather than to satisfy the traditional SPC objective of detecting assignable causes, two important and useful techniques can be employed. One method uses *modified* (or *reject*) control limits, and the second uses the acceptance control chart.

8-2.1 Modified Control Limits for the $\bar{x}$ Chart

Modified control limits are generally used in situations where the 6-sigma spread of the process is smaller than the spread in the specification limits; that is, PCR > 1. This situation occurs frequently in practice. In fact, this should be the natural eventual result of a strong quality-improvement program—reduction of process variability with a corresponding increase in the process-capability ratio. Suppose, for example, that the specification limits on the fill volume of a carbonated beverage container are LSL $= 10.00$ oz and USL $= 10.20$ oz, but as the result of a program of engineering and operating refinements, the filling machine can operate with a standard deviation of fill volume of approximately $\sigma = 0.01$ oz. Therefore, the distance USL $-$ LSL is approximately 20-sigma, or much greater than the 6-sigma natural tolerance limits on the process, and the process-capability ratio is PCR $=$ (USL $-$ LSL)$/6\sigma = 0.20/[6(0.01)] = 3.33$.

In situations where 6-sigma is much smaller than the spread in the specifications (USL $-$ LSL), the process mean can sometimes be allowed to vary over a reasonably wide range without appreciably affecting the fraction of nonconforming product produced.[1] For example, see Figure 8-2. When this situation occurs, we can use a *modified* control chart for $\bar{x}$ instead of the usual $\bar{x}$ chart. The modified $\bar{x}$ control chart is concerned only with detecting whether the true process mean μ is located such that the process is producing a fraction nonconforming in excess

---

[1] There are also cases where the mean should not be allowed to vary even if the PCR is considerably larger than unity. The conventional $\bar{x}$ chart should be used in such situations.

of some specified value δ. In effect, μ is allowed to vary over an interval, say $\mu_L \leq \mu \leq \mu_U$, where μ_L and μ_U are chosen as the smallest and largest permissible values of μ, respectively, consistent with producing a fraction nonconforming of at most δ. We will assume that the process variability σ is in control. Good general discussions of the modified control chart are in Hill (1956) and Duncan (1974). As noted in Duncan (1974), the procedure is sometimes used when a process is subject to tool wear (see Section 8-9).

To specify the control limits for a modified $\bar{x}$ chart, we will assume that the process output is normally distributed. For the process fraction nonconforming to be less than δ, we must require that the true process mean is in the interval $\mu_L \leq \mu \leq \mu_U$. Consequently, we see from Figure 8-3a that we must have

$$\mu_L = \text{LSL} + Z_\delta \sigma \qquad (8\text{-}1a)$$

and

$$\mu_U = \text{USL} - Z_\delta \sigma \qquad (8\text{-}1b)$$

where Z_δ is the upper $100(1 - \delta)$ percentage point of the standard normal distribution. Now if we specify a type I error of α, the upper and lower control limits are

$$
\begin{aligned}
\text{UCL} &= \mu_U + \frac{Z_\alpha \sigma}{\sqrt{n}} \\
&= \text{USL} - Z_\delta \sigma + \frac{Z_\alpha \sigma}{\sqrt{n}} \\
&= \text{USL} - \left(Z_\delta - \frac{Z_\alpha}{\sqrt{n}} \right) \sigma \qquad (8\text{-}2a)
\end{aligned}
$$

and

$$
\begin{aligned}
\text{LCL} &= \mu_L - \frac{Z_\alpha \sigma}{\sqrt{n}} \\
&= \text{LSL} + Z_\delta \sigma - \frac{Z_\alpha \sigma}{\sqrt{n}} \\
&= \text{LSL} + \left(Z_\delta - \frac{Z_\alpha}{\sqrt{n}} \right) \sigma \qquad (8\text{-}2b)
\end{aligned}
$$

respectively. The control limits are shown on the distribution of $\bar{x}$ in Figure 8-3b. Instead of specifying a type I error, one may use

$$\text{UCL} = \text{USL} - \left(Z_\delta - \frac{3}{\sqrt{n}} \right) \sigma \qquad (8\text{-}3a)$$

and

$$\text{LCL} = \text{LSL} + \left(Z_\delta - \frac{3}{\sqrt{n}} \right) \sigma \qquad (8\text{-}3b)$$

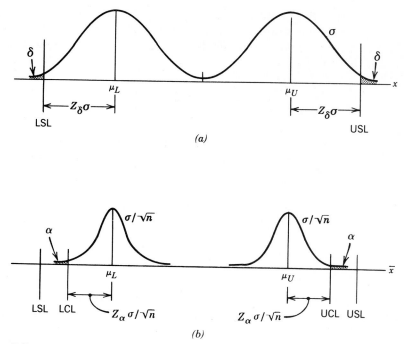

Figure 8-3

Control limits on a modified control chart. (a) Distribution of process output.
(b) Distribution of the sample mean $\bar{x}$.

Some quality engineers recommend the use of 2-sigma limits on the modified control chart, arguing that the tighter control limits afford better protection (smaller β-risk) against critical shifts in the mean at little loss in the α-risk. A discussion of this subject is in Freund (1957). Noticee that the modified control chart is equivalent to testing the hypothesis that the process mean lies in the interval $\mu_L \le \mu \le \mu_U$.

To design a modified control chart, we must have a good estimate of σ available. If the process variability shifts, then the modified control limits are not appropriate. Consequently, an R or an S chart should always be used in conjunction with the modified control chart. Furthermore, the initial estimate of σ required to set up the modified control chart would usually be obtained from an R or an S chart.

8-2.2 Acceptance Control Charts

The second approach to using an $\bar{x}$ chart to control the fraction of nonconforming units, or the fraction of units exceeding specifications, is called the acceptance control chart. In the modified control chart design of Section 8-2.1, the chart was based on a specified sample size n, a process fraction nonconforming δ, and type I error probability α. Thus, we interpret δ as a process fraction nonconforming that we will accept with probability $1 - \alpha$. Freund (1957) developed the acceptance control chart to take into account both the risk of rejecting a process operating at a satisfactory level (type I error or α-risk) and the risk of accepting a process that is operating at an unsatisfactory level (type II error or β-risk).

There are two ways to design the control chart. In the first approach, we design the control chart based on a specified n and a process fraction nonconforming γ that we would like to reject with probability $1 - \beta$. In this case, the control limits for the chart are

$$\text{UCL} = \mu_U - \frac{Z_\beta \sigma}{\sqrt{n}}$$

$$= \text{USL} - Z_\gamma \sigma - \frac{Z_\beta \sigma}{\sqrt{n}}$$

$$= \text{USL} - \left(Z_\gamma + \frac{Z_\beta}{\sqrt{n}} \right) \sigma \qquad (8\text{-}4a)$$

and

$$\text{LCL} = \mu_L + \frac{Z_\beta \sigma}{\sqrt{n}}$$

$$= \text{LSL} + Z_\gamma \sigma + \frac{Z_\beta \sigma}{\sqrt{n}}$$

$$= \text{LSL} + \left(Z_\gamma + \frac{Z_\beta}{\sqrt{n}} \right) \sigma \qquad (8\text{-}4b)$$

Note that when n, γ, and $1 - \beta$ (or β) are specified, the control limits are inside the μ_L and μ_U values that produce the fraction nonconforming γ. In contrast, when n, δ, and α are specified, the lower control limit falls between μ_L and LSL and the upper control limit falls between μ_U and USL.

It is also possible to choose a sample size for an acceptance control chart so that specified values of δ, α, γ, and β are obtained. By equating the upper control limits (say) for a specified δ and α [Equation (8-2a)] and a specified γ and β [Equation (8-4a)], we obtain

$$\text{USL} - \left(Z_\delta - \frac{Z_\alpha}{\sqrt{n}} \right) \sigma = \text{USL} - \left(Z_\gamma + \frac{Z_\beta}{\sqrt{n}} \right) \sigma$$

Therefore, a sample size of

$$n = \left(\frac{Z_\alpha + Z_\beta}{Z_\delta - Z_\gamma} \right)^2 \qquad (8\text{-}5)$$

will yield the required values of δ, α, γ, and β. For example, if $\delta = 0.01$, $\alpha = 0.00135$, $\gamma = 0.05$, and $\beta = 0.20$, we must use a sample of size

$$n = \left(\frac{Z_{0.00135} + Z_{0.20}}{Z_{0.01} - Z_{0.05}} \right)^2 = \left(\frac{3.00 + 0.84}{2.33 - 1.645} \right)^2 = 31.43 \simeq 32$$

on the acceptance control chart. Obviously, to use this approach, n must not be seriously restricted by cost or other factors.

8-3 GROUP CONTROL CHARTS FOR MULTIPLE-STREAM PROCESSES

Many processes have several sources or streams of output. For example, a machine may have several heads, with each head producing (we hope) identical units of product. In such situations several possible control procedures may be followed. One possibility is to use separate control charts on each stream. This approach usually results in a prohibitively large number of control charts. If the output streams are highly correlated, say nearly perfectly correlated, then control charts on only one stream may be adequate.

When the output streams are not highly correlated, the group control chart can be a very effective procedure. To illustrate the methods of construction and use, suppose that the process has six streams and that each stream has the same target value and inherent variability. Variables measurement is made on the items produced, and the distribution of the measurement is well approximated by the normal. The objective of the control procedure is twofold:

1. To detect when the output of one stream has shifted away from target.
2. To detect when the output of all streams has shifted away from target.

In the first case, we are trying to detect an assignable cause that affects only one stream, while in the second, we are looking for an assignable cause that impacts *all* streams (such as a change in raw materials).

To establish a group control chart, the sampling is performed just as if separate control charts were to be set up on each stream. Suppose, for purposes of illustration, that a sample size of $n = 4$ is used. This means that 4 units will be taken from each of the six streams over a short period of time. This will be repeated until about 20 such groups of samples have been taken. At this point we would have $20 \times 6 = 120$ averages of $n = 4$ observations each and 120 corresponding ranges. These averages and ranges would be averaged to produce a grand average $\bar{\bar{x}}$ and an average range $\bar{R}$. The limits on the group control charts would be at

$$\text{UCL} = \bar{\bar{x}} + A_2\bar{R}$$
$$\text{LCL} = \bar{\bar{x}} - A_2\bar{R}$$

for the $\bar{x}$ chart and at

$$\text{UCL} = D_4\bar{R}$$
$$\text{LCL} = D_3\bar{R}$$

for the R chart, with $A_2 = 0.729$, $D_3 = 0$, and $D_4 = 2.282$. Notice that the sample size $n = 4$ determines the control chart constants.

When the group control chart is used to control the process, we plot only the largest and smallest of the six means observed at any time period on the $\bar{x}$ chart. If these means are inside the control limits, then all other means will also lie inside the limits. Similarly, only the largest range will be plotted on the range chart. Each plotted point is identified on the chart by the number of the stream that produced it. The process is out of control if a point exceeds a 3-sigma limit. Runs tests cannot be applied to these charts, because the conventional runs tests were not developed to test averages or ranges that are the extremes of a group of averages or ranges.

It is useful to examine the stream numbers on the chart. In general, if a stream consistently gives the largest (or smallest) value several times in a row, that may constitute evidence that this stream is different from the others. If the process has s streams and if r is the number of consecutive times that a particular stream is the largest or smallest value, then the average run length for this event is

$$\text{ARL} = \frac{s^r - 1}{s - 1} \qquad (8\text{-}6)$$

if all streams are identical. To illustrate the use of this equation, if $s = 6$ and $r = 4$ then

$$\text{ARL} = \frac{6^4 - 1}{6 - 1} = 259$$

That is, if the process is in control, we will expect to see the same stream producing an extreme value on the group control chart four times in a row only once every 259 samples.

One way to choose a good value of r to detect the presence of one stream that is different from the others is to use Equation (8-6) to find an ARL that is roughly consistent with the ARL of a conventional control chart. The ARL for an in-control process for a single point beyond the upper control limit (say) is 740. Thus, using $r = 4$ for a six-stream process results in an ARL that is too short and that will give too many false alarms. A better choice is $r = 5$, since

$$\text{ARL} = \frac{6^5 - 1}{6 - 1} = 1555$$

Thus, if we have six streams and if the same stream produces an extreme value on the control chart in five consecutive samples, then that is strong evidence that this stream is different from the others.

Using Equation (8-6), we can generate some general guidelines for choosing r given the number of streams s. Suitable pairs (s, r) would include (3, 7), (4, 6), (5–6, 5), and (7–10, 4). All these combinations give good ARL performance when the process is in control.

8-4 MULTIVARIATE QUALITY CONTROL

There are many situations in which the simultaneous control of two or more related quality characteristics is necessary. For example, suppose that a bearing has both an inner diameter (x_1) and an outer diameter (x_2) that together determine the usefulness of the part. Suppose that x_1 and x_2 have a bivariate normal distribution. As both quality characteristics are measurements, they could be controlled by applying the usual $\bar{x}$ chart to each characteristic, as illustrated in Figure 8-4. The process is considered to be in control only if the sample means $\bar{x}_1$ and $\bar{x}_2$ fall within their respective control limits. This is equivalent to the pair of means ($\bar{x}_1, \bar{x}_2$) plotting within the shaded region in Figure 8-5.

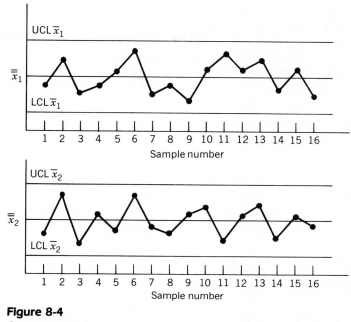

Figure 8-4
Control charts for inner $(\bar{x}_1)$ and outer $(\bar{x}_2)$ bearing diameters.

Controlling these two quality characteristics independently can be very misleading. The probability that either $\bar{x}_1$ or $\bar{x}_2$ exceeds 3-sigma control limits is 0.0027. However, the joint probability that both variables exceed their control limits simultaneously when they are both in control is $(0.0027)(0.0027) = 0.00000729$, which is considerably smaller than 0.0027. Furthermore, the probability that both $\bar{x}_1$ and $\bar{x}_2$ will simultaneously plot inside the control limits when the process is really in control is $(0.9973)(0.9973) = 0.99460729$. Therefore, the use of two independent

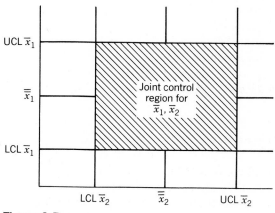

Figure 8-5
Control region using independent control limits for $\bar{x}_1$ and $\bar{x}_2$.

$\bar{x}$ charts has distorted the simultaneous control of $\bar{x}_1$ and $\bar{x}_2$, in that the type I error and the probability of a point correctly plotting in control are not equal to their advertised levels for the individual control charts.

This distortion in the control procedure increases as the number of quality characteristics increases. In general, if there are p statistically independent quality characteristics for a particular product and if an $\bar{x}$ chart with $P\{\text{type I error}\} = \alpha$ is maintained on each, then the true probability of type I error for the joint control procedure is

$$\alpha' = 1 - (1 - \alpha)^p \tag{8-7}$$

and the probability that all p means will simultaneously plot inside their control limits when the process is in control is

$$P\{\text{all } p \text{ means plot in control}\} = (1 - \alpha)^p \tag{8-8}$$

Clearly, the distortion in the joint control procedure can be severe, even for moderate values of p. Furthermore, if the p quality characteristics are not independent, which would usually be the case if they relate to the same product, then Equations (8-7) and (8-8) do not hold, and we have no easy way even to measure the distortion in the joint control procedure.

Quality-control problems in which several related variables are of interest are sometimes called *multivariate* quality-control problems. The original work in multivariate quality control was done by Hotelling (1947), who applied his procedures to bombsight data during World War II. Subsequent papers dealing with control procedures for several related variables include Hicks (1955), Jackson (1956) (1959), Montgomery and Wadsworth (1972), and Alt (1985). This subject is particularly important today, as automatic inspection procedures make it relatively easy to measure many parameters on each unit of product manufactured.

8-4.1 Control of Means

Suppose that two quality characteristics x_1 and x_2 are jointly distributed according to the bivariate normal distribution. Let μ_1 and μ_2 be the mean values of the quality characteristics, and let σ_1 and σ_2 be the standard deviations of x_1 and x_2, respectively. The covariance between x_1 and x_2 is a measure of dependence between x_1 and x_2, and is denoted by σ_{12}. We assume that σ_1, σ_2, and σ_{12} are known. If $\bar{x}_1$ and $\bar{x}_2$ are the sample averages of the two quality characteristics computed from a sample of size n, then the statistic

$$\chi_0^2 = \frac{n}{\sigma_1^2 \sigma_2^2 - \sigma_{12}^2} \left[\sigma_2^2 (\bar{x}_1 - \mu_1)^2 + \sigma_1^2 (\bar{x}_2 - \mu_2)^2 - 2\sigma_{12}(\bar{x}_1 - \mu_1)(\bar{x}_2 - \mu_2) \right] \tag{8-9}$$

will have a chi-square distribution with 2 degrees of freedom. This equation can be used as the basis of a control chart for the process means μ_1 and μ_2. If the process means remain at the values μ_1 and μ_2, then values of χ_0^2 should be less than $\chi_{\alpha,2}^2$, where $\chi_{\alpha,2}^2$ is the upper α percentage point of the chi-square distribution with 2 degrees of freedom. If at least one of the means shifts to some new (out-of-control) value, then we will expect to find $\chi_0^2 > \chi_{\alpha,2}^2$.

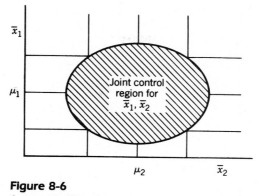

Figure 8-6
A control ellipse for two independent variables.

The control procedure may be represented graphically. Consider the case in which the two random variables x_1 and x_2 are independent; that is, $\sigma_{12} = 0$. If $\sigma_{12} = 0$, then Equation (8-9) defines an ellipse centered at (μ_1, μ_2) with principal axes parallel to the $\bar{x}_1, \bar{x}_2$ axes, as shown in Figure 8-6. Taking χ_0^2 in (8-9) equal to $\chi_{\alpha,2}^2$ implies that a pair of sample averages $(\bar{x}_1, \bar{x}_2)$ yielding a value of χ_0^2 plotting inside the ellipse indicates that the process is in control, while if the corresponding value of χ_0^2 plots outside the ellipse the process is out of control. Figure 8-6 is often called a *control* ellipse.

Compare the region of joint control for $\bar{x}_1$ and $\bar{x}_2$ in the control ellipse with the region of joint control for $\bar{x}_1$ and $\bar{x}_2$ when two independent $\bar{x}$ charts are used (Figure 8-5). If the two quality characteristics are dependent, then $\sigma_{12} \neq 0$, and the corresponding control ellipse is shown in Figure 8-7. Note that when the two variables are dependent, the principal axes of the ellipse are no longer parallel to the $\bar{x}_1, \bar{x}_2$ axes.

Two disadvantages are associated with the control ellipse. The first is that the time sequence of the plotted points is lost; consequently, runs tests and other related procedures cannot be easily applied. The second disadvantage is that it is difficult to construct the ellipse for more than two quality characteristics. To avoid these difficulties, it is customary to plot the values of χ_0^2 computed from Equation

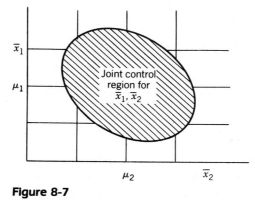

Figure 8-7
A control ellipse for two dependent variables.

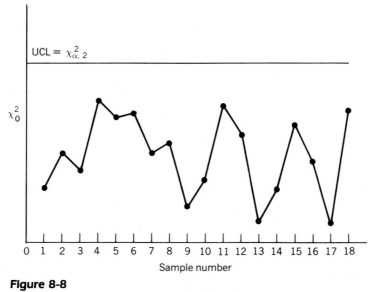

Figure 8-8
A χ^2 control chart for $p = 2$ quality characteristics.

(8-9) for each sample on a control chart with only an upper control limit at $\chi^2_{\alpha,2}$, as shown in Figure 8-8. This control chart is usually called the χ^2 control chart. Notice that the time sequence of the data is preserved by this control chart, so that runs or other nonrandom patterns can be investigated. Furthermore, it has the additional advantage that the "state" of the process is characterized by a single number (the value of the statistic χ^2_0). This is particularly helpful when there are two or more quality characteristics of interest.

It is possible to extend these results to the case where p related quality characteristics are controlled jointly. It is assumed that the joint probability distribution of the p quality characteristics is the p-variate normal distribution. The procedure requires computing the sample mean for each of the p quality characteristics from a sample of size n. This set of quality characteristic means is represented by the $p \times 1$ vector

$$\bar{x} = \begin{bmatrix} \bar{x}_1 \\ \bar{x}_2 \\ \vdots \\ \bar{x}_p \end{bmatrix}$$

The test statistic plotted on the control chart for each sample is

$$\chi^2_0 = n(\bar{x} - \mu)' \sum{}^{-1} (\bar{x} - \mu) \tag{8-10}$$

where $\mu' = [\mu_1, \mu_2, \ldots, \mu_p]$ is the vector of in-control means for each quality characteristic and $\sum$ is the covariance matrix. The upper limit on the control chart is

$$UCL = \chi^2_{\alpha,p} \tag{8-11}$$

In practice, it is usually necessary to estimate μ and $\sum$ from the analysis of preliminary samples of size n, taken when the process is assumed to be in control. Suppose that m such samples are available. The sample means and variances are calculated from each sample as usual; that is

$$\bar{x}_{jk} = \frac{1}{n} \sum_{i=1}^{n} x_{ijk} \qquad \begin{cases} j = 1, 2, \ldots, p \\ k = 1, 2, \ldots, m \end{cases} \qquad (8\text{-}12)$$

$$S_{jk}^2 = \frac{1}{n-1} \sum_{i=1}^{n} (x_{ijk} - \bar{x}_{jk})^2 \qquad \begin{cases} j = 1, 2, \ldots, p \\ k = 1, 2, \ldots, m \end{cases} \qquad (8\text{-}13)$$

where x_{ijk} is the ith observation on the jth quality characteristic in the kth sample. The covariance between quality characteristic j and quality characteristic h in the kth sample is

$$S_{jhk} = \frac{1}{n-1} \sum_{i=1}^{n} (x_{ijk} - \bar{x}_{jk})(x_{ihk} - \bar{x}_{hk}) \qquad \begin{cases} k = 1, 2, \ldots, m \\ j \neq h \end{cases} \qquad (8\text{-}14)$$

The statistics $\bar{x}_{jk}$, S_{jk}^2, and S_{jhk} are then averaged over all m samples to obtain

$$\bar{\bar{x}}_j = \frac{1}{m} \sum_{k=1}^{m} \bar{x}_{jk} \qquad j = 1, 2, \ldots, p \qquad (8\text{-}15a)$$

$$S_j^2 = \frac{1}{m} \sum_{k=1}^{m} S_{jk}^2 \qquad j = 1, 2, \ldots, p \qquad (8\text{-}15b)$$

and

$$S_{jh} = \frac{1}{m} \sum_{k=1}^{m} S_{jhk} \qquad j \neq h \qquad (8\text{-}15c)$$

The $\{\bar{\bar{x}}_j\}$ are the elements of the vector $\bar{\bar{x}}$, and the $p \times p$ sample covariance matrix S is formed as

$$S = \begin{bmatrix} S_1^2 & S_{12} & S_{13} & \cdots & S_{1p} \\ & S_2^2 & S_{23} & \cdots & S_{2p} \\ & & \ddots & & \vdots \\ & & & & S_p^2 \end{bmatrix} \qquad (8\text{-}16)$$

Now we would replace μ with $\bar{\bar{x}}$ and $\sum$ with S in Equation (8-10). The test statistic now becomes

$$T^2 = n(\bar{x} - \bar{\bar{x}})'S^{-1}(\bar{x} - \bar{\bar{x}}) \qquad (8\text{-}17)$$

in this form, the procedure is usually called the Hotelling T^2 control chart. If μ and $\sum$ are estimated from a relatively large number of preliminary samples (say $m \geq 20$ or 25), then it is customary to use UCL $= \chi_{\alpha, p}^2$ as the upper control limit on the Hotelling T^2 chart. If this is not the case, then an upper control limit can be based on the T^2 distribution (which is related to the F distribution; see Alt (1985) for details).

Table 8-3

Data for Example 8-1

Sample Number k	(a) Sample Means		(b) Variances and Covariances			(c) Control Chart Statistics	
	Tensile Strength ($\bar{x}_{1k}$)	Diameter ($\bar{x}_{2k}$)	S_{1k}^2	S_{2k}^2	S_{12k}	T_k^2	$|S_k|$
1	115.25	1.04	1.25	0.87	0.80	2.16	0.45
2	115.91	1.06	1.26	0.85	0.81	2.14	0.41
3	115.05	1.09	1.30	0.90	0.82	6.77	0.50
4	116.21	1.05	1.02	0.85	0.81	8.29	0.21
5	115.90	1.07	1.16	0.73	0.80	1.89	0.21
6	115.55	1.06	1.01	0.80	0.76	0.03	0.23
7	114.98	1.05	1.25	0.78	0.75	7.54	0.41
8	115.25	1.10	1.40	0.83	0.80	3.01	0.52
9	116.15	1.09	1.19	0.87	0.83	5.92	0.35
10	115.92	1.05	1.17	0.86	0.95	2.41	0.10
11	115.75	0.99	1.45	0.79	0.78	1.13	0.54
12	114.90	1.06	1.24	0.82	0.81	9.96	0.36
13	116.01	1.05	1.26	0.55	0.72	3.86	0.17
14	115.83	1.07	1.17	0.76	0.75	1.11	0.33
15	115.29	1.11	1.23	0.89	0.82	2.56	0.42
16	115.63	1.04	1.24	0.91	0.83	0.07	0.44
17	115.47	1.03	1.20	0.95	0.70	0.19	0.65
18	115.58	1.05	1.18	0.83	0.79	0.00	0.36
19	115.72	1.06	1.31	0.89	0.76	0.35	0.59
20	115.40	1.04	1.29	0.85	0.68	0.62	0.63
Averages	$\bar{\bar{x}}_1 = 115.59$	$\bar{\bar{x}}_2 = 1.06$	$S_1^2 = 1.23$	$S_2^2 = 0.83$	$S_{12} = 0.79$		

Example 8-1

The tensile strength and diameter of a textile fiber are two important quality characteristics that are to be jointly controlled. The quality engineer has decided to use $n = 10$ fiber specimens in each sample. He has taken 20 preliminary samples, and on the basis of these data he concludes that $\bar{\bar{x}}_1 = 115.59$ psi, $\bar{\bar{x}}_2 = 1.06$ ($\times 10^{-2}$) inch, $S_1^2 = 1.23$, $S_2^2 = 0.83$, and $S_{12} = 0.79$. Therefore, the statistic he will use for process control purposes is

$$T^2 = \frac{10}{(1.23)(0.83) - (0.79)^2} \left[0.83(\bar{x}_1 - 115.59)^2 + 1.23(\bar{x}_2 - 1.06)^2 \right. $$
$$\left. - 2(0.79)(\bar{x}_1 - 115.59)(\bar{x}_2 - 1.06) \right]$$

The data used in this analysis and the summary statistics are in Table 8-3, panels (a) and (b).

Figure 8-9 presents the Hotelling T^2 control chart for this example. We have used UCL $= \chi^2_{0.001, 2} = 13.815$ as the upper control limit. No points plot outside the limits, so we would conclude that the process mean vector is in control.

One difficulty encountered with the use of either the χ^2 or T^2 control chart is practical interpretation of an out-of-control signal. Specifically, which of the p variables (or which *subset* of them) is responsible for the signal? This question is not always easy to answer. The standard practice is to plot *univariate* $\bar{x}$ charts on the individual variables $x_1, x_2, \ldots, x_p$. However, this approach may not be successful, for reasons discussed previously. Alt (1985) suggests using $\bar{x}$ charts with Bonferroni-type control limits [i.e., replace $Z_{\alpha/2}$ in the $\bar{x}$ chart control limit calculation with $Z_{\alpha/(2p)}$]. Jackson (1980) recommends using control charts based on the p

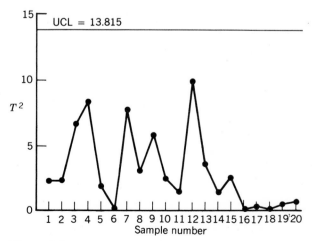

Figure 8-9
The Hotelling T^2 control chart for tensile strength and diameter, Example 8-1.

principal components (which are linear combinations of the original variables). These plots do not always lend themselves to a clear interpretation of the situation with respect to the original variables. A procedure Murphy (1987) has suggested based on discriminant analysis seems promising.

8-4.2 Control of Process Variability

Just as it is important to control the process mean vector μ in the multivariate case, it is also important to control process variability. Process variability is summarized by the $p \times p$ *covariance matrix* $\sum$. The main diagonal elements of this matrix are the variances of the individual process variables, and the off-diagonal elements are the covariances. Alt (1985) gives a nice introduction to the problem and presents two useful procedures.

The first procedure is a direct extension of the univariate S^2 control chart. The procedure is equivalent to repeated tests of significance of the hypothesis that the process covariance matrix is equal to a particular matrix of constants $\sum$. If this approach is used, the statistic plotted on the control chart for the ith sample is

$$W_i = -pn + pn \, ln(n) - n \, ln(|\mathbf{A}_i|/|\sum|) + tr(\sum^{-1} \mathbf{A}_i) \tag{8-18}$$

where $\mathbf{A}_i = (n - 1)\mathbf{S}_i$, $\mathbf{S}_i$ is the sample covariance matrix for sample i, and tr is the trace operator. (The trace of a matrix is the sum of the main diagonal elements.) If the value of W_i plots above the upper control limit UCL $= \chi^2_{\alpha, \, p(p+1)/2}$, the process is out of control.

The second approach is based on the sample *generalized* variance, $|\mathbf{S}|$. This statistic, which is the determinant of the sample covariance matrix, is a widely used measure of multivariate dispersion. Montgomery and Wadsworth (1972) used an asymptotic normal approximation to develop a control chart for $|\mathbf{S}|$. Another method would be to use the mean and variance of $|\mathbf{S}|$, that is, $E(|\mathbf{S}|)$ and $V(|\mathbf{S}|)$, and the property that most of the probability distribution of $|\mathbf{S}|$ is contained in the interval $E|\mathbf{S}| \pm 3\sqrt{V(|\mathbf{S}|)}$. It can be shown that

$$E(|\mathbf{S}|) = b_1|\sum| \tag{8-19}$$

and

$$V(|\mathbf{S}|) = b_2|\sum|^2 \tag{8-20}$$

where

$$b_1 = \frac{1}{(n - 1)^p} \prod_{i=1}^{p} (n - i) \tag{8-21}$$

and

$$b_2 = \frac{1}{(n - 1)^{2p}} \prod_{i=1}^{p} (n - i) \left[\prod_{i=1}^{p} (n - j + 2) - \prod_{i=1}^{p} (n - j) \right] \tag{8-22}$$

Therefore, the parameters of the control chart for $|S|$ would be

$$\text{UCL} = |\Sigma|(b_1 + 3b_2^{1/2})$$
$$\text{CL} = b_1|\Sigma| \qquad\qquad (8\text{-}23)$$
$$\text{LCL} = |\Sigma|(b_1 - 3b_2^{1/2})$$

The lower control limit in (8-23) is replaced with zero if the calculated value is less than zero.

Usually, in practice Σ will be estimated by a sample covariance matrix S, based on the analysis of preliminary samples. If this is the case, we should replace $|\Sigma|$ in Equation (8-23) by $|S|/b_1$, since Equation (8-19) has shown that $|S|/b_1$ is an unbiased estimator of $|\Sigma|$.

Example 8-2

To illustrate controlling process variability in the multivariate case, we will return to Example 8-1 and construct a control chart for the generalized variance. Based on the 20 preliminary samples, the sample covariance matrix is

$$S = \begin{bmatrix} 1.23 & 0.79 \\ 0.79 & 0.83 \end{bmatrix}$$

so

$$|S| = 0.3968$$

The constants b_1 and b_2 are

$$b_1 = \frac{1}{81}(9)(8) = 0.8889$$

$$b_3 = \frac{1}{6561}(9)(8)[(11)(10) - (9)(8)] = 0.4170$$

Therefore, replacing $|\Sigma|$ in (8-23) by $|S|/b_1 = 0.3968/0.8889 = 0.4464$, we find that the control chart parameters are

$$\text{UCL} = (|S|/b_1)(b_1 + 3b_2^{1/2}) = 0.4464[0.8889 + 3(0.4170)^{1/2}]$$
$$= 1.26$$
$$\text{CL} = |S| = 0.3968$$
$$\text{LCL} = (|S|/b_1)(b_1 - 3b_2^{1/2}) = 0.4464[0.8889 - 3(0.4170)^{1/2}]$$
$$= -0.47 = 0$$

Figure 8-10 presents the control chart. The values of $|S_i|$ for each sample are shown in the last column of panel (c) of Table 8-3.

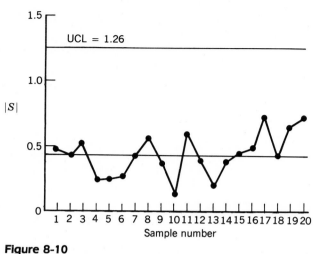

Figure 8-10
A control chart for the sample generalized variance, Example 8-2.

While the sample generalized variance is a widely used measure of multivariate dispersion, remember it is a relatively simplistic scalar representation of a complex multivariable problem, and it is easy to be fooled if all we look at is $|\mathbf{S}|$. For example, consider the three covariance matrices:

$$\mathbf{S}_1 = \begin{bmatrix} 1 & 0 \\ 0 & 1 \end{bmatrix}$$

$$\mathbf{S}_2 = \begin{bmatrix} 2.32 & 0.40 \\ 0.40 & 0.50 \end{bmatrix}$$

$$\mathbf{S}_3 = \begin{bmatrix} 1.68 & -0.40 \\ -0.40 & 0.50 \end{bmatrix}$$

Now $|\mathbf{S}_1| = |\mathbf{S}_2| = |\mathbf{S}_3| = 1$, yet the three matrices convey considerably different information about process variability and the correlation between the two variables. It is probably a good idea to use univariate control charts for variability in conjunction with the control chart for $|\mathbf{S}|$.

8-5 PRE-CONTROL

PRE-control is a technique that is used to detect shifts or upsets in the process that may result in the production of nonconforming units. The technique differs from statistical process control in that conventional control charts are designed to detect shifts in process parameters that are statistically significant, and PRE-control requires no plotting of graphs and no computations. PRE-control uses the normal distribution in determining changes in the process mean or standard deviation that could result in increased production of nonconforming units. Only three units are required to give control information.

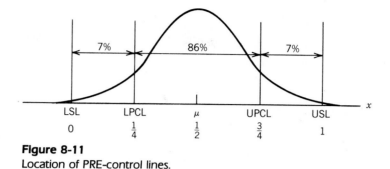

Figure 8-11
Location of PRE-control lines.

To demonstrate the procedure, suppose that the quality characteristic is normally distributed and that the natural tolerance limits ($\mu \pm 3\sigma$) exactly coincide with the specification limits. Furthermore, the process average μ is halfway between the specifications, so that the process is producing 0.27% fallout. Construct two PRE-control limits (called upper and lower PC lines), each of which is one-fourth the distance in from the modified limit, as in Figure 8-11. Since the distribution of the quality characteristic is normal, approximately 86% of the process output will lie inside the PC lines, and approximately 7% will lie in each of the regions between the PC line and specification limit. This means that only about one item in 14 will fall outside a PC line if the process mean and standard deviation are on the target values.

If the probability is one-fourteenth that one unit falls outside a PC line, the probability that two consecutive units fall outside a PC line is $(\frac{1}{14})(\frac{1}{14}) = \frac{1}{196} \simeq \frac{1}{200}$. That is, if the process is operating correctly, the probability of finding two consecutive units outside of a given PC line is only about $\frac{1}{200}$. When two such consecutive units are found, it is likely that the process has shifted to an out-of-control state. Similarly, it is unlikely to find the first unit beyond one PC line and the next beyond the other PC line. In this case, we suspect that process variability has increased.

Below is a set of rules that describe the operation of PRE-control. These rules assume that 1 to 3% nonconforming production is acceptable and that the process-capability ratio is at least 1.15.

1. Start the process. If the first item is outside specifications, reset and start again.
2. If an item is inside specifications but outside a PC line, check the next item.
3. If the second item is outside the same PC line, reset the process.
4. If the second item is inside the PC line, continue. Process is reset only when two consecutive items are outside a given PC line.
5. If one item is outside a PC line and the next item is outside the other PC line, the process variability is out of control.
6. When five consecutive units are inside the PC lines, shift to frequency gaging.
7. When frequency gaging, do not adjust process until an item exceeds a PC line. Then examine the next consecutive item, and proceed as in step 4.
8. When process is reset, five consecutive items must fall inside the PC line before frequency gaging can be resumed.

9. If the operator samples from the process more than 25 times without having to reset the process, reduce the gaging frequency so that more units are manufactured between samples. If we must rest before 25 samples are taken, increase the gaging frequency. An average of 25 samples to a reset indicates that the sampling frequency is satisfactory.

PRE-control is an example of a technique called *narrow-limit gaging* (or *compressed-limit gaging*), in which inspection procedures are determined using tightened limits located so as to meet established risks of accepting nonconforming product. Narrow-limit gaging is discussed in more general terms in Section 14-4.4 and by Ott (1975).

While PRE-control has the advantage of simplicity, it should not be used indiscriminately. The procedure has several serious drawbacks. First, because no control chart is usually constructed, all the sensitizing rules and pattern-recognition procedures associated with the control chart cannot be used. Thus, the diagnostic information about the process contained in the pattern of points on the control chart, along with the logbook aspect of the chart, is lost. Second, the small sample sizes greatly reduce the ability of the procedure to detect even moderate-to-large shifts. Third, PRE-control does not provide information that is helpful in bringing the process into control, or that would be helpful in reducing variability (which is the goal of statistical process control). Finally, the assumption of an in-control process and adequate process capability is extremely important. PRE-control should only be considered in manufacturing processes where the process-capability ratio is much greater than one (perhaps at least two or three), and where a near-zero defects environment has been achieved.

8-6 STATISTICAL ALTERNATIVES TO CONTROL CHARTS

We have noted previously that the control chart is statistically equivalent to testing a hypothesis. In fact, it is possible to use various statistical hypothesis-testing procedures as alternatives to control charts. For example, contingency tables can be used instead of the fraction nonconforming control chart to study a set of preliminary samples for lack of control. The contingency table can also be used to study defects per unit in preliminary samples, instead of c charts or u charts. Duncan (1974) has pointed out that there is little difference in the two approaches, except that it is customary to compute the OC curve for a contingency table in terms of an average difference from the nominal value of the parameter in question (say p), while in the control chart analysis, we usually tabulate the OC curve in terms of a single sample having a value of the parameter that exceeds the nominal value.

The analysis of variance may be substituted for the usual $\bar{x}$ and R charts when examining preliminary samples for lack of control. However, the two procedures do not always produce identical results. For example, a single $\bar{x}$ exceeds the control limits on the $\bar{x}$ chart, yet the remaining values of $\bar{x}$ may be close enough to $\bar{\bar{x}}$ that the F-test in the analysis of variance does not indicate lack of control. On the other hand, it is possible that no individual $\bar{x}$ exceeds the control limits, yet they collectively deviate enough from $\bar{\bar{x}}$ so that the analysis of variance rejects the hypothesis of control. Futhermore, we should remember that the control chart is a visual display, and frequently, pattern recognition and process diagnosis or troubleshooting are the most important parts of the analysis. The analysis of variance is a tabular display; it would be the difficult to analyze the data for runs, cyclic patterns, and so forth, without plotting graphs that would be roughly equivalent to $\bar{x}$ and R charts.

8-7 EVOLUTIONARY OPERATION[2]

Most process-control techniques measure one or more output quality characteristics, and if these quality characteristics are satisfactory, no modification of the process is made. However, in some situations where there is a strong relationship between one or more controllable *independent* process variable and the observed quality characteristic or *dependent* variable, other process-control methods can sometimes be employed. For example, suppose that a chemical engineer wishes to maximize the yield of the process. The yield is a function of two controllable process variables, temperature (x_1) and pressure (x_2), say,

$$y = f(x_1, x_2) + \epsilon$$

where ϵ is a random error component. The chemical engineer has found a set of operating conditions or levels for x_1 and x_2 that maximizes yield and provides acceptable values for all other quality characteristics. However, even if the plant operates continuously at these levels, it will eventually "drift" away from the optimum as a result of variations in the incoming raw materials, environmental changes, operating personnel, and the like.

A method is needed for continuous operation and monitoring of a process with the goal of moving the operating conditions toward the optimum or following a "drift." The method should not require large or sudden changes in operating conditions that might disrupt production. Evolutionary operation (EVOP) was proposed by Box (1957) as such an operating procedure. It is designed as a method of routine plant operation that is carried out by operating personnel with minimum assistance from the quality or manufacturing engineering staff. EVOP makes use of principles of experimental design, which is usually an "off-line" quality-control method. Thus, it is an on-line application of designed experiments.

EVOP consists of systematically introducing small changes in the levels of the process-operating variables. The procedure requires that each independent process variable be assigned a "high" and a "low" level. The changes in the variables are assumed to be small enough so that serious disturbances in product quality will not occur, yet large enough so that potential improvements in process performance

---

[2] The material in this section is adapted from D. C. Montgomery, *Design and Analysis of Experiments*, 2nd ed., John Wiley, New York, 1984, with permission of the publisher.

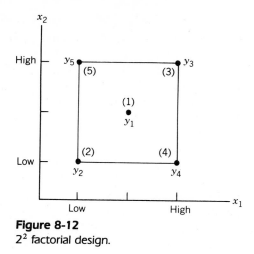

Figure 8-12
2^2 factorial design.

will eventually be discovered. For two variables x_1 and x_2, the four possible combinations of high and low levels are shown in Figure 8-12. This arrangement of points is called a 2^2 *factorial design*. We have also included a point at the center of the design. Typically, the 2^2 design would be centered about the best current estimate of the optimum operating conditions.

The points in the 2^2 design are numbered 1, 2, 3, 4, and 5. Let y_1, y_2, y_3, y_4, and y_5 be the observed values of the dependent or response variable corresponding to these points. After one observation has been run at each point in the design, a *cycle* is said to have been completed. The main effect of a factor is defined as the average change in response produced by a change from the low level to the high level of the factor. Thus, the effect of x_1 is the average difference between the responses on the right-hand side of the design in Figure 8-12 and the responses on the left-hand side, or

$$x_1 \text{ effect} = \tfrac{1}{2}[y_3 + y_4) - (y_2 - y_5)]$$
$$= \tfrac{1}{2}[y_3 + y_4 - y_2 - y_5] \tag{8-24}$$

Similarly, the effect of x_2 is found by computing the average difference in the responses on the top of the design in Figure 8-12 and the responses on the bottom; that is,

$$x_2 \text{ effect} = \tfrac{1}{2}[y_3 + y_5) - (y_2 + y_4)]$$
$$= \tfrac{1}{2}[y_3 + y_5 - y_2 - y_4] \tag{8-25}$$

If the change from the low to the high level of x_1 produces an effect that is different at the two levels of x_2, then we say that there is an *interaction* between x_1 and x_2. The interaction effect is

$$x_1 \times x_2 \text{ interaction} = \tfrac{1}{2}[y_2 + y_3 - y_4 - y_5] \tag{8-26}$$

or just the average difference between the diagonal totals in Figure 8-12. After n cycles, there will be n observations at each of the five design points. The effects of

x_1, x_2, and their interaction are then computed by replacing the individual observations y_i in Equations (8-24), (8-25), and (8-26) by the averages $\bar{y}_i$ of the n observations at each point.

After several cycles have been completed, the effect of one or more process variables, or their interaction, may appear to have a significant effect on the response variable y. When this occurs, a decision may be made to change the basic operating conditions to improve the process output. When improved conditions are detected, a *phase* is said to have been completed.

In testing the significance of process variables and interactions, an estimate of experimental error is required. This is calculated from the cycle data. By comparing the response at the center point with the 2^k points in the factorial portion, we may check on the *change in mean* (CIM); that is, if the process is really centered at the maximum (say), then the response at the center should be significantly greater than the responses at the 2^k peripheral points.

In theory, EVOP can be applied to k process variables. In practice, only two or three variables are usually considered at a time. We will give an example of the procedure for two variables. Box and Draper (1969) give a discussion of the three-variable case, including necessary forms and worksheets.

Example 8-3

Consider a chemical process whose yield is a function of temperature (x_1) and pressure (x_2). The current operating conditions are $x_1 = 250°$ F and $x_2 = 145$ psi. The EVOP procedure uses the 2^2 design plus the center point shown in Figure 8-13. The cycle is completed by running each design point in numerical order (1, 2, 3, 4, 5). The yields in the first cycle are shown in Figure 8-13.

The yields from the first cycle are entered in the EVOP calculation sheet shown in Table 8-4. At the end of the first cycle, no estimate of the standard deviation can be made. The calculation of the main effects of temperature and pressure and their interaction are shown in the bottom half of Table 8-4.

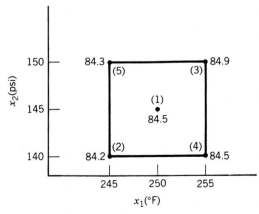

Figure 8-13
2^2 design for Example 8-3.

Table 8-4
EVOP calculation sheet—Example 8-3, $n = 1$

<table>
<tr><td>

```
5┌──────┐3
 │      │
 │  1   │
 │      │
2└──────┘4
```

</td><td>Cycle: $n = 1$
Response: Yield</td><td>Phase 1
Date: 6-14-89</td></tr>
</table>

	Calculation of Averages					Calculation of Standard Deviation
	(1)	(2)	(3)	(4)	(5)	
Operating Conditions						
(i) Previous cycle sum						Previous sum $S =$
(ii) Previous cycle average						Previous average $S =$
(iii) New observations	84.5	84.2	84.9	84.5	84.3	New $S = $ range $\times f_{5,n} =$
(iv) Differences [(ii) − (iii)]						Range of (iv) =
(v) New sums [(i) + (iii)]	84.5	84.2	84.9	84.5	84.3	New sum $S =$
(vi) New averages $[\bar{y}_i = (v)/n]$	84.5	84.2	84.9	84.5	84.3	New average $S = \dfrac{\text{new sum } S}{n-1}$

Calculation of Effects	Calculation of Error Limits
Temperature effect $= \frac{1}{2}(\bar{y}_3 + \bar{y}_4 - \bar{y}_2 - \bar{y}_5) = 0.45$	For new average $\dfrac{2}{\sqrt{n}} S =$
Pressure effect $= \frac{1}{2}(\bar{y}_3 + \bar{y}_5 - \bar{y}_2 - \bar{y}_4) = 0.25$	For new effects $\dfrac{2}{\sqrt{n}} S =$
$T \times P$ interaction effect $= \frac{1}{2}(\bar{y}_2 + \bar{y}_3 - \bar{y}_4 - \bar{y}_5) = 0.15$	
Change-in-mean effect	
$\frac{1}{5}(\bar{y}_2 + \bar{y}_3 + \bar{y}_4 + \bar{y}_5 - 4\bar{y}_1) = -0.02$	For change in mean $\dfrac{1.78}{\sqrt{n}} S =$

A second cycle is then run, and the yield data are entered in another EVOP calculation sheet shown in Table 8-5. At the end of the second cycle, the experimental error can be estimated and the estimates of the effects compared to approximate 95% (two standard deviations) limits. Note that the range refers to the range of the differences in row (iv); thus, the range is $+1.0 - (-1.0) = 2.0$. Since none of the effects in Table 8-5 exceeds their error limits, the true effect is probably zero, and no changes in operating conditions are contemplated.

The results of a third cycle are shown in Table 8-6. The effect of pressure now exceeds its error limit, and the temperature effect is equal to the error limits. A change in operating conditions is now probably justified.

In light of the results, it seems reasonable to begin a new EVOP phase about point (3). Thus, $x_1 = 225°$ F and $x_2 = 150$ psi would become the center of the 2^2 design in the second phase.

An important aspect of EVOP is feeding the information generated back to the process operators and supervisors. This is accomplished by a prominently

Table 8-5

EVOP calculation sheet—Example 8-3, $n = 2$

| Cycle: $n = 2$ | Phase 1 |
| Response: Yield | Date: 6-14-89 |

		Calculation of Averages				Calculation of Standard Deviation
Operating Conditions	(1)	(2)	(3)	(4)	(5)	
(i) Previous cycle sum	84.5	84.2	84.9	84.5	84.3	Previous sum $S =$
(ii) Previous cycle average	84.5	84.2	84.9	84.5	84.3	Previous average $S =$
(iii) New observations	84.9	84.6	85.9	83.5	84.0	New $S =$ range $\times f_{5,n}$ $= 0.60$
(iv) Differences [(ii) − (iii)]	−0.4	−0.4	−1.0	+1.0	0.3	Range of (iv) $= 2.0$
(v) New sums [(i) + (iii)]	169.4	168.8	170.8	168.0	168.3	New sum $S = 0.60$
(vi) New averages $[\bar{y}_i = (v)/n]$	84.70	84.40	85.40	84.00	84.15	New average S $= \dfrac{\text{New sum } S}{n-1} = 0.60$

Temperature effect $= \frac{1}{2}(\bar{y}_3 + \bar{y}_4 - \bar{y}_2 - \bar{y}_5) = 0.43$

For new average
$$\frac{2}{\sqrt{n}} S = 0.85$$

Pressure effect $= \frac{1}{2}(\bar{y}_3 + \bar{y}_5 - \bar{y}_2 - \bar{y}_4) = 0.58$

For new effects
$$\frac{2}{\sqrt{n}} S = 0.85$$

$T \times P$ interaction effect $= \frac{1}{2}(\bar{y}_2 + \bar{y}_3 - \bar{y}_4 - \bar{y}_5) = 0.83$

Change-in-mean effect $= \frac{1}{5}(\bar{y}_2 + \bar{y}_3 + \bar{y}_4 + \bar{y}_5 - 4\bar{y}_1) = -0.17$

For change in mean
$$\frac{1.78}{\sqrt{n}} S = 0.76$$

displayed EVOP information board. The information board for this example at the end of cycle three is shown in Table 8-7.

Most of the quantities on the EVOP calculation sheet follow directly from the analysis of the 2^k factorial design. For example, the variance of any effect such as $\frac{1}{2}(\bar{y}_3 + \bar{y}_5 - \bar{y}_2 - \bar{y}_4)$ is simply

$$V[\tfrac{1}{2}(\bar{y}_3 + \bar{y}_5 - \bar{y}_2 - \bar{y}_4)] = \tfrac{1}{4}(\sigma_{\bar{y}_3}^2 + \sigma_{\bar{y}_5}^2 + \sigma_{\bar{y}_2}^2 + \sigma_{\bar{y}_4}^2)$$

$$= \tfrac{1}{4}(4\sigma_{\bar{y}}^2) = \frac{\sigma^2}{n}$$

where σ^2 is the variance of the observations (y). Thus, two standard deviation (corresponding to 95%) error limits on any effect would be $\pm 2\sigma/\sqrt{n}$. The variance

Table 8-6
EVOP calculation sheet—Example 8-3, $n = 3$

	Cycle: $n = 3$ Response: Yield	Phase 1 Date: 6-14-89

5 ⌐————¬ 3
   │ 1 │
2 └————┘ 4

		Calculation of Averages				Calculation of Standard Deviation
Operating Conditions	(1)	(2)	(3)	(4)	(5)	
(i) Previous cycle sum	169.4	168.8	170.8	168.0	168.3	Previous sum $S = 0.60$
(ii) Previous cycle average		84.70	84.40	85.40	84.00	84.15	Previous average $S = 0.60$
(iii) New observations	85.0	84.0	86.6	84.9	85.2	New S = range $\times f_{5,n}$ = 0.56
(iv) Differences $[(ii) - (iii)]$	-0.30	$+0.40$	-1.20	-0.90	-1.05	Range of (iv) = 1.60
(v) New sums $[(i) + (iii)]$	254.4	252.8	257.4	252.9	253.5	New sum $S = 1.16$
(vi) New averages $[\bar{y}_i = (v)/n]$	84.80	84.27	85.80	84.30	84.50	New average S = $\dfrac{\text{New sum } s}{n-1}$ = 0.58

Calculation of Effects	Calculation of Error Limits
Temperature effect = $\frac{1}{2}(\bar{y}_3 + \bar{y}_4 - \bar{y}_2 - \bar{y}_5) = 0.67$	For new average $\dfrac{2}{\sqrt{n}}S = 0.67$
Pressure effect = $\frac{1}{2}(\bar{y}_3 + \bar{y}_5 - \bar{y}_2 - \bar{y}_4) = 0.87$	For new effects $\dfrac{2}{\sqrt{n}}S = 0.67$
$T \times P$ interaction effect = $\frac{1}{2}(\bar{y}_2 + \bar{y}_3 - \bar{y}_4 - \bar{y}_5) = 0.64$ Change-in-mean effect = $\frac{1}{5}(\bar{y}_2 + \bar{y}_3 + \bar{y}_4 + \bar{y}_5 - 4\bar{y}_1) = -0.07$	For change in mean $\dfrac{1.78}{\sqrt{n}}S = 0.60$

Table 8-7
EVOP information board—cycle three

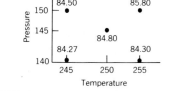

Response: Percent yield
Requirement: Maximize

Effects with 95% Error Limits	Error Limits for Averages: ± 0.67	
Temperature	0.67	± 0.67
Pressure	0.87	± 0.67
$T \times P$	0.64	± 0.67
Change in mean	0.07	± 0.60

Standard deviation: 0.58

Table 8-8
Values of $f_{k,n}$

$n =$	2	3	4	5	6	7	8	9	10
$k = 5$	0.30	0.35	0.37	0.38	0.39	0.40	0.40	0.40	0.41
9	0.24	0.27	0.29	0.30	0.31	0.31	0.31	0.32	0.32
10	0.23	0.26	0.28	0.29	0.30	0.30	0.30	0.31	0.31

of the change in mean is

$$V(\text{CIM}) = V[\tfrac{1}{5}(\bar{y}_2 + \bar{y}_3 + \bar{y}_4 + \bar{y}_5 - 4\bar{y}_1)]$$

$$= \tfrac{1}{25}(4\sigma_{\bar{y}}^2 + 16\sigma_{\bar{y}}^2) = \frac{20}{25}\frac{\sigma^2}{n}$$

Thus, two standard deviation error limits on the CIM are $\pm 2\sigma\sqrt{20(25)/n} = \pm 1.78\sigma/\sqrt{n}$. For more information on the 2^k factorial design, see Montgomery (1984) and Part III.

The standard deviation σ is estimated by the range method. Let $y_i(n)$ denote the observation at the ith design point in cycle n, and $\bar{y}_i(n)$ the corresponding average of $y_i(n)$ after n cycles. The quantities in row (iv) of the EVOP calculation sheet are the differences $y_i(n) - \bar{y}_i(n-1)$. The variance of these differences is $V[y_i(n) - \bar{y}_i(n-1)] \equiv \sigma^2[n/(n-1)]$. The range of the differences, say R_D, is related to the estimate of the distribution of the differences by $\hat{\sigma}_D = R_D/d_2$. Now $R_D/d_2 = \hat{\sigma}\sqrt{n/(n-1)}$, so

$$\hat{\sigma} = \sqrt{\frac{(n-1)}{n}}\frac{R_D}{d_2} = (f_{k,n})R_D \equiv S$$

can be used to estimate the standard deviation of the observations, where k denotes the number of points used in the design. For a 2^2 with one center point we have $k = 5$, and for a 2^3 with one center point we have $k = 9$. Values of $f_{k,n}$ are given in Table 8-8.

8-8 SPC WITH CORRELATED PROCESS DATA

The standard assumptions that are usually cited in justifying the use of control charts are that the data generated by the process when it is in control are normally and independently distributed with mean μ and standard deviation σ. Both μ and σ are considered fixed and unknown. An out-of-control condition is a change in μ or σ (or both) to some different value. Therefore, we could say that the quality characteristic at time t, x_t, is represented by the model

$$x_t = \mu + \epsilon_t \qquad t = 1, 2, \ldots \qquad (8\text{-}27)$$

where ϵ_t is normally and independently distributed with mean zero and standard deviation σ.

When these assumptions are satisfied, one may apply conventional control charts as and draw conclusions about the state of control of the process. Furthermore, the statistical properties of the control chart, such as the false-alarm rate with 3-sigma control limits, or the average run length, can be easily determined and used to provide guidance for chart interpretation. Even in situations where the normality assumption is violated to a slight or moderate degree, these control charts will still work reasonably well.

The most important of these assumptions is that of independence of the observations, for conventional control charts do not work well if the quality characteristic exhibits even low levels of correlation over time. Specifically, these control charts will give misleading results in the form of too many false alarms if the data are correlated. Unfortunately, the assumption of uncorrelated or independent observations is not even approximately satisfied in some manufacturing processes. Examples include chemical processes where consecutive measurements on process or product characteristics are often highly correlated, or automated test and inspection procedures, where every quality characteristic is measured on every unit in time order of production. Basically, all manufacturing processes are driven by inertial elements, and when the interval between samples becomes small relative to these forces, the observations on the process will be correlated over time.

As an example, consider the data in Figure 8-14. This graph plots 100 observations on the deviation from nominal diameter (in mm $\times\ 10^{-5}$) of a cable harness hole drilled in a wing leading edge rib. The hole is drilled by a computer-controlled machine, and a sensor is probed into the hole immediately after the drilling operation is complete, providing automatic data capture. A control chart for individuals

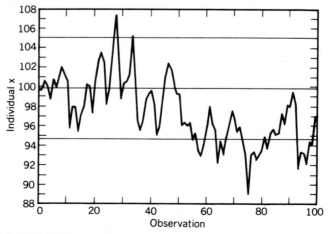

Figure 8-14
Hole diameter data with a control chart for individuals.

has been applied to the data, with the limits calculated from the first 50 observations. Notice that the process is apparently out of control, particularly from about sample 50 onward, where it seems that a downward shift in the process mean has occurred. However, there are several out-of-control signals during samples 20–40 as well. It would be of interest to know whether the out-of-control signals are indicating real problems or whether they are false alarms.

The correlation over a series of time-oriented observations is measured by the autocorrelation function

$$\rho_k = \frac{\text{cov}(x_t, x_{t-k})}{V(x_t)}, \qquad k = 0, 1, \ldots$$

where $\text{cov}(x_t, x_{t-k})$ is the covariance of observations that are k times periods apart, and we have assumed that the observations have constance variance given by $V(x_t)$. We usually estimate the values with the sample autocorrelation function.

$$\hat{\rho}_k = \frac{\sum_{t=1}^{n-k} (x_t - \bar{x})(x_{t-k} - \bar{x})}{\sum_{t=1}^{n} (x_t - \bar{x})2}, \qquad k = 0, 1, \ldots$$

As a general rule, we usually need to compute values of $\hat{\rho}_k$ for a few values of k, $k \leq n/4$. Many software programs for statistical data analysis can perform these calculations.

The sample autocorrelation function for the hole diameter data is shown in Figure 8-15. Notice that there is a strong positive correlation at *lag* 1; that is, observations that are one period apart are positively correlated with $\hat{\rho}_1 = 0.61$. This level of autocorrelation is sufficiently high to distort greatly the performance of a Shewhart control chart. In particular, because we know that positive correlation greatly increases the frequency of false alarms, we should be very suspicious about the out-of-control signals on the control chart in Figure 8-14.

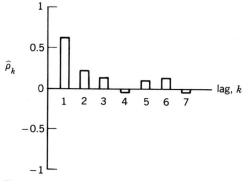

Figure 8-15
Sample autocorrelation function for the hole diameter data.

One approach that has proved useful in dealing with autocorrelated data is to directly model the correlative structure, use that model to remove the autocorrelation from the data, and apply control charts to the *residuals*. For example, suppose that we could model the quality characteristic x_t as

$$x_t = \xi + \phi x_{t-1} + \epsilon_t$$

where ξ and $\phi (-1 < \phi < 1)$ are unknown constants, and ϵ_t is normally and independently distributed with mean zero and standard deviation σ. This is called a *first-order autoregressive model*; the observations x_t from such a model have mean $\xi/(1 - \phi)$, standard deviation $\sigma/(1 - \phi^2)^{1/2}$, and the observations that are k periods apart (x_t and x_{t+k}) have correlation coefficient ϕ^k. Suppose that $\hat{\phi}$ is an estimate of ϕ, obtained from analysis of sample data from the process, and $\hat{x}_t$ is the fitted value of x_t. Then the residuals

$$e_t = x_t - \hat{x}_t$$

are normally and independently distributed with mean zero and constant variance. Now conventional control charts could be applied to the sequence of residuals. Points out of control or unusual patterns on such charts would indicate that the parameter ϕ had changed, implying that the original variable x_t was out of control. Models such as this one for autocorrelated data are usually called time series models. For details of identifying and fitting these models, see Montgomery and Johnson (1976) and Box and Jenkins (1976).

Montgomery and Friedman (1989) show that a reasonable model for the first 50 observations on the hole diameter data in Figure 8-14 is a second-order autoregressive model

$$\hat{x}_t = 50 + 0.8x_{t-1} - 0.3x_{t-2}$$

Figure 8-16 presents a control chart for individuals applied to the residuals from this model. It is now apparent that the process is in control until about observation 50 and that the out-of-control signals during that period observed in Figure 8-14 were false alarms. Furthermore, there has been a downward shift in the process beginning at about sample 50.

It is also sometimes possible to use a suitably modified cusum control chart with autocorrelated data, where the modification allows the control chart in some sense to compensate for the autocorrelative structure of the data. For example, if a cusum is applied to autocorrelated data such as shown in the first 50 observations in Figure 8-14, the primary effect of the autocorrelation is to increase the frequency of false alarms. That is, the in-control ARL of the cusum will be too small, but the out-of-control ARL will not be greatly affected. One modification that seems to work well in compensating for autocorrelation is to increase the reference value of the cusum. More specifically, use of a reference value that is about twice the reference value that would be used for uncorrelated data is recommended. Thus, if the cusum would be defined with $H = 10$ and $K = 2$ for uncorrelated data, then using $H = 10$ and $K = 4$ would be a reasonably good approximate method for compensating for correlated data. This increase in K will make the in-control ARL larger while having relatively little effect on the out-of-control ARL.

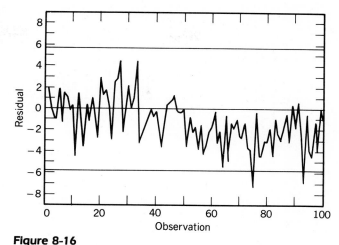

Figure 8-16

Control chart for individuals applied to residuals from $\hat{x}_t = 50 + 0.8x_{t-1} - 0.3x_{t-2}$, hole diameter data.

In this discussion we have assumed that the process is well-modeled by Equation (8-27); that is, the process mean is constant at some value μ and, it is the noise process that contains the autocorrelative structure. In many processes that exhibit autocorrelation the mean is not constant. This behavior is frequently observed in the chemical and process industries, for example. In these types of processes a more realistic model than (8-27) is

$$x_t = \mu_t + \epsilon_t \tag{8-28}$$

where the mean of the process μ_t may wander over time and is not fixed at a constant level. For example, Figure 8-17 shows a run chart of a critical characteristic

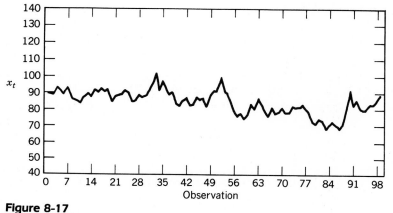

Figure 8-17

Critical characteristic for a chemical process.

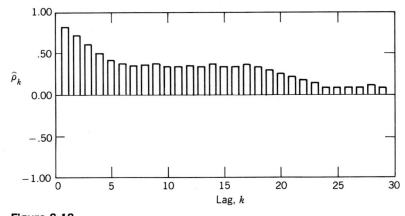

Figure 8-18
Sample autocorrelation function for the process data in Figure 8-17.

from a chemical process. Note the tendency of the mean to drift slowly or "wander" in this process.

This motion in the mean is likely caused by autocorrelation. The sample autocorrelation function for this variable is shown in Figure 8-18. Notice there is high autocorrelation present even at long lags. When there is motion in the process mean, such as is illustrated in Figure 8-17, the usual Shewhart-type control charts will be ineffective. To illustrate this, Figure 8-19 presents the results of applying a control chart for individuals (with the moving range used to estimate the process standard deviation) to the process data from Figure 8-17. The limits on this chart are virtually meaningless, and from this illustration it is almost impossible to derive any meaningful interpretation about the state of control of the process. Notice that the moving-range method will be very ineffective in estimating the process standard deviation when the data are autocorrelated. Generally, when the data

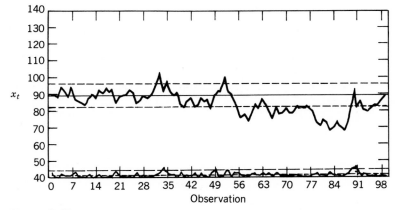

Figure 8-19
Applying Shewhart control charts (individuals and moving range) to the data from Figure 8-17.

are positively autocorrelated, the moving-range method will produce an estimate of the process standard deviation that is too small. This will result in control limits that are too narrow, and will further impact the tendency of the control chart to produce too many false alarms.

It is frequently necessary to apply statistical process control to processes with a wandering mean. One approach would be to build a time series model that accounts for this type of behavior and control chart the residuals. These autoregressive integrated moving-average (ARIMA) models are discussed in Montgomery and Johnson (1976) and Box and Jenkins (1976). Another useful approach in some cases is to apply an EWMA control chart directly to the process data. The EWMA is a general control scheme that is useful for many processes where the observations are positively autocorrelated and the mean does not drift too fast. The control limits for this EWMA control chart must be determined using a method different from the one described in Chapter 7.

Since the EWMA statistic z_t can be viewed as a one-step-ahead forecast of the process mean for the next period, we can use the one-step-ahead prediction error

$$e_1(t) = x_t - z_{t-1}$$

to establish control limits for the EWMA. If the EWMA is a good one-step-ahead predictor, the sequence of one-step-ahead prediction errors is uncorrelated. Two procedures may be used to generate the standard deviation of these one-step-ahead prediction errors. One method is to apply an EWMA to the absolute value of the prediction error

$$\Delta(t) = \alpha|e_1(t)| + (1 - \alpha)\,\Delta(t - 1) \tag{8-29}$$

Since $\sigma \simeq 1.25\,\Delta(t)$ for a normal distribution, we can use $\pm 3[1.25\,\Delta(t)]$ as the upper and lower control limits on the EWMA control chart. This will provide a set of control limits that are based on a more reliable variance estimate than the one produced by the moving-range method applied to the original observations.

A second approach is to use the smoothed variance of the prediction error

$$\hat{\sigma}_p^2(t) = \alpha[e_1(t)]^2 + (1 - \alpha)\hat{\sigma}_p^2(t - 1) \tag{8-30}$$

As before, we would base the control limits on the standard deviation of the prediction error, that is, $\pm 3\hat{\sigma}_p(t)$.

If the process mean does not wander, we can use the process mean μ (or a suitable estimate, say $\bar{x}$) as the center line of this EWMA control chart. If the process mean does wander, as in Figure 8-17, we should use the EWMA statistic z_t as the center line of the control chart. Remembering that z_t is the forecast of the mean at period $t + 1$, we will actually use

$$\begin{aligned} \text{UCL}_{t+1} &= z_t + 3\hat{\sigma}_p(t) \\ \text{CL}_{t+1} &= z_t \\ \text{LCL}_{t+1} &= z_t - 3\hat{\sigma}_p(t) \end{aligned} \tag{8-31}$$

as the EWMA control chart parameters at time period $t + 1$. Notice that we have used the square root of the smoothed prediction error variance from Equation

(8-30) to determine the control limits. If one wishes to use the smoothed absolute prediction error method (Equation 8-29), the control chart parameters at time $t + 1$ are

$$\text{UCL}_{t+1} = z_t + 4.75 \, \Delta(t)$$
$$\text{CL}_{t+1} = z_t \qquad\qquad (8\text{-}32)$$
$$\text{LCL}_{t+1} = z_t - 4.75 \, \Delta(t)$$

Figure 8-20*a* presents the results of applying the EWMA scheme described in Equation (8-31) to the chemical process data from Figure 8-17. In constructing these control charts we have used $\lambda = 0.2$ for the EWMA and $\alpha = 0.1$ in Equation (8-30). We observe that this chart provides a much more reasonable set of control limits and leads to much more useful information about the state of control of the process. Figure 8-20*b* presents the results of using the EWMA control scheme

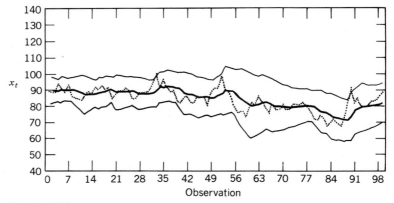

Figure 8-20a
The EWMA control chart with smoothed prediction error variance control limits applied to the chemical process data from Figure 8-17.

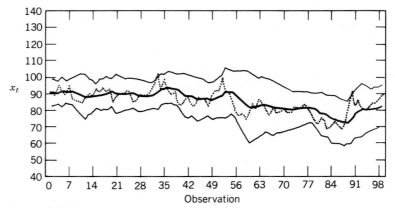

Figure 8-20b
The EWMA control chart with smoothed absolute prediction error control limits applied to the chemical process data from Figure 8-17.

with control limits based on the smoothed absolute prediction error to the data from Figure 8-17. Notice that the control limits in Figures 8-20a and 8-20b are essentially equivalent. This is because the two prediction error estimation methods [smoothed variance, Equation (8-30), and smoothed absolute error, Equation (8-29)] are equivalent.

The EWMA is a very flexible statistic for statistical process control applications. As we showed in Chapter 7, when applied to uncorrelated data the EWMA is a good alternative to the cumulative sum control chart. In this section we have shown that if process data are autocorrelated, the EWMA can be adapted to form a control chart that eliminates the excessive false alarm problem associated with traditional control charts. We should caution the reader that the EWMA procedure described in this section is not applicable to all situations with autocorrelated data. Technically, the EWMA with $\lambda = 1 - \theta$ is an optimal one-step-ahead predictor for a process where the data is generated by

$$x_t = x_{t-1} + \epsilon_t - \theta\epsilon_{t-1}$$

This is called an integrated-moving-average process of order one [IMA(1,1)]. In practice, we have found that the EWMA often works well as a one-step-ahead predictor even when the underlying process is not the IMA(1,1) model above. If the process observations are positively correlated, then the EWMA will usually work reasonably well as a predictor, and the control chart described in this section will provide a good basis for process control.

The selection of an appropriate value of λ for the EWMA chart requires careful attention. The procedures mentioned in Chapter 7 were developed for uncorrelated data, and are not suitable for the control chart described in this section. If the IMA(1,1) model above is the correct model for the process, then we could fit that model (by using non-linear least squares techniques) and set $\lambda = 1 - \theta$. When the IMA(1,1) model is not the exact process model, a reasonable procedure is to select the value of λ that minimizes the sum of squares of the one-step-ahead prediction errors. We have found that this works reasonably well in a wide variety of practical situations.

We must also choose a value for α in either Equation (8-29) or (8-30) for smoothing the prediction errors. The choice of α essentially controls how much of the historical process data is to be used in estimating the standard deviation of prediction error. Large values of α put most of the weight on recent periods, whereas smaller values of α apply substantially more weight to older observations. Practical experience with the procedure indicates that small values of α, say in the interval $0.01 \leq \alpha \leq 0.1$ work well.

Figure 8-21 presents some guidelines for applying control charts to both correlated and uncorrelated data. The correlated data branch of the flow chart assumes that the sample size is $n = 1$.

Figure 8-22 summarizes several situations where various types of control charts are useful. On the left axis we find that as the interval between samples increases, the Shewhart control chart becomes the appropriate choice. This is because the larger sampling interval negates the effects of autocorrelation. As the interval between samples gets smaller, autocorrelation plays a much more important role, which leads to the ARIMA or EWMA approach. On the right axis we find that as the cost of process adjustment increases, we are driven to the Shewhart chart. On the other hand, if the adjustment cost is low, we are driven to some type of

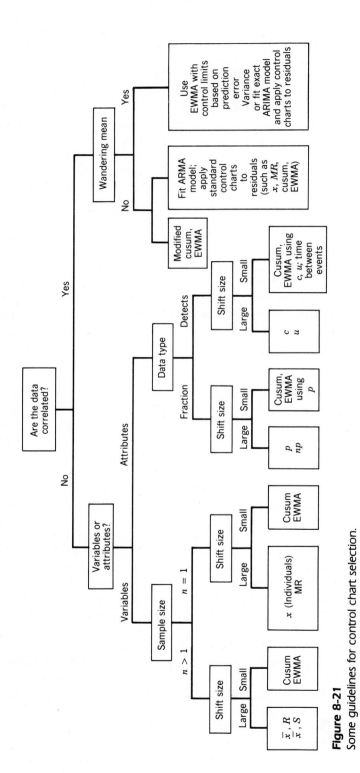

Figure 8-21

Some guidelines for control chart selection.

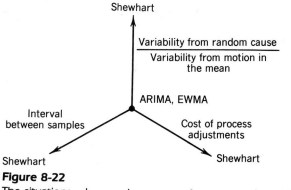

Figure 8-22
The situations where various types of control charts are useful.

engineering process control system, which may use an EWMA or ARIMA procedure on the adjustments to the process to identify upsets. Finally, on the vertical axis, we see that as the variability owing to random causes or noise dominates any motion in the mean, the Shewhart chart becomes more appropriate. However, if the motion in the mean is large relative to random noise, we are driven once again to ARIMA- or EWMA-type procedures.

8-9 OVERVIEW OF OTHER PROCEDURES

There are many useful process-control techniques in addition to those presented previously. This section gives a brief overview of some of these methods, along with some basic references. The selection of topics is far from exhaustive but does reflect a collection of ideas that are useful in practice.

Tool Wear

Many production processes are subject to tool wear. When tool wear occurs, we usually find that the process variability at any one point in time is considerably less than the allowable variability over the entire life of the tool. Furthermore, as the tool wears out, there will generally be an upward drift or trend in the mean caused by the worn tool producing larger dimensions. In such cases, the distance between specification limits is generally much greater than, say 6σ. Consequently, the modified control chart concept can be applied to the tool-wear problem. The procedure is illustrated in Figure 8-23.

The initial setting for the tool is at some multiple of σ_x above the lower specification limit, say $3\sigma_x$, and the maximum permissible process average is at the same multiple of σ_x below the upper specification limit. If the rate of wear is known, or can be estimated from the data, we can construct a set of slanting control limits about the tool-wear trend line. If the sample values of $\bar{x}$ fall within these limits, the tool wear is in control. When the trend line exceeds the maximum permissible process average, the process should be reset or the tool replaced.

Control charts for tool wear are discussed in more detail by Duncan (1974) and Manuele (1945). The regression control chart [see Mandel (1969)] can also be adapted to the tool-wear problem. Quesenberry (1988) points out that these

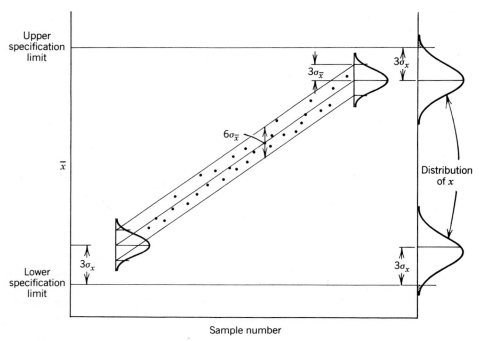

Figure 8-23
Control chart for tool wear.

approaches essentially assume that resetting the process is expensive and that they attempt to minimize the number of adjustments made to keep the parts within specifications rather than reducing overall variability. Quesenberry develops a two-part tool-wear compensator that centers the process periodically and protects against assignable causes, as well as adjusting for the estimated mean tool wear since the previous adjustment.

Control Charts Based on Other Sample Statistics

Some authors have suggested the use of sample statistics other than the average and range (or standard deviation) for construction of control charts. For example, Ferrell (1953) proposed that subgroup midranges and ranges be used, with control limits determined by the median midrange and the median range. The author noted that ease of computation would be a feature of such control charts and that they would do a better job of detecting "outlier" points than would conventional control charts. The median has been used frequently instead of $\bar{x}$ as a center line on charts of individuals when the underlying distribution is skewed. Similarly, medians of R and S have been proposed as the center lines of those charts so that the asymmetrical distribution of these statistics will not influence the number of runs above and below the center line.

The recent interest in robust statistical methods has generated some application of these ideas to control charts. Generally speaking, the presence of assignable causes produces "outlier" values that stretch or extend the control limits, thereby reducing the sensitivity of the control chart. One approach to this problem has been to develop control charts using statistics that are themselves outlier-resistant. Examples include the median and midrange control charts [see Clifford (1959)], and plotting subgroup boxplots [(see Inglewitz and Hoaglin (1987) and White and Schroeder (1987)]. These procedures are typically not as effective in assignable-cause or outlier detection as are conventional $\bar{x}$ and R (or S) charts.

A better approach is to plot a sample statistic that is sensitive to assignable causes ($\bar{x}$ and R or S), but to base the control limits on some outlier-resistant method. The paper by Ferrell (1953) mentioned above is an example of this approach, as is plotting $\bar{x}$ and R on charts with control limits determined by the trimmed mean of the sample means and the trimmed mean of the ranges, as suggested by Langenberg and Inglewitz (1986).

Rocke (1989) has reported that plotting an outlier-sensitive statistic on a control chart with control limits determined using an outlier-resistant method works well in practice. The suggested procedures in Ferrell (1953), Langenberg and Inglewitz (1986), and his own method are very effective in detecting assignable causes. Interestingly enough, Rocke also notes that the widely used two-stage method of setting control limits, wherein the initial limits are treated as trial control limits, the samples that plot outside these trial limits are then removed, and a final set of limits are then calculated, performs nearly as well as the more complex robust methods. In other words, the use of this two-stage method creates a robust control chart. For an example of this two-stage procedure, refer to Example 5-1.

In addition to issues of robustness, other authors have suggested control charts for other sample statistics for process-specific reasons. For example, when pairs of measurements are made on each unit, or when comparison with a standard unit is desired, one may plot the difference $x_{1j} - x_{2j}$ on a *difference control chart* [see Grubbs (1946)]. In some cases, the largest and smallest sample values may be of interest. These charts have been developed by Howell (1949).

Selecting the Optimum Target Value for a Process

An important problem in manufacturing involves determining the optimal target level for the process. For example, suppose that there is a lower specification limit on the weight of a package. In many manufacturing processes, each package is weighted using an automatic weighing machine. If the package weighs less than the lower specification limit, say, LSL, it is automatically rejected. We wish to determine a target fill value $T > \text{LSL}$ that is in some sense optimal.

Hunter and Kartha (1977) have given an interesting formulation of this problem. Let x be the observed value of the quality characteristic (weight or volume), and let $T = \text{LSL} + \delta$ be the target value for the process. Suppose that the selling price of a good unit of product ($x \geq \text{LSL}$) is a and that the selling price of a defective unit of product ($x < \text{LSL}$) is r. Let g be the cost of excess quality per unit measure for a good item. For example, g could be the cost in dollars per ounce for the excess product above 12 oz in a 12-oz can of soft drink. Note that $a > r$, and $g > 0$. Assume that the distribution of x is normal with mean T and variance σ^2.

The net income per unit product is

$$I = \begin{cases} a - g(x - \text{LSL}) & \text{if } x \geq \text{LSL} \\ r & \text{if } x < \text{LSL} \end{cases}$$

The expected net income is

$$E(I) = a \int_{\text{LSL}}^{\infty} f(x)\, dx - g \int_{\text{LSL}}^{\infty} (x - \text{LSL}) f(x)\, dx + r \int_{-\infty}^{\text{LSL}} f(x)\, dx \quad (8\text{-}33)$$

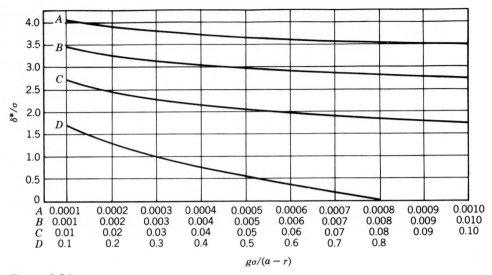

Figure 8-24
Four-cycle arithmetic graph for determining δ^*/σ given $g\sigma/(a-r)$. (From L. S. Nelson, "Best Target Value for a Production Process," *Journal of Quality Technology*, vol. 10, 1978, with permission of the American Society for Quality Control.)

where $f(x)$ is the normal distribution with mean $T = \text{LSL} + \delta$ and variance σ^2. Equation (8-33) may be written as

$$E(I) = a\Phi\left(\frac{\delta}{\sigma}\right) - g\int_{\text{LSL}}^{\infty} (x - \text{LSL})f(x)\,dx + r\Phi\left(\frac{-\delta}{\sigma}\right) \qquad (8\text{-}34)$$

Note that δ is the average amount of product that must be "given away"; that is, it is the distance above the lower specification limit LSL to the target value T at which the process must be operated.

The optimal value of δ is the solution to

$$\frac{dE(I)}{d\delta} = \frac{a}{\sigma}\,\phi\left(\frac{\delta}{\sigma}\right) - g\Phi\left(\frac{\delta}{\sigma}\right) - \frac{r}{\sigma}\,\phi\left(\frac{-\delta}{\sigma}\right) = 0 \qquad (8\text{-}35)$$

where $\phi(z) = (2\pi)^{-1/2}\exp(-z^2/2)$. The solution to (8-35) is

$$\frac{\phi(\delta/\sigma)}{\Phi(\delta/\sigma)} = \frac{g\sigma}{a - r} \qquad (8\text{-}36)$$

For specified values of a, r, g, and σ, Equation (8-36) can be solved for the optimal δ^* by trial and error with the aid of a table of the standard normal cumulative distribution. Alternatively, one can read the solution to (8-36) directly from Figure 8-24. The procedure is illustrated by the following example.

Example 8-4

A machine is used to fill aluminum cans with a carbonated soft drink beverage. The nominal fill volume is 12.0 fl oz. The cost of the beverage is \$0.01/fl oz. The wholesale selling price of a can is \$0.20. An automatic weighing machine is used to reject cans with low fills. All underfilled cans are used in-plant and are sold at $0.10 each. $\bar{x}$ and R charts based on samples of size five have been maintained on this process. Both charts exhibit control, and the center line of the R chart is 0.15. Consequently, the process standard deviation may be estimated by

$$\hat{\sigma} = \frac{\bar{R}}{d_2} = \frac{0.15}{2.326} = 0.0645$$

To find the optimum target mean fill volume, note that

$$\frac{g\sigma}{a - r} = \frac{(0.01)(0.0645)}{0.20 - 0.10} = 0.0065$$

Using 0.0065 as the abscissa value in Figure 8-24, we find the corresponding ordinate value is approximately 2.85. Therefore, since $\delta^*/\sigma = 2.85$, we have

$$\delta^* = 2.85\sigma = 2.85(0.0645) = 0.1838$$

Therefore, the economically optimum mean fill volume for this process is

$$T = \text{LSL} + \delta^* = 12 + 0.1838 = 12.1838 \text{ fl oz}$$

Bisgaard, Hunter, and Pallesen (1984) have extended the Hunter and Kartha procedure to a more general economic model in which the selling price of each underfilled unit is proportional to the actual fill, and given detailed solutions for normal, lognormal, and Poisson distributions of the quality characteristic. When the secondary market price equals the production cost, the two models agree exactly. Furthermore, when δ^*/σ is greater than two, the two models produce very similar results.

Fill Control Problems

Many products are filled on a high-speed, multiple-head circular filling machine that operates continuously. It is not unusual to find machines in the beverage industry that have from 40 to 72 heads and operate at speeds of from 800 to 1000 bottles per minute. In such cases, it is difficult to sample products from specific heads because there is no automatic method of identifying a filled container with its filling head. Furthermore, in addition to assignable causes that affect all filling heads simultaneously, some assignable causes affect only certain heads. Special sampling and control charting methods are needed for these types of fill control problems. Ott and Snee (1973) present some techniques useful for this problem, particularly for filling machines with a moderate number of heads.

The Interface Between Statistical Process Control and Engineering Process Control

The control chart is a useful technique for reduction of process variability; however, it is not always the best method for reducing variability around a target. For example, in the chemical and process industries engineering process control has been very effectively used for this purpose. Much of engineering control theory is based on the idea that if we can (1) predict the next observation on the process, (2) have some other variable that we can manipulate in order to affect the process output and (3) know the effect of this manipulated variable so that we can determine how much control action to apply, then we can make the adjustment in the manipulated variable at time t that is most likely to produce an ontarget value of the process output in period $t + 1$. Clearly, this requires good knowledge of the relationship between the output or controlled variable and the manipulated variable, as well as an understanding of process dynamics. We must also be able to easily change the manipulated variable. In fact, if the cost of taking control action is negligible, then the variability in the process output is minimized by taking control action every period. Notice that this is in sharp contrast with SPC, where "control action" or a process adjustment is taken only when there is statistical evidence that the process is out of control. This statistical evidence is usually a point outside the limits on a control chart.

There are many processes where some type of feedback-control scheme would be preferable to a control chart. For example, consider the process of driving a car, with the objective of keeping it in the center of the right-hand lane (or equivalently, minimizing variation around the center of the right-hand lane). The driver can easily see the road ahead, and process adjustments (corrections to the steering wheel position) can be made at any time with negligible cost. Consequently, if the driver knew the relationship between the output variable (car position) and the manipulated variable (steering wheel adjustment), he would likely prefer to use a feedback-control scheme to control car position, rather than a statistical control chart (driving a car with a Shewhart control chart may be an interesting idea, but the author doesn't want to be in the car during the experiment).

On the other hand, engineering process control makes no attempt to identify assignable causes that may impact the process. The elimination of assignable causes

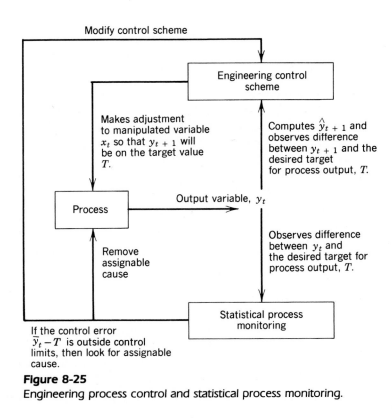

Figure 8-25
Engineering process control and statistical process monitoring.

can result in significant process improvement. All feedback-control schemes do is react to process upsets, they do not make any effort to remove the root causes. Consequently, in processes where feedback control is used there may be substantial improvement if control charts are also used for statistical process *monitoring* (as opposed to *control*; the control actions are based on the engineering control scheme). The control chart should not be applied to the output or controlled variable. Instead, it is more useful to apply control charts to either the control error (the difference between the controlled variable and the target) or to the sequence of adjustments to the manipulated variable. Points that lie outside the control limits on these charts would identify periods where the control errors are large or where large changes to the manipulated variable are being made. These periods would likely be good opportunities to search for assignable causes. Figure 8-25 illustrates how such a combination of engineering process control and statistical process monitoring might be employed.

8-10 Exercises

8-1 Use the data below to set up short-run $\bar{x}$ and R charts. The nominal dimensions for each part are $N_A = 100$, $N_B = 60$, $N_C = 75$, and $N_D = 50$

Sample Number	Part Number	x_1	x_2	x_3
1	A	105	102	103
2	A	101	98	100
3	A	103	100	99
4	A	101	104	97
5	A	106	102	100
6	B	57	60	59
7	B	61	64	63
8	B	60	58	62
9	C	73	75	77
10	C	78	75	76
11	C	77	75	74
12	C	75	72	79
13	C	74	75	77
14	C	73	76	75
15	D	50	51	49
16	D	46	50	50
17	D	51	46	50
18	D	49	50	53
19	D	50	52	51
20	D	53	51	50

8-2 Printed circuit boards used in several different avionics devices are 100% tested for defects. The batch size for each board type is relatively small, and management wishes to establish SPC using a short-run version of the c chart. Defect data from the last two weeks of production are shown below. What chart would you recommend? Set up the chart and examine the process for control.

Production Day	Part Number	Total Number of Defects
245	1261	16
	1261	10
	1261	15
246	1261	8
	1261	11
	1385	24
	1395	21
247	1385	28
	1385	35
	1261	10
248	1261	8
	8611	47
	8611	45
249	8611	53
	8611	41
	1385	21
250	1385	25
	1385	29
	1385	30
	4610	6
	4610	8
251	4610	10
	4610	0
	1261	20
	1261	21
252	1261	15
	1261	8
	1261	10
	1130	64
	1130	75
	1130	53
253	1055	16
	1055	15
	1055	10
259	1055	12
	8611	47
	8611	60
255	8611	51
	8611	57
	4010	0
	4610	4

8-3 A machine has four heads. Samples of $n = 3$ units are selected from each head, and the $\bar{x}$ and R values are computed. The data are shown below. Set up group control charts for this process.

Sample Number	Head 1 $\bar{x}$	1 R	2 $\bar{x}$	2 R	3 $\bar{x}$	3 R	4 $\bar{x}$	4 R
1	53	2	54	1	56	2	55	3
2	51	1	55	2	54	4	54	4
3	54	2	52	5	53	3	57	2
4	55	3	54	3	52	1	51	5
5	54	1	50	2	51	2	53	1
6	53	2	51	1	54	2	52	2
7	51	1	53	2	58	5	54	1
8	52	2	24	4	51	2	55	2
9	50	2	52	3	52	1	51	3
10	51	1	55	1	53	3	53	5
11	52	3	57	2	52	4	55	1
12	51	2	55	1	54	2	58	2
13	54	4	58	2	51	1	53	1
14	53	1	54	4	50	3	54	2
15	55	2	52	3	54	2	52	6
16	54	4	51	1	53	2	58	5
17	53	3	50	2	57	1	53	1
18	52	1	49	1	52	1	49	2
19	51	2	53	3	51	2	50	3
20	52	4	52	2	50	3	52	2

8-4 The $\bar{x}$ and R values for 20 samples of size five are shown below. Specifications on this product have been established as 0.550 ± 0.02.

Sample Number	$\bar{x}$	R	Sample Number	$\bar{x}$	R
1	0.549	0.0025	11	0.547	0.0020
2	0.548	0.0021	12	0.545	0.0030
3	0.548	0.0023	13	0.549	0.0031
4	0.551	0.0029	14	0.552	0.0022
5	0.553	0.0018	15	0.550	0.0023
6	0.552	0.0017	16	0.548	0.0021
7	0.550	0.0020	17	0.556	0.0019
8	0.551	0.0024	18	0.546	0.0018
9	0.553	0.0022	19	0.550	0.0021
10	0.556	0.0028	20	0.551	0.0022

a. Construct a modified control chart with 3-sigma limits, assuming that if the true process fraction nonconforming is as large as 1%, the process is unacceptable.

b. Suppose that if the true process fraction nonconforming is as large as 1%, we would like an acceptance control chart to detect this out-of-control condition with probability 0.90. Construct this acceptance control chart, and compare it to the chart obtained in part (a).

8-5 A sample of five units is taken from a process every half hour. It is known that the process standard deviation is in control with $\sigma = 2.0$. The $\bar{x}$ values for the last 20 samples are:

Sample Number	$\bar{x}$	Sample Number	$\bar{x}$
1	41.5	11	40.6
2	42.7	12	39.4
3	40.5	13	38.6
4	39.8	14	42.5
5	41.6	15	41.8
6	44.7	16	40.7
7	39.6	17	42.8
8	40.2	18	43.4
9	41.4	19	42.0
10	43.9	20	41.9

Specifications on the product are 40 ± 8.

a. Set up a modified control chart on this process. Use 3-sigma limits on the chart and assume that the largest fraction nonconforming that is tolerable is 0.1%.

b. Reconstruct the chart in part (a) using 2-sigma limits. Is there any difference in the analysis of the data?

c. Suppose that if the true process fraction nonconforming is 5%, we would like to detect this condition with probability 0.95. Construct the corresponding acceptance control chart.

8-6 A manufacturing process operates with an in-control fraction of nonconforming production of at most 0.1%, which management is willing to accept 95% of the time; however, if the fraction nonconforming increases to 2% or more, management wishes to detect this shift with probability 0.90. Design an appropriate acceptance control chart for this process.

8-7 Consider a modified control chart with center line at $\mu = 0$, and $\sigma = 1.0$ (known). If $n = 5$, the tolerable fraction nonconforming is $\delta = 0.00135$, and the control limits are at 3-sigma, sketch the OC curve for the chart. On the same set of axes, sketch the OC curve corresponding to the chart with 2-sigma limits.

8-8 Specifications on a bearing diameter are established at 8.00 ± 0.01 cm. Samples of size $n = 8$ are used, and a control chart for s shows statistical control, with the best current estimate of the population standard deviation $s = 0.001$. If the fraction of nonconforming product that is barely acceptable is 0.135%, find the 3-sigma limits on the modified control chart for this process.

8-9 An $\bar{x}$ chart is to be designed for a quality characteristic assumed to be normal with a standard deviation of 4. Specifications on the product quality characteristics are 50 ± 20. The control chart is to be designed so that if the fraction nonconforming is 1% the probability of a point falling inside the control limits will be 0.995. The sample size is $n = 4$. What are the control limits and center line for the chart?

8-10 An $\bar{x}$ chart is to be established to control a quality characteristic assumed to be normally distributed with a standard deviation of 4. Specifications on the quality characteristic are 800 ± 20. The control chart is to be designed so that if the fraction nonconforming is 1%, the probability of a point falling inside the control limits will be 0.90. The sample size is $n = 4$. What are the control limits and center line for the chart?

8-11 A normally distributed quality characteristic is controlled by $\bar{x}$ and R charts having the following parameters ($n = 4$, both charts are in-control):

R Chart	$\bar{x}$ Chart
UCL = 18.795	UCL = 626.00
Center line = 8.236	Center line = 620.00
LCL = 0	LCL = 614.00

a. What is the estimated standard deviation of the quality characteristic x?

b. If specifications are 610 ± 15, what is your estimate of the fraction of nonconforming material produced by this process when it is in control at the given level?

c. Suppose you wish to establish a modified $\bar{x}$ chart to substitute for the original $\bar{x}$ chart. The process mean is to be controlled so that the fraction nonconforming is less than 0.005. The probability of type I error is to be 0.01. What control limits do you recommend?

8-12 The data shown below come from a production process with two observable quality characteristics, x_1 and x_2. The data are sample means of each quality characteristic, based on samples of size $n = 25$. Assume that the nominal value of the quality characteristics and the covariance matrix are

$$\bar{\bar{x}} = \begin{bmatrix} 55 \\ 30 \end{bmatrix} \qquad S = \begin{bmatrix} 200 & 130 \\ 130 & 120 \end{bmatrix}$$

Construct a T^2 control chart using these data.

Sample Number	$\bar{x}_1$	$\bar{x}_2$
1	58	32
2	60	33
3	50	27
4	54	31
5	63	38
6	53	30
7	42	20
8	55	31
9	46	25
10	50	29
11	49	27
12	57	30
13	58	33
14	75	45
15	55	27

8-13 A product has three quality characteristics. The nominal values of these quality characteristics and their sample covariance matrix have been determined from the analysis of preliminary samples of size $n = 10$ as follows:

$$\bar{\bar{x}} = \begin{bmatrix} 3.0 \\ 3.5 \\ 2.8 \end{bmatrix} \qquad S = \begin{bmatrix} 1.40 & 1.02 & 1.05 \\ 1.02 & 1.35 & 0.98 \\ 1.05 & 0.98 & 1.20 \end{bmatrix}$$

The sample means for each quality characteristic for 15 additional samples of size $n = 10$ are shown below. Is the process in statistical control?

Sample Number	$\bar{x}_1$	$\bar{x}_2$	$\bar{x}_3$
1	3.1	3.7	3.0
2	3.3	3.9	3.1
3	2.6	3.0	2.4
4	2.8	3.0	2.5
5	3.0	3.3	2.8
6	4.0	4.6	3.5
7	3.8	4.2	3.0
8	3.0	3.3	2.7
9	2.4	3.0	2.2
10	2.0	2.6	1.8
11	3.2	3.9	3.0
12	3.7	4.0	3.0
13	4.1	4.7	3.2
14	3.8	4.0	2.9
15	3.2	3.6	2.8

8-14 Yield from the first four cycles of a chemical process is shown below. The variables are percent concentration (x_1) at levels 30, 31, and 32, and temperature (x_2) at 140°, 142°, and 144° F. Analyze these data by EVOP methods.

Cycle	Conditions				
	(1)	**(2)**	**(3)**	**(4)**	**(5)**
1	60.7	59.8	60.2	64.2	57.5
2	59.1	62.8	62.5	64.6	58.3
3	56.6	59.1	59.0	62.3	61.1
4	60.5	59.8	64.5	61.0	60.1

8-15 A control chart for tool wear. A sample of five units of product is taken from a production process every hour. The following results are obtained.

Sample Number	$\bar{x}$	R
1	1.0020	0.0008
2	1.0022	0.0009
3	1.0025	0.0006
4	1.0028	0.0007
5	1.0029	0.0005
6	1.0032	0.0006

Tool Reset

7	1.0018	0.0005
8	1.0021	0.0006
9	1.0024	0.0005
10	1.0026	0.0008
11	1.0029	0.0005
12	1.0031	0.0007

Assume that the specifications on this quality characteristic are at 1.0015 and 1.0035. Set up the R chart on this process. Set up a control chart to monitor the tool wear.

8-16 An automatic machine is used to fill cans with coffee. The nominal weight of each can is 16.0 oz. The standard deviation of the fill weight is known to be 0.10 oz. Cans are automatically inspected, and all underfilled cans are rejected. The selling price of a can of coffee is $3. Underfilled cans can be sold for $1.75. The cost of the coffee is $0.10 per ounce. Determine the optimum mean target level for the filling machine.

8-17 Five-gallon stainless steel containers are filled with soft drink syrup on an automatic machine. The filling process is monitored by $\bar{x}$ and R charts, based on samples of size six. These charts indicate that the process is in control, and the center line of the R chart is 0.20 fluid ounces. The filled containers are inspected, and all underfilled containers are rejected. A container is sold for $10; however, an underfilled container must be refilled to the correct volume. The additional labor cost associated with this refilling operation is $2. The product cost is $0.10 per fluid ounce. What is the optimum mean target level for the filling machine?

8-18 The viscosity of a chemical product is read every two minutes. Some data from this process are shown below.

a. Is there a serious problem with autocorrelation in these data?

b. Set up a control chart for individuals with a moving range used to estimate process variability. What conclusion can you draw from this chart?

c. Design a cusum control scheme for this process, assuming that the observations are uncorrelated. How does the cusum perform?

d. Set up an EWMA control chart with $\lambda = 0.15$ for the process. How does this chart perform?

e. Discuss how you would modify both the cusum and EWMA control chart to handle the autocorrelation in the viscosity data. Implement these changes on the control charts from parts (c) and (d) above. How effective are these charts?

f. Suppose that a reasonable model for the viscosity data is $\hat{x}_t = 20.62 + 0.777x_{t-1} - 0.492x_{t-2}$.

How could this model be used to assist in the development of a statistical process-control procedure for viscosity? Set up an appropriate control chart and use it to assess the current state of statistical control.

OBS.	Viscosity	OBS.	Viscosity
1	29.330	51	27.990
2	19.980	52	24.130
3	25.760	53	29.200
4	29.000	54	34.300
5	31.030	55	26.410
6	32.680	56	28.780
7	33.560	57	21.280
8	27.500	58	21.710

OBS.	Viscosity	OBS.	Viscosity
9	26.750	59	21.470
10	30.550	60	24.710
11	28.940	61	33.610
12	28.500	62	36.540
13	28.190	63	35.700
14	26.130	64	33.680
15	27.790	65	29.290
16	27.630	66	25.120
17	29.890	67	27.230
18	28.180	68	30.610
19	26.650	69	29.060
20	30.010	70	28.480
21	30.800	71	32.010
22	30.450	72	31.890
23	36.610	73	31.720
24	31.400	74	29.090
25	30.830	75	31.920
26	33.220	76	24.280
27	30.150	77	22.690
28	27.080	78	26.600
29	33.660	79	28.860
30	36.580	80	28.270
31	29.040	81	28.170
32	28.080	82	28.580
33	30.280	83	30.760
34	29.350	84	30.620
35	33.600	85	20.840
36	30.290	86	16.560
37	20.110	87	25.230
38	17.510	88	31.790
39	23.710	89	32.520
40	24.220	90	30.280
41	32.430	91	26.140
42	32.440	92	19.030
43	29.390	93	24.340
44	23.450	94	31.530
45	23.620	95	31.950
46	28.120	96	31.680
47	29.940	97	29.100
48	30.560	98	23.150
49	32.300	99	26.740
50	31.580	100	32.440

Chapter 9

Process-Capability Analysis

9-1 INTRODUCTION

Statistical techniques can be helpful throughout the product cycle, including development activities prior to manufacturing, in quantifying process variability, in analyzing this variability relative to product requirements or specifications, and in assisting development and manufacturing in eliminating or greatly reducing this variability. This general activity is called *process-capability analysis*. In this chapter, we describe several statistical methods helpful in process-capability studies and show how the information so generated is useful in setting specifications on individual discrete parts or components.

   Process capability refers to the *uniformity* of the process. Obviously, the variability in the process is a measure of the uniformity of output. There are two ways to think of this variability:

1. The natural or inherent variability at a specified time; that is, "instantaneous" variability.
2. The variability over time.

We present methods for investigating and assessing both aspects of process capability.

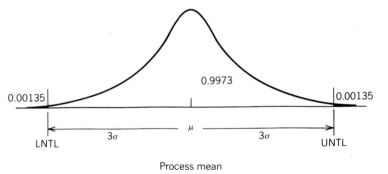

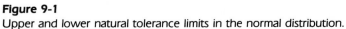

Figure 9-1
Upper and lower natural tolerance limits in the normal distribution.

It is customary to take the 6-sigma spread in the distribution of the product quality characteristic as a measure of process capability. Figure 9-1 shows a process for which the quality characteristic has a normal distribution with mean μ and standard deviation σ. The upper and lower "natural tolerance limits" of the process fall at $\mu + 3\sigma$ and $\mu - 3\sigma$, respectively. That is,

$$\text{UNTL} = \mu + 3\sigma$$
$$\text{LNTL} = \mu - 3\sigma$$

For a normal distribution, the natural tolerance limits include 99.73% of the variable, or put another way, only 0.27% of the process output will fall outside the natural tolerance limits. Two points should be remembered:

1. 0.27% outside the natural tolerances sounds small, but this corresponds to 2700 nonconforming parts per million.
2. If the distribution of process output is nonnormal, then the percentage of output falling outside $\mu \pm 3\sigma$ may differ considerably from 0.27%.

We define *process-capability analysis* as an engineering study to estimate process capability. The estimate of process capability may be in the form of a probability distribution having a specified shape, center (mean), and spread (standard deviation). For example, we may determine that the process output is normally distributed with mean $\mu = 1.0$ cm and standard deviation $\sigma = 0.001$ cm. In this sense, a process-capability analysis may be performed *without regard to specifications on the quality characteristic*. Alternatively, we may express process capability as a percentage outside of specifications. However, specifications are not *necessary* to perform a process-capability analysis.

A process-capability study usually measures functional parameters on the product, not the process itself. When the analyst can directly observe the process and can control or monitor the data-collection activity, the study is a true process-capability study, because by controlling the data collection and knowing the time sequence of the data, inferences can be made about the stability of the process over time. However, when we have available only sample units of product, perhaps supplied by the vendor or obtained via receiving inspection, and there is no direct observation of the process or time history of production, then the study is more properly called *product characterization*. In a product characterization study we can only estimate the distribution of the product quality characteristic or the process yield (fraction conforming to specifications); we can say nothing about the dynamic behavior of the process or its state of statistical control.

Process-capability analysis is a vital part of an overall quality-improvement program. Among the major uses of data from a process-capability analysis are the following:

1. Predicting how well the process will hold the tolerances.
2. Assisting product developers/designers in selecting or modifying a process.
3. Assisting in establishing an interval between sampling for process controls.
4. Specifying performance requirements for new equipment.
5. Selecting between competing vendors.
6. Planning the sequence of production processes when there is an interactive effect of processes on tolerances.
7. Reducing the variability in a manufacturing process.

Thus, process-capability analysis is a technique that has application in many segments of the product cycle, including product and process design, vendor sourcing, production or manufacturing planning, and manufacturing.

Three primary techniques are used in process-capability analysis: histograms or probability plots, control charts, and designed experiments. We will discuss and illustrate each of these methods in the next three sections. We will also discuss the process-capability ratio (PCR) introduced in Chapter 6 and some useful variations of this ratio.

9-2 PROCESS-CAPABILITY ANALYSIS USING A HISTOGRAM OR A PROBABILITY PLOT

9-2.1 Using the Histogram

The frequency distribution can be helpful in estimating process capability. At least 100 or more observations should be available in order for the histogram to be moderately stable so that a reasonably reliable estimate of process capability may be obtained. If the quality engineer has access to the process and can control the data-collection effort, the following steps should be followed prior to data collection:

1. Choose the machine or machines to be used. If the results based on one (or a few) machines are to be extended to a larger population of machines, the machine selected should be representative of those in the population. Furthermore, if the machine has multiple work stations or heads, it may be important to collect the data so that head-to-head variability can be isolated. This may imply that designed experiments should be used (see Section 9-4).
2. Select the process operating conditions. Carefully define conditions, such as cutting speeds, feed rates, and temperatures, for future reference. It may be important to study the effects of varying these factors on process capability.
3. Select a representative operator. In some studies, it may be important to estimate *operator* variability. In these cases, the operators should be selected at random from the population of operators.

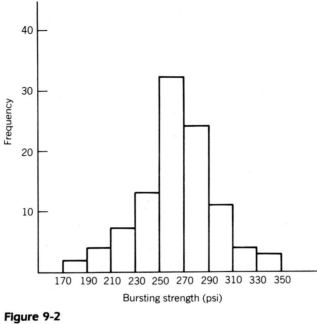

Figure 9-2
Histogram for the bursting-strength data.

4. Carefully monitor the data-collection process, and record the time order in which each unit is produced.

The histogram, along with the sample average $\bar{x}$ and sample standard deviation S, provides information about process capability. You may wish to review the guidelines for constructing histograms in Chapter 2.

Example 9-1

To illustrate the use of a histogram to estimate process capability, consider Figure 9-2 which presents a histogram of the bursting strength of 100 glass 1-liter soft drink bottles. The data are shown in Table 9-1, and the frequency distribution is

Table 9-1
Bursting strengths for 100 1-liter glass soft drink bottles

265	197	346	280	265	200	221	265	261	278
205	286	317	242	254	235	176	262	248	250
263	274	242	260	281	246	248	271	260	265
307	243	258	321	294	328	263	245	274	270
220	231	276	228	223	296	231	301	337	298
268	267	300	250	260	276	334	280	250	257
260	281	208	299	308	264	280	274	278	210
234	265	187	258	235	269	265	253	254	280
299	214	264	267	283	235	272	287	274	269
215	318	271	293	277	290	283	258	275	251

Table 9-2
Frequency distribution for the bursting-strength data

Class Interval (psi)	Frequency	Relative Frequency	Cumulative Relative Frequency
$170 \leq x < 190$	2	0.02	0.02
$190 \leq x < 210$	4	0.04	0.06
$210 \leq x < 230$	7	0.07	0.13
$230 \leq x < 250$	13	0.13	0.26
$250 \leq x < 270$	32	0.32	0.58
$270 \leq x < 290$	24	0.24	0.82
$290 \leq x < 310$	11	0.11	0.93
$310 \leq x < 330$	4	0.04	0.97
$330 \leq x < 350$	3	0.03	1.00
	100	1.00	

shown in Table 9-2. Analysis of the 100 observations gives

$$\bar{x} = 264.06 \qquad S = 32.02$$

Consequently, the process capability would be estimated as

$$\bar{x} \pm 3S$$

or

$$264.06 \pm 3(32.02) \simeq 264 \pm 96 \text{ psi}$$

Furthermore, the shape of the histogram implies that the distribution of bursting strength is approximately normal. Thus, we can estimate that approximately 99.73% of the bottles manufactured by this process will burst between 168 and 360 psi. Note that we can estimate process capability *independent of the specifications on bursting strength*.

An advantage of using the histogram to estimate process capability is that it gives an immediate, visual impression of process performance. It may also immediately show the reason for poor process performance. For example, Figure 9-3*a* shows a process with adequate potential capability, but the process target is poorly located, whereas Figure 9-3*b* shows a process with poor capability resulting from excess variability.

9-2.2 Process-Capability Ratios

It is frequently convenient to have a simple, quantitative way to express process capability. One way to do so is through the process-capability ratio PCR[1] first

---

[1] Some authors use the Japanese terminology C_p instead of PCR.

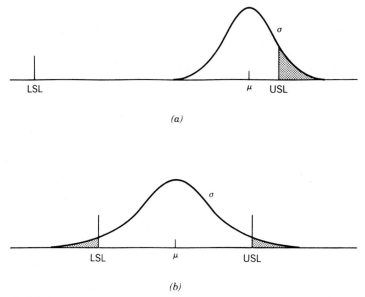

(a)

(b)

Figure 9-3
Some reasons for poor process capability. (a) Poor process
centering. (b) Excess process variability.

introduced in Chapter 6. Recall that

$$PCR = \frac{USL - LSL}{6\sigma} \qquad (9\text{-}1)$$

where USL and LSL are the upper and lower specification limits, respectively. Usually, the process standard deviation σ is unknown and must be replaced by an estimate $\hat{\sigma}$. To estimate σ we typically use either the *sample standard deviation S* or $\bar{R}/d_2$ (when variables control charts are used in the capability study). This results in an estimate of the PCR, say

$$\widehat{PCR} = \frac{USL - LSL}{6\hat{\sigma}} \qquad (9\text{-}2)$$

To illustrate the calculation of the PCR, recall the diameter of automobile engine piston rings, first analyzed in Example 6-1 using $\bar{x}$ and R charts. The specifications on piston-ring diameter are USL = 74.05 mm and LSL = 73.95 mm, and from the R chart we estimated $\hat{\sigma} = \bar{R}/d_2 = 0.0099$. Thus, our estimate of the PCR is

$$
\begin{aligned}
\widehat{PCR} &= \frac{USL - LSL}{6\hat{\sigma}} \\
&= \frac{74.05 - 73.95}{6(0.0099)} \\
&= 1.68
\end{aligned}
$$

In Chapter 6, we assumed that piston-ring diameter is approximately normally distributed (a reasonable assumption, based on the histogram in Figure 2-1) and the cumulative normal distribution table in the Appendix was used to estimate that the process produces approximately 20 PPM (parts per million) defective.

The PCR in Equation (9-1) has a useful practical interpretation, namely

$$P = \left(\frac{1}{PCR}\right)100 \tag{9-3}$$

is the percentage of the specification band used up by the process. The piston-ring process uses

$$P = \left(\frac{1}{1.68}\right)100$$
$$= 59.5$$

percent of the specification band.

Equations (9-1) and (9-2) assume that the process has both upper and lower specification limits. For one-sided specifications, we define the PCR as

$$PCR_U = \frac{USL - \mu}{3\sigma} \qquad \text{(upper specification only)} \tag{9-4}$$

or

$$PCR_L = \frac{\mu - LSL}{3\sigma} \qquad \text{(lower specification only)} \tag{9-5}$$

Estimates $\widehat{PCR}_U$ and $\widehat{PCR}_L$ would be obtained by replacing μ and σ in Equations (9-4) and (9-5) by estimates $\hat{\mu}$ and $\hat{\sigma}$, respectively.

Example 9-2

To illustrate the use of the one-sided process-capability ratios, consider the bottle-bursting strength data in Example 9-1. Suppose that the lower specification limit on bursting strength is 200 psi. We will use $\bar{x} = 264$ and $S = 32$ as estimates of μ and σ, respectively, and the resulting estimate of the one-sided lower process-capability ratio is

$$\widehat{PCR}_L = \frac{\hat{\mu} - LSL}{3\hat{\sigma}}$$
$$= \frac{264 - 200}{3(32)}$$
$$= \frac{64}{96}$$
$$= 0.67$$

The fraction of defective bottles produced by this process is estimated by finding the area to the left of $Z = (\mu - \text{LSL})/\sigma = (264 - 200)/32 = 2$ under the standard normal distribution. The estimated fallout is about 2.28% defective, or about 22,800 nonconforming bottles per million. Notice that if the normal distribution was an inappropriate model for strength, then this last calculation would have to be performed using the appropriate probability distribution.

The process-capability ratio is a measure of the ability of the process to manufacture product that meets specifications. Table 9-3 shows several values of the PCR, along with the associated values of process fallout, expressed in defective or nonconforming parts per million (PPM). These process fallouts were calculated assuming a normal distribution for the quality characteristic, and in the case of two-sided specifications, assuming the process mean is centered between the upper and lower specification limits. To illustrate the use of the table, notice that a PCR of 1.00 implies a fallout rate of 2700 PPM for two-sided specifications, while a PCR of 1.50 implies a fallout rate of 4 PPM for one-sided specifications.

Table 9-4 presents some recommended guidelines for minimum values of the PCR. The bottle-strength characteristic is a parameter closely related to the safety of the product; bottles with inadequate pressure strength may fail and injure consumers. This implies that the PCR should be at least 1.45. Perhaps one way the PCR could be improved would be by increasing the mean strength of the bottles, say by pouring more glass in the mold.

Table 9-3
Values of the process-capability ratio (PCR) and associated process fallout for a normally distributed process (in defective PPM)

	Process Fallout (in defective PPM)	
PCR	One-Sided Specifications	Two-Sided Specifications
0.25	226,628	453,255
0.50	66,807	133,614
0.60	35,931	71,861
0.70	17,865	35,729
0.80	8,198	16,395
0.90	3,467	6,934
1.00	1,350	2,700
1.10	484	967
1.20	159	318
1.30	48	96
1.40	14	27
1.50	4	7
1.60	1	2
1.70	0.17	0.34
1.80	0.03	0.06
2.00	0.0009	0.0018

Table 9-4

Recommended minimum values of the process-capability ratio

	Two-Sided Specifications	One-Sided Specifications
Existing processes	1.33	1.25
New processes	1.50	1.45
Safety, strength, or critical parameter, existing process	1.50	1.45
Safety, strength, or critical parameter, new process	1.67	1.60

Process-Capability Ratio for an Off-Center Process

The process-capability ratio (PCR) does not take into account *where* the process mean is located relative to the specifications. PCR simply measures the spread of the specifications relative to the 6-sigma spread in the process. For example, the top two normal distributions in Figure 9-4 both have PCR = 2.0, but the process in panel (*b*) of the figure clearly has lower capability than the process in panel (*a*) because it is not operating at the midpoint of the interval between the specifications.

This situation may be more accurately reflected by defining a new process-capability ratio that takes process centering into account, say

$$PCR_k = \min(PCR_U, PCR_L) \tag{9-6}$$

Notice that PCR_k is just the one-sided PCR for the specification limit nearest to the process average. For the process shown in Figure 9-4*b*, we would have

$$PCR_k = \min(PCR_U, PCR_L)$$

$$= \min\left(PCR_U = \frac{USL - \mu}{3\sigma}, PCR_L = \frac{\mu - LSL}{3\sigma} \right)$$

$$= \min\left(PCR_U = \frac{62 - 53}{3(2)} = 1.5, PCR_L = \frac{53 - 38}{3(2)} = 2.5 \right)$$

$$= 1.5$$

Generally, if PCR = PCR_k, the process is centered at the midpoint of the specifications, and when PCR_k < PCR the process is off-center.

The magnitude of PCR_k relative to PCR is a direct measure of how off-center the process is operating. Several commonly encountered cases are illustrated in Figure 9-4. Note in panel (*c*) of Figure 9-4 that PCR_k = 1.0 while PCR = 2.0. One can use Table 9-3 to get a quick estimate of potential improvement that would be possible by centering the process. If we take PCR = 1.0 in Table 9-3 and read the fallout from the one-sided specifications column, we can estimate the *actual* fallout as 1350 PPM. However, if we can center the process, then PCR = 2.0 can be achieved, and Table 9-3 (using PCR = 2.0 and two-sided specifications) suggests that the *potential* fallout is 0.0018 PPM, an improvement of several orders

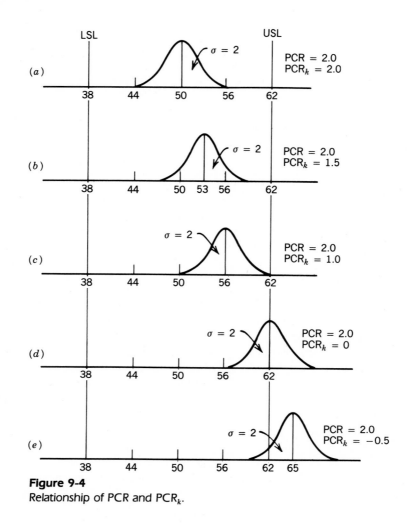

Figure 9-4
Relationship of PCR and PCR_k.

of magnitude in process performance. Thus, we usually say that PCR measures *potential capability* in the process, while PCR_k measures *actual* capability.

Panel (*d*) of Figure 9-4 illustrates the case in which the process mean is exactly equal to one of the specification limits, leading to $PCR_k = 0$. As panel (*e*) illustrates, when $PCR_k < 0$ the implication is that the process mean lies outside the specifications. Clearly, if $PCR_k < -1$, the entire process lies outside the specification limits. Some authors define PCR_k to be nonnegative, so that values less than zero are defined as zero.

A Confidence Interval Estimate of PCR

Replacing σ by S in the equation for PCR produces a point estimate $\widehat{PCR}$ of PCR. In some cases, a confidence interval estimate may be helpful. A $100(1 - \alpha)\%$ confidence interval estimate of PCR may be obtained from

$$\frac{\text{USL} - \text{LSL}}{6S}\sqrt{\frac{\chi^2_{1-\alpha/2,n-1}}{n-1}} \leq \text{PCR} \leq \frac{\text{USL} - \text{LSL}}{6S}\sqrt{\frac{\chi^2_{\alpha/2,n-1}}{n-1}} \qquad (9\text{-}7)$$

or

$$\widehat{PCR} \sqrt{\frac{\chi^2_{1-\alpha/2,n-1}}{n-1}} \le PCR \le \widehat{PCR} \sqrt{\frac{\chi^2_{\alpha/2,n-1}}{n-1}}$$

where $\chi^2_{1-\alpha/2,n-1}$ and $\chi^2_{\alpha/2,n-1}$ are the lower $\alpha/2$ and upper $\alpha/2$ percentage points of the chi-square distribution with $n-1$ degrees of freedom. These percentage points are tabulated in Appendix Table III.

Example 9-3

Suppose that a process has upper and lower specifications at USL = 62 and LSL = 38. A sample of size $n = 20$ from this process reveals that the process mean is centered approximately at the midpoint of the tolerance interval and that the sample standard deviation $S = 1.75$. Therefore, a point estimate of PCR is

$$\widehat{PCR} = \frac{USL - LSL}{6S}$$
$$= \frac{62 - 38}{6(1.75)}$$
$$= 2.29$$

The 95 percent confidence interval on PCR is found from Equation (9-7) as follows:

$$\frac{USL - LSL}{6S} \sqrt{\frac{\chi^2_{1-\alpha/2,n-1}}{n-1}} \le PCR \le \frac{USL - LSL}{6S} \sqrt{\frac{\chi^2_{\alpha/2,n-1}}{n-1}}$$
$$2.29 \sqrt{\frac{8.91}{19}} \le PCR \le 2.29 \sqrt{\frac{32.85}{19}}$$
$$1.57 \le PCR \le 3.01,$$

where $\chi^2_{0.975,19} = 8.91$ and $\chi^2_{0.025,19} = 32.85$ were taken from Appendix Table III.

The confidence interval on PCR in Example 9-3 is relatively wide because the sample standard deviation S exhibits considerable fluctuation in small to moderately large samples.

Testing Hypotheses About PCR

A practice that is becoming increasingly common in industry is to require a supplier to demonstrate process capability as part of the contractual agreement. Thus, it is frequently necessary to demonstrate that the process-capability ratio meets or exceeds some particular target value, say PCR_0. This problem may be formulated as a hypothesis-testing problem

$$H_0: \quad PCR < PCR_0 \text{ (or the process is not capable)}$$
$$H_1: \quad PCR \ge PCR_0 \text{ (or the process is capable)}$$

Table 9-5
Sample size and critical value determination for testing PCR

Sample Size, n	(a) $\alpha = \beta = 0.10$		(b) $\alpha = \beta = 0.05$	
	PCR(High)/ PCR(Low)	C/PCR(Low)	PCR(High)/ PCR(Low)	C/PCR(Low)
10	1.88	1.27	2.26	1.37
20	1.53	1.20	1.73	1.26
30	1.41	1.16	1.55	1.21
40	1.34	1.14	1.46	1.18
50	1.30	1.13	1.40	1.16
60	1.27	1.11	1.36	1.15
70	1.25	1.10	1.33	1.14
80	1.23	1.10	1.30	1.13
90	1.21	1.10	1.28	1.12
100	1.20	1.09	1.26	1.11

Source: Adapted from Kane (1986), with permission of the American Society for Quality Control.

We would like to reject H_0 (recall that rejection of H_0 is always a strong conclusion), thereby demonstrating that the process is capable. We can formulate the statistical test in terms of $\widehat{PCR}$, so that we will reject H_0 if $\widehat{PCR}$ exceeds a critical value C.

Kane (1986) has investigated this test, and provides a table of sample sizes and critical values C to assist in testing process capability. We may define PCR(High) as a process capability that we would like to accept with probability $1 - \alpha$ and PCR(Low) as a process capability that we would like to reject with probability $1 - \beta$. Table 9-5 gives values of PCR(High)/PCR(Low) and C/PCR(Low) for varying sample sizes and $\alpha = \beta = 0.05$ or $\alpha = \beta = 0.10$. The following example illustrates the use of this table.

Example 9-4

A customer has told his supplier that, in order to qualify for business with his company, the supplier must demonstrate that his process capability exceeds PCR = 1.33. Thus, the supplier is interested in establishing a procedure to test the hypotheses

$$H_0: \quad PCR \leq 1.33$$
$$H_1: \quad PCR > 1.33$$

The supplier wants to be sure that if the process capability is below 1.33 there will be a high probability of detecting this (say 0.90), while if the process capability exceeds 1.66 there will be a high probability of judging the process capable (again, say 0.90). This would imply that PCR(Low) = 1.33, PCR(High) = 1.66, and $\alpha =$

$\beta = 0.10$. To find the sample size and critical value C from Table 9-5, compute

$$\frac{\text{PCR(High)}}{\text{PCR(Low)}} = \frac{1.66}{1.33} = 1.25$$

and enter the table in panel (a) where $\alpha = \beta = 0.10$. This yields

$$n = 70$$

and

$$C/\text{PCR(Low)} = 1.10$$

from which we calculate

$$\begin{aligned} C &= \text{PCR(Low)}1.10 \\ &= 1.33(1.10) \\ &= 1.46 \end{aligned}$$

Thus, to demonstrate capability, the supplier must take a sample of $n = 70$ parts, and the sample process-capability ratio $\widehat{\text{PCR}}$ must exceed $C = 1.46$.

This example shows that, in order to demonstrate that process capability is at least equal to 1.33, the *observed sample* $\widehat{\text{PCR}}$ will have to exceed 1.33 by a considerable amount. This illustrates that some common industrial practices may be questionable statistically. For example, it is fairly common practice to accept as capable at the level $\text{PCR} \geq 1.33$ if the *sample* $\widehat{\text{PCR}} \geq 1.33$ based on a sample size of $30 \leq n \leq 50$ parts. Clearly, this procedure does not account for sampling variation in the estimate of σ, and larger values of n and/or higher acceptable values of $\widehat{\text{PCR}}$ may be necessary in practice.

Normality and the Process-Capability Ratio

An important assumption underlying our discussion of process capability and the ratios PCR and PCR_k is that their usual interpretation is based on a normal distribution of process output. If the underlying distribution is nonnormal, then the statements about expected process fallout attributed to a particular value of PCR or PCR_k may be in error.

To illustrate this point, consider the data in Figure 9-5, which is a histogram of 80 measurements of surface roughness on a machined part (measured in microinches). The upper specification limit is at USL = 32 microinches. The sample average and standard deviation are $\bar{x} = 10.44$ and $S = 3.053$, implying that $\text{PCR}_U = 2.35$, and Table 9-3 would suggest that the fallout is less than one part per billion. However, since the histogram is highly skewed, we are fairly certain that the distribution is nonnormal. Thus, this estimate of capability is unlikely to be correct.

One approach to dealing with this situation is to transform the data so that in the new, transformed metric the data have a normal distribution appearance. There

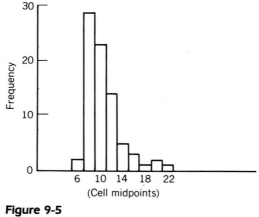

Figure 9-5
Surface roughness in microinches for a machined part.

are various graphical and analytical approaches to selecting a transformation. In this example, a reciprocal transformation was used. Figure 9-6 presents a histogram of the reciprocal values $x^* = 1/x$. In the transformed scale, $\bar{x}^* = 0.1025$ and $S^* = 0.0244$, and the upper specification limit is USL $= 1/32 = 0.03125$. This gives $PCR_U = 0.97$, which implies that about 1350 PPM are outside of specifications. This estimate of process performance is clearly much more realistic than the one resulting from the usual "normal theory" assumption.

More About Process Centering

The process-capability ratio PCR_k was initially developed because PCR does not adequately deal with the case of a process with mean μ that is not centered between the specification limits. However, PCR_k *alone* is still an inadequate measure of process centering. For example, consider the two processes shown in Figure 9-7. Both processes A and B have $PCR_k = 1.0$, yet their centering is clearly different. To characterize process centering satisfactorily, PCR_k must be compared to PCR. For Process A, $PCR_k = PCR = 1.0$, implying that the process is centered, while

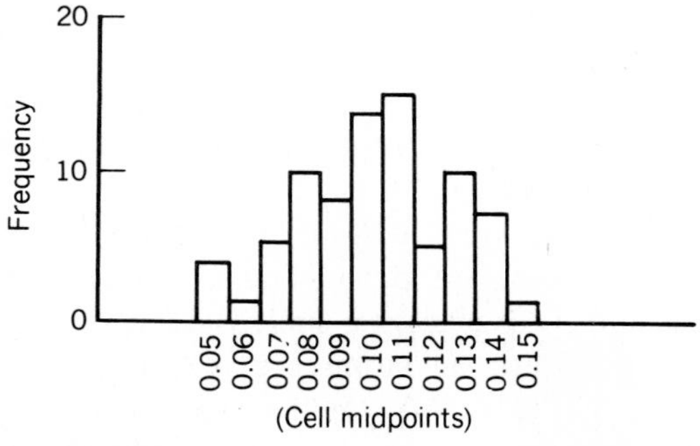

Figure 9-6
Reciprocals of surface roughness. (Adapted from data in the "Statistics Corner" Column in *Quality Progress*, March 1989, with permission of the American Society for Quality Control.)

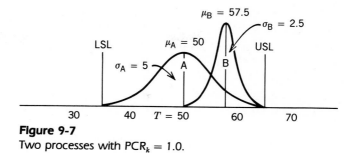

Figure 9-7
Two processes with PCR$_k$ = 1.0.

for process B, PCR $= 2.0 >$ PCR$_k = 1.0$, implying that the process is off-center. For any fixed value of μ in the interval from LSL to USL, PCR$_k$ depends inversely on σ and becomes large as σ approaches zero. This characteristic can make PCR$_k$ unsuitable as a measure of centering. That is, a large value of PCR$_k$ does not really tell us anything about the location of the mean in the interval from LSL to USL.

One way to address this difficulty is to use a process-capability ratio that is a better indicator of centering. One such ratio is

$$\text{PCR}_{km} = \frac{\text{USL} - \text{LSL}}{6\tau} \tag{9-8}$$

where τ is the square root of expected squared deviation from target $T = \frac{1}{2}(\text{USL} - \text{LSL})$,

$$\begin{aligned} \tau^2 &= E[(x - T)^2] \\ &= E[(x - \mu)^2] + (\mu - T)^2 \\ &= \sigma^2 + (\mu - T)^2 \end{aligned}$$

Thus, (9-8) can be written as

$$\begin{aligned} \text{PCR}_{km} &= \frac{\text{USL} - \text{LSL}}{6\sqrt{\sigma^2 + (\mu - T)^2}} \\ &= \frac{\text{PCR}}{\sqrt{1 + \xi^2}} \end{aligned} \tag{9-9}$$

where

$$\xi = \frac{T - \mu}{\sigma} \tag{9-10}$$

A logical way to estimate PCR$_{km}$ is by

$$\widehat{\text{PCR}}_{km} = \frac{\widehat{\text{PCR}}}{\sqrt{1 + V^2}} \tag{9-11}$$

where

$$V = \frac{T - \bar{x}}{S} \tag{9-12}$$

Chan et al. (1988) discuss this ratio, various estimators of PCR_{km}, and their sampling properties. Boyles (1989) has provided a definitive analysis of PCR_{km} and its usefulness in measuring process centering. He notes that both PCR_k and PCR_{km} coincide with PCR when $\mu = T$ and decrease as μ moves away from T. However, $PCR_k < 0$ for $\mu > \text{USL}$ or $\mu < \text{LSL}$, while PCR_{km} approaches zero asymptotically as $|\mu - T| \to \infty$. Boyles also shows that the PCR_{km} of a process with $|\mu - T| = \Delta > 0$ is strictly bounded above by the PCR value of a process with $\sigma = \Delta$. That is,

$$PCR_{km} < \frac{\text{USL} - \text{LSL}}{6|\mu - T|} \tag{9-13}$$

Thus, a necessary condition for $PCR_{km} \geq 1$ is

$$|\mu - T| < \tfrac{1}{6}(\text{USL} - \text{LSL})$$

This statistic says that if the target value T is the midpoint of the specifications, a PCR_{km} of one or greater implies that the mean μ lies within the middle third of the specification band. A similar statement can be made for any value of PCR_{km}. For instance, $PCR_{km} \geq \tfrac{4}{3}$ implies that $|\mu - T| < \tfrac{1}{8}(\text{USL} - \text{LSL})$. Thus, a given value of PCR_{km} places a constraint on the difference between μ and the target value T.

Example 9-5

To illustrate the use of PCR_{km}, consider the two processes A and B in Figure 9-5. For process A we find that

$$PCR_{km} = \frac{PCR}{\sqrt{1 + \xi^2}} = \frac{1.0}{\sqrt{1 + 0}} = 1.0$$

since process A is centered at the target value $T = 50$. Note that $PCR_{km} = PCR_k$ for process A. Now consider process B:

$$PCR_{km} = \frac{PCR}{\sqrt{1 + \xi^2}} = \frac{2.0}{\sqrt{1 + (-3)^2}} = 0.63$$

If we use Equation (9-13), this is equivalent to saying that the process mean lies approximately within the middle half of the specification range. Visual examination of Figure 9-7 reveals this to be the case.

9-2.3 Probability Plotting

Probability plotting is an alternative to the histogram that can be used to determine the shape, center, and spread of the distribution. It has the advantage that it is unnecessary to divide the range of the variable into class intervals, and it often produces reasonable results for moderately small samples (which the histogram will not). A probability plot is a graph of the ranked data versus the sample cumulative frequency on special paper with a vertical scale chosen so that the cumulative distribution of the assumed type is a straight line. Probability papers are available for the normal, exponential, Weibull, and several other distributions. If, for example, data for a normal distribution are plotted on normal probability paper, then the points will fall almost exactly along a straight line.

To illustrate the procedure, consider the 20 observations on bottle-bursting strength shown below in rank order:

Rank, j	Strength, x_j	Plotting Position, P_j
1.	197	0.025
2.	200	0.075
3.	215	0.125
4.	221	0.175
5.	231	0.225
6.	242	0.275
7.	245	0.325
8.	258	0.375
9.	265	0.425
10.	265	0.475
11.	271	0.525
12.	275	0.575
13.	277	0.625
14.	278	0.675
15.	280	0.725
16.	283	0.775
17.	290	0.825
18.	301	0.875
19.	318	0.925
20.	346	0.975

The plotting position P_j of the observation with rank j is calculated as follows:

$$P_j = \frac{j - \frac{1}{2}}{n} \tag{9-14}$$

where n is the sample size. For example, the plotting position of point 1 is

$$P_1 = \frac{1 - \frac{1}{2}}{20} = \frac{0.5}{20} = 0.025$$

Figure 9-8 is the plot of P_j versus strength x_j on normal probability paper. Notice that the data lie nearly along a straight line, implying that the distribution of bursting strength is normal. The straight line in Figure 9-8 was fit by eye. When drawing the line, it is best to give more emphasis to the central points on the graph, rather than the extremes.

The mean of the normal distribution is the fiftieth percentile, which we may estimate from Figure 9-8 as approximately 260 psi. The standard deviation of the distribution is the *slope* of the straight line. It is convenient to estimate the standard deviation as the difference between the eighty-fourth and the fiftieth percentiles. For the strength data, this yields

$$\hat{\sigma} = 84\text{th percentile} - 50\text{th percentile}$$
$$= 298 - 260 \text{ psi}$$
$$= 38 \text{ psi}$$

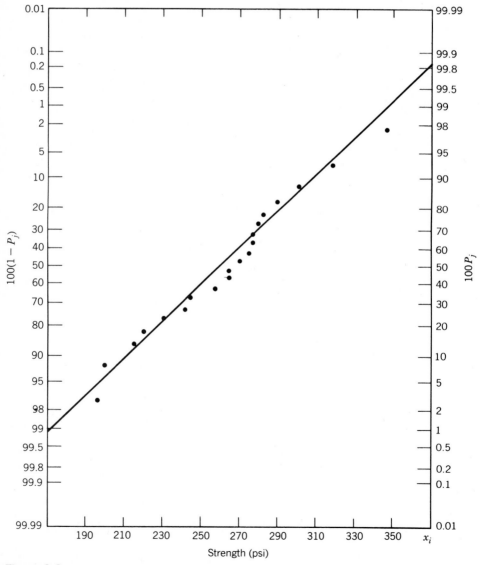

Figure 9-8
Normal probability plot for the strength data.

Notice that $\hat{\mu} = 260$ psi and $\hat{\sigma} = 38$ psi are not far from the sample average $\bar{x} = 264.06$ and standard deviation $S = 32.02$.

The normal probability plot can also be used to estimate process yields and fallouts. For example, the specification on bottle strength is LSL = 200 psi. From Figure 9-8, we would estimate that about 5% of the bottles manufactured by this process would burst below this limit.

Care should be exercised in using probability plots. If the data do not come from the assumed distribution, inferences about process capability drawn from the plot may be seriously in error. Figure 9-9 presents a normal probability plot of nonnormal data. From examining this plot, we can see that the distribution of

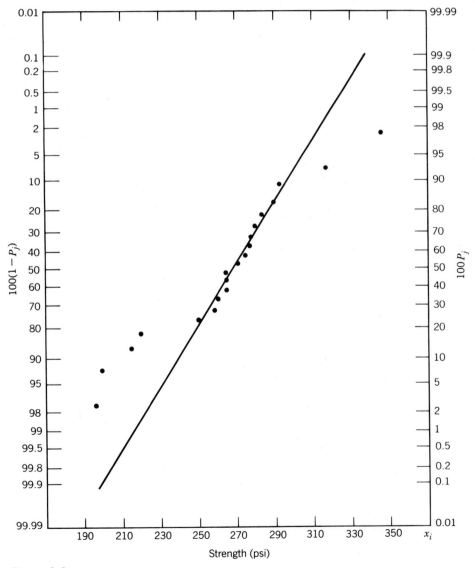

Figure 9-9
Plot of nonnormal data on a normal probability plot.

these data has somewhat "heavier" tails than the normal. That is, the extreme values are larger than one would expect in the normal model. Consequently, more area lies outside the 3-sigma limits than in the normal distribution.

An obvious disadvantage of probability plotting is that it is not an objective procedure. It is possible for two analysts to arrive at different conclusions using the same data. For this reason, it is often desirable to supplement probability plots with more formal statistically based goodness-of-fit tests. A good introduction to these tests is in Shapiro (1980). Choosing the distribution to fit the data is also an important step in probability plotting. Sometimes we can use our knowledge of the physical phenomena or past experience to suggest the choice of distribution. In other situations, the display in Figure 9-10 may be useful in selecting a distribution that describes the data. This figure shows the regions in the β_1, β_2 plane for several standard probability distributions, where β_1 and β_2 are the measures of *skewness* and *kurtosis*, respectively. To use Figure 9-10, calculate estimates of

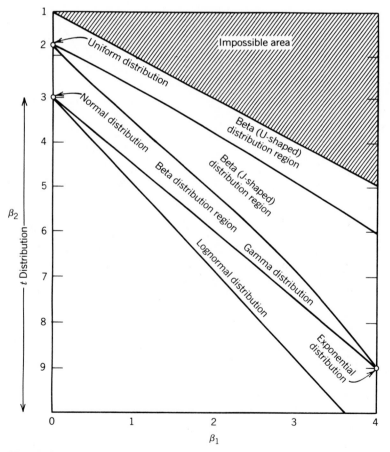

Figure 9-10
Regions in (β_1, β_2) plane for various distributions. (From G. J. Hahn and S. S. Shapiro, *Statistical Models in Engineering,* John Wiley, New York, 1967.)

skewness and kurtosis from the sample, say

$$\sqrt{\hat{\beta}_1} = \frac{M_3}{(M_2)^{3/2}} \qquad (9\text{-}15)$$

and

$$\hat{\beta}_2 = \frac{M_4}{M_2^2} \qquad (9\text{-}16)$$

where

$$M_j = \frac{\sum_{i=1}^{n} (x_i - \bar{x})^j}{n} \qquad j = 1, 2, 3, 4 \qquad (9\text{-}17)$$

and plot the point $(\hat{\beta}_1, \hat{\beta}_2)$ on the graph. If the plotted point falls close to a point, line, or region that corresponds to one of the distributions in the figure, then this distribution is a logical choice to use as a model for the data. If the point falls in regions of the β_1, β_2 plane were *none* of the distributions seems appropriate, other, more general probability distributions, such as the Johnson or Pearson families of distributions, may be required. Procedures similar to Figure 9-10 for fitting these distributions and graphs are in Hahn and Shapiro (1967).

9-3 PROCESS-CAPABILITY ANALYSIS USING A CONTROL CHART

Histograms and probability plots summarize the performance of the process. They do not necessarily display the *potential* capability of the process because they do not address the issue of *statistical control*, or show systematic patterns in process output which, if eliminated, would reduce the variability in the quality characteristic. Control charts are very effective in this regard. The control chart should be regarded as the primary technique of process-capability analysis.

Both attributes and variables control charts can be used in process-capability analysis. The $\bar{x}$ and R chart should be used whenever possible, because of the greater power and better information they provide relative to attributes charts. However, both p charts and c (or u) charts are useful in analyzing process capability. Techniques for constructing and using these charts are given in Chapters 5 and 6. Remember that to use the p chart, there must be specifications on the product characteristics. The $\bar{x}$ and R charts allow us to study processes without regard to specifications.

The $\bar{x}$ and R control charts allow both the instantaneous variability (short-term process capability) and variability across time (long-term process capability) to be analyzed. It is particularly helpful if the data for a process capability study are collected in two to three different time periods (such as different shifts, different days, etc.).

Table 9-6
Bottle-strength data

Sample	Data					$\bar{x}$	R
1	265	205	263	307	220	252.0	102
2	268	260	234	299	215	255.2	84
3	197	286	274	243	231	246.2	89
4	267	281	265	214	318	269.0	104
5	346	317	242	258	276	287.8	104
6	300	208	187	264	271	246.0	113
7	280	242	260	321	228	266.2	93
8	250	299	258	267	293	273.4	49
9	265	254	281	294	223	263.4	71
10	260	308	235	283	277	272.6	73
11	200	235	246	328	296	261.0	128
12	276	264	269	235	290	266.8	55
13	221	176	248	263	231	227.8	87
14	334	280	265	272	283	286.8	69
15	265	262	271	245	301	268.8	56
16	280	274	253	287	258	270.4	34
17	261	248	260	274	337 ·	276.0	89
18	250	278	254	274	275	266.2	28
19	278	250	265	270	298	272.2	48
20	257	210	280	269	251	253.4	70
						$\bar{\bar{x}} = 264.06$	$\bar{R} = 77.3$

Table 9-6 presents the soft drink bottle bursting-strength data in 20 samples of five observations each. The calculations for the $\bar{x}$ and R charts are summarized below:

R-Chart

Center line $= \bar{R} = 77.3$

$$\text{UCL} = D_4\bar{R} = (2.115)(77.3) = 163.49$$
$$\text{LCL} = D_3\bar{R} = (0)(77.3) = 0$$

$\bar{x}$-Chart

Center line $= \bar{\bar{x}} = 264.06$

$$\text{UCL} = \bar{\bar{x}} + A_2\bar{R} = 264.06 + (0.577)(77.3) = 308.66$$
$$\text{LCL} = \bar{\bar{x}} - A_2\bar{R} = 264.06 - (0.577)(77.3) = 219.46$$

Figure 9-11 presents the $\bar{x}$ and R charts for the 20 samples in Table 9-6. Both charts exhibit statistical control. The process parameters may be estimated from the control chart as

$$\hat{\mu} = \bar{\bar{x}} = 264.06$$
$$\hat{\sigma} = \frac{\bar{R}}{d_2} = \frac{77.3}{2.326} = 33.23$$

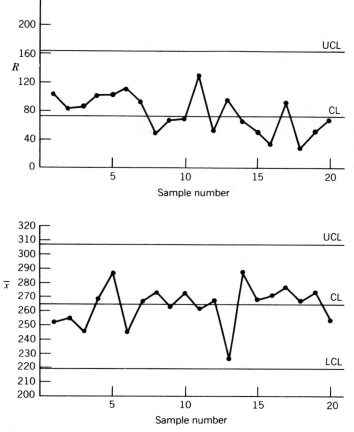

Figure 9-11
$\bar{x}$ and R charts for the bottle-strength data.

Thus, the one-sided lower process-capability ratio is estimated by

$$\widehat{\text{PCR}}_L = \frac{\mu - \text{LSL}}{3\hat{\sigma}}$$

$$= \frac{264.06 - 200}{3(33.23)}$$

$$= 0.64$$

Clearly, since strength is a safety-related parameter, the process capability is inadequate.

This example illustrates a process that is in control but operating at an unacceptable level. There is no evidence to indicate that the production of nonconforming units is *operator-controllable*. Management intervention will be required either to improve the process or to change the requirements if the quality problems with the bottles are to be solved. The objective of these interventions is to increase the process-capability ratio to at least a minimum acceptable level. The control chart can be used as a monitoring device or logbook to show the effect of changes in the process on process performance.

Sometimes the process-capability analysis indicates an out-of-control process. It is unsafe to estimate process capability in such cases. The process must be stable in order to produce a reliable estimate of process capability. When the process is out of control in the early stages of process-capability analysis, the first objective is finding and eliminating the assignable causes in order to bring the process into an in-control state.

9-4 PROCESS-CAPABILITY ANALYSIS USING DESIGNED EXPERIMENTS

The design of experiments is a systematic approach to varying the input *controllable* variables in the process and analyzing the effects of these process variables on the output. Designed experiments are also useful in discovering *which* set of process variables are influential on the output, and at what levels these variables should be held to optimize process performance. Thus, design of experiments is useful in more general manufacturing and development problems than just estimating process capability. For an introduction to design of experiments, see Montgomery (1984). Part III of this textbook (Chapters 11 and 12) provides more information on experimental design methods and on their use in process improvement.

One of the major uses of designed experiments is in isolating and estimating the *sources* of variability in a process. For example, consider a machine that fills bottles with a soft drink beverage. Each machine has a large number of filling heads that must be independently adjusted. The quality characteristic measured is the syrup content (in degrees brix) of the finished product. There can be variation in the observed brix (σ_B^2) because of machine variability (σ_M^2), head variability (σ_H^2), and analytical test variability (σ_A^2). The variability in the observed brix value is

$$\sigma_B^2 = \sigma_M^2 + \sigma_H^2 + \sigma_A^2$$

An experiment can be designed, involving sampling from several machines and several heads on each machine, and making several analyses on each bottle, which would allow estimation of the variances σ_M^2, σ_H^2, and σ_A^2. Suppose that the results appear as in Figure 9-12. Since a substantial portion of the total variability in observed brix is due to variability between heads, this indicates that the process can perhaps best be improved by reducing the head-to-head variability. This could be done by more careful set-up or by more careful control of the operation of the machine.

Example 9-6

In his book *Design and Analysis of Experiments* (2nd ed., Wiley, 1984) D. C. Montgomery describes an experiment to investigate the hand-insertion of electronic components on printed circuit boards to reduce the number of defective boards produced. The engineer responsible for the process has designed three assembly fixtures and two workplace layouts that seem promising. Operators are required to perform the assembly, and it is decided to randomly select four operators for each fixture-layout combination. However, because the workplaces are

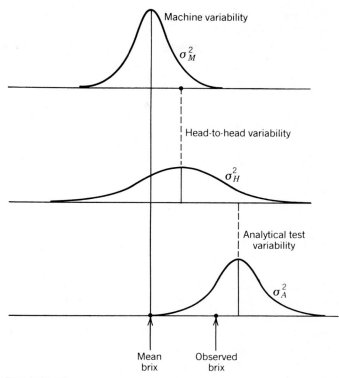

Figure 9-12
Sources of variability in the bottling line example.

in different locations within the plant, it is difficult to use the *same* four operators for each layout. Therefore, the four operators chosen for layout 1 are different individuals from the four operators chosen for layout 2. These are shown in Table 9-7.

The technique used to partition total variability into its various component parts is the *analysis of variance*. The results of applying this procedure to the printed

Table 9-7
Defect data for printed circuit board example

Operator	Layout 1				Layout 2				Fixture Totals
	1	2	3	4	1	2	3	4	
Fixture 1	22	23	28	25	26	27	28	24	404
	24	24	29	23	28	25	25	23	
Fixture 2	30	29	30	27	29	30	24	28	447
	27	28	32	25	28	27	23	30	
Fixture 3	25	24	27	26	27	26	24	28	401
	21	22	25	23	25	24	27	27	
Operator totals	149	150	171	149	163	159	151	160	
Layout totals		619				633			1252

Table 9-8
Analysis of variance for the printed circuit board defect data

Source of Variation	Sum of Squares	Degrees of Freedom	Mean Square	F_0
Fixtures (F)	82.80	2	41.40	7.54[b]
Layouts (L)	4.08	1	4.08	0.34
Operators (within layouts), $O(L)$	71.91	6	11.99	5.15[b]
FL	19.04	2	9.52	1.73
$FO(L)$	65.84	12	5.49	2.36[a]
Error	56.00	24	2.33	
Total	299.67	47		

[a] Significant at 5%.
[b] Significant at 1%.

circuit board defect data are shown in Table 9-8. The analysis of variance indicates that the assembly fixtures differ significantly in their effect on hand-insertion-caused defects but that workplace layouts do not. Because different operators were used in each layout, we can isolate a source of variability due to *operations within layouts*; this source is also statistically significant, indicating that there is an operator effect. There is also a significant interaction between fixtures and operators within layouts, indicating that the effect of the different fixtures is not the same for all operators. Therefore, to reduce the number of hand-insertion defects, we should concentrate on fixture types 1 and 3. (Note that the fixture totals in Table 9-7 are smaller for fixture types 1 and 3 than for type 2.) Furthermore, the interaction between operators and fixtures implies that some operators are more effective than others using the same fixtures. Engineering studies could be performed to determine why some operators are better than others, and possibly this information could be used to improve the performance of the other operators.

9-5 GAGE CAPABILITY STUDIES

An important aspect of many statistical process-control implementation efforts is ensuring adequate gage and inspection system capability. In any problem involving measurements, some of the observed variability will be due to variability in the product itself, and some will be due to measurement error or gage variability. Expressed mathematically,

$$\sigma_{total}^2 = \sigma_{product}^2 + \sigma_{gage}^2$$

where σ_{total}^2 is the total observed variance, $\sigma_{product}^2$ is the component of variance due to the product, and σ_{gage}^2 is the component of variance due to measurement error. Control charts and other statistical methods can be used to separate these components of variance, as well as to give an assessment of gage capability.

Example 9-7

Measuring Gage Capability

An instrument is to be used as part of a proposed SPC implementation. The quality-improvement team involved in designing the SPC system would like to get an assessment of gage capability. Twenty units of the product are obtained, and the process operator who will actually take the measurements for the control chart uses the instrument to measure each unit of product twice. The data are shown in Table 9-9.

Figure 9-13 shows the $\bar{x}$ and R charts for these data. Notice that the $\bar{x}$ chart exhibits many out-of-control points. This is to be expected, as in this situation the $\bar{x}$ chart has an interpretation that is somewhat different from the usual interpretation. The $\bar{x}$ chart in this example shows the discriminating power of the instrument—literally, the ability of the gage to distinguish between units of product. The R chart directly shows the magnitude of measurement error, or the gage capability. The R values represent the difference between measurements made on the same unit using the same instrument. In this example, the R chart is in control. This indicates that the operator is having no difficulty in making consistent measurements. Out-of-control points on the R chart would indicate that the operator is having difficulty using the instrument.

Table 9-9
Parts measurement data

Part Number	Measurements 1	2	$\bar{x}$	R
1	21	20	20.5	1
2	24	23	23.5	1
3	20	21	20.5	1
4	27	27	27.0	0
5	19	18	18.5	1
6	23	21	22.0	2
7	22	21	21.5	1
8	19	17	18.0	2
9	24	23	23.5	1
10	25	23	24.0	2
11	21	20	20.5	1
12	18	19	18.5	1
13	23	25	24.0	2
14	24	24	24.0	0
15	29	30	29.5	1
16	26	26	26.0	0
17	20	20	20.0	0
18	19	21	20.0	2
19	25	26	25.5	1
20	19	19	19.0	0

$$\bar{\bar{x}} = 22.3 \qquad \bar{R} = 1.0$$

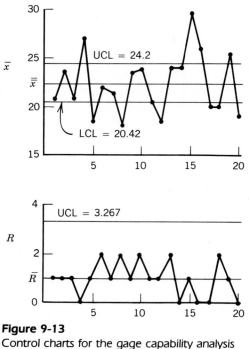

Figure 9-13
Control charts for the gage capability analysis
in Example 9-7.

The standard deviation of measurement error, σ_{gage}, can be estimated as follows:

$$\hat{\sigma}_{\text{gage}} = \frac{\bar{R}}{d_2} = \frac{1.0}{1.128} = 0.887$$

The distribution of measurement error is usually well approximated by the normal. Thus, $6\hat{\sigma}_{\text{gage}}$ is a good estimate of gage capability. In our problem, this is

$$6\hat{\sigma}_{\text{gage}} = 6(0.887) = 5.32$$

Individual measurements can be expected to vary as much as $\pm 3\hat{\sigma}_{\text{gage}}$ (± 2.66) owing to gage error. It is sometimes useful to compare gage capability to the total specification or tolerance band (USL − LSL) for the part. The ratio of $6\hat{\sigma}_{\text{gage}}$ to the total tolerance band is often called the precision-to-tolerance or P/T ratio:

$$\frac{P}{T} = \frac{6\hat{\sigma}_{\text{gage}}}{\text{USL} - \text{LSL}}$$

The part used in this example has USL = 60 and LSL = 5. Therefore,

$$\frac{P}{T} = \frac{6(0.887)}{60 - 5} = \frac{5.32}{55} = 0.097$$

Values of P/T of 0.1 or less generally imply adequate gage capability. This is based on the generally used rule that requires a measurement device to be calibrated in units one-tenth as large as the accuracy required in the final measurement.

We can use the data from the gage capability experiment in Example 9-7 to estimate the variance components associated with total observed variability. From the actual sample measurements in Table 9-9, we can calculate $S = 6.20$. This is an estimate of the standard deviation of *total* variability, including both product variability and gage variability. Therefore,

$$\hat{\sigma}^2_{total} = S^2 = (6.20)^2 = 38.44$$

Since

$$\sigma^2_{total} = \sigma^2_{product} + \sigma^2_{gage}$$

and since we have an estimate of $\sigma^2_{gage} = (0.887)^2 = 0.79$, we can obtain an estimate of $\sigma^2_{product}$ as

$$\hat{\sigma}^2_{product} = \hat{\sigma}^2_{total} - \hat{\sigma}^2_{gage}$$
$$= 38.44 - 0.79$$
$$= 37.65$$

Therefore, the standard deviation of the product characteristic is

$$\hat{\sigma}_{product} = \sqrt{37.65} = 6.14$$

The measurement error can also be expressed as a percentage of the product characteristic variability, or

$$\frac{\hat{\sigma}_{gage}}{\hat{\sigma}_{product}} \times 100 = \frac{0.887}{6.14} \times 100 = 14.4\%$$

Example 9-8

Components of Measurement Error

We now extend the gage capability study of Example 9-7 to include two components of measurement error—the repeatability and reproducibility of the gage. We define reproducibility as being due to different operators using the gage, and repeatability as reflecting the basic inherent precision of the gage itself. That is,

$$\sigma^2_{measurement\ error} = \sigma^2_{gage} = \sigma^2_{repeatability} + \sigma^2_{reproducibility}$$

To measure these two components of measurement error, the original study was repeated using two additional operators who would also be involved in the work cell where the parts would be produced. The data from the completed measurement error study are shown in Table 9-10.

The estimate of gage repeatability is obtained from the average of the three average ranges, say

$$\bar{\bar{R}} = \tfrac{1}{3}(\bar{R}_1 + \bar{R}_2 + \bar{R}_3)$$
$$= \tfrac{1}{3}(1.00 + 1.25 + 1.20)$$
$$= 1.15$$

as follows:

$$\hat{\sigma}_{\text{repeatability}} = \frac{\bar{\bar{R}}}{d_2}$$
$$= \frac{1.15}{1.128}$$
$$= 1.02$$

Notice that we have used the d_2 factor for samples of size two because each range was calculated from two repeat measurements on the same part made by the same operator.

Gage reproducibility is essentially variability that arises because of differences among the three operators. If the $\bar{\bar{x}}_i$ values differ, the reason will be operator bias, since all three operators measure the same parts. Therefore, to estimate gage reproducibility let

$$\bar{\bar{x}}_{\text{max}} = \max(\bar{\bar{x}}_1, \bar{\bar{x}}_2, \bar{\bar{x}}_3)$$
$$\bar{\bar{x}}_{\text{min}} = \min(\bar{\bar{x}}_1, \bar{\bar{x}}_2, \bar{\bar{x}}_3)$$
$$R_{\bar{\bar{x}}} = \bar{\bar{x}}_{\text{max}} - \bar{\bar{x}}_{\text{min}}$$

and

$$\hat{\sigma}_{\text{reproducibility}} = \frac{R_{\bar{\bar{x}}}}{d_2}$$

where we would use $d_2 = 1.693$, because $R_{\bar{\bar{x}}}$ is the range of a sample of size three. Since for our example, $\bar{\bar{x}}_{\text{max}} = 22.60$, $\bar{\bar{x}}_{\text{min}} = 22.28$, $R_{\bar{\bar{x}}} = 0.32$, and

$$\hat{\sigma}_{\text{reproducibility}} = \frac{0.32}{1.693}$$
$$= 0.19$$

We have now estimated both components of the measurement error standard deviation, σ_{gage}. Therefore,

$$\hat{\sigma}^2_{\text{gage}} = \hat{\sigma}^2_{\text{repeatability}} + \hat{\sigma}^2_{\text{reproducibility}}$$
$$= (1.02)^2 + (0.19)^2$$
$$= 1.08$$

Table 9-10
Data for the repeatability and reproducibility study in Example 9-8

Part Number	Operator 1 Measurements 1	2	$\bar{x}$	R	Operator 2 Measurements 1	2	$\bar{x}$	R	Operator 3 Measurements 1	2	$\bar{x}$	R
1	21	20	20.5	1	20	20	20.0	0	19	21	20.0	2
2	24	23	23.5	1	24	24	24.0	0	23	24	23.5	1
3	20	21	20.5	1	19	21	20.0	2	20	22	21.0	2
4	27	27	27.0	0	28	26	27.0	2	27	28	27.5	1
5	19	18	18.5	1	19	18	18.5	1	18	21	19.5	3
6	23	21	22.0	2	24	21	22.5	3	23	22	22.5	1
7	22	21	21.5	1	22	24	23.0	2	22	20	21.0	2
8	19	17	18.0	2	18	20	19.0	2	19	18	18.5	1
9	24	23	23.5	1	25	23	24.0	2	24	24	24.0	0
10	25	23	24.0	2	26	25	25.5	1	24	25	24.5	1
11	21	20	20.5	1	20	20	20.0	0	21	20	20.5	1
12	18	19	18.5	1	17	19	18.0	2	18	19	18.5	1
13	23	25	24.0	2	25	25	25.0	0	25	25	25.0	0
14	24	24	24.0	0	23	25	24.0	2	24	25	24.5	1
15	29	30	29.5	1	30	28	29.0	2	31	30	30.5	1
16	26	26	26.0	0	25	26	25.5	1	25	27	26.0	2
17	20	20	20.0	0	19	20	19.5	1	20	20	20.0	0
18	19	21	20.0	2	19	19	19.0	0	21	23	22.0	2
19	25	26	25.5	1	25	24	24.5	1	25	25	25.0	0
20	19	19	19.0	0	18	17	17.5	1	19	17	18.0	2
	$\bar{\bar{x}}_1 = 22.30$		$\bar{R}_1 = 1.00$		$\bar{\bar{x}}_2 = 22.28$		$\bar{R}_2 = 1.25$		$\bar{\bar{x}}_3 = 22.60$		$\bar{R}_3 = 1.20$	

and $\hat{\sigma}_{gage} = \sqrt{1.08} = 1.04$. Notice that when both repeatability and reproducibility are taken into account, the standard deviation of measurement error increases. (Recall that the estimate of the standard deviation of measurement error based on a single operator was $\hat{\sigma}_{gage} = 0.887$ from Example 9-7.) The P/T ratio for this gage would be

$$
\begin{aligned}
\frac{P}{T} &= \frac{6\hat{\sigma}_{gage}}{USL - LSL} \\
&= \frac{6(1.08)}{60 - 5} \\
&= 0.12
\end{aligned}
$$

Notice that when both repeatability and reproducibility are taken into account, the gage capability is not as good as we would like. (Recall that P/T should be ≤ 0.10.) Training the operators to produce more uniform work methods in using the gage would help reduce $\sigma_{reproducibility}$, but since $\sigma_{repeatability}$ is the largest component of σ_{gage}, some effort should also be directed toward finding another inspection device.

9-6 SETTING SPECIFICATION LIMITS ON DISCRETE COMPONENTS

It is often necessary to use information from a process-capability study to set specifications on discrete parts or components that interact with other components to form the final product. This is particularly important in complex assemblies, or, where there are many interacting dimensions, to prevent "tolerance stack-up." This section discusses some aspects of setting specifications on components to ensure that the final product meets specifications.

9-6.1 Linear Combinations

In many cases, the dimension of an item is a linear combination of the dimensions of the component parts. That is, if the dimensions of the components are $x_1, x_2, \ldots, x_n$, then the dimension of the final assembly is

$$y = a_1 x_1 + a_2 x_2 + \cdots + a_n x_n \tag{9-18}$$

If the x_i are normally and independently distributed with mean μ_i and variance σ_i^2, then y is normally distributed with mean $\mu_y = \sum_{i=1}^{n} a_i \mu_i$ and variance $\sigma_y^2 = \sum_{i=1}^{n} a_i^2 \sigma_i^2$. Therefore, if μ_i and σ_i^2 are known for each component, the fraction of assembled items falling outside the specifications can be determined.

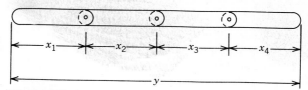

Figure 9-14
A linkage assembly with four components.

Example 9-9

A linkage consists of four components as shown in Figure 9-14. The lengths of x_1, x_2, x_3, and x_4 are known to be $x_1 \sim N(2.0, 0.0004)$, $x_2 \sim N(4.5, 0.0009)$, $x_3 \sim N(3.0, 0.0004)$, and $x_4 \sim N(2.5, 0.0001)$. The lengths of the components can be assumed independent, as they are produced on different machines. All lengths are in inches.

The design specifications on the length of the assembled linkage are 12.00 ± 0.10. To find the fraction of linkages that fall within these specification limits, note that y is normally distributed with mean

$$\mu_y = 2.0 + 4.5 + 3.0 + 2.5 = 12.0$$

and variance

$$\sigma_y^2 = 0.0004 + 0.0009 + 0.0004 + 0.0001 = 0.0018$$

To find the fraction of linkages that are within specification, we must evaluate

$$P\{11.90 \leq y \leq 12.10\} = P\{y \leq 12.10\} - P\{y \leq 11.90\}$$
$$= \Phi\left(\frac{12.10 - 12.00}{\sqrt{0.0018}}\right) - \Phi\left(\frac{11.90 - 12.00}{\sqrt{0.0018}}\right)$$
$$= \Phi(2.36) - \Phi(-2.36)$$
$$= 0.99086 - 0.00914$$
$$= 0.98172$$

Therefore, we conclude that 98.172% of the assembled linkages will fall within the specification limits.

Sometimes it is necessary to determine specification limits on the individual components of an assembly so that specification limits on the final assembly will be satisfied. This is demonstrated in the following example.

Example 9-10

Consider the assembly shown in Figure 9-15. Suppose that the specifications on this assembly are 6.00 ± 0.06 in. Let each component x_1, x_2, and x_3 be normally and independently distributed with means $\mu_1 = 1.00$ in., $\mu_2 = 3.00$ in., and $\mu_3 = 2.00$ in., respectively. Suppose that the natural tolerance limits for each component as well as the final assembly are defined such that the fraction of components or final assemblies falling outside these limits is 0.0027. Furthermore, we want the specification limits to fall at the natural tolerance limits of the process for the final assembly so that PCR = 1.0, approximately, for the final assembly.

The length of the final assembly is normally distributed. Furthermore, if the allowable fraction of assemblies nonconforming to specifications is 0.0027, this implies that the natural tolerance limits must be located at $\mu_y \pm 3.00\sigma_y$. Now $\mu_y = \mu_1 + \mu_2 + \mu_3 = 1.00 + 3.00 + 2.00 = 6.00$, so the process is centered at the nominal value. Therefore, the maximum possible value of σ_y that would place the natural tolerance limits of the final assembly just equal to the specification limits (PCR = 1) is

$$\sigma_y = \frac{0.06}{3.00} = 0.02$$

That is, if $\sigma_y \le 0.02$, then the specification will either be equal to or outside the natural tolerance limits of the process, and the fraction of nonconforming assemblies produced will be less than or equal to 0.0027.

Now let us see how this affects the specifications on the individual components. The variance of the length of the final assembly is

$$\sigma_y^2 = \sigma_1^2 + \sigma_2^2 + \sigma_3^2 \le (0.02)^2 = 0.0004$$

Suppose that the variances of the component lengths are all equal, that is, $\sigma_1^2 = \sigma_2^2 = \sigma_3^2 = \sigma^2$ (say). Then

$$\sigma_y^2 = 3\sigma^2$$

and the maximum possible value for the variance of the length of any component is

$$\sigma^2 = \frac{\sigma_y^2}{3} = \frac{0.0004}{3} = 0.000133$$

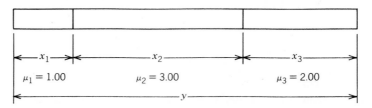

Figure 9-15
Assembly for Example 9-10.

Effectively, if $\sigma^2 \leq 0.000133$ for each component, then the natural tolerance limits for the final assembly will either be equal to or slightly inside the specification limits.

This can be translated into specification limits on the individual components. If we assume that the natural tolerance limits and the specification limits for the components are to coincide exactly, then the specification limits for each component are as follows:

$$x_1: \quad 1.00 \pm 3.00\sqrt{0.000133} = 1.00 \pm 0.0346$$
$$x_2: \quad 3.00 \pm 3.00\sqrt{0.000133} = 3.00 \pm 0.0346$$
$$x_3: \quad 2.00 \pm 3.00\sqrt{0.000133} = 2.00 \pm 0.0346$$

It is possible to give a general solution to the problem in Example 9-10. Let the assembly consist of n components having common variance σ^2. If the natural tolerances of the assembly are defined so that no more than $\alpha\%$ of the assemblies will fall outside these limits, and $2W$ is the width of the specification limits, then

$$\sigma_y^{2*} = \left(\frac{W}{Z_{\alpha/2}}\right)^2$$

is the maximum possible value for the variance of the final assembly that will permit the natural tolerance limits and the specification limits to coincide. Consequently, the maximum permissible value of the variance for the individual components is

$$\sigma^{2*} = \frac{\sigma_y^{2*}}{n}$$

Example 9-11

A shaft is to be assembled into a bearing. The internal diameter of the bearing is a normal random variable, say x_1, with mean $\mu_1 = 1.500$ in. and standard deviation $\sigma_1 = 0.0020$ in. The external diameter of the shaft, say x_2, is normally distributed with mean $\mu_2 = 1.480$ in. and standard deviation $\sigma_2 = 0.0040$ in. The assembly is shown in Figure 9-16.

When the two parts are assembled, interference will occur if the shaft diameter is larger than the bearing diameter, that is, if

$$y = x_1 - x_2 < 0$$

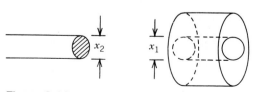

Figure 9-16
Assembly of a shaft and a bearing.

Note that the distribution of y is normal with mean

$$\mu_y = \mu_1 - \mu_2 = 1.500 - 1.480 = 0.020$$

and variance

$$\sigma_y^2 = \sigma_1^2 + \sigma_2^2 = (0.0020)^2 + (0.0040)^2 = 0.00002$$

Therefore, the probability of interference is

$$
\begin{aligned}
P\{\text{interference}\} &= P\{y < 0\} \\
&= \Phi\left(\frac{0 - 0.020}{\sqrt{0.00002}}\right) \\
&= \Phi(-4.47) \\
&= .000004 \ (4 \ \text{PPM})
\end{aligned}
$$

This indicates that very few assemblies with have interence.

In problems of this type, we occasionally define a minimum clearance, say C, such that

$$P\{\text{clearance} < C\} = \alpha$$

Thus, C becomes the natural tolerance for the assembly and can be compared with the design specification. In our example, if we establish $\alpha = 0.0001$ (i.e., only 1 out of 10,000 assemblies or 100 PPM will have clearance less than or equal to C), then we have

$$\frac{C - \mu_y}{\sigma_y} = -Z_{0.0001}$$

or

$$\frac{C - 0.020}{\sqrt{0.00002}} = -3.71$$

which implies that $C = 0.020 - (3.71)\sqrt{0.00002} = 0.0034$. That is, only 1 out of 10,000 assemblies will have clearance less than 0.0034 in.

9-6.2 Nonlinear Combinations

In some problems, the dimension of interest may be a nonlinear function of the n component dimensions $x_1, x_2, \ldots, x_n$, say

$$y = g(x_1, x_2, \ldots, x_n) \qquad (9\text{-}19)$$

In problems of this type, the usual approach is to approximate the nonlinear function g by a linear function of the x_i in the region of interest. If $\mu_1, \mu_2, \ldots, \mu_n$ are the nominal dimensions associated with the components $x_1, x_2, \ldots, x_n$, then by expanding the right-hand side of Equation (9-19) in a Taylor series about μ_1, $\mu_2, \ldots, \mu_n$, we obtain

$$y = g(x_1, x_2, \ldots, x_n)$$

$$= g(\mu_1, \mu_2, \ldots, \mu_n) + \sum_{i=1}^{n} (x_i - \mu_i) \frac{\partial g}{\partial x_i}\bigg|_{\mu_1, \mu_2, \ldots, \mu_n} + R \qquad (9\text{-}20)$$

where R represents the higher order terms. Neglecting the terms of higher order, we have

$$\mu_y \simeq g(\mu_1, \mu_2, \ldots, \mu_n) \qquad (9\text{-}21)$$

and

$$\sigma_y^2 \simeq \sum_{i=1}^{n} \left(\frac{\partial g}{\partial x_i}\bigg|_{\mu_1, \mu_2, \ldots, \mu_n}\right)^2 \sigma_i^2 \qquad (9\text{-}22)$$

The following example illustrates how these results are useful in tolerance problems.

Example 9-12

Consider the simple DC circuit components shown in Figure 9-17. Suppose that the voltage across the points (a, b) is required to be 100 ± 2 V. The specifications on the current and the resistance in the circuit are shown in Figure 9-17. We assume that the component random variables I and R are normally and independently distributed with means equal to their nominal values.

From Ohm's law, we know that the voltage is

$$V = IR$$

Since this involves a nonlinear combination, we expand V in a Taylor series about mean current μ_I and mean resistance μ_R, yielding

$$V \simeq \mu_I \mu_R + (I - \mu_I)\mu_R + (R - \mu_R)\mu_I$$

neglecting the terms of higher order. Now the mean and variance of voltage are

$$\mu_V \simeq \mu_I \mu_R$$

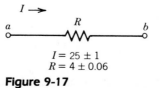

$$I = 25 \pm 1$$
$$R = 4 \pm 0.06$$

Figure 9-17
Electrical circuit for Example 9-12.

and

$$\sigma_V^2 \simeq \mu_R^2 \sigma_I^2 + \mu_I^2 \sigma_R^2$$

approximately, where σ_I^2 and σ_R^2 are the variances of I and R, respectively.

Now suppose that I and R are centered at their nominal values and that the natural tolerance limits are defined so that $\alpha = 0.0027$ is the fraction of values of each component falling outside these limits. Assume also that the specification limits are exactly equal to the natural tolerance limits. For the current I we have $I = 25 \pm 1$ A. That is, $24 \leq I \leq 26$ A correspond to the natural tolerance limits *and* the specifications. Since $I \sim N(25, \sigma_I^2)$, and since $Z_{\alpha/2} = Z_{0.00135} = 3.00$, we have

$$\frac{26 - 25}{\sigma_I} = 3.00$$

or $\sigma_I = 0.33$. For the resistance, we have $R = 4 \pm 0.06$ ohm as the specification limits *and* the natural tolerance limits. Thus,

$$\frac{4.06 - 4.00}{\sigma_R} = 3.00$$

and $\sigma_R = 0.02$. Note that σ_I and σ_R are the largest possible values of the component standard deviations consistent with the natural tolerance limits falling inside or equal to the specification limits.

Using these results, and if we assume that the voltage V is approximately normally distributed, then

$$\mu_V \simeq \mu_I \mu_R = (25)(4) = 100 \text{ V}$$

and

$$\sigma_V^2 \simeq \mu_R^2 \sigma_I^2 + \mu_I^2 \sigma_R^2$$
$$= (4)^2 (0.33)^2 + (25)^2 (0.02)^2 = 1.99$$

approximately. Thus, $\sigma_V = \sqrt{1.99} = 1.41$. Therefore, the probability that the voltage will fall within the design specifications is

$$P\{98 \leq V \leq 102\} = P\{V \leq 102\} - P\{V \leq 98\}$$
$$= \Phi\left(\frac{102 - 100}{1.41}\right) - \Phi\left(\frac{98 - 100}{1.41}\right)$$
$$= \Phi(1.42) - \Phi(-1.42)$$
$$= 0.92219 - 0.07781$$
$$= 0.84438$$

That is, only 84% of the observed output voltages will fall within the design specifications. Notice that the natural tolerance limits or process capability for the output voltage is

$$\mu_V \pm 3.00\sigma_V$$

or

$$100 \pm 4.23 \text{ V}$$

In this problem the process-capability ratio is

$$PCR = \frac{USL - LSL}{6\sigma}$$

$$= \frac{102 - 98}{6(1.41)} = 0.47$$

Notice that, although the individual current and resistance variations are not excessive relative to their specifications, because of "tolerance stack-up," they interact to produce a circuit whose performance relative to the voltage specifications is very poor.

9-7 ESTIMATING THE NATURAL TOLERANCE LIMITS OF A PROCESS

In many types of production processes, it is customary to think of the natural tolerance limits as those limits that contain a certain fraction, say $1 - \alpha$, of the distribution. In this section we present some approaches to estimating the natural tolerance limits of a process.

If the underlying distribution of the quality characteristic and its parameters are known, say on the basis of long experience, then the tolerance limits may be readily established. For example, in Section 9-6, we studied several problems involving tolerances where the quality characteristic was normally distributed with known mean μ and known variance σ^2. If in this case we define the tolerance limits as those limits that contain $100(1 - \alpha)\%$ of the distribution of this quality characteristic, then these limits are simply $\mu \pm Z_{\alpha/2}\sigma$. If $\alpha = 0.05$ (say), then the tolerance limits are given by $\mu \pm 1.96\sigma$.

In most practical problems, both the form of the distribution and its parameters will be unknown. However, the parameters may usually be estimated from sample data. In certain cases, then, it is possible to estimate the tolerance limits of the process by use of these sample statistics. We will discuss two procedures for estimating natural tolerance limits, one for those situations in which the normality assumption is reasonable, and a nonparametric approach useful in cases where the normality assumption is inappropriate.

The estimation of the natural tolerance limits of a process is an important problem with many significant practical implications. As noted previously, unless the product specifications exactly coincide with or exceed the natural tolerance limits of the process (PCR ≥ 1), an extremely high percentage of the production will be outside specifications, resulting in a high loss or rework rate.

9-7.1 Tolerance Limits Based on the Normal Distribution

Suppose a random variable x is normally distributed with mean μ and variance σ^2, both unknown. From a random sample of n observations, the sample mean $\bar{x}$ and sample variance S^2 may be computed. A logical procedure for estimating the natural tolerance limits $\mu \pm Z_{\alpha/2}\sigma$ is to replace μ by $\bar{x}$ and σ by S, yielding

$$\bar{x} \pm Z_{\alpha/2}S$$

Since $\bar{x}$ and S are only *estimates* and not the *true* parameter values, we cannot say that the above interval always contains $100(1 - \alpha)\%$ of the distribution. However, one may determine a constant K, such that in a large number of samples a fraction γ of the intervals $\bar{x} \pm KS$ will include at least $100(1 - \alpha)\%$ of the distribution. Values of K for $2 \le n \le 1000$, $\gamma = 0.90, 0.95, 0.99$, and $\alpha = 0.10, 0.05$, and 0.01 are given in Appendix Table VII.

Example 9-13

The manufacturer of a solid-fuel rocket propellant is interested in finding the tolerance limits of the process such that 95% of the burning rates will lie within these limits with probability 0.99. It is known from previous experience that the burning rate is normally distributed. A random sample of 25 observations shows that the sample mean and variance of burning rate are $\bar{x} = 40.75$ and $S^2 = 1.87$, respectively. Since $\alpha = 0.05$, $\gamma = 0.99$, and $n = 25$, we find $K = 2.972$ from Appendix Table VII. Therefore, the required tolerance limits are found as $\bar{x} \pm 2.972S = 40.75 \pm (2.972)(1.37) = 40.75 \pm 4.06 = [36.69, 44.81]$.

We note that there is a fundamental difference between confidence limits and tolerance limits. *Confidence limits* are used to provide an interval estimate of the parameter of a distribution, while *tolerance limits* are used to indicate the limits between which we can expect to find a specified proportion of a population. Note that as n approaches infinity, the length of a confidence interval approaches zero, while the tolerance limits approach the corresponding value for the population. Thus, in Appendix Table VII, as n approaches infinity for $\alpha = 0.05$, say, K approaches 1.96.

It is also possible to specify one-sided tolerance limits based on the normal distribution. That is, we may wish to state that with probability γ at least $100(1 - \alpha)\%$ of the distribution is greater than the lower tolerance limit $\bar{x} - KS$, or less than the upper tolerance limit $\bar{x} + KS$. Values of K for these one-sided tolerance limits for $2 \le n \le 1000$, $\gamma = 0.90, 0.95, 0.99$, and $\alpha = 0.10, 0.05$, and 0.01 are given in Appendix Table VIII.

9-7.2 Nonparametric Tolerance Limits

It is possible to construct nonparametric (or distribution-free) tolerance limits that are valid for any continuous probability distribution. These intervals are based on the distribution of the extreme values (largest and smallest sample observation) in a sample from an arbitrary continuous distribution. For two-sided tolerance limits, the number of observations that must be taken to ensure that with probability γ at least $100(1 - \alpha)\%$ of the distribution will lie between the largest and smallest observations obtained in the sample is

$$n \simeq \frac{1}{2} + \left(\frac{2 - \alpha}{\alpha}\right)\frac{\chi^2_{1-\gamma, 4}}{4}$$

approximately. Thus, to be 99% certain that at least 95% of the population will be included between the sample extreme values, we have $\alpha = 0.05$, $\gamma = 0.99$, and consequently,

$$n \simeq \frac{1}{2} + \left(\frac{1.95}{0.05}\right)\frac{13.28}{4} = 130$$

For one-sided nonparametric tolerance limits such that with probability γ at least $100(1 - \alpha)\%$ of the population exceeds the smallest sample value (or is less than the largest sample value), we must take a sample of

$$n = \frac{\log(1 - \gamma)}{\log(1 - \alpha)}$$

observations. Thus, the upper nonparametric tolerance limit that contains at least 90% of the population with probability at least 0.95 ($\alpha = 0.10$ and $\gamma = 0.95$) is the largest observation in a sample of

$$n = \frac{\log(1 - \gamma)}{\log(1 - \alpha)} = \frac{\log(0.05)}{\log(0.90)} = 28$$

observations.

In general, nonparametric tolerance limits have limited practical value, as in order to construct suitable intervals that contain a relatively large fraction of the distribution with high probability, large samples are required. In some cases, the sample sizes required may be so large as to prohibit their use. If one can specify the *form* of the distribution, it is possible for a given sample size to construct tolerance intervals that are narrower than those obtained from the nonparametric approach.

9-8 Exercises

9-1 Consider the piston-ring data in Table 6-1. Estimate the process capability assuming that specifications are 74.00 ± 0.035 mm.

9-2 Perform a process-capability analysis using $\bar{x}$ and R charts for the data in Exercise 6-1.

9-3 Estimate process capability using $\bar{x}$ and R charts for the power supply voltage data in Exercise 6-2. If specifications are at 350 ± 5 V, calculate PCR, PCR_k, and PCR_{km}. Interpret these capability ratios.

9-4 Consider the hole diameter data in Exercise 6-3. Estimate process capability using $\bar{x}$ and R charts. If specifications are at 0 ± 0.01, calculate PCR, PCR_k, and PCR_{km}. Interpret these ratios.

9-5 A process is in control with $\bar{\bar{x}} = 100$ and $\bar{S} = 1.05$. The process specifications are at 95 ± 10.

  a. Estimate the potential capability.

  b. Estimate the actual capability.

  c. How much could be fallout in the process be reduced if the process were corrected to operate at the nominal specification?

9-6 A process is in control with $\bar{\bar{x}} = 75$ and $\bar{S} = 2$. The process specifications are at 80 ± 8.

  a. Estimate the potential capability.

  b. Estimate the actual capability.

  c. How much could process fallout be reduced by shifting the mean to the nominal dimension?

9-7 Consider the two processes shown below:

Process A	Process B
$\bar{x}_A = 100$	$\bar{x}_B = 105$
$\bar{S}_A = 3$	$\bar{S}_B = 1$

Specifications are at 100 ± 10. Calculate PCR, PCR_k, and PCR_{km} and interpret these ratios. Which process would you prefer to use?

9-8 Suppose that 20 of the parts manufactured by the processes in Exercise 9-7 were assembled so that their dimensions were additive; that is,

$$x = x_1 + x_2 + \cdots + x_{20}$$

Specifications on x are 2000 ± 200. Would you prefer to produce the parts using process A or process B? Why? Do the capability ratios computed in Exercise 9-7 provide any guidance for process selection?

9-9 The weights of nominal 1-lb containers of a concentrated chemical ingredient are shown below. Prepare a normal probability plot of the data and estimate process capability.

0.9475	0.9775	0.9965	1.0075	1.0180
0.9705	0.9860	0.9975	1.0100	1.0200
0.9770	0.9960	1.0050	1.0175	1.0250

9-10 Consider the hardness data in Exercise 6-41. Use a probability plot to assess normality. Estimate process capability.

9-11 The failure time in hours of 10 LSI memory devices is shown below. Plot the data on normal probability paper and, if appropriate, estimate process capability. Is it safe to estimate the proportion of circuits that fail below 1200 h?

1210	2105
1275	2230
1400	2250
1695	2500
1900	2625

9-12 An operator–instrument combination is known to test parts with an average error of zero; however, the standard deviation of measurement error is estimated to be 3. Samples from a controlled process were analyzed, and the total variability was estimated to be $\hat{\sigma} = 5$. What is the true process standard deviation?

9-13 Consider the situation in Example 9-7. A new gage is being evaluated for this process. The same operator measures the same 20 parts twice using the new gage and obtains the data shown below.

   a. What can you say about the performance of the new gage relative to the old one?
   b. If specifications are at 25 ± 15, what is the P/T ratio for the new gage?

Part Number	Measurements 1	2
1	19	23
2	22	28
3	19	24
4	28	23
5	16	19
6	20	19
7	21	24
8	17	15
9	24	26
10	25	23
11	20	25
12	16	15
13	25	24
14	24	22
15	31	27
16	24	23
17	20	24
18	17	19
19	25	23
20	17	16

9-14 Ten parts are measured three times by the same operator in a gage capability study. The data are shown below.

Part Number	Measurements 1	2	3
1	100	101	100
2	95	93	97
3	101	103	100
4	96	95	97
5	98	98	96
6	99	98	98
7	95	97	98
8	100	99	98
9	100	100	97
10	100	98	99

   a. Describe the measurement error that results from the use of this gage.
   b. Estimate total variability and product variability.

c. What percentage of total variability is due to the gage?

d. If specifications on the part are at 100 ± 15, find the P/T ratio for this gage. Comment on the adequacy of the gage.

9-15 In a study to isolate both gage repeatability and gage reproducibility, two operators use the same gage to measure 10 parts three times each. The data are shown below.

Part Number	Operator 1 Measurements			Operator 2 Measurements		
	1	2	3	1	2	3
1	50	49	50	50	48	51
2	52	52	51	51	51	51
3	53	50	50	54	52	51
4	49	51	50	48	50	51
5	48	49	48	48	49	48
6	52	50	50	52	50	50
7	51	51	51	51	50	50
8	52	50	49	53	48	50
9	50	51	50	51	48	49
10	47	46	49	46	47	48

a. Estimate gage repeatability and reproducibility.

b. Estimate the standard deviation of measurement error.

c. If the specifications are at 50 ± 10, what can you say about gage capability?

9-16 The data below were taken by one operator during a gage capability study.

Part Number	Measurements	
	1	2
1	20	20
2	19	20
3	21	21
4	24	20
5	21	21
6	25	26
7	18	17
8	16	15
9	20	20
10	23	22
11	28	22
12	19	25
13	21	20
14	20	21
15	18	18

a. Estimate gage capability.

b. Does the control chart analysis of these data indicate any potential gaging problems?

9-17 Three parts are assembled in series so that their critical dimensions x_1, x_2, and x_3 add. The dimensions of each part are normally distributed with the following parameters: $\mu_1 = 100$, $\sigma_1 = 4$, $\mu_2 = 75$, $\sigma_2 = 4$, $\mu_3 = 75$, and $\sigma_3 = 2$. What is the probability that an assembly chosen at random will have a combined dimension in excess of 262?

9-18 Two parts are assembled as shown below. The distributions of x_1 and x_2 are normal, with $\mu_1 = 20$, $\sigma_1 = 0.3$, $\mu_2 = 19.6$ and $\sigma_2 = 0.4$. The specifications of the clearance between the mating parts are 0.5 ± 0.4. What fraction of assemblies will fail to meet specifications if assembly is at random?

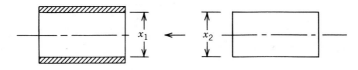

9-19 A product is packaged by filling a container completely full. This container is shaped as shown below. The process that produces these containers is examined, and the following information collected on the three critical dimensions:

Variable	Mean	Variance
L—Length	6.0	0.01
H—Height	3.0	0.01
W—Width	4.0	0.01

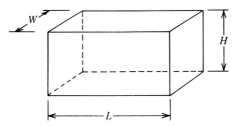

Assuming the variables to be independent, what are approximate values for the mean and variance of container volume?

9-20 A rectangular piece of metal of width W and length L is cut from a plate of thickness T. If W, L, and T are independent random variables with means and standard deviations as given below and the density of the metal is 0.08 g/cm^3, what would be the estimated mean and standard deviation of the weights of pieces produced by this process?

Variable	Mean	Standard Deviation
W	10 cm	0.2 cm
L	20 cm	0.3 cm
T	3 cm	0.1 cm

9-21 The surface tension of a chemical product, measured on a coded scale, is given by the relationship

$$s = (3 + 0.05x)^2$$

where x is a component of the product with probability distribution

$$f(x) = \tfrac{1}{32}(5x - 2) \qquad 2 \le x \le 4$$

Find the mean and variance of s.

9-22 Two resistors are connected to a battery as shown below. Find approximate expressions for the mean and variance of the resulting current (I). E, R_1, and R_2 are random variables with means μ_E, μ_{R_1}, μ_{R_2}, and variances σ_E^2, $\sigma_{R_1}^2$, and $\sigma_{R_2}^2$, respectively.

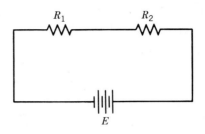

9-23 Two mating parts have critical dimensions x_1 and x_2 as shown below. Assume that x_1 and x_2 are normally distributed with means μ_1 and μ_2 and standard deviations $\sigma_1 = 0.400$ and $\sigma_2 = 0.300$. If it is desired that the probability of a smaller clearance (i.e., $x_1 - x_2$) than 0.09 should be 0.006, what distance between the average dimension of the two parts (i.e., $\mu_1 - \mu_2$) should be specified by the designer?

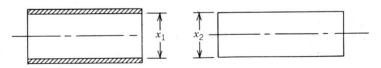

9-24 An assembly of two parts is formed by fitting a shaft into a bearing. It is known that the inside diameters of bearings are normally distributed with mean 2.010 cm and standard deviation 0.002 cm, and that the outside diameters of the shafts are normally distributed with mean 2.004 cm and standard deviation 0.001 cm. Determine the distribution of clearance between the parts if random assembly is used. What is the probability that the clearance is positive?

9-25 We wish to estimate a two-sided natural tolerance interval that will include 99% of the values of a random variable with probability 0.80. If nothing is known about the distribution of the random variable, how large should the sample be?

9-26 A sample of 10 items from a normal population had a mean of 300 and a standard deviation of 10. Using these data, estimate a value for the random variable such that the probability is 0.95 that 90% of the measurements on this random variable will lie below the value.

9-27 A sample of 25 measurements on a normally distributed quality characteristic has a mean of 85 and a standard deviation of 1. Using a confidence probability of 0.95, find a value such that 90% of the future measurements on this quality characteristic will lie above it.

9-28 A sample of 20 measurements on a normally distributed quality characteristic had $\bar{x} = 350$ and $S = 10$. Find an upper natural tolerance limit that has probability 0.90 of containing 95% of the distribution of this quality characteristic.

9-29 How large a sample is required to obtain a natural tolerance interval that has probability 0.90 of containing 95% percent of the distribution? After the data are collected, how would you construct the interval?

9-30 A random sample of $n = 40$ pipe sections resulted in a mean wall thickness of 0.1264 in. and a standard deviation of 0.0003 in. We assume that wall thickness is normally distributed.

   a. Between what limits can we say with 95% confidence that 95% of the wall thicknesses should fall?

   b. Construct a 95% confidence interval on the true mean thickness. Explain the difference between this interval and the one constructed in part (a).

9-31 Find the sample size required to construct an upper nonparametric tolerance limit that contains at least 95% of the population with probability at least 0.95. How would this limit actually be computed from sample data?

Chapter 10

Economic Design
of Control Charts

10-1 INTRODUCTION[1]

Control charts are widely used to establish and maintain statistical control of a process. They are also effective devices for estimating process parameters, particularly in process-capability studies. The use of a control chart requires that the engineer or analyst select a sample size, a sampling frequency or interval between samples, and the control limits for the chart. Selection of these three parameters is usually called the *design* of the control chart.

Traditionally, control charts have been designed with respect to statistical criteria only. This usually involves selecting the sample size and control limits such that the power of the test to detect a particular shift in the quality characteristic and the type I error probability are equal to specified values. The frequency of sampling is rarely treated analytically, and usually the practitioner is advised to consider such factors as the production rate, the expected frequency of shifts to an out-of-control state, and the possible consequences of such process shifts in selecting the sampling interval. The use of statistical criteria and practical experience have led, in many cases, to general guidelines for the design of control charts. Many of these guidelines, as well as the approach used in developing them, have been discussed for specific types of control charts in Chapters 5, 6, 7, and 8.

---

[1] This chapter uses more advanced statistical concepts than the rest of the book, and may be omitted on first reading without loss of continuity.

The design of a control chart has economic consequences in that the costs of sampling and testing, costs associated with investigating out-of-control signals and possibly correcting assignable causes, and costs of allowing nonconforming units to reach the consumer are all affected by the choice of the control chart parameters. Therefore, it is logical to consider the design of a control chart from an economic viewpoint. In recent years, considerable research has been devoted to this problem. This chapter will present several models for the optimal economic design of control charts. Some of the practical implications of these models will also be discussed.

10-1.1 Process Characteristics

To formulate an economic model for the design of a control chart, it is necessary to make certain assumptions about the behavior of the process. The assumptions summarized below are relatively standard in that most economic models incorporate them to some degree. In later sections we see how these assumptions are used in building specific models, and we discuss their relative importance.

The process is assumed to be characterized by a single in-control state. For example, if the process has one measurable quality characteristic, then the in-control state will correspond to the mean of this quality characteristic when no assignable causes are present. Similarly, when the quality characteristic is an attribute, the in-control state will be represented by the fraction nonconforming (say) produced by the process when no assignable causes are present. The process may have, in general, $s \geq 1$ out-of-control states. Each out-of-control state is usually associated with a particular type of assignable cause.

Determining the nature of the transitions between the in-control and out-of-control states requires certain assumptions. It is customary to assume that assignable causes occur during an interval of time according to a Poisson process. This implies that the length of time the process remains in the in-control state, given that it begins in control, is an exponential random variable. This assumption allows considerable simplification in the development of economic models, and in some situations results in a Markov chain model structure. The nature in which process shifts occur is sometimes called the *process-failure mechanism*. We will see subsequently that this can be a very critical assumption. We also observe that the assumption of discrete states and the nature of the failure mechanism imply that process transitions between states are instantaneous. Processes that "drift" slowly from an in-control state—as, for example, in the case of tool wear—have received little analytical attention.

It is also usually assumed that the process is not self-correcting. That is, once a transition to an out-of-control state has occurred, the process can be returned to the in-control condition only by management intervention following an appropriate out-of-control signal on the control chart. In some cases, however, transitions between different out-of-control states are allowed, provided the transitions are always consistent with further quality deterioration.

10-1.2 Cost Parameters

Three categories of costs are customarily considered in the economic design of control charts: the costs of sampling and testing, the costs associated with investigating an out-of-control signal and with the repair or correction of any assignable causes found, and the costs associated with the production of nonconforming items.

The costs of sampling and testing include the out-of-pocket expenses of inspectors' and technicians' salaries and wages, the costs of any necessary test equipment, and, in the case of destructive testing, the unit cost of the items sampled. Usually, the cost of sampling and testing is assumed to consist of both fixed and variable components, say a_1 and a_2, respectively, such that the total cost of sampling and testing is

$$a_1 + a_2 n$$

Because of the difficulty of obtaining and evaluating cost information, use of more complex relationships is probably inappropriate.

The costs of investigating and possibly correcting the process following an out-of-control signal have been treated in several ways. Some authors have suggested that the costs of investigating false alarms will differ from the costs of correcting assignable causes; consequently, these two situations must be represented in the model by different cost coefficients. Furthermore, the cost of repairing or correcting the process could depend on the type of assignable cause present. Thus, in models having s out-of-control states, $s + 1$ cost coefficients might be necessary to model the search and adjustment procedures associated without out-of-control signals. Usually, these cost coefficients would be chosen so that larger process shifts incurred larger costs of repair or adjustment. Other authors have argued that this level of modeling detail is unnecessary because in many cases small shifts are difficult to find but easy to correct, whereas large shifts are easy to find but difficult to correct. Hence, one loses little accuracy by using a single cost coefficient to represent the *average* cost of investigating and possibly correcting out-of-control signals.

The costs associated with producing nonconforming items consist of typical *failure* costs—that is, the costs of rework or scrap for internal failures, or replacement or repair costs for units covered by warranties in the case of external failures. With external failures, there may also be secondary effects from the production of nonconforming items if the customer's dissatisfaction with the product causes an alteration in future purchases of the product or other products manufactured by the company. Finally, there may be losses resulting from product liability claims against the company. Most authors model these costs with a single, average cost coefficient, expressed on either a per unit time or per item basis.

Economic models are generally formulated using a total cost function, which expresses the relationships between the control chart design parameters and the three types of costs discussed above. The production, monitoring, and adjustment process may be thought of as a series of independent cycles over time. Each cycle begins with the production process in the in-control state and continues until process monitoring via the control chart results in an out-of-control signal. Following an adjustment in which the process is returned to the in-control state, a new cycle begins. Let $E(T)$ be the *expected length* (that is, the *long-term average length*, or *mean length*) of a cycle, and let $E(C)$ be the expected total cost incurred during a cycle. Then the expected cost per unit time is

$$E(A) = \frac{E(C)}{E(T)} \tag{10-1}$$

Optimization techniques are then applied to Equation (10-1) to determine the economically optimal control chart design. Minor variations in (10-1) have appeared in the literature. For example, some authors have elected to replace $E(T)$ in (10-1) by the expected number of units produced during the cycle, resulting in the expected cost expressed on a per item rather than a per unit time basis. In other studies, a somewhat different definition of a cycle is used, depending on whether the process is shut down or allowed to continue operation while out-of-control signals are investigated.

The general model structure in (10-1) has a disturbing appearance. Note that C and T are dependent random variables, yet we have represented the expected value of their ratio $E(A)$ by the ratio of expectations $E(C)/E(T)$. Now it is well known that the expected value of a ratio is not equal to the ratio of expected values (even for independent random variables), so some further explanation of the structure of (10-1) seems warranted. The sequence of production–monitoring–adjustment, with accumulation of costs over the cycle, can be represented by a particular type of stochastic process called a *renewal reward process* [see Ross (1970)]. Stochastic processes of this type have the property that their average time cost is given by the ratio of the expected reward per cycle to the expected cycle length, as shown in (10-1).

10-1.3 Early Work and Semieconomic Designs

A fundamental paper in the area of cost modeling of quality-control systems was published by Girshick and Rubin (1952). They consider a process model in which a machine producing items characterized by a measurable quality characteristic x can be in one of four states. States 1 and 2 are production states, and, in state i the output quality characteristic is described by the probability density function $f_i(x)$, $i = 1, 2$. State 1 is the "in-control" state. While in state 1, there is a constant probability of a shift state 2. The process is not self-correcting; repair is necessary to return the process to state 1. States $j = 3$ and $j = 4$ are repair states, if we assume that the machine was previously in state $j - 2$. In state $j = 3, 4$, n_j units of time are required for repair, where a time unit is defined as the time to produce one unit of product. Girshick and Rubin treat both 100% inspection and periodic inspection rules. The economic criterion is to maximize the expected income from the process. The optimal control rules are difficult to derive, as they depend on the solution to complex integral equations. Consequently, the model's use in practice has been very limited.

Although it has had little or no practical application, Girshick and Rubin's work is of significant theoretical value. They were the first researchers to propose the expected cost (or income) per unit time criterion (10-1), and rigorously show its appropriateness for this problem. Later analysts' use of the criterion (10-1) rests directly on its development by Girshick and Rubin. Other researchers have investigated generalized formulations of the Girshick–Rubin model, including Bather (1963), Ross (1971), Savage (1962), and White (1974). Again, their results are primarily of theoretical interest, as they do not lead to process-control rules easily implemented by practitioners.

Economic design of conventional Shewhart control charts was investigated by several early researchers. Most of their work could be classified as semieconomic design procedures, in that either the proposed model did not consider all relevant costs or no formal optimization techniques were applied to the cost function. Weiler (1952) suggested that for an $\bar{x}$ chart, the optimum sample size should minimize the total amount of inspection required to detect a specified shift. If the shift is from an in-control state μ_0 to an out-of-control state $\mu_1 = \mu_0 + \delta\sigma$, then Weiler shows that the optimal sample size is

$$n = \frac{12.0}{\delta^2} \quad \text{when } \pm 3.09\text{-sigma control limits are used}$$

$$n = \frac{11.1}{\delta^2} \quad \text{when } \pm 3\text{-sigma control limits are used}$$

$$n = \frac{6.65}{\delta^2} \quad \text{when } \pm 2.58\text{-sigma control limits are used}$$

$$n = \frac{4.4}{\delta^2} \quad \text{when } \pm 2.33\text{-sigma control limits are used}$$

Note that Weiler did not formally consider costs; the implication is that minimizing total inspection will minimize total costs. A similar approach was used by Weiler in studies of other control charts (1953, 1954), as well as by Aroian and Levine (1950).

Other semieconomic analyses have been reported by Cowden (1957) and Barish and Hauser (1963). Cowden (1957) considered all three major categories of costs but offered no structured approach to optimization. His results consisted of a comparison of several simple $\bar{x}$ control chart design strategies, based on numerical evaluation of the cost function. Barish and Hauser (1963) employed Monte Carlo simulation to investigate several different $\bar{x}$ control chart designs, including a number of process-adjustment strategies. Formal optimization methods were not employed. In addition to the expected cost per unit, they also evaluated the number of process adjustments required and the fraction nonconforming produced.

Taylor (1965) has shown that control procedures based on taking a sample of constant size at fixed intervals of time is nonoptimal. He suggests that sample size and sampling frequency should be determined at each point in time based on the posterior probability that the process is in an out-of-control state. Dynamic programming-type methods are utilized extensively in the development. In a subsequent paper, Taylor (1967) derives the optimal control rule for a two-state process with a normally distributed quality characteristic. Although Taylor's work has indicated their nonoptimality, fixed sample size–fixed sampling interval control rules are widely used in practice because of their administrative simplicity. Consequently, most researchers have concentrated on the optimal economic design of such procedures. We devote the remainder of this chapter to the development and analysis of these models.

10-2 ECONOMIC MODELS OF THE $\bar{X}$ CONTROL CHART

Much of the research in the development of economic models of control charts has been devoted to the $\bar{x}$ chart. The interest of analysts in this control chart follows directly from its widespread use in practice. In this section, we discuss some of the economic models currently available.

10-2.1 Single Assignable-Cause Models

In 1956, Duncan (1956) proposed an economic model for the optimum economic design of the $\bar{x}$ control chart. His paper was the first to deal with a fully economic model of a Shewhart-type control chart and to incorporate formal optimization methodology into determining the control chart parameters. Duncan's paper was the stimulus for much of the subsequent research in this area.

Duncan drew on the earlier work of Girshick and Rubin (1952) in that he utilized a design criterion that maximized the expected net income per unit of time from the process. In the development of the cost model, Duncan assumes that the process is characterized by an in-control state μ_0 and that a single assignable cause of magnitude δ, which occurs at random, results in a shift in the mean from μ_0 to either $\mu_0 + \delta\sigma$ or $\mu_0 - \delta\sigma$. The process is monitored by an $\bar{x}$ chart with center line μ_0 and upper and lower control limits $\mu_0 \pm k(\sigma/\sqrt{n})$. Samples are to be taken at intervals of h hours. When one point exceeds the control limits, a search for the assignable cause is initiated. During the search for the assignable cause, the process is allowed to continue in operation. Furthermore, it is assumed that the cost of adjustment or repairs (if necessary) is not charged against the net income from the process. The parameters μ_0, δ, and σ are assumed known, while n, k, and h are to be determined.

The assignable cause is assumed to occur according to a Poisson process with an intensity of λ occurrences per hour. That is, assuming that the process begins in the in-process state, the time interval that the process remains in control is an exponential random variable with mean $1/\lambda$ h. Therefore, given the occurrence of the assignable cause between the jth and $(j + 1)$st samples, the expected time of occurrence within this interval is

$$\tau = \frac{\int_{jh}^{(j+1)h} e^{-\lambda t}\lambda(t - jh)\, dt}{\int_{jh}^{(j+1)h} e^{-\lambda t}\lambda\, dt} = \frac{1 - (1 + \lambda h)\, e^{-\lambda h}}{\lambda(1 - e^{-\lambda h})} \tag{10-2}$$

When the assignable cause occurs, the probability that it will be detected on any subsequent sample is

$$1 - \beta = \int_{-\infty}^{-k-\delta\sqrt{n}} \phi(z)\, dz + \int_{k-\delta\sqrt{n}}^{\infty} \phi(z)\, dz \tag{10-3}$$

where $\phi(z) = (2\pi)^{-1/2} \exp(-z^2/2)$ is the standard normal density. The quantity $1 - \beta$ is the power of the test, and β is the type II error probability. The probability of a false alarm is

$$\alpha = 2 \int_{k}^{\infty} \phi(z)\, dz \tag{10-4}$$

A production cycle is defined as the interval of time from the start of production (the process is assumed to start in the in-control state) following an adjustment to the detection and elimination of the assignable cause. The cycle consists of four periods: (1) the in-control period, (2) the out-of-control period, (3) the time to take a sample and interpret the results, and (4) the time to find the assignable cause. The expected length of the in-control period is $1/\lambda$. Noting that the number of samples required to produce an out-of-control signal given that the process is actually out of control is a geometric random variable with mean $1/(1 - \beta)$, we conclude that the expected length of the out-of-control period is $h/(1 - \beta) - \tau$. The time required to take a sample and interpret the results is a constant g proportional to the sample size, so that gn is the length of this segment of the cycle. The time required to find the assignable cause following an action signal is a constant D. Therefore, the expected length of a cycle is

$$E(T) = \frac{1}{\lambda} + \frac{h}{1 - \beta} - \tau + gn + D \tag{10-5}$$

The net income per hour of operation in the in-control state is V_0, and the net income per hour of operation in the out-of-control state is V_1. The cost of taking a sample of size n is assumed to be of the form $a_1 + a_2 n$; that is, a_1 and a_2 represent, respectively, the fixed and variable components of sampling cost. The expected number of samples taken within a cycle is the expected cycle length divided by the interval between samples, or $E(T)/h$. The cost of finding an assignable cause is a_3, and the cost of investigating a false alarm is a'_3. The expected number of false alarms generated during a cycle is α times the expected number of samples taken before the shift, or

$$\alpha \sum_{j=0}^{\infty} \int_{jh}^{(j+1)h} je^{-\lambda t} \, dt = \frac{\alpha e^{-\lambda h}}{1 - e^{-\lambda h}} \tag{10-6}$$

Therefore, the expected net income per cycle is

$$E(C) = V_0 \frac{1}{\lambda} + V_1 \left(\frac{h}{1 - \beta} - \tau + gn + D \right) - a_3 - \frac{a'_3 e^{-\lambda h}}{1 - e^{-\lambda h}}$$
$$- (a_1 + a_2 n) \frac{E(T)}{h} \tag{10-7}$$

The expected net income per hour is found by dividing the expected net income per cycle (10-7) by the expected cycle length (10-5), resulting in

$$E(A) = \frac{E(C)}{E(T)}$$
$$= \frac{V_0(1/\lambda) + V_1[h/(1 - \beta) - \tau + gn + D] - a_3 - a'_3 \alpha e^{-\lambda h}/(1 - e^{-\lambda h})}{1/\lambda + h/(1 - \beta) - \tau + gn + D}$$
$$- \frac{a_1 + a_2 n}{h} \tag{10-8}$$

Let $a_4 = V_0 - V_1$; that is, a_4 represents the hourly penalty cost associated with production in the out-of-control state. Then (10-8) may be rewritten as

$$E(A) = V_0 - \frac{a_1 + a_2 n}{h}$$
$$- \frac{a_4[h/(1 - \beta) - \tau + gn + D] + a_3 + a'_3 \alpha e^{-\lambda h}/(1 - e^{-\lambda h})}{1/\lambda + h/(1 - \beta) - \tau + gn + D} \tag{10-9}$$

or

$$E(A) = V_0 - E(L)$$

where

$$E(L) = \frac{a_1 + a_2 n}{h}$$

$$+ \frac{a_4[h/(1-\beta) - \tau + gn + D] + a_3 + a_3'\alpha e^{-\lambda h}/(1 - e^{-\lambda h})}{1/\lambda + h/(1-\beta) - \tau + gn + D} \quad (10\text{-}10)$$

The expression $E(L)$ represents the expected loss per hour incurred by the process. $E(L)$ is a function of the control chart parameters n, k, and h. Clearly, maximizing the expected net income per hour is equivalent to minimizing $E(L)$.

Duncan introduces several approximations to develop an optimization procedure for this model.[2] The optimization procedure suggested is based on solving numerical approximations to the system of first partial derivatives of $E(L)$ with respect to n, k, and h. An iterative procedure is required to solve for the optimal n and k. A closed-form solution for h is given using the optimal values of n and k.

Several authors have reported optimization methods for Duncan's model. Goel, Jain, and Wu (1968) have devised an iterative procedure for minimizing $E(L)$ that will produce the exact optimum solution. Their procedure is superior to Duncan's approximate optimization technique in situations where either a_4 or g is large, or where δ is small. (Duncan ignored some terms involving these quantities in developing his solution technique.) This paper also contains an extensive sensitivity analysis. Chiu and Wetherill (1974) have developed a simple, approximate procedure for optimizing Duncan's model. Their procedure utilizes a constraint on the power of the test $(1 - \beta)$. The recommended values are either $1 - \beta = 0.90$ or $1 - \beta = 0.95$. Tables are provided to generate the optimum design subject to this constraint. This procedure usually produces a design close to the true optimum. We also note that $E(L)$ could be easily minimized by using an unconstrained optimization or search technique coupled with a digital computer program for repeated evaluations of the cost function. This is the approach to optimization most frequently used.

Example 10-1

A manufacturer produces nonreturnable glass bottles for packaging a carbonated soft drink beverage. The wall thickness of the bottles is an important quality characteristic. If the wall is too thin, internal pressure generated during filling will cause the bottle to burst. The manufacturer has used $\bar{x}$ and R charts for process surveillance for some time. These control charts have been designed with respect to statistical criteria. However, in an effort to reduce costs, the manufacturer wishes to design an economically optimum $\bar{x}$ chart for the process.

---

[2] Several numerical approximations are also introduced in the actual structure of the model. Approximations used are for $\tau \simeq h/2 - \lambda h^2/12$, and for the expected number of false alarms $\alpha e^{-\lambda h}/(1 - e^{-\lambda h}) \simeq \alpha/\lambda h$.

Based on an analysis of quality-control technicians' salaries and the costs of test equipment, it is estimated that the fixed cost of taking a sample is $1. The variable cost of sampling is estimated to be $0.10 per bottle, and it takes approximately 1 min (0.0167 h) to measure and record the wall thickness of a bottle.

The process is subject to several different types of assignable causes. However, on the average, when the process goes out of control, the magnitude of the shift is approximately two standard deviations. Process shifts occur at random with a frequency of about one every 20 h of operation. Thus, the exponential distribution with parameter $\lambda = 0.05$ is a reasonable model of the run length in control. The average time required to investigate an out-of-control signal is 1 h. The cost of investigating an action signal that results in the elimination of an assignable cause is $25, while the cost of investigating a false alarm is $50.

The bottles are sold to a soft drink bottler. If the walls are too thin, an excessive number of bottles will burst when they are filled. When this happens, the bottler's standard practice is to backcharge the manufacturer for the costs of cleanup and lost production. Based on this practice, the manufacturer estimates that the penalty cost of operating in the out-of-control state for one hour is $100.

The expected cost per hour associated with the use of an $\bar{x}$ chart for this process is given by Equation (10-10), with $a_1 = \$1$, $a_2 = \$0.10$, $a_3 = \$25$, $a_3' = \$50$, $a_4 = \$100$, $\lambda = 0.05$, $\delta = 2.0$, $g = 0.0167$, and $D = 1.0$. A FORTRAN computer program for optimization of this cost model is given in Appendix 10A at the end of this chapter. The output from this program, using the values of the model parameters given above, is shown in Figure 10-1. The program calculates the optimal control limit width k and sampling frequency h for several values of n, and computes the value of the cost function (10-10). The corresponding α risk and power for each combination of n, k, and h are also provided. The optimal control chart design may be found by inspecting the values of the cost function to find the minimum. From Figure 10-1, we note that the minimum cost is $10.38 per hour, and the economically optimal $\bar{x}$ chart would use samples of size $n = 5$, the control limits would be located at $\pm k\sigma$, with $k = 2.99$, and samples would be

N	OPTIMUM K	OPTIMUM H	ALPHA	POWER	COST
1	2.30	.45	.0214	.3821	14.71
2	2.52	.57	.0117	.6211	11.91
3	2.68	.66	.0074	.7835	10.90
4	2.84	.71	.0045	.8770	10.51
5	2.99	.76	.0028	.9308	10.38
6	3.13	.79	.0017	.9616	10.39
7	3.27	.82	.0011	.9784	10.48
8	3.40	.85	.0007	.9880	10.60
9	3.53	.87	.0004	.9932	10.75
10	3.66	.89	.0003	.9961	10.90
11	3.78	.92	.0002	.9978	11.06
12	3.90	.94	.0001	.9988	11.23
13	4.02	.96	.0001	.9993	11.39
14	4.14	.98	.0000	.9996	11.56
15	4.25	1.00	.0000	.9998	11.72

Figure 10-1
Optimum solution to Example 10-1.

N	OPTIMUM K	OPTIMUM H	ALPHA	POWER	COST
1	2.31	.37	.0209	.3783	19.17
2	2.52	.46	.0117	.6211	15.71
3	2.68	.54	.0074	.7835	14.48
4	2.84	.58	.0045	.8770	14.01
5	2.99	.62	.0028	.9308	13.88
6	3.13	.65	.0017	.9616	13.91
7	3.27	.67	.0011	.9784	14.04
8	3.40	.69	.0007	.9880	14.21
9	3.53	.71	.0004	.9932	14.41
10	3.66	.73	.0003	.9961	14.62
11	3.78	.75	.0002	.9978	14.84
12	3.90	.77	.0001	.9988	15.06
13	4.02	.78	.0001	.9993	15.28
14	4.14	.80	.0000	.9996	15.50

Figure 10-2
Optimum $\bar{x}$ chart design for Example 10-1 with $a_4 = \$150$.

taken at intervals of $h = 0.76$ h (approximately every 45 min). The α risk for this control chart is $\alpha = 0.0028$, and the power of the test is $1 - \beta = 0.9308$.

After studying the optimal $\bar{x}$ chart design, the bottle manufacturer suspects that the penalty cost of operating out of control (a_4) may not have been precisely estimated. At worst, a_4 may have been underestimated by about 50%. Therefore, it is decided to return the computer program with $a_4 = \$150$ to investigate the effect of misspecifying this parameter. The results of this additional run are shown in Figure 10-2. We see that the optimal solution is now $n = 5$, $k = 2.99$, and $h = 0.62$, and the cost per hour is $13.88. Note that the optimal sample size and control limit width are unchanged. The primary effect of increasing a_4 by 50% is to reduce the optimal sampling frequency from 0.76 h to 0.62 h (i.e., from 45 min to 37 min). Based on this analysis, the manufacturer decides to adopt a sampling frequency of 45 min because of its administrative convenience.

From analysis of numerical problems such as those in Example 10-1, it is possible to draw several general conclusions about the optimum economic design of the $\bar{x}$ control chart. Some of these conclusions are illustrated below.

1. The optimum sample size is largely determined by the magnitude of the shift δ. For example, Figure 10-3 illustrates the solution to the problem in Example 10-1 with $\delta = 1.0$. Note that the optimum sample size has increased considerably to $n = 14$. The optimum control limits are now slightly narrower, and the optimum sampling interval is slightly greater. In general, relatively large shifts, say $\delta \geq 2$, often result in relatively small optimum sample size, say $2 \leq n \leq 10$. Smaller shifts require much larger samples, with $1 \leq \delta \leq 2$ frequently producing optimum sample sizes in the range $10 \leq n \leq 20$. Very small shifts, say $\delta \leq 0.5$, may require sample sizes as large as $n \geq 40$.

2. The hourly penalty cost for production in the out-of-control state a_4 mainly affects the interval between samples h. Larger values of a_4 imply smaller values

N	OPTIMUM K	OPTIMUM H	ALPHA	POWER	COST
4	2.22	.53	.0264	.4129	15.47
5	2.27	.58	.0232	.4865	14.57
6	2.31	.64	.0209	.5555	13.95
7	2.35	.69	.0188	.6163	13.50
8	2.39	.73	.0168	.6695	13.18
9	2.43	.77	.0151	.7157	12.95
10	2.47	.81	.0135	.7556	12.79
11	2.50	.85	.0124	.7929	12.69
12	2.54	.88	.0111	.8223	12.62
13	2.58	.91	.0099	.8474	12.59
14	2.61	.94	.0091	.8711	12.59
15	2.65	.96	.0080	.8893	12.61
16	2.69	.99	.0071	.9049	12.65
17	2.72	1.02	.0065	.9197	12.71
18	2.76	1.04	.0058	.9309	12.77
19	2.79	1.06	.0053	.9417	12.85
20	2.83	1.08	.0047	.9497	12.94
21	2.87	1.10	.0041	.9566	13.03
22	2.90	1.12	.0037	.9633	13.13
23	2.94	1.14	.0033	.9683	13.24
24	2.97	1.16	.0030	.9731	13.35

Figure 10-3
Optimum $\bar{x}$ chart design for Example 9-1 with $\delta = 1.0$.

of h (more frequent sampling), while smaller values of a_4 imply larger values of h (less frequent sampling). The effect of increasing a_4 is illustrated in Figures 10-1 and 10-2 for the data in Example 10-1.

3. The costs associated with looking for assignable causes (a_3 and a'_3) mainly affect the width of the control limits. They also have a slight effect on the sample size n. Figure 10-4 shows the solution to Example 10-1 with $a_3 = a'_3 = \$100$.

N	OPTIMUM K	OPTIMUM H	ALPHA	POWER	COST
1	2.53	.40	.0114	.2981	19.59
2	2.72	.53	.0065	.5432	16.03
3	2.87	.62	.0041	.7238	14.74
4	3.00	.70	.0027	.8413	14.20
5	3.13	.75	.0017	.9102	13.99
6	3.27	.78	.0011	.9483	13.95
7	3.40	.82	.0007	.9707	14.00
8	3.52	.84	.0004	.9837	14.10
9	3.65	.87	.0003	.9906	14.24
10	3.77	.89	.0002	.9947	14.38
11	3.89	.92	.0001	.9970	14.53
12	4.00	.94	.0001	.9983	14.69
13	4.12	.96	.0000	.9990	14.85
14	4.23	.98	.0000	.9994	15.01
15	4.34	1.00	.0000	.9997	15.17

Figure 10-4
Optimum $\bar{x}$ chart design for Example 10-1 with $a_3 = a'_3 = \$100$.

Note that the optimal $\bar{x}$ chart design is now $n = 6$, $k = 3.27$, and $h = 0.78$. The increased width of the control limits and the small change in n have decreased the α risk considerably to 0.0011 and increased the power of the test slightly to 0.9483. This is intuitively appealing; as the costs of investigating action signals increase, we would want to reduce the incidence of false alarms (i.e., reduce α).

4. Variation in the costs of sampling affects all three design parameters. Increasing the fixed cost of sampling increases the interval between samples. It also usually results in slightly larger samples. Figure 10-5 presents the solution to Example 10-1 with $a_1 = \$2$. Note that in the optimum solution, the sampling frequency has increased to $h = 1.01$ h, while the sample size and control limit width have increased to $n = 6$ and $k = 3.03$, respectively. Large values of a_2, the variable cost of sampling, imply small, relatively infrequent samples, and narrow control limits. Figure 10-6 gives the solution to Example 10-1 with $a_1 = \$0.5$. Note that the optimum sample size has decreased to 4, the optimum frequency of sampling has increased to $h = 1.07$, and the optimum control limit width has decreased to $k = 2.65$.

5. Changes in the mean number of occurrences of the assignable cause per hour primarily affect the interval between samples. Figure 10-7 presents the optimum solution to Example 10-1 with $\lambda = 0.01$ (i.e., the mean duration in control is 100 h). Note that the optimum sampling interval has increased considerably to 1.76 h. The optimum sample size and control limits have also increased slightly.

6. The optimum economic design is relatively insensitive to errors in estimating the cost coefficients. That is, the cost surface is relatively flat in the vicinity of the optimum. This may be seen in one dimension by examining Figures 10-1 through 10-7. Note that as n varies, there is little change in the optimum cost.

N	OPTIMUM K	OPTIMUM H	ALPHA	POWER	COST
1	2.07	.71	.0385	.4721	16.31
2	2.33	.82	.0198	.6909	13.25
3	2.53	.90	.0114	.8249	12.10
4	2.71	.95	.0067	.9015	11.63
5	2.87	.98	.0041	.9454	11.45
6	3.03	1.01	.0024	.9692	11.43
7	3.18	1.04	.0015	.9826	11.48
8	3.32	1.06	.0009	.9903	11.58
9	3.46	1.08	.0005	.9945	11.70
10	3.59	1.10	.0003	.9969	11.84
11	3.72	1.11	.0002	.9982	11.98
12	3.85	1.13	.0001	.9990	12.12
13	3.97	1.15	.0001	.9994	12.27
14	4.09	1.17	.0000	.9997	12.42
15	4.21	1.18	.0000	.9998	12.56

Figure 10-5
Optimum $\bar{x}$ chart design for Example 10-1 with $a_1 = \$2$.

N	OPTIMUM K	OPTIMUM H	ALPHA	POWER	COST
1	2.19	.56	.0285	.4247	15.44
2	2.36	.78	.0183	.6803	13.02
3	2.51	.94	.0121	.8300	12.31
4	2.65	1.07	.0080	.9115	12.18
5	2.80	1.17	.0051	.9528	12.31
6	2.94	1.26	.0033	.9749	12.57
7	3.08	1.34	.0021	.9865	12.89
8	3.22	1.41	.0013	.9926	13.23
9	3.35	1.48	.0008	.9960	13.58
10	3.48	1.55	.0005	.9978	13.93
11	3.61	1.61	.0003	.9987	14.28
12	3.74	1.67	.0002	.9993	14.62
13	3.86	1.73	.0001	.9996	14.95
14	3.98	1.79	.0001	.9998	15.28

Figure 10-6
Optimum $\bar{x}$ chart design for Example 10-1 with $a_2 = \$0.5$.

There is some indication that the cost surface is steeper near the origin, so that it would be preferable to overestimate the optimum n slightly, rather than underestimate it. The optimum economic design is relatively sensitive to errors in estimating the magnitude of the shift (δ), the in-control state (μ_0), and the process standard deviation (σ).

7. One should exercise caution in using arbitrarily designed $\bar{x}$ control charts. Duncan (1956) has compared the optimum economic design with the arbitrary design $n = 5$, $k = 3.00$, and $h = 1$, for several sets of system parameters. Depending on the values of the system parameters, very large economic penalties may result from the use of the arbitrary design.

N	OPTIMUM K	OPTIMUM H	ALPHA	POWER	COST
1	2.33	.98	.0198	.3707	5.42
2	2.54	1.25	.0111	.6135	4.03
3	2.70	1.45	.0069	.7776	3.52
4	2.85	1.59	.0044	.8749	3.31
6	3.14	1.76	.0017	.9607	3.21
7	3.28	1.83	.0010	.9779	3.24
8	3.41	1.89	.0006	.9877	3.28
9	3.54	1.95	.0004	.9931	3.33
10	3.76	2.00	.0002	.9960	3.38
11	3.79	2.05	.0002	.9978	3.44
12	3.91	2.10	.0001	.9987	3.50
13	4.03	2.14	.0001	.9993	3.56
14	4.15	2.19	.0000	.9996	3.62
15	4.26	2.24	.0000	.9998	3.68

Figure 10-7
Optimum $\bar{x}$ chart design for Example 10-1 with $\lambda = 0.01$.

Other Process Models

Two fundamental assumptions are made in the development of the economic model (10-10): the process is allowed to continue in operation during the search for an assignable cause, and the cost of eliminating the assignable cause is not charged against the net income for the period. In many processes, these restrictions are unrealistic, and it would be of interest to formulate a cost model based on somewhat different assumptions. Suppose that following an out-of-control signal, the process is stopped while a search for the assignable cause is performed. If the signal is a false alarm, an expected time of D_0 hours elapses and an expected cost of a'_3 is incurred. If the assignable cause is present, an expected time of D_1 hours is required to locate and eliminate it, and an expected cost of $a_3 + \Delta$ incurred. Note that a_3 is the cost of finding the assignable cause, and Δ is the cost of eliminating it. After the search has been completed, the production process is restarted.

The production cycle for this process model consists of four periods: (1) the in-control period, with expected length $1/\lambda$; (2) the out-of-control period, with expected length $h/(1 - \beta) - \tau$; (3) the search periods due to false alarms, with expected length $\alpha D_0 e^{-\lambda h}/(1 - e^{-\lambda h})$; and (4) the search and process-adjustment period due to the assignable cause, with expected length D_1. Therefore, the average length of a production cycle is

$$E(T) = \frac{1}{\lambda} + \frac{h}{1 - \beta} - \tau + \frac{\alpha D_0 e^{-\lambda h}}{1 - e^{-\lambda h}} + D_1 \tag{10-11}$$

The expected net income during a cycle is, by analogy with Equation (10-7),

$$E(C) = V_0(1/\lambda) + V_1[h/(1 - \beta) - \tau] - \frac{a'_3 \alpha e^{-\lambda h}}{(1 - e^{-\lambda h})}$$
$$- (a_3 + \Delta) - \frac{(a_1 + a_2 n)[1/\lambda + h/(1 - \beta) - \tau]}{h} \tag{10-12}$$

The expected net income per hour is

$$\begin{aligned}
E(A) &= \frac{E(C)}{E(T)} \\
&= \{V_0(1/\lambda) + V_1[h/(1 - \beta) - \tau] - a'_3 \alpha e^{-\lambda h}/(1 - e^{-\lambda h}) \\
&\quad - (a_3 + \Delta) - (a_1 + a_2 n)[1/\lambda + h/(1 - \beta) - \tau]/h\} \\
&\quad \div \{1/\lambda + h/(1 - \beta) - \tau + \alpha D_0 e^{-\lambda h}/(1 - e^{-\lambda h}) + D_1\}
\end{aligned} \tag{10-13}$$

Letting $a_4 = V_0 - V_1$, (10-13) can be written as $E(A) = V_0 - E(L)$, where

$$\begin{aligned}
E(L) &= \{(a_1 - a_2 n)[1/\lambda + h/(1 - \beta) - \tau]/h + a_3 + \Delta \\
&\quad + [\alpha e^{-\lambda h}/(1 - e^{-\lambda h})](V_0 D_0 + a'_3) + V_0 D_0 + a_4[h/(1 - \beta) - \tau]\} \\
&\quad \div \{1/\lambda + h/(1 - \beta) - \tau + \alpha D_0 e^{-\lambda h}/(1 - e^{-\lambda h}) + D_1\}
\end{aligned} \tag{10-14}$$

The expression $E(L)$ represents the expected loss per hour for the process. Note that (10-14) is a function of the control chart design parameters n, k, and h. It can be easily minimized by direct search methods.

Panagos, Heikes, and Montgomery (1985) report on a numerical study of this model, and compare it to the Duncan-type model in which the process is allowed to continue in operation during the searches for the assignable cause. They report that the model in (10-14) always results in optimum economic designs having larger sample sizes, wider control limits, and a longer sampling interval than produced by the Duncan-type model. Furthermore, there is always a penalty for model mis-specification. That is, if one uses the optimum economic design for Duncan's model in a process that must be stopped to search for the assignable cause, then the actual cost incurred is greater than the expected lost, and this penalty can be high. This emphasizes the importance of choosing the correct process model.

The process models discussed above assume that the process-failure mechanism (the time that the process remains in the in-control state) is an exponential random variable. Baker (1971) has proposed a process model that allows this assumption to be investigated. He develops two discrete-time models in which a sample of size n is taken at the end of each period and the test statistic plotted on a control chart with k-sigma limits. The first model utilizes the geometric distribution with range space 0, 1, 2, ... to model the number of periods the process remains in the in-control state. (Note that the geometric distribution is the discrete-time analog of the exponential distribution.) A cycle is defined as the sum of the number of periods the process remains in control and the number of periods the process runs out of control until the assignable cause is detected. If p is the parameter of the geometric distribution (i.e., the probability that the process will shift out of control at the start of period $t + 1$, given that it is in control at the end of period t), then the expected length of the cycle is

$$E(T) = \frac{1 - p}{p} + \frac{1}{1 - \beta}$$

The expected cost incurred during the cycle is the sum of expected sampling costs, the expected cost of investigating out-of-control signals, and the expected cost of operating out of control. If there are M false alarms in a cycle, then the expected cost incurred during the cycle is

$$E(C) = a_2 n[(1 - p)/p + 1/(1 - \beta)] + a_3[1 + E(M)] + a_4[1/(1 - \beta)]$$

Note that the model does not include a fixed cost of sampling (a_1), as the sampling frequency is not a decision variable. Consequently, the expected cost incurred per unit of time is

$$E(A) = \frac{E(C)}{E(T)} = a_2 n + \frac{a_3[1 + E(M)] + a_4[1/(1 - \beta)]}{(1 - p)/p + 1/(1 - \beta)} \tag{10-15}$$

Since the expected number of false alarms in a cycle is $E(M) = \alpha(1 - p)/p$, the expected cost per unit time is

$$E(A) = a_2 n + \frac{a_3[(1 - \beta)p + (1 - \beta)\alpha(1 - p)] + a_4 p}{(1 - \beta)(1 - p) + p} \tag{10-16}$$

Baker's second process model allows the use of any discrete probability function $p(t)$ to model the process-failure mechanism, that is, the number of periods the process remains in control. In this model, a cycle is defined as the number of periods following the conclusion of a search for the assignable cause until the next out-of-control signal. Let T^* denote the length of the cycle, and let S denote the number of periods the process is in the out-of-control state. The expected cost incurred during the cycle is

$$E(C) = a_2 n T^* + a_3 + a_4 E(S)$$

Consequently, the expected cost per unit time is

$$E(A) = \frac{E(C)}{E(T^*)} = a_2 n + \frac{a_3 + a_4 E(S)}{E(T^*)} \qquad (10\text{-}17)$$

It can be shown that

$$E(S) = \sum_{t=0}^{\infty} \frac{(1 - \alpha)^t p(t)}{1 - \beta}$$

$$E(T^*) = \sum_{t=0}^{\infty} \left[\frac{1}{\alpha} - (1 - \alpha)^t \left(\frac{1}{\alpha} - \frac{1}{1 - \beta} \right) \right] p(t)$$

The cost function (10-17) is a general expression that can be specialized depending on the choice of process-failure mechanism $p(t)$. Baker (1971) investigates in some detail the case where $p(t)$ is Poisson, and he compares it to the usual geometric process model (10-16). He notes that if the process-failure mechanism is Poisson, smaller sample sizes and narrower control limits result than would be economically optimal in the geometric case. The narrower control limits arise because false alarms can be beneficial. That is, a false alarm can postpone a true shift, because the run length in control does not have the "memoryless" property of the geometric distribution. It is also observed that the optimal economic control chart design is relatively sensitive to the choice of process-failure mechanism. Substantial cost penalties may be incurred if an incorrect process-failure mechanism is assumed.

Banerjee and Rahim (1988) generalize the Baker model to treat the case of a Weibull process-failure mechanism. They enrich the approach above by incorporating a variable-sampling-interval strategy. This model seems appropriate for many processes where the failure mechanism is driven by wear or fatigue considerations. Banerjee and Rahim assume that the length of the sampling intervals is chosen so that the probability of a process shift in an interval, given no shift until the start of the interval, is constant for all intervals. They illustrate numerically that the variable-sampling-interval strategy is superior to the traditional uniform-sampling-interval approach.

Gibra (1971) has proposed a single assignable-cause economic model of the $\bar{x}$ chart. His process model is similar to Duncan's (1956) in that the process is assumed to continue in operation during searches for the assignable cause. It is assumed that the time required to take and inspect a sample, interpret the results, and search for and eliminate the assignable cause is an Erlang random variable. In the development of the cost model, the concept of worst cycle quality level (WCQL) was proposed. A quality cycle is defined as the interval between two successive in-control periods, and the WCQL is the permissible expected number of nonconforming units produced during this period. Thus, the WCQL is an upper limit on the expected number of nonconforming units produced during out-of-control production periods. The parameters of the $\bar{x}$ chart were selected so as to minimize the expected cost subject to the constraint of obtaining a particular WCQL.

Gibra (1967) has also investigated the optimal economic design of $\bar{x}$ charts used to monitor a process in which the mean of the quality characteristic exhibits a linear trend over time. This would be a suitable model for processes involving tool wear. The optimal control procedure determines decision rules for shutting the process down for adjustment due to drift, as well as for the occurrence of an assignable cause. The control rules minimize adjustment costs and costs due to the production of nonconforming items.

The Lorenzen and Vance Model

Lorenzen and Vance (1986) have developed an economic model for the design of control charts that uses a somewhat different approach than those above. The principal feature of their model is that it is developed in terms of the in-control and out-of-control average run lengths, rather than the α and β risks. This model has the advantage that it allows other control charts to be incorporated simply by changing the probability distributions that generate the ARLs.

10-2.2 Multiple Assignable-Cause Models

The models of the previous section treat the case where a single assignable-cause of known effect occurs randomly. Many production processes are affected by several assignable causes, and in such situations, a single assignable-cause model would seem inappropriate. In this section, we present economic models designed to incorporate the occurrence of several assignable causes. Two distinctly different modeling approaches to the multiple assignable-cause problem have been developed—one by Duncan (1971) and the other by Knappenberger and Grandage (1969).

Duncan's Multiple Assignable-Cause Model

Duncan's (1971) multiple assignable-cause model is a generalization of his assignable-cause model (1956). There is one in-control state μ_0. When the process shifts out of control, it does so as a result of the occurrence of an assignable cause $\delta_j, j = 1, 2, \ldots, s$, of known magnitude. The effort of this shift is to modify the process mean to $\mu_j = \mu_0 + \delta_j\sigma, j = 1, 2, \ldots, s$. When the process shifts to an out-of-control state, it remains in that state without further quality deterioration until detected. The process is assumed to continue in operation during the search of an assignable cause.

The occurrence times of the assignable causes are assumed to be independent exponential random variables with means $1/\lambda_j, j = 1, 2, \ldots, s$. Therefore, the time duration of the process in the in-control state is distributed as the minimum of s independent exponential random variables. This is an exponential random variable with mean $1/\lambda = 1/\sum_{j=1}^{s} \lambda_j$. The power of the control chart test to detect the jth assignable cause once it has occurred is

$$1 - \beta_j = \int_{-\infty}^{-k - \delta_j\sqrt{n}} \phi(z) \, dz + \int_{k - \delta_j\sqrt{n}}^{\infty} \phi(z) \, dz \qquad (10\text{-}18)$$

Thus, the expected number of samples taken following the occurrence of the jth assignable cause is $1/(1 - \beta_j)$. Furthermore, an assignable cause may occur between any two successive samples with mean interoccurrence time

$$\tau_j = \frac{\int_{uh}^{(u+1)h} e^{-\lambda_j t} \lambda_j(t - uh) \, dt}{\int_{uh}^{(u+1)h} e^{-\lambda_j t} \lambda_j \, dt} = \frac{1 - (1 + \lambda_j h)e^{-\lambda_j h}}{\lambda_j(1 - e^{-\lambda_j h})} \tag{10-19}$$

Therefore, the time required for an out-of-control signal to be generated following the occurrence of the jth assignable cause is $h/(1 - \beta_j) - \tau_j$.

The production cycle consists of four periods: (1) the in-control period, with expected length $1/\lambda$; (2) the out-of-control period, with expected length $\sum_{j=1}^{s} \lambda_j[h/(1 - \beta_j) - \tau_j]/\lambda$; (3) the time for taking and analyzing a sample of size n; and (4) the time required to find the assignable cause. If D_j hours are required to discover the jth assignable cause, then the expected length of time per cycle for discovery of the assignable cause is $\sum_{j=1}^{s} \lambda_j D_j/\lambda$. Consequently, the expected length of a cycle is

$$E(T) = \frac{1}{\lambda} + \frac{\sum_{j=1}^{s} \lambda_j[h/(1 - \beta_j) - \tau_j]}{\lambda} + gn + \frac{\sum_{j=1}^{s} \lambda_j D_j}{\lambda}$$

$$= \frac{1 + \sum_{j=1}^{s} \lambda_j[h/(1 - \beta_j) - \tau_j + gn + D_j]}{\lambda} \tag{10-20}$$

Let a_{3j} be the cost of discovering the jth assignable cause, and a_{4j} be the hourly penalty cost of producing nonconforming items when the jth assignable cause is present. Then the expected cost incurred during a cycle is

$$E(C) = \frac{\sum_{j=1}^{s} a_{4j} \lambda_j[h/(1 - \beta_j) - \tau_j + gn + D_j] + \sum_{j=1}^{s} \lambda_j a_{3j}}{\lambda}$$

$$+ \frac{a_3' \alpha e^{-\lambda h}}{(1 - e^{-\lambda h})} + \frac{(a_1 + a_2 n)E(T)}{h} \tag{10-21}$$

Therefore, the expected cost per unit time is

$$E(A) = \frac{E(C)}{E(T)} = \frac{a_1 + a_2 n}{h}$$

$$+ \left\{ \sum_{j=1}^{s} a_{4j} \lambda_j[h/(1 - \beta_j) - \tau_j + gn + D_j] \middle/ \lambda \right.$$

$$+ \sum_{j=1}^{s} \lambda_j a_{3j}/\lambda + a_3' \alpha e^{-\lambda h} \middle/ (1 - e^{-\lambda h}) \right\}$$

$$\div \left\{ 1/\lambda + \sum_{j=1}^{s} \lambda_j[h/(1 - \beta_j) - \tau_j + gn + D_j] \middle/ \lambda \right\} \tag{10-22}$$

Note that the cost function (10-22) is a function of the control chart design parameters n, k, and h.

Duncan employs direct search methods to find the values of n, k, and h that minimize (10-22). He presents the solution to several example problems and conducts a sensitivity analysis of the model. Chiu (1973) has noted that some of the numerical results in Duncan's paper are in error. The discrepancies seem to result from errors in Duncan's computer program and from the use of single-precision arithmetic to calculate τ_j. Chiu suggests the use of double-precision arithmetic or numerical approximations as employed in Duncan's original paper (1956) in calculating small numbers such as the τ_j. The numerical errors do not seem to have seriously affected the general analysis and conclusions drawn from the model.

The model (10-22) is not completely realistic in that once the process shifts to an out-of-control state, no further quality deterioration can occur. In the same paper, Duncan (1971) extends (10-22) to a "double occurrence" model. In this formulation it is assumed that following an initial shift, a second occurrence of an assignable cause is possible. The joint effect of the two assignable causes is always to produce a shift of constant magnitude, say $\Delta\sigma$, regardless of what two assignable causes have occurred. Duncan concluded that this modification in the process model has little effect on the minimum cost solution, although some changes in the behavior of the cost surface were noted.

Knappenberger and Grandage's Multiple Assignable-Cause Model

Knappenberger and Grandage (1969) have also developed a model for the optimum economic design of an $\bar{x}$ chart when the process is affected by several assignable causes. The in-control state is μ_0, and the out-of-control states are $\mu_1, \mu_2, \ldots, \mu_s$, where $\mu_j > \mu_i$ if $j > i$. Their model differs considerably from Duncan's (1971), in that transitions between the s out-of-control states are possible, and a simplified cost structure is assumed. It is also assumed that the process is stopped while out-of-control signals are investigated. Following the completion of a search, the process is restarted. The objective function is to minimize the expected cost of the process-control procedure per unit of product, say

$$E(C) = E(C_1) + E(C_2) + E(C_3) \tag{10-23}$$

where $E(C_1)$ is the expected cost per unit of sampling and testing, $E(C_2)$ is the expected cost of investigating out-of-control signals and possibly correcting the process, and $E(C_3)$ is the expected penalty cost per unit of producing nonconforming product. The design parameters in the control chart are taken to be the sample size n, the number of units produced between successive samples m, and the width of the control limits k, expressed as a multiple of σ.

The cost of sampling and testing is

$$E(C_1) = \frac{a_1 + a_2 n}{m} \tag{10-24}$$

Note that m is the number of units produced between the first items included in successive samples. If R is the production rate in units per hour, then the number of hours between samples is just $h = m/R$.

Let a_3 be the cost of investigating an out-of-control signal and adjusting the process, if it is necessary. Since the process is stopped during searches, a_3 should also include the opportunity losses resulting from lost production during a search.

Note that the assumption is that the cost of investigating real and false alarms is the same. Let Z be an indicator random variable defined such that $Z = 1$ if $\bar{x}$ plots out of control. Then, if no searches for an assignable cause are made when $\bar{x}$ plots in control, the expected cost per unit of investigating and possible adjusting the process is

$$E(C_2) = \frac{a_3 P\{Z = 1\}}{m}$$

Define $\alpha_j, j = 0, 1, \ldots, s$, as the probability that $\bar{x}$ plots out of control given that the process is in state μ_j. That is, α_0 is the probability of type I error and α_j, $j = 1, 2, \ldots, s$, is the power of the test. [$\alpha_j = 1 - \beta_j$ is defined in (10-18).] Also let $q_j, j = 1, 2, \ldots, s$, be the steady-state probability that the process is in state μ_j at the time a sample is taken. Then, since $P\{Z = 1\} = \sum_{j=0}^{s} \alpha_j q_j$, we have

$$E(C_2) = \frac{a_3 \displaystyle\sum_{j=0}^{s} \alpha_j q_j}{m} \tag{10-25}$$

Let W be an indicator random variable defined such that $W = 0$ if a unit conforms to requirements, and $W = 1$ if a unit is nonconforming. Define $f_j, j = 0, 1, \ldots, s$, as the probability that a unit is nonconforming given that the process is in state μ_j. If LSL and USL are the lower and upper specification limits on the product, then

$$f_j = 1 - \int_{LSL}^{USL} \frac{1}{\sigma\sqrt{2\pi}} e^{-\frac{1}{2}\left(\frac{x - \mu_j}{\sigma}\right)^2} dx$$

Let γ_j be the probability that the process is in state μ_j at any point in time. Then the expected penalty cost associated with the production of nonconforming units is

$$E(C_3) = a_4 P\{W = 1\} = a_4 \sum_{j=0}^{s} f_j \gamma_j \tag{10-26}$$

The expected total cost per unit is found by summing (10-24), (10-25), and (10-26), yielding

$$E(C) = \frac{a_1 + a_2 n}{m} + \frac{a_3 \displaystyle\sum_{j=0}^{s} \alpha_j q_j}{m} + a_4 \sum_{j=0}^{s} f_j \gamma_j \tag{10-27}$$

The cost coefficients $\{a_i\}$ and the probabilities $\{f_j\}$ are independent of the control chart design parameters n, m, and k. However $\{\alpha_j\}$, $\{q_j\}$, and $\{\gamma_j\}$ depend on the control chart design. The elements of $\{\alpha_j\}$ have been defined previously. We will now determine the $\{q_j\}$ and $\{\gamma_j\}$.

The elements $\{q_j\}$ are the steady-state probabilities that the process is in state μ_j at the time a sample is taken. These probabilities are generated through a transition matrix $\mathbf{B}$. Let the elements of $\mathbf{B} = \{b_{ij}\}$ represent the probability of the process shifting from state μ_i to state μ_j during the production of m units. Assuming that the run length of the process in control, given that it starts in the in-control state, is an exponential random variable with mean $1/\lambda$, then we observe that the probability of remaining in the in-control state during the production of m units is

$$p_{00} = 1 - \int_0^{m/R} \lambda e^{-\lambda t}\, dt = e^{-\lambda m/R}$$

It is necessary to devise a method for allocating the remaining probability $1 - e^{-\lambda m/R}$ of shifting directly from state μ_0 to state μ_j. Knappenberger and Grandage (1969) suggest letting

$$p_{0j} = \binom{s}{j} \frac{(1 - e^{-\lambda m/R})\theta^j(1 - \theta)^{s-j}}{1 - (1 - \theta)^s} \qquad j = 1, 2, \ldots, s \qquad (10\text{-}28)$$

Thus, the probability distribution $\{p_{00}, p_{01}, p_{02}, \ldots, p_{0s}\}$ defines the probabilities of shifting from state μ_0 directly to an out-of-control state μ_j. The shape of this distribution is controlled by the parameter θ; large values of θ result in negative skew (i.e., relatively larger probabilities assigned to higher numbered states), while small values of θ result in positive skew (i.e., relatively larger probabilities assigned to lower numbered states). The probability of a drift from an out-of-control state μ_i to another out-of-control state μ_j ($j > i$) is denoted by p_{ij}. Knappenberger and Grandage assume that the probability of a shift from μ_i to μ_j is proportional to the probability of a shift from μ_0 to μ_j. Therefore

$$p_{ij} = \begin{cases} \dfrac{p_{0j}}{1 - p_{00}} & 0 < i < j \\[2ex] \dfrac{\sum\limits_{r=1}^{j} p_{0r}}{1 - p_{00}} & i = j > 0 \\[2ex] 0 & 0 < i > j \end{cases} \qquad (10\text{-}29)$$

These assumptions regarding the $\{p_{ij}\}$ seem very elaborate. However, numerical evidence suggests that they do not play an important role in the performance of the model. In practice, the $\{p_{ij}\}$ could be determined empirically by the manufacturing or quality engineer based on his or her experience with the process.

Using the $\{p_{ij}\}$, we may define the elements of the transition matrix **B**. In addition to the usual assumption that the process cannot correct itself, it is assumed that only one shift can occur between successive samples and the probability of a shift occurring while a sample is being taken is zero. The probability b_{0j} is the probability that the process is in state μ_0 at the time of the uth sample and in state μ_j at the time of the $(u + 1)$st sample. By definition, this is

$$b_{0j} = p_{0j} \qquad j \geq 0$$

When $0 \leq j < i$, b_{ij} is the probability that the process is in state μ_i at the time of the uth sample and is in a better state μ_j at the time of the $(u + 1)$st sample. This is equal to the probability that the state μ_i is detected at the uth sample times the probability of shifting from μ_0 to state μ_j during the production of the next m units, or

$$b_{ij} = \alpha_i p_{0j} \qquad 0 \leq j < i$$

For $j \geq i$, b_{ij} is the probability that the process is in state μ_i at the time of the uth sample and has deteriorated either to the same state or to a worse state μ_j at the time of the next sample. This is the probability that state μ_i is detected at the uth sample times the probability of a shift from state μ_0 to state μ_j before the next sample, plus the probability that state μ_i is not detected at the uth sample and the process shifts from state μ_i to state μ_j before the next sample. That is,

$$b_{ij} = \alpha_i p_{0j} + (1 - \alpha_i) p_{ij} \qquad j \geq i$$

The $(s + 1) \times (s + 1)$ matrix **B** is the transition matrix of an aperiodic positive recurrent Markov chain. Therefore, the steady-state probability of the process being in state μ_j at the time a sample is taken is the solution to

$$\mathbf{q}' = \mathbf{q}'\mathbf{B} \tag{10-30}$$

where $\mathbf{q}' = [q_0, q_1, q_2, \ldots, q_s]$ is a row vector with $s + 1$ elements. To find the elements $\{q_j\}$, we may solve any s of the $s + 1$ equations in (10-30) along with constraint

$$\sum_{j=0}^{s} q_j = 1$$

The $\{\gamma_j\}$ are the probabilities of the process being in state μ_j at any point in time. Note that γ_0 depends on the probability that the process is in state μ_0 at the time of the uth sample and remains in that state until the next sample is taken, and the probability that the process is in state μ_0 at the time of the uth sample but shifts out of control before the next sample. Consequently,

$$\gamma_0 = q_0 p_{00} + \tau q_0 (1 - p_{00}) \tag{10-31}$$

where τ is the time elapsed before the shift occurs, given a process shift between the uth and $(u + 1)$st samples. For $\gamma_j, j > 0$, Knappenberger and Grandage (1969) assume that

$$\gamma_j = q_j p_{jj} + (1 - \tau) q_0 p_{0j} + (1 - \tau) \sum_{l=1}^{j-1} q_l p_{lj} + \tau q_j \sum_{h=j+1}^{s} p_{jh} \qquad j > 0 \tag{10-32}$$

That is, the fraction of time the process spends in the lower numbered state when a transition to a higher numbered state occurs is the same fraction of time τ that the process spends in state μ_0 given that a shift to state μ_j has occurred. The third term in (10-32) is zero if $j = 1$ because state μ_1 can only be reached from state μ_0, and the last term in (10-32) is zero when $j = s$ because no further transitions to higher numbered states are possible.

Knappenberger and Grandage suggest a two-stage grid search method to minimize (10-27). The first stage is a coarse grid, followed by a fine grid search in the second stage. They present the solutions to 81 example problems, having a variety of cost coefficients and other model parameters. A limited sensitivity analysis is conducted.

Comparison of Model Structure

We may make a number of interesting comparisons between the single assignable-cause and multiple assignable-cause models, as well as between Duncan's (1971) and Knappenberger and Grandage's (1969) multiple assignable-cause models. We note that multiple assignable-cause models are considerably more complex than single assignable-cause models. Furthermore, the multiple assignable-cause models have more unknown parameters that the user must specify in order to determine the optimum control chart design. Thus, it is of considerable practical importance to investigate the model's sensitivity to the number of out-of-control states. From a practical viewpoint, it is difficult to characterize out-of-control states in the precise fashion required by the models. One would hope that a production process characterized by many out-of-control states could be adequately approximated by a single out-of-control state model.

Duncan (1971) reports that a single assignable-cause model that matches the true multiple assignable-cause system in certain important ways produced very good results. He suggested that the magnitude of the shift for the single assignable-cause model should be equal to the average shift for the multiple assignable-cause system; that is,

$$\delta = \sum_{j=1}^{s} \frac{\lambda_j \delta_j}{\lambda}$$

Furthermore, one should use $\lambda = \sum_{j=1}^{s} \lambda_j$ as the mean duration in control for the single assignable-cause model, and one should choose the penalty cost a_4 such that

$$a_4 = \sum_{j=1}^{s} \frac{\lambda_j a_{4j}}{\lambda}$$

Knappenberger and Grandage (1969) also reported similar experiences. Therefore, it seems reasonable to conclude that very complex multistate processes can be satisfactorily approximated by a model containing only a few states, provided those states can be properly defined.

The Duncan (1971) and Knappenberger and Grandage (1969) multiple-cause models have different objective functions. Duncan's model minimizes cost per unit time, where the cycle length can be defined to allow either continued operation of the process during the investigation of action signals or production stoppage during searches. Knappenberger and Grandage's model minimizes cost per unit produced, and the process is assumed to stop when an action signal is generated. By appropriate definition of the search cost a_3, the two models can be made to give consistent results.

Duncan's multiple-cause model seems to have a more realistic cost structure than the Knappenberger and Grandage model, in that the different costs associated with searching for different assignable causes are explicitly treated in the model. However, the Knappenberger and Grandage model allows continued deterioration of quality beyond the initial shift, which is probably a more realistic portrayal of the behavior of actual production processes than the single- or double-shift multiple-cause Duncan model. Furthermore, the Knappenberger and Grandage model has fewer parameters to estimate than Duncan's. This has important implications for practitioners.

10-2.3 Joint Economic Design of $\bar{x}$ and R Control Charts

As $\bar{x}$ and R charts are usually employed together for process control, it seems necessary to consider their joint economic design. Saniga (1978) has presented a model for the joint economic design of $\bar{x}$ and R control charts. He assumes that the process is characterized by three states: an in-control and two out-of-control states. In the in-control state, the process mean and standard deviation are μ_0 and σ_0, respectively. Two assignable causes generate the out-of-control states. The first assignable cause results in a shift of the process mean from μ_0 to μ_1, but does not affect the process standard deviation. The second assignable cause results in a shift in the process standard deviation from σ_0 to σ_1. Thus, the two out-of-control states are described by $\mu_1 > \mu_0$ and σ_0, and μ_0 and $\sigma_1 > \sigma_0$, respectively. A simultaneous shift in both the process mean and the process standard deviation is not considered. The control chart design parameters are the sample size n, the number of units produced between successive samples m, the width of the control limits on the $\bar{x}$ chart in standard deviation units, $k_{\bar{x}}$, and the upper control limit factor on the R chart k_R, where $\text{UCL}_R = k_R \sigma_0$.

The general modeling approach is similar to Knappenberger and Grandage (1969). In that model structure, Equation (10-27), the $\{\alpha_j\}$, $j = 0, 1, 2$, are defined as the conditional probability that at least one control chart produces an action signal given that the process is in state j. Let $\alpha_0(\bar{x})$ and $\alpha_0(R)$ be the individual type I error probabilities of the $\bar{x}$ and R charts, respectively, and also let $\alpha_j(\bar{x})$ and $\alpha_j(R)$, $j > 0$, be the powers of the two control charts when the process is in state j. Then, since $\bar{x}$ are R are independent random variables,

$$\alpha_0 = \alpha_0(\bar{x}) + \alpha_0(R) - \alpha_0(\bar{x})\alpha_0(R)$$
$$\alpha_j = \alpha_j(\bar{x}) + \alpha_j(R) - \alpha_j(\bar{x})\alpha_j(R) \qquad j = 1, 2$$

Note that α_0 is the probability of a type I error resulting from the joint use of the $\bar{x}$ and R chart, while similarly, α_j, $j > 0$, is the corresponding power of the test. The function $\alpha_j(\bar{x})$, $j \geq 0$, may be evaluated directly from the cumulative standard normal distribution, while $\alpha_j(R)$, $j \geq 0$, is obtained from the distribution of the relative range.

Pattern search was used to find the economically optimum parameters n, m, $k_{\bar{x}}$, and k_R. Saniga noted that the cost surface is not convex, although the local minimum was in a realistic region as far as the control chart parameters were concerned. The cost surface is also relatively flat in the vicinity of the optimum, so that moderate errors in estimating the cost coefficients and other model parameters would not seriously effect the results. The solutions to 81 numerical examples are reported. All of the examples utilize relatively large process shifts. These examples indicate that somewhat less frequent samples are optimum when the $\bar{x}$ and R charts are optimized jointly than in the case where only the $\bar{x}$ chart is optimized. This is probably due to the increased power of the test resulting from the joint use of the two control charts.

Saniga also gives a cost comparison to the arbitrary control chart design $n = 5$, $k_{\bar{x}} = 3.0$, and $k_R = 5.4$. When an economically optimum value of the sampling frequency m is used in conjunction with these parameter values, the difference in expected cost between the arbitrary control chart design and the fully optimum design is between 0.4% and 8.2%. However, when nonoptimum values of m are used, much larger economic penalties are incurred by the arbitrary design. Furthermore, the numerical comparisons all involve problems with process shifts of two standard deviations and very small penalty costs of operating in the out-of-control state. If smaller process shifts and/or larger penalty costs for producing defectives are experienced, then the difference between the optimum economic design and the arbitrary design will be much greater.

10-3 ECONOMIC DESIGN OF THE CONTROL CHART FOR FRACTION NONCONFORMING

The models developed in Section 10-2 can be easily adapted for use with the control chart for fraction nonconforming. We assume that the control chart has center line at p_0, which corresponds to the fraction nonconforming produced when the process is in control, and has upper and lower control limits given by

$$\text{UCL} = p_0 + k\sqrt{\frac{p_0(1 - p_0)}{n}}$$
$$\text{LCL} = p_0 - k\sqrt{\frac{p_0(1 - p_0)}{n}} \tag{10-33}$$

when n is the sample size and k is the width of the control limits in standard deviation units. The design parameters are n, k, and the sampling frequency.

From Chapter 5, we recall that the test statistic is

$$\hat{p} = \frac{D}{n}$$

where D is the number of nonconforming units found in the sample size n. The hypothesis of statistical control is reflected if $\hat{p}$ exceeds either the UCL or the LCL. It is also possible to design the decision rule using an *acceptance number c* such that if $D \leq c$, the process is assumed to be in control and if $D > c$, the process is assumed to be out of control. The relationship between k and c is

$$\frac{c}{n} \bigg/ \sqrt{\frac{p_0(1 - p_0)}{n}} < k \leq \frac{c + 1}{n} \bigg/ \sqrt{\frac{p_0(1 - p_0)}{n}} \tag{10-34}$$

Note that (10-34) implies a range of values for k corresponding to a particular choice of n and c. This phenomenon occurs because the test statistic $\hat{p}$ is a discrete random variable with range space $\{0, 1/n, 2/n, \ldots, (n - 1)/n, 1\}$. For example, if the in-control state is $p_0 = 0.01$, the sample size is $n = 27$, and the acceptance number is $c = 2$, then any value of k in the interval $3.87 < k \leq 5.80$ can be used on the control chart. This has led several authors to choose c as a design parameter instead of k. Using this approach, we may write the α- and β-risks for the control chart for fraction nonconforming as

$$\alpha = 1 - \sum_{x=0}^{c} \binom{n}{x} p_0^x (1 - p_0)^{n-x} \tag{10-35}$$

and

$$\beta = \sum_{x=0}^{c} \binom{n}{x} p_1^x (1 - p_1)^{n-x} \qquad (10\text{-}36)$$

respectively, where p_1 is the fraction nonconforming produced when the process is out of control.

Several authors have investigated single assignable-cause economic models of the fraction nonconforming control chart. Ladany (1973) proposed a somewhat different modeling approach than that employed in Section 10-2. He formulated the total cost of sampling, searching for assignable causes, process adjustment, and production in the out-of-control state over a fixed time period. This time period is assumed to start and end with a scheduled process "set-up" or adjustment that places the process in the in-control state. He does not report any numerical results, and he recommends direct search methods to optimize the control chart parameters. Ladany and Alperovitch (1975) develop a similar model involving unscheduled set-ups, and suggest that by comparison of the two models, an economically optimal set-up and control strategy can be determined. Chiu (1975) has formulated a cost model, using the variation of Duncan's (1956) $\bar{x}$ chart model structure given in Equation (10-14). He has elected to work with the np chart instead of the usual fraction nonconforming or p chart. (See Chapter 5 for discussion of the equivalence of the np and p charts.) He uses a variation of Fibonacci search to find the economically optimal design. He also proposes an approximately optimal design procedure similar to that reported in Chiu and Wetherill (1974) for the $\bar{x}$ chart. A brief sensitivity analysis of this model is reported. The model is relatively insensitive to errors in estimating the cost coefficients, but requires more precise estimates of p_0 and p_1. Gibra (1978) has also investigated the economic design of np charts. He develops two different process models, one assuming that the process continues in operation during a search, and the other assuming that the process is shut down during a search. The general modeling approach is similar to Duncan's (1956). Direct search techniques are used to optimize the objective function.

Two papers have treated multiple assignable-cause economic models of the control chart for fraction nonconforming. Montgomery, Heikes, and Mance (1975) have developed a model using the general approach of Knappenberger and Grandage [see Equation (10-27)]. They use both grid search methods and pattern search to minimize the cost function. The paper contains solutions to approximately 100 numerical examples, and the results of a sensitivity analysis are reported. They note that the shape of the distribution of $\hat{p}$ depends on the true value p_0 and $p_j, j = 1, 2, \ldots, s$ (the fractions nonconforming in the out-of-control states) and not simply the magnitude of the shift, as would be the case for the $\bar{x}$ chart. Consequently, different control chart designs would be required to optimally detect a shift from $p_0 = 0.01$ to $p_1 = 0.06$ versus a shift from $p_0 = 0.05$ to $p_1 = 0.10$, although the magnitude of the shift $\delta = 0.05$ is the same in both cases. The model is not extremely sensitive to the number of out-of-control states used, and a properly chosen single-cause model would often be a suitable approximation for a complex multiple-cause process. They also examine the cost response surface, and report that it is convex and relatively flat in the vicinity of the optimum. Consequently, the effect of moderate errors in estimating the model parameters is slight.

Chiu (1976a) has also investigated a multiple assignable-cause economic model of the np chart. His model is similar in structure to Duncan's multiple-cause $\bar{x}$ chart model [Equation (10-22)], except that the process is assumed to stop while action signals are investigated. He uses grid search procedures to determine the economically optimum parameters of the control chart.

An extensive sensitivity analysis of the control chart for fraction nonconforming with a single assignable cause has been reported by Duncan (1978). The model structure is similar to the one employed in his study of the $\bar{x}$ chart, and his results are based on the solutions to 237 problems. Duncan observes that the optimal fraction defective control chart design is not stable for all shifts of magnitude δ, but depends on the specific process levels p_0 and p_1. However, he reports that if the magnitude of the shift is expressed in process standard deviation units of $\delta\sigma_0 = \delta\sqrt{p_0(1 - p_0)}$, reasonable stabilization does occur so that some general conclusions may be drawn. These conclusions may be summarized as follows.

1. For small process shifts on the order of $0.1\sigma_0$, the acceptance number generally will be zero. These small shifts are typically accompanied by larger sample sizes and longer sampling intervals than optimal for cases in which the shift is large. There is little support for widespread use of arbitrary sample sizes such as $n = 50$, as is often recommended.

2. Changes in the cost coefficients and other model parameters produce changes in the optimal control chart design that are generally what one would anticipate. For example, increasing inspection costs reduces the sample size and increases the sampling interval.

3. The more frequently the assignable cause occurs, the shorter the optimal sampling interval should be, although in general each sample should be smaller. The impact of a more frequently occurring shift is to increase the sampling intensity.

4. The numerical results obtained basically agree with other reported results.

Montgomery and Heikes (1976) have investigated the assumptions regarding the process-failure mechanism for the control chart for fraction nonconforming. Specifically, they consider discrete-time models similar to (10-16) and (10-17), and investigate the use of the geometric, Poisson, and logarithmic series distributions to model the duration in control. They note that the choice of process-failure mechanism is an important aspect of optimum control chart design, and the misspecification of this property can result in significant economic penalties.

10-4 OTHER ASPECTS OF THE ECONOMIC DESIGN OF CONTROL CHARTS

The development of economic models for the design of control charts has concentrated on the $\bar{x}$ chart and the control chart for fraction nonconforming. However, the general approach has been extended to other types of control charts. This section briefly summarizes some of this work.

The economic design of cumulative-sum control charts was first investigated by Taylor (1968). His model expresses the expected cost per unit of time as a function of the sample size n, sampling interval h, and the V-mask design parameters d and θ. He assumes that a single assignable cause of magnitude δ occurs according to a Poisson process. To solve the model, however, he assumes that n and h are specified.

Goel and Wu (1973) have also developed a single assignable-cause model for the optimum economic design of cumulative-sum control charts. They utilize a cost model similar in structure to Duncan's single-cause $\bar{x}$ chart model. Both V-mask and decision interval schemes are discussed (see Chapter 7 for a discussion of cumulative-sum control charts). Pattern search is employed to determine the economically optimum control chart design. Their paper reports the results of a sensitivity analysis on some of the model parameters. The magnitude of the shift affects the optimum design parameters in that smaller shifts imply larger samples at longer sampling intervals with a decreasing decision limit. Sampling costs tend to affect the sampling frequency primarily, with increases in both the fixed and variable costs of sampling resulting in less frequent samples being economically optimal. Decreases in the parameter λ also lead to longer sampling intervals.

Goel (1968) has compared economically optimal $\bar{x}$ and cumulative-sum charts. He reports that, in general, there is little difference between the two types of charts, with respect to optimum system cost. However, if a smaller than optimum sample size is used, the resulting economic penalties are more severe for the $\bar{x}$ chart. Furthermore, the cumulative-sum chart is not quite as sensitive to errors in specifying the magnitude of the shift as is the $\bar{x}$ chart.

Chiu (1974) has also developed a single assignable-cause economic model of the cumulative-sum chart, following the general modeling strategy of Duncan's $\bar{x}$ chart model. He does not consider V-mask schemes but chooses to optimize the decision interval instead. Both a numerical optimization method and a simplified approximate-solution procedure are presented. A brief sensitivity analysis and a discussion of an extension of the model to a multiple-cause system are given.

The economic design of $\bar{x}$ charts with warning limits has been discussed by several authors. In all cases, research has been confined to single assignable-cause systems. Tiago de Oliveira and Littauer (1966) have developed a procedure for selecting the parameters of the control chart on an economic basis. They utilized the mean action time, that is, the mean number of samples between action signals, in the procedure. Assuming that the mean action times in both the in-control and out-of-control states are known, they determine an economically optimal sample size and sampling interval.

Gordon and Weindling (1975) have also studied the optimal economic design of control charts with warning limits. They propose the average cost per good unit produced as an objective function. The design parameters in their model are the sample size n, the sampling frequency h, the width of the outer (or action) control limits k_a, the width of the warning limits k_w, and the run length r of sample means between the warning and action limits that would constitute an action signal. Their model formulation is general and can be adapted to any type of control chart. A numerical example for the $\bar{x}$ chart is given. Grid search is used to optimize the model.

Chiu and Cheung (1977) formulate an economic model of the $\bar{x}$ chart with warning limits, using the expected cost per unit time as the objective function. Their treatment of the problem is mathematically simpler than Gordon and Weindling's (1975), and the resulting model structure is similar to Duncan's conventional $\bar{x}$ chart model. They also compare the economically optimal $\bar{x}$ chart with warning limits to economically optimal conventional $\bar{x}$ charts and economically optimal cumulative-sum charts, noting that economically optimal $\bar{x}$ charts with warning limits and economically optimal cumulative-sum charts are nearly equivalent, and both are only slightly better than an economically optimal conventional $\bar{x}$ chart. They also observe that the common industrial practice of setting the ratio of warning limit width to action limit width (k_w/k_a) equal to $\frac{2}{3}$ is not desirable from an economic viewpoint. A better choice in many cases is $k_w/k_a = 0.85$. Thus, this research provides a good argument for the use in practice of the two-out-of-three and four-out-of five sensitizing rules discussed in earlier chapters.

The optimal economic design of T^2 control charts, the multivariate analog of the $\bar{x}$ chart, has been investigated by Montgomery and Klatt (1972a, 1972b). These authors employ a single assignable-cause version of the Knappenberger and Grandage model structure. Their numerical results are restricted to the case of two quality characteristics. The sensitivity of the model to estimates of the cost coefficients and the estimate of the population covariance matrix is investigated, and it is concluded that the optimum control chart parameters are relatively insensitive to errors in estimating these parameters. It is noted that both the magnitude of the shift and the sign of the correlation coefficient relating the two quality characteristics affect the optimum economic design. In general, if the shift in both quality characteristics is in the same direction, negative correlation between the quality characteristics leads to smaller samples than would be required if this correlation were positive. This occurs because negative correlation always leads to a more powerful test if the process shift is in the same direction for both quality characteristics. Heikes, Montgomery, and Yeung (1974) have also investigated the choice of process-failure mechanism in the economic design of T^2 control charts, concluding that this is a critical assumption.

Recently, Woodall (1986, 1987) has criticized the economic design of control charts, noting that in many economic designs the Type I error of the control chart is considerably higher than it would usually be in a statistical design, and that this will lead to more false alarms—an undesirable situation. The occurrence of excessive false alarms is always a problem, as managers will be reluctant to shut down a process if the control scheme has a history of many false alarms. Furthermore, if the Type I error is high, then this could lead to excessive process adjustment, which often increases the variability of the quality characteristic. Woodall also notes that economic models assign a cost to passing defective items, which would include liability claims and customer dissatisfaction costs, among other components, and this is counter to Deming's philosophy that these costs cannot be measured and that customer satisfaction is necessary to staying in business.

These concerns are easily overcome. An economic design should always be checked for statistical properties, such as Type I and Type II errors, average run lengths, and so forth. If any of these properties are at undesirable levels, this may indicate that inappropriate costs have been assigned, or that a constrained solution is necessary. It is recommended to optimize the cost function with suitable constraints on Type I error, Type II error, average run length, or other statistical properties. Saniga (1989) has reported such a study relating to the joint economic statistical design of $\bar{x}$ and R charts. Saniga uses constraints on Type I error, power, and the average time to signal for the charts. His economic statistical designs have higher cost than the pure economic designs, but give superior protection over a wider range of process shifts and also have statistical properties that are as good as control charts designed entirely from statistical considerations.

10-5 SUMMARY

Procedures for the optimal economic design of control charts are well developed. Most of the standard types of control charts, such as the $\bar{x}$ chart, the p chart, and the cumulative-sum chart, have been extensively investigated. Several different process models have been studied, and the practitioner can choose one that best describes any particular production operation. Optimization of these models is relatively straightforward, with direct search techniques probably being the most popular approach. The widespread availability of digital computers should play a major role in the development and implementation of these procedures.

Several authors have conducted sensitivity analyses on these economic models. In general, it seems that multiple assignable-cause processes can usually be well approximated by an appropriately chosen single assignable-cause model. This is an important finding, as single assignable-cause models have fewer parameters to estimate and are much simpler to use than multiple assignable-cause models. Furthermore, the models reported in the literature are relatively insensitive to errors in estimating the cost coefficients. This result is of considerable practical importance, as some of the cost coefficients are difficult to determine precisely, such as the cost of producing defective units. The cost surfaces studied are generally flat in the vicinity of the optimum. However, they are steeper near the origin. Consequently, it is better to overestimate a parameter than to underestimate it. The models are sensitive to estimates of the in-control and out-of-control states, and the magnitude of the shift. These parameters are usually easier to estimate than the costs. Chiu (1976b) discusses parameter estimation in the economic design of $\bar{x}$ charts.

It is also important to model the occurrence of assignable causes properly. Most of the currently available models assume that assignable causes occur according to a Poisson process; that is, the duration of the process in control given that it starts in the in-control state is an exponential random variable. If the occurrence of assignable causes can be thought of as random "shocks' acting on the system—in other words, the probability of a process shift within any small interval of time is directly proportional to the length of the interval—then this assumption is probably appropriate. However, if assignable causes occur as a result of the cumulative effects of heat, vibration, shock, and other similar phenomena, or as a result of improper set-up or excessive stress during process start-up, then use of the exponential distribution to model the duration in-control may not be appropriate. Serious economic consequences may result from misuse of this model assumption.

Saniga and Shirland (1977) and Chiu and Wetherill (1975) report that very few practitioners have implemented economic models for the design of control charts. This is somewhat surprising, as most quality engineers claim that a major objective in the use of statistical process-control procedures is to reduce costs. There are at least two reasons for the lack of practical implementation of this methodology. First, the mathematical models and their associated optimization schemes are relatively complex, and are often presented in a manner that is difficult for the practitioner to understand and use. The availability of computer programs for these models and the development of simplified optimization procedures and methods for handling constraints is increasing. The availability of microcomputers and the ease with which these applications may be implemented on them should alleviate this problem. A second problem is the difficulty in estimating costs and other model parameters. Fortunately, costs do not have to be estimated with high precision, although other model components, such as the magnitude of the shift, require relatively accurate determination. Sensitivity analysis of the specific model could help the practitioner decide which parameters are critical in the problem.

As a guideline to implementation of these models, it is suggested that the cost or value of the items be evaluated and initial efforts in economic design of the control procedures be devoted to the products of greatest value. Frequently, we find that a relatively small percentage of the products produced account for most of the cost of production or sales revenue. In inventory control, the "*ABC* system" defines these as "*A* items", while "*B* items" and "*C* items" are more numerous but account for proportionately less value to the company. Usually, more sophisticated inventory-control techniques would be concentrated on the *A* items. Similarly, these items are probably appropriate candidates for the optimum economic design of their process-control procedure.

Appendix 10A

A Computer Program for the Economic Design of the x̄ Control Chart[3]

DESCRIPTION

This computer program will find the economically optimal sample size n, control limit factor k, and sampling interval h for an $\bar{x}$ control chart. Duncan's (1956) process model is assumed; that is, the objective function minimized is Equation (10-10). The program is interactive and requests the user to input values of the parameters a_1, a_2, a_3, a_3', a_4, λ, δ, g, and D. Use of the program, as well as a sample of the output, is given in Example 10-1.

The approximation suggested by Duncan (1956) and Chiu and Wetherill (1974) for the optimum sampling interval h is employed in the program. An exact closed-form solution for the optimum value of h given n and k has been derived by Goel, Jain, and Wu (1968). If desired, this more exact method of determining h could be used instead of the present approximation.

---

[3] From Douglas C. Montgomery, "Economic Design of an $\bar{x}$ Control Chart," *Journal of Quality Technology*, Vol. 14, No. 1, 1982, with permission of the publisher.

PROGRAM LISTING

```
        READ (5, 2) A1, A2, A3, A3P, A4, XLAM, DELT, G, D
   2    FORMAT (9F8.0)
        WRITE (6, 3)
   3    FORMAT (1H0, 3X, 'N', 5X, 'OPTIMUM K', 3X, 'OPTIMUM H'
       &6X, 'ALPHA', 5X, 'POWER', 4X, 'COST')
        AA=DELT**2*A3P/(A2+XLAM*A4*G)
        XK=0.
        DO 4 I=1, 10
        RHS=(1.2826+XK)/ORDN(XK)
        IF (RHS.GT.AA) GO TO 5
   4    XK=XK+0.5
   5    XK=XK-0.5
        IF (XK.LT.0) XK=0.
        N=((1.286+XK)/DELT)**2+0.5
        NMIN=N-10
        IF (NMIN.LE.0) NMIN=1
        NMAX=N+10
        DO 9 I=NMIN, NMAX
        XN=1
        XK=0.5
        STEP=0.5
        DO 8 J=1, 3
        BESTFN=1.0E+38
        IF (J.EQ.2) STEP=0.1
        IF (J.EQ.3) STEP=0.01
   6    ARG=-1.0*XK
        A=2.0*PNORM (ARG)
        ARG=DELT*SQRT(XN)-XK
        P=PNORM (ARG)
        H=SQRT ((A*A3P+A1+A2*XN)/(XLAM*A4*(1./P-0.5)))
        B=H*(1./P-0.5+XLAM*H/12.)+G*XN+D
        OBJFN=(A4*XLAM*B+A3P/H+XLAM*A3)/(XLAM*B+1.0)
       &+(A1+A2*XN)/H
        IF (OBJFN.GT.BESTFN) GO TO 7
        BESTFN=OBJFN
        BESTA=A
        BESTP=P
        BESTK=XK
        BESTH=H
        XK=XK+STEP
        GO TO 6
   7    IF (J.EQ.3) GO TO 8
        XK=BESTK-STEP
   8    CONTINUE
   9    WRITE (6, 10) I,BESTK,BESTH,BESTA,BESTP,BESTFN
  10    FORMAT (1H,14,2(5X,F7.2),3X,2(3X,F7.4),4X,F7.2)
        STOP
        END
```

```
FUNCTION ORDN(Z)
ORDN=0.39894228*EXP(-Z*Z/2)
RETURN
END
FUNCTION PNORM(X)
DIMENSION C(7)
DATA C/.319381530,-.356563782,1.781477937,
&-1.821255978,1.330274429,.2316419,2.506628725/
Y=X
IF (X.LT.0.) Y=-X
T=1./(1.+C(6)*Y)
S=(((( C(5)*T+C(4))*T+C(3))*T+C(2))*T+C(1))*T
PNORM=S*EXP(-Y*Y/2)/C(7)
IF (X.GT.0.) PNORM=1.-PNORM
RETURN
END
```

10-6 Exercises

10-1 An $\bar{x}$ chart is used to maintain current control of a process. A single assignable cause of magnitude 2σ occurs, and the duration of the process in control is an exponential random variable with mean 100 h. Suppose that sampling costs are $0.50 per sample and $0.10 per unit, it costs $5 to investigate a false alarm, $2.50 to find the assignable cause, and $100 is the penalty cost per hour to operate in the out-of-control state. The time required to collect and evaluate a sample is 0.05 h, and it takes 2 h to locate the assignable cause. Assume that the process is allowed to continue operating during searches for the assignable cause.

   a. What is the cost associated with the arbitrary control chart design $n = 5$, $k = 3$, and $h = 1$?

   b. Find the control chart design that minimizes the cost function given by Equation (10-1).

10-2 An $\bar{x}$ chart is used to maintain current control of a process. The cost parameters are $a_1 = \$0.50$, $a_2 = \$0.10$, $a_3 = \$25$, $a'_3 = \$50$, and $a_4 = \$100$. A single assignable cause of magnitude $\delta = 2$ occurs, and the duration of the process in control is an exponential random variable with mean 100 h. Sampling and testing require 0.05 h, and it takes 2 h to locate the assignable cause. Assume that Equation (10-10) is the appropriate process model.

   a. Evaluate the cost of the arbitrary control chart design $n = 5$, $k = 3$, $h = 1$.

   b. Evaluate the cost of the arbitrary control chart design $n = 5$, $k = 3$, $h = 0.5$.

   c. Determine the economically optimum design.

10-3 Consider the cost information given in Exercise 10-1. Suppose that the process model represented by Equation (10-14) is appropriate. It requires 2 h to investigate a false alarm, the profit per hour of operating in the in-control state is $500, and it costs $25 to eliminate the assignable cause. Evaluate the cost of the arbitrary control chart design $n = 5$, $k = 3$, and $h = 1$.

10-4 An $\bar{x}$ chart is used to maintain current control of a process. The cost parameters are $a_1 = \$2$, $a_2 = \$0.50$, $a_3 = \$50$, $a'_3 = \$75$, and $a_4 = \$200$. A single assignable cause occurs, with magnitude $\delta = 1$, and the run length of the process in control is exponentially distributed with mean 100 h. It requires 0.05 h to sample and test, and

1 h to locate the assignable cause. Assume that the process is allowed to continue operating during searches for the assignable cause.

a. Evaluate the cost of the arbitrary $\bar{x}$ chart design $n = 5$, $k = 3$, and $h = 0.5$.

b. Determine the economically optimum design.

10-5 Suppose that a measurable quality characteristic is subject to a single assignable cause that occurs at random, with a mean rate of occurrence equal to one every $1/\lambda$ hours of operation. The effect of the assignable cause is to increase the mean μ_0 by δ_t, where $\delta > 0$ and t is operating time. Develop an economic model for the $\bar{x}$ chart used to monitor and control this process.

10-6 A new tool that costs $100 can be resharpened at a cost of $1 an average of 100 times. The tool life between sharpening can be assumed to be normally distributed with mean 6 h and standard deviation 2 h. It costs $3 to install a new tool, which results in 0.5 h of lost production time, while no time is lost when the tool is resharpened. The production rate is 100 units per hour. The production costs are $0.25 per unit, and the sales revenue is $0.50 per unit. When the tool fails, all parts produced subsequently are defective. It costs $0.50 to inspect the process. When defective parts are found, all units produced since the last inspection are examined at a cost of $0.01 per unit, and defectives removed. The quality-control procedure consists of inspecting the process every h hours and automatically resharpening the tool at intervals of $r = kh$ hours, where k is a positive integer.

a. Find k and h that minimize total production costs per hour.

b. Determine another control procedure that would be superior in terms of minimum production costs per hour.

10-7 **A Simplified Method for the Economic Design of $\bar{x}$ Charts.** Chiu and Wetherill (1974) have suggested a procedure for the approximate economic design of $\bar{x}$ charts using the process model given by Equation (10-10). Their procedure utilizes certain simplifications in the cost function and its partial derivatives, and imposes a constraint on the power of the test $(1 - \beta)$. To implement their procedure, we must solve the following equations:

$$1 - \beta = \Phi(\delta\sqrt{n} - k) \tag{1}$$

or

$$\delta\sqrt{n} - k = a$$

where $a = 1.2826$ if $1 - \beta = 0.90$ and $a = 1.6449$ if $1 - \beta = 0.95$,

$$\frac{a + k}{\phi(k)} = \frac{\delta^2 a'_3}{a_2 + \lambda g a_4} \tag{2}$$

and

$$h = \left\{ \frac{\alpha a'_3 + a_1 + a_2 n}{\lambda a_4 [(1 - \beta)^{-1} - 0.5]} \right\}^{1/2} \tag{3}$$

where $\phi(z) = (2\pi)^{-1/2} \exp(-z^2/2)$. The solution procedure consists of selecting a value for $1 - \beta$, solving (2) for k, using this value of k in (1) to solve for n, then solving (3) with these values of k and n for h. Apply this procedure to the data of Exercise 10-1. Compare the answer obtained to the exact optimal solution.

10-8 A production process produces items at a rate of R units per hour. When in control, all the parts produced are within specifications. However, an assignable cause occurs randomly at a rate of λ occurrences per hour. When this assignable cause occurs, not all of the product produced meets requirements. Let a_4 be the cost of each nonconforming item, and let a_1 be the cost of inspecting the process. The quality-control rule consists of inspecting the process every h hours. If the process is out of control, then the assignable cause is removed and all nonconforming units produced since the last inspection are discarded.

a. Write an appropriate cost function for this process.

b. Discuss how to find the optimum value of h.

c. Find the standard deviation of h in terms of σ_R, σ_λ, σ_{a_1}, and σ_{a_4}. Discuss the effect of these standard deviations on the standard deviation of h.

10-9 Show that Equation (10-16) can be derived from Equation (10-14) by assuming that samples are taken every $h = 1$ units of time and that $a_1 = a_3' = \Delta = D_0 = D_1 = \tau = 0$.

10-10 A production process is monitored by an $\bar{x}$ chart with samples of size n taken every hour. The test statistic is plotted on a control chart with k-sigma control limits. The number of periods the process remains in the in-control state before a shift occurs is a geometric random variable with parameter $p = 0.0385$. The magnitude of the shift is $\delta = 1.5$. If the cost of sampling is $\$0.5$ per period, the cost of searching for and possibly eliminating assignable causes is $\$50$, and the cost of operating out of control for one period is $\$5$, evaluate the cost of the arbitrary control procedure $n = 8$ and $k = 2.50$.

10-11 Consider the process model given by Equation (10-17). Evaluate $E(S)$ and $E(T^*)$ for the case where the number of periods the process remains in control is Poisson with parameter θ.

a. Using the cost information in Exercise 10-10, evaluate the cost of the control procedure $n = 8$ and $k = 2.50$, assuming that $\theta = 25$.

b. Evaluate the cost function using $n = 2$ and $k = 1.45$. Is this a better control procedure?

c. Describe a production process for which the Poisson distribution would be a reasonable model for the process-failure mechanism.

10-12 Consider the process model given by Equation (10-17). Show that (10-17) reduces to (10-16) when $p(t)$ is the geometric distribution, that is,

$$p(t) = p(1 - p)^t \qquad t = 0, 1, \ldots$$

10-13 Derive the general expressions for $E(S)$ and $E(T^*)$ used in Equation (10-17).

10-14 Assume that $p(t)$ is the logarithmic series distribution

$$p(t) = \begin{cases} \rho & t = 0 \\ \dfrac{\gamma\theta(1 - \rho)}{t} & t = 1, 2, \ldots \end{cases}$$

where $0 < \theta < 1$ and $\gamma = -[\ln(1 - \theta)]^{-1}$.

a. Find the mean of this distribution.

b. Assuming that this distribution represents the duration the process is in control, determine the form of the process model (10-17).

c. Evaluate the cost of the control procedure $n = 8$ and $h = 2.50$ using the cost information in Exercise 10-10. Match the mean time in control with the mean time in control given in Exercise 10-10.

d. Describe a process for which the logarithmic series distribution would be a reasonable process-failure mechanism.

10-15 A process is monitored by an $\bar{x}$ chart. Two assignable causes can occur, with magnitudes $\delta_1 = 0.5$ and $\delta_2 = 2.0$, and with mean occurrence times $1/\lambda_1 = 5.0$ and $1/\lambda_2 = 100$ h. The times to discover these causes are $D_1 = 1$ and $D_2 = 1.5$ h, and the delay time for sampling is $g = 0.05$. The cost coefficients are $a_1 = \$0.50$, $a_2 = \$0.10$, $a_{31} = \$10$, $a_{32} = \$50$, $a_3' = \$25$, $a_{41} = \$100$, and $a_{42} = \$500$.

    a. Using Equation (10-22), evaluate the cost of the control procedure $n = 5$, $k = 3$, and $h = 1$.

    b. Determine the matched single-cause approximate model for this situation. Evaluate the cost of the control procedure given in part (a). Does the matched single-cause model adequately approximate the two assignable-cause process in this case?

    c. Apply the approximate optimization procedure in Exercise 10-7 to the matched single-cause model in part (b).

    d. Determine the optimum solution to the matched single-cause model. Compare this solution to the approximate solution in part (c).

10-16 Develop a process model with multiple assignable causes that is an extension of Equation (10-14). That is, assume that the process is stopped during searches for an assignable cause. Let D_0 be the search time for a false alarm, and D_j, $j = 1, 2, \ldots,$ s, be the search time for the jth assignable cause. Assume that the adjustment cost is Δ_j, if the jth assignable cause is present.

10-17 A process is controlled by a control chart for fraction nonconforming, with parameters $n = 25$, $k = 3$, and $h = 1$. The in-control state is $p_0 = 0.01$, and when the single assignable cause occurs, the process shifts to $p_1 = 0.10$. The mean occurrence time of the assignable cause is $1/\lambda = 100$ h. Assuming that $g = 0.01$, $D = 0.5$, $a_1 = \$0.50$, $a_2 = \$0.05$, $a_3 = \$25$, $a_3' = \$50$, and $a_4 = \$100$, find the expected cost per hour of the control procedure.

10-18 A control chart for fraction nonconforming, with $n = 25$, $k = 3$, and $h = 1$, is used to monitor a process with two states, $p_0 = 0.05$ and $p_1 = 0.10$. The mean occurrence time for the assignable cause is $1/\lambda = 50$ h. The costs and other parameters are $a_1 = \$0.50$, $a_2 = \$0.05$, $a_3' = 75$, $a_4 = \$150$, $g = 0.01$, and $D = 1$.

    a. Find the cost per hour of the control procedure.

    b. Suppose the sample size is increased to $n = 50$. What is the effect on the cost per hour?

    c. Suppose the sampling frequency is changed to $h = 0.5$. What is the effect on the cost per hour?

10-19 Consider the cost model (10-27) for the special case $s = 1$. Write our the cost model in detail for this case. Solve for the steady-state probabilities q_1 and q_2. Suppose that an $\bar{x}$ chart, with $n = 5$, $k = 3$, and $m = 250$, is used. If the production rate is $R = 500$ units per hour, the magnitude of the shift is $\delta = 1.5$, the mean occurrence time of the assignable cause is $1/\lambda = 50$ h, specifications are at $\mu_0 \pm 3\sigma$, and the costs are $a_1 = \$1$, $a_2 = \$0.25$, $a_3 = \$25$, and $a_4 = \$100$, evaluate the cost per unit of the control procedure.

10-20 Suppose that the cost model (10-27) is to be modified for use with the fraction nonconforming control chart. Describe the changes that are required in the model.

PART III

Process Improvement
with Designed Experiments

Quality and productivity improvement is most effective when it is an integral part of the product and process development cycle. In particular, the formal introduction of experimental design methodology at the earliest stage of the development cycle, where new products are designed, existing product designs improved, and manufacturing processes optimized, is often the key to overall product success. This principle has been established in many different industries, including electronics and semiconductors, aerospace, automotive, medical devices, food and pharmaceuticals, and the chemical and process industries. The effective use of sound statistical experimental design methodology can lead to products that are easier to manufacture, have higher reliability, and enhanced field performance. Experimental design can also greatly enhance process development and trouble-shooting activities. This is the primary focus of this section.

Chapter 11 is an introduction to the fundamental concepts of experimental design. The ideas of randomization and blocking are introduced, and the analysis of variance, along with some simple graphical techniques, is presented and used to examine the data from designed experiments. Factorial and fractional factorial designs are introduced in Chapter 12, along with a brief example of response surface methods for process optimization. This chapter also summarizes the contributions of Taguchi to quality engineering and offers a critique of his methodology along with suggested modifications.

The material in this section is not a substitute for a full course on experimental design. The reader who is interested in applying experimental design to process improvement will need additional background, but hopefully this presentation will serve to effectively illustrate some of the many applications of this powerful tool. In many industries, the effective use of statistical experimental design is the key to higher yields, reduced variability, reduced development lead times, better products, and a satisfied customer.

Chapter 11

The Fundamentals
of Experimental Design

11-1 WHAT IS EXPERIMENTAL DESIGN?

As indicated in Chapter 1, a designed experiment is a test or series of tests in which purposeful changes are made to the input variables of a process so that we may observe and identify corresponding changes in the output response. The process, as shown in Figure 11-1, can be visualized as some combination of machines, methods and people that transforms an input material into an output product. This output product has one or more observable quality characteristics or responses. Some of the process variables $x_1 x_2, \ldots, x_p$ are controllable, while others $z_1, z_2, \ldots, z_q$ are uncontrollable (although they may be controllable for purposes of the test). Sometimes these uncontrollable factors are called *noise* factors. The objectives of the experiment may include

1. Determining which variables are most influential on the response, y.
2. Determining where to set the influential x's so that y is near the nominal requirement.
3. Determining where to set the influential x's so that variability in y is small.
4. Determining where to set the influential x's so that the effects of the uncontrollable variables z are minimized.

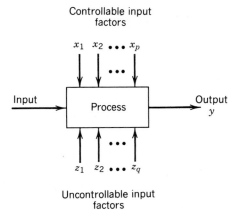

Figure 11-1
General model of a process.

Thus, experimental design methods may be used either in process development or process troubleshooting to improve process performance or to obtain a process that is *robust* or insensitive to external sources of variability.

Statistical process control methods and experimental design, two very powerful tools for the improvement and optimization of processes, are closely interrelated. For example, if a process is in statistical control but still has poor capability, then to improve process capability it will be necessary to reduce variability. Experiment design may offer a more effective way to do this than SPC. Essentially, SPC is a *passive* statistical method: we watch the process and wait for some information that will lead to a useful change. However, if the process is in control, passive observation may not produce much useful information. On the other hand, experimental design is an *active* statistical method: we will actually perform a series of tests on the process making changes in the inputs and observing the corresponding changes in the outputs, and this will produce information that can lead to process improvement.

Experimental design methods can also be very useful in establishing statistical control of a process. For example, suppose that a control chart indicates that the process is out of control, and the process has many controllable input variables. Unless we know *which* input variables are the important ones, it may be very difficult to bring the process under control. Experimental design methods can be used to identify these influential process variables.

Experimental design is a critically important engineering tool for improving a manufacturing process. It also has extensive application in the development of new processes. Application of these techniques early in process development can result in

1. Improved yield.
2. Reduced variability and closer conformance to nominal.
3. Reduced development time.
4. Reduced overall costs.

Experimental design methods can also play a major role in engineering *design* activities, where new *products* are developed and existing ones improved. Some applications of statistical experimental design in engineering design include

1. Evaluation and comparison of basic design configurations.
2. Evaluation of material alternatives.
3. Determination of key product design parameters that impact performance.

Use of experimental design in these areas can result in improved manufacturability of the product, enhanced field performance and reliability, lower product cost, and shorter product development time.

11-2 EXAMPLES OF EXPERIMENTAL DESIGN IN QUALITY AND PROCESS IMPROVEMENT

In this section, we present several examples that illustrate the application of designed experiments in improving process and product quality. In subsequent sections, we will demonstrate the statistical methods used to analyze the data and draw conclusions from experiments such as these.

Example 11-1

Characterizing a Process

A manufacturing engineer has applied SPC to a process for soldering electronic components to printed circuit boards. Through the use of u charts and Pareto analysis he has established statistical control of the flow solder process and has reduced the average number of defective solder joints per board to around 1%. However, since the average board contains over 2000 solder joints, even 1% defective presents far too many solder joints requiring rework. The engineer would like to reduce defect levels even further; however, since the process is in statistical control, it is not obvious what machine adjustments will be necessary.

The flow solder machine has several variables that can be controlled. They include:

1. Solder temperature
2. Preheat temperature
3. Conveyor speed
4. Flux type
5. Flux specific gravity
6. Solder wave depth
7. Conveyor angle

In addition to these controllable factors, several others cannot be easily controlled during routine manufacturing, although they could be controlled for purposes of a test. They are

1. Thickness of the printed circuit board

2. Types of components used on the board
3. Layout of the components on the board
4. Operator
5. Production rate

In this situation, the engineer is interested in *characterizing* the flow solder machine; that is, he wants to determine which factors (both controllable and uncontrollable) affect the occurrence of defects on the printed circuit boards. To accomplish this task he can design an experiment that will enable him to estimate the magnitude and direction of the factor effects. That is, how much does the response variable (defects per unit) change when each factor is changed, and does changing the factors *together* produce different results than are obtained from individual factor adjustments? Sometimes we call this kind of experiment a *screening* experiment.

The information from this screening or characterization experiment will be used to identify the critical process factors and to determine the direction of adjustment for these factors to further reduce the number of defects per unit. The experiment may also provide information about which factors should be more carefully controlled during routine manufacturing to prevent high defect levels and erratic process performance. Thus, one result of the experiment could be the application of control charts to one or more *process* variables (such as solder temperature) in addition to the *u* chart on process output. Over time, if the process is sufficiently improved, it may be possible to base most of the process control plan on controlling process input variables instead of control charting the output.

Example 11-2

Optimizing a Process

In a characterization experiment, we are usually interested in determining which process variables affect the response. A logical next step is to optimize, that is, to determine the region in the important factors that lead to the best possible response. For example, if the response is yield, we will look for a region of maximum yield, and if the response is variability in a critical product dimension, we will look for a region of minimum variability.

Suppose we are interested in improving the yield of a chemical process. We know from the results of a characterization experiment (say) that the two most important process variables that influence yield are operating temperature and reaction time. The process currently runs at 155° F and 1.7 h of reaction time, producing yields around 75%. Figure 11-2 shows a view of the time–temperature region from above. In this graph the lines of constant yield are connected to form response *contours*, and we have shown the contour lines for 60, 70, 80, 90, and 95% yield.

To locate the optimum, it is necessary to perform an experiment that varies time and temperature together. This type of experiment is called a *factorial* experiment; an example of a factorial experiment with both time and temperature run at two levels is shown in Figure 11-2. The responses observed at the four

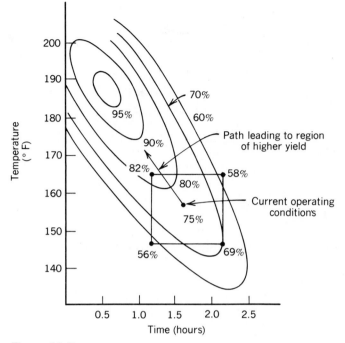

Figure 11-2
Contour plot of yield as a function of reaction time and
reaction temperature, illustrating an optimization experiment.

corners of the square indicate that we should move in the general direction of increased temperature and decreased reaction time to increase yield. A few additional runs could be performed in this direction which would be sufficient to locate the region of maximum yield.

Example 11-3

A Product Design Example

Experimental design methods can often be applied in the product design process. To illustrate, suppose that a group of engineers are designing a door hinge for an automobile. The quality characteristic of interest is the check effort, or the holding ability of the door latch that prevents the door from swinging closed when the vehicle is parked on a hill. The check mechanism consists of a spring and a roller. When the door is opened, the roller travels through an arc causing the leaf spring to be compressed. To close the door, the spring must be forced aside, which creates the check effort. The engineering team believes the check effort is a function of the following factors:

1. Roller travel distance
2. Spring height pivot to base

3. Horizontal distance from pivot to spring

4. Free height of the reinforcement spring

5. Free height of the main spring

The engineers build a prototype hinge mechanism in which all these factors can be varied over certain ranges. Once appropriate levels for these five factors are identified, an experiment can be designed consisting of various combinations of the factor levels, and the prototype hinge can be tested at these combinations. This will produce information concerning which factors are most influential on latch check effort, and through use of this information the design can be improved.

Example 11-4

Determining System and Component Tolerances

The Wheatstone bridge shown in Figure 11-3 is a device used for measuring an unknown resistance, Y. The adjustable resistor B is manipulated until a particular current flow is obtained through the ammeter (usually $X = 0$). Then the unknown resistance is calculated as

$$Y = \frac{BD}{C} - \frac{X^2}{C^2 E} [A(D + C) + D(B + C)][B(C + D) + F(B + C)] \quad (11\text{-}1)$$

The engineer wants to design the circuit so that overall gage capability is good; that is, he would like the standard deviation of measurement error to be small. He has decided that $A = 20\Omega$, $C = 2\Omega$, $D = 50\Omega$, $E = 1.5$ V, and $F = 2\Omega$ is the best choice of the design parameters as far as gage capability is concerned, but the overall measurement error is still too high. This is likely due to the tolerances that have been specified on the circuit components. These tolerances are $\pm 1\%$ for each resistor A, B, C, D, and F, and $\pm 5\%$ for the power supply E. These tolerance bands can be used to define appropriate factor levels, and an experiment can be

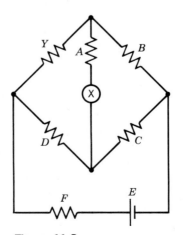

Figure 11-3
A wheatstone bridge.

performed to determine which circuit components have the most critical tolerances and how much they must be tightened to produce adequate gage capability. The information from this experiment will result in a design specification that tightens only the most critical tolerances the minimum amount possible consistent with desired measurement capability. Consequently, a lower cost design that is easier to manufacture will be possible.

Notice that in this experiment it is unnecessary actually to build hardware, since the response from the circuit can be calculated via Equation (11-1). The actual response variable for the experiment should be the standard deviation of Y. However, an equation for the transmitted variation in Y from the circuit can be found using the methods of Section 9-6.2. Therefore, the entire experiment can be performed using a computer model of the Wheatstone bridge.

11-3 EXPERIMENTS WITH ONE FACTOR

In this section, we begin a more detailed presentation of experimental design methods and introduce the appropriate methods of analyzing the resulting data. Initially, we will consider the simplest type of experiment—one with a single factor of interest.

11-3.1 An Example

A manufacturer of paper used for making grocery bags is interested in improving the tensile strength of the product. The manufacturing process specifications currently call for 10% hardwood concentration in the pulp, and at this level, the paper has an average tensile strength of about 15 psi. The process is in statistical control, as evidenced by the control charts shown in Figure 11-4.

The process engineer and the operators suspect that tensile strength is a function of pulp hardwood concentration and that tensile strength should be high at higher hardwood concentration. Process economics dictates that the range of practical interest on hardwood concentration is between 5 and 20%. The process engineer decides to investigate four levels of hardwood concentration: 5%, 10%, 15%, and 20%. She also decides to make up six test specimens at each concentration level, using a pilot plant. All 24 specimens are tested on a laboratory tensile tester, in random order. The data from this experiment are shown in Table 11-1.

This is an example of a completely randomized single-factor experiment with four levels of the factor. Each factor level has six observations or *replicates*. The role of *randomization* in this experiment is extremely important. By randomizing the order of the 24 runs, the effect of any nuisance variable that may impact the observed tensile strength is approximately balanced out. For example, suppose that there is a warm-up effect on the tensile-tester; that is, the longer the machine is on, the greater the observed tensile strength. If the 24 runs are made in order of increasing hardwood concentration (that is, all six 5% concentration specimens are tested first, followed by all six 10% concentration specimens, etc.), then any observed differences in hardwood concentration may also be due to the warm-up effect.

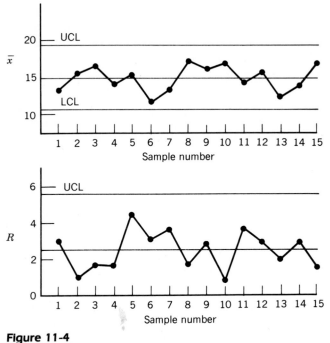

Figure 11-4
$\bar{x}$ and R charts for the paper manufacturing process.

It is important to analyze graphically the data from a designed experiment. Figure 11-5 presents box plots of tensile strength at the four hardwood concentration levels. These plots indicate that changing the hardwood concentration has a strong effect on tensile strength; specifically, higher hardwood concentrations produce higher observed tensile strength. Furthermore, the distribution of tensile strength at a particular hardwood level is reasonably symmetrical, and the variability in tensile strength does not change very much as the hardwood concentration changes.

Graphical interpretation of the data is always a good idea. Box plots show the variability of the observations *within* a factor level and the variability *between* factor levels. We now show how the data from a single-factor randomized experiment can be analyzed statistically.

Table 11-1
Tensile strength of paper (psi)

Hardwood Concentration (%)	Observations						Totals	Averages
	1	2	3	4	5	6		
5	7	8	15	11	9	10	60	10.00
10	12	17	13	18	19	15	94	15.67
15	14	18	19	17	16	18	102	17.00
20	19	25	22	23	18	20	127	21.17
							383	15.96

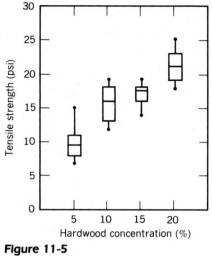

Figure 11-5
Box plots of hardwood concentration
data.

11-3.2 The Analysis of Variance

Suppose we have *a* different levels of a single factor that we wish to compare. The observed response at each of the factor levels is a random variable. The data would appear as in Table 11-2. An entry in Table 11-2, say y_{ij}, represents the *j*th observation taken under factor level *i*. We consider the case where there are an equal number of observations, *n*, at each factor level.

We may describe the observations in Table 11-2 by the model

$$y_{ij} = \mu + \tau_i + \epsilon_{ij} \begin{cases} i = 1, 2, \ldots, a \\ j = 1, 2, \ldots, n \end{cases} \tag{11-2}$$

where y_{ij} is the (*ij*)th observation, μ is a parameter common to all factors called the overall mean, τ_i is a parameter associated with the *i*th factor level called the *i*th factor effect, and ϵ_{ij} is a random error component. We would like to test certain hypotheses about factor effects and to estimate them. For hypothesis testing, the model errors are assumed to be normally and independently distributed random variables with mean zero and variance σ^2 [abbreviated NID(0, σ^2)]. The variance

Table 11-2
Typical data for a single-factor experiment

Factor Level	Observation				Totals	Averages
1	y_{11}	y_{12}	$\cdots$	y_{1n}	$y_{1.}$	$\bar{y}_{1.}$
2	y_{21}	y_{22}	$\cdots$	y_{2n}	$y_{2.}$	$\bar{y}_{2.}$
$\vdots$	$\vdots$	$\vdots$	$\cdots$	$\vdots$	$\vdots$	$\vdots$
a	y_{a1}	y_{a2}	$\cdots$	y_{an}	$y_{a.}$	$\bar{y}_{a.}$
					$y_{..}$	$\bar{y}_{..}$

σ^2 is assumed constant for all levels of the factor. Typically, the model errors result from measurement error, the effects of variables not included in the experiment, variation due to chance causes in the process, and so on.

The model of Equation (11-2) is called the *one-way* analysis of variance model, because only one factor is investigated. Furthermore, we will require that the observations be taken in random order so that the environment in which the factors are used (often called the experimental units) is as uniform as possible. This is called a completely randomized experimental design. The *a* factor levels in the experiment can be chosen in two different ways. First, they can be specifically chosen by the experimenter. In this situation we wish to test hypotheses about the τ_i, and conclusions will apply only to the factor levels considered in the analysis. The conclusions cannot be extended to similar factor levels that were not considered. This is called the *fixed effects* model. Alternatively, the *a* factor levels can be a random sample from a larger population of levels. In this situation we want to be able to extend the conclusions (which are based on the sample) to *all* factor levels in the population, whether or not they are explicitly considered in the analysis. Here the τ_i are random variables, and knowledge about the particular ones investigated is relatively useless. Instead, we test hypotheses about the variability of the τ_i and try to estimate this variability. This is called the *random effects*, or *components-of-variance*, model. We give an example of this type of experiment in Section 11-3.5.

In this section we will present the analysis of variance for the single-factor fixed effects model. In the fixed effects model, the factor effects τ_i are usually defined as deviations from the overall mean, so that

$$\sum_{i=1}^{a} \tau_i = 0 \qquad (11\text{-}3)$$

Let $y_{i.}$ represent the total of the observations for the *i*th factor level and $\bar{y}_{i.}$ represent the average of the observations under the *i*th factor level. Similarly, let $y_{..}$ represent the grand total of all observations and $\bar{y}_{..}$ represent the grand average of all observations. Expressed mathematically,

$$y_{i.} = \sum_{j=1}^{n} y_{ij} \qquad \bar{y}_{i.} = y_{i.}/n \qquad i = 1, 2, \ldots, a$$

$$y_{..} = \sum_{i=1}^{a} \sum_{j=1}^{n} y_{ij} \qquad \bar{y}_{..} = y_{..}/N \qquad (11\text{-}4)$$

where $N = an$ is the total number of observations. Thus, the "dot" subscript notation implies summation over the subscript that it replaces.

We are interested in testing the equality of the *a* factor level means. Using Equation (11-3), we find that the appropriate hypotheses are

$$H_0: \quad \tau_1 = \tau_2 = \cdots = \tau_a = 0$$
$$H_1: \quad \tau_i \neq 0 \text{ for at least one } i \qquad (11\text{-}5)$$

That is, if the null hypothesis is true, then each observation is made up of the overall mean μ plus a realization of the random error ϵ_{ij}.

The test procedure for the hypotheses in Equation (11-5) is called the analysis of variance. The term "analysis of variance" results from partitioning total variability in the data into its component parts. The total corrected sum of squares, which is a measure of total variability in the data, may be written as

$$\sum_{i=1}^{a} \sum_{j=1}^{n} (y_{ij} - \bar{y}_{..})^2 = \sum_{i=1}^{a} \sum_{j=1}^{n} [(\bar{y}_{i.} - \bar{y}_{..}) + (y_{ij} - \bar{y}_{i.})]^2 \qquad (11\text{-}6)$$

or

$$\sum_{i=1}^{a} \sum_{j=1}^{n} (y_{ij} - \bar{y}_{..})^2 = n \sum_{i=1}^{a} (\bar{y}_{i.} - \bar{y}_{..})^2 + \sum_{i=1}^{a} \sum_{j=1}^{n} (y_{ij} - \bar{y}_{i.})^2$$
$$+ 2 \sum_{i=1}^{a} \sum_{j=1}^{n} (\bar{y}_{i.} - \bar{y}_{..})(y_{ij} - \bar{y}_{i.}) \qquad (11\text{-}7)$$

The cross-product term in Equation (11-7) is zero, so

$$\sum_{i=1}^{a} \sum_{j=1}^{n} (y_{ij} - \bar{y}_{..})^2 = n \sum_{i=1}^{a} (\bar{y}_{i.} - \bar{y}_{..})^2 + \sum_{i=1}^{a} \sum_{j=1}^{n} (y_{ij} - \bar{y}_{i.})^2 \qquad (11\text{-}8)$$

Equation (11-8) shows that the total variability in the data, measured by the total corrected sum of squares, can be partitioned into a sum of squares of differences between factor-level averages and the grand average and a sum of squares of differences of observations within a specific factor level and the factor-level average. Differences between observed factor-level averages and the grand average measures the differences between factor levels, while differences of observations within a factor level from the factor-level average can be due only to random error. Therefore, we write Equation (11-8) symbolically as

$$SS_T = SS_{\text{Factor}} + SS_E$$

where SS_T is the total sum of squares, SS_{Factor} is called the sum of squares due to the factor, and SS_E is called the sum of squares due to error.

If SS_{Factor} is large, it is due to differences among the means at the different factor levels. Thus, by comparing the magnitude of SS_{Factor} to SS_E we can see how much variability is due to changing factor levels and how much is due to error. This comparison is facilitated if we first scale these sums of squares by dividing them by their number of degrees of freedom. There are $an = N$ total observations; thus, SS_T has $N - 1$ degrees of freedom. There are a levels of the factor, so SS_{Factor} has $a - 1$ degrees of freedom. Finally, within any factor level there are n replicates providing $n - 1$ degrees of freedom with which to estimate the experimental error. Since there are a factor levels, we have $a(n - 1) = an - a = N - a$ degrees of freedom for error.

The ratio of a sum of squares to its number of degrees of freedom is called a mean square; thus

$$MS_{\text{Factor}} = \frac{SS_{\text{Factor}}}{a - 1}$$

and

$$MS_E = \frac{SS_E}{a(n - 1)}$$

Table 11-3
Analysis of variance for a single-factor experiment

Source of Variation	Sum of Squares	Degrees of Freedom	Mean Square	F_0
Between factor levels	SS_{Factor}	$a - 1$	MS_{Factor}	$F_0 = \dfrac{MS_{\text{Factor}}}{MS_E}$
Error (within factor levels)	SS_E	$a(n - 1)$	MS_E	
Total	SS_T	$an - 1$		

It can be shown that the mean square error MS_E estimates the variance of the experimental error, σ^2. In addition, MS_{Factor} estimates σ^2 only if all factor-level means are equal, but the value of MS_{Factor} will be greater than σ^2 if the factor-level means are different. This leads to a statistical test based on the F distribution for the equality of the factor means using the test statistic

$$F_0 = \frac{MS_{\text{Factor}}}{MS_E}$$

If $F_0 > F_{\alpha,\,a-1,\,a(n-1)}$, we may conclude that the factor-level means are different. The test procedure is usually summarized in an analysis of variance table, such as Table 11-3.

An analysis of variance computer program is usually employed to analyze the data from a designed experiment, so that manual computation of the test statistic F_0 is unnecessary. However, for completeness, convenient computing formulas for the sums of squares are

$$SS_T = \sum_{i=1}^{a} \sum_{j=1}^{n} y_{ij}^2 - \frac{y_{..}^2}{an} \tag{11-9}$$

and

$$SS_{\text{Factor}} = \sum_{i=1}^{a} \frac{y_{i.}^2}{n} - \frac{y_{..}^2}{an} \tag{11-10}$$

The error sum of squares is obtained by subtraction as

$$SS_E = SS_T - SS_{\text{Factor}} \tag{11-11}$$

Example 11-5

Consider the hardwood concentration experiment described in Section 11-3.1. We can use the analysis of variance to test the hypothesis that different hardwood concentrations do not affect the mean tensile strength of the paper. The sums of squares for analysis of variance are computed from Equations (11-9), (11-10), and

Table 11-4
Analysis of variance for the tensile strength data

Source of Variation	Sum of Squares	Degrees of Freedom	Mean Square	F_0
Hardwood concentration	382.79	3	127.60	$F_0 = 19.61$
Error	130.17	20	6.51	
Total	512.96	23		

(11-11) as follows:

$$SS_T = \sum_{i=1}^{4} \sum_{j=1}^{4} y_{ij}^2 - \frac{y_{..}^2}{an}$$

$$= (7)^2 + (8)^2 + \cdots + (20)^2 - \frac{(383)^2}{24} = 512.96$$

$$SS_{\text{Factor}} = \sum_{i=1}^{4} \frac{y_{i.}^2}{n} - \frac{y_{..}^2}{an}$$

$$= \frac{(60)^2 + (94)^2 + (102)^2 + (127)^2}{6} - \frac{(383)^2}{24} = 382.79$$

$$SS_E = SS_T - SS_{\text{Factor}}$$
$$= 512.96 - 382.79 = 130.17$$

Typically, this analysis would be performed using a computer, not manually. The analysis of variance is summarized in Table 11-4. Since $F_{0.01,3,20} = 4.94$, we would conclude that changing pulp hardwood concentration affects the tensile strength of the paper. Coupled with inspection of Figure 11-5, the statistical analysis of this experiment implies that by increasing hardwood concentration to 20%, we can increase tensile strength significantly, to an average level of about 20 psi. The engineer and the operators make the change, and the control charts on tensile strength following the increase in pulp hardwood concentration that are shown in Figure 11-6 confirm that mean tensile strength has increased. There has been no apparent change in process variability.

11-3.3 Residual Analysis

The analysis of variance assumes that the observations are normally and independently distributed with the same variance in each factor level. These assumptions should be checked by examining the residuals. We define a residual as the difference between the actual observation y_{ij} and the value $\hat{y}_{ij}$ that would be obtained from a least-squares fit of the underlying analysis of variance model to the sample data. For the type of experimental design in this situation, the value $\hat{y}_{ij}$ is just the factor-level mean $\bar{y}_{i.}$. Therefore, the residual is $e_{ij} = y_{ij} - \bar{y}_{i.}$; that is, the difference between an observation and the corresponding factor-level mean. The residuals for the hardwood percentage experiment are shown in Table 11-5.

The normality assumption can be checked by plotting the residuals on normal probability paper. To check the assumption of equal variances at each factor level, plot the residuals against the factor levels and compare the spread in the residuals.

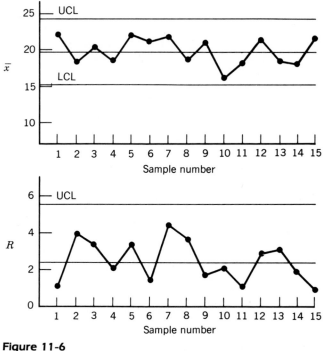

Figure 11-6
Control charts on tensile strength after changing pulp
hardwood concentration.

It is also useful to plot the residuals against $\bar{y}_{i.}$ (sometimes called the *fitted value*); the variability in the residuals should not depend in any way on the value of $\bar{y}_{i.}$. When a pattern appears in these plots, it usually suggests the need for data *transformation*, that is, analyzing the data in a different metric. For example, if the variability in the residuals increases with $\bar{y}_{i.}$ then a transformation such as log y or $\sqrt{y}$ should be considered. In some problems the dependency of residual scatter on $\bar{y}_{i.}$ is very important information. It may be desirable to select the factor level that results in maximum y; however, this level may also cause more variation in response from run to run.

The independence assumption can be checked by plotting the residuals against the run order in which the experiment was performed. A pattern in this plot, such as sequences of positive and negative residuals, may indicate that the observations are not independent. This suggests that run order is important or that variables that change over time are important and have not been included in the experimental design.

Table 11-5
Residuals for the hardwood experiment

Hardwood Concentration	Residuals					
5%	−3.00	−2.00	5.00	1.00	1.00	0.00
10%	−3.37	1.33	−2.67	2.33	−3.33	0.67
15%	−3.00	1.00	2.00	0.00	−1.00	1.00
20%	−2.17	3.83	0.83	1.83	−3.17	−1.17

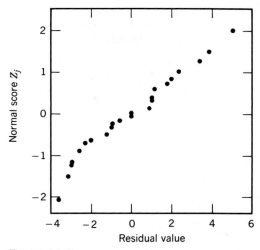

Figure 11-7
Normal probability plot of residuals from the
hardwood concentration experiment. In this
plot the vertical axis is the normal score z_j
corresponding to the probability p_j. Many
computer programs produce normal
probability plots using this choice of scaling.

A normal probability plot of the residuals from the hardwood concentration experiment is shown in Figure 11-7. Figures 11-8 and 11-9 present the residuals plotted against the factor levels and the fitted value $\bar{y}_{i.}$. These plots do not reveal any model inadequacy or unusual problem with the assumptions.

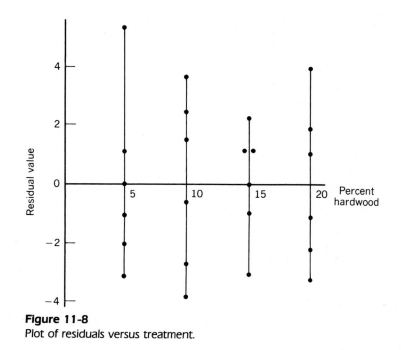

Figure 11-8
Plot of residuals versus treatment.

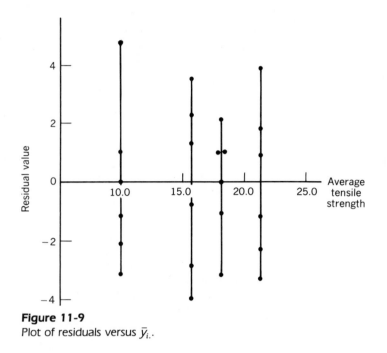

Figure 11-9
Plot of residuals versus $\bar{y}_{i.}$.

11-3.4 Comparison of Individual Means

In the tensile strength example of the previous two sections, we used the statistical results of the analysis of variance and the graphical interpretation of Figure 11-5 to conclude that increasing the hardwood concentration in the pulp to 20% would increase average tensile strength. In some problems it is important to have a less subjective method for comparing factor-level means.

If we know σ, any factor level average will have standard deviation $\sigma/\sqrt{n}$. Consequently, if all factor-level means were the same, the $\bar{y}_{i.}$ values would behave as if they were a set of a observations from the same normal distribution with standard deviation $\sigma/\sqrt{n}$. Visualize a normal distribution that can slide along a horizontal axis on which the values $\bar{y}_{1.}, \bar{y}_{2.}, \ldots, \bar{y}_{a.}$ are plotted. There should be some position for this normal distribution that makes it seem obvious that the $\bar{y}_{i.}$ values were all generated from this distribution. If not, the $\bar{y}_{i.}$ that appear not to have been drawn from this distribution are associated with factor levels that produce different mean response.

Since σ is unknown, as an approximation we may replace it with $\sqrt{MS_E}$ from the analysis of variance and use a t distribution with scale factor $\sqrt{MS_E/n}$. Such an arrangement for the tensile strength data of Example 11-5 is shown in Figure 11-10.

To sketch the t distribution in Figure 11-10, simply multiply the abscissa t value by the scale factor $\sqrt{MS_E/n} = \sqrt{6.51/6} = 1.04$ and plot this against the ordinate of t at that point. Since the t looks much like the normal, except that it is a little flatter near the center and has longer tails, this sketch is usually easily constructed by eye. The distribution can have an arbitrary origin, although it is best to choose one in the region of the $\bar{y}_{i.}$ values to be compared. In Figure 11-10, the origin is 15 psi.

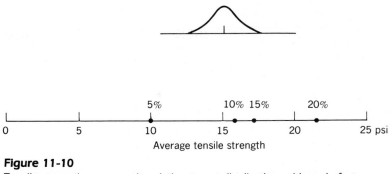

Figure 11-10
Tensile strength averages in relation to a *t* distribution with scale factor $\sqrt{MS_E/n} = \sqrt{6.51/6} = 1.04$.

Now visualize sliding the distribution in Figure 11-10 along the horizontal axis, and examine the four sample means plotted in the figure. Note that there is no place to locate the distribution so that all four averages seem to be typical randomly selected observations. This implies that all four means are not equal; thus, the figure is a graphical display of the *results* of the analysis of variance. The figure *does*, however, make it very clear that 5% concentration would produce much lower tensile strengths than would 10 or 15% concentrations (which are about equivalent), and that 20% concentration would produce the largest mean tensile strength for the product.

The procedure that we have just outlined is a rough but effective form of *multiple comparison*. More formal methods of making multiple comparisons are available and are described in experimental design texts [for example, see Montgomery (1984)]. In many practical cases, the simple graphical method described here works very well.

11-3.5 A Components-of-Variance Model

In many experiments, the factor of interest has a large number of possible levels. The analyst is interested in drawing conclusions about the entire *population* of factor levels. If the experimenter randomly selects *a* of these levels from the population of factor levels, then we say that the factor is a *random* factor. Because the levels of the factor actually used in the experiment were chosen randomly, the conclusions reached will be valid about the entire population of factor levels. We will assume that the population of factor levels is either of infinite size or is large enough to be considered infinite.

The underlying model is still

$$y_{ij} = \mu + \tau_i + \epsilon_{ij} \begin{cases} i = 1, 2, \ldots, a \\ j = 1, 2, \ldots, n \end{cases} \qquad (11\text{-}12)$$

where τ_i and ϵ_{ij} are independent random variables. Note that the model is identical in structure to the fixed effects case, but the parameters have a different interpretation. If the variance of τ_i is σ_τ^2, then the variance of any observation is

$$\sigma_y^2 = \sigma_\tau^2 + \sigma^2$$

The variances σ_τ^2 and σ^2 are called *variance components*, and the model, Equation (11-12), is called the *components-of-variance* or the *random effects* model. To test hypotheses in this model, we require that the $\{\epsilon_{ij}\}$ are NID$(0, \sigma^2)$, that the $\{\tau_i\}$ are NID$(0, \sigma_\tau^2)$, and that τ_i and ϵ_{ij} are independent.

The sum of squares identity

$$SS_T = SS_{\text{Factor}} + SS_E \tag{11-13}$$

and all analysis of variance calculations are identical to the fixed effects case discussed previously. However, in the components-of-variance case, the ratio

$$F_0 = \frac{MS_{\text{Factor}}}{MS_E}$$

tests the hypotheses

$$H_0: \quad \sigma_\tau^2 = 0$$
$$H_i: \quad \sigma_\tau^2 > 0$$

If $\sigma_\tau^2 = 0$, all factor levels are identical; but if $\sigma_\tau^2 > 0$, then factor levels differ. Reasonable estimates of the variance components are

$$\hat{\sigma}^2 = MS_E \tag{11-14}$$

and

$$\hat{\sigma}_\tau^2 = \frac{MS_{\text{Factor}} - MS_E}{n} \tag{11-15}$$

Example 11-6

In his book *Design and Analysis of Experiments*, 2nd ed. (John Wiley, 1984), D. C. Montgomery describes a single-factor experiment involving variance components. A textile manufacturing company weaves a fabric on a large number of looms. The company is interested in loom-to-loom variability in tensile strength. To investigate this possibility, a manufacturing engineer selects four looms at random and makes four strength determinations on fabric samples chosen at random from each loom. The data are shown in Table 11-6, and the analysis of variance is summarized in Table 11-7.

From the analysis of variance, we conclude that the looms in the plant differ significantly in their ability to produce fabric of uniform strength. The variance components are estimated by $\hat{\sigma}^2 = 1.90$ and

$$\hat{\sigma}_\tau^2 = \frac{29.73 - 1.90}{4} = 6.96$$

Table 11-6
Strength data for Example 11-6

Loom	Observations				Total	Average
	1	2	3	4		
1	98	97	99	96	390	97.5
2	91	90	93	92	366	91.5
3	96	95	97	95	383	95.8
4	95	96	99	98	388	97.0
					1527	95.4

Therefore, the variance of strength in the *manufacturing process* is estimated by

$$\hat{\sigma}_y^2 = \hat{\sigma}_\tau^2 + \hat{\sigma}^2$$
$$= 6.96 + 1.90$$
$$= 8.86$$

Most of this variability is attributable to differences *between* looms.

This example illustrates an important application of analysis of variance—the isolation of different sources of variability in a manufacturing process. Problems of excessive variability in critical functional parameters or properties frequently arise in quality-improvement programs. For example, in the fabric strength example above, the process mean is estimated by $\bar{y}_{..} = 95.45$ psi and the process standard deviation is estimated by $\hat{\sigma}_y = \sqrt{\hat{V}(y_{ij})} = \sqrt{8.86} = 2.98$ psi. If strength is approximately normally distributed, this would imply a distribution of strength in the outgoing product that looks like the normal distribution in Figure 11-11a. If the lower specification limit (LSL) on strength is at 90 psi, then a substantial proportion of the production is *fallout*. This fallout is directly related to the excess variability resulting from *differences between looms*. Variability in loom performance can be caused by faulty set-up, poor maintenance, inadequate supervision, poorly trained operators, and so forth. The engineer or manager responsible for quality improvement must identify and remove these sources of variability from the process. If he can do so, then strength variability will be greatly reduced, perhaps

Table 11-7
Analysis of variance for the strength data

Source of Variation	Sum of Squares	Degrees of Freedom	Mean Square	F_0
Looms	89.19	3	29.73	15.68
Error	22.75	12	1.90	
Total	111.94	15		

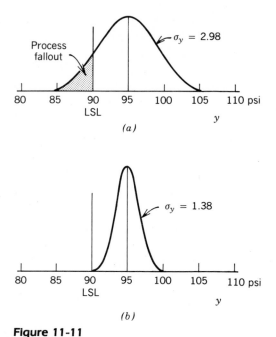

Figure 11-11
The distribution of fabric strength.
(*a*) Distribution of fabric strength, current process. (*b*) The distribution of fabric strength, improved process.

as low as $\hat{\sigma}_y = \hat{\sigma} = \sqrt{1.90} = 1.38$ psi, as shown in Figure 11*b*. In this improved process, reducing the variability in strength has greatly reduced the fallout and increased overall process capability. The ultimate result is a more satisfied customer.

11-4 BLOCKING AND NUISANCE FACTORS

11-4.1 The Randomized Block Design

In many experimental problems it is necessary to design the experiment so that variability arising from nuisance variables can be controlled. As an example, suppose we wish to compare the effect of four different chemicals on the strength of a particular fabric. It is known that the effect of these chemicals varies considerably from one fabric specimen to another. Therefore, we can select several pieces of fabric and compare all four chemicals within the relatively homogeneous conditions provided by each piece of fabric. This will remove any variation due to the fabric. This type of experimental design is called a randomized complete block design.

The general procedure for a randomized complete block design consists of selecting *b* blocks and running a complete replicate of the experiment in each block. There will be a observations (one per factor level) in each block, and the order in which these observations are run is randomly assigned within the block.

We will briefly outline the statistical analysis for a randomized block design. Suppose that a single factor with a levels is of interest, and the experiment is run in b blocks. The observations may be represented by the model

$$y_{ij} = \mu + \tau_i + \beta_j + \epsilon_{ij} \begin{cases} i = 1, 2, \ldots, a \\ j = 1, 2, \ldots, b \end{cases} \tag{11-16}$$

where μ is an overall mean, τ_i is the effect of the ith factor level, β_j is the effect of the jth block, and ϵ_{ij} is the usual NID$(0, \sigma^2)$ random error term. Factors and blocks will be considered initially as fixed factors. Furthermore, the factor and block effects are defined as deviations from the overall mean, so that $\sum_{i=1}^{a} \tau_i = 0$ and $\sum_{j=1}^{b} \beta_j = 0$. We are interested in testing the equality of the factor effects. That is,

$$H_0: \quad \tau_1 = \tau_2 = \cdots = \tau_a = 0$$
$$H_1: \quad \tau_i \neq 0 \text{ at least one } i$$

Let $y_{i.}$ be the total of all observations taken under factor level i; $y_{.j}$ be the total of all observations in block j; $y_{..}$ be the grand total of all observations; and $N = ab$ be the total number of observations. Similarly, $\bar{y}_{i.}$ is the average of the observations taken under factor i; $\bar{y}_{.j}$ is the average of the observations in block j; and $\bar{y}_{..}$ is the grand average of all observations. The total corrected sum of squares is

$$\sum_{i=1}^{a} \sum_{j=1}^{b} (y_{ij} - \bar{y}_{..})^2 = \sum_{i=1}^{a} \sum_{i=1}^{b} [(\bar{y}_{i.} - \bar{y}_{..}) + (\bar{y}_{.j} - \bar{y}_{..}) + (y_{ij} - \bar{y}_{i.} - \bar{y}_{.j} + \bar{y}_{..})]^2 \tag{11-17}$$

Expanding the right-hand side of Equation (11-17) yields

$$\sum_{i=1}^{a} \sum_{j=1}^{b} (y_{ij} - \bar{y}_{..})^2 = b \sum_{i=1}^{a} (\bar{y}_{i.} - \bar{y}_{..})^2 + a \sum_{j=1}^{b} (\bar{y}_{.j} - \bar{y}_{..})^2$$
$$+ \sum_{i=1}^{a} \sum_{j=1}^{b} (y_{ij} - \bar{y}_{.j} - \bar{y}_{i.} + \bar{y}_{..})^2 \tag{11-18}$$

or, symbolically,

$$SS_T = SS_{\text{Factor}} + SS_{\text{Blocks}} + SS_E \tag{11-19}$$

The degree of freedom breakdown corresponding to Equation (11-19) is

$$ab - 1 = (a - 1) + (b - 1) + (a - 1)(b - 1) \tag{11-20}$$

The null hypothesis of no difference in factor level means ($H_0: \tau_i = 0$) is tested by the F ratio MS_{Factor}/MS_E. The analysis of variance is summarized in Table 11-8. Computing formulas for the sums of squares are also shown in this table. The same test procedure is used in cases where factors and/or blocks are random.

Table 11-8
Analysis of variance for randomized complete block design

Source of Variation	Sum of Squares	Degrees of Freedom	Mean Square	F_0
Factor	$\sum_{i=1}^{a} \dfrac{y_{i.}^2}{b} - \dfrac{y_{..}^2}{ab}$	$a-1$	$\dfrac{SS_{\text{Factor}}}{a-1}$	$\dfrac{MS_{\text{Factor}}}{MS_E}$
Blocks	$\sum_{j=1}^{b} \dfrac{y_{.j}^2}{a} - \dfrac{y_{..}^2}{ab}$	$b-1$	$\dfrac{SS_{\text{blocks}}}{b-1}$	
Error	SS_E (by subtraction)	$(a-1)(b-1)$	$\dfrac{SS_E}{(a-1)(b-1)}$	
Total	$\sum_{i=1}^{a} \sum_{j=1}^{b} y_{ij}^2 - \dfrac{y_{..}^2}{ab}$	$ab-1$		

Example 11-7

An experiment was performed to determine the effect of four different chemicals on the strength of a fabric. These chemicals are used as part of the permanent press finishing process. Five fabric samples were selected, and a randomized block design was run by testing each chemical type once in random order on each fabric sample. The data are shown in Table 11-9.

The sums of squares for the analysis of variance are computed as follows:

$$SS_T = \sum_{i=1}^{4} \sum_{j=1}^{5} y_{ij}^2 - \frac{y_{..}^2}{ab}$$

$$= (1.3)^2 + (1.6)^2 + \cdots + (3.4)^2 - \frac{(39.2)^2}{20} = 25.69$$

$$SS_{\text{Chemicals}} = \sum_{i=1}^{4} \frac{y_{i.}^2}{b} - \frac{y_{..}^2}{ab}$$

$$= \frac{(5.7)^2 + (8.8)^2 + (6.9)^2 + (17.8)^2}{5} - \frac{(39.2)^2}{20} = 18.04$$

$$SS_{\text{Blocks}} = \sum_{j=1}^{5} \frac{y_{.j}^2}{a} - \frac{y_{..}^2}{ab}$$

$$= \frac{(9.2)^2 + (10.1)^2 + (3.5)^2 + (8.8)^2 + (7.6)^2}{4} - \frac{(39.2)^2}{20} = 6.69$$

$$SS_E = SS_T - SS_{\text{Blocks}} - SS_{\text{Chemicals}}$$
$$= 25.69 - 6.69 - 18.04 = 0.96$$

The analysis of variance is summarized in Table 11-10. We would conclude that there is a significant difference in the chemical types so far as their effect on fabric strength is concerned.

Table 11-9
Fabric strength data—randomized block design

| Chemical Type | Fabric Sample | | | | | Row Totals $y_{i.}$ | Row Averages $\bar{y}_{i.}$ |
	1	2	3	4	5		
1	1.3	1.6	0.5	1.2	1.1	5.7	1.14
2	2.2	2.4	0.4	2.0	1.8	8.8	1.76
3	1.8	1.7	0.6	1.5	1.3	6.9	1.38
4	3.9	4.4	2.0	4.1	3.4	17.8	3.56
Column Totals $y_{.j}$	9.2	10.1	3.5	8.8	7.6	39.2	1.96
Column Averages $\bar{y}_{.j}$	2.30	2.53	0.88	2.20	1.90	$(y_{..})$	$(\bar{y}_{..})$

Table 11-10
Analysis of variance for the randomized block experiment

Source of Variation	Sums of Squares	Degrees of Freedom	Mean Square	F_0
Chemical types	18.04	3	6.01	75.13
Fabric sample (Blocks)	6.69	4	1.67	
Error	0.96	12	0.08	
Total	25.69	19		

Following the formal analysis of variance, we may use the procedure described in Section 11-3.4 to compare the effects of individual chemical types on mean fabric strength. The t distribution would be scaled by $\sqrt{MS_E/b} = \sqrt{0.08/5} = 0.13$. Figure 11-12 plots the observed average tensile strength for the four chemical types and the corresponding scaled t distribution. Inspection of this plot indicates that chemical type 4 results in much higher tensile strengths than do the other three chemical types and that chemical types 1, 2, and 3 are approximately equivalent.

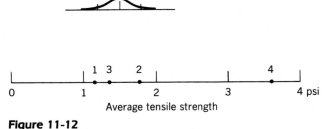

Figure 11-12
Plot of average tensile strength for the four chemical types in relation to a t distribution with scale factor $\sqrt{MS_E/b} = \sqrt{0.08/5} = 0.13$.

Table 11-11
Residuals from the randomized block design

Chemical Type	Fabric Sample				
	1	2	3	4	5
1	−0.18	−0.11	0.44	−0.18	0.02
2	0.10	0.07	−0.27	0.00	0.10
3	0.08	−0.24	0.30	−0.12	−0.02
4	0.00	0.27	−0.48	0.30	−0.10

11-4.2 Residual Analysis

In any designed experiment, it is always important to examine the residuals and check for violations of basic assumptions that could invalidate the results. The residuals for the randomized block design are just the difference between the observed and fitted values,

$$e_{ij} = y_{ij} - \hat{y}_{ij}$$

and the fitted values are

$$\hat{y}_{ij} = \bar{y}_{i.} + \bar{y}_{.j} - \bar{y}_{..} \tag{11-21}$$

The fitted value represents the estimate of the mean response when the ith treatment is run in the jth block. The residuals from this experiment are shown in Table 11-11.

Figures 11-13, 11-14, 11-15, and 11-16 present the important residual plots for the experiment. There is some indication that fabric sample (block) 3 has greater variability in strength when treated with the four chemicals than the other samples.

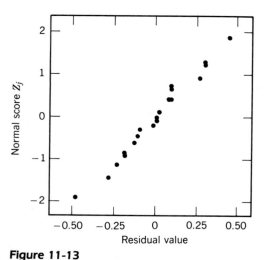

Figure 11-13
Normal probability plot of residuals from the randomized block design.

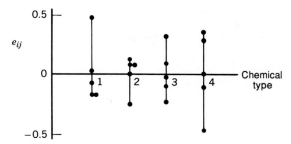

Figure 11-14
Residuals by chemical type.

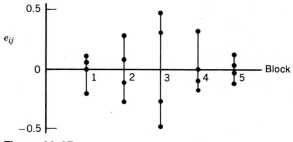

Figure 11-15
Residuals by block.

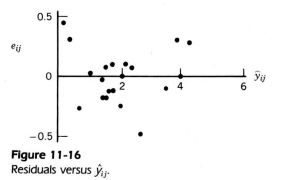

Figure 11-16
Residuals versus $\hat{y}_{ij}$.

In addition, chemical type 4, which provides the greatest strength, also has somewhat more variability in strength. Follow-up experiments may be necessary to confirm these findings, if they are potentially important.

11-5 GUIDELINES FOR DESIGNING EXPERIMENTS

Experimental design methods are a powerful approach to improving a process. In order to use this approach, it is necessary that everyone involved in the experiment have a clear idea in advance of the objective of the experiment, exactly what factors are to be studied, how the experiment is to be conducted, and at least a qualitative understanding of how the data will be analyzed. Montgomery (1984)

1. Recognition of and statement of the problem
2. Choice of factors and levels
3. Selection of the response variable
4. Choice of experimental design
5. Performing the experiment
6. Data analysis
7. Conclusions and recommendations

Figure 11-17
Procedure for designing an experiment.

gives an outline of the recommended procedure, reproduced in Figure 11-17. We now briefly amplify each point in this checklist.

1. Recognition of and statement of the problem. In practice, it is often difficult to realize that a problem requiring formal designed experiments exists, so it may not be easy to develop a clear and generally accepted statement of the problem. However, it is absolutely essential to fully develop all ideas about the problem and about the specific objectives of the experiment. Usually, it is important to solicit input from all concerned parties—engineering, quality, marketing, the customer, management, and the operators (who usually have much insight and who are too often ignored). A clear statement of the problem and the objectives of the experiment often contribute substantially to better process understanding and eventual solution of the problem.

2. Choice of factors and levels. The experimenter must choose the factors to be varied in the experiment, the ranges over which these factors will be varied, and the specific levels at which runs will be made. Process knowledge is required to do this. This process knowledge is usually a combination of practical experience and theoretical understanding. It is important to investigate all factors that may be of importance and to avoid being overly influenced by past experience, particularly when we are in the early stages of experimentation or when the process is not very mature. When the objective is factor screening or process characterization, it is usually best to keep the number of factor levels low. (Most often two levels are used.)

3. Selection of the response variable. In selecting the response variable, the experimenter should be certain that the variable really provides useful information about the process under study. Most often the average or standard deviation (or both) of the measured characteristic will be the response variable. Multiple responses are not unusual. Gage capability is also an important factor. If gage capability is poor, then only relatively large factor effects will be detected by the experiment, or additional replication will be required.

4. Choice of experimental design. If the first three steps are done correctly, this step is relatively easy. Choice of design involves consideration of sample size (number of replicates), selection of a suitable run order for the experimental trials, and whether or not blocking or other randomization restrictions are involved. The next chapter illustrates some of the more important types of experimental designs.

5. Performing the experiment. When running the experiment, it is vital to carefully monitor the process to ensure that everything is being done according to plan. Errors in experimental procedure at this stage will usually destroy experimental validity. Up-front planning is crucial to success. It is easy to underestimate the logistical and planning aspects of running a designed experiment in a complex manufacturing environment.

6. Data analysis. Statistical methods should be used to analyze the data so that results and conclusions are objective rather than judgmental. If the experiment has been designed correctly and if it has been performed according to the design, then the type of statistical methods required is not elaborate. Many excellent software packages are available to assist in the data analysis, and simple graphical methods play an important role in data interpretation. Residual analysis and model validity checking are also important.

7. Conclusions and recommendations. Once the data have been analyzed, the experimenter must draw *practical* conclusions about the results and recommend a course of action. Graphical methods are often useful in this stage, particularly in presenting the results to others. Follow-up runs and confirmation testing should also be performed to validate the conclusions from the experiment.

Throughout this entire process, it is important to keep in mind that experimentation is an important part of the learning process, where we tentatively formulate hypotheses about a system, perform experiments to investigate these hypotheses, and on the basis of the results formulate new hypotheses, and so on. This suggests that experimentation is *iterative*. It is usually a major mistake to design a single, large comprehensive experiment at the start of a study. A successful experiment requires knowledge of the important factors, the ranges over which these factors should be varied, the appropriate number of levels to use, and the proper units of measurement for these variables. Generally, we do not perfectly know the answers to these questions, but we learn about them as we go along. As an experimental program progresses, we often drop some variables, add others, change the region of exploration for some factors, or add new response variables. Consequently, we usually experiment *sequentially*, and as a general rule, no more than about 25% of the available resources should be invested in the first experiment. This will insure that sufficient resources are available to accomplish the final objective of the experiment.

11-6 Exercises

11-1 An article in *Solid State Technology* (May 1987) describes an experiment to determine the effect of C_2F_6 flow rate on etch uniformity on a silicon wafer used in integrated-circuit manufacturing. Three flow rates are tested, and the resulting uniformity (in percent) is observed for six test units at each flow rate. The data are shown in the following table.

C_2F_6 Flow (SCCM)	Observations					
	1	2	3	4	5	6
125	2.7	2.6	4.6	3.2	3.0	3.8
160	4.6	4.9	5.0	4.2	3.6	4.2
200	4.6	2.9	3.4	3.5	4.1	5.1

a. Does C_2F_6 flow rate affect etch uniformity?

b. Plot the residuals versus predicted C_2F_6 flow. Interpret this plot.

c. Does the normality assumption seem reasonable in this problem?

d. Where would you run the process to get the best etch uniformity (a small percentage is best)?

11-2 Compare the mean etch uniformity values at each of the C_2F_6 flow rates from Exercise 11-1 with a scaled t distribution. Does this analysis indicate that there are differences in mean etch uniformity at the different flow rates? Which flows produce different results?

11-3 Consider the etch uniformity experiment in Exercise 11-1. Suppose that the manufacturer selects 125 SCCM as the optimal C_2F_6 flow. He plans to control the process using a control chart for individuals. Use the data from the designed experiment to set up the center line and control limits on the control chart.

11-4 Rework Exercise 11-3 assuming that the manufacturer plans to use $\bar{x}$ and R charts based on a sample of five wafers.

11-5 An aluminum producer manufactuers carbon anodes and bakes them in a ring furnace prior to use in the smelting operation. The baked density of the anode is an important quality characteristic, as it may affect anode life. One of the process engineers suspects that firing temperature in the ring furnace affects baked anode density. An experiment was run at four different temperature levels, and six anodes were baked at each temperature level. The data from the experiment follow.

Temperature (°C)	Density					
500	41.8	41.9	41.7	41.6	41.5	41.7
525	41.4	41.3	41.7	41.6	41.7	41.8
550	41.2	41.0	41.6	41.9	41.7	41.3
575	41.0	40.6	41.8	41.2	41.9	41.5

a. Does firing temperature in the ring furnace affect mean baked anode density?

b. Find the residuals for this experiment and plot them on a normal probability scale. Comment on the plot.

c. What firing temperature would you recommend using?

11-6 Plot the residuals from Exercise 11-5 against the firing temperatures. Is there any indication that variability in baked anode density depends on the firing temperature? What firing temperature would you recommend using?

11-7 In his book *Design and Analysis of Experiments*, 2nd ed. (John Wiley & Sons, 1984), D. C. Montgomery describes an experiment to determine whether there is any difference in mean hardness readings for four different types of tips used on a hardness tester. Four test coupons from a paticular type of alloy are obtained, and each tip is tested once on each coupon, producing the following data

Type of Tip	Coupon			
	1	2	3	4
1	9.3	9.4	9.6	10.0
2	9.4	9.3	9.8	9.9
3	9.2	9.4	9.5	9.7
4	9.7	9.6	10.0	10.2

    a. Is there any difference in mean hardness readings between the tips?

    b. Analyze the residuals from this experiment.

11-8 Consider the hardness testing experiment in Exercise 11-7. If the tips tested can be viewed as a random sample of the available tips, what is your estimate of measurement error in the hardness testing process?

11-9 For the hardness testing experiment in Exercise 11-7, use a scaled t distribution to determine which tips differ.

11-10 In an experiment to improve the performance of a water-jet cutting tool, five nozzle shapes were tested. Each nozzle shape was used to make test cuts in a standard metal sheet. The experiment was repeated four times, and the time (in minutes) to make each test cut was recorded. The data are shown below.

| Nozzle | Test Sheet | | | |
Shape	1	2	3	4
1	1.1	1.2	1.3	1.0
2	1.4	1.3	1.1	1.2
3	1.3	1.2	1.1	1.1
4	1.4	1.5	1.2	1.3
5	1.1	1.0	1.2	1.1

    a. Is there any indication that nozzle shape has any effect on mean cutting time?

    b. Analyze the residuals from this experiment.

11-11 Consider the cutting time data in Exercise 11-10. Compare the average cutting times for each nozzle shape to a scaled t distribution to determine which nozzle shapes produce the best results.

11-12 Consider the hardness testing experiment in Exercise 11-7. Suppose the experimenter had analyzed the data as if the test had been completely randomized (i.e., no blocking). How would this erroneous analysis affect the conclusions from the experiment?

Chapter 12

Factorial Experiments and Other Methods for Process Improvement

Most experiments for process troubleshooting and improvement involve several variables. Factorial experimental designs, and their variations, are used in such situations. This chapter gives a brief introduction to factorial designs as well as some other methods that are frequently useful for process and quality improvement. The chapter concludes with an overview of the contributions of Professor Genechi Taguchi to quality engineering.

12-1 FACTORIAL EXPERIMENTS

When there are several factors of interest in an experiment, a *factorial design* should be used. In some designs factors are varied together. Specifically, by a factorial experiment we mean that in each complete trial or replicate of the experiment all possible combinations of the levels of the factors are investigated. Thus, if there are two factors A and B with a levels of factor A and b levels of factor B, then each replicate contains all ab possible combinations.

The effect of a factor is defined as the change in response produced by a change in the level of the factor. This is called a *main effect* because it refers to

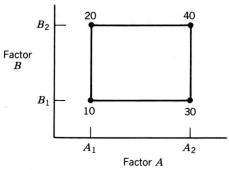

Figure 12-1
A factorial experiment with two factors.

the primary factors in the study. For example, consider the data in Figure 12-1. The main effect of factor A is the difference between the average response at the first level of A and the average response at the second level of A, or

$$A = \frac{30 + 40}{2} - \frac{10 + 20}{2} = 20$$

That is, changing factor A from level 1 to level 2 causes an average response increase of 20 units. Similarly, the main effect of B is

$$B = \frac{20 + 40}{2} - \frac{10 + 30}{2} = 10$$

In some experiments, the difference in response between the levels of one factor is not the same at all levels of the other factors. When this occurs, there is an *interaction* between the factors. For example, consider the data in Figure 12-2. At the first level of factor B, the A effect is

$$A = 30 - 10 = 20$$

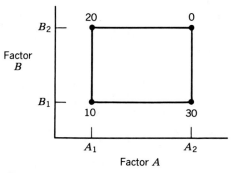

Figure 12-2
A factorial experiment with interaction.

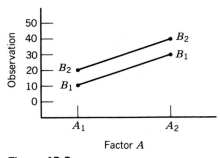

Figure 12-3
Factorial experiment, no interaction.

and at the second level of factor B, the A effect is

$$A = 0 - 20 = -20$$

Since the effect of A depends on the level chosen for factor B, there is interaction between A and B.

When an interaction is large, the corresponding main effects have little meaning. For example, by using the data in Figure 12-2, we find the main effect of A as

$$A = \frac{30 + 0}{2} - \frac{10 + 20}{2} = 0$$

and we would be tempted to conclude that there is no A effect. However, when we examined the effects of A at *different levels of factor B*, we saw that this was not the case. The effect of factor A depends on the levels of factor B. Thus, knowledge of the AB interaction is more useful than knowledge of the main effect. A significant interaction can mask the significance of main effects.

The concept of interaction can be illustrated graphically. Figure 12-3 plots the data in Figure 11-1 against the levels of A for both levels of B. Note that the B_1 and B_2 lines are roughly parallel, indicating that factors A and B do not interact significantly. Figure 12-4 plots the data in Figure 12-2. In this graph, the B_1 and B_2 lines are not parallel, indicating the interaction between factors A and B. Such graphical displays are often useful in presenting the results of experiments.

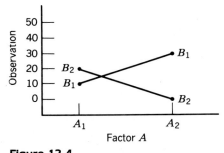

Figure 12-4
Factorial experiment, with interaction.

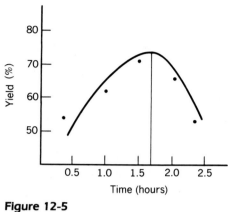

Figure 12-5
Yield versus reaction time with
temperature constant at 155° F.

An alternative to the factorial design that is (unfortunately) used in practice is to change the factors one at a time rather than to vary them simultaneously. To illustrate the one-factor-at-a-time procedure, consider the optimization experiment described earlier in Example 11-2. The engineer is interested in finding the values of temperature and pressure that maximize yield. Suppose that we fix temperature at 155° F (the current operating level) and perform five runs at different levels of time, say 0.5 h, 1.0 h, 1.5 h, 2.0 h, and 2.5 h. The results of this series of runs are shown in Figure 12-5. This figure indicates that maximum yield is achieved at about 1.7 h of reaction time. To optimize temperature, the engineer fixes time at 1.7 h (the apparent optimum) and performs five runs at different temperatures, say 140° F, 150° F, 160° F, 170° F, and 180° F. The results of this set of runs are plotted in Figure 12-6. Maximum yield occurs at about 155° F. Therefore, we would conclude that running the process at 155° F and 1.7 h is the best set of operating conditions, resulting in yields around 75%.

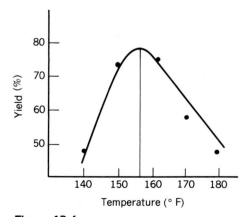

Figure 12-6
Yield versus temperature with reaction
time constant at 1.7 hr.

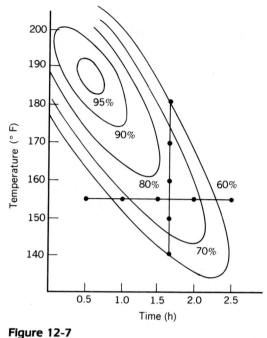

Figure 12-7
Optimization experiment using the
one-factor-at-a-time method.

Figure 12-7 displays the contour plot of yield as a function of temperature and time with the one-factor-at-a-time experiment shown on the contours. Clearly, the one-factor-at-a-time design has failed dramatically here, as the true optimum is at least 20 yield points higher and occurs at much lower reaction times and higher temperatures. The failure to discover the shorter reaction times is particularly important as it could have significant impact on production volume or capacity, production planning, manufacturing cost, and total productivity.

The one-factor-at-a-time method has failed here because it fails to detect the interaction between temperature and time. Factorial experiments are the only way to detect interactions. Furthermore, the one-factor-at-a-time method is inefficient; it will require more experimentation than a factorial, and as we have just seen, there is no assurance that it will produce the correct results. The experiment shown in Figure 11-2 that produced the information pointing to the region of the optimum is a simple example of a factorial experiment.

12-1.1 An Example

Aircraft primer paints are applied to aluminum surfaces by two methods—dipping and spraying. The purpose of the primer is to improve paint adhesion; some parts can be primed using either application method. An engineer interested in learning whether three different primers differ in their adhesion properties performed a factorial experiment to investigate the effect of paint primer type and application method on paint adhesion. Three specimens were painted with each primer using each application method, a finish paint was applied, and the adhesion force was

Table 12-1
Adhesion force data

Primer Type	Application Method			$y_{i..}$
	Dipping		Spraying	
1	4.0, 4.5, 4.3	(12.8)	5.4, 4.9, 5.6 (15.9)	28.7
2	5.6, 4.9, 5.4	(15.9)	5.8, 6.1, 6.3 (18.2)	34.1
3	3.8, 3.7, 4.0	(11.5)	5.5, 5.0, 5.0 (15.5)	27.0
$y_{.j.}$	40.2		49.6	$89.8 = y_{...}$

measured. The 18 runs from this experiment were run in random order. The resulting data are shown in Table 12-1. The circled numbers in the cells are the cell totals. The objective of the experiment was to determine which combination of primer paint and application method produced the highest adhesion force. It would be desirable if at least one of the primers produced high-adhesion force *regardless* of application method, as this would add some flexibility to the manufacturing process.

12-1.2 Statistical Analysis

The analysis of variance described in Chapter 11 can be extended to handle the two-factor factorial experiment. Let the two factors be denoted A and B, with a levels of factor A and b levels of B. If the experiment is replicated n times, the data layout will look like Table 12-2. In general, the observation in the ijth cell in the kth replicate is y_{ijk}. In collecting the data, the abn observations would be run in *random* order. Thus, like the single-factor experiment studied in Chapter 11, the two-factor factorial is a *completely randomized design*.

Table 12-2
Data for a two-factor factorial design

		Factor B			
		1	2	$\cdots$	b
	1	$y_{111}, y_{112},$ $\ldots, y_{11n}$	$y_{121}, y_{122},$ $\ldots, y_{12n}$		$y_{1b1}, y_{1b2},$ $\ldots, y_{1bn}$
	2	$y_{211}, y_{212},$ $\ldots, y_{21n}$	$y_{221}, y_{222},$ $\ldots, y_{22n}$		$y_{2b1}, y_{2b2},$ $\ldots, y_{2bn}$
Factor A	$\vdots$				
	a	$y_{a11}, y_{a12},$ $\ldots, y_{a1n}$	$y_{a21}, y_{a22},$ $\ldots, y_{a2n}$		$y_{ab1}, y_{ab2},$ $\ldots, y_{abn}$

The observations may be described by the model

$$y_{ijk} = \mu + \tau_i + \beta_j + (\tau\beta)_{ij} + \epsilon_{ijk} \begin{cases} i = 1, 2, \ldots, a \\ j = 1, 2, \ldots, b \\ k = 1, 2, \ldots, n \end{cases} \tag{12-1}$$

where μ is the overall mean effect, τ_i is the effect of the ith level of factor A, β_j is the effect of the jth level of factor B, $(\tau\beta)_{ij}$ is the effect of the interaction between A and B, and ϵ_{ijk} is a NID$(0, \sigma^2)$ random error component. We are interested in testing the hypotheses of no significant factor A effect, no significant factor B effect, and no significant AB interaction.

Let $y_{i..}$ denote the total of the observations under the ith level of factor A, $y_{.j.}$ denote the total of the observations under the jth level of factor B, $y_{ij.}$ denote the total of the observations in the ijth cell of Table 12-2, and $y_{...}$ denote the grand total of all the observations. Define $\bar{y}_{i..}$, $\bar{y}_{.j.}$, $\bar{y}_{ij.}$, and $\bar{y}_{...}$ as the corresponding row, column, cell and grand averages. That is,

$$\begin{aligned} y_{i..} &= \sum_{j=1}^{b} \sum_{k=1}^{n} y_{ijk} & \bar{y}_{i..} &= \frac{y_{i..}}{bn} & i = 1, 2, \ldots, a \\ y_{.j.} &= \sum_{i=1}^{a} \sum_{k=1}^{n} y_{ijk} & \bar{y}_{.j.} &= \frac{y_{.j.}}{an} & j = 1, 2, \ldots, b \\ y_{ij.} &= \sum_{k=1}^{n} y_{ijk} & \bar{y}_{ij.} &= \frac{y_{ij.}}{n} & \begin{array}{l} i = 1, 2, \ldots, a \\ j = 1, 2, \ldots, b \end{array} \\ y_{...} &= \sum_{i=1}^{a} \sum_{j=1}^{b} \sum_{k=1}^{n} y_{ijk} & \bar{y}_{...} &= \frac{y_{...}}{abn} \end{aligned} \tag{12-2}$$

The analysis of variance decomposes the total corrected sum of squares

$$SS_T = \sum_{i=1}^{a} \sum_{j=1}^{b} \sum_{k=1}^{n} (y_{ijk} - \bar{y}_{...})^2$$

as follows:

$$\begin{aligned} \sum_{i=1}^{a} \sum_{j=1}^{b} \sum_{k=1}^{n} (y_{ijk} - \bar{y}_{...})^2 &= bn \sum_{i=1}^{a} (\bar{y}_{i..} - \bar{y}_{...})^2 + an \sum_{j=1}^{b} (\bar{y}_{.j.} - \bar{y}_{...})^2 \\ &\quad + n \sum_{i=1}^{a} \sum_{j=1}^{b} (\bar{y}_{ij.} - \bar{y}_{i..} - \bar{y}_{.j.} + \bar{y}_{...})^2 \\ &\quad + \sum_{i=1}^{a} \sum_{j=1}^{b} \sum_{k=1}^{n} (y_{ijk} - \bar{y}_{ij.})^2 \end{aligned}$$

or symbolically,

$$SS_T = SS_A + SS_B + SS_{AB} + SS_E \tag{12-3}$$

The corresponding degree of freedom decomposition is

$$abn - 1 = (a - 1) + (b - 1) + (a - 1)(b - 1) + ab(n - 1) \tag{12-4}$$

Table 12-3
The analysis of variance table for a two-factor factorial, fixed effects model

Source of Variation	Sum of Squares	Degrees of Freedom	Mean Square	F_0
A	SS_A	$a - 1$	$MS_A = \dfrac{SS_A}{a - 1}$	$F_0 = \dfrac{MS_A}{MS_E}$
B	SS_B	$b - 1$	$MS_B = \dfrac{SS_B}{b - 1}$	$F_0 = \dfrac{MS_B}{MS_E}$
Interaction	SS_{AB}	$(a - 1)(b - 1)$	$MS_{AB} = \dfrac{SS_{AB}}{(a - 1)(b - 1)}$	$F_0 = \dfrac{MS_{AB}}{MS_E}$
Error	SS_E	$ab(n - 1)$	$MS_E = \dfrac{SS_E}{ab(n - 1)}$	
Total	SS_T	$abn - 1$		

This decomposition is usually summarized in an analysis of variance table such as the one shown in Table 12-3.

To test for no row factor effects, no column factor effects, and no interaction effects, we would divide the corresponding mean square by mean square error. Each of these ratios will follow an F distribution, with numerator degrees of freedom equal to the number of degrees of freedom for the numerator mean square and $ab(n - 1)$ denominator degrees of freedom. We would reject the corresponding hypothesis if the computed F exceeded the tabular value.

The analysis is usually done using a computer, although simple computing formulas for the sums of squares may be obtained easily. The total sum of squares is computed from

$$SS_T = \sum_{i=1}^{a} \sum_{j=1}^{b} \sum_{k=1}^{n} y_{ijk}^2 - \frac{y_{...}^2}{abn} \tag{12-5}$$

The sums of squares for main effects are

$$SS_A = \sum_{i=1}^{a} \frac{y_{i..}^2}{bn} - \frac{y_{...}^2}{abn} \tag{12-6}$$

and

$$SS_B = \sum_{j=1}^{b} \frac{y_{.j.}^2}{an} - \frac{y_{...}^2}{abn} \tag{12-7}$$

We usually calculate the SS_{AB} in two steps. First, we compute the sum of squares between the ab cell totals, called the sum of squares due to "subtotals."

$$SS_{\text{subtotals}} = \sum_{i=1}^{a} \sum_{j=1}^{b} \frac{y_{ij.}^2}{n} - \frac{y_{...}^2}{abn}$$

This sum of squares also contains SS_A and SS_B. Therefore, the second step is to compute SS_{AB} as

$$SS_{AB} = SS_{\text{subtotals}} - SS_A - SS_B \qquad (12\text{-}8)$$

The error sum of square is found by subtraction as either

$$SS_E = SS_T - SS_{AB} - SS_A - SS_B \qquad (12\text{-}9a)$$

or

$$SS_E = SS_T - SS_{\text{subtotals}} \qquad (12\text{-}9b)$$

Example 12-1

The Aircraft Primer Paint Problem

The analysis of variance described above may be applied to the aircraft primer paint experiment described in Section 12-1. The sums of squares required to perform the analysis of variance are

$$SS_T = \sum_{i=1}^{a} \sum_{j=1}^{b} \sum_{k=1}^{n} y_{ijk}^2 - \frac{y_{...}^2}{abn}$$

$$= (4.0)^2 + (4.5)^2 + \cdots + (5.0)^2 - \frac{(89.8)^2}{18} = 10.72$$

$$SS_{\text{primers}} = \sum_{i=1}^{a} \frac{y_{i..}^2}{bn} - \frac{y_{...}^2}{abn}$$

$$= \frac{(28.7)^2 + (34.1)^2 + (27.0)^2}{6} - \frac{(89.8)^2}{18} = 4.58$$

$$SS_{\text{methods}} = \sum_{j=1}^{b} \frac{y_{.j.}^2}{an} - \frac{y_{...}^2}{abn}$$

$$= \frac{(40.2)^2 + (49.6)^2}{9} - \frac{(89.8)^2}{18} = 4.91$$

$$SS_{\text{interaction}} = \sum_{i=1}^{a} \sum_{j=1}^{b} \frac{y_{ij.}^2}{n} - \frac{y_{...}^2}{abn} - SS_{\text{primers}} - SS_{\text{methods}}$$

$$= \frac{(12.8)^2 + (15.9)^2 + (11.5)^2 + (15.9)^2 + (18.2)^2 + (15.5)^2}{3}$$

$$- \frac{(89.8)^2}{18} - 4.58 - 4.91 = 0.24$$

and

$$SS_E = SS_T - SS_{\text{primers}} - SS_{\text{method}} - SS_{\text{interaction}}$$
$$= 10.72 - 4.58 - 4.91 - 0.24 = 0.99$$

Table 12-4
Analysis of variance for Example 12-1

Source of Variation	Sum of Squares	Degrees of Freedom	Mean Square	F_0
Primer types	4.58	2	2.29	28.63
Application methods	4.91	1	4.91	61.38
Interaction	0.24	2	0.12	1.5
Error	0.99	12	0.08	
Total	10.72	17		

The analysis of variance is summarized in Table 12-4. Since $F_{0.05,2,12} = 3.89$ and $F_{0.05,1,12} = 4.75$, we conclude that primer type and application method affect adhesion force. Furthermore, since $1.5 < F_{0.05,2,12}$, there is no indication of interaction between these factors.

A graph of the cell adhesion force averages $\{\bar{y}_{ij.}\}$ versus the levels of primer type for each application method is shown in Figure 12-8. The absence of interaction is evident in the parallelism of the two lines. Furthermore, since a large response indicates greater adhesion force, we conclude that spraying is a superior application method and that primer type 2 is most effective. Therefore, if we wish to operate the process so as to attain maximum adhesion force, we should use primer type 2 and spray all parts.

12-1.3 Residual Analysis

Just as in the single-factor experiments discussed in Chapter 11, the residuals from a factorial experiment play an important role in assessing model adequacy. The residuals from a two-factor factorial are

$$e_{ijk} = y_{ijk} - \hat{y}_{ijk}$$
$$= y_{ijk} - \bar{y}_{ij.}$$

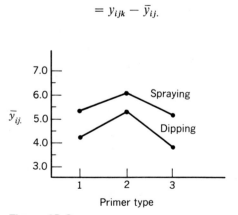

Figure 12-8
Graph of average adhesion force versus primer types for Example 12-1.

Table 12-5
Residuals for the aircraft primer paint experiment

Primer Type	Application Method	
	Dipping	Spraying
1	-0.26, 0.23, 0.03	0.10, -0.40, 0.30
2	0.30, -0.40, 0.10	-0.26, 0.03, 0.23
3	-0.03, -0.13, 0.16	0.34, -0.17, -0.17

That is, the residuals are just the difference between the observations and the corresponding cell averages.

Table 12-5 presents the residuals for the aircraft primer paint data in Example 12-1. The normal probability plot of these residuals is shown in Figure 12-9. This plot has tails that do not fall exactly along a straight line passing through the center of the plot, indicating some potential problems with the normality assumption, but the deviation from normality is not serious. Figure 12-10 and 12-11

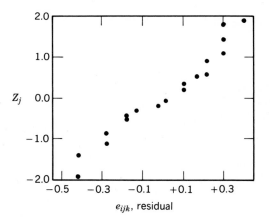

Figure 12-9
Normal probability plot of the residuals from Example 12-1.

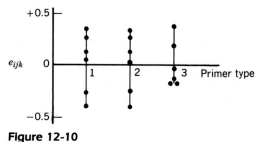

Figure 12-10
Plot of residuals versus primer type.

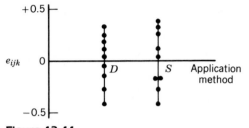

Figure 12-11
Plot of residuals versus application method.

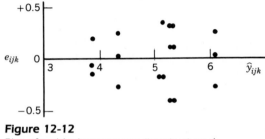

Figure 12-12
Plot of residuals versus predicted values $\hat{y}_{ijk}$.

plot the residuals versus the levels of primer types and application methods, respectively. There is some indication that primer type 3 results in slightly lower variability in adhesion force than the other two primers. The graph of residuals versus fitted values in Figure 12-12 does not reveal any unusual or diagnostic pattern.

12-2 THE 2^k FACTORIAL DESIGN

Certain special types of factorial designs are very useful in process development and improvement. One of these is a factorial design with k factors, each at two levels. Because each complete replicate of the design has 2^k runs, the arrangement is called a 2^k factorial design. These designs have a greatly simplified analysis, and they also form the basis of many other useful designs.

12-2.1 The 2^2 Design

The simplest type of 2^k design is the 2^2—that is, two factors A and B, each at two levels. We usually think of these levels as the "low" and "high" levels of the factor. The 2^2 design is shown in Figure 12-13. Note that the design can be represented geometrically as a square with the $2^2 = 4$ runs forming the corners of the square.

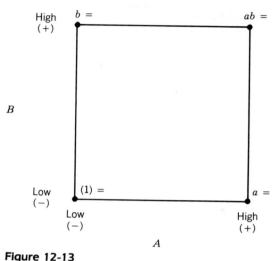

Figure 12-13
The 2^2 factorial design.

A special notation is used to represent the runs. In general, a run is represented by a series of lower case letters. If a letter is present, then the corresponding factor is set at the high level in that run; if it is absent, the factor is run at its low level. For example, run a indicates that factor A is at the high level and factor B is at the low level. The run with both factors at the low level is represented by (1). This notation is used throughout the 2^k design series. For example, the run in a 2^4 with A and C at the high level and B and D at the low level is denoted by ac.

The effects of interest in the 2^2 design are the main effects A and B and the two-factor interaction AB. Let the letters (1), a, b, and ab also represent the totals of all n observations taken at these design points. It is easy to estimate the effects of these factors. To estimate the main effect of A, we would average the observations on the right side of the square when A is at the high level and subtract from this the average of the observations on the left side of the square where A is at the low level, or

$$A = \frac{a + ab}{2n} - \frac{b + (1)}{2n}$$

$$= \frac{1}{2n}[a + ab - b - (1)] \tag{12-10}$$

Similarly, the main effect of B is found by averaging the observations on the top of the square where B is at the high level and subtracting the average of the observations on the bottom of the square where B is at the low level,

$$B = \frac{b + ab}{2n} - \frac{a + (1)}{2n}$$

$$= \frac{1}{2n}[b + ab - a - (1)] \tag{12-11}$$

Finally, the AB interaction is estimated by taking the difference in the diagonal averages in Figure 12-13, or

$$AB = \frac{ab + (1)}{2n} - \frac{a + b}{2n}$$

$$= \frac{1}{2n}[ab + (1) - a - b] \qquad (12\text{-}12)$$

The quantities in brackets in Equations (12-10), (12-11), and (12-12) are called *contrasts*. For example, the A contrast is

$$\text{Contrast}_A = a + ab - b - (1).$$

In these equations, the contrast coefficients are always either $+1$ or -1. A table of plus and minus signs, such as Table 12-6, can be used to determine the sign on each run for a particular contrast. The column headings for the table are the main effects A and B, the AB interaction, and I, which represents the total. The row headings are the runs. Note that the signs in the AB column are the product of signs from columns A and B. To generate a contrast from this table, multiply the signs in the appropriate column of Table 12-6 by the runs listed in the rows and add.

To obtain the sums of squares for A, B, and AB, we use

$$SS = \frac{(\text{contrast})^2}{n \sum (\text{contrast coefficients})^2} \qquad (12\text{-}13)$$

Therefore, the sums of squares for A, B, and AB are

$$SS_A = \frac{[a + ab - b - (1)]^2}{4n}$$

$$SS_B = \frac{[b + ab - a - (1)^2]}{4n} \qquad (12\text{-}14)$$

$$SS_{AB} = \frac{[ab + (1) - a - b]^2}{4n}$$

Table 12-6
Signs for effects in the 2^2 design

Run		I	A	B	AB
			Factorial Effect		
1	(1)	+	−	−	+
2	a	+	+	−	−
3	b	+	−	+	−
4	ab	+	+	+	+

The analysis of variance is completed by computing the total sum of squares SS_T (with $4n - 1$ degrees of freedom) as usual, and obtaining the error sum of squares SS_E [with $4(n - 1)$ degrees of freedom] by subtraction.

Example 12-2

The Router Experiment

A router is used to cut registration notches in printed circuit boards. The average notch dimension is satisfactory, and the process is in statistical control (see the $\bar{x}$ and R control charts in Figure 12-14), but there is too much variability in the process. This excess variability leads to problems in board assembly. The components are inserted into the board using automatic equipment, and the variability in notch dimension causes improper board registration. As a result, the auto-insertion equipment does not work properly.

Since the process is in statistical control, the quality-improvement team assigned to this project decided to use a designed experiment to study the process. The team considered two factors: bit size (A) and speed (B). Two levels were chosen for each factor (bit size A at $\frac{1}{16}''$ and $\frac{1}{8}''$ and speed B at 40 rpm and 80 rpm) and a 2^2 design was set up. Since variation in notch dimension was difficult to measure directly, the team decided to measure it indirectly. Sixteen test boards were instrumented with accelerometers that allowed vibration on the (X, Y, Z) coordinate axes to be measured. The resultant vector of these three components was used as

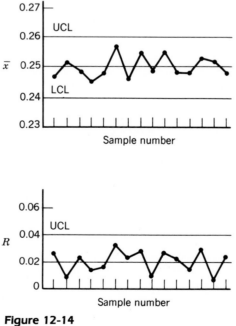

Figure 12-14
$\bar{x}$ and R control charts on notch dimension, Example 12-2.

Table 12-7
Data from the router experiment

Run		Factors A	B	Vibration				Total
1	(1)	−	−	18.2	18.9	12.9	14.4	64.4
2	a	+		27.2	24.0	22.4	22.5	96.1
3	b	−	+	15.9	14.5	15.1	14.2	59.7
4	ab	+	+	41.0	43.9	36.3	39.9	161.7

the response variable. Since vibration at the surface of the board when it is cut is directly related to variability in notch dimension, reducing vibration levels will also reduce the variability in notch dimension.

Four boards were tested at each of the four runs in the experiment, and the resulting data are shown in Table 12-7. Using Equations (12-10), (12-11), and (12-12), we can compute the factor effect estimates as follows:

$$A = \frac{1}{2n} [a + ab - b - (1)]$$

$$= \frac{1}{2(4)} [96.1 + 161.1 - 59.7 - 64.4] = 16.64$$

$$B = \frac{2}{2n} [b + ab - a - (1)]$$

$$= \frac{1}{2(4)} [59.7 + 161.1 - 96.1 - 64.4] = 7.54$$

$$AB = \frac{1}{2n} [ab + (1) - a - b]$$

$$= \frac{1}{2(4)} [161.1 + 64.4 - 96.1 - 59.7] = 8.71$$

All the numerical effect estimates seem large. For example, when we change factor A from the low level to the high level (bit size from $\frac{1}{16}''$ to $\frac{1}{8}''$), the average vibration level increases by 16.64 cps.

The magnitude of these factor effects may be confirmed with the analysis of variance, which is summarized in Table 12-8. This confirms our conclusions obtained by initially examining the magnitude and direction of effects; both bit size and speed are important, and there is interaction between the two variables.

Residual Analysis

It is easy to obtain the residuals from a 2^k design by fitting a regression model to the data. For the router experiment, the regression model is

$$y = \beta_0 + \beta_1 x_1 + \beta_2 x_2 + \beta_3 x_1 x_2 + \epsilon$$

Table 12-8
Analysis of variance for the router experiment

Source of Variation	Sum of Squares	Degrees of Freedom	Mean Square	F_0
Bit Size (A)	1107.226	1	1107.226	185.25
Speed (B)	227.256	1	227.256	38.03
AB	303.631	1	303.631	50.80
Error	71.723	12	5.977	
Total	1709.836	15		

where factors A and B are represented by coded variables x_1 and x_2, and the AB interaction is x_1x_2. The low and high levels of each factor are assigned the values $x_j = -1$ and $x_j = +1$, respectively. The fitted model is

$$\hat{y} = 23.83 + \left(\frac{16.64}{2}\right)x_1 + \left(\frac{7.54}{2}\right)x_2 + \left(\frac{8.71}{2}\right)x_1x_2$$

where the intercept is the grand average of all 16 observations ($\bar{y}$) and the slopes $\hat{\beta}_j$ are one-half the effect estimate for the corresponding factor. [Each regression coefficient is one-half the effect estimate because regression coefficients measure the effect of a unit change in x_i on the mean of y, and the effect estimate is based on a two-unit change (from -1 to $+1$)].

This model can be used to obtain the predicted values of vibration level at the four points in the design. For example, consider the point with the small bit ($x_1 = -1$) and low speed ($x_2 = -1$). The predicted vibration level is

$$\hat{y} = 23.83 + \left(\frac{16.64}{2}\right)(-1) + \left(\frac{7.54}{2}\right)(-1) + \left(\frac{8.71}{2}\right)(-1)(-1)$$
$$= 16.1$$

The four residuals at this run would be

$$e_1 = 18.2 - 16.1 = 2.1 \qquad e_3 = 12.9 - 16.1 = -3.2$$
$$e_2 = 18.9 - 16.1 = 2.8 \qquad e_4 = 14.4 - 16.1 = -1.7$$

The residuals at the other three runs would be computed similarly.

Figures 12-15 and 12-16 present the normal probability plot and the plot of residuals versus the fitted values, respectively. The normal probability plot is satisfactory, as is the plot of residuals versus $\hat{y}$, although this latter plot does give some indication that there may be less variability in the data at the point of lowest predicted vibration level.

Practical Interpretation

Since both factors A (bit size) and B (speed) have large, positive effects, we could reduce vibration levels by running both factors at the low level. However, with both bit size and speed at the low level, the production rate will be unacceptably

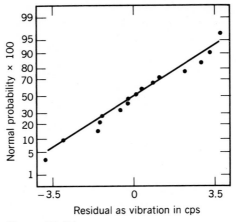

Figure 12-15
Normal probability plot, Example 12-2.

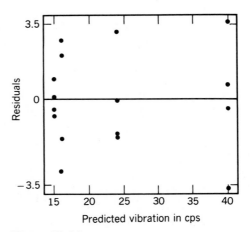

Figure 12-16
Plot of residuals versus $\hat{y}$, Example 12-2.

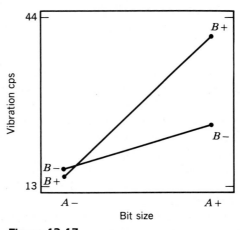

Figure 12-17
AB interaction plot.

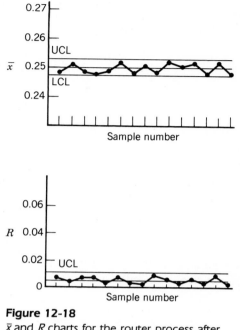

Figure 12-18
$\bar{x}$ and R charts for the router process after the experiment.

low. The AB interaction provides a solution to this dilemma. Figure 12-17 presents the two-factor AB interaction plot. Notice that the large positive effect of speed occurs primarily when bit size is at the high level. If we use the small bit, then either speed level will provide lower vibration levels. If we run with speed high and use the small bit, the production rate will be satisfactory.

When manufacturing implemented this set of operating conditions, the result was a dramatic reduction in variability in the registration notch dimension. The process remained in statistical control, as the control charts in Figure 12-18 imply, and the reduced variability dramatically improved the performance of the auto-insertion process.

12-2.2 The 2^k Design for $k \geq 3$ Factors

The methods presented in the previous section for factorial designs with $k = 2$ factors each at two levels can be easily extended to more than two factors. For example, consider $k = 3$ factors, each at two levels. This design is a 2^3 factorial design, and it has eight factor-level combinations. Geometrically, the design is a cube as shown in Figure 12-19, with the eight runs forming the corners of the cube. This design allows three main effects to be estimated (A, B, and C) along with three two-factor interactions (AB, AC, and BC) and a three-factor interaction (ABC).

The main effects can be estimated easily. Remember that the lower case letters (1), a, b, ab, c, ac, bc, and abc represent the total of all n replicates at each of the eight runs in the design. Referring to the cube in Figure 12-19, we would estimate the main effect of A by averaging the four runs on the right side of the cube where

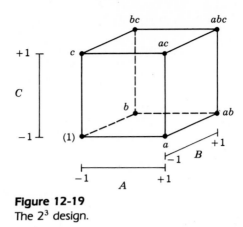

Figure 12-19
The 2^3 design.

A is at the high level and subtracting from that quantity the average of the four runs on the left side of the cube where A is at the low level. This gives

$$A = \frac{1}{4n} [a + ab + ac + abc - b - c - bc - (1)] \qquad (12\text{-}15)$$

In a similar manner, the effect of B is the average difference of the four runs in the back face of the cube and the four in the front, or

$$B = \frac{1}{4n} [b + ab + bc + abc - a - c - ac - (1)] \qquad (12\text{-}16)$$

and the effect of C is the average difference between the four runs in the top face of the cube and the four in the bottom, or

$$C = \frac{1}{4n} [c + ac + bc + abc - a - b - ab - (1)] \qquad (12\text{-}17)$$

Now consider the two-factor interaction AB. When C is at the low level, AB is just the average difference in the A effect at the two levels of B, or

$$AB \,(C \text{ low}) = \frac{1}{2n} [ab - b] - \frac{1}{2n} [a - (1)]$$

Similarly, when C is at the high level, the AB interaction is

$$AB \,(C \text{ high}) = \frac{1}{2n} [abc - bc] - \frac{1}{2n} [ac - c]$$

The AB interaction is just the average of these two components, or

$$AB = \frac{1}{4n} [ab + (1) + abc + c - b - a - bc - ac] \qquad (12\text{-}18)$$

Notice that the *AB* interaction is just the difference in averages on two diagonal planes in the cube (Figure 12-19).

Using a similar approach, we can show that the *AC* and *BC* interaction effect estimates are as follows:

$$AC = \frac{1}{4n}\left[ac + (1) + abc + b - a - c - ab - bc\right] \qquad (12\text{-}19)$$

$$BC = \frac{1}{4n}\left[bc + (1) + abc + a - b - c - ab - ac\right] \qquad (12\text{-}20)$$

The *ABC* interaction effect is the average difference between the *AB* interaction at the two levels of *C*. Thus

$$ABC = \frac{1}{4n}\left\{[abc - bc] - [ac - c] - [ab - b] + [a - (1)]\right\}$$

$$= \frac{1}{4n}\left[abc - bc - ac + c - ab + b + a - (1)\right] \qquad (12\text{-}21)$$

The quantities in brackets in Equations (12-15) through (12-21) are contrasts in the eight factor-level combinations. These contrasts can be obtained from a table of plus and minus signs for the 2^3 design, shown in Table 12-9. Signs for the main effects (columns *A*, *B*, and *C*) are obtained by associating a plus with the high level and a minus with the low level. Once the signs for the main effects have been established, the signs for the remaining columns are found by multiplying the appropriate preceding columns, row by row. For example, the signs in column *AB* are the product of the signs in column *A* and *B*.

Table 12-9 has several interesting properties:

1. Except for the identity column *I*, each column has an equal number of plus and minus signs.

Table 12-9
Signs for effects in the 2^3 design

Treatment Combination		Factorial Effect						
	I	*A*	*B*	*AB*	*C*	*AC*	*BC*	*ABC*
(1)	+	−	−	+	−	+	+	−
a	+	+	−	−	−	−	+	+
b	+	−	+	−	−	+	−	+
ab	+	+	+	+	−	−	−	−
c	+	−	−	+	+	−	−	+
ac	+	+	−	−	+	+	−	−
bc	+	−	+	−	+	−	+	−
abc	+	+	+	+	+	+	+	+

2. The sum of products of signs in any two columns is zero; that is, the columns in the table are *orthogonal*.

3. Multiplying any column by column *I* leaves the column unchanged; that is, *I* is an *identity element*.

4. The product of any two columns yields a column in the table, for example, $A \times B = AB$, and $AB \times ABC = A^2B^2C = C$, since any column multiplied by itself is the identity column.

The estimate of any main effect or interaction is determined by multiplying the factor-level combinations in the first column of the table by the signs in the corresponding main effect or interaction column, adding the result to produce a contrast, and then dividing the contrast by one-half the total number of runs in the experiment. Expressed mathematically,

$$\text{Effect} = \frac{\text{Contrast}}{n2^{k-1}} \tag{12-22}$$

The sum of squares for any effect is

$$SS = \frac{(\text{Contrast})^2}{n2^k} \tag{12-23}$$

Example 12-3

An experiment was performed to investigate the surface finish of a metal part. The experiment is a 2^3 factorial design in the factors feed rate (*A*), depth of cut (*B*), and tool angle (*C*), with $n = 2$ replicates. Table 12-10 presents the observed surface-finish data.

The main effects may be estimated using Equations (12-15) through (12-21). The effect of *A*, for example, is

$$A = \frac{1}{4n}\left[a + ab + ac + abc - b - c - bc - (1)\right]$$

$$= \frac{1}{4(2)}\left[22 + 27 + 23 + 30 - 20 - 21 - 18 - 16\right]$$

$$= \frac{1}{8}[27] = 3.375$$

and the sum of squares for *A* is found using Equation (12-23):

$$SS_A = \frac{(\text{Contrast}_A)^2}{n2^k}$$

$$= \frac{(27)^2}{2(8)} = 45.5625$$

Table 12-10
Surface-finish data for Example 12-3

Runs		Design Factors A	B	C	Surface Finish	Totals
1	(1)	−1	−1	−1	9, 7	16
2	a	1	−1	−1	10, 12	22
3	b	−1	1	−1	9, 11	20
4	ab	1	1	−1	12, 15	27
5	c	−1	−1	1	11, 10	21
6	ac	1	−1	1	10, 13	23
7	bc	−1	1	1	10, 8	18
8	abc	1	1	1	16, 14	30

It is easy to verify that the other effects are

$$B = 1.625$$
$$C = 0.875$$
$$AB = 1.375$$
$$AC = 0.125$$
$$BC = -0.625$$
$$ABC = 1.125$$

From examining the magnitude of the effects, clearly feed rate (factor A) is dominant, followed by depth of cut (B) and the AB interaction, although the interaction effect is relatively small. The analysis of variance is summarized in Table 12-11, and it confirms our interpretation of the effect estimates. Since both active factors have positive effects, surface roughness can be reduced by running feed rate (A) and depth of cut (B) at the low level.

Table 12-11
Analysis of variance for the surface-finish experiment

Source of Variation	Sum of Squares	Degrees of Freedom	Mean Square	F_0
A	45.5625	1	45.5625	18.69
B	10.5625	1	10.5625	4.33
C	3.0625	1	3.0625	1.26
AB	7.5625	1	7.5625	3.10
AC	0.0625	1	0.0625	0.03
BC	1.5625	1	1.5625	0.64
ABC	5.5625	1	5.5625	2.08
Error	19.5000	8	2.4375	
Total	92.9375	15		

Other Methods for Judging the Significance of Effects

The analysis of variance is a formal way to determine which effects are nonzero. Two other methods are useful. In the first method, we can calculate the standard errors of the effects and compare the magnitude of the effects to their standard errors. The second method uses normal probability plots to assess the importance of the effects.

The standard error of an effect is easy to find. If we assume that there are n replicates at each of the 2^k runs in the design, and if $y_{i1}, y_{i2}, \ldots, y_{in}$ are the observations at the ith run, then

$$S_i^2 = \frac{1}{n-1} \sum_{j=1}^{n} (y_{ij} - \bar{y}_i)^2, \qquad i = 1, 2, \ldots, 2^k$$

is an estimate of the variance at the ith run. The 2^k variance estimates can be pooled to give an overall variance estimate

$$S^2 = \frac{1}{2^k(n-1)} \sum_{i=1}^{2^k} \sum_{j=1}^{n} (y_{ij} - \bar{y}_i)^2 \tag{12-24}$$

This is also the variance estimate given by the error mean square from the analysis of variance procedure. Each effect estimate has variance given by

$$V(\text{Effect}) = \frac{1}{n2^{k-2}} \sigma^2 \tag{12-25}$$

The estimated standard error of an effect would be found by replacing σ^2 by its estimate S^2 and taking the square root of (12-25).

As an illustration for the surface-finish experiment, we find that $S^2 = 2.4375$, and the standard error of each effect is

$$s.e\,(\text{Effect}) = \sqrt{\frac{1}{n2^{k-2}} S^2}$$

$$= \sqrt{\frac{1}{(2)2^{3-2}} (2.4375)}$$

$$= 0.78$$

Therefore two standard deviation limits on the effect estimates are

$$\begin{aligned}
A:&\quad 3.375 \pm 1.56 \\
B:&\quad 1.625 \pm 1.56 \\
C:&\quad 0.875 \pm 1.56 \\
AB:&\quad 1.375 \pm 1.56 \\
AC:&\quad 0.125 \pm 1.56 \\
BC:&\quad 0.625 \pm 1.56 \\
ABC:&\quad 1.125 \pm 1.56
\end{aligned}$$

These intervals are approximate 95% confidence intervals. They indicate that the two main effects A and B are important but that the other effects are not, since the intervals for all effects except A and B include zero.

Normal probability plots can also be used to judge the significance of effects. We will illustrate that method in the next section.

Projection of 2^k Designs

Any 2^k design will collapse or project into another 2^k design in fewer variables if one or more of the original factors are dropped. Sometimes this can provide additional insight into the remaining factors. For example, consider the surface-finish experiment. Since factor C and all its interactions are negligible, we could eliminate factor C from the design. The result is to collapse the cube in Figure 13-17 into a square in the A-B plane; however, each of the four runs in the new design has four replicates. In general, if we delete h factors so that $r = k - h$ factors remain, the original 2^k design with n replicates will project into a 2^r design with $n2^h$ replicates.

Residual Analysis

We may obtain the residuals from a 2^k design by using the method demonstrated earlier from the 2^2 design. As an example, consider the surface-finish experiment. The three largest effects are A, B, and the AB interaction. The regression model used to obtain the predicted values is

$$\hat{y} = \hat{\beta}_0 + \hat{\beta}_1 x_1 + \hat{\beta}_2 x_2 + \hat{\beta}_{12} x_1 x_2$$

where x_1 represents factor A, x_2 represents factor B, and $x_1 x_2$ represents the AB interaction. The regression coefficients $\hat{\beta}_1$, $\hat{\beta}_2$, and $\hat{\beta}_{12}$ are one-half the corresponding effect estimates and $\hat{\beta}_0$ is the grand average. Thus

$$\hat{y} = 11.0625 + \left(\frac{3.375}{2}\right)x_1 + \left(\frac{1.625}{2}\right)x_2 + \left(\frac{1.375}{2}\right)x_1 x_2$$

The predicted values would be obtained by substituting the low and high levels of A and B into this equation. To illustrate, at the treatment combination where A, B, and C are all at the low level, the predicted value is

$$\hat{y} = 11.0625 + \left(\frac{3.375}{2}\right)(-1) + \left(\frac{1.625}{2}\right)(-1) + \left(\frac{1.375}{2}\right)(-1)(-1)$$

$$= 9.25$$

The observed values at this run are 9 and 7, so the residuals are $9 - 9.25 = -0.25$ and $7 - 9.25 = -2.25$. Residuals for the other seven runs are obtained similarly.

A normal probability plot of the residuals is shown in Figure 12-20. Since the residuals lie approximately along a straight line, we do not suspect any severe nonnormality in the data. There are no indications of severe outliers. It would also be helpful to plot the residuals versus the predicted values and against each of the factors A, B, and C.

12-2.3 A Single Replicate of the 2^k Design

As the number of factors in a factorial experiment grows, the number of effects that can be estimated also grows. For example, a 2^4 experiment has 4 main effects, 6 two-factor interactions, 4 three-factor interactions, and 1 four-factor interaction,

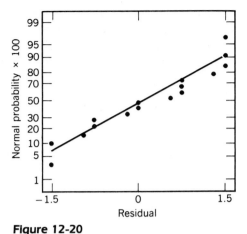

Figure 12-20
Normal probability plot of residuals,
Example 12-3.

while a 2^6 experiment has 6 main effects, 15 two-factor interactions, 20 three-factor interactions, 15 four-factor interactions, 6 five-factor interactions, and 1 six-factor interaction. In most situations the *sparsity of effects principle* applies; that is, the system is usually dominated by the main effects and low-order interactions. Three-factor and higher interactions are usually negligible. Therefore, when the number of factors is moderately large, say $k \geq 4$ or 5, a common practice is to run only a single replicate of the 2^k design and then pool or combine the higher order interactions as an estimate of error.

Example 12-4

An article in *Solid State Technology* ("Orthogonal Design for Process Optimization and Its Application in Plasma Etching," May 1987, pp. 127–132) describes the application of factorial designs in developing a nitride etch process on a single-wafer plasma etcher. The process uses C_2F_6 as the reactant gas. It is possible to vary the gas flow, the power applied to the cathode, the pressure in the reactor chamber, and the spacing between the anode and the cathode (gap). Several response variables would usually be of interest in this process, but in this example we will concentrate on etch rate for silicon nitride.

We will use a single replicate of a 2^4 design to investigate this process. Since it is unlikely that the three-factor and four-factor interactions are significant, we will tentatively plan to combine them as an estimate of error. The factor levels used in the design are shown below:

Design factor

Level	Gap A (cm)	Pressure B (m Torr)	C_2F_6 Flow C (SCCM)	Power D (W)
Low ($-$)	0.80	450	125	275
High ($+$)	1.20	550	200	325

Table 12-12
The 2^4 design for the plasma etch experiment

Run	A (Gap)	B (Pressure)	C (C_2F_6 Flow)	D (Power)	Etch Rate (Å/min)
1	−1	−1	−1	−1	550
2	1	−1	−1	−1	669
3	−1	1	−1	−1	604
4	1	1	−1	−1	650
5	−1	−1	1	−1	633
6	1	−1	1	−1	642
7	−1	1	1	−1	601
8	1	1	1	−1	635
9	−1	−1	−1	1	1037
10	1	−1	−1	1	749
11	−1	1	−1	1	1052
12	1	1	−1	1	868
13	−1	−1	1	1	1075
14	1	−1	1	1	860
15	−1	1	1	1	1063
16	1	1	1	1	729

Table 12-12 presents the data from the 16 runs of the 2^4 design. Table 12-13 is the table of plus and minus sign for the 2^4 design. The signs in the columns of this table can be used to estimate the factor effects. To illustrate, the estimate of A is

$$A = \tfrac{1}{8}[a + ab + ac + abc + ad + abd + acd + abcd - (1) - b$$
$$- c - d - bc - bd - cd - bcd]$$
$$= \tfrac{1}{8}[669 + 650 + 642 + 635 + 749 + 868 + 860 + 729 - 550$$
$$- 604 - 633 - 601 - 1037 - 1052 - 1075 - 1063]$$
$$= -101.625$$

Thus, the effect of increasing the gap between the anode and the cathode from 0.80 cm to 1.20 cm is to decrease the etch rate by 101.625 angstroms per minute. It is easy to verify that the complete set of effect estimates is

$$
\begin{aligned}
A &= -101.625 & AD &= -153.625 \\
B &= -1.625 & BD &= -0.625 \\
AB &= -7.875 & ABD &= 4.125 \\
C &= 7.375 & CD &= -2.125 \\
AC &= -24.875 & ACD &= 5.625 \\
BC &= -43.875 & BCD &= -25.375 \\
ABC &= -15.625 & ABCD &= -40.125 \\
D &= 306.125
\end{aligned}
$$

Table 12-13
Contrast constants for the 2^4 design

Run		A	B	AB	C	AC	BC	ABC	D	AD	BD	ABD	CD	ACD	BCD	ABCD
1	(1)	−	−	+	−	+	+	−	−	+	+	−	+	−	−	+
2	a	+	−	−	−	−	+	+	−	−	+	+	+	+	−	−
3	b	−	+	−	−	+	−	+	−	+	−	+	+	−	+	−
4	ab	+	+	+	−	−	−	−	−	−	−	−	+	+	+	+
5	c	−	−	+	+	−	−	+	−	+	+	−	−	+	+	−
6	ac	+	−	−	+	+	−	−	−	−	+	+	−	−	+	+
7	bc	−	+	−	+	−	+	−	−	+	−	+	−	+	−	+
8	abc	+	+	+	+	+	+	+	−	−	−	−	−	−	−	−
9	d	−	−	+	−	+	+	−	+	−	−	+	−	+	+	−
10	ad	+	−	−	−	−	+	+	+	+	−	−	−	−	+	+
11	bd	−	+	−	−	+	−	+	+	−	+	−	−	+	−	+
12	abd	+	+	+	−	−	−	−	+	+	+	+	−	−	−	−
13	cd	−	−	+	+	−	−	+	+	−	−	+	+	−	−	+
14	acd	+	−	−	+	+	−	−	+	+	−	−	+	+	−	−
15	bcd	−	+	−	+	−	+	−	+	−	+	−	+	−	+	−
16	abcd	+	+	+	+	+	+	+	+	+	+	+	+	+	+	+

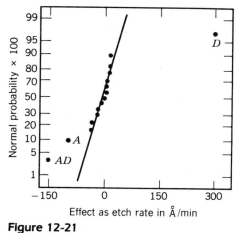

Figure 12-21
Normal probability plot of effects,
Example 12-4.

A very helpful method in judging the significance of factors in a 2^k experiment is to construct a normal probability plot of the effect estimates. If none of the effects is significant, then the estimates will behave like a random sample drawn from a normal distribution with zero mean, and the plotted effects will lie approximately along a straight line. Those effects that do not plot on the line are significant factors.

The normal probability plot of effect estimates from the plasma etch experiment is shown in Figure 12-21. Clearly, the main effects of A and D and the AD interaction are significant, as they fall far from the line passing through the other points. The analysis of variance summarized in Table 12-14 confirms these findings. Notice that in the analysis of variance we have pooled the three- and four-factor interactions to form the error mean square. If the normal probability plot had indicated that any of these interactions were important, they then would not be included in the error term.

Table 12-14
Analysis of variance for the plasma etch experiment

Source of Variation	Sum of Squares	Degrees of Freedom	Mean Square	F_0
A	41,310.563	1	41,310.563	20.28
B	10.563	1	10.563	<1
C	217.563	1	217.563	<1
D	374,850.063	1	374,850.063	183.99
AB	248.063	1	248.063	<1
AC	2,475.063	1	2,475.063	1.21
AD	94,402.563	1	99,402.563	48.79
BC	7,700.063	1	7,700.063	3.78
BD	1.563	1	1.563	<1
CD	18.063	1	18.063	<1
Error	10,186.815	5	2,037.363	
Total	531,420.938	15		

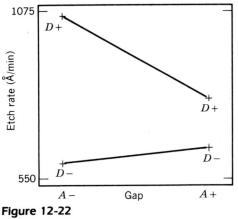

Figure 12-22
AD interaction in the plasma etch experiment.

Since $A = -101.625$, the effect of increasing the gap between the cathode and anode is to decrease the etch rate. However, $D = 306.125$, so applying higher power levels will increase the etch rate. Figure 12-22 is a plot of the AD interaction. This plot indicates that the effect of changing the gap width at low power settings is small, but that increasing the gap at high power settings dramatically reduces the etch rate. High etch rates are obtained at high power settings and narrow gap widths.

The residuals from the experiment can be obtained from the regression model

$$\hat{y} = 776.0625 - \left(\frac{101.625}{2}\right)x_1 + \left(\frac{306.125}{2}\right)x_4 - \left(\frac{153.625}{2}\right)x_1x_4$$

For example, when both A and D are at the low level, the predicted value is

$$\hat{y} = 776.0625 - \left(\frac{101.625}{2}\right)(-1) + \left(\frac{306.125}{2}\right)(-1) - \left(\frac{153.625}{2}\right)(-1)(-1)$$
$$= 597$$

and the four residuals at this run are

$$e_1 = 550 - 597 = -47$$
$$e_2 = 604 - 597 = \quad 7$$
$$e_3 = 638 - 597 = \quad 36$$
$$e_4 = 601 - 597 = \quad 4$$

The residuals at the other three runs (A high, D low), (A low, D high), and (A high, D high) are obtained similarly. A normal probability plot of the residuals is shown in Figure 12-23. The plot is satisfactory.

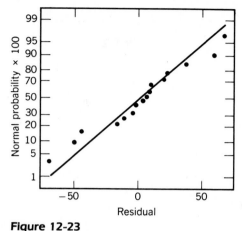

Figure 12-23
Normal probability plot of residuals,
Example 12-4.

12-2.4 Blocking and Confounding in the 2^k Design

It is often impossible to run a complete replicate of a factorial design under homogeneous experimental conditions. *Confounding* is a design technique for running a factorial experiment in blocks, where the block size is smaller than the number of runs in one complete replicate. The technique causes certain interactions to be indistinguishable from or *confounded* with blocks. We will illustrate confounding in the 2^k factorial design in 2^p blocks, where $p < k$.

Consider a 2^2 design. Suppose that each of the $2^2 = 4$ runs requires four hours of laboratory analysis. Thus, two days are required to perform the experiment. If days are considered as blocks, then we must assign two of the four runs to each day.

Consider the design shown in Figure 12-24. Notice that block 1 contains the runs (1) and ab, and that block 2 contains a and b. The contrasts for estimating the main effects A and B are

$$\text{Contrast}_A = ab + a - b - (1)$$
$$\text{Contrast}_B = ab + b - a - (1)$$

Note that these contrasts are unaffected by blocking since in each contrast there is one plus and one minus run from each block. That is, any difference between block 1 and block 2 will cancel out. The contrast for the AB interaction is

$$\text{Contrast}_{AB} = ab + (1) - a - b$$

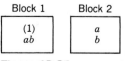

Figure 12-24
The 2^2 design in
two blocks.

Figure 12-25
The 2^3 design in two
blocks, *ABC* confounded.

Since the two runs with the plus sign, *ab* and (1), are in block 1 and the two with the minus sign, *a* and *b*, are in block 2, the block effect and the *AB* interaction are identical. That is, *AB* is confounded with blocks.

The reason for this is apparent from the table of plus and minus signs for the 2^2 design, shown in Table 12-6. From this table, we see that all runs that have a plus on *AB* are assigned to block 1, while all runs that have a minus sign on *AB* are assigned to block 2.

This scheme can be used to confound any 2^k design in two blocks. As a second example, consider a 2^3 design, run in two blocks. Suppose we wish to confound the three-factor interaction *ABC* with blocks. From the table of plus and minus signs, shown in Table 12-9, we assign the runs that are minus on *ABC* to block 1 and those that are plus on *ABC* to block 2. The resulting design is shown in Figure 12-25.

For more information on confounding, refer to Montgomery (1984, Chapter 10). This book contains guidelines for selecting factors to confound with blocks so that main effects and low-order interactions are not confounded. In particular, the book contains a table of suggested confounding schemes for designs with up to seven factors and a range of block sizes, some as small as two runs.

12-3 FRACTIONAL REPLICATION OF THE 2^k DESIGN

As the number of factors in a 2^k increases, the number of runs required increases rapidly. For example, a 2^5 requires 32 runs. In this design, only 5 degrees of freedom correspond to main effects and 10 degrees of freedom correspond to two-factor interactions. If we can assume that certain high-order interactions are negligible, then a fractional factorial design involving fewer that the complete set of 2^k runs can be used to obtain information on the main effects and low-order interactions. In this section, we will introduce fractional replication of the 2^k design. For a more complete treatment, see Montgomery (1984, Chapter 11).

12-3.1 The One-Half Fraction of the 2^k

A one-half fraction of the 2^k design contains 2^{k-1} runs and is often called a 2^{k-1} fractional factorial design. As an example, consider the 2^{3-1} design, that is, a one-half fraction of the 2^3. The table of plus and minus signs for the 2^3 design is shown in Table 12-15. Suppose we select the four runs *a*, *b*, *c*, and *abc* as our one-half fraction. These runs are shown in the top half of Table 12-15. We will use both the

Table 12-15
Plus and minus signs for the 2^3 factorial design

Run	I	A	B	C	AB	AC	BC	ABC
					Factorial Effect			
a	+	+	−	−	−	−	+	+
b	+	−	+	−	−	+	−	+
c	+	−	−	+	+	−	−	+
abc	+	+	+	+	+	+	+	+
ab	+	+	+	−	+	−	−	−
ac	+	+	−	+	−	+	−	−
bc	+	−	+	+	−	−	+	−
(1)	+	−	−	−	+	+	+	−

conventional notation $(a, b, c, \ldots)$ and the plus and minus notation for the runs. The equivalence between the two is as follows:

Notation 1	Notation 2
a	$+ - -$
b	$- + -$
c	$- - +$
abc	$+ + +$

Notice that the 2^{3-1} design is formed by selecting only those runs that yield a plus on the ABC effect. Thus, ABC is called the *generator* of this particular fraction. Furthermore, the identity element I is also plus for the four runs, so we call

$$I = ABC$$

the defining relation for the design.

The runs in the 2^{3-1} designs yield three degrees of freedom associated with the main effects. From Table 12-15, we obtain the estimates of the main effects as

$$A = \tfrac{1}{2}[a - b - c + abc]$$
$$B = \tfrac{1}{2}[-a + b - c + abc]$$
$$C = \tfrac{1}{2}[-a - b + c + abc]$$

It is also easy to verify that the estimates of the two-factor interactions are

$$BC = \tfrac{1}{2}[a - b - c + abc]$$
$$AC = \tfrac{1}{2}[-a + b - c + abc]$$
$$AB = \tfrac{1}{2}[-a - b + c + abc]$$

Thus, the linear combination of observations in column A, say ℓ_A, estimates $A + BC$. Similarly, ℓ_B estimates $B + AC$, and ℓ_C estimates $C + AB$. Two or more effects that have this property are called *aliases*. In our 2^{3-1} design, A and BC

are aliases, B and AC are aliases, and C and AB are aliases. Aliasing is the direct result of fractional replication. In many practical situations, it will be possible to select the fraction so that the main effects and low-order interactions of interest will be aliased with high-order interactions (which are probably negligible).

The alias structure for this design is found by using the defining relation $I = ABC$. Multiplying any effect by the defining relation yields the aliases for that effect. In our example, the alias of A

$$A = A \cdot ABC = A^2BC = BC$$

since $A \cdot I = A$ and $A^2 = I$. The aliases of B and C are

$$B = B \cdot ABC = AB^2C = AC$$

and

$$C = C \cdot ABC = ABC^2 = AB$$

Now suppose that we had chosen the other one-half fraction, that is, the runs in Table 12-15 associated with minus on ABC. The defining relation for this design is $I = -ABC$. The aliases are $A = -BC$, $B = -AC$, and $C = -AB$. Thus, the effects A, B, and C with this particular fraction really estimate $A - BC$, $B - AC$, and $C - AB$. In practice, it usually does not matter which one-half fraction we select. The fraction with the plus sign in the defining relation is usually called the *principal fraction*; the other fraction is usually called the *alternate fraction*.

Sometimes we use *sequences* of fractional factorial designs to estimate effects. For example, suppose we had run the principal fraction of the 2^{3-1} design. From this design we have the following effect estimates:

$$\ell_A = A + BC$$
$$\ell_B = B + AC$$
$$\ell_C = C + AB$$

Suppose that we are willing to assume at this point that the two-factor interactions are negligible. If they are, then the 2^{3-1} design has produced estimates of the three main effects A, B, and C. However, if after running the principal fraction we are uncertain about the interactions, it is possible to estimate them by running the *alternate* fraction. The alternate fraction produces the following effect estimates:

$$\ell'_A = A - BC$$
$$\ell'_B = B - AC$$
$$\ell'_C = C - AC$$

If we combine the estimates from the two fractions, we obtain the following:

Effect, i	from $\frac{1}{2}(\ell_i - \ell'_i)$	from $\frac{1}{2}(\ell_i + \ell'_i)$
$i = A$	$\frac{1}{2}(A + BC + A - BC) = A$	$\frac{1}{2}[A + BC - (A - BC)] = BC$
$i = B$	$\frac{1}{2}(B + AC + B - AC) = B$	$\frac{1}{2}[B + AC - (B - AC)] = AC$
$i = C$	$\frac{1}{2}(C + AB + C - AB) = C$	$\frac{1}{2}[C + AB - (C - AB)] = AB$

Thus, by combining a sequence of two fractional factorial designs, we can isolate both the main effects and the two-factor interactions. This property makes the fractional factorial design highly useful in experimental problems as we can run sequences of small, efficient experiments, combine information across *several* experiments, and take advantage of learning about the process we are experimenting with as we go along.

A 2^{k-1} design may be constructed by writing down the treatment combinations for a full factorial in $k - 1$ factors and then adding the kth factor by identifying its plus and minus levels with the plus and minus signs of the highest order interaction $\pm ABC \cdots (K - 1)$. Therefore, a 2^{3-1} fractional factorial is obtained by writing down the full 2^2 factorial and then equating factor C to the $\pm AB$ interaction. Thus, to generate the principal fraction, we would use $C = +AB$ as follows:

Full 2^2		$2^{3-1}, I = ABC$		
A	B	A	B	$C = AB$
−	−	−	−	+
+	−	+	−	−
−	+	−	+	−
+	+	+	+	+

To generate the alternate fraction we would equate the last column to $C = -AB$.

Example 12-5

To illustrate the use of a one-half fraction, consider the plasma etch experiment described in Example 12-4. Suppose we decide to use a 2^{4-1} design with $I = ABCD$ to investigate the four factors gap (A), pressure (B), C_2F_6 flow rate (C), and power setting (D). This design would be constructed by writing down a 2^3 in the factors A, B, and C and then setting $D = ABC$. The design and the resulting etch rates are shown in Table 12-16.

Table 12-16
The 2^{4-1} design with defining relation $I = ABCD$

Run		A	B	C	$D = ABC$	Etch Rate
1.	(1)	−	−	−	−	550
2.	ad	+	−	−	+	749
3.	bd	−	+	−	+	1052
4.	ab	+	+	−	−	650
5.	cd	−	−	+	+	1075
6.	ac	+	−	+	−	642
7.	bc	−	+	+	−	601
8.	$abcd$	+	+	+	+	729

In this design, the main effects are aliased with the three-factor interactions; note that the alias of A is

$$A \cdot I = A \cdot ABCD$$
$$A = A^2BCD$$
$$A = BCD$$

Similarly,

$$B = ACD$$
$$C = ABD$$
$$D = ABC$$

The two-factor interactions are aliased with each other. For example, the alias of AB is CD:

$$AB \cdot I = AB \cdot ABCD$$
$$AB = A^2B^2CD$$
$$AB = CD$$

The other aliases are

$$AC = BD$$
$$AD = BC$$

The estimates of the main effects and their aliases are found using the four columns of signs in Table 12-16. For example, from column A we obtain

$$\ell_A = A + BCD = \tfrac{1}{4}(-550 + 749 - 1052 + 650 - 1075 + 642 - 601 + 729)$$
$$= -127.00$$

The other columns produce

$$\ell_B = B + ACD = 4.00$$
$$\ell_C = C + ABD = 11.50$$

and

$$\ell_D = D + ABC = 290.51$$

Clearly, ℓ_A and ℓ_D are large, and if we believe that the three-factor interactions are negligible, then the main effects A (gap) and D (power setting) significantly affect the etch rate.

The interactions are estimated by forming the AB, AC, and AD columns and adding them to the table. The signs in the AB column are $+$, $-$, $-$, $+$, $+$, $-$, $-$, $+$, and this column produces the estimate

$$\ell_{AB} = AB + CD = \tfrac{1}{4}(550 - 749 - 1052 + 650 + 1075 - 642 - 601 + 729)$$
$$= -10.00$$

From the AC and AD columns we find

$$\ell_{AC} = AC + BD = -25.50$$
$$\ell_{AD} = AD + BD = -197.50$$

The ℓ_{AD} estimate is large; the most straightforward interpretation of the results is that this is the A and D interaction. Thus, the results obtained from the 2^{4-1} design agree with the full factorial results in Example 12-4.

Normal Probability Plots and Residuals

The normal probability plot is very useful in assessing the significance of effects from a fractional factorial, especially when many effects are to be estimated. Residuals can be obtained from a fractional factorial by the regression model method shown previously. These residuals should be plotted against the predicted values, against the levels of the factors, and on normal probability paper as we have discussed before, both to assess the validity of the underlying model assumptions and to gain additional insight into the experimental situation.

Projection of the 2^{k-1} Design

If one or more factors from a one-half fraction of a 2^k can be dropped, the design will project into a full fractional design. For example, Figure 12-26 presents a 2^{3-1} design. Notice that this design will project into a full factorial in any two of the three original factors. Thus, if we think that at most two of the three factors are important, the 2^{3-1} design is an excellent design for identifying the significant factors. Sometimes experiments that seek to identify a relatively few significant factors from a larger number of factors are called *screening experiments*. This projection property is highly useful in factor screening as it allows negligible factors to be eliminated, resulting in a stronger experiment in the active factors that remain.

In the 2^{4-1} design used in the plasma etch experiment in Example 12-5, we found that two of the four factors (B and C) could be dropped. If we eliminate

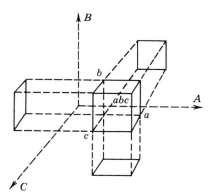

Figure 12-26
Projection of a 2^{3-1} design into three 2^2 designs.

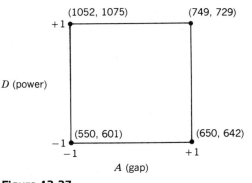

Figure 12-27
The 2^2 design obtained by dropping factors B and C from the plasma etch experiment.

these two factors, the remaining columns in Table 12-16 form a 2^2 design in the factors A and D, with two replicates. This design is shown in Figure 12-27.

Design Resolution

The concept of design resolution is a useful way to catalog fractional factorial designs according to the alias patterns they produce. Designs of resolution III, IV, and V are particularly important. The definitions of these terms and an example of each follow.

1. **Resolution III designs.** In these designs no main effects are aliased with any other main effect, but main effects are aliased with two-factor interactions and two-factor interactions may be aliased with each other. The 2^{3-1} design with $I = ABC$ is of resolution III. We usually employ a subscript Roman numeral to indicate design resolution; thus, this one-half fraction is a 2^{3-1}_{III} design.

2. **Resolution IV designs.** In these designs no main effect is aliased with any other main effect or two-factor interaction, but two-factor interactions are aliased with each other. The 2^{4-1} design with $I = ABCD$ used in Example 12-5 is of resolution IV (2^{4-1}_{IV}).

3. **Resolution V designs.** In these designs no main effect or two-factor interaction is aliased with any other main effect or two-factor interaction, but two-factor interactions are aliased with three-factor interactions. A 2^{5-1} design with $I = ABCDE$ is of resolution V (2^{5-1}_V).

Resolution III and IV designs are particularly useful in factor screening experiments. The resolution IV design provides very good information about main effects and will provide some information about two-factor interactions.

12-3.2 Smaller Fractions: The 2^{k-p} Fractional Factorial Design

While the 2^{k-1} design is valuable in reducing the number of runs required for an experiment, we frequently find that smaller fractions will provide almost as much useful information at even greater economy. In general, a 2^k design may be run in a $1/2^p$ fraction called a 2^{k-p} fractional factorial design. Thus, a $\frac{1}{4}$ fraction is called a 2^{k-2} fractional factorial design, a $\frac{1}{8}$ fraction is called a 2^{k-3} design, a $\frac{1}{16}$ fraction is called a 2^{k-4} design, and so on.

To illustrate a $\frac{1}{4}$ fraction, consider an experiment with six factors and suppose that the engineer is interested primarily in main effects but would also like to get some information about the two-factor interactions. A 2^{6-1} design would require 32 runs and would have 31 degrees of freedom for estimation of effects. Since there are only 6 main effects and 15 two-factor interactions, the one-half fraction is inefficient—it requires too many runs. Suppose we consider a $\frac{1}{4}$ fraction, or a 2^{6-2} design. This design contains 16 runs and with 15 degrees of freedom will alow estimation of all six main effects, with some capability for examination of the two-factor interactions. To generate this design we would write down a 2^4 design in the factors A, B, C, and D, and then add two columns for E and F. To find the new columns, we would select the two *design generators* $I = ABCE$ and $I = BCDF$. Thus, column E would be found from $E = ABC$ and column F would be $F = BCD$. Thus, columns $ABCE$ and $BCDF$ are equal to the identity column. However, we know that the product of any two columns in the table of plus and minus signs for a 2^k is just another column in the table; therefore, the product of $ABCE$ and $BCDF$ or $ABCE(ACDF) = AB^2C^2DEF = ADEF$ is also an identity column. Consequently, the *complete defining relation* for the 2^{6-2} design is

$$I = ABCE = BCDF = ADEF$$

To find the alias of any effect, simply multiply the effect by each word in the above defining relation. The complete alias structure is shown here.

$$A = BCE = DEF = ABCDF \qquad AB = CE = ACDF = BDEF$$
$$B = ACE = CDF = ABDEF \qquad AC = BE = ABDF = CDEF$$
$$C = ABE = BDF = ACDEF \qquad AD = EF = BCDE = ABCF$$
$$D = BCF = AEF = ABCDE \qquad AE = BC = DF = ABCDEF$$
$$E = ABC = ADF = BCDEF \qquad AF = DE = BCEF = ABCD$$
$$F = BCD = ADE = ABCEF \qquad BD = CF = ACDE = ABEF$$
$$ABD = CDE = ACF = BEF \qquad BF = CD = ACEF = ABDE$$
$$ACD = BDE = ABF = CEF$$

Notice that this is a resolution IV design; the main effects are aliased with three-factor and higher interactions, and two-factor interactions are aliased with each other. This design would provide very good information on the main effects and give some idea about the strength of the two-factor interactions. The construction of the design is shown in Table 12-17.

Selection of Design Generators
In the foregoing example, we selected $I = ABCD$ and $I = BCDF$ as the generators to construct the 2^{6-2} fractional factorial design. This choice is not arbitrary; some generators will produce designs with more attractive alias structures than will other generators. For a given number of factors and number of runs we wish to make, we want to select the generators so that the design has the highest possible

Table 12-17

Construction of the 2^{6-2} design with generators $I = ABCE$
and $I = BCDF$

Run	A	B	C	D	$E = ABC$	$F = BCD$
1	−	−	−	−	−	−
2	+	−	−	−	+	−
3	−	+	−	−	+	+
4	+	+	−	−	−	+
5	−	−	+	−	+	+
6	+	−	+	−	−	+
7	−	+	+	−	−	−
8	+	+	+	−	+	−
9	−	−	−	+	−	+
10	+	−	−	+	+	+
11	−	+	−	+	+	−
12	+	+	−	+	−	−
13	−	−	+	+	+	−
14	+	−	+	+	−	−
15	−	+	+	+	−	+
16	+	+	+	+	+	+

resolution. Montgomery (1984) presents a set of designs of maximum resolution
for 2^{k-p} designs with $p \le 10$ factors. This table is reproduced in Table 12-18. In
this table, each choice of generator is shown with a $\pm$ sign. If all generators are
selected with a positive sign (as above) the principal fraction will result; selection
of one or more negative signs will produce an alternate fraction.

Table 12-18

Selected 2^{k-p} Fractional Factorial Designs (from *Design and
Analysis of Experiments*, 2nd ed., by D. C. Montgomery,
John Wiley & Sons, 1984).

Number of Factors k	Fraction	Number of Runs	Design Generators
3	2^{3-1}_{III}	4	$C = \pm AB$
4	2^{4-1}_{IV}	8	$D = \pm ABC$
5	2^{5-1}_{V}	16	$E = \pm ABCD$
	2^{5-2}_{III}	8	$D = \pm AB$
			$E = \pm AC$
6	2^{6-1}_{VI}	32	$F = \pm ABCDE$
	2^{6-2}_{IV}	16	$E = \pm ABC$
			$F = \pm BCD$
	2^{6-3}_{III}	8	$D = \pm AB$
			$E = \pm AC$
			$F = \pm BC$

(continued)

Table 12-18 (Continued)

Number of Factors k	Fraction	Number of Runs	Design Generators
7	2_{VII}^{7-1}	64	$G = \pm ABCDEF$
	2_{IV}^{7-2}	32	$F = \pm ABCD$
			$G = \pm ABDE$
	2_{IV}^{7-3}	16	$E = \pm ABC$
			$F = \pm BCD$
			$G = \pm ACD$
	2_{III}^{7-4}	8	$D = \pm AB$
			$E = \pm AC$
			$F = \pm BC$
			$G = \pm ABC$
8	2_{V}^{8-2}	64	$G = \pm ABCD$
			$H = \pm ABEF$
	2_{IV}^{8-3}	32	$F = \pm ABC$
			$G = \pm ABD$
			$H = \pm BCDE$
	2_{IV}^{8-4}	16	$E = \pm BCD$
			$F = \pm ACD$
			$G = \pm ABC$
			$H = \pm ABD$
9	2_{VI}^{9-2}	128	$H = \pm ACDFG$
			$J = \pm BCEFG$
	2_{IV}^{9-3}	64	$G = \pm ABCD$
			$H = \pm ACEF$
			$J = \pm CDEF$
	2_{IV}^{9-4}	32	$F = \pm CDEF$
			$G = ACDE$
			$H = \pm ABDE$
			$J = ABCE$
	2_{III}^{9-5}	16	$E = \pm ABC$
			$F = \pm BCD$
			$G = \pm ACD$
			$H = \pm ABD$
			$J = \pm ABCD$
10	2_{V}^{10-3}	128	$H = \pm ABCG$
			$J = \pm ACDE$
			$K = \pm ACDF$
	2_{V}^{10-4}	64	$G = \pm BCDF$
			$H = \pm ACDF$
			$J = \pm ABDE$
			$K = \pm ABCE$
	2_{IV}^{10-5}	32	$F = \pm ABCD$
			$G = \pm ABCE$
			$H = \pm ABDE$
			$J = \pm ACDE$
			$K = \pm BCDE$
	2_{III}^{10-6}	16	$E = \pm ABC$
			$F = \pm BCD$
			$G = \pm ACD$
			$H = \pm ABD$
			$J = \pm ABCD$
			$K = \pm AB$

Example 12-6

Parts manufactured in an injection-molding process are experiencing excessive shrinkage. This is causing problems in assembly operations upstream from the injection-molding area. A quality-improvement team has decided to use a designed experiment to study the injection-molding process so that shrinkage can be reduced. The team decides to investigate seven factors: mold temperature (A), screw speed (B), holding time (C), cycle time (D), moisture content (E), gate size (F), and holding pressure (G). Each is examined at two levels, with the objective of learning how each factor affects shrinkage, as well as about how the factors interact.

The team decides to use a 16-run two-level fractional factorial design. Table 12-18 indicates that the appropriate design is a 2_{IV}^{7-3} design, with generators $I = ABCE$, $I = BCDF$, and $I = ACDG$. The design is shown in Table 12-19 and the alias structure for the design is shown in Table 12-20. The last column of Table 12-19 gives the observed shrinkage $\times 10$ for the test part produced at each of the 16 runs in the design.

A normal probability plot of the effect estimates from this experiment is shown in Figure 12-28. The only large effects are A(mold temperature), B(screw speed), and the AB interaction. In light of the alias relationships in Table 12-20, it seems reasonable to tentatively adopt those conclusions. The AB interaction plot in Figure 12-29 shows that the process is very insensitive to temperature if screw speed is at the low level, but is very temperature-sensitive if screw speed is at the high level. With screw speed at the low level, the process should operate with average shrinkage around 10%, regardless of the temperature level chosen.

Based on this initial analysis, the team decided to set both mold temperature and screw speed at the low level. This set of conditions will reduce *mean* parts shrinkage to around 10%. However, the variability in shrinkage from part to part

Table 12-19

2_{IV}^{7-3} design for the injection-molding experiment, Example 12-6

Run	A	B	C	D	$E(=ABC)$	$F(=BCD)$	$G(=ACD)$	Observed Shrinkage ($\times 10$)
1	−	−	−	−	−	−	−	6
2	+	−	−	−	+	−	+	10
3	−	+	−	−	+	+	−	32
4	+	+	−	−	−	+	+	60
5	−	−	+	−	+	+	+	4
6	+	−	+	−	−	+	−	15
7	−	+	+	−	−	−	+	26
8	+	+	+	−	+	−	−	60
9	−	−	−	+	−	+	+	8
10	+	−	−	+	+	+	−	12
11	−	+	−	+	+	−	+	34
12	+	+	−	+	−	−	−	60
13	−	−	+	+	+	−	−	16
14	+	−	+	+	−	−	+	5
15	−	+	+	+	−	+	−	37
16	+	+	+	+	+	+	+	52

Table 12-20

Aliases for the 2_{IV}^{7-3} design used in Example 12-6

$A = BCE = DEF = CDG = BFG$	$AB = CE = FG$
$B = ACE = CDF = DEG = AFG$	$AC = BE = DG$
$C = ABE = BDF = ADG = EFG$	$AD = EF = CG$
$D = BCF = AEF = ACG = BEG$	$AE = BC = DF$
$E = ABC = ADF = BDG = CFG$	$AF = DE = BG$
$F = BCD = ADE = ABG = CEG$	$AG = CD = BF$
$G = ACD = BDE = ABF = CEF$	$BD = CF = EG$

$$ABD = CDE = ACF = BEF = BCG = AEG = DFG$$

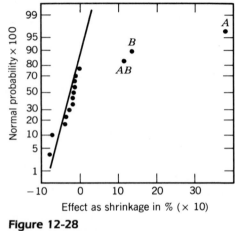

Figure 12-28
Normal probability plot of effects,
Example 12-6.

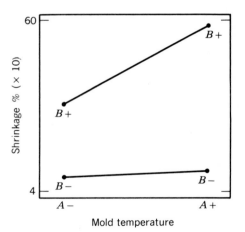

Figure 12-29
AB or mold temperature—screw speed
interaction plot, Example 12-6.

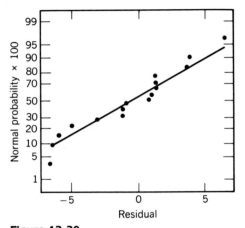

Figure 12-30
Normal probability plot of residuals,
Example 12-6.

is still a potential problem. In effect, the mean shrinkage can be reduced effectively to nearly zero by appropriate modification of the tool; but the part-to-part variability in shrinkage over a production run could still cause problems in assembly, even if the average shrinkage over the run was nearly zero. One way to address this issue is to see if any of the process variables affect *variability* in parts shrinkage.

Figure 12-30 presents the normal probability plot of the residuals. This plot appears satisfactory. The plots of residuals versus each variable were then constructed. One of these plots, that for residuals versus factor C (holding time), is shown in Figure 12-31. The plot reveals that there is much less scatter in the residuals at low holding time than at high holding time. Now the residuals were obtained by first fitting a model for predicted shrinkage

$$\hat{y} = \hat{\beta}_0 + \hat{\beta}_1 x_1 + \hat{\beta}_2 x_2 + \hat{\beta}_{12} x_1 x_2$$

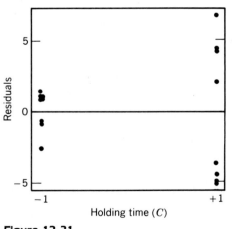

Figure 12-31
Residuals versus holding time (c),
Example 12-6.

where x_1, x_2, and x_1x_2 are coded variables that correspond to the factors A, B, and the AB interaction. The residuals are then

$$e = y - \hat{y}$$

The regression model used to produce the residuals essentially removes the *location* effects of A, B, and AB from the data; the residuals therefore contain information about unexplained variability. Figure 12-28 indicates that there is a *pattern* in that variability and that variability in parts shrinkage may be smaller when holding time is at the low level.

This is further amplified by the analysis of residuals in Table 12-21. In this table, the residuals are arranged at the low $(-)$ and high $(+)$ levels of each factor, and the standard deviation of the residuals at the low and high levels of each factor is calculated. Note that the standard deviation of the residuals with C at the low level $[S(C^-) = 1.63$ in Table 12-21] is considerably smaller than the standard deviation of the residuals with C at the high level $[S(C^+) = 5.70]$.

The bottom portion of Table 12-21 presents a statistic

$$F_i^* = \ln \frac{S^2(i^+)}{S^2(i^-)} \tag{12-26}$$

Table 12-21
Residuals at each level of the factors, Example 12-6

-2.50	-0.50	-0.50	1.50	-2.50	-0.50	-0.25	1.75
-0.25	1.75	2.00	2.00	-0.50	1.50	2.00	2.00
-4.50	7.50	4.50	-5.50	-4.50	7.50	-6.25	4.75
-6.25	4.75	2.00	-6.00	4.50	-5.50	2.00	-6.00

	$-$	Factor A	$+$		$-$	Factor B	$+$
	$S(A^-) = 4.59$		$S(A^+) = 3.80$		$S(B^-) = 4.41$		$S(B^+) = 4.01$

-2.50	-0.50	4.50	7.50	-2.50	-4.50	-0.50	7.50
-0.50	1.50	-4.50	-5.50	-0.50	4.50	1.50	-5.50
-0.25	1.75	-6.25	4.75	-0.25	-6.25	1.75	4.75
2.00	2.00	2.00	-6.00	2.00	2.00	2.00	-6.00

	$-$	Factor C	$+$		$-$	Factor D	$+$
	$S(C^-) = 1.63$		$S(C^+) = 5.70$		$S(D^-) = 3.59$		$S(D^+) = 4.62$

-0.50	-0.50	-2.50	1.50
-0.25	2.00	2.00	1.75
-4.50	-5.50	4.50	7.50
2.00	4.75	-6.25	-6.00

	$-$	Factor E	$+$
	$S(E^-) = 3.40$		$S(E^+) = 4.87$

$$F_i^* = \ln \frac{S^2(i^+)}{S^2(i^-)} \sim N(0, 1)$$

$$F_A^* = -0.38 \qquad F_D^* = 0.50$$

$$F_B^* = -0.19 \qquad F_E^* = 0.72$$

$$F_C^* = 2.50$$

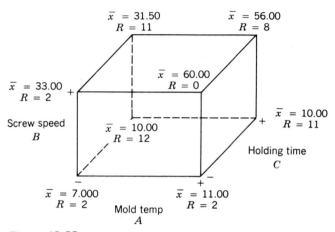

Figure 12-32
Average and range of shrinkage in factors A, B, C,
Example 12-6.

the log of the ratio of the sample variances for factor i, when i is at the high $(+)$ and low $(-)$ levels. This ratio is approximately normally distributed with mean zero and unit standard deviation, so it can be used to judge the difference in the standard deviation at the two levels of factor i. Since the ratio F_C^* exceeds the upper $2\frac{1}{2}\%$ point $Z_{0.025} = 1.96$, we can conclude that the apparent *dispersion* or variability effect observed in Figure 12-28 is real, and setting holding time at its low level would contribute to reducing the variability in shrinkage from part to part during a production run. An alternate way to look for dispersion effects is to examine a normal probability plot of the F_i^* values.

Figure 12-32 shows the data from this experiment projected onto a cube in the factors A, B, and C. The average observed shrinkage and the range of observed shrinkage are shown at each corner of the cube. From inspection of this graph, we see that running the process with screw speed (B) at the low level is the key to reducing average parts shrinkage. If B is low, virtually any combination of temperature (A) and holding time (C) will result in low values of average parts shrinkage. However, from examining the ranges of the shrinkage values at each corner of the cube, it is immediately clear that holding time (C) at the low level is the only reasonable choice if we wish to keep the part-to-part variability in shrinkage low during a production run.

12-4 RESPONSE SURFACE METHODS

Response surface methods are a collection of mathematical and statistical techniques that can be used to improve processes where several variables $x_1, x_2, \ldots, x_k$ influence a process output or *response y*, and the goal is to *optimize* that response. For example, consider the injection-molding process discussed in Example 12-6 in the preceding section. The team assigned to improving this process has identified three process variables that affect parts shrinkage: mold temperature, screw speed, and holding time. Their objective now might be to determine exactly *which* levels of these factors will give the *lowest* levels of parts shrinkage.

The approach used in response surface analysis can be summarized as follows:

1. Step up and conduct a series of experiments that will give reliable data on the process.
2. Fit a mathematical model that describes the relationship between the process variables $x_1, x_2, \ldots, x_k$ and the response y.
3. Use the mathematical model to determine the optimal levels of the process variables; that is, what levels of the x's should be used to produce a maximum (or minimum) value of y?

Response surface methodology usually involves *sequential* experimentation. In the initial stages of the analysis, we usually focus on identifying the important process variables, determining if the process is operating near the optimum, and if it is not, moving the process toward the vicinity of the optimum. In the final stage, contour plotting and other analyses are performed to locate the optimum more precisely and to provide in-depth process understanding. An introduction to response surface methods is in Montgomery (1984, Chapter 15). Two excellent book-length treatments of the subject are Box and Draper (1986) and Cornell and Khuri (1987).

Example 12-7

To illustrate one aspect of response surface methods, we will return to the injection-molding process investigated in Example 12-6. The improvement team in that example has discovered three variables that have some effect on parts shrinkage. Mold/temperature and screw speed primarily affect mean shrinkage, and holding time affects the variability in parts shrinkage. The preliminary indication is that running all three variables at the low level will reduce overall parts shrinkage the most.

The team decides to expand this experiment to determine more precisely what region in this three-variable space would be the best operating point. They decide to use the standard deviation of parts shrinkage as the response variable, and they run an experiment that will allow them to model this response over the region of interest. The team runs the experiment design shown in Figure 12-33. This type of design is called a central composite design. It is constructed by adding the axial (or star) runs and the center points to a standard 2^3 factorial design.

The quality-improvement team used the central composite design in Figure 12-33 for the injection-molding process and produced 35 parts for each run in the design. They used the log standard deviation of parts shrinkage as the response variable. The data from this experiment are shown in Table 12-22. Using the data from this experiment, the improvement team modeled log standard deviation of parts shrinkage (y) as

$$\hat{y} = 0.1040 + 0.0356x_1 + 0.0904x_2 + 0.1469x_3$$
$$+ 0.1316x_1^2 + 0.0609x_2^2 + 0.1546x_3^2$$
$$- 0.0113x_1x_2 + 0.0063x_1x_3 - 0.0413x_2x_3$$

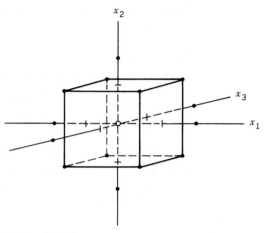

Figure 12-33
Central composite design in three variables.

This equation is often called a second-order response surface model. The central composite design is an important design used to identify and fit these models.

Since the regression coefficients involving x_2 seem relatively small, the team decided that screw speed x_2 does not contribute as much to this model as mold temperature (x_1) and holding time (x_3). Figure 12-34 presents a response surface contour plot of $\hat{y}$ as a function of mold temperature and holding time when screw

Table 12-22
The central composite design for Example 12-7

	Mold Temperature x_1	Screw Speed x_2	Holding Time x_3	Log Standard Deviation of Parts Shrinkage
Cube or factorial design points	−1	−1	−1	0.02
	1	−1	−1	0.14
	−1	1	−1	0.22
	1	1	−1	0.31
	−1	−1	1	0.50
	1	−1	1	0.66
	−1	1	1	0.55
	1	1	1	0.65
Star or axial design points	−1.682	0	0	0.57
	1.682	0	0	0.58
	0	−1.682	0	0.13
	0	1.682	0	0.62
	0	0	−1.682	0.54
	0	0	1.682	0.74
Center points	0	0	0	0.08
	0	0	0	0.04
	0	0	0	0.11
	0	0	0	0.14
	0	0	0	0.09
	0	0	0	0.13

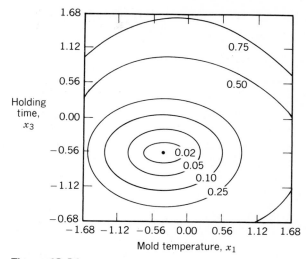

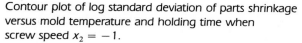

Figure 12-34
Contour plot of log standard deviation of parts shrinkage
versus mold temperature and holding time when
screw speed $x_2 = -1$.

speed takes on the level $x_2 = -1$. Inspection of this figure reveals that lowering mold temperature and using shorter holding times can greatly reduce the standard deviation of parts shrinkage.

This example briefly illustrates only one aspect of response surface methods, using a second-order model to map the response in a region of the process variables thought to contain the optimum. Response surface methods are one of the most powerful experimental design tools available for process development, improvement, and optimization.

12-5 TAGUCHI'S CONTRIBUTIONS TO QUALITY ENGINEERING

In this chapter (and Chapter 11) we have emphasized the importance of moving quality-improvement efforts upstream from the manufacturing process. The goal of quality engineering is to design quality into every product and the processes that build them. Statistically designed experiments are a major element of this activity.

Unfortunately, the principles of experimental design (and statistical methods, in general) have not been as widely used in the West as they have been in Japan. Japanese engineers have had much greater exposure to these concepts, and consequently, experimental design methods have become more of an engineering tool than they have in the United States. In the early 1980s Professor Genechi Taguchi introduced his approach to using experimental design for

1. Designing products or processes so that they are robust to environmental conditions.

2. Designing/developing products so that they are robust to component variation.

3. Minimizing variation around a target value.

See Taguchi and Wu (1980), and Taguchi (1986). By robust, we mean that the product or process performs consistently on target and is relatively insensitive to factors that are difficult to control. Taguchi refers to the three activities described above as *parameter design.*

The philosophy Taguchi recommends is sound and should be included in the quality-improvement process of any organization. However, some novel methods of statistical analysis and some approaches to the design of experiments which he advocates are unnecessarily complicated, inefficient, and sometimes ineffective. In this section, we will briefly overview Taguchi's philosophy regarding quality engineering and present an example of this approach to parameter design. We will use this example to highlight the problems with his technical methods. As we will see, his sound engineering concepts can be combined with more efficient and effective experiment design and statistical data analysis methods.

12-5.1 The Taguchi Philosophy

Professor Taguchi's philosophy about quality engineering is broadly applicable. He considers three stages in a product's (or process's) development: system design, parameter design, and tolerance design. In system design, the engineer uses scientific and engineering principles to determine the basic configuration. For example, if we wish to measure an unknown resistance, we may use knowledge of electrical circuits to determine that the basic system should be configured as a Wheatstone bridge. If we are designing a process to assemble printed circuit boards, the process designer will determine the need for axial insertion machines, surface-mount placement machines, flow solder machines, and so forth.

In the parameter design stage, the specific values for the system parameters are determined. This involves choosing the nominal resistor and power supply values for the Wheatstone bridge, the number and type of component placement machines for the printed circuit board assembly process, and so forth. Usually, the objective is to specify these parameter nominal values in order to minimize variability transmitted from uncontrollable (or noise) variables.

Tolerance design is used to determine the best tolerances for the parameters. For example, in the Wheatstone bridge, tolerance design methods would reveal which components were most sensitive in the design and where the tolerances should be set. If a component does not have much effect on the performance of the circuit, it can be specified with a wide tolerance.

Taguchi recommends that statistical experimental design methods be employed to assist in quality improvement, particularly during parameter design and tolerance design. In this section, we will focus on parameter design. Experimental design methods can be used to find a best product or process design. By "best" here we mean a product or process that is robust or insensitive to uncontrollable factors that will influence the product or process once it is in routine operation.

The notion of *robust design* is not new; engineers have always tried to design products so that they will work well under uncontrollable conditions. For example, commercial transport aircraft fly nearly as well in a thunderstorm as they do in clear air. Taguchi deserves recognition for realizing that experimental design can

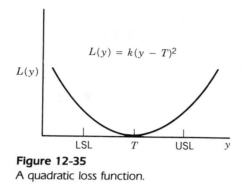

Figure 12-35
A quadratic loss function.

be used as a formal part of the *engineering design process* to help accomplish this objective.

A key component of Taguchi's philosophy is *reduction of variability*. We often require that each quality characteristic have a target or *nominal* value. The objective is to reduce variability around this target. Taguchi models the departures that may occur from this target value with a *loss function*. The loss refers to the cost that is incurred by *society* when the consumer uses a product whose quality characteristics differ from the nominal. The concept of societal loss is a departure from traditional thinking. Taguchi imposes a quadratic loss function of the form

$$L(y) = k(y - T)^2 \tag{12-27}$$

shown in Figure 12-35. Clearly, this type of function will penalize even small departures of y from the target T. Again, this is a departure from traditional Western thinking, which usually only attaches penalties to the case where y is outside of specifications (say $y > USL$ or $y < LSL$ in Figure 12-35). However, the Taguchi philosophy regarding reduction of variability is entirely consistent with the continuous improvement philosophy of Deming and Juran.

In summary Taguchi's philosophy involves three central ideas:

1. Products and processes should be designed so that they are robust to external sources of variability.
2. Experimental design methods are an engineering tool to help accomplish this objective.
3. Operation on target is more important than conformance to specifications.

These are sound concepts, and their value should be readily apparent. Furthermore, they are supportive of and consistent with the philosophy of quality improvement expressed in previous chapters of this book.

We now turn to a discussion of the specific methods that Professor Taguchi recommends for carrying this philosophy into practice. As we will see, his approach to experimental design and data analysis can be improved.

12-5.2 The Taguchi Approach to Parameter Design

We will use an example to illustrate Professor Taguchi's approach to parameter design. The example was published in *Quality Progress* in December 1987. (See

"The Taguchi Approach to Parameter Design," by D. M. Byrne and S. Taguchi, *Quality Progress*, December 1987, pp. 19–26.)

The Problem

The experiment involves finding a method to assemble an elastometric connector to a nylon tube that would deliver the required pull-off performance to be suitable for use in an automotive engine application. The specific objective of the experiment is to maximize pull-off force. Four controllable and three uncontrollable noise factors were identified. These factors are defined in Table 12-23. We want to find the levels of the controllable factors that are least influenced by the noise factors and that provide maximum pull-off force. Notice that, while the noise factors are not controllable during routine operations, they can be controlled for purposes of a test. Each controllable factor is tested at three levels, and each noise factor is tested at two levels.

The Experimental Design

Following the Taguchi parameter design methodology, one experimental design is selected for the controllable factors and another for the noise or uncontrollable factors. These designs are shown in Table 12-24. Panel (a) of Table 12-24 contains an L_9 orthogonal array, a table of integers whose column elements (1, 2, 3) represent the low, medium, and high levels of the column factors. Each row of the orthogonal array represents a run; that is, a specific set of factor levels to be tested. The L_9 orthogonal array will accommodate four factors at three levels each in nine runs. Panel (b) of Table 12-24 contains the L_8 orthogonal array—a design for up to seven factors at two levels each in eight runs. Because the L_8 array in this example contains only three factors, E, F, and G, the remaining columns can be used to estimate interactions. The purpose of the noise factor array (L_8) is to create noise so that we can identify the controllable factor levels that are least sensitive to it.

The two designs are combined, as shown in Table 12-25. In this complete *parameter design layout*, the L_9 array containing the controllable factors is called the *inner* array, and the L_8 array containing the noise factors is called the *outer* array. Literally, each of the nine runs from the inner array is tested across the eight runs from the inner array, for a total required sample size of 72. The observed pull-off force is reported in Table 12-25.

Data Analysis and Conclusions

The data from this experiment may now be analyzed. Taguchi recommends analyzing the mean response for each run in the inner array (see Table 12-25); he also suggests analyzing variation using an appropriately chosen signal-to-noise ratio (SN). These signal-to-noise ratios are derived from the quadratic loss function, and three of them are considered "standard" and widely applicable. They are:

Nominal the best

$$SN_N = 10 \log(\bar{y}^2/S^2) \qquad (12\text{-}28)$$

Larger the better

$$SN_L = -10 \log\left(\frac{1}{n} \sum_{i=1}^{n} \frac{1}{y_i^2}\right) \qquad (12\text{-}29)$$

Table 12-23

Factors and levels for the parameter design example

Controllable Factors		Levels	
A. Interference	Low	Medium	High
B. Connector wall thickness	Thin	Medium	Thick
C. Insertion depth	Shallow	Medium	Deep
D. Percent adhesive in connector pre-dip	Low	Medium	High

Uncontrollable Factors	Levels	
E. Conditioning time	24 h	120 h
F. Conditioning temperature	72° F	150° F
G. Conditioning relative humidity	25%	75%

Table 12-24

Designs for the controllable and uncontrollable factors

(a)
L_9 Orthogonal Array for
the Controllable Factors

	Variable			
Run	A	B	C	D
1	1	1	1	1
2	1	2	2	2
3	1	3	3	3
4	2	1	2	3
5	2	2	3	1
6	2	3	1	2
7	3	1	3	2
8	3	2	1	3
9	3	3	2	1

(b)
L_8 Orthogonal Array for
the Uncontrollable Factors

	Variable						
Run	E	F	$E \times F$	G	$E \times G$	$F \times G$	e
1	1	1	1	1	1	1	1
2	1	1	1	2	2	2	2
3	1	2	2	1	1	2	2
4	1	2	2	2	2	1	1
5	2	1	2	1	2	1	2
6	2	1	2	2	1	2	1
7	2	2	1	1	2	2	1
8	2	2	1	2	1	1	2

Table 12-25

Parameter design with both inner and outer arrays

				Outer E	1	1	1	1	2	2	2	2		
			Array (L_8) F		1	1	2	2	1	1	2	2		
				G	1	2	1	2	1	2	1	2		
Inner Array (L_9)													Responses	
Run	A	B	C	D									$\bar{y}$	SN_L
1	1	1	1	1	15.6	9.5	16.9	19.9	19.6	19.6	20.0	19.1	17.525	24.025
2	1	2	2	2	15.0	16.2	19.4	19.2	19.7	19.8	24.2	21.9	19.475	25.522
3	1	3	3	3	16.3	16.7	19.1	15.6	22.6	18.2	23.3	20.4	19.025	25.335
4	2	1	2	3	18.3	17.4	18.9	18.6	21.0	18.9	23.2	24.7	20.125	25.904
5	2	2	3	1	19.7	18.6	19.4	25.1	25.6	21.4	27.5	25.3	22.825	26.908
6	2	3	1	2	16.2	16.3	20.0	19.8	14.7	19.6	22.5	24.7	19.225	25.326
7	3	1	3	2	16.4	19.1	18.4	23.6	16.8	18.6	24.3	21.6	19.850	25.711
8	3	2	1	3	14.2	15.6	15.1	16.8	17.8	19.6	23.2	24.2	18.338	24.852
9	3	3	2	1	16.1	19.9	19.3	17.3	23.1	22.7	22.6	28.6	21.200	26.152

Smaller the better

$$SN_S = -10 \log\left(\frac{1}{n}\sum_{i=1}^{n} y_i^2\right) \qquad (12\text{-}30)$$

Notice that these SN ratios are expressed in a decibel scale. We use SN_N if the objective is to reduce variability around a specific target, SN_L if the system is optimized when the response is as large as possible, and SN_S if the system is optimized when the response is as small as possible. Factor levels that maximize the appropriate SN ratio are optimal.

In our problem we use SN_L as our objective is to maximize pull-off force. The last *two* columns of Table 12-25 contain $\bar{y}$ and SN_L for each of the nine inner-array runs. Taguchi-oriented practitioners often use the analysis of variance to determine which factors influence $\bar{y}$ and which influence the signal-to-noise ratio. They also employ graphs of the "marginal means" of each factor, such as the ones shown in Figures 12-36 and 12-37. The usual approach is to examine the graphs and "pick the winner." In this case, factors A and C have larger effects than do B and D, and in terms of maximizing SN_L we would select A_{medium}, C_{deep}, B_{medium}, and D_{low}. In terms of maximizing average pull-off force y, we would choose A_{medium}, C_{medium}, B_{medium}, and D_{low}. Notice that there is almost no difference between C_{medium} and C_{deep}. The implication is that this choice of levels will maximize mean pull-off force and reduce variability in pull-off force.

Taguchi claims that the use of the SN ratio generally eliminates the need to examine specific interactions between the controllable and noise factors, although sometimes looking at these interactions improves process understanding. The authors of this study found that the AG and DE interactions were strong. Analysis of these interactions, shown in Figure 12-38, suggests that A_{medium} is best (highest

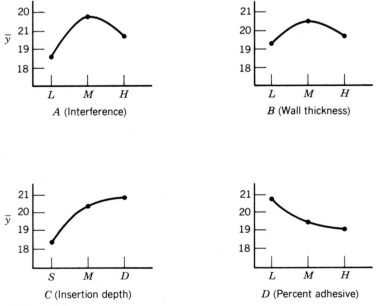

Figure 12-36
Effects of controllable factors on mean response.

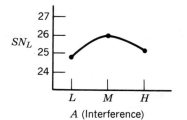

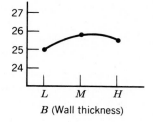

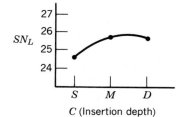

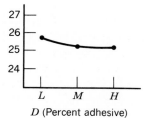

Figure 12-37
Effects of controllable factors on SN_L.

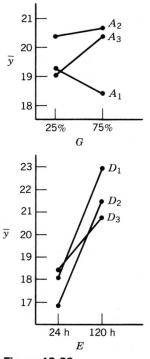

Figure 12-38
AG and AE interactions.

pull-off force and a slope close to zero, indicating that if we choose A_{medium} the effect of relative humidity is minimized) and that D_{low} gives the highest pull-off force, regardless of the conditioning time.

When cost and other factors were taken into account, the experimenters in this example finally decided to use A_{medium}, B_{low}, C_{medium}, and D_{low}. (B_{low} was much less expensive than B_{medium}, and C_{medium} was felt to give slightly less variability that C_{deep}.) Since this is not a run in the original nine inner-array trials, five additional tests were made at this set of conditions as a *confirmation experiment*. For this confirmation experiment, the levels used on the noise variables were E_{low}, F_{low}, and G_{low}. The authors report that good results were obtained during the confirmation test.

Critique of Experimental Designs

The advocates of Taguchi's approach to parameter design utilize the orthogonal array designs, two of which were presented in the foregoing example (the L_8 and the L_9). Many of these designs are just simple two-level fractional factorials (the L_8 is a 2_{III}^{7-4} design), but others are three-level fractional factorials that have very messy alias structures. Furthermore, Taguchi usually selects the designs so that interactions between control factors are aliased with their main effects.

Taguchi argues that we do not need explicitly to consider two-factor interactions, either by correctly specifying the response and design factors or by using a sliding setting approach to eliminate the interaction. As an example of the second approach, consider two factors—pressure and temperature. Varying these factors independently will probably produce an interaction. However, if temperature levels are chosen contingent on the pressure levels, then the interaction effect can be minimized. In practice, these two approaches are usually difficult to implement unless we have an unusually high level of process knowledge. The lack of provision for adequately dealing with potential interactions between the controllable process factors is a major weakness of the Taguchi approach to parameter design.

Instead of designing the experiment to investigate potential interactions, Taguchi prefers to use three-level factors to estimate curvature. A much safer strategy is to identify potential effects and interactions that may be important and then consider curvature only in the important variables, if there is evidence that the curvature is important. This will usually lead to fewer experiments, simpler interpretation of the data, and better overall process understanding.

Another criticism of the Taguchi approach to parameter design is that the inner- and outer-array structure usually leads to a very large experiment. For example, in the foregoing application, the authors used 72 tests to investigate only seven factors, and still they could not estimate any of the two-factor interactions between the four controllable factors. Several alternative experimental designs would be superior to the inner and outer-array method used in this example. Suppose that we run all seven factors at two levels. Consider the 2_{IV}^{7-2} design in Table 12-18. The alias relationships for this design are shown in the top half of Table 12-26. Notice that this design requires only 32 runs (as compared to 72). In the bottom half of Table 12-26 two different possible assignments of process controllable variables and noise variables to the letters $A–G$ are shown. The first assignment scheme allows all interactions between controllable and noise factors to be estimated while providing estimates of all main effects that are clear of two-factor interactions. The second assignment scheme allows all controllable factor main effects and their two-factor interactions to be estimated; provides estimates

Table 12-26
An alternative parameter design

$\frac{1}{4}$ fraction of 7 factors in 32 runs	Resolution IV

$$I = ABCDF = ABDEG = CEFG$$

ALIASES

A	$AF = BCD$	$CG = EF$
B	$AG = BDE$	$DE = ABG$
$C = EFG$	$BC = ADF$	$DF = ABC$
D	$BD = ACF = AEG$	$DG = ABE$
$E = CFG$	$BE = ADG$	$ACE = AFG$
$F = CEG$	$BF = ACD$	$ACG = AEF$
$G = CEF$	$BG = ADE$	$BCE = BFG$
$AB = CDF = DEG$	$CD = ABF$	$BCG = BEF$
$AC = BDF$	$CE = FG$	$CDE = DFG$
$AD = BCF = BEG$	$CF = ABD = EG$	$CDG = DEF$
$AE = BDG$		

ASSIGNMENT OF FACTORS

1. Controllable factors are assigned to letters C, E, F, and G. Noise factors are assigned to letters A, B, and D. All interactions between controllable and noise factors can be estimated, and all controllable factor main effects can be estimated clear of two-factor interactions.

2. Controllable factors are assigned to letters A, B, C, and D. Noise factors are assigned to letters E, F, and G. All controllable factor main effects and two factor interactions can be estimated; only the CE, CF, and CG interactions are aliased with interactions of the noise factors.

of all noise factor main effects that are clear of two-factor interactions; and aliases only three controllable-noise factor interactions with a single two-factor interaction between two noise factors. This is a much cleaner alias relationship than that obtained from the original inner- and outer-array parameter design that required over twice as many runs.

In general, the inner- and outer-array approach is unnecessary. A better strategy is to use a single design (Taguchi advocates would call it an inner array only) and incorporate both controllable and noise factors in this design. Now this design must be chosen with a high enough resolution to estimate all the interactions of interest. (Usually the design must be resolution IV or higher.) This approach will almost always lead to a dramatic reduction in the size of the experiment. At the same time, it will produce information that is more likely to improve process understanding.

A final aspect of design is Taguchi's use of linear graphs to assign factors to the columns of the orthogonal array. A set of linear graphs for the L_8 design is shown in Figure 12-39. In these graphs, each number is a column in the design. A line segment on the graph corresponds to interaction between the nodes it connects. To assign variables to columns in an orthogonal array, assign the variables to nodes first; then when the nodes are used up, assign the variables to the line segments. When you assign variables to the nodes, strike out any line segments that

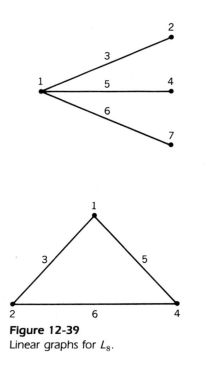

Figure 12-39
Linear graphs for L_8.

correspond to interactions that might be important. The linear graphs in Figure 12-39 imply that column 3 contains the interaction between columns 1 and 2 in the L_8, column 5 contains the interaction between columns 1 and 4, and so forth. If we had four factors, we could assign them to columns 1, 2, 4, and 7. This would insure that each main effect was clear of two-factor interactions. What is *not* clear is the two-factor interaction aliasing. If the main effects are in columns 1, 2, 4, and 7, then column 3 contains the 1–2 *and* the 4–7 interaction, column 5 contains the 1–4 *and* the 2–7 interaction, and column 6 contains the 1–7 *and* the 2–4 interaction. This is clearly the case, because four variables in eight runs is a resolution IV plan with all pairs of two-factor interactions aliased. For a complete picture of the aliasing, refer to the plasma etch experiment in Example 12-5, which utilized this design. In order to fully understand the two-factor interaction aliasing, Taguchi would refer the experiment designer to a supplementary interaction table.

Taguchi (1986) gives a collection of linear graphs for each of his recommended orthogonal array designs. These linear graphs seem to have been developed heuristically. Unfortunately, their use can lead to inefficient designs. For example, see his car engine experiment [Taguchi and Wu (1980)] and his cutting tool experiment [Taguchi (1986)]. Both of these are 16-run designs which he sets up as resolution III designs, having main effects aliased with two-factor interactions. Conventional methods for setting up these designs would have resulted in resolution IV plans, with the main effects clear of the two-factor interactions. For the quality engineer who simply wants to generate a good design, the linear graph approach may not produce the best result. A better approach is to use a simple table that gives the design and its full alias structures. These tables are easy to construct or can be generated by several widely available and inexpensive computer programs.

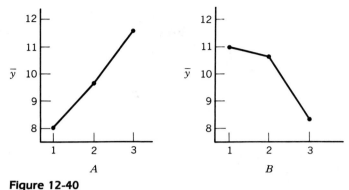

Figure 12-40
"Marginal means" plots for the data in Table 12-27.

Critique of Data Analysis Methods

Several of Taguchi's data analysis methods are questionable. For example, he recommends some variations of the analysis of variance that are known to produce spurious results, and he also proposes some unique methods for the analysis of attribute and life testing data. For a discussion of these methods, refer to Box et al. (1988) and the references contained therein.

In this section we focus on only two aspects of data analysis used in the example: use of "marginal means" plots to optimize the factor settings, and the signal-to-noise ratios. Consider the use of "marginal means" plots and the associated "pick the winner" optimization that was demonstrated previously in the pull-off force problem. To keep the situation simple, suppose that we have two factors A and B, each at three levels. The marginal means plots are shown in Figure 12-40. From looking at these graphs, we would select A_3 and B_1 as the optimum, assuming that we wish to maximize y. However, this is the wrong answer: direct inspection of Table 12-27 or the AB interaction plot in Figure 12-41 shows that A_3 and B_2 produce the maximum value of y. In general, playing "pick the winner" with marginal averages can never be guaranteed to produce the optimum. Now the Taguchi advocates recommend that a confirmation experiment be run, although this approach offers no guarantees either. We might be confirming a response that differs dramatically from the optimum. The best way to find a set of optimum conditions is with response surface methods, as discussed in Section 12-4.

Table 12-27
Data for the "marginal means" plots in Figure 12-37

| | | | A | | Averages |
		1	2	3	for B
	1	10	10	13	11.00
B	2	8	10	14	10.67
	3	6	9	10	8.33
Averages for A		8.00	9.67	11.67	

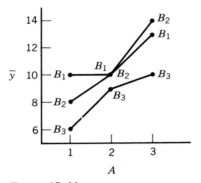

Figure 12-41
The *AB* interaction plot for the
data in Table 12-27.

Taguchi's signal-to-noise ratios SN_N, SN_L, and SN_S [see Equations (12-28), (12-29), and (12-30)] are his recommended performance measures in a wide variety of situations. By maximizing the appropriate SN ratio, it is claimed that variability is minimized.

Consider first the SN_N ratio. It can be used as the performance measure if we wish to minimize variability around a target value. Since we can write

$$SN_N = 10 \log(\bar{y}^2/S^2)$$
$$= 10 \log(\bar{y}^2) - 10 \log(S^2)$$

maximizing this ratio for a fixed target value (estimated by $\bar{y}$) would be equivalent to minimizing $\log(S^2)$. This requires fewer calculations, is more intuitively appealing, and provides a clearer understanding of the relationship involving the factors that influence process variability—in other words better process understanding. Furthermore, if we minimize $\log(S^2)$ directly, we eliminate the risk of obtaining wrong answers from maximization of SN_N if some of the manipulated factors drive the mean $\bar{y}$ upward instead of driving S^2 downward. There is no guarantee that the transformation $10 \log(\bar{y}^2/S^2)$ uncouples *location* and *dispersion* effects. As Hunter (1985) points out, other data transformations might be more appropriate.

The ratios SN_L and SN_S are even more troublesome. Schmidt and Boudot (1989) have conducted a simulation study that addresses the effectiveness of these signal-to-noise ratios in detecting dispersion or variability effects. They show that SN_L and SN_S are completely *ineffective* in identifying dispersion effects, although they may serve to identify *location* effects—factors that drive the mean. The reason for this is easy to see. Consider the smaller-the-better signal-to-noise ratio

$$SN_S = -10 \log\left(\frac{1}{n} \sum_{i=1}^{n} y_i^2\right)$$

Ignoring the -10 scale factor and the logarithm transformation, we can write

$$\frac{1}{n} \sum_{i=1}^{n} y_i^2 = \bar{y}^2 + \frac{(n-1)}{n} S^2$$

where S^2 is the sample variance. Thus, SN_S directly confounds location and dispersion effects. To some extent we observed this confounding of location and dispersion effects in the analysis of the SN_L ratio in the pull-off force example. Notice in Figures 12-33 and 12-34 that the plots of $\bar{y}$ and SN_L versus each factor have approximately the same shape, implying that both responses measure location. In fact, it can be shown that *none* of the factors A–D in this example has *any* major effect on process variability. (Refer to Exercise 12-15.) Furthermore, since these ratios involve y^2 and $(1/y^2)$, they will be very sensitive to outliers or values near zero, and they are not invariant to linear transformation of the original response. Hunter (1987) strongly recommends that these signal-to-noise ratios not be used. This is excellent advice.

A better approach for isolating location and dispersion and location effects is to analyze $\bar{y}$ and $\log(S)$ as separate responses. For an example of using $\log(S)$ as a response variable, see Example 12-7. If no replication is available to estimate variability at each run in the design, methods for analyzing residuals can be used. Refer to Example 12-6.

Some Final Remarks

In this section we have directed some major criticisms toward the specific methods of experimental design and data analysis used in the Taguchi approach to parameter design. Remember that these comments have focused on technical issues and that the broad philosophy recommended by Taguchi is inherently sound.

On the other hand, many companies have reported success with the use of Taguchi's parameter design methods. If the methods are flawed, why do they produce successful results? Taguchi advocates often refute criticism with the remark that "they work." We must remember that the "best guess" and "one-factor-at-a-time" methods will also work, and occasionally they produce good results. This is no reason to claim they are good methods. Most successful applications of Taguchi's technical methods have been in industries without a history of good experimental design practice. Designers and developers were using the best guess and one-factor-at-a-time methods (or other unstructured approaches), and since the Taguchi approach is based on the factorial design concept, it will often produce better results than the methods it replaces. In other words, the factorial design is so powerful that even when it is used inefficiently, it will work better than almost anything else.

As pointed out earlier, the Taguchi approach to parameter design often leads to *large comprehensive* experiments, with 70 or more runs. Most of the successful applications of this approach have been in industries characterized by a high-volume, low-cost manufacturing environment. In such situations, large designs may not be a real problem, as it is really no more difficult to make 72 runs than to make 16 or 32 runs. On the other hand, in industries characterized by low-volume, high-cost manufacturing, (such as aerospace, chemical and process industries, electronics and semiconductor, etc.), these methodological inefficiencies can be significant.

A final point concerns the learning process. If the Taguchi approach to parameter design works and yields good results, we may still not know what has caused the result, because of aliasing of critical interactions. In other words, we may have solved a problem (a short-term success), but we may not have gained *process knowledge*, which could be invaluable in future problems.

In summary, we should support Taguchi's philosophy of quality engineering. However, in order to carry this philosophy into practice, we must rely on methods that are simpler, more efficient, and easier to learn and apply.

12-6 Exercises

12-1 An article in *Industrial Quality Control* (1956, pp. 5–8) describes an experiment to investigate the effect of glass type and phosphor type on the brightness of a television tube. The response measured is the current necessary (in microamps) to obtain a specified brightness level. The data are shown below. Analyze the data and draw conclusions.

	Phosphor Type		
Glass Type	1	2	3
1	280	300	290
	290	310	285
	285	295	290
2	230	260	220
	235	240	225
	240	235	230

12-2 A process engineer is trying to improve the life of a cutting tool. He has run a 2^3 experiment using cutting speed (A), metal hardness (B), and cutting angle (C) as the factors. The data from two replicates are shown below.

	Replicate	
Run	I	II
(1)	221	311
a	325	435
b	354	348
ab	552	472
c	440	453
ac	406	377
bc	605	500
abc	392	419

a. Do any of the three factors affect tool life?

b. What combination of factor levels produces the longest tool life?

c. Is there a combination of cutting speed and cutting angle that always gives good results regardless of metal hardness?

12-3 Find the residuals from the tool life experiment in Exericse 12-2. Construct a normal probability plot of the residuals. Plot the residuals versus the predicted values. Comment on the plots.

12-4 Four factors are thought to possibly influence the taste of a soft drink beverage; type of sweetener (A), ratio of syrup to water (B), carbonation level (C), and temperature (D). Each factor can be run at two levels, producing a 2^4 design. At each run in the design, samples of the beverage are given to a test panel consisting of 20 people. Each tester assigns a point score from 1 to 10 to the beverage. Total score is the response variable, and the objective is to find a formulation that maximizes total score. Two replicates of this design are run, and the results shown here. Analyze the data and draw conclusions.

Treatment Combination	Replicate I	Replicate II	Treatment Combination	Replicate I	Replicate II
(1)	190	193	d	198	195
a	174	178	ad	172	176
b	181	185	bd	187	183
ab	183	180	abd	185	186
c	177	178	cd	199	190
ac	181	180	acd	179	175
bc	188	182	bcd	187	184
abc	173	170	abcd	180	180

12-5 Consider the experiment in Exercise 12-4. Plot the residuals against the levels of factors A, B, C, and D. Also construct a normal probability plot of the residuals. Comment on these plots.

12-6 Find the standard error of the effects for the experiment in Exercise 12-4. Using the standard errors as a guide, what factors appear significant?

12-7 Suppose that only the data from replicate I in Exercise 12-4 were available. Analyze the data and draw appropriate conclusions.

12-8 Suppose that only one replicate of the 2^4 design in Exercise 12-4 could be run, and we could only conduct eight tests each day. Set up a design that would block out the day effect. Show specifically which runs would be made on each day.

12-9 Show how a 2^5 experiment could be set up in two blocks of 16 runs each. Specifically, which runs would be made in each block?

12-10 R. D. Snee ("Experimenting with a Large Number of Variables," in *Experiments in Industry: Design, Analysis and Interpretation of Results*, by R. D. Snee, L. B. Hare, and J. B. Trout, Editors, ASQC, 1985) describes an experiment in which a 2^{5-1} design with $I = ABCDE$ was used to investigate the effects of five factors on the color of a chemical product. The factors were A = solvent/reactant, B = catalyst/reactant, C = temperature, D = reactant purity, and E = reactant pH. The results obtained are as follows:

$$e = -0.63 \qquad d = 6.79$$
$$a = 2.51 \qquad ade = 6.47$$
$$b = -2.68 \qquad bde = 3.45$$
$$abe = 1.66 \qquad abd = 5.68$$
$$c = 2.06 \qquad cde = 5.22$$
$$ace = 1.22 \qquad acd = 4.38$$
$$bce = -2.09 \qquad bcd = 4.30$$
$$abc = 1.93 \qquad abcde = 4.05$$

a. Prepare a normal probability plot of the effects. Which effects seem active?

b. Calculate the residuals. Construct a normal probability plot of the residuals and plot the residuals versus the fitted values. Comment on the plots.

c. If any factors are negligible, collapse the 2^{5-1} design into a full factorial in the active factors. Comment on the resulting design and interpret the results.

12-11 An article in the *Journal of Quality Technology* (Vol. 17, 1985, pp. 198–206) describes the use of a replicated fractional factorial to investigate the effect of five factors on the free height of leaf springs used in an automotive application. The factors are A = furnace temperature, B = heating time, C = transfer time, D = hold down time, and E = quench oil temperature. The data are shown below.

A	B	C	D	E			
−	−	−	−	−	7.78,	7.78,	7.81
+	−	−	+	−	8.15,	8.18,	7.88
−	+	−	+	−	7.50,	7.56,	7.50
+	+	−	−	−	7.59,	7.56,	7.75
−	−	+	+	−	7.54,	8.00,	7.88
+	−	+	−	−	7.69,	8.09,	8.06
−	+	+	−	−	7.56,	7.52,	7.44
+	+	+	+	−	7.56,	7.81,	7.69
−	−	−	−	+	7.50,	7.25,	7.12
+	−	−	+	+	7.88,	7.88,	7.44
−	+	−	+	+	7.50,	7.56,	7.50
+	+	−	−	+	7.63,	7.75,	7.56
−	−	+	+	+	7.32,	7.44,	7.44
+	−	+	−	+	7.56,	7.69,	7.62
−	+	+	−	+	7.18,	7.18,	7.25
+	+	+	+	+	7.81,	7.50, ·	7.59

a. Write out the alias structure for this design. What is the resolution of this design?

b. Analyze the data. What factors influence mean free height?

c. Calculate the range and standard deviation of free height for each run. Is there any indication that any of these factors affects variability in free height?

d. Analyze the residuals from this experiment and comment on your findings.

e. Is this the best possible design for five factors in 16 runs? Specifically, can you find a fractional design for five factors in 16 runs with higher resolution than this one?

12-12 An article in *Industrial and Engineering Chemistry* ("More on Planning Experiments to Increase Research Efficiency," 1970, pp. 60–65) uses a 2^{5-2} design to investigate the effect of A = condensation temperature, B = amount of materials, C = solvent volume, D = condensation time, and E = amount of material 2, on yield. The results obtained are as follows:

$$e = 23.2 \qquad ad = 16.9 \qquad cd = 23.8 \qquad bde = 16.8$$
$$ab = 15.5 \qquad bc = 16.2 \qquad ace = 23.4 \qquad abcde = 18.1$$

a. Verify that the design generators used were $I = ACE$ and $I = BDE$.

b. Write down the complete defining relation and the aliases from this design.

c. Estimate the main effects.

d. Prepare an analysis of variance table. Verify that the AB and AD interactions are available to use as error.

e. Plot the residuals versus the fitted values. Also construct a normal probability plot of the residuals. Comment on the results.

12-13 Consider the leaf spring experiment in Exercise 12-11. Suppose that factor E (quench oil temperature) is very difficult to control during manufacturing. Where would you set factors A, B, C, and D to reduce variability in free height as much as possible regardless of the quench oil temperature used?

12-14 Consider the leaf spring experiment in Exercise 12-11. Put factors A, B, C, and D into an inner array and factor E into an outer array. Write out the resulting Taguchi parameter design.

    a. Calculate the average free height and the type SN_N signal-to-noise ratio for each point in the inner array.

    b. Compute effect estimates using $\bar{y}$ and SN_N as response variables. Is there evidence that any of the factors affects $\bar{y}$ or SN_N?

    c. Repeat the analysis in part (b) using $\log(S^2)$ as the response instead of SN_N. What are your conclusions, and do they differ from those in part (b)?

12-15 Consider the data from the pull-off force experiment described in Table 12-25. Calculate $\bar{y}$ and S for each of the nine runs in the inner array.

    a. Plot $\log S$ versus $\log \bar{y}$ for each of the nine runs. It can be shown that if the slope of the line passing through these points is zero, then the variability of y is unrelated to the mean of y [see Montgomery (1984), Chapter 4]. What are your conclusions after examining this plot?

    b. Can you find any indication that any of the four factors A, B, C, and D affects the variability of pull-off force?

PART IV

Acceptance Sampling

Inspection of raw materials, semifinished products, or finished products is an important part of quality assurance. When inspection is for the purpose of acceptance or rejection of a product, based on adherence to a standard, the type of inspection proceduce employed is usually called acceptance sampling. This section presents three chapters that deal with the design and use of sampling plans, schemes, and systems. The primary focus is on lot-by-lot acceptance sampling.

Chapter 13 presents lot-by-lot acceptance sampling plans for attributes. Included in this chapter is a discussion of MIL STD 105D and its civilian counterpart ANSI/ASQC Z1.4. Variables sampling plans are presented in Chapter 14, and MIL STD 414 and its civilian counterpart, ANSI/ASQC Z1.9, are discussed. Various aspects of the relationship between the military and civilian standard sampling plans are also discussed. Chapter 15 presents a survey of several useful topics in acceptance sampling, including chain-sampling plans, sampling plans for continuous production, skip-lot sampling plans, the effect of inspection error on acceptance sampling, and the economic design of acceptance-sampling plans.

The underlying philosophy here is that acceptance sampling is not a substitute for adequate process controls. In fact, it is our opinion that the successful use of process-control techniques at the early stages of manufacturing, including the installation of such statistical controls at the vendor or supplier level, can greatly reduce and in some cases eliminate the need for extensive sampling inspection.

Chapter 13

Lot-by-Lot Acceptance Sampling for Attributes

13-1 THE ACCEPTANCE-SAMPLING PROBLEM

Acceptance sampling is a major field of statistical quality control. A typical application of acceptance sampling is as follows: A company receives a shipment of product from a vendor. This product is often a component or raw material used in the company's manufacturing process. A sample is taken from the lot, and some quality characteristic of the units in the sample is inspected. On the basis of the information in this sample, a decision is made regarding lot disposition. Usually, this decision is either to accept or to reject the lot. Sometimes we refer to this decision as *lot sentencing*. Accepted lots are put into production; rejected lots may be returned to the vendor or may be subjected to some other *lot-disposition action*.

While it is customary to think of acceptance sampling as a receiving inspection activity, there are other uses of sampling methods. For example, frequently a manufacturer will sample and inspect its own product at various stages of production. Lots that are accepted are sent forward for further processing, while rejected lots may be reworked or scrapped.

Three aspects of sampling are important:

1. It is the purpose of acceptance sampling to sentence lots, not to estimate the lot quality. Most acceptance-sampling plans are not designed for estimation purposes.

2. Acceptance-sampling plans do not provide any *direct* form of quality control. Acceptance sampling simply accepts and rejects lots. Even if all lots are of the same quality, sampling will accept some lots and reject others, the accepted lots being no better than the rejected ones. Process controls are used to control and systematically improve quality, but acceptance sampling is not.

3. The most effective use of acceptance sampling is *not* to "inspect quality into the product," but rather as an audit tool to ensure that the output of a process conforms to requirements.

Generally, there are three approaches to lot sentencing: (1) accept with no inspection; (2) 100% inspection—that is, inspect every item in the lot, removing all defective[1] units found (defectives may be returned to the vendor, reworked, replaced with known good items, or discarded); and (3) acceptance sampling. The no-inspection alternative is useful in situations where either the vendor's process is so good that defective units are almost never encountered or where there is no economic justification to look for defective units. For example, if the vendor's process-capability ratio is 3 or 4, acceptance sampling is unlikely to discover any defective units. We generally use 100% inspection in situations where the component is extremely critical and passing any defectives would result in an unacceptably high failure cost at subsequent stages, or where the vendor's process capability is inadequate to meet specifications. Acceptance sampling is most likely to be useful in the following situations:

1. When testing is destructive.

2. When the cost of 100% inspection is extremely high.

3. When 100% inspection is not technologically feasible or would require so much calendar time that production scheduling would be seriously impacted.

4. When there are many items to be inspected and the inspection error rate is sufficiently high that 100% inspection might cause a higher percentage of defective units to be passed than would occur with the use of a sampling plan.

5. When the vendor has an excellent quality history, and some reduction in inspection from 100% is desired, but the vendor's process-capability ratio is sufficiently low to make no inspection an unsatisfactory alternative.

6. When there are potentially serious product liability risks, and although the vendor's process is satisfactory, a program for continuously monitoring the product is necessary.

---

[1] In previous chapters, the terms "nonconforming" and "nonconformity" were used instead of defective and defect. This is because the popular meanings of defective and defect differ from their technical meanings and have caused considerable misunderstanding, particularly in product liability litigation. In the field of sampling inspection, however, "defective" and "defect" continue to be used in their technical sense—that is, nonconformance to requirements.

13-1.1 Advantages and Disadvantages of Sampling

When acceptance sampling is contrasted with 100% inspection, it has the following advantages:

1. It is usually less expensive because there is less inspection.
2. There is less handling of the product, hence reduced damage.
3. It is applicable to destructive testing.
4. Fewer personnel are involved in inspection activities.
5. It often greatly reduces the amount of inspection error.
6. The rejection of entire lots as opposed to the simple return of defectives often provides a stronger motivation to the vendor for quality improvements.

Acceptance sampling also has several disadvantages, however. These include the following:

1. There are risks of accepting "bad" lots and rejecting "good" lots.
2. Less information is usually generated about the product or about the process that manufactured the product.
3. Acceptance sampling requires planning and documentation of the acceptance-sampling procedure whereas 100% inspection does not.

While this last point is often mentioned as a disadvantage of acceptance sampling, proper design of an acceptance-sampling plan usually requires study of the actual level of quality required by the consumer. This resulting knowledge is often a useful input into the overall quality planning and engineering process. Thus, in many applications, it may not be a significant disadvantage.

We have pointed out that acceptance sampling is a "middle ground" between the extremes of 100% inspection and no inspection. If often provides a methodology for moving between these extremes as sufficient information is obtained on the control of the manufacturing process that produces the product. While there is no direct control of quality in the application of an acceptance-sampling plan to an isolated lot, when that plan is applied to a stream of lots from a vendor, it becomes a means of providing protection for both the producer of the lot and the consumer. It also provides for an accumulation of quality history regarding the process that produces the lot, and it may provide feedback that is useful in process control, such as determining when process controls at the vendor's plant are not adequate. Finally, it may place economic or psychological pressure on the vendor to improve the production process.

13-1.2 Types of Sampling Plans

There are a number of different ways to classify acceptance-sampling plans. One major classification is by attributes and variables. *Variables*, of course, are quality characteristics that are measured on a numerical scale. *Attributes* are quality characteristics that are expressed on a "go, no-go" basis. This chapter deals with lot-by-lot acceptance sampling plans for attributes. Variables sampling plans are the subject of Chapter 14. A number of special acceptance-sampling procedures are discussed in Chapter 15.

A single sampling plan is a lot-sentencing procedure in which one sample of n units is selected at random from the lot, and the disposition of the lot is determined based on the information contained in that sample. For example, a single-sampling plan for attributes would consist of a sample size n and an acceptance number c. The procedure would operate as follows: Select n items at random from the lot. If there are c or fewer defectives in the sample, accept the lot, and if there are more than c defective items in the sample, reject the lot. We investigate this type of sampling plan extensively in Section 13-2.

Double-sampling plans are somewhat more complicated. Following an initial sample, a decision based on the information in that sample is made either to (1) accept the lot, (2) reject the lot, or (3) take a second sample. If the second sample is taken, the information from both the first and second sample is combined in order to reach a decision whether to accept or reject the lot. Double-sampling plans are discussed in Section 13-3.

A multiple-sampling plan is an extension of the double-sampling concept, in that more than two samples may be required in order to reach a decision regarding the disposition of the lot. Sample sizes in multiple sampling are usually smaller than they are in either single or double sampling. The ultimate extension of multiple sampling is sequential sampling, in which units are selected from the lot one at a time, and following inspection of each unit, a decision is made either to accept the lot, reject the lot, or select another unit. Multiple- and sequential-sampling plans are also discussed in Section 13-3.

Single-, double-, multiple-, and sequential-sampling plans can be designed so that they produce equivalent results. That is, these procedures can be designed so that a lot of specified quality has exactly the same probability of acceptance under all four types of sampling plans. Consequently, when selecting the type of sampling procedure, one must consider factors such as the administrative efficiency, the type of information produced by the plan, the average amount of inspection required by the procedure, and the impact that a given procedure may have on the material flow in the manufacturing organization. These issues are discussed in more detail in Section 13-3.

13-1.3 Lot Formation

How the lot is formed can influence the effectiveness of the aceeptance-sampling plan. There are a number of important considerations in forming lots for inspection. Some of these are as follows:

1. **Lots should be homogeneous.** The units in the lot should be produced by the same machines, the same operators, and from common raw materials, at approximately the same time. When lots are nonhomogeneous, such as when the output of two different production lines is mixed, the acceptance-sampling scheme may not function as effectively as it could. Nonhomogeneous lots also make it more difficult to take corrective action to eliminate the source of defective products.

2. **Larger lots are preferred over smaller ones.** It is usually more economically efficient to inspect large lots than small ones.

3. Lots should be conformable to the materials-handling systems used in both the vendor and consumer facilities. In addition, the items in the lots should be packaged so as to minimize shipping and handling risks, and so as to make selection of the units in the sample relatively easy.

13-1.4 Random Sampling

The units selected for inspection from the lot should be chosen at random, and they should be representative of all the items in the lot. The random-sampling concept is extremely important in acceptance sampling. Unless random samples are used, bias will be introduced. For example, the vendor may ensure that the units packaged on the top of the lot are of extremely good quality, knowing that the inspector will select the sample from the top layer. "Salting" a lot in this manner is not a common practice, but if it occurs and nonrandom-sampling methods are used, the effectiveness of the inspection process is destroyed.

The technique often suggested to draw a random sample is to assign a number to each item in the lot. Then *n* random numbers are drawn, where the range of these numbers is from 1 to the maximum number of units in the lot. This sequence of random numbers determines which units in the lot will constitute the sample. Random numbers can be conveniently generated from a computer, from many hand-held calculators, or from tables of random numbers such as in Appendix IX. If products have serial or other code numbers, these numbers can be used to avoid the process of actually assigning numbers to each unit. Another possibility would be to use a three-digit random number to represent the length, width, and depth in a container. For example, the random number 482 could represent the unit located on the fourth level, eighth row, and second column of the container.

In situations where we cannot assign a number to each unit, utilize serial or code numbers, or randomly determine the location of the sample unit, some other technique must be employed to ensure that the sample is random or representative. Sometimes the inspector may "stratify" the lot. This consists of dividing the lot into strata or layers and then subdividing each strata into cubes, as shown in Figure 13-1. Units are then selected from within each cube. While this stratification of the lot is usually an imaginary activity performed by the inspector and does

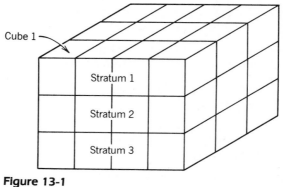

Figure 13-1
Stratifying a lot.

not necessarily ensure random samples, at least it ensures that units are selected from all locations in the lot.

We cannot over emphasize the importance of random sampling. If judgment methods are used to select the sample, the statistical basis of the acceptance-sampling procedure is lost.

13-1.5 Guidelines for Using Acceptance Sampling

An acceptance-sampling plan is a statement of the sample size to be used and the associated acceptance or rejection criteria for sentencing individual lots. A sampling scheme is defined as a set of procedures consisting of acceptance-sampling plans in which lot sizes, sample sizes, and acceptance or rejection criteria along with the amount of 100% inspection and sampling are related. Finally, a sampling system is a unified collection of one or more acceptance-sampling schemes. In this chapter, we see examples of sampling plans, sampling schemes, and sampling systems.

The major types of acceptance-sampling procedures and their applications are shown in Table 13-1. In general, the selection of an acceptance-sampling procedure depends both on the objective of the sampling organization and the history of the organization whose product is sampled. Furthermore, the application of sampling methodology is not static. That is, there is a natural evolution from one level of sampling effort to another. For example, if we are dealing with a vendor who enjoys an excellent quality history, we might begin with an attributes sampling plan. As our experience with the vendor grows, and its good-quality reputation is proved by the results of our sampling activities, we might transition to a sampling procedure that requires much less inspection, such as skip-lot sampling. Finally, after extensive experience with the vendor, and if its process capability is extremely good, we might stop all acceptance-sampling activities on the product.

Table 13-1
Acceptance-sampling procedures

Objective	Attribute Procedure	Variables Procedure
Assure quality levels for consumer/producer	Select plan for specific OC curve	Select plan for specific OC curve
Maintain quality at a target	AQL System; MIL STD 105D, ANSI/ASQC Z1.4	AQL System; MIL STD 414, ANSI/ASQC Z1.9
Assure average outgoing quality level	AOQL System; Dodge-Romig plans	AOQL System
Reduce inspection, with small sample sizes, good-quality history	Chain sampling	Narrow-limit gaging
Reduce inspection after good-quality history	Skip-lot sampling; double sampling	Skip-lot sampling; double sampling
Assure quality no worse than target	LTPD plan; Dodge-Romig plans	LTPD Plan; hypothesis testing

In another situation, where we have little knowledge of or experience with the vendor's quality-assurance efforts, we might begin with attributes sampling using a plan that assures us that the quality of accepted lots is no worse than a specified target value. If this plan proves successful, and if the vendor's performance is satisfactory, we might transition from attributes to variables inspection, particularly as we learn more about the nature of the vendor's process. Finally, we might use the information gathered in variables sampling plans in conjunction with efforts directly at the vendor's manufacturing facility to assist in the installation of process controls. A successful program of process controls at the vendor level might improve the vendor's process capability to the point where inspection could be discontinued.

These examples illustrate that there is a life cycle of application of acceptance-sampling techniques. This was also reflected in the phase diagram, Figure 1-2, which presented the percentage of application of various quality-assurance techniques as a function of the maturity of the business organization. Typically, we find that organizations with relatively new quality-assurance efforts place a great deal of reliance on acceptance sampling. As their maturity grows and the quality organization develops, they begin to rely less on acceptance sampling and more on statistical process control and experimental design.

The importance of quality in component parts and raw materials has caused many manufacturing organizations to exert considerable pressure on their vendors and suppliers to improve quality. The proper use of acceptance-sampling plans is an integral aspect of this activity. Remember, however, that quality must be built into a product. An article in the *Wall Street Journal*[2] states that

> . . . *some manufacturers have pursuaded their suppliers to install a management tool called statistical process control. Managers and engineers set standards for the quality of parts or materials, such as the minimum and maximum width of steel sheet. Then products are tested as they are being made; when the quality varies too much, the process is corrected. That sounds like common sense, but engineers says the mix of computers, statistics and immediate information lets companies catch problems as they occur.*

In effect, we must rely more on adequate process controls at the vendor level to ensure quality, and use acceptance sampling as an audit or compliance tool, not as a technique for attempting to inspect quality into the product or sort good lots from bad ones.

Manufacturers are also trying to improve the quality of their products by reducing the number of vendors from whom they buy their components, and by working more closely with the ones they retain. Once again, the key tool in this effort to improve quality is statistical process control. Acceptance sampling will always be an important ingredient of any quality-assurance program; however, remember that it is an activity that you are trying to avoid doing. It is much more cost effective to use adequate process controls at the appropriate stage of the manufacturing process. Sampling methods will be a tool that you employ along the road to that ultimate goal.

---

[2] "Concerns' Push to Improve Quality of Products Puts Heat on Suppliers," *The Wall Street Journal*, September 20, 1983.

13-2 SINGLE-SAMPLING PLANS FOR ATTRIBUTES

13-2.1 Definition of a Single-Sampling Plan

Suppose that a lot of size N has been submitted for inspection. A single-sampling plan is defined by the sample size n and the acceptance number c. Thus, if the lot size is $N = 10,000$, then the sampling plan

$$n = 89$$
$$c = 2$$

means that from a lot of size 10,000 a random sample of $n = 89$ units is inspected and the number of nonconforming or defective items d observed. If the number of observed defectives d is less than or equal to $c = 2$, the lot will be accepted. If the number of observed defectives d is greater than 2, the lot will be rejected. Since the quality characteristic inspected is an attribute, each unit in the sample is judged to be either conforming or nonconforming. One or several attributes can be inspected in the same sample; generally, a unit that is nonconforming to specifications on one or more attributes is said to be a defective unit. This procedure is called a single-sampling plan because the lot is sentenced based on the information contained in one sample of size n.

13-2.2 The OC Curve

An important measure of the performance of an acceptance-sampling plan is the operating-characteristic (OC) curve. This curve plots the probability of accepting the lot versus the lot fraction defective. Thus, the OC curve displays the discriminatory power of the sampling plan. That is, it shows the probability that a lot submitted with a certain fraction defective will be either accepted or rejected. The OC curve of the sampling plan $n = 89$, $c = 2$ is shown in Figure 13-2. It is easy to demonstrate how the points on this curve are obtained. Suppose that the lot size N is large (theoretically infinite). Under this condition, the distribution of the number of defectives d in a random sample of n items is binomial with parameters n and p, where p is the fraction of defective items in the lot. An equivalent way to conceptualize this is to draw lots of N items at random from a theoretically infinite process, and then to draw random samples of n from these lots. Sampling from the lot in this manner is the equivalent of sampling directly from the process. The probability of observing exactly d defectives is

$$P\{d \text{ defectives}\} = f(d) = \frac{n!}{d!(n-d)!} p^d(1-p)^{n-d} \tag{13-1}$$

The probability of acceptance is just the probability that d is less than or equal to c, or

$$P_a = P\{d \le c\} = \sum_{d=0}^{c} \frac{n!}{d!(n-d)!} p^d(1-p)^{n-d} \tag{13-2}$$

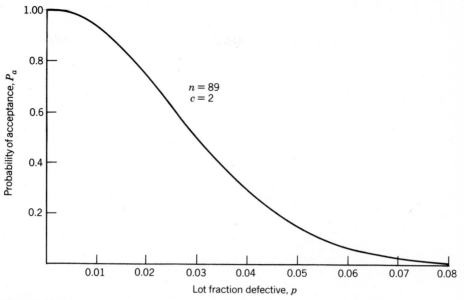

Figure 13-2
OC curve of the single-sampling plan, $n = 89$, $c = 2$.

For example, if the lot fraction defective is $p = 0.01$, $n = 89$ and $c = 2$, then

$$P_a = P\{d \leq 2\} = \sum_{d=0}^{2} \frac{89!}{d!(89 - d)!} (0.01)^d(0.99)^{89-d}$$

$$= \frac{89!}{0!89!} (0.01)^0(0.99)^{89} + \frac{89!}{1!88!} (0.01)^1(0.99)^{88} + \frac{89!}{2!(87)!} (0.01)^2(0.99)^{87}$$

$$= 0.9397$$

The OC curve is developed by evaluating (13-2) for various values of p. Table 13-2 displays the calculated value of several points on the curve.

Table 13-2
Probabilities of acceptance for the
single-sampling plan $n = 89$, $c = 2$

Fraction Defective, p	Probability of Acceptance, P_a
0.005	0.9897
0.010	0.9397
0.020	0.7366
0.030	0.4985
0.040	0.3042
0.050	0.1721
0.060	0.0919
0.070	0.0468
0.080	0.0230
0.090	0.0109

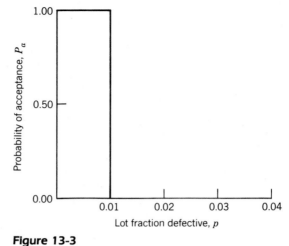

Figure 13-3
Ideal OC curve.

The OC curve shows the discriminatory power of the sampling plan. For example, in the sampling plan $n = 89$, $c = 2$, if the lots are 2% defective, the probability of acceptance is approximately 0.74. This means that if 100 lots from a process that manufactures 2% defective product are submitted to this sampling plan, we will expect to accept 74 of the lots and reject 26 of them.

Effect of *n* and *c* on OC Curves

A sampling plan that discriminated perfectly between good and bad lots would have an OC curve that looks like Figure 13-3. The OC curve runs horizontally at a probability of acceptance $P_a = 1.00$ until a level of lot quality that is considered

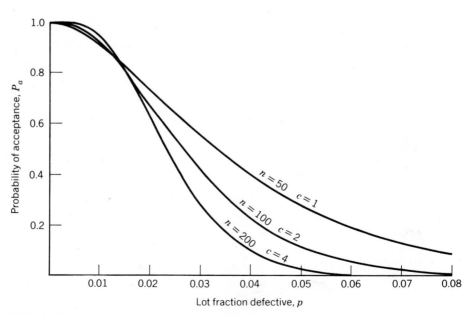

Figure 13-4
OC curves for different sample sizes.

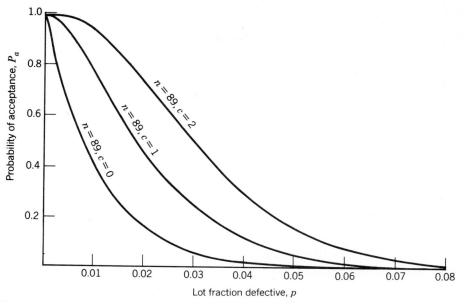

Figure 13-5
The effect of changing the acceptance number on the OC curve.

"bad" is reached, at which point the curve drops vertically to a probability of acceptance $P_a = 0.00$, and then the curve runs horizontally again for all lot fraction defectives greater than the undesirable level. If such a sampling plan could be employed, all lots of "bad" quality would be rejected, and all lots of "good" quality would be accepted.

Unfortunately, the ideal OC curve in Figure 13-3 can almost never be obtained in practice. In theory, it could be realized by 100% inspection, if the inspection were error free. The ideal OC curve shape can be approached, however, by increasing the sample size. Figure 13-4 shows that the OC curve becomes more like the idealized OC curve shape as the sample size increases. (Note that the acceptance number c is kept proportional to n.) Thus, the precision with which a sampling plan differentiates between good and bad lots increases with the size of the sample. The greater the slope of the OC curve, the greater the discriminatory power.

Figure 13-5 shows how the OC curve changes as the acceptance number changes. Generally, changing the acceptance number does not dramatically change the slope of the OC curve. As the acceptance number is decreased, the OC curve is shifted to the left. Plans with smaller values of c provide discrimination at lower levels of lot fraction defective than do plans with larger values of c.

Specific Points on the OC Curve

Frequently, the quality engineer's interest focuses on certain points on the OC curve. The vendor or supplier is usually interested in knowing what level of lot or process quality would yield a high probability of acceptance. For example, the vendor might be interested in the 0.95 probability of acceptance point. This would indicate the level of process fallout that could be experienced and still have a 95% chance that the lots would be accepted. Conversely, the consumer might be interested in the other end of the OC curve. That is, what level of lot or process quality will yield a low probability of acceptance?

A consumer often establishes a sampling plan for a continuing supply of components or raw material with reference to an *acceptable quality level* or AQL. The AQL represents the poorest level of quality for the vendor's process that the consumer would consider to be acceptable as a process average. Note that the AQL is a property of the vendor's manufacturing process; it is not a property of the sampling plan. The consumer will often design the sampling procedure so that the OC curve gives a high probability of acceptance at the AQL. Furthermore, the AQL is not usually intended to be a specification on the product, nor is it a target value for the vendor's production process. It is simply a standard against which to judge the lots. It is hoped that the vendor's process will operate at a fallout level that is considerably better than the AQL.

The consumer will also be interested in the other end of the OC curve, that is, in the protection that is obtained for individual lots of poor quality. In such a situation, the consumer may establish a *lot tolerance percent defective* (LTPD). The LTPD is the poorest level of quality that the consumer is willing to accept in an individual lot. Note that the lot tolerance percent defective is not a characteristic of the sampling plan, but is a level of lot quality specified by the consumer. Alternate names for the LTPD are the *rejectable quality level* (RQL) and the *limiting quality level* (LQL). It is possible to design acceptance-sampling plans that give specified probabilities of acceptance at the LTPD point. Subsequently, we will see how to design sampling plans that have specified performance at the AQL and LTPD points.

Type-A and Type-B OC Curves

The OC curves that were constructed in the previous examples are called type-B OC curves. In the construction of the OC curve it was assumed that the samples came from a large lot or that we were sampling from a stream of lots selected at random from a process. In this situation, the binomial distribution is the exact probability distribution for calculating the probability of lot acceptance. Such an OC curve is referred to as a type-B OC curve.

The type-A OC curve is used to calculate probabilities of acceptance for an isolated lot of finite size. Suppose that the lot size is N, the sample size is n, and the acceptance number is c. The exact sampling distribution of the number of defective items in the sample is the hypergeometric distribution.

Figure 13-6 shows the type-A OC curve for a single-sampling plan with $n = 50$, $c = 1$, where the lot size is $N = 500$. The probabilities of acceptance defining the OC curve were calculated using the hypergeometric distribution. Also shown on this graph is the type-A OC curve for $N = 2000$, $n = 50$, and $c = 1$. Note that the two OC curves are very similar. Generally, as the size of the lot increases, the lot size has a decreasing impact on the OC curve. In fact, if the lot size is at least 10 times the sample size ($n/N \leq 0.10$), the type-A and type-B OC curves are virtually indistinguishable. As an illustration, the type-B OC curve for the sampling plan $n = 50$, $c = 1$ is also shown in Figure 13-6. Notice that it is identical to the type-A OC curve based on a lot size of $N = 2000$.

The type-A OC curve will always lie below the type-B OC curve. That is, if a type-B OC curve is used as an approximation for a type-A curve, the probabilities of acceptance calculated for the type-B curve will always be higher than they would have been if the type-A curve had been used instead. However, this difference is only significant when the lot size is small relative to the sample size. Unless otherwise stated, all discussion of OC curves in this text is in terms of the type-B OC curve.

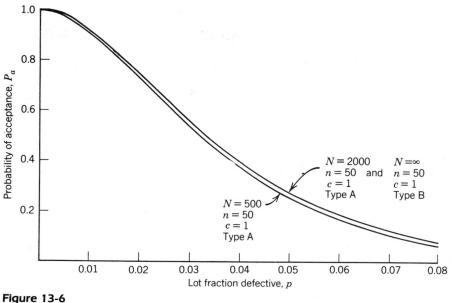

Figure 13-6
Type-A and type-B OC curves.

Other Aspects of OC Curve Behavior

Two approaches to designing sampling plans that are encountered in practice have certain implications for the behavior of the OC curve. Since not all of these implications are positive, it is worthwhile to briefly mention these two approaches to sampling plan design. These approaches are the use of sampling plans with zero acceptance numbers ($c = 0$) and the use of sample sizes that are a fixed percentage of the lot size.

Figure 13-7 shows several OC curves for acceptance-sampling plans with $c = 0$. By comparing Figure 13-7 with Figure 13-5, it is easy to see that plans with zero acceptance numbers have OC curves that have a very different shape than the OC curves of sampling plans for which $c > 0$. Generally, sampling plans with $c = 0$ have OC curves that are convex throughout their range. As a result of this shape, the probability of acceptance begins to drop very rapidly, even for small values of the lot fraction defective. This is extremely hard on the vendor, and in some circumstances, it may be extremely uneconomical for the consumer. For example, consider the sampling plans in Figure 13-5. Suppose the acceptable quality level is 1%. This implies that we would like to accept lots that are 1% defective or better. Notice that if sampling plan $n = 89$, $c = 1$, is used, the probability of lot acceptance at the AQL is about 0.78. On the other hand, if the plan $n = 89$, $c = 0$, is used, the probability of acceptance at the AQL is approximately 0.41. That is, nearly 60% of the lots of AQL quality will be rejected if we use an acceptance number of zero. If rejected lots are returned to the vendor, then a large number of lots will be unnecessarily returned, perhaps creating production delays at the consumer's manufacturing site. If the consumer screens or 100% inspects all rejected lots, a large number of lots that are of acceptable quality will be screened. This is, at best, an inefficient use of sampling resources. In Chapter 15, we suggest an alternative approach to using zero acceptance numbers called *chain-sampling*

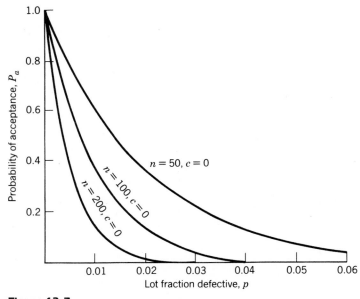

Figure 13-7
OC curves for single-sampling plan with $c = 0$.

plans. Under certain circumstances, chain sampling works considerably better than acceptance-sampling plans with $c = 0$.

Figure 13-8 presents the OC curves for sampling plans in which the sample size is a fixed percentage of the lot size. The principal disadvantage of this approach is that the different sample sizes offer different levels of protection. It is illogical

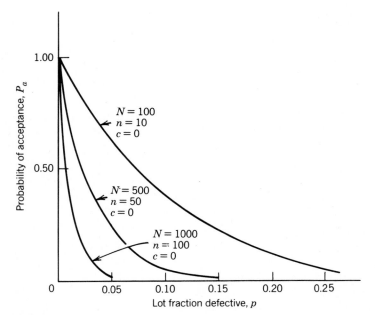

Figure 13-8
OC curves for sampling plans where sample size n is 10% of the lot size.

for the level of protection that the consumer enjoys for a critical part or component to vary as the size of the lot varies. While sampling procedures such as this
one were in wide use before the statistical principles of acceptance sampling were
generally known, their use has (unfortunately) not entirely disappeared.

13-2.3 Designing a Single-Sampling Plan with a Specified OC Curve

A common approach to the design of an acceptance-sampling plan is to require
that the OC curve pass through two designated points. Note that one point is not
enough to fully specify the sampling plan; however, two points are sufficient. In
general, it does not matter which two points are specified.

Suppose that we wish to construct a sampling plan such that the probability
of acceptance is $1 - \alpha$ for lots with fraction defective p_1, and the probability of
acceptance is β for lots with fraction defective p_2. Assuming that binomial sampling (with type-B OC curves) is appropriate, we see that the sample size n and
acceptance number c are the solution to

$$1 - \alpha = \sum_{d=0}^{c} \frac{n!}{d!(n-d)!} p_1^d (1 - p_1)^{n-d}$$

$$\beta = \sum_{d=0}^{c} \frac{n!}{d!(n-d)!} p_2^d (1 - p_2)^{n-d}$$
(13-3)

Equation (13-3) was obtained by writing out the two points on the OC curve using
the binomial distribution. The two simultaneous equations in (13-3) are nonlinear,
and there is no simple, direct solution.

The nomograph in Figure 13-9 can be used for solving these equations. The
procedure for using the nomograph is very simple. Two lines are drawn on the
nomograph, one connecting p_1 and $1 - \alpha$, and the other connecting p_2 and β.
The intersection of these two lines gives the region of the nomograph in which the
desired sampling plan is located. To illustrate the use of the nomograph, suppose
we wish to construct a sampling plan for which $p_1 = 0.01$, $\alpha = 0.05$, $p_2 = 0.06$, and
$\beta = 0.10$. Locating the intersection of the lines connecting $(p_1 = 0.01, 1 - \alpha = 0.95)$
and $(p_2 = 0.06$ and $\beta = 0.10)$ on the nomograph indicates that the plan $n = 89$,
$c = 2$ is very close to passing through these two points on the OC curve. Obviously,
since n and c must be integer, this procedure will actually produce several plans
that have OC curves that pass close to the desired points. For instance, if the first
line is followed either to the c-line just above the intersection point or to the c-line
just below it, and the alternate sample sizes are read from the chart, this will produce two plans that pass almost exactly through the $p_1, 1 - \alpha$ point, but may deviate somewhat from the p_2, β point. A similar procedure could be followed with
the p_2, β-line. The result of following both of these lines would be four plans that
pass approximately through the two points specified on the OC curve.

In addition to the graphical procedure that we have described for designing
sampling plans with specified OC curves, tabular procedures are also available
for the same purpose. Duncan (1974) gives a good description of these techniques.

While any two points on the OC curve could be used to define the sampling
plan, it is customary in many industries to use the AQL and LTPD points for this
purpose. When the levels of lot quality specified are $p_1 = $ AQL and $p_2 = $ LTPD,
the corresponding points on the OC curve are usually referred to as the producer's

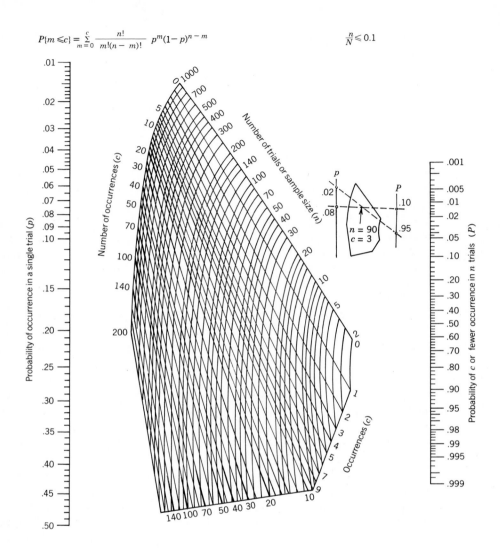

$$P\{m \leqslant c\} = \sum_{m=0}^{c} \frac{n!}{m!(n-m)!} \; p^m(1-p)^{n-m} \qquad \frac{n}{N} \leqslant 0.1$$

Note:
If p is less than 0.01, set $k \times p$ on the p-scale and multiply the values on the n-scale by k, where $k = 0.01/p$ (taking k to the next higher integer).

Figure 13-9
Binomial nomograph.

risk point and the consumer's risk point, respectively. Thus, $1 - \alpha$ would be called the producer's risk and β would be called the consumer's risk.

13-2.4 Rectifying Inspection

Acceptance-sampling programs usually require corrective action when lots are rejected. This generally takes the form of 100% inspection or *screening* of rejected lots, with all discovered defective items either removed for subsequent rework or return to the vendor, or replaced from a stock of known good items. Such sampling

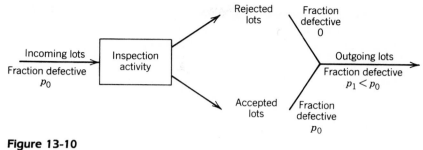

Figure 13-10
Rectifying inspection.

programs are called *rectifying inspection programs*, because the inspection activity affects the final quality of the outgoing product. This is illustrated in Figure 13-10. Suppose that incoming lots to the inspection activity have fraction defective p_0. Some of these lots will be accepted, and others will be rejected. The rejected lots will be screened, and their final fraction defective will be zero. However, accepted lots have fraction defective p_0. Consequently, the outgoing lots from the inspection activity are a mixture of lots with fraction defective p_0 and fraction defective zero, so the average fraction defective in the stream of outgoing lots is p_1, which is less than p_0. Thus, a rectifying inspection program serves to "correct" lot quality.

Rectifying inspection programs are not new. Such programs were developed by Harold F. Dodge and Harry G. Romig at the Bell Telephone Laboratories and used at Western Electric before World War II. Rectifying inspection programs are used in situations where the manufacturer wishes to know the average level of quality that is likely to result at a given stage of the manufacturing operations. Thus, rectifying inspection programs are used either at receiving inspection, in-process inspection of semifinished products, or at final inspection of finished goods. The objective of in-plant usage is to give assurance regarding the average quality of material used in the next stage of the manufacturing operations.

Rejected lots may be handled in a number of ways. The best approach is to return rejected lots to the vendor, and require it to perform the screening and re-work activities. This has the psychological effect of making the vendor responsible for poor quality and may exert pressure on the vendor to improve its manufacturing processes or to install better process controls. However, in many situations, because the components or raw materials are required in order to meet production schedules, screening and rework take place at the consumer level. This is not the most desirable situation.

Average outgoing quality is widely used for the evaluation of a rectifying sampling plan. The average outgoing quality is the quality in the lot that results from the application of rectifying inspection. It is the average value of lot quality that would be obtained over a long sequence of lots from a process with fraction defective p. It is simple to develop a formula for average outgoing quality (AOQ). Assume that the lot size is N and that all defectives are replaced with good units. Then in lots of size N, we have

1. n items in the sample which, after inspection, contain no defectives, because all discovered defectives are replaced.

2. $N - n$ items which, if the lot is rejected, also contain no defectives.

3. $N - n$ items which, if the lot is accepted, contain $p(N - n)$ defectives.

Thus, lots in the outgoing stage of inspection have an expected number of defective units equal to $P_a p(N - n)$, which we may express as an *average fraction defective*, called the average outgoing quality or

$$AOQ = \frac{P_a p(N - n)}{N} \qquad (13\text{-}4)$$

To illustrate the use of (13-4) suppose that $N = 10,000$, $n = 89$, and $c = 2$, and that the incoming lots are of quality $p = 0.01$. Now at $p = 0.01$, we have $P_a = 0.9397$, and the AOQ is

$$
\begin{aligned}
AOQ &= \frac{P_a p(N - n)}{N} \\
&= \frac{(0.9397)(0.01)(10,000 - 89)}{10,000} \\
&= 0.0093
\end{aligned}
$$

That is, the average outgoing quality is 0.93% defective. Note that as the lot size N becomes large relative to the sample size n, we may write (13-4) as

$$AOQ \simeq P_a p \qquad (13\text{-}5)$$

Now average outgoing quality will vary as the fraction defective of the incoming lots varies. The curve that plots average outgoing quality against incoming lot quality is called an *AOQ curve*. The AOQ curve for the sampling plan $n = 89$, $c = 2$ is shown in Figure 13-11. From examining this curve we note that when the incoming quality is very good, the average outgoing quality is also very good. In contrast, when the incoming lot quality is very bad, most of the lots are rejected and screened, which leads to a very good level of quality in the outgoing lots. In between these extremes, the AOQ curve rises, passes through a maximum, and descends. The maximum ordinate on the AOQ curve represents the worst possible average quality that would result from the rectifying inspection program, and this point is called the *average outgoing quality limit* (AOQL). From examining Figure 13-11, the AOQL is seen to be approximately 0.0155. That is, no matter how bad the fraction defective is in the incoming lots, the outgoing lots will never have a worse quality level on the average than 1.55% defective. Let us emphasize that this AOQL is an *average level of quality*, *across a large stream of lots*. It does not give assurance that an isolated lot will have quality no worse than 1.55% defective.

Another important measure relative to rectifying inspection is the total amount of inspection required by the sampling program. If the lots contain no defective items, no lots will be rejected, and the amount of inspection per lot will be the sample size n. If the items are all defective, every lot will be submitted to 100% inspection, and the amount of inspection per lot will be the lot size N. If the lot quality is $0 < p < 1$, the average amount of inspection per lot will vary between the sample size n and the lot size N. If the lot is of quality p and the probability of lot acceptance is P_a, then the average total inspection per lot will be

$$ATI = n + (1 - P_a)(N - n) \qquad (13\text{-}6)$$

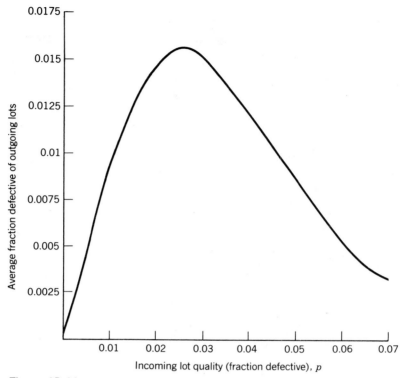

Figure 13-11
Average outgoing quality curve for $n = 89$, $c = 2$.

To illustrate the use of (13-6), consider our previous example with $N = 10,000$, $n = 89$, $c = 2$, and $p = 0.01$. Then, since $P_a = 0.9397$, we have

$$\begin{aligned} \text{ATI} &= n + (1 - P_a)(N - n) \\ &= 89 + (1 - 0.9397)(10,000 - 89) \\ &= 687 \end{aligned}$$

Remember that this is an average number of units inspected over *many* lots with fraction defective $p = 0.01$.

It is possible to draw a curve of average total inspection as a function of lot quality. Average total inspection curves for the sampling plan $n = 89$, $c = 2$, for lot sizes of 1000, 5000, and 10,000 are shown in Figure 13-12.

The AOQL of a rectifying inspection plan is a very important characteristic. It is possible to design rectifying inspection programs that have specified values of AOQL. However, specification of the AOQL is not sufficient to determine a unique sampling plan. Therefore, it is relatively common practice to choose the sampling plan that has a specified AOQL and, in addition, yields a minimum ATI at a particular level of lot quality. The level of lot quality usually chosen is the most likely level of incoming lot quality, which is generally called the *process average*. The procedure for generating these plans is relatively straightforward and is illustrated in Duncan (1974). Generally, it is unnecessary to go through this procedure, as tables of sampling plans that minimize ATI for a given AOQL and

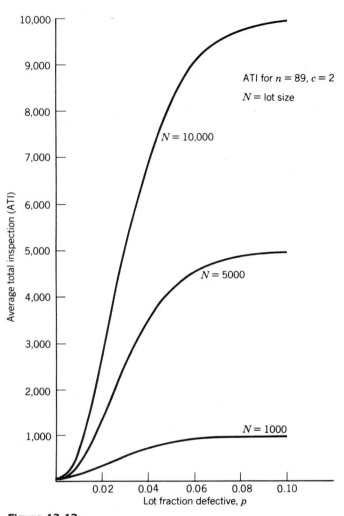

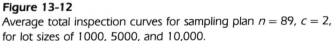

Figure 13-12
Average total inspection curves for sampling plan $n = 89$, $c = 2$, for lot sizes of 1000, 5000, and 10,000.

a specified process average p have been developed by Dodge and Romig. We describe the use of these tables in Section 13-6.

It is also possible to design a rectifying inspection program that gives a specified level of protection at the LTPD point and that minimizes the average total inspection for a specified process average p. The Dodge-Romig sampling inspection tables also provide these LTPD plans. Section 13-6 discusses the use of the Dodge-Romig tables to find plans that offer specified LTPD protection.

13-3 DOUBLE, MULTIPLE, AND SEQUENTIAL SAMPLING

A number of extensions of single-sampling plans for attributes are useful. These include double-sampling plans, multiple-sampling plans, and sequential-sampling plans. This section discusses the design and application of these sampling plans.

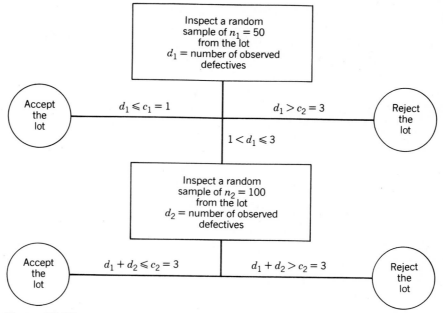

Figure 13-13
Operation of the double-sampling plan, $n_1 = 50$, $c_1 = 1$, $n_2 = 100$, $c_2 = 3$.

13-3.1 Double-Sampling Plans

A double-sampling plan is a procedure in which, under certain circumstances, a second sample is required before the lot can be sentenced. A double-sampling plan is defined by four parameters:[3]

$$n_1 = \text{sample size on the first sample}$$
$$c_1 = \text{acceptance number of the first sample}$$
$$n_2 = \text{sample size on the second sample}$$
$$c_2 = \text{acceptance number for both samples}$$

As an example, suppose $n_1 = 50$, $c_1 = 1$, $n_2 = 100$, and $c_2 = 3$. Thus, a random sample of $n_1 = 50$ items is selected from the lot, and the number of defectives in the sample, d_1, observed. If $d_1 \leq c_1 = 1$, the lot is accepted on the first sample. If $d_1 > c_2 = 3$, the lot is rejected on the first sample. If $c_1 < d_1 \leq c_2$, a second random sample of size $n_2 = 100$ is drawn from the lot, and the number of defectives in this second sample, d_2, observed. Now the combined number of observed defectives from both the first and second sample, $d_1 + d_2$, is used to determine the lot sentence. If $d_1 + d_2 \leq c_2 = 3$, the lot is accepted. However, if $d_1 + d_2 > c_2 = 3$, the lot is rejected. The operation of this double-sampling plan is illustrated graphically in Figure 13-13.

---

[3] Some authors prefer the notation n_1, Ac_1, Re_1, n_2, Ac_2, $Re_2 = Ac_2 + 1$. Since the rejection number on the first sample Re_1 is not necessarily equal to Re_2, this gives some additional flexibility in designing double-sampling plans. MIL STD 105D and ANSI/ASQC Z1.4 currently use this notation. However, because assuming that $Re_1 = Re_2$ does not significantly affect the plans obtained, we have chosen to discuss this slightly simpler system.

The principal advantage of a double-sampling plan with respect to single sampling is that it may reduce the total amount of required inspection. Suppose that the first sample taken under a double-sampling plan is smaller than the sample that would be required using a single-sampling plan that offers the consumer the same protection. In all cases, then, in which a lot is accepted or rejected on the first sample, the cost of inspection will be lower for double sampling than it would be for single sampling. It is also possible to reject a lot without complete inspection of the second sample. (This is called *curtailment* on the second sample.) Consequently, the use of double sampling can often result in lower total inspection costs. Furthermore, in some situations, a double-sampling plan has the psychological advantage of giving a lot a second chance. This may have some appeal to the vendor. However, there is no real advantage to double sampling in this regard, because single- and double-sampling plans can be chosen so that they have the same OC curves. Thus, both plans would offer the same risks of accepting or rejecting lots of specified quality.

Double sampling has two potential disadvantages. First, unless curtailment is used on the second sample, under some circumstances double sampling may require more total inspection than would be required in a single-sampling plan that offers the same protection. Next, unless double sampling is used carefully, its potential economic advantage may be lost. The second disadvantage of double sampling is that it is administratively more complex, which may increase the opportunity for the occurrence of inspection errors. Furthermore, there may be problems in storing and handling raw materials or component parts for which one sample has been taken, but which are awaiting a second sample before a final lot dispositioning decision can be made.

The OC Curve

The performance of a double sampling plan can be conveniently summarized by means of its operating-characteristic (OC) curve. The OC curve for a double-sampling plan is somewhat more involved than the OC curve for single sampling. In this section, we describe the construction of type-B OC curves for double sampling. A double-sampling plan has a primary OC curve that gives the probability of acceptance as a function of lot or process quality. It also has supplementary OC curves that show the probability of and acceptance and rejection on the first sample. The OC curve for the probability of rejection on the first sample is just the OC curve for the single-sampling plan $n = n_1$ and $c = c_2$. Primary and supplementary OC curves for the plan $n_1 = 50$, $c_1 = 1$, $n_2 = 100$, $c_2 = 3$ are shown in Figure 13-14.

We now illustrate the computation of the OC curve for the plan $n_1 = 50$, $c_1 = 1$, $n_2 = 100$, $c_2 = 3$. If P_a denotes the probability of acceptance on the combined samples, and P_a^I and P_a^{II} denote the probability of acceptance on the first and second samples, respectively, then

$$P_a = P_a^I + P_a^{II}$$

Now P_a^I is just the probability that we will observe $d_1 \leq c_1 = 1$ defectives out of a random sample of $n_1 = 50$ items. Thus

$$P_a^I = \sum_{d_1=0}^{1} \frac{50!}{d_1!(50 - d_1)!} p^{d_1}(1 - p)^{50 - d_1}$$

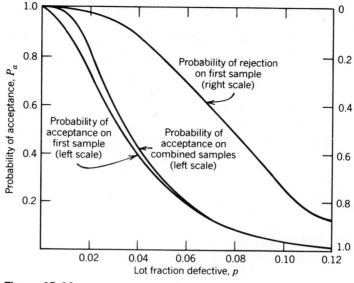

Figure 13-14
OC curves for the double-sampling plan, $n_1 = 50$, $c_1 = 1$, $n_2 = 100$, $c_2 = 3$.

If $p = 0.05$ is the fraction defective in the incoming lot, then

$$P_a^I = \sum_{d_1=0}^{1} \frac{50!}{d_1!(50 - d_1)}(0.05)^{d_1}(0.95)^{50-d_1} = 0.279$$

To obtain the probability of acceptance on the second sample, we must list the number of ways the second sample can be obtained. A second sample is drawn *only* if there are two or three defectives on the first sample, that is, if $c_1 < d_1 \le c_2$. The lot is accepted on the second sample *only* if:

1. $d_1 = 2$ *and* $d_2 = 0$ or 1; that is, we find two defectives on the first sample and one or less defectives on the second sample. The probability of this is

$$P\{d_1 = 2, d_2 \le 1\} = P\{d_1 = 2\} \cdot P\{d_2 \le 1\}$$

$$= \frac{50!}{2!48!}(0.05)^2(0.95)^{48}$$

$$\times \sum_{d_2=0}^{1} \frac{100!}{d_2!(100 - d_2)!}(0.05)^{d_2}(0.95)^{100-d_2}$$

$$= (0.261)(0.037)$$

$$= 0.009$$

2. $d_1 = 3$ *and* $d_2 = 0$; that is, we find three defectives on the first sample and no defectives on the second sample. The probability of this is

$$P\{d_1 = 3, d_2 = 0\} = P\{d_1 = 3\} \cdot P\{d_2 = 0\}$$

$$= \frac{50!}{3!(47)!}(0.05)^3(0.95)^{47}\frac{100!}{0!100!}(0.05)^0(0.95)^{100}$$

$$= (0.220)(0.0059)$$

$$= 0.001$$

Thus, the probability of acceptance on the second sample is

$$P_a^{II} = P\{d_1 = 2, d_2 \le 1\} + P\{d_1 = 3, d_2 = 0\}$$
$$= 0.009 + 0.001$$
$$= 0.010$$

The probability of acceptance of a lot that has fraction defective $p = 0.05$ is therefore

$$P_a = P_a^{I} + P_a^{II}$$
$$= 0.279 + 0.010$$
$$= 0.289$$

Other points on the OC curve are calculated similarly.

The Average Sample Number Curve

The average sample number curve of a double-sampling plan is also usually of interest to the quality engineer. In single sampling, the size of the sample inspected from the lot is always constant, while in double sampling, the size of the sample selected depends on whether or not the second sample is necessary. The probability of drawing a second sample varies with the fraction defective in the incoming lot. With complete inspection of the second sample, the average sample size in double sampling is equal to the size of the first sample times the probability that there will only be one sample plus the size of the combined samples times the probability that a second sample will be necessary. Therefore, a general formula for the average sample number in double sampling, if we assume complete inspection of the second sample, is

$$\text{ASN} = n_1 P_{\text{I}} + (n_1 + n_2)(1 - P_{\text{I}})$$
$$= n_1 + n_2(1 - P_{\text{I}}) \tag{13-7}$$

where P_{I} is the probability of making a lot-dispositioning decision on the *first* sample. This is

$$P_{\text{I}} = P \text{ \{lot is accepted on the first sample\}}$$
$$+ P \text{ \{lot is rejected on the first sample\}}$$

If Equation (13-7) is evaluated for various values of lot fraction defective p, the plot of ASN versus p is called an *average sample number curve*.

In practice, inspection of the second sample is usually terminated and the lot rejected as soon as the number of observed defective items in the combined sample exceeds the second acceptance number c_2. This is referred to as curtailment of the second sample. The use of curtailed inspection lowers the average sample number required in double sampling. It is not recommended that curtailment be used in single sampling, or in the first sample of double sampling, because it is usually desirable to have complete inspection of a fixed sample size in order to secure an unbiased estimate of the quality of the material supplied by the vendor. If curtailed inspection is used in single sampling or on the first sample of double sampling, the estimate of lot or process fallout obtained from these data is biased. For instance, suppose that the acceptance number is one. If the first two items in the sample are defective, and the inspection process is curtailed, the estimate of lot or process fraction defective is 100%. Based on this information, even nonstatistically trained managers or engineers will be very reluctant to believe that the lot is really 100% defective.

The ASN curve formula for a double-sampling plan with curtailment on the second sample is

$$ASN = n_1 + \sum_{j=c_1+1}^{c_2} P(n_1, j) \left[n_2 P_L(n_2, c_2 - j) \right.$$
$$\left. + \frac{c_2 - j + 1}{p} P_M(n_2 + 1, c_2 - j + 2) \right] \qquad (13\text{-}8)$$

In Equation (13-8), $P(n_1, j)$ is the probability of observing exactly j defectives in a sample of size n_1, $P_L(n_2, c_2 - j)$ is the probability of observing $c_2 - j$ or less defectives in a sample of size n_2, and $P_M(n_2 + 1, c_2 - j + 2)$ is the probability of observing $c_2 - j + 2$ defectives in a sample of size $n_2 + 1$.

Figure 13-15 compares the average sample number curves for complete and curtailed inspection for the double-sampling plan $n_1 = 60$, $c_1 = 2$, $n_2 = 120$, $c_2 = 3$, and the average sample number that would be used in single sampling with $n = 89$, $c = 2$. Obviously, the sample size in the single-sampling plan is always constant. This double-sampling plan has been selected because it has an OC curve that is nearly identical to the OC curve for the single-sampling plan. That is, both plans offer equivalent protection to the producer and the consumer. Notice from inspection of Figure 13-15 that the ASN curve for double sampling without curtailment on the second sample is not lower than the sample size used in single sampling throughout the entire range of lot fraction defective. If lots are of very good quality, they will usually be accepted on the first sample, whereas if lots are of very bad

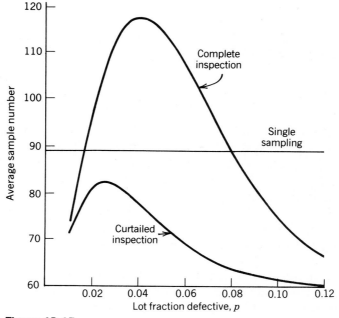

Figure 13-15
Average sample number curves for single and double sampling.

quality, they will usually be rejected on the first sample. This gives an ASN for double sampling that is smaller than the sample size used in single sampling for lots that are either very good or very bad. However, if lots are of intermediate quality, the second sample will be required in a large number of cases before a lot disposition decision can be made. In this range of lot quality, the ASN performance of double sampling is worse than single sampling.

This example points out that it is important to use double sampling very carefully. Unless care is exercised to ensure that lot or process quality is in the range where double sampling is most effective, then the economic advantages of double sampling relative to single sampling may be lost. It is a good idea to maintain a running estimate of the vendor's lot or process fallout, so that if it shifts into a range where double sampling is not economically effective, a change to single sampling (or some other appropriate strategy) can be made. Another way to do this would be to record the proportion of times that the second sample is required in order to make a decision.

Figure 13-15 also shows the ASN curve using curtailment on the second sample. Note that if curtailment is used, the average sample number curve for double sampling always lies below the sample size used in single sampling.

Designing Double-Sampling Plans with Specified p_1, $1 - \alpha$, p_2, and β

It is often necessary to be able to design a double-sampling plan that has a specified OC curve. Let $(p_1, 1 - \alpha)$ and (p_2, β) be the two points of interest on the OC curve. If, in addition, we impose another relationship on the parameters of the sampling plan, then a very simple procedure can be used to obtain such plans. The most common constraint is to require that n_2 is a multiple of n_1. Tables 13-3 and 13-4 allow construction of these plans for the cases where $\alpha = 0.05$ and $\beta = 0.10$. Table 13-3 is for the case $n_1 = n_2$, and Table 13-4 for the case $n_2 = 2n_1$. We often refer to such tables as Grubbs'-type tables (after Frank E. Grubbs, who suggested their use in single sampling). We now illustrate the use of these tables.

Suppose that we wish to find a double-sampling plan with $p_1 = 0.01$, $\alpha = 0.05$, $p_2 = 0.06$, $\beta = 0.10$, and $n_2 = 2n_1$. Since we have chosen $n_2 = 2n_1$, Table 13-4 is used. The plans in the tables are indexed on the ratio

$$R = p_2/p_1$$

For our example, we find $R = p_2/p_1 = 0.06/0.01 = 6$. Now find the plan with R closest to the calculated R. For our example, this is plan 3, with $c_1 = 1$ and $c_2 = 3$. The value of n_1 is determined from either of the two columns headed pn_1. The two columns are associated with holding α constant at 0.05 (giving $P_a = 0.95$) and holding β constant at 0.10 (giving $P_a = 0.10$). For our problem, if we hold α constant at 0.05, we obtain $pn_1 = 0.60$. Thus,

$$n_1 = pn_1/p_1 = 0.60/0.01 = 60$$

and so the desired sampling plan is

$$n_1 = 60 \qquad c_1 = 1 \qquad n_2 = 120 \qquad c_3 = 3$$

If we hold β constant at 0.10, we obtain $pn_1 = 3.89$, and

$$n_1 = pn_1/p_2 = 3.89/0.06 = 65$$

Table 13-3
Grubbs' tables for $n_1 = n_2$ ($\alpha = 0.05$, $\beta = 0.10$)

Plan Number	$R = p_2/p_1$	Acceptance Numbers		Approximate Values of pn_1 for	
		c_1	c_2	$P = 0.95$	$P = 0.10$
1	11.90	0	1	0.21	2.50
2	7.54	1	2	0.52	3.92
3	6.79	0	2	0.43	2.96
4	5.39	1	3	0.76	4.11
5	4.65	2	4	1.16	5.39
6	4.25	1	4	1.04	4.42
7	3.88	2	5	1.43	5.55
8	3.63	3	6	1.87	6.78
9	3.38	2	6	1.72	5.82
10	3.21	3	7	2.15	6.91
11	3.09	4	8	2.62	8.10
12	2.85	4	9	2.90	8.26
13	2.60	5	11	3.68	9.56
14	2.44	5	12	4.00	9.77
15	2.32	5	13	4.35	10.08
16	2.22	5	14	4.70	10.45
17	2.12	5	16	5.39	11.41

Source: Format adapted with permission from A. J. Duncan, *Quality Control and Industrial Statistics*, 4th ed., Irwin, Homewood, Ill. 1974. Values adapted from Chemical Corps Engineering Agency, Manual No. 2, *Master Sampling Plans for Single, Duplicate, Double and Multiple Sampling*, Army Chemical Center, Edgewood Arsenal, Md., 1953.

Thus, the desired sampling plan is

$$n_1 = 65 \qquad c_1 = 1 \qquad n_2 = 130 \qquad c_2 = 3$$

Either of these plans will pass approximately through the two required points on the OC curve.

Rectifying Inspection
When rectifying inspection is performed with double sampling, the AOQ curve is given by

$$\text{AOQ} = \frac{[P_a^I(N - n_1) + P_a^{II}(N - n_1 - n_2)]p}{N} \tag{13-9}$$

assuming that all defective items discovered, either in sampling or 100% inspection, are replaced with good ones. The average total inspection curve is given by

$$\text{ATI} = n_1 P_a^I + (n_1 + n_2)P_a^{II} + N(1 - P_a) \tag{13-10}$$

Remember that $P_a = P_a^I = P_a^{II}$ is the probability of final lot acceptance and that the acceptance probabilities depend on the level of lot or process quality p.

Table 13-4
Grubbs' tables for $n_2 = 2n_1$ ($\alpha = 0.05$, $\beta = 0.10$)

Plan Number	$R = p_2/p_1$	Acceptance Numbers c_1	Acceptance Numbers c_2	Approximate Values of pn_1 for $P = 0.95$	Approximate Values of pn_1 for $P = 0.10$
1	14.50	0	1	0.16	2.32
2	8.07	0	2	0.30	2.42
3	6.48	1	3	0.60	3.89
4	5.39	0	3	0.49	2.64
5	5.09	1	4	0.77	3.92
6	4.31	0	4	0.68	2.93
7	4.19	1	5	0.96	4.02
8	3.60	1	6	1.16	4.17
9	3.26	2	8	1.68	5.47
10	2.96	3	10	2.27	6.72
11	2.77	3	11	2.46	6.82
12	2.62	4	13	3.07	8.05
13	2.46	4	14	3.29	8.11
14	2.21	3	15	3.41	7.55
15	1.97	4	20	4.75	9.35
16	1.74	6	30	7.45	12.96

Source: Format adapted with permission from A. J. Duncan, *Quality Control and Industrial Statistics*, 4th ed., Irwin, Homewood, Ill. 1974. Values are taken, in part, from Chemical Corps Engineering Agency, Manual No. 2, *Master Sampling Plans for Single, Duplicate, Double and Multiple Sampling*, Army Chemical Center, Edgewood Arsenal, Md., 1953, and adapted, in part, from H. C. Hamaker, "The Theory of Sampling Inspection Plans," *Philips Technical Review*, Vol. XI, p. 266, 1950.

13-3.2 Multiple-Sampling Plans

A multiple-sampling plan is an extension of double sampling in that more than two samples can be required to sentence a lot. An example of a multiple-sampling plan with five stages follows.

Cumulative-Sample Size	Acceptance Number	Rejection Number
20	0	3
40	1	4
60	3	5
80	5	7
100	8	9

This plan will operate as follows: If, at the completion of any stage of sampling, the number of defective items is less than or equal to the acceptance number, the lot is accepted. If, during any stage, the number of defective items equals or exceeds the reflection number, the lot is rejected; otherwise the next sample is taken. This multiple-sampling procedure continues until the fifth sample is taken, at which time a lot disposition decision must be made. The first sample is usually inspected 100%, although subsequent samples are usually subject to curtailment.

The construction of OC curves for multiple sampling is a straightforward extension of the approach used in double sampling. Similarly, it is also possible to compute the average sample number curve of multiple-sampling plans. One may also construct Grubbs'-type tables to design a multiple-sampling plan when specified values of p_1, $1 - \alpha$, p_2, and β. For an extensive discussion of these techniques, see Duncan (1974).

The principal advantage of multiple-sampling plans is that the samples required at each stage are usually smaller than those in single or double sampling; thus, some economic efficiency is connected with the use of the procedure. However, multiple sampling is much more complex to administer.

13-3.3 Sequential-Sampling Plans

Sequential sampling is an extension of the double-sampling and multiple-sampling concept. In sequential sampling, we take a sequence of samples from the lot and allow the number of samples to be determined entirely by the results of the sampling process. In practice, sequential sampling can theoretically continue indefinitely, until the lot is inspected 100%. In practice, sequential-sampling plans are usually truncated after the number inspected is equal to three times the number that would have been inspected using a corresponding single-sampling plan. If the sample size selected at each stage is greater than one, the process is usually called *group* sequential sampling. If the sample size inspected at each stage is one, the procedure is usually called *item-by-item* sequential sampling.

Item-by-item sequential sampling is based on the sequential probability ratio test (SPRT), developed by Wald (1947). The operation of an item-by-item sequential-sampling plan is illustrated in Figure 13-16. The cumulative observed number

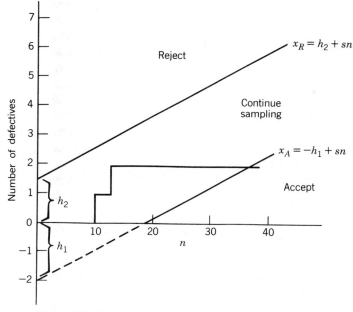

Figure 13-16
Graphical performance of sequential sampling.

of defectives is plotted on the chart. For each point, the abscissa is the total number of items selected up to that time, and the ordinate is the total number of observed defectives. If the plotted points stay within the boundaries of the acceptance and rejection lines, another sample must be drawn. As soon as a point falls on or above the upper line, the lot is rejected. When a sample point falls on or below the lower line, the lot is accepted. The equations for the two limit lines for specified values of p_1, $1 - \alpha$, p_2, and β are:

$$X_A = -h_1 + sn \qquad \text{(acceptance line)} \qquad \text{(13-11a)}$$
$$X_R = h_2 + sn \qquad \text{(rejection line)} \qquad \text{(13-11b)}$$

where

$$h_1 = \left(\log \frac{1 - \alpha}{\beta} \right) \bigg/ k \qquad \text{(13-12)}$$

$$h_2 = \left(\log \frac{1 - \beta}{\alpha} \right) \bigg/ k \qquad \text{(13-13)}$$

$$k = \log \frac{p_2(1 - p_1)}{p_1(1 - p_2)} \qquad \text{(13-14)}$$

$$s = (\log[(1 - p_1)/(1 - p_2)])/k \qquad \text{(13-15)}$$

To illustrate the use of these equations, suppose we wish to find a sequential-sampling plan for which $p_1 = 0.01$, $\alpha = 0.05$, $p_2 = 0.06$, and $\beta = 0.10$. Thus,

$$k = \log \frac{p_2(1 - p_1)}{p_1(1 - p_2)}$$
$$= \log \frac{(0.06)(0.99)}{(0.01)(0.94)}$$
$$= 0.80066$$

$$h_1 = \left(\log \frac{1 - \alpha}{\beta} \right) \bigg/ k$$
$$= \left(\log \frac{0.95}{0.10} \right) \bigg/ 0.80066$$
$$= 1.22$$

$$h_2 = \left(\log \frac{1 - \beta}{\alpha} \right) \bigg/ k$$
$$= \left(\log \frac{0.90}{0.05} \right) \bigg/ 0.80066$$
$$= 1.57$$

$$s = \log[(1 - p_1)/(1 - p_2)]/k$$
$$= (\log[0.99/0.94])/0.80066$$
$$= 0.028$$

Therefore, the limit lines are

$$X_A = -1.22 + 0.028n \qquad \text{(accept)}$$

and

$$X_R = 1.57 + 0.028n \qquad \text{(reject)}$$

Instead of using a graph to determine the lot disposition, the sequential-sampling plan can be displayed in a table such as Table 13-5. The entries in the table are found by substituting values of n into the equations for the acceptance and rejection lines and calculating acceptance and rejection numbers. For example, the calculations for $n = 45$ are:

$$\begin{aligned} X_A &= -1.22 + 0.028n \\ &= -1.22 + 0.028(45) = 0.04 \qquad \text{(accept)} \\ X_R &= 1.57 + 0.028n \\ &= 1.57 + 0.028(45) = 2.83 \qquad \text{(reject)} \end{aligned}$$

Now acceptance and rejection numbers must be integers, so the acceptance number is the next integer less than or equal to X_A, and the rejection number is the next integer greater than or equal to X_R. Thus, for $n = 45$, the acceptance number is

Table 13-5

Item-by-item sequential-sampling plan $p_1 = 0.01$, $\alpha = 0.05$, $p_2 = 0.06$, $\beta = 0.10$ (First 46 units only)

Number of Items Inspected, n	Acceptance Number	Rejection Number	Number of Items Inspected, n	Acceptance Number	Rejection Number
1	a	b	24	a	3
2	a	2	25	a	3
3	a	2	26	a	3
4	a	2	27	a	3
5	a	2	28	a	3
6	a	2	29	a	3
7	a	2	30	a	3
8	a	2	31	a	3
9	a	2	32	a	3
10	a	2	33	a	3
11	a	2	34	a	3
12	a	2	35	a	3
13	a	2	36	a	3
14	a	2	37	a	3
15	a	2	38	a	3
16	a	3	39	a	3
17	a	3	40	a	3
18	a	3	41	a	3
19	a	3	42	a	3
20	a	3	43	a	3
21	a	3	44	0	3
22	a	3	45	0	3
23	a	3	46	0	3

[a] means acceptance not possible.

[b] means rejection not possible.

0 and the rejection number is 3. Note that the lot cannot be accepted until at least 44 units have been tested. Table 13-5 shows only the first 46 units. Normally, the plan would be truncated after the inspection of 267 units, which is three times the sample size required for an equivalent single-sampling plan.

The OC Curve and ANS Curve for Sequential Sampling

The OC curve for sequential sampling can be easily obtained. Two points on the curve are $(p_1, 1 - \alpha)$ and (p_2, β). A third point, near the middle of the curve is $p = s$ and $p_a = h_2/(h_1 + h_2)$.

The average sample number taken under sequential sampling is

$$\text{ASN} = P_a\left(\frac{A}{C}\right) + (1 - P_a)\frac{B}{C} \tag{13-16}$$

where

$$A = \log \frac{\beta}{1 - \alpha}$$

$$B = \log \frac{1 - \beta}{\alpha}$$

and

$$C = p \log\left(\frac{p_2}{p_1}\right) + (1 - p) \log\left(\frac{1 - p_2}{1 - p_1}\right)$$

Rectifying Inspection

The average outgoing quality (AOQ) for sequential sampling is given approximately by

$$\text{AOQ} \simeq P_a p \tag{13-17}$$

The average total inspection is also easily obtained. Note that the amount of sampling is A/C when a lot is accepted and N when it is rejected. Therefore, the average total inspection is

$$\text{ATI} = P_a\left(\frac{A}{C}\right) + (1 - P_a)N \tag{13-18}$$

13-4 A LOT-SENSITIVE COMPLIANCE (LTPD) SAMPLING PLAN

In this section, we present a sampling plan that is applicable in general acceptance sampling but that is particularly useful in compliance testing or sampling for safety-related product characteristics. The procedure is also useful in any situation where minimum sample sizes are required. The plans provide for rejection of the lot if any defective items are found in the sample. They are also based on a well-defined relationship between the sampling plan and the size of the lots submitted for inspection. The sampling procedure gives the proportion of the lot that must be sampled to guarantee that the fraction defective in the lot is less than a prescribed limit with probability 0.90. That is, for a specified LTPD, the probability of lot acceptance is 0.10. Sample sizes are based on the hypergeometric distribution.

Remember that acceptance-sampling plans with zero acceptance number have operating-characteristic curves with a very undesirable shape at low fractions non-conforming. Since lot acceptance is permitted only when the number of observed defectives in the sample is zero, the manufacturer's process must operate at a fall-out level that is less than about 5% of the LTPD to ensure a reasonably small prob-ability (about 0.1) of a good lot being rejected. When the LTPD value is closer than this to the vendor's process average, acceptance-sampling plans with $c = 0$ are not appropriate. When the LTPD is close to the process fallout level, sampling plans that permit lot acceptance on one or more defects in the sample should be used. The Dodge-Romig plans, described in Section 13-6, would be good sampling pro-cedures to implement in these cases. These plans require much larger sample sizes than the lot-sensitive compliance sampling plans presented in this section.

Table 13-6 is used to derive the lot-sensitive compliance sampling plan. This table may be used as follows:

1. Determine the lot size N.

2. Specify the LTPD quality level p_L. This is the level of quality to be protected against with the plan.

3. Compute the product $D = Np_L$.

4. Enter the body of Table 13-6 at the nearest value of D and read the corre-sponding value of f as the sum of the associated row and column headings.

$$f = \text{fraction of the lot inspected}$$

5. The sampling plan is

$$n = \text{sample size} = fN$$
$$c = \text{acceptance number} = 0$$

Round the value of n up in computing the sample size. The plan is then applied by selecting a random sample of n items out of the lot of N items; the lot is rejected if any defective units are found in the sample.

To illustrate the use of this table, suppose that $N = 100$ and LTPD $= p_L = 0.10$. Then $D = Np_L = 100(0.10) = 10$. Table 13-6 then gives $f = 0.21$ closest to $D = 10$. The desired sampling plan then is

$$n = 0.21(100) = 21$$
$$c = 0$$

Thus, the sampling plan is to randomly select 21 items from the lot of size 100 and to reject the lot if one or more defectives are found.

If rectifying inspection is used, the AOQL can be computed for lot-sensitive compliance sampling plans as

$$\text{AOQL} = \frac{0.3679}{N}\left(\frac{1}{f} - 1\right)$$

If the lot contains all nondefective items, its probability of acceptance is one; thus, the producer's risk for such a lot will be zero. If the lot contains only one defective

Table 13-6
Values of $D = Np_L$ corresponding to f

f	0.00	0.01	0.02	0.03	0.04	0.05	0.06	0.07	0.08	0.09
0.9	1.0000	0.9562	0.9117	0.8659	0.8184	0.7686	0.7153	0.6567	0.5886	0.5000
0.8	1.4307	1.3865	1.3428	1.2995	1.2565	1.2137	1.1711	1.1286	1.0860	1.0432
0.7	1.9125	1.8601	1.8088	1.7586	1.7093	1.6610	1.6135	1.5667	1.5207	1.4754
0.6	2.5129	2.4454	2.3797	2.3159	2.2538	2.1933	2.1344	2.0769	2.0208	1.9660
0.5	3.3219	3.2278	3.1372	3.0497	2.9652	2.8836	2.8047	2.7283	2.6543	2.5825
0.4	4.5076	4.3640	4.2270	4.0963	3.9712	3.8515	3.7368	3.6268	3.5212	3.4196
0.3	6.4557	6.2054	5.9705	5.7496	5.5415	5.3451	5.1594	4.9836	4.8168	4.6583
0.2	10.3189	9.7682	9.2674	8.8099	8.3902	8.0039	7.6471	7.3165	7.0093	6.7231
0.1	21.8543	19.7589	18.0124	16.5342	15.2668	14.1681	13.2064	12.3576	11.6028	10.9272
0.0	a	229.1053	113.9741	75.5957	56.4055	44.8906	37.2133	31.7289	27.6150	24.4149

(Adapted from E. G. Schilling, "A Lot Sensitive Sampling Plan for Compliance Testing and Acceptance Inspection," *Journal of Quality Technology*, Vol. 10, No. 2, 1978, with permission of the American Society for Quality Control.)

[a] For values of $f < 0.01$, use $f = 2.303/D$; for infinite lot size, use sample size $n = 2.303/p_L$.

item, the probability of acceptance of the lot is just

$$P_a = 1 - f$$

The producer's risk of such a lot is

$$1 - P_a = f$$

Thus, in the above example, where the fraction of the lot inspected is $f = 0.21$, and the lot is of size 100, the probability of acceptance of a lot with 1% defective (that is, one defective item) is

$$P_a = 1 - f$$
$$= 1 - 0.21 = 0.79$$

Thus, the producer's risk for this lot is

$$1 - P_a = 0.21$$

This is a lower bound on the producer's risk, since a lot containing more than one defective item would have a higher probability of rejection.

Remember that sampling plans that have zero acceptance numbers should not be used indiscriminately. Such plans should only be used for lot sentencing when the manufacturing process is operating in a near-zero-defects environment.

13-5 MILITARY STANDARD 105D (ANSI/ASQC Z1.4)

13-5.1 Description of the Standard

Standard sampling procedures for inspection by attributes were developed during World War II. MIL STD 105D is the most widely used acceptance-sampling system for attributes in the world today. The original version of the standard, MIL STD 105A, was issued in 1950. Since then, there have been three revisions; the latest version, MIL STD 105D, was issued in 1963.

The sampling plans discussed in previous sections of this chapter are individual sampling plans. A sampling scheme is an overall strategy specifying the way in which sampling plans are to be used. MIL STD 105D is a collection of sampling schemes; therefore, it is an acceptance-sampling system. Our discussion will focus primarily on MIL STD 105D; however, there is a derivative civilian standard ANSI/ASQC Z1.4, which is quite similar to the military standard.

The standard provides for three types of sampling: single sampling, double sampling, and multiple sampling. For each type of sampling plan, a provision is made for either normal inspection, tightened inspection, or reduced inspection. Normal inspection is used at the start of the inspection activity. Tightened inspection is instituted when the vendor's recent quality history has deteriorated. Acceptance requirements for lots under tightened inspection are more stringent than under normal inspection. Reduced inspection is instituted when the vendor's recent quality history has been exceptionally good. The sample size generally used under reduced inspection is less than that under normal inspection.

The primary focal point of MIL STD 105D is the acceptable quality level (AQL). The standard is indexed with respect to a series of AQLs. When the standard is used for percent defective plans, the AQLs range from 0.10% to 10%. For defects per units plans, there are an additional 10 AQLs running up to 1000 defects per 100 units. It should be noted that for the smaller AQL levels, the same sampling plan can be used to control either a fraction defective or a number of defects per unit. The AQLs are arranged in a progression, each AQL being approximately 1.585 times the preceding one.

The AQL is generally specified in the contract or by the authority responsible for sampling. Different AQLs may be designated for different types of defects. For example, the standard differentiates critical defects, major defects, and minor defects. It is relatively common practice to choose an AQL of 1% for major defects and an AQL of 2.5% for minor defects. No critical defects would be acceptable.

The sample size used in MIL STD 105D is determined by the lot size and by the choice of inspection level. Three general levels of inspection are provided. Level II is designated as normal. Level I requires about one-half the amount of inspection as Level II and may be used when less discrimination is needed. Level III requires about twice as much inspection as Level II and should be used when more discrimination is needed. There are also four special inspection levels, S1, S2, S3, and S4. The special inspection levels use very small samples, and should only be employed when the small sample sizes are necessary and when large sampling risks can or must be tolerated.

For a specified AQL and inspection level and a given lot size, MIL STD 105D provides a normal sampling plan that is to be used as long as the supplier is producing the product at AQL quality or better. It also provides a procedure for switching to tightened and reduced inspection whenever there is an indication that the vendor's quality has changed. The switching procedures between normal, tightened, and reduced inspection are illustrated graphically in Figure 13-17 and are described below:

1. **Normal to tightened.** When normal inspection is in effect, tightened inspection is instituted when two out of five consecutive lots have been rejected on original submission.

2. **Tightened to normal.** When tightened inspection is in effect, normal inspection is instituted when five consecutive lots or batches are accepted on original inspection.

3. **Normal to reduced.** When normal inspection is in effect, reduced inspection is instituted provided all four of the following conditions are satisfied.

   a. The preceding 10 lots have been on normal inspection, and none of the lots has been rejected on original inspection.

   b. The total number of defectives in the samples from the preceding 10 lots is less than or equal to the applicable number given in Table 13-17 later in this chapter.

   c. Production is at a steady rate; that is, no difficulty such as machine breakdowns, material shortages, or other problems have recently occurred.

   d. Reduced inspection is considered desirable by the authority responsible for sampling.

4. **Reduced to normal.** When reduced inspection is in effect, normal inspection is instituted provided any of the four conditions below are satisfied.

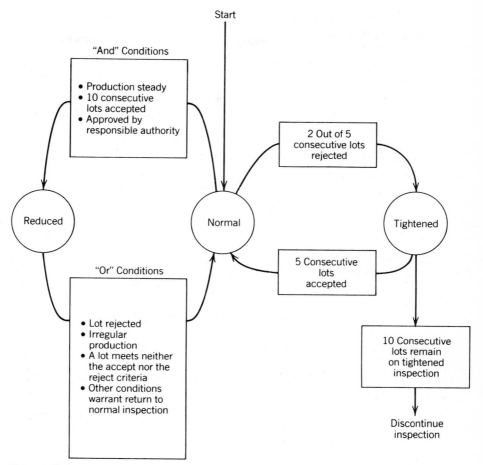

Figure 13-17
Switching rules for normal, tightened, and reduced inspection, MIL STD 105D.

    a. A lot or batch is rejected.

    b. When the sampling procedure terminates with neither acceptance nor rejection criteria having been met, the lot or batch is accepted, but normal inspection is reinstituted starting with the next lot.

    c. Production is irregular or delayed.

    d. Other conditions warrant that normal inspection be instituted.

5. Discontinuance of inspection. In the event that ten consecutive lots remain on tightened inspection, inspection under the provision of MIL STD 105D should be terminated, and action should be taken at the vendor level to improve the quality of submitted lots.

13-5.2 Procedure

A step-by-step procedure for using MIL STD 105D is as follows:

1. Choose the AQL.

2. Choose the inspection level.
3. Determine the lot size.
4. Find the appropriate sample size code letter from Table 13-7.
5. Determine the appropriate type of sampling plan to use (single, double, multiple).
6. Enter the appropriate table to find the type of plan to be used.
7. Determine the corresponding normal and reduced inspection plans to be used when required.

Table 13-7 presents the sample size code letters for MIL STD 105D. Tables 13-8, 13-9, and 13-10 present the single-sampling plans for normal inspection, tightened inspection, and reduced inspection, respectively. The double-sampling plans for normal, tightened, and reduced inspection are shown in Tables 13-11, 13-12, and 13-13. The multiple-sampling plans for normal, tightened, and reduced inspection are shown in Tables 13-14, 13-15, and 13-16. Table 13-17 presents the limit numbers for reduced inspection.

To illustrate the use of MIL STD 105D, suppose that a product is submitted in lots of size $N = 2000$. The acceptable quality level is 0.65%. We will use the standard to generate normal, tightened, and reduced single-sampling plans for this situation. For lots of size 2000 under general inspection level II, Table 13-7 indicates that the appropriate sample size code letter is K. Therefore, from Table 13-8, for single-sampling plans under normal inspection, the normal inspection plan is $n = 125$, $c = 2$. Table 13-9 indicates that the corresponding tightened inspection plan is $n = 125$, $c = 1$. Notice that in switching from normal to tightened inspection, the sample size remains the same, but the acceptance number is reduced by

Table 13-7
Sample size code letters (MIL STD 105D, Table 1)

Lot or Batch Size	Special Inspection Levels				General Inspection Levels		
	S-1	S-2	S-3	S-4	I	II	III
2 to 8	A	A	A	A	A	A	B
9 to 15	A	A	A	A	A	B	C
16 to 25	A	A	B	B	B	C	D
26 to 50	A	B	B	C	C	D	E
51 to 90	B	B	C	C	C	E	F
91 to 150	B	B	C	D	D	F	G
151 to 280	B	C	D	E	E	G	H
281 to 500	B	C	D	E	F	H	J
501 to 1200	C	C	E	F	G	J	K
1201 to 3200	C	D	E	G	H	K	L
3201 to 10000	C	D	F	G	J	L	M
10001 to 35000	C	D	F	H	K	M	N
35001 to 150000	D	E	G	J	L	N	P
150001 to 500000	D	E	G	J	M	P	Q
500001 and over	D	E	H	K	N	Q	R

Table 13-8

Master table for normal inspection—single sampling (MIL STD 105D, Table II-A)

Acceptable Quality Levels (normal inspection)

Sample size code letter	Sample size	0.010		0.015		0.025		0.040		0.065		0.10		0.15		0.25		0.40		0.65		1.0		1.5		2.5		4.0		6.5		10		15		25		40		65		100		150		250		400		650		1000	
		Ac	Re	Ac	Re	Ac	Re	Ac	Re	Ac	Re	Ac	Re	Ac	Re	Ac	Re	Ac	Re	Ac	Re	Ac	Re	Ac	Re	Ac	Re	Ac	Re	Ac	Re	Ac	Re	Ac	Re	Ac	Re	Ac	Re	Ac	Re	Ac	Re	Ac	Re	Ac	Re	Ac	Re	Ac	Re	Ac	Re
A	2	↓		↓		↓		↓		↓		↓		↓		↓		↓		↓		↓		↓		↓		↓		↓		↓		0	1	1	2	2	3	3	4	5	6	7	8	10	11	14	15	21	22	30	31
B	3	↓		↓		↓		↓		↓		↓		↓		↓		↓		↓		↓		↓		↓		↓		↓		0	1	1	2	2	3	3	4	5	6	7	8	10	11	14	15	21	22	30	31	44	45
C	5	↓		↓		↓		↓		↓		↓		↓		↓		↓		↓		↓		↓		↓		↓		0	1	1	2	2	3	3	4	5	6	7	8	10	11	14	15	21	22	30	31	44	45	↑	
D	8	↓		↓		↓		↓		↓		↓		↓		↓		↓		↓		↓		↓		↓		0	1	1	2	2	3	3	4	5	6	7	8	10	11	14	15	21	22	30	31	44	45	↑		↑	
E	13	↓		↓		↓		↓		↓		↓		↓		↓		↓		↓		↓		↓		0	1	1	2	2	3	3	4	5	6	7	8	10	11	14	15	21	22	30	31	44	45	↑		↑		↑	
F	20	↓		↓		↓		↓		↓		↓		↓		↓		↓		↓		↓		0	1	1	2	2	3	3	4	5	6	7	8	10	11	14	15	21	22	30	31	44	45	↑		↑		↑		↑	
G	32	↓		↓		↓		↓		↓		↓		↓		↓		↓		↓		0	1	1	2	2	3	3	4	5	6	7	8	10	11	14	15	21	22	↑		↑		↑		↑		↑		↑		↑	
H	50	↓		↓		↓		↓		↓		↓		↓		↓		↓		0	1	1	2	2	3	3	4	5	6	7	8	10	11	14	15	21	22	↑		↑		↑		↑		↑		↑		↑		↑	
J	80	↓		↓		↓		↓		↓		↓		↓		↓		0	1	1	2	2	3	3	4	5	6	7	8	10	11	14	15	21	22	↑		↑		↑		↑		↑		↑		↑		↑		↑	
K	125	↓		↓		↓		↓		↓		↓		↓		0	1	1	2	2	3	3	4	5	6	7	8	10	11	14	15	21	22	↑		↑		↑		↑		↑		↑		↑		↑		↑		↑	
L	200	↓		↓		↓		↓		↓		↓		0	1	1	2	2	3	3	4	5	6	7	8	10	11	14	15	21	22	↑		↑		↑		↑		↑		↑		↑		↑		↑		↑		↑	
M	315	↓		↓		↓		↓		↓		0	1	1	2	2	3	3	4	5	6	7	8	10	11	14	15	21	22	↑		↑		↑		↑		↑		↑		↑		↑		↑		↑		↑		↑	
N	500	↓		↓		↓		↓		0	1	1	2	2	3	3	4	5	6	7	8	10	11	14	15	21	22	↑		↑		↑		↑		↑		↑		↑		↑		↑		↑		↑		↑		↑	
P	800	↓		↓		↓		0	1	1	2	2	3	3	4	5	6	7	8	10	11	14	15	21	22	↑		↑		↑		↑		↑		↑		↑		↑		↑		↑		↑		↑		↑		↑	
Q	1250	↓		↓		0	1	1	2	2	3	3	4	5	6	7	8	10	11	14	15	21	22	↑		↑		↑		↑		↑		↑		↑		↑		↑		↑		↑		↑		↑		↑		↑	
R	2000	↓		0	1	1	2	2	3	3	4	5	6	7	8	10	11	14	15	21	22	↑		↑		↑		↑		↑		↑		↑		↑		↑		↑		↑		↑		↑		↑		↑		↑	

⇩ = Use first sampling plan below arrow. If sample size size equals, or exceeds, lot or batch size, do 100 percent inspection.

⇧ = Use first sampling plan above arrow.

Ac = Acceptance number.

Re = Rejection number.

Table 13-9
Master table for tightened inspection—single sampling (MIL STD 105D, Table II-B)

Each Acceptable Quality Level cell shows "Ac Re" (acceptance number / rejection number). ↓ = use first sampling plan below arrow. ↑ = use first sampling plan above arrow.

Sample size code letter	Sample size	Acceptable Quality Levels (tightened inspection)																									
		0.010	0.015	0.025	0.040	0.065	0.10	0.15	0.25	0.40	0.65	1.0	1.5	2.5	4.0	6.5	10	15	25	40	65	100	150	250	400	650	1000
A	2	↓	↓	↓	↓	↓	↓	↓	↓	↓	↓	↓	↓	↓	↓	↓	↓	↓	0 1	1 2	2 3	3 4	5 6	8 9	12 13	18 19	27 28
B	3	↓	↓	↓	↓	↓	↓	↓	↓	↓	↓	↓	↓	↓	↓	↓	↓	0 1	1 2	2 3	3 4	5 6	8 9	12 13	18 19	27 28	41 42
C	5	↓	↓	↓	↓	↓	↓	↓	↓	↓	↓	↓	↓	↓	↓	↓	0 1	1 2	2 3	3 4	5 6	8 9	12 13	18 19	27 28	41 42	↑
D	8	↓	↓	↓	↓	↓	↓	↓	↓	↓	↓	↓	↓	↓	↓	0 1	1 2	2 3	3 4	5 6	8 9	12 13	18 19	27 28	41 42	↑	↑
E	13	↓	↓	↓	↓	↓	↓	↓	↓	↓	↓	↓	↓	↓	0 1	1 2	2 3	3 4	5 6	8 9	12 13	18 19	27 28	41 42	↑	↑	↑
F	20	↓	↓	↓	↓	↓	↓	↓	↓	↓	↓	↓	↓	0 1	1 2	2 3	3 4	5 6	8 9	12 13	18 19	27 28	41 42	↑	↑	↑	↑
G	32	↓	↓	↓	↓	↓	↓	↓	↓	↓	↓	↓	0 1	1 2	2 3	3 4	5 6	8 9	12 13	18 19	27 28	41 42	↑	↑	↑	↑	↑
H	50	↓	↓	↓	↓	↓	↓	↓	↓	↓	↓	0 1	1 2	2 3	3 4	5 6	8 9	12 13	18 19	27 28	41 42	↑	↑	↑	↑	↑	↑
J	80	↓	↓	↓	↓	↓	↓	↓	↓	↓	0 1	1 2	2 3	3 4	5 6	8 9	12 13	18 19	27 28	41 42	↑	↑	↑	↑	↑	↑	↑
K	125	↓	↓	↓	↓	↓	↓	↓	↓	0 1	1 2	2 3	3 4	5 6	8 9	12 13	18 19	27 28	41 42	↑	↑	↑	↑	↑	↑	↑	↑
L	200	↓	↓	↓	↓	↓	↓	↓	0 1	1 2	2 3	3 4	5 6	8 9	12 13	18 19	27 28	41 42	↑	↑	↑	↑	↑	↑	↑	↑	↑
M	315	↓	↓	↓	↓	↓	↓	0 1	1 2	2 3	3 4	5 6	8 9	12 13	18 19	27 28	41 42	↑	↑	↑	↑	↑	↑	↑	↑	↑	↑
N	500	↓	↓	↓	↓	↓	0 1	1 2	2 3	3 4	5 6	8 9	12 13	18 19	27 28	41 42	↑	↑	↑	↑	↑	↑	↑	↑	↑	↑	↑
P	800	↓	↓	↓	↓	0 1	1 2	2 3	3 4	5 6	8 9	12 13	18 19	27 28	41 42	↑	↑	↑	↑	↑	↑	↑	↑	↑	↑	↑	↑
Q	1250	↓	↓	↓	0 1	1 2	2 3	3 4	5 6	8 9	12 13	18 19	27 28	41 42	↑	↑	↑	↑	↑	↑	↑	↑	↑	↑	↑	↑	↑
R	2000	↓	↓	0 1	1 2	2 3	3 4	5 6	8 9	12 13	18 19	27 28	41 42	↑	↑	↑	↑	↑	↑	↑	↑	↑	↑	↑	↑	↑	↑
S	3150	↓	0 1	1 2	2 3	3 4	5 6	8 9	12 13	18 19	27 28	41 42	↑	↑	↑	↑	↑	↑	↑	↑	↑	↑	↑	↑	↑	↑	↑

⇩ = Use first sampling plan below arrow. If sample size equals or exceeds lot or batch size, do 100 percent inspection.
⇧ = Use first sampling plan above arrow.
Ac = Acceptance number.
Re = Rejection number.

Table 13-10
Master table for reduced inspection—single sampling (MIL STD 105D, Table II-C)†

Each data cell below shows the acceptance number (Ac) and rejection number (Re) as "Ac Re". Arrows: ↓ = use first sampling plan below arrow; ↑ = use first sampling plan above arrow.

Acceptable Quality Levels (reduced inspection)†

Code	Sample size	0.010	0.015	0.025	0.040	0.065	0.10	0.15	0.25	0.40	0.65	1.0
A	2	↓	↓	↓	↓	↓	↓	↓	↓	↓	↓	↓
B	2	↓	↓	↓	↓	↓	↓	↓	↓	↓	↓	↓
C	2	↓	↓	↓	↓	↓	↓	↓	↓	↓	↓	↓
D	3	↓	↓	↓	↓	↓	↓	↓	↓	↓	↓	↓
E	5	↓	↓	↓	↓	↓	↓	↓	↓	↓	↓	↓
F	8	↓	↓	↓	↓	↓	↓	↓	↓	↓	↓	0 1
G	13	↓	↓	↓	↓	↓	↓	↓	↓	↓	0 1	1 2
H	20	↓	↓	↓	↓	↓	↓	↓	↓	0 1	1 2	1 3
J	32	↓	↓	↓	↓	↓	↓	↓	0 1	1 2	1 3	1 4
K	50	↓	↓	↓	↓	↓	↓	0 1	1 2	1 3	1 4	2 5
L	80	↓	↓	↓	↓	↓	0 1	1 2	1 3	1 4	2 5	3 6
M	125	↓	↓	↓	↓	0 1	1 2	1 3	1 4	2 5	3 6	5 8
N	200	↓	↓	↓	0 1	1 2	1 3	1 4	2 5	3 6	5 8	7 10
P	315	↓	↓	0 1	1 2	1 3	1 4	2 5	3 6	5 8	7 10	10 13
Q	500	↓	0 1	1 2	1 3	1 4	2 5	3 6	5 8	7 10	10 13	14 17
R	800	0 1	1 2	1 3	1 4	2 5	3 6	5 8	7 10	10 13	14 17	21 24

Code	Sample size	1.5	2.5	4.0	6.5	10	15	25	40	65	100	150	250	400	650	1000
A	2	↓	↓	↓	↓	↓	↓	1 2	2 3	3 4	5 6	7 8	10 11	14 15	21 22	30 31
B	2	↓	↓	↓	↓	↓	0 2	1 3	2 4	3 5	5 6	7 8	10 11	14 15	21 22	30 31
C	2	↓	↓	↓	0 1	1 2	1 3	1 4	2 5	3 6	5 8	7 10	10 13	14 17	21 24	↑
D	3	↓	↓	0 1	1 2	1 3	1 4	2 5	3 6	5 8	7 10	10 13	14 17	21 24	↑	↑
E	5	↓	0 1	1 2	1 3	1 4	2 5	3 6	5 8	7 10	10 13	14 17	21 24	↑	↑	↑
F	8	1 2	1 3	1 4	2 5	3 6	5 8	7 10	10 13	14 17	21 24	↑	↑	↑	↑	↑
G	13	1 3	1 4	2 5	3 6	5 8	7 10	10 13	14 17	21 24	↑	↑	↑	↑	↑	↑
H	20	1 4	2 5	3 6	5 8	7 10	10 13	14 17	21 24	↑	↑	↑	↑	↑	↑	↑
J	32	2 5	3 6	5 8	7 10	10 13	14 17	21 24	↑	↑	↑	↑	↑	↑	↑	↑
K	50	3 6	5 8	7 10	10 13	14 17	21 24	↑	↑	↑	↑	↑	↑	↑	↑	↑
L	80	5 8	7 10	10 13	14 17	21 24	↑	↑	↑	↑	↑	↑	↑	↑	↑	↑
M	125	7 10	10 13	14 17	21 24	↑	↑	↑	↑	↑	↑	↑	↑	↑	↑	↑
N	200	10 13	14 17	21 24	↑	↑	↑	↑	↑	↑	↑	↑	↑	↑	↑	↑
P	315	14 17	21 24	↑	↑	↑	↑	↑	↑	↑	↑	↑	↑	↑	↑	↑
Q	500	21 24	↑	↑	↑	↑	↑	↑	↑	↑	↑	↑	↑	↑	↑	↑
R	800	↑	↑	↑	↑	↑	↑	↑	↑	↑	↑	↑	↑	↑	↑	↑

↓ = Use first sampling plan below arrow. If sample size equals or exceeds lot or batch size, do 100 percent inspection.

↑ = Use first sampling plan above arrow.

Ac = Acceptance number.

Re = Rejection number.

† = If the acceptance number has been exceeded, but the rejection number has not been reached, accept the lot, but reinstate normal inspection.

591

Table 13-11

Master table for normal inspection—double sampling (MIL STD 105D, Table III-A)

Acceptable Quality Levels (normal inspection). Each Acceptable Quality Level column contains two values: Ac (acceptance number) and Re (rejection number), shown as "Ac Re".

Sample size code letter	Sample	Sample size	Cumulative sample size	0.010	0.015	0.025	0.040	0.065	0.10	0.15	0.25	0.40	0.65	1.0	1.5	2.5	4.0	6.5	10	15	25	40	65	100	150	250	400	650	1000
A				↓	↓	↓	↓	↓	↓	↓	↓	↓	↓	↓	↓	↓	↓	↓	↓	↓	↓	↓	↓	↓	↓	↓	↓	↓	↓
B	First	2	2	↓	↓	↓	↓	↓	↓	↓	↓	↓	↓	↓	↓	↓	↓	↓	•	0 2	0 3	1 4	2 5	3 7	5 9	7 11	11 16	17 22	25 31
B	Second	2	4																	1 2	3 4	4 5	6 7	8 9	12 13	18 19	26 27	37 38	56 57
C	First	3	3	↓	↓	↓	↓	↓	↓	↓	↓	↓	↓	↓	↓	↓	↓	•	0 2	0 3	1 4	2 5	3 7	5 9	7 11	11 16	17 22	25 31	↑
C	Second	3	6																1 2	3 4	4 5	6 7	8 9	12 13	18 19	26 27	37 38	56 57	
D	First	5	5	↓	↓	↓	↓	↓	↓	↓	↓	↓	↓	↓	↓	↓	•	0 2	0 3	1 4	2 5	3 7	5 9	7 11	11 16	17 22	25 31	↑	↑
D	Second	5	10															1 2	3 4	4 5	6 7	8 9	12 13	18 19	26 27	37 38	56 57		
E	First	8	8	↓	↓	↓	↓	↓	↓	↓	↓	↓	↓	↓	↓	•	0 2	0 3	1 4	2 5	3 7	5 9	7 11	11 16	17 22	25 31	↑	↑	↑
E	Second	8	16														1 2	3 4	4 5	6 7	8 9	12 13	18 19	26 27	37 38	56 57			
F	First	13	13	↓	↓	↓	↓	↓	↓	↓	↓	↓	↓	↓	•	0 2	0 3	1 4	2 5	3 7	5 9	7 11	11 16	17 22	25 31	↑	↑	↑	↑
F	Second	13	26													1 2	3 4	4 5	6 7	8 9	12 13	18 19	26 27	37 38	56 57				
G	First	20	20	↓	↓	↓	↓	↓	↓	↓	↓	↓	↓	•	0 2	0 3	1 4	2 5	3 7	5 9	7 11	11 16	17 22	25 31	↑	↑	↑	↑	↑
G	Second	20	40												1 2	3 4	4 5	6 7	8 9	12 13	18 19	26 27	37 38	56 57					
H	First	32	32	↓	↓	↓	↓	↓	↓	↓	↓	↓	•	0 2	0 3	1 4	2 5	3 7	5 9	7 11	11 16	17 22	25 31	↑	↑	↑	↑	↑	↑
H	Second	32	64											1 2	3 4	4 5	6 7	8 9	12 13	18 19	26 27	37 38	56 57						
J	First	50	50	↓	↓	↓	↓	↓	↓	↓	↓	•	0 2	0 3	1 4	2 5	3 7	5 9	7 11	11 16	17 22	25 31	↑	↑	↑	↑	↑	↑	↑
J	Second	50	100										1 2	3 4	4 5	6 7	8 9	12 13	18 19	26 27	37 38	56 57							
K	First	80	80	↓	↓	↓	↓	↓	↓	↓	•	0 2	0 3	1 4	2 5	3 7	5 9	7 11	11 16	17 22	25 31	↑	↑	↑	↑	↑	↑	↑	↑
K	Second	80	160									1 2	3 4	4 5	6 7	8 9	12 13	18 19	26 27	37 38	56 57								
L	First	125	125	↓	↓	↓	↓	↓	↓	•	0 2	0 3	1 4	2 5	3 7	5 9	7 11	11 16	17 22	25 31	↑	↑	↑	↑	↑	↑	↑	↑	↑
L	Second	125	250								1 2	3 4	4 5	6 7	8 9	12 13	18 19	26 27	37 38	56 57									
M	First	200	200	↓	↓	↓	↓	↓	•	0 2	0 3	1 4	2 5	3 7	5 9	7 11	11 16	17 22	25 31	↑	↑	↑	↑	↑	↑	↑	↑	↑	↑
M	Second	200	400							1 2	3 4	4 5	6 7	8 9	12 13	18 19	26 27	37 38	56 57										
N	First	315	315	↓	↓	↓	↓	•	0 2	0 3	1 4	2 5	3 7	5 9	7 11	11 16	17 22	25 31	↑	↑	↑	↑	↑	↑	↑	↑	↑	↑	↑
N	Second	315	630						1 2	3 4	4 5	6 7	8 9	12 13	18 19	26 27	37 38	56 57											
P	First	500	500	↓	↓	↓	•	0 2	0 3	1 4	2 5	3 7	5 9	7 11	11 16	17 22	25 31	↑	↑	↑	↑	↑	↑	↑	↑	↑	↑	↑	↑
P	Second	500	1000					1 2	3 4	4 5	6 7	8 9	12 13	18 19	26 27	37 38	56 57												
Q	First	800	800	↓	↓	•	0 2	0 3	1 4	2 5	3 7	5 9	7 11	11 16	17 22	25 31	↑	↑	↑	↑	↑	↑	↑	↑	↑	↑	↑	↑	↑
Q	Second	800	1600				1 2	3 4	4 5	6 7	8 9	12 13	18 19	26 27	37 38	56 57													
R	First	1250	1250	↓	•	0 2	0 3	1 4	2 5	3 7	5 9	7 11	11 16	17 22	25 31	↑	↑	↑	↑	↑	↑	↑	↑	↑	↑	↑	↑	↑	↑
R	Second	1250	2500			1 2	3 4	4 5	6 7	8 9	12 13	18 19	26 27	37 38	56 57														

↓ = Use first sampling plan below arrow. If sample size equals or exceeds lot or batch size, do 100 percent inspection.

↑ = Use first sampling plan above arrow.

Ac = Acceptance number

Re = Rejection number

• = Use corresponding single sampling plan (or alternatively, use double sampling plan below, where available).

Table 13-12
Master table for tightened inspection—double sampling (MIL STD 105D, Table III-B)

Acceptable Quality Levels (tightened inspection)

In the data body below, each cell shows **Ac Re** (acceptance number and rejection number). The "First" sub-row is the first sample; the "Second" sub-row is the cumulative (second) sample. ↓ = use first sampling plan below arrow; ↑ = use first sampling plan above arrow; · = use corresponding single sampling plan.

Code	Sample	Sample size	Cum. sample size	0.010	0.015	0.025	0.040	0.065	0.10	0.15	0.25	0.40	0.65	1.0	1.5	2.5	4.0	6.5	10	15	25	40	65	100	150	250	400	650	1000
A				↓	↓	↓	↓	↓	↓	↓	↓	↓	↓	↓	↓	↓	↓	↓	↓	↓	↓	↓	↓	↓	↓	↓	↓	↓	·
B	First	2	2	↓	↓	↓	↓	↓	↓	↓	↓	↓	↓	↓	↓	↓	↓	↓	·	0 2	0 3	1 4	2 5	3 7	6 10	9 14	15 20	23 29	↑
	Second	2	4																	1 2	3 4	4 5	6 7	11 12	15 16	23 24	34 35	52 53	
C	First	3	3	↓	↓	↓	↓	↓	↓	↓	↓	↓	↓	↓	↓	↓	↓	·	0 2	0 3	1 4	2 5	3 7	6 10	9 14	15 20	23 29	↑	↑
	Second	3	6																1 2	3 4	4 5	6 7	11 12	15 16	23 24	34 35	52 53		
D	First	5	5	↓	↓	↓	↓	↓	↓	↓	↓	↓	↓	↓	↓	↓	·	0 2	0 3	1 4	2 5	3 7	6 10	9 14	15 20	23 29	↑	↑	↑
	Second	5	10															1 2	3 4	4 5	6 7	11 12	15 16	23 24	34 35	52 53			
E	First	8	8	↓	↓	↓	↓	↓	↓	↓	↓	↓	↓	↓	↓	·	0 2	0 3	1 4	2 5	3 7	6 10	9 14	15 20	23 29	↑	↑	↑	↑
	Second	8	16														1 2	3 4	4 5	6 7	11 12	15 16	23 24	34 35	52 53				
F	First	13	13	↓	↓	↓	↓	↓	↓	↓	↓	↓	↓	↓	·	0 2	0 3	1 4	2 5	3 7	6 10	9 14	15 20	23 29	↑	↑	↑	↑	↑
	Second	13	26													1 2	3 4	4 5	6 7	11 12	15 16	23 24	34 35	52 53					
G	First	20	20	↓	↓	↓	↓	↓	↓	↓	↓	↓	↓	·	0 2	0 3	1 4	2 5	3 7	6 10	9 14	15 20	23 29	↑	↑	↑	↑	↑	↑
	Second	20	40												1 2	3 4	4 5	6 7	11 12	15 16	23 24	34 35	52 53						
H	First	32	32	↓	↓	↓	↓	↓	↓	↓	↓	↓	·	0 2	0 3	1 4	2 5	3 7	6 10	9 14	15 20	23 29	↑	↑	↑	↑	↑	↑	↑
	Second	32	64											1 2	3 4	4 5	6 7	11 12	15 16	23 24	34 35	52 53							
J	First	50	50	↓	↓	↓	↓	↓	↓	↓	↓	·	0 2	0 3	1 4	2 5	3 7	6 10	9 14	15 20	23 29	↑	↑	↑	↑	↑	↑	↑	↑
	Second	50	100										1 2	3 4	4 5	6 7	11 12	15 16	23 24	34 35	52 53								
K	First	80	80	↓	↓	↓	↓	↓	↓	↓	·	0 2	0 3	1 4	2 5	3 7	6 10	9 14	15 20	23 29	↑	↑	↑	↑	↑	↑	↑	↑	↑
	Second	80	160									1 2	3 4	4 5	6 7	11 12	15 16	23 24	34 35	52 53									
L	First	125	125	↓	↓	↓	↓	↓	↓	·	0 2	0 3	1 4	2 5	3 7	6 10	9 14	15 20	23 29	↑	↑	↑	↑	↑	↑	↑	↑	↑	↑
	Second	125	250								1 2	3 4	4 5	6 7	11 12	15 16	23 24	34 35	52 53										
M	First	200	200	↓	↓	↓	↓	↓	·	0 2	0 3	1 4	2 5	3 7	6 10	9 14	15 20	23 29	↑	↑	↑	↑	↑	↑	↑	↑	↑	↑	↑
	Second	200	400							1 2	3 4	4 5	6 7	11 12	15 16	23 24	34 35	52 53											
N	First	315	315	↓	↓	↓	↓	·	0 2	0 3	1 4	2 5	3 7	6 10	9 14	15 20	23 29	↑	↑	↑	↑	↑	↑	↑	↑	↑	↑	↑	↑
	Second	315	630						1 2	3 4	4 5	6 7	11 12	15 16	23 24	34 35	52 53												
P	First	500	500	↓	↓	↓	·	0 2	0 3	1 4	2 5	3 7	6 10	9 14	15 20	23 29	↑	↑	↑	↑	↑	↑	↑	↑	↑	↑	↑	↑	↑
	Second	500	1000					1 2	3 4	4 5	6 7	11 12	15 16	23 24	34 35	52 53													
Q	First	800	800	↓	↓	·	0 2	0 3	1 4	2 5	3 7	6 10	9 14	15 20	23 29	↑	↑	↑	↑	↑	↑	↑	↑	↑	↑	↑	↑	↑	↑
	Second	800	1600				1 2	3 4	4 5	6 7	11 12	15 16	23 24	34 35	52 53														
R	First	1250	1250	↓	·	0 2	0 3	1 4	2 5	3 7	6 10	9 14	15 20	23 29	↑	↑	↑	↑	↑	↑	↑	↑	↑	↑	↑	↑	↑	↑	↑
	Second	1250	2500			1 2	3 4	4 5	6 7	11 12	15 16	23 24	34 35	52 53															
S	First	2000	2000	·	0 2	0 3	1 4	2 5	3 7	6 10	9 14	15 20	23 29	↑	↑	↑	↑	↑	↑	↑	↑	↑	↑	↑	↑	↑	↑	↑	↑
	Second	2000	4000		1 2	3 4	4 5	6 7	11 12	15 16	23 24	34 35	52 53																

↓ = Use first sampling plan below arrow. If sample size equals or exceeds lot or batch size, do 100 percent inspection.

↑ = Use first sampling plan above arrow.

Ac = Acceptance number

Re = Rejection number

· = Use corresponding single sampling plan (or, alternatively, use double sampling plan below, where available).

Table 13-13
Master table for reduced inspection—double sampling (MIL STD 105D, Table III-C) †

Acceptable Quality Levels (reduced inspection). Each AQL entry is given as **Ac Re** (Ac = Acceptance number, Re = Rejection number). ↓ = use first sampling plan below arrow; ↑ = use first sampling plan above arrow; • = use corresponding single sampling plan.

Sample size code letter	Sample	Sample size	Cumulative sample size	0.010	0.015	0.025	0.040	0.065	0.10	0.15	0.25	0.40	0.65	1.0	1.5	2.5	4.0	6.5	10	15	25	40	65	100	150	250	400	650	1000
A				↓	↓	↓	↓	↓	↓	↓	↓	↓	↓	↓	↓	↓	↓	↓	↓	↓	•	•	•	•	•	•	•	•	•
B				↓	↓	↓	↓	↓	↓	↓	↓	↓	↓	↓	↓	↓	↓	↓	↓	•	•	•	•	•	•	•	•	•	•
C				↓	↓	↓	↓	↓	↓	↓	↓	↓	↓	↓	↓	↓	↓	↓	•	•	•	•	•	•	•	•	•	•	•
D	First	2	2	↓	↓	↓	↓	↓	↓	↓	↓	↓	↓	↓	↓	↓	•	0 2	0 3	0 4	0 4	1 5	2 7	3 8	5 10	7 12	11 17	↑	↑
D	Second	2	4	↓	↓	↓	↓	↓	↓	↓	↓	↓	↓	↓	↓	↓	•	0 2	0 4	1 5	3 6	4 7	6 9	8 12	12 16	18 22	26 30	↑	↑
E	First	3	3	↓	↓	↓	↓	↓	↓	↓	↓	↓	↓	↓	↓	•	0 2	0 3	0 4	0 4	1 5	2 7	3 8	5 10	7 12	11 17	↑	↑	↑
E	Second	3	6	↓	↓	↓	↓	↓	↓	↓	↓	↓	↓	↓	↓	•	0 2	0 4	1 5	3 6	4 7	6 9	8 12	12 16	18 22	26 30	↑	↑	↑
F	First	5	5	↓	↓	↓	↓	↓	↓	↓	↓	↓	↓	↓	•	0 2	0 3	0 4	0 4	1 5	2 7	3 8	5 10	7 12	11 17	↑	↑	↑	↑
F	Second	5	10	↓	↓	↓	↓	↓	↓	↓	↓	↓	↓	↓	•	0 2	0 4	1 5	3 6	4 7	6 9	8 12	12 16	18 22	26 30	↑	↑	↑	↑
G	First	8	8	↓	↓	↓	↓	↓	↓	↓	↓	↓	↓	•	0 2	0 3	0 4	0 4	1 5	2 7	3 8	5 10	7 12	11 17	↑	↑	↑	↑	↑
G	Second	8	16	↓	↓	↓	↓	↓	↓	↓	↓	↓	↓	•	0 2	0 4	1 5	3 6	4 7	6 9	8 12	12 16	18 22	26 30	↑	↑	↑	↑	↑
H	First	13	13	↓	↓	↓	↓	↓	↓	↓	↓	↓	•	0 2	0 3	0 4	0 4	1 5	2 7	3 8	5 10	7 12	11 17	↑	↑	↑	↑	↑	↑
H	Second	13	26	↓	↓	↓	↓	↓	↓	↓	↓	↓	•	0 2	0 4	1 5	3 6	4 7	6 9	8 12	12 16	18 22	26 30	↑	↑	↑	↑	↑	↑
J	First	20	20	↓	↓	↓	↓	↓	↓	↓	↓	•	0 2	0 3	0 4	0 4	1 5	2 7	3 8	5 10	7 12	11 17	↑	↑	↑	↑	↑	↑	↑
J	Second	20	40	↓	↓	↓	↓	↓	↓	↓	↓	•	0 2	0 4	1 5	3 6	4 7	6 9	8 12	12 16	18 22	26 30	↑	↑	↑	↑	↑	↑	↑
K	First	32	32	↓	↓	↓	↓	↓	↓	↓	•	0 2	0 3	0 4	0 4	1 5	2 7	3 8	5 10	7 12	11 17	↑	↑	↑	↑	↑	↑	↑	↑
K	Second	32	64	↓	↓	↓	↓	↓	↓	↓	•	0 2	0 4	1 5	3 6	4 7	6 9	8 12	12 16	18 22	26 30	↑	↑	↑	↑	↑	↑	↑	↑
L	First	50	50	↓	↓	↓	↓	↓	↓	•	0 2	0 3	0 4	0 4	1 5	2 7	3 8	5 10	7 12	11 17	↑	↑	↑	↑	↑	↑	↑	↑	↑
L	Second	50	100	↓	↓	↓	↓	↓	↓	•	0 2	0 4	1 5	3 6	4 7	6 9	8 12	12 16	18 22	26 30	↑	↑	↑	↑	↑	↑	↑	↑	↑
M	First	80	80	↓	↓	↓	↓	↓	•	0 2	0 3	0 4	0 4	1 5	2 7	3 8	5 10	7 12	11 17	↑	↑	↑	↑	↑	↑	↑	↑	↑	↑
M	Second	80	160	↓	↓	↓	↓	↓	•	0 2	0 4	1 5	3 6	4 7	6 9	8 12	12 16	18 22	26 30	↑	↑	↑	↑	↑	↑	↑	↑	↑	↑
N	First	125	125	↓	↓	↓	↓	•	0 2	0 3	0 4	0 4	1 5	2 7	3 8	5 10	7 12	11 17	↑	↑	↑	↑	↑	↑	↑	↑	↑	↑	↑
N	Second	125	250	↓	↓	↓	↓	•	0 2	0 4	1 5	3 6	4 7	6 9	8 12	12 16	18 22	26 30	↑	↑	↑	↑	↑	↑	↑	↑	↑	↑	↑
P	First	200	200	↓	↓	↓	•	0 2	0 3	0 4	0 4	1 5	2 7	3 8	5 10	7 12	11 17	↑	↑	↑	↑	↑	↑	↑	↑	↑	↑	↑	↑
P	Second	200	400	↓	↓	↓	•	0 2	0 4	1 5	3 6	4 7	6 9	8 12	12 16	18 22	26 30	↑	↑	↑	↑	↑	↑	↑	↑	↑	↑	↑	↑
Q	First	315	315	↓	↓	•	0 2	0 3	0 4	0 4	1 5	2 7	3 8	5 10	7 12	11 17	↑	↑	↑	↑	↑	↑	↑	↑	↑	↑	↑	↑	↑
Q	Second	315	630	↓	↓	•	0 2	0 4	1 5	3 6	4 7	6 9	8 12	12 16	18 22	26 30	↑	↑	↑	↑	↑	↑	↑	↑	↑	↑	↑	↑	↑
R	First	500	500	↓	•	0 2	0 3	0 4	0 4	1 5	2 7	3 8	5 10	7 12	11 17	↑	↑	↑	↑	↑	↑	↑	↑	↑	↑	↑	↑	↑	↑
R	Second	500	1000	↓	•	0 2	0 4	1 5	3 6	4 7	6 9	8 12	12 16	18 22	26 30	↑	↑	↑	↑	↑	↑	↑	↑	↑	↑	↑	↑	↑	↑

Legend:

- ↓ = Use first sampling plan below arrow. If sample size equals or exceeds lot or batch size, do 100 percent inspection.
- ↑ = Use first sampling plan above arrow.
- Ac = Acceptance number.
- Re = Rejection number.
- • = Use corresponding single sampling plan (or alternatively, use double sampling plan below, when available.)
- † = If, after the second sample, the acceptance number has been exceeded, but the rejection number has not been reached, accept the lot, but reinstate normal inspection

Table 13-14
Master table for normal inspection—multiple sampling (MIL STD 105D, Table IV-A)

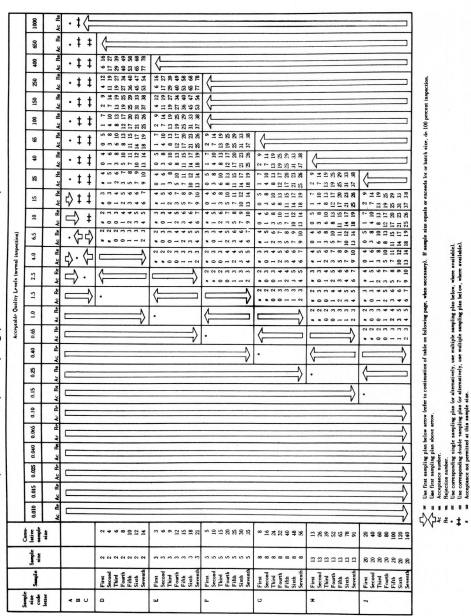

Use first sampling plan below arrow (refer to continuation of table on following page, when necessary). If sample size equals or exceeds lot or batch size, do 100 percent inspection.

Use first sampling plan above arrow.

Ac = Acceptance number.

Re = Rejection number.

‡ = Use corresponding single sampling plan (or alternatively, use multiple sampling plan below, where available).
‡ = Use corresponding double sampling plan (or alternatively, use multiple sampling plan below, where available).

* = Acceptance not permitted at this sample size.

(continued)

595

Table 13-14 (Continued)

Acceptable Quality Levels (normal inspection)

Note: For Acceptable Quality Levels 15, 25, 40, 65, 100, 150, 250, 400, 650, and 1000, all rows in this portion of the table show an upward arrow (↑ = use first sampling plan above arrow). The data‑bearing columns (0.010 through 10) are shown below. (↓ = use first sampling plan below arrow; ↑ = use first sampling plan above arrow.)

Code	Sample	Sample size	Cum. sample size	0.010 Ac Re	0.015 Ac Re	0.025 Ac Re	0.040 Ac Re	0.065 Ac Re	0.10 Ac Re	0.15 Ac Re	0.25 Ac Re	0.40 Ac Re	0.65 Ac Re	1.0 Ac Re	1.5 Ac Re	2.5 Ac Re	4.0 Ac Re	6.5 Ac Re	10 Ac Re
K	First	32	32	↓	↓	↓	↓	↓	↓	# 2	# 2	# 3	# 3	0 4	0 4	# 4	0 5	1 7	2 9
	Second	32	64	↓	↓	↓	↓	↓	↓	# 2	# 2	0 3	0 4	1 5	1 6	1 6	3 8	4 10	7 14
	Third	32	96	↓	↓	↓	↓	↓	↓	0 2	0 2	0 3	1 5	2 6	3 8	3 8	6 10	8 13	13 19
	Fourth	32	128	↓	↓	↓	↓	↓	↓	0 3	0 3	1 4	1 5	3 6	5 9	5 10	8 13	12 17	19 25
	Fifth	32	160	↓	↓	↓	↓	↓	↓	0 3	0 3	1 4	2 5	4 6	6 10	7 11	11 15	17 20	25 29
	Sixth	32	192	↓	↓	↓	↓	↓	↓	1 3	1 3	2 4	3 5	5 7	8 10	10 13	14 17	21 23	31 33
	Seventh	32	224	↓	↓	↓	↓	↓	↓	1 2	2 3	3 4	4 5	6 7	9 10	13 14	18 19	25 26	37 38
L	First	50	50	↓	↓	↓	↓	↓	# 2	# 2	# 3	# 3	0 4	0 4	# 4	0 5	1 7	2 9	↑
	Second	50	100	↓	↓	↓	↓	↓	# 2	# 2	0 3	0 4	1 5	1 6	1 6	3 8	4 10	7 14	↑
	Third	50	150	↓	↓	↓	↓	↓	0 2	0 2	0 3	1 5	2 6	3 8	3 8	6 10	8 13	13 19	↑
	Fourth	50	200	↓	↓	↓	↓	↓	0 3	0 3	1 4	1 5	3 6	5 9	5 10	8 13	12 17	19 25	↑
	Fifth	50	250	↓	↓	↓	↓	↓	0 3	0 3	1 4	2 5	4 6	6 10	7 11	11 15	17 20	25 29	↑
	Sixth	50	300	↓	↓	↓	↓	↓	1 3	1 3	2 4	3 5	5 7	8 10	10 13	14 17	21 23	31 33	↑
	Seventh	50	350	↓	↓	↓	↓	↓	1 2	2 3	3 4	4 5	6 7	9 10	13 14	18 19	25 26	37 38	↑
M	First	80	80	↓	↓	↓	↓	# 2	# 2	# 3	# 3	0 4	0 4	# 4	0 5	1 7	2 9	↑	↑
	Second	80	160	↓	↓	↓	↓	# 2	# 2	0 3	0 4	1 5	1 6	1 6	3 8	4 10	7 14	↑	↑
	Third	80	240	↓	↓	↓	↓	0 2	0 2	0 3	1 5	2 6	3 8	3 8	6 10	8 13	13 19	↑	↑
	Fourth	80	320	↓	↓	↓	↓	0 3	0 3	1 4	1 5	3 6	5 9	5 10	8 13	12 17	19 25	↑	↑
	Fifth	80	400	↓	↓	↓	↓	0 3	0 3	1 4	2 5	4 6	6 10	7 11	11 15	17 20	25 29	↑	↑
	Sixth	80	480	↓	↓	↓	↓	1 3	1 3	2 4	3 5	5 7	8 10	10 13	14 17	21 23	31 33	↑	↑
	Seventh	80	560	↓	↓	↓	↓	1 2	2 3	3 4	4 5	6 7	9 10	13 14	18 19	25 26	37 38	↑	↑
N	First	125	125	↓	↓	↓	# 2	# 2	# 3	# 3	0 4	0 4	# 4	0 5	1 7	2 9	↑	↑	↑
	Second	125	250	↓	↓	↓	# 2	# 2	0 3	0 4	1 5	1 6	1 6	3 8	4 10	7 14	↑	↑	↑
	Third	125	375	↓	↓	↓	0 2	0 2	0 3	1 5	2 6	3 8	3 8	6 10	8 13	13 19	↑	↑	↑
	Fourth	125	500	↓	↓	↓	0 3	0 3	1 4	1 5	3 6	5 9	5 10	8 13	12 17	19 25	↑	↑	↑
	Fifth	125	625	↓	↓	↓	0 3	0 3	1 4	2 5	4 6	6 10	7 11	11 15	17 20	25 29	↑	↑	↑
	Sixth	125	750	↓	↓	↓	1 3	1 3	2 4	3 5	5 7	8 10	10 13	14 17	21 23	31 33	↑	↑	↑
	Seventh	125	875	↓	↓	↓	1 2	2 3	3 4	4 5	6 7	9 10	13 14	18 19	25 26	37 38	↑	↑	↑
P	First	200	200	↓	↓	# 2	# 2	# 3	# 3	0 4	0 4	# 4	0 5	1 7	2 9	↑	↑	↑	↑
	Second	200	400	↓	↓	# 2	# 2	0 3	0 4	1 5	1 6	1 6	3 8	4 10	7 14	↑	↑	↑	↑
	Third	200	600	↓	↓	0 2	0 2	0 3	1 5	2 6	3 8	3 8	6 10	8 13	13 19	↑	↑	↑	↑
	Fourth	200	800	↓	↓	0 3	0 3	1 4	1 5	3 6	5 9	5 10	8 13	12 17	19 25	↑	↑	↑	↑
	Fifth	200	1000	↓	↓	0 3	0 3	1 4	2 5	4 6	6 10	7 11	11 15	17 20	25 29	↑	↑	↑	↑
	Sixth	200	1200	↓	↓	1 3	1 3	2 4	3 5	5 7	8 10	10 13	14 17	21 23	31 33	↑	↑	↑	↑
	Seventh	200	1400	↓	↓	1 2	2 3	3 4	4 5	6 7	9 10	13 14	18 19	25 26	37 38	↑	↑	↑	↑
Q	First	315	315	↓	# 2	# 2	# 3	# 3	0 4	0 4	# 4	0 5	1 7	2 9	↑	↑	↑	↑	↑
	Second	315	630	↓	# 2	# 2	0 3	0 4	1 5	1 6	1 6	3 8	4 10	7 14	↑	↑	↑	↑	↑
	Third	315	945	↓	0 2	0 2	0 3	1 5	2 6	3 8	3 8	6 10	8 13	13 19	↑	↑	↑	↑	↑
	Fourth	315	1260	↓	0 3	0 3	1 4	1 5	3 6	5 9	5 10	8 13	12 17	19 25	↑	↑	↑	↑	↑
	Fifth	315	1575	↓	0 3	0 3	1 4	2 5	4 6	6 10	7 11	11 15	17 20	25 29	↑	↑	↑	↑	↑
	Sixth	315	1890	↓	1 3	1 3	2 4	3 5	5 7	8 10	10 13	14 17	21 23	31 33	↑	↑	↑	↑	↑
	Seventh	315	2205	↓	1 2	2 3	3 4	4 5	6 7	9 10	13 14	18 19	25 26	37 38	↑	↑	↑	↑	↑
R	First	500	500	# 2	# 2	# 3	# 3	0 4	0 4	# 4	0 5	1 7	2 9	↑	↑	↑	↑	↑	↑
	Second	500	1000	# 2	# 2	0 3	0 4	1 5	1 6	1 6	3 8	4 10	7 14	↑	↑	↑	↑	↑	↑
	Third	500	1500	0 2	0 2	0 3	1 5	2 6	3 8	3 8	6 10	8 13	13 19	↑	↑	↑	↑	↑	↑
	Fourth	500	2000	0 3	0 3	1 4	1 5	3 6	5 9	5 10	8 13	12 17	19 25	↑	↑	↑	↑	↑	↑
	Fifth	500	2500	0 3	0 3	1 4	2 5	4 6	6 10	7 11	11 15	17 20	25 29	↑	↑	↑	↑	↑	↑
	Sixth	500	3000	1 3	1 3	2 4	3 5	5 7	8 10	10 13	14 17	21 23	31 33	↑	↑	↑	↑	↑	↑
	Seventh	500	3500	1 2	2 3	3 4	4 5	6 7	9 10	13 14	18 19	25 26	37 38	↑	↑	↑	↑	↑	↑

↓ = Use first sampling plan below arrow. If sample size equals or exceeds lot or batch size, do 100 percent inspection.

↑ = Use first sampling plan above arrow (refer to preceding page, when necessary).

Ac = Acceptance number.

Re = Rejection number.

⬍ = Use corresponding single sampling plan (or alternatively, use multiple plan below, where available).

* = Acceptance not permitted at this sample size.

Table 13-15
Master table for tightened inspection—multiple sampling (MIL STD 105D, Table IV-B)

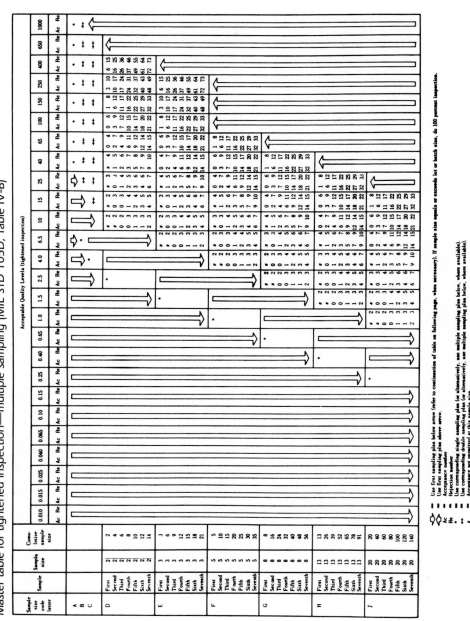

(continued)

Table 13-15 (Continued)

Acceptable Quality Levels (tightened inspection)

Sample size code letter	Sample	Sample size	Cumulative sample size
K	First	32	32
	Second	32	64
	Third	32	96
	Fourth	32	128
	Fifth	32	160
	Sixth	32	192
	Seventh	32	224
L	First	50	50
	Second	50	100
	Third	50	150
	Fourth	50	200
	Fifth	50	250
	Sixth	50	300
	Seventh	50	350
M	First	80	80
	Second	80	160
	Third	80	240
	Fourth	80	320
	Fifth	80	400
	Sixth	80	480
	Seventh	80	560
N	First	125	125
	Second	125	250
	Third	125	375
	Fourth	125	500
	Fifth	125	625
	Sixth	125	750
	Seventh	125	875
P	First	200	200
	Second	200	400
	Third	200	600
	Fourth	200	800
	Fifth	200	1000
	Sixth	200	1200
	Seventh	200	1400
Q	First	315	315
	Second	315	630
	Third	315	945
	Fourth	315	1260
	Fifth	315	1575
	Sixth	315	1890
	Seventh	315	2205
R	First	500	500
	Second	500	1000
	Third	500	1500
	Fourth	500	2000
	Fifth	500	2500
	Sixth	500	3000
	Seventh	500	3500
S	First	800	800
	Second	800	1600
	Third	800	2400
	Fourth	800	3200
	Fifth	800	4000
	Sixth	800	4800
	Seventh	800	5600

The Acceptable Quality Level columns (each with Ac and Re sub-columns) are: 0.010, 0.015, 0.025, 0.040, 0.065, 0.10, 0.15, 0.25, 0.40, 0.65, 1.0, 1.5, 2.5, 4.0, 6.5, 10, 15, 25, 40, 65, 100, 150, 250, 400, 650, 1000.

⇩ = Use first sampling plan below arrow. If sample size equals or exceeds lot or batch size, do 100 percent inspection.
⇧ = Use first sampling plan above arrow (refer to preceding page, when necessary).
Ac = Acceptance number
Re = Rejection number
∗ = Use corresponding single sampling plan (or alternatively, use multiple sampling plan below, where available).
✦ = Acceptance not permitted at this sample size.

Table 13-16
Master table for reduced inspectors—multiple sampling (MIL STD 105D, Table IV-C) †

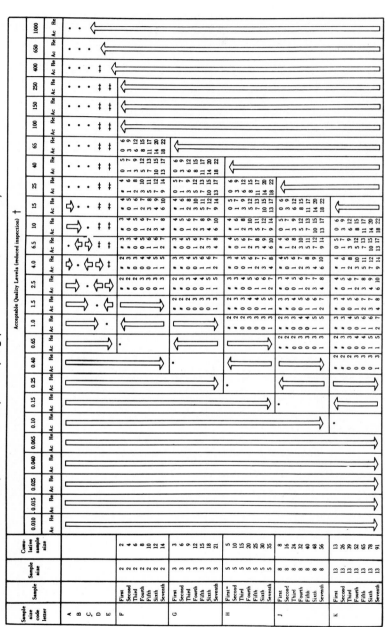

(continued)

Table 13-16 *(Continued)*

Sample size code letter	Sample	Sample size	Cumulative sample size	0.010 Ac Re	0.015 Ac Re	0.025 Ac Re	0.040 Ac Re	0.065 Ac Re	0.10 Ac Re	0.15 Ac Re	0.25 Ac Re	0.40 Ac Re	0.65 Ac Re	1.0 Ac Re	1.5 Ac Re	2.5 Ac Re	4.0 Ac Re	6.5 Ac Re	10 Ac Re	15 Ac Re	25 Ac Re	40 Ac Re	65 Ac Re	100 Ac Re	150 Ac Re	250 Ac Re	400 Ac Re	650 Ac Re	1000 Ac Re
L	First	20	20	↓	↓	↓	↓	•	↑	↓	# 2	# 2	# 3	# 3	# 4	# 4	0 5	0 6	↑	↑	↑	↑	↑	↑	↑	↑	↑	↑	↑
	Second	20	40								# 2	# 3	# 3	0 4	0 5	1 6	1 7	3 9											
	Third	20	60								0 2	0 3	0 4	0 5	1 6	2 8	3 9	6 12											
	Fourth	20	80								0 3	0 4	0 5	1 6	2 7	3 10	5 12	8 15											
	Fifth	20	100								0 3	0 4	1 6	2 7	3 8	5 11	7 13	11 17											
	Sixth	20	120								0 3	1 5	1 6	3 7	4 9	7 12	10 15	14 20											
	Seventh	20	140								1 3	1 5	2 7	4 8	6 10	9 14	13 17	18 22											
M	First	32	32				•	↑	↓	# 2	# 2	# 3	# 3	# 4	# 4	0 5	0 6	↑											
	Second	32	64							# 2	# 3	# 3	0 4	0 5	1 6	1 7	3 9												
	Third	32	96							0 2	0 3	0 4	0 5	1 6	2 8	3 9	6 12												
	Fourth	32	128							0 3	0 4	0 5	1 6	2 7	3 10	5 12	8 15												
	Fifth	32	160							0 3	0 4	1 6	2 7	3 8	5 11	7 13	11 17												
	Sixth	32	192							0 3	1 5	1 6	3 7	4 9	7 12	10 15	14 20												
	Seventh	32	224							1 3	1 5	2 7	4 8	6 10	9 14	13 17	18 22												
N	First	50	50			•	↑	↓	# 2	# 2	# 3	# 3	# 4	# 4	0 5	0 6	↑												
	Second	50	100						# 2	# 3	# 3	0 4	0 5	1 6	1 7	3 9													
	Third	50	150						0 2	0 3	0 4	0 5	1 6	2 8	3 9	6 12													
	Fourth	50	200						0 3	0 4	0 5	1 6	2 7	3 10	5 12	8 15													
	Fifth	50	250						0 3	0 4	1 6	2 7	3 8	5 11	7 13	11 17													
	Sixth	50	300						0 3	1 5	1 6	3 7	4 9	7 12	10 15	14 20													
	Seventh	50	350						1 3	1 5	2 7	4 8	6 10	9 14	13 17	18 22													
P	First	80	80		•	↑	↓	# 2	# 2	# 3	# 3	# 4	# 4	0 5	0 6	↑													
	Second	80	160					# 2	# 3	# 3	0 4	0 5	1 6	1 7	3 9														
	Third	80	240					0 2	0 3	0 4	0 5	1 6	2 8	3 9	6 12														
	Fourth	80	320					0 3	0 4	0 5	1 6	2 7	3 10	5 12	8 15														
	Fifth	80	400					0 3	0 4	1 6	2 7	3 8	5 11	7 13	11 17														
	Sixth	80	480					0 3	1 5	1 6	3 7	4 9	7 12	10 15	14 20														
	Seventh	80	560					1 3	1 5	2 7	4 8	6 10	9 14	13 17	18 22														
Q	First	125	125	•	↑	↓	# 2	# 2	# 3	# 3	# 4	# 4	0 5	0 6	↑														
	Second	125	250				# 2	# 3	# 3	0 4	0 5	1 6	1 7	3 9															
	Third	125	375				0 2	0 3	0 4	0 5	1 6	2 8	3 9	6 12															
	Fourth	125	500				0 3	0 4	0 5	1 6	2 7	3 10	5 12	8 15															
	Fifth	125	625				0 3	0 4	1 6	2 7	3 8	5 11	7 13	11 17															
	Sixth	125	750				0 3	1 5	1 6	3 7	4 9	7 12	10 15	14 20															
	Seventh	125	875				1 3	1 5	2 7	4 8	6 10	9 14	13 17	18 22															
R	First	200	200	↑		# 2	# 2	# 3	# 3	# 4	# 4	0 5	0 6	↑															
	Second	200	400			# 2	# 3	# 3	0 4	0 5	1 6	1 7	3 9																
	Third	200	600			0 2	0 3	0 4	0 5	1 6	2 8	3 9	6 12																
	Fourth	200	800			0 3	0 4	0 5	1 6	2 7	3 10	5 12	8 15																
	Fifth	200	1000			0 3	0 4	1 6	2 7	3 8	5 11	7 13	11 17																
	Sixth	200	1200			0 3	1 5	1 6	3 7	4 9	7 12	10 15	14 20																
	Seventh	200	1400			1 3	1 5	2 7	4 8	6 10	9 14	13 17	18 22																

(Column heads: Acceptable Quality Levels (reduced inspection)†)

↓ = Use first sampling plan below arrow. If sample size equals, or exceeds, lot or batch size, do 100 percent inspection.
↑ = Use first sampling plan above arrow (refer to preceding page when necessary).
Ac = Acceptance number
Re = Rejection number
# = Acceptance not permitted at this sample size.
† = If, after the final sample, the acceptance number has been exceeded, but the rejection number has not been reached, accept the lot, but reinstate normal inspection

Table 13-17

Limit numbers for reduced inspection (MIL STD 105D, Table VIII)

Number of Sample Units from Last 10 Lots or Batches	Acceptable Quality Level																									
	0.010	0.015	0.025	0.040	0.065	0.10	0.15	0.25	0.40	0.65	1.0	1.5	2.5	4.0	6.5	10	15	25	40	65	100	150	250	400	650	1000
20 – 29	*	*	*	*	*	*	*	*	*	*	*	*	*	*	*	0	0	2	4	8	14	22	40	68	115	
30 – 49	*	*	*	*	*	*	*	*	*	*	*	*	*	*	0	0	1	3	7	13	22	36	63	105	178	
50 – 79	*	*	*	*	*	*	*	*	*	*	*	*	*	0	0	2	3	7	14	25	40	63	110	181	301	
80 – 129	*	*	*	*	*	*	*	*	*	*	*	*	0	0	2	4	7	14	24	42	68	105	181	297		
130 – 199	*	*	*	*	*	*	*	*	*	*	*	0	0	2	4	7	13	25	42	72	115	177	301	490		
200 – 319	*	*	*	*	*	*	*	*	*	*	0	0	2	4	8	14	22	40	68	115	181	277	471			
320 – 499	*	*	*	*	*	*	*	*	*	0	0	1	4	8	14	24	39	68	113	189						
500 – 799	*	*	*	*	*	*	*	*	0	0	2	3	7	14	25	40	63	110	181							
800 – 1249	*	*	*	*	*	*	*	0	0	2	4	7	14	24	42	68	105	181								
1250 – 1999	*	*	*	*	*	*	0	0	2	4	7	13	24	40	69	110	169									
2000 – 3149	*	*	*	*	*	0	0	2	4	8	14	22	40	68	115	181										
3150 – 4999	*	*	*	*	0	0	1	4	8	14	24	38	67	111	186											
5000 – 7999	*	*	*	0	0	2	3	7	14	25	40	63														
8000 – 12499	*	*	0	0	2	4	7	14	24	42	68	105														
12500 – 19999	*	0	0	2	4	7	13	24	40	69	110	169														
20000 – 31499	0	0	2	4	8	14	22	40	68	115	181															
31500 – 49999	0	1	4	8	14	24	38	67	111	186																
50000 & Over	2	3	7	14	25	40	63	110	181	301																

* Denotes that the number of sample units from the last ten lots or batches is not sufficient for reduced inspection for this AQL. In this instance more than ten lots or batches may be used for the calculation, provided that the lots or batches used are the most recent ones in sequence, that they have all been on normal inspection, and that none has been rejected while on original inspection.

one. This general strategy is used throughout MIL STD 105D for a transition to tightened inspection. If the normal inspection acceptance number is 1, 2, or 3, the acceptance number for the corresponding tightened inspection plan is reduced by one. If the normal inspection acceptance number is 5, 7, 10, or 14, the reduction in acceptance number for tightened inspection is two. For a normal acceptance number of 21, the reduction is three. Table 13-10 indicates that under reduced inspection, the sample size for this example would be $n = 50$, the acceptance number would be $c = 1$, and the rejection number would be $r = 3$. Thus, if two defectives were encountered, the lot would be accepted, but the next lot would be inspected under normal inspection.

In examining the tables, notice that if a vertical arrow is encountered the first sampling plan above or below the arrow should be used. When this occurs, the sample size code letter and the sample size change. For example, if a single-sampling plan is indexed by an AQL of 1.5% and a sample size code letter of F, the code letter changes to G and the sample size changes from 20 to 32.

As a second example, consider finding a double-sampling scheme from MIL STD 105D for the case when $N = 2000$, AQL $= 0.65$, and general inspection level II. The sample size code letter is still K, and from Table 13-11, 13-12, and 13-13, we may find the normal, tightened, and reduced sampling plans as follows:

Normal Inspection

Sample Size	Acceptance Number	Rejection Number
80	0	3
80	3	4

Thus, from a lot of $N = 2000$, inspect a random sample of $n_1 = 80$ units. If there are no defectives, accept the lot. If there are three or more defectives, reject the lot. If there are one or two defectives, take a second sample of $n_2 = 80$ units. If the combined number of defectives is three or less, accept the lot. If there are four or more total defectives, reject the lot.

Tightened Inspection

Sample Size	Acceptance Number	Rejection Number
80	0	2
80	1	2

On tightened inspection, a random sample of $n_1 = 80$ units is drawn from the lot. If there are no defectives, the lot is accepted, and if there are two or more defectives, the lot is rejected. If there is one defective, a second sample of $n_2 = 80$ units is drawn. If the total number of defectives is one, the lot is accepted, while if there are two or more total defectives, the lot is rejected.

Reduced Inspection

Sample Size	Acceptance Number	Rejection Number
32	0	3
32	0	4

When on reduced inspection, a random sample of $n_1 = 32$ is drawn from the lot. If there are no defectives the lot is accepted, and if there are three or more defectives, the lot is rejected and we return to normal inspection. If there are one or two defectives in the first sample, select a second sample of $n_2 = 32$ units. Now notice that the second acceptance number is zero, and the corresponding rejection number is four. This implies that if there are one, two, or three *total* defectives (note that there *cannot* be zero total defectives after the second sample), then accept the lot but return to normal inspection. If there are four or more defectives, reject the lot and reinstate normal inspection.

13-5.3 Discussion

MIL STD 105D presents the OC curves for single-sampling plans. These are all type-B OC curves. The OC curves for the matching double- and multiple-sampling plans are roughly comparable with those for the corresponding single-sampling plans. Figure 13-18 presents an example of these curves for code letter K. The OC

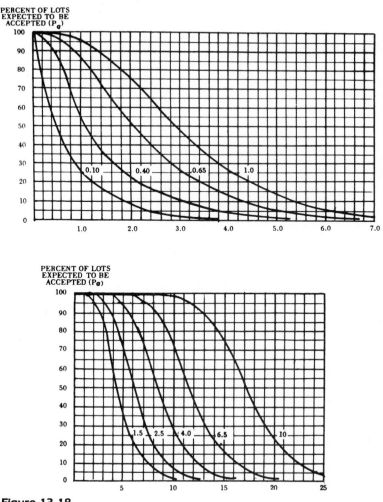

Figure 13-18
OC curves for sample size code letter K, MIL STD 105D.

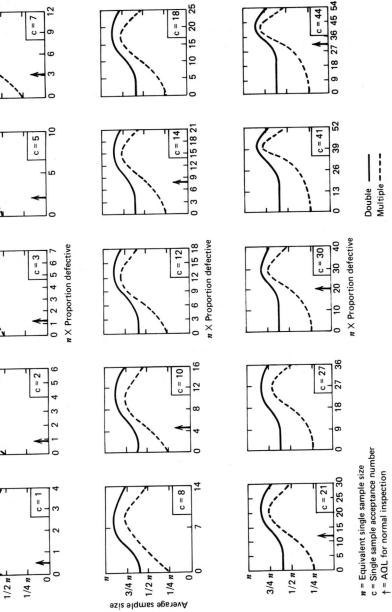

Figure 13-19
ANS curves for double and multiple sampling, MIL STD 105D.

n = Equivalent single sample size
c = Single sample acceptance number
↑ = AQL for normal inspection

Double ——
Multiple - - - -

curves presented in the standard are for the initial sampling plan only. They are not the OC curves for the overall inspection program,[4] including shifts to and from tightened inspection.

Average sample number curves for double and multiple sampling are given, assuming that no curtailment is used. These curves are shown in Figure 13-19 and are useful in evaluating the average sample sizes that may be expected to occur under the various sampling plans for a given lot or process quality.

The standard also has supplementary tables giving the 10% and 5% point of the OC curves. Table 13-18 presents these values for sample size code letter K. These are included for the benefit of individuals who are interested in controlling the risk of acceptance for individual lots worse than a specified LTPD. In addition, there is a table of AOQL values for normal and tightened inspection plans, so that the performance of an individual acceptance sampling plan in rectifying inspection can be evaluated.

There are several points about MIL STD 105D that should be emphasized. These include the following. One, MIL STD 105D is AQL-oriented. It focuses attention on the producer's risk end of the OC curve. The only control over the discriminatory power of the sampling plan (i.e., the steepness of the OC curve) is through the choice of inspection level.

Two, the sample sizes selected for use in MIL STD 105D are 2, 3, 5, 8, 13, 20, 32, 50, 80, 125, 200, 315, 500, 800, 1250, and 2000. Thus, not all sample sizes are possible. Notice that there are some rather significant gaps, such as between 125 and 200, and between 200 and 315.

Three, the sample sizes in MIL STD 105D are related to the lot sizes. To see the nature of this relationship, calculate the midpoint of each lot size range, and plot the logarithm of the sample size for that lot size range against the logarithm of the lot size range midpoint. Such a plot will follow roughly a straight line up to $n = 80$, and thereafter another straight line with a shallower slope. Thus, the sample size will increase as the lot size increases. However, the ratio of sample size to lot size will decrease rapidly. This gives significant economy in inspection costs per unit when the vendor submits large lots. For a given AQL, the effect of this increase in sample size as the lot size increases is to increase the probability of acceptance for submitted lots of AQL quality. The probability of acceptance at a given AQL will vary with increasing sample size from about 0.91 to about 0.99. This feature of the standard was and still is subject to some controversy. The argument in favor of the approach in MIL STD 105D is that rejection of a large lot has more serious consequences for the vendor than rejection of a small lot, and if the probability of acceptance at the AQL increases with sample size, this reduces the risk of false rejection of a large lot. Furthermore, the large sample also gives a more discriminating OC curve, which means that the protection that the consumer receives against accepting an isolated bad lot will also be increased.

Four, the switching rules from normal to tightened inspection and from tightened to normal inspection are also subject to some criticism. In particular, Japanese quality-control engineers dislike the switching rules because, they argue, there is often a considerable amount of misswitching from normal to tightened or

---

[4] ANSI/ASQC Z1.4 presents the scheme performance of the standard, giving scheme OC curves and the corresponding percentage points.

Table 13-18

Values of OC curves for sample size code letter K (MIL STD 105D, Table X-K-1)

P_a	Acceptable Quality Levels (normal inspection)											
	0.10	0.40	0.65	1.0	1.5	2.5	✕	4.0	✕	6.5	✕	10
	p (in percent defective or defects per hundred units)											
99.0	0.0081	0.119	0.349	0.658	1.43	2.33	2.81	3.82	4.88	5.98	8.28	10.1
95.0	0.0410	0.284	0.654	1.09	2.09	3.19	3.76	4.94	6.15	7.40	9.95	11.9
90.0	0.0840	0.426	0.882	1.40	2.52	3.73	4.35	5.62	6.92	8.24	10.9	13.0
75.0	0.230	0.769	1.38	2.03	3.38	4.77	5.47	6.90	8.34	9.79	12.7	14.9
50.0	0.554	1.34	2.14	2.94	4.54	6.14	6.94	8.53	10.1	11.7	14.9	17.3
25.0	1.11	2.15	3.14	4.09	5.94	7.75	8.64	10.4	12.2	13.9	17.4	20.0
10.0	1.84	3.11	4.26	5.35	7.42	9.42	10.4	12.3	14.2	16.1	19.8	22.5
5.0	2.40	3.80	5.04	6.20	8.41	10.5	11.5	13.6	15.6	17.5	21.4	24.2
1.0	3.68	5.31	6.73	8.04	10.5	12.8	13.6	16.1	18.3	20.4	24.5	27.5
	0.15	0.65	1.0	1.5	2.5	4.0	✕	6.5	✕	10	✕	✕
	Acceptable Quality Levels (tightened inspection)											

Note: All values given in above table based on Poisson distribution as an approximation to the binomial.

normal to reduced inspection when the process is actually producing lots of AQL quality. They have also pointed out that there is a significant probability that production would even be discontinued, even though there has been no actual quality deterioration. Since the Japanese view of tightened inspection is that it is a dishonorable situation, the MIL STD 105D switching rules are not used in Japan. The Japanese switching rules use a procedure in which the process average is estimated over the last five lots. This is similar to the switching rules used in older versions of MIL STD 105D. It should be pointed out that the AQL is a maximum acceptable percent defective, and the process average should actually be less than the AQL. Switching rules that encourage production at the AQL, such as the rules used in Japan, reduce protection to the consumer when the process average moves above the AQL.

Five, a flagrant and common abuse of MIL STD 105D is failure to use the switching rules at all. When this is done, it results in ineffective and deceptive inspection and a substantial increase in the consumer's risk. It is not recommended that MIL STD 105D be implemented without use of the switching rules from normal to tightened and normal to reduced inspection.

As mentioned previously, a civilian standard, ANSI/ASQC Z1.4, is the counterpart of MIL STD 105D. It seems appropriate to conclude our discussion of MIL STD 105D with a comparison of the military and civilian standards. ANSI/ASQC Z1.4 was adopted in 1981. Aspects of ANSI/ASQC Z1.4 that differ from MIL STD 105D are presented below.

1. The terminology "nonconformity," "nonconformance," and "percent nonconforming" is used.
2. The switching rules were changed slightly to provide an option for reduced inspection without the use of limit numbers.
3. Several tables that show measures of scheme performance (*including* the switching rules) were introduced. Some of these performance measures include AOQL, limiting quality for which $P_a = 0.10$ and $P_a = 0.05$, ASN, and operating-characteristic curves.
4. A section was added describing proper use of individual sampling plans when extracted from the system.
5. A figure illustrating the switching rules was added.

These revisions modernize the terminology and emphasize the system concept of the standard. All tables, numbers, and procedures used in MIL STD 105D are retained in ANSI/ASQC Z1.4.

13-6 THE DODGE-ROMIG SAMPLING PLANS

H. F. Dodge and H. G. Romig have developed a set of sampling inspection tables for lot-by-lot inspection of product by attributes. These plans were developed in the 1920s and enjoy extensive industrial use. Two types of sampling plans are presented in the tables—plans for lot tolerance percent defective (LTPD) protection, and plans that provide a specified average outgoing quality limit (AOQL).

For each of these approaches to sampling plan design, there are tables for single and double sampling.

Sampling plans that emphasize LTPD protection, such as the Dodge-Romig plans and the lot-sensitive compliance plans in Section 13-4, are often preferred to AQL-oriented sampling plans, such as those in MIL STD 105D, particularly for critical components and parts. Many manufacturers feel that they have relied too much on AQLs in the past, and they are now emphasizing other measures of performance, such as defective parts per million (ppm). Consider the following:

AQL	Defective Parts per Million
10%	100,000
1%	10,000
0.1%	1,000
0.01%	100
0.001%	10
0.0001%	1

Thus, even very small AQLs imply large numbers of defective ppm. In complex products, the effect of this can be devastating. For example, suppose that a printed circuit board contains 100 elements, each manufactured by a process operating at 0.5% defective. If the AQLs for these elements are 0.5% and if all elements on the printed curcuit board must operate for the card to function properly, then the probability that a board works is

$$P(\text{function properly}) = (0.995)^{100} = 0.6058$$

Thus, there is an obvious need for sampling plans that emphasize LTPD protection, even when the process average fallout is low. The Dodge-Romig plans are often useful in these situations.

The Dodge-Romig AOQL plans are designed so that the average total inspection for a given AOQL and a specified process average p will be minimized. Similarly, the LTPD plans are designed so that the average total inspection is a minimum. This makes the Dodge-Romig plans very useful for in-plant inspection of semifinished product.

The Dodge-Romig plans apply only to programs that submit rejected lots to 100% inspection. Unless rectifying inspection is used, the AOQL concept is meaningless. Furthermore, in order to use the plans, we must know the process average—that is, the average fraction nonconforming of the incoming product. When a vendor is relatively new, we usually do not know its process fallout. Sometimes this may be estimated from a preliminary sample or from data provided by the vendor. Alternatively, the largest possible process average in the table can be used until enough information has been generated to provide a more accurate estimate of the vendor's process fallout. Obtaining a more accurate estimate of the incoming fraction nonconforming or process average will allow a more appropriate sampling plan to be adopted. It is not uncommon to find that sampling inspection begins with one plan, and after sufficient information is generated to reestimate the vendor's process fallout, a new plan is adopted. We discuss estimation of the process average in more detail in Section 13-6.3.

13-6.1 AOQL Plans

The Dodge-Romig [1959] tables give AOQL sampling plans for AOQL values of 0.1%, 0.25%, 0.5%, 0.75%, 1%, 1.5%, 2%, 2.5%, 3%, 4%, 5%, 7%, and 10%. For each of these AOQL values, six classes of values for the process average are specified. Tables are provided for both single and double sampling. These plans have been designed so that the average total inspection at the given AOQL and process average is approximately a minimum.

A selection of the Dodge-Romig sampling plans are shown in Tables 13-19,[5] 13-20, 13-21, and 13-22. Tables 13-19 through 13-21 are single-sampling plans for AOQL values of 2%, 2.5%, and 3%. Table 13-22 is a double-sampling table for an AOQL of 3%.

To illustrate the use of the Dodge-Romig AOQL tables, suppose that we are inspecting LSI memory elements for a personal computer and that the elements are shipped in lots of size $N = 5000$. The vendor's process average fallout is 1% nonconforming. We wish to find a single-sampling plan with an AOQL = 3%. From Table 13-21, we find that the plan is

$$n = 65 \qquad c = 3$$

Table 13-21 also indicates that the LTPD for this sampling plan is 10.3%. This is the point on the OC curve for which $P_a = 0.10$. Therefore, the sampling plan $n = 65$, $c = 3$, gives an AOQL of 3% nonconforming and provides assurance that 90% of incoming lots that are as bad as 10.3% defective will be rejected. Assuming that incoming quality is equal to the process average and that the probability of lot acceptance at this level of quality is $P_a = 0.9957$, we find that the average total inspection for this plan is:

$$
\begin{aligned}
\text{ATI} &= n + (1 - P_a)(N - n) \\
&= 65 + (1 - 0.9957)(5000 - 65) \\
&= 86.22
\end{aligned}
$$

Thus, we will inspect approximately 86 units, on the average, in order to sentence a lot.

13-6.2 LTPD Plans

The Dodge-Romig LTPD tables are designed so that the probability of lot acceptance at the LTPD is 0.1. Tables are provided for LTPD values of 0.5%, 1%, 2%, 3%, 4%, 5%, 7%, and 10%. Tables 13-23 through 13-26 are a representative set of Dodge-Romig tables. Single-sampling plans for LTPD values of 1%, 2%, and 5% are shown in Tables 13-23, 13-24, and 13-25, respectively. Double-sampling plans for an LTPD of 1% defective are shown in Table 13-26.

---

[5] Tables 13-19 through 13-26 are adapted from H. F. Dodge and H. G. Romig, *Sampling Inspection Tables, Single and Double Sampling*, 2nd ed., John Wiley & Sons, New York, 1959, with the permission of the publisher.

Table 13-19

Dodge-Romig inspection tables—Single-sampling plans AOQL = 2.0%

	Process Average																	
	0–0.04%			0.05–0.40%			0.41–0.80%			0.81–1.20%			1.21–1.60%			1.61–2.00%		
Lot Size	n	c	LTPD %	n	c	LTPD %	n	c	LTPD %	n	c	LTPD %	n	c	LTPD %	n	c	LTPD %
1–15	All	0	—	All	0	—	All	0	—	All	0	—	All	0	—	All	0	—
16–50	14	0	13.6	14	0	13.6	14	0	13.6	14	0	13.6	14	0	13.6	14	0	13.6
51–100	16	0	12.4	16	0	12.4	16	0	12.4	16	0	12.4	16	0	12.4	16	0	12.4
101–200	17	0	12.2	17	0	12.2	17	0	12.2	17	0	12.2	35	1	10.5	35	1	10.5
201–300	17	0	12.3	17	0	12.3	17	0	12.3	37	1	10.2	37	1	10.2	37	1	10.2
301–400	18	0	11.8	18	0	11.8	38	1	10.0	38	1	10.0	38	1	10.0	60	2	8.5
401–500	18	0	11.9	18	0	11.9	39	1	9.8	39	1	9.8	60	2	8.6	60	2	8.6
501–600	18	0	11.9	18	0	11.9	39	1	9.8	39	1	9.8	60	2	8.6	60	2	8.6
601–800	18	0	11.9	40	1	9.6	40	1	9.6	65	2	8.0	65	2	8.0	85	3	7.5
801–1000	18	0	12.0	40	1	9.6	40	1	9.6	65	2	8.1	65	2	8.1	90	3	7.4
1001–2000	18	0	12.0	41	1	9.4	65	2	8.2	65	2	8.2	95	3	7.0	120	4	6.5
2001–3000	18	0	12.0	41	1	9.4	65	2	8.2	95	3	7.0	120	4	6.5	180	6	5.8
3001–4000	18	0	12.0	42	1	9.3	65	2	8.2	95	3	7.0	155	5	6.0	210	7	5.5
4001–5000	18	0	12.0	42	1	9.3	70	2	7.5	125	4	6.4	155	5	6.0	245	8	5.3
5001–7000	18	0	12.0	42	1	9.3	95	3	7.0	125	4	6.4	185	6	5.6	280	9	5.1
7001–10,000	42	1	9.3	70	2	7.5	95	3	7.0	155	5	6.0	220	7	5.4	350	11	4.8
10,001–20,000	42	1	9.3	70	2	7.6	95	3	7.0	190	6	5.6	290	9	4.9	460	14	4.4
20,001–50,000	42	1	9.3	70	2	7.6	125	4	6.4	220	7	5.4	395	12	4.5	720	21	3.9
50,001–100,000	42	1	9.3	95	3	7.0	160	5	5.9	290	9	4.9	505	15	4.2	955	27	3.7

Table 13-20

Dodge-Romig inspection tables—Single-sampling plans AOQL = 2.5%

| | Process Average | | | | | | | | | | | | | | | | | |
| Lot Size | 0–0.05% | | | 0.06–0.50% | | | 0.51–1.00% | | | 1.01–1.50% | | | 1.51–2.00% | | | 2.01–2.50% | | |
	n	c	LTPD %	n	c	LTPD %	n	c	LTPD %	n	c	LTPD %	n	c	LTPD %	n	c	LTPD %
1–10	All	0	—	All	0	—	All	0	—	All	0	—	All	0	—	All	0	—
11–50	11	0	17.6	11	0	17.6	11	0	17.6	11	0	17.6	11	0	17.6	11	0	17.6
51–100	13	0	15.3	13	0	15.3	13	0	15.3	13	0	15.3	13	0	15.3	13	0	15.3
101–200	14	0	14.7	14	0	14.7	14	0	14.7	29	1	12.9	29	1	12.9	29	1	12.9
202–300	14	0	14.9	14	0	14.9	30	1	12.7	30	1	12.7	30	1	12.7	30	1	12.7
301–400	14	0	15.0	14	0	15.0	31	1	12.3	31	1	12.3	31	1	12.3	48	2	10.7
401–500	14	0	15.0	14	0	15.0	32	1	12.0	32	1	12.0	49	2	10.6	49	2	10.6
501–600	14	0	15.1	32	1	12.0	32	1	12.0	50	2	10.4	50	2	10.4	70	3	9.3
601–800	14	0	15.1	32	1	12.0	32	1	12.0	50	2	10.5	50	2	10.5	70	3	9.4
801–1000	15	0	14.2	33	1	11.7	33	1	11.7	50	2	10.6	70	3	9.4	90	4	8.5
1001–2000	15	0	14.2	33	1	11.7	55	2	9.3	75	3	8.8	95	4	8.0	120	5	7.6
2001–3000	15	0	14.2	33	1	11.8	55	2	9.4	75	3	8.8	120	5	7.6	145	6	7.2
3001–4000	15	0	14.3	33	1	11.8	55	2	9.5	100	4	7.9	125	5	7.4	195	8	6.6
4001–5000	15	0	14.3	33	1	11.8	75	3	8.9	100	4	7.9	150	6	7.0	225	9	6.3
5001–7000	33	1	11.8	55	2	9.7	75	3	8.9	125	5	7.4	175	7	6.7	250	10	6.1
7001–10,000	34	1	11.4	55	2	9.7	75	3	8.9	125	5	7.4	200	8	6.4	310	12	5.8
10,001–20,000	34	1	11.4	55	2	9.7	100	4	8.0	150	6	7.0	260	10	6.0	425	16	5.3
20,001–50,000	34	1	11.4	55	2	9.7	100	4	8.0	180	7	6.7	345	13	5.5	640	23	4.8
50,001–100,000	34	1	11.4	80	3	8.4	125	5	7.4	235	9	6.1	435	16	5.2	800	28	4.5

Table 13-21

Dodge-Romig inspection table—Single-sampling plans AOQL = 3.0%

Lot Size	0–0.06%			0.07–0.60%			0.61–1.20%			1.21–1.80%			1.81–2.40%			2.41–3.00%		
	n	c	LTPD %	n	c	LTPD %	n	c	LTPD %	n	c	LTPD %	n	c	LTPD %	n	c	LTPD %
1–10	All	0	—	All	0	—	All	0	—	All	0	—	All	0	—	All	0	—
11–50	10	0	19.0	10	0	19.0	10	0	19.0	10	0	19.0	10	0	19.0	10	0	19.0
51–100	11	0	18.0	11	0	18.0	11	0	18.0	11	0	18.0	11	0	18.0	22	1	16.4
101–200	12	0	17.0	12	0	17.0	12	0	17.0	25	1	15.1	25	1	15.1	25	1	15.1
201–300	12	0	17.0	12	0	17.0	26	1	14.6	26	1	14.6	26	1	14.6	40	2	12.8
301–400	12	0	17.1	12	0	17.1	26	1	14.7	26	1	14.7	41	2	12.7	41	2	12.7
401–500	12	0	17.2	27	1	14.1	27	1	14.1	42	2	12.4	42	2	12.4	42	2	12.4
501–600	12	0	17.3	27	1	14.2	27	1	14.2	42	2	12.4	42	2	12.4	60	3	10.8
601–800	12	0	17.3	27	1	14.2	27	1	14.2	43	2	12.1	60	3	10.9	60	3	10.9
801–1,000	12	0	17.4	27	1	14.2	44	2	11.8	44	2	11.8	60	3	11.0	80	4	9.8
1,001–2,000	12	0	17.5	28	1	13.8	45	2	11.7	65	3	10.2	80	4	9.8	100	5	9.1
2,001–3,000	12	0	17.5	28	1	13.8	45	2	11.7	65	3	10.2	100	5	9.1	140	7	8.2
3,001–4,000	12	0	17.5	28	1	13.8	65	3	10.3	85	4	9.5	125	6	8.4	165	8	7.8
4,001–5,000	28	1	13.8	28	1	13.8	65	3	10.3	85	4	9.5	125	6	8.4	210	10	7.4
5,001–7,000	28	1	13.8	45	2	11.8	65	3	10.3	105	5	8.8	145	7	8.1	235	11	7.1
7,001–10,000	28	1	13.9	46	2	11.6	65	3	10.3	105	5	8.8	170	8	7.6	280	13	6.8
10,001–20,000	28	1	13.9	46	2	11.7	85	4	9.5	125	6	8.4	215	10	7.2	380	17	6.2
20,001–50,000	28	1	13.9	65	3	10.3	105	5	8.8	170	8	7.6	310	14	6.5	560	24	5.7
50,001–100,000	28	1	13.9	65	3	10.3	125	6	8.4	215	10	7.2	385	17	6.2	690	29	5.4

Process Average

Table 13-22

Dodge-Romig inspection table—Double-sampling plans AOQL = 3.0%

Lot Size	Process Average																	
	0–0.06%						0.07–0.60%						0.61–1.20%					
	Trial 1		Trial 2			LTPD %	Trial 1		Trial 2			LTPD %	Trial 1		Trial 2			LTPD %
	n_1	c_1	n_2	$n_1 + n_2$	c_2		n_1	c_1	n_2	$n_1 + n_2$	c_2		n_1	c_1	n_2	$n_1 + n_2$	c_2	
1–10	All	0	—	—	—	—	All	0	—	—	—	—	All	0	—	—	—	—
11–50	10	0	—	—	—	19.0	10	0	—	—	—	19.0	10	0	—	—	—	19.0
51–100	16	0	9	25	1	16.4	16	0	9	25	1	16.4	16	0	9	25	1	16.4
101–200	17	0	9	26	1	16.0	17	0	9	26	1	16.0	17	0	9	26	1	16.0
201–300	18	0	10	28	1	15.5	18	0	10	28	1	15.5	21	0	23	44	2	13.3
301–400	18	0	11	29	1	15.2	21	0	24	45	2	13.2	23	0	37	60	3	12.0
401–500	18	0	11	29	1	15.2	21	0	25	46	2	13.0	24	0	36	60	3	11.7
501–600	18	0	12	30	1	15.0	21	0	25	46	2	13.0	24	0	41	65	3	11.5
601–800	21	0	25	46	2	13.0	21	0	25	46	2	13.0	24	0	41	65	3	11.5
801–1,000	21	0	26	47	2	12.8	21	0	26	47	2	12.8	25	0	40	65	3	11.4
1,001–2,000	22	0	26	48	2	12.6	22	0	26	48	2	12.6	27	0	58	85	4	10.3
2,001–3,000	22	0	26	48	2	12.6	25	0	40	65	3	11.4	28	0	62	90	4	10.0
3,001–4,000	23	0	26	49	2	12.4	25	0	45	70	3	11.0	29	0	76	105	5	9.6
4,001–5,000	23	0	26	49	2	12.4	26	0	44	70	3	11.0	30	0	75	105	5	9.5
5,001–7,000	23	0	27	50	2	12.2	26	0	44	70	3	11.0	30	0	80	110	5	9.4
7,001–10,000	23	0	27	50	2	12.2	27	0	43	70	3	11.0	30	0	80	110	5	9.4
10,001–20,000	23	0	27	50	2	12.2	27	0	43	70	3	11.0	31	0	94	125	6	9.2
20,001–50,000	23	0	27	50	2	12.2	28	0	67	95	4	9.7	55	1	120	175	8	8.0
50,001–100,000	23	0	27	50	2	12.2	31	0	84	115	5	9.0	60	1	140	200	9	7.6

(continued)

Table 13-22 (Continued)

Lot Size	Process Average																			
	1.21–1.80%						1.81–2.40%						2.41–3.00%						
	Trial 1		Trial 2			LTPD	Trial 1		Trial 2			LTPD	Trial 1		Trial 2			LTPD
	n_1	c_1	n_2	$n_1 + n_2$	c_2	%	n_1	c_1	n_2	$n_1 + n_2$	c_2	%	n_1	c_1	n_2	$n_1 + n_2$	c_2	%
1–10	All	0	—	—	—	—	All	0	—	—	—	—	All	0	—	—	—	—
11–50	10	0	—	—	—	19.0	10	0	—	—	—	19.0	10	0	—	—	—	19.0
51–100	17	0	17	34	2	15.8	17	0	17	34	2	15.8	17	0	17	34	2	15.8
101–200	20	0	21	41	2	13.7	22	0	33	55	3	12.4	22	0	33	55	3	12.4
201–300	23	0	37	60	3	12.0	23	0	37	60	3	12.0	24	0	51	75	4	11.1
301–400	23	0	37	60	3	12.0	25	0	55	80	4	10.8	42	1	63	105	6	10.4
401–500	24	0	36	60	3	11.7	25	0	55	80	4	10.8	46	1	79	125	7	9.7
501–600	26	0	54	80	4	10.7	46	1	69	115	6	9.7	48	1	97	145	8	9.2
601–800	26	0	54	80	4	10.7	49	1	81	130	7	9.4	50	1	115	165	9	8.9
801–1,000	27	0	58	85	4	10.3	49	1	86	135	7	9.2	70	2	120	190	10	8.4
1,001–2,000	49	1	76	125	6	9.1	50	1	150	200	10	8.0	100	3	180	280	14	7.5
2,001–3,000	50	1	95	145	7	8.7	80	2	165	245	12	7.6	130	4	260	390	19	6.9
3,001–4,000	55	1	110	165	8	8.5	105	3	200	305	14	7.0	155	5	330	485	23	6.5
4,001–5,000	60	1	135	195	9	7.8	110	3	225	335	15	6.7	215	7	390	605	27	6.0
5,001–7,000	60	1	165	225	10	7.3	110	3	250	360	16	6.6	270	9	505	775	34	5.7
7,001–10,000	85	2	160	245	11	7.2	115	3	290	405	18	6.5	285	9	680	965	41	5.4
10,001–20,000	85	2	180	265	12	7.2	140	4	315	455	20	6.3	315	10	805	1,120	47	5.3
20,001–50,000	85	2	205	290	13	7.0	170	5	420	590	26	6.0	390	13	940	1,330	56	5.2
50,001–100,000	90	2	245	335	15	6.8	200	6	505	705	30	5.7	445	15	1,105	1,550	65	5.1

Table 13-23

Dodge-Romig single-sampling table for lot tolerance percent defective (LTPD) = 1.0%

| | Process Average | | | | | | | | | | | | | | | | | |
| | 0–0.010% | | | 0.011–0.10% | | | 0.11–0.20% | | | 0.21–0.30% | | | 0.31–0.40% | | | 0.41–0.50% | | |
Lot Size	n	c	AOQL %	n	c	AOQL %	n	c	AOQL %	n	c	AOQL %	n	c	AOQL %	n	c	AOQL %
1–120	All	0	0	All	0	0	All	0	0	All	0	0	All	0	0	All	0	0
121–150	120	0	0.06	120	0	0.06	120	0	0.06	120	0	0.06	120	0	0.06	120	0	0.06
151–200	140	0	0.08	140	0	0.08	140	0	0.08	140	0	0.08	140	0	0.08	140	0	0.08
201–300	165	0	0.10	165	0	0.10	165	0	0.10	165	0	0.10	165	0	0.10	165	0	0.10
301–400	175	0	0.12	175	0	0.12	175	0	0.12	175	0	0.12	175	0	0.12	175	0	0.12
401–500	180	0	0.13	180	0	0.13	180	0	0.13	180	0	0.13	180	0	0.13	180	0	0.13
501–600	190	0	0.13	190	0	0.13	190	0	0.13	190	0	0.13	190	0	0.13	305	1	0.14
601–800	200	0	0.14	200	0	0.14	200	0	0.14	330	1	0.15	330	1	0.15	330	1	0.15
801–1,000	205	0	0.14	205	0	0.14	205	0	0.14	335	1	0.17	335	1	0.17	335	1	0.17
1,001–2,000	220	0	0.15	220	0	0.15	360	1	0.19	490	2	0.21	490	2	0.21	610	3	0.22
2,001–3,000	220	0	0.15	375	1	0.20	505	2	0.23	630	3	0.24	745	4	0.26	870	5	0.26
3,001–4,000	225	0	0.15	380	1	0.20	510	2	0.24	645	3	0.25	880	5	0.28	1,000	6	0.29
4,001–5,000	225	0	0.16	380	1	0.20	520	2	0.24	770	4	0.28	895	5	0.29	1,120	7	0.31
5,001–7,000	230	0	0.16	385	1	0.21	655	3	0.27	780	4	0.29	1,020	6	0.32	1,260	8	0.34
7,001–10,000	230	0	0.16	520	2	0.25	660	3	0.28	910	5	0.32	1,150	7	0.34	1,500	10	0.37
10,001–20,000	390	1	0.21	525	2	0.26	785	4	0.31	1,040	6	0.35	1,400	9	0.39	1,980	14	0.43
20,001–50,000	390	1	0.21	530	2	0.26	920	5	0.34	1,300	8	0.39	1,890	13	0.44	2,570	19	0.48
50,001–100,000	390	1	0.21	670	3	0.29	1,040	6	0.36	1,420	9	0.41	2,120	15	0.47	3,150	23	0.50

Table 13-24

Dodge-Romig single-sampling table for lot tolerance percent defective (LTPD) = 2.0%

	Process Average																	
	0–0.02%			0.03–0.20%			0.21–0.40%			0.41–0.60%			0.61–0.80%			0.81–1.00%		
Lot Size	n	c	AOQL %	n	c	AOQL %	n	c	AOQL %	n	c	AOQL %	n	c	AOQL %	n	c	AOQL %
1–75	All	0	0	All	0	0	All	0	0	All	0	0	All	0	0	All	0	0
76–100	70	0	0.16	70	0	0.16	70	0	0.16	70	0	0.16	70	0	0.16	70	0	0.16
101–200	85	0	0.25	85	0	0.25	85	0	0.25	85	0	0.25	85	0	0.25	85	0	0.25
201–300	95	0	0.26	95	0	0.26	95	0	0.26	95	0	0.26	95	0	0.26	95	0	0.26
301–400	100	0	0.28	100	0	0.28	100	0	0.28	160	1	0.32	160	1	0.32	160	1	0.32
401–500	105	0	0.28	105	0	0.28	105	0	0.28	165	1	0.34	165	1	0.34	165	1	0.34
501–600	105	0	0.29	105	0	0.29	175	1	0.34	175	1	0.34	175	1	0.34	235	2	0.36
601–800	110	0	0.29	110	0	0.29	180	1	0.36	240	2	0.40	240	2	0.40	300	3	0.41
801–1000	115	0	0.28	115	0	0.28	185	1	0.37	245	2	0.42	305	3	0.44	305	3	0.44
1001–2000	115	0	0.30	190	1	0.40	255	2	0.47	325	3	0.50	380	4	0.54	440	5	0.56
2001–3000	115	0	0.31	190	1	0.41	260	2	0.48	380	4	0.58	450	5	0.60	565	7	0.64
3001–4000	115	0	0.31	195	1	0.41	330	3	0.54	450	5	0.63	510	6	0.65	690	9	0.70
4001–5000	195	1	0.41	260	2	0.50	335	3	0.54	455	5	0.63	575	7	0.69	750	10	0.74
5001–7000	195	1	0.42	265	2	0.50	335	3	0.55	515	6	0.69	640	8	0.73	870	12	0.80
7001–10,000	195	1	0.42	265	2	0.50	395	4	0.62	520	6	0.69	760	10	0.79	1050	15	0.86
10,001–20,000	200	1	0.42	265	2	0.51	460	5	0.67	650	8	0.77	885	12	0.86	1230	18	0.94
20,001–50,000	200	1	0.42	335	3	0.58	520	6	0.73	710	9	0.81	1060	15	0.93	1520	23	1.0
50,001–100,000	200	1	0.42	335	3	0.58	585	7	0.76	770	10	0.84	1180	17	0.97	1690	26	1.1

Table 13-25

Dodge-Romig single-sampling table for lot tolerance percent defective (LTPD) = 5.0%

Lot Size	Process Average																
	0–0.05%			0.06–0.50%			0.51–1.00%			1.01–1.50%			1.51–2.00%			2.01–2.50%		
	n	c	AOQL %	n	c	AOQL %	n	c	AOQL %	n	c	AOQL %	n	c	AOQL %	n	c	AOQL %
1–30	All	0	0	All	0	0	All	0	0	All	0	0	All	0	0	All	0	0
31–50	30	0	0.49	30	0	0.49	30	0	0.49	30	0	0.49	30	0	0.49	30	0	0.49
51–100	37	0	0.63	37	0	0.63	37	0	0.63	37	0	0.63	37	0	0.63	37	0	0.63
101–200	40	0	0.74	40	0	0.74	40	0	0.74	40	0	0.74	40	0	0.74	40	0	0.74
201–300	43	0	0.74	43	0	0.74	70	1	0.92	70	1	0.92	95	2	0.99	95	2	0.99
301–400	44	0	0.74	44	0	0.74	70	1	0.99	100	2	1.0	120	3	1.1	145	4	1.1
401–500	45	0	0.75	75	1	0.95	100	2	1.1	100	2	1.1	125	3	1.2	150	4	1.2
501–600	45	0	0.76	75	1	0.98	100	2	1.1	125	3	1.2	150	4	1.3	175	5	1.3
601–800	45	0	0.77	75	1	1.0	100	2	1.2	130	3	1.2	175	5	1.4	200	6	1.4
801–1000	45	0	0.78	75	1	1.0	105	2	1.2	155	4	1.4	180	5	1.4	225	7	1.5
1001–2000	45	0	0.80	75	1	1.0	130	3	1.4	180	5	1.6	230	7	1.7	280	9	1.8
2001–3000	75	1	1.1	105	2	1.3	135	3	1.4	210	6	1.7	280	9	1.9	370	13	2.1
3001–4000	75	1	1.1	105	2	1.3	160	4	1.5	210	6	1.7	305	10	2.0	420	15	2.2
4001–5000	75	1	1.1	105	2	1.3	160	4	1.5	235	7	1.8	330	11	2.0	440	16	2.2
5001–7000	75	1	1.1	105	2	1.3	185	5	1.7	260	8	1.9	350	12	2.2	490	18	2.4
7001–10,000	75	1	1.1	105	2	1.3	185	5	1.7	260	8	1.9	380	13	2.2	535	20	2.5
10,001–20,000	75	1	1.1	135	3	1.4	210	6	1.8	285	9	2.0	425	15	2.3	610	23	2.6
20,001–50,000	75	1	1.1	135	3	1.4	235	7	1.9	305	10	2.1	470	17	2.4	700	27	2.7
50,001–100,000	75	1	1.1	160	4	1.6	235	7	1.9	355	12	2.2	515	19	2.5	770	30	2.8

Table 13-26

Dodge-Romig double-sampling table for lot tolerance percent defective (LTPD) = 1%

Lot Size	Process Average																	
	0–0.010%						0.011–0.10%						0.11–0.20%					
	Trial 1		Trial 2			AOQL %	Trial 1		Trial 2			AOQL %	Trial 1		Trial 2			AOQL %
	n_1	c_1	n_2	n_1+n_2	c_2		n_1	c_1	n_2	n_1+n_2	c_1		n_1	c_1	n_2	n_1+n_2	c_2	
1–120	All	0	—	—	—	0	All	0	—	—	—	0	All	0	—	—	—	0
121–150	120	0	—	—	—	0.06	120	0	—	—	—	0.06	120	0	—	—	—	0.06
151–200	140	0	—	—	—	0.08	140	0	—	—	—	0.08	140	0	—	—	—	0.08
201–260	165	0	—	—	—	0.10	165	0	—	—	—	0.10	165	0	—	—	—	0.10
261–300	180	0	75	255	1	0.10	180	0	75	255	1	0.10	180	0	75	255	1	0.10
301–400	200	0	90	290	1	0.12	200	0	90	290	1	0.12	200	0	90	290	1	0.12
401–500	215	0	100	315	1	0.14	215	0	100	315	1	0.14	215	0	100	315	1	0.14
501–600	225	0	115	340	1	0.15	225	0	115	340	1	0.15	225	0	115	340	1	0.15
601–800	235	0	125	360	1	0.16	235	0	125	360	1	0.16	235	0	125	360	1	0.16
801–1,000	245	0	135	380	1	0.17	245	0	135	380	1	0.17	245	0	250	495	2	0.19
1,001–2,000	265	0	155	420	1	0.18	265	0	155	420	1	0.18	265	0	285	550	2	0.21
2,001–3,000	270	0	160	430	1	0.19	270	0	300	570	2	0.22	270	0	420	690	3	0.25
3,001–4,000	275	0	160	435	1	0.19	275	0	305	580	2	0.22	275	0	435	710	3	0.25
4,001–5,000	275	0	165	440	1	0.19	275	0	310	585	2	0.23	275	0	565	840	4	0.28
5,001–7,000	275	0	170	445	1	0.20	275	0	315	590	2	0.23	275	0	580	855	4	0.29
7,001–10,000	280	0	320	600	1	0.24	280	0	460	740	3	0.26	280	0	590	870	4	0.30
10,001–20,000	280	0	325	605	1	0.24	280	0	465	745	3	0.27	450	1	700	1,150	6	0.33
20,001–50,000	280	0	325	605	1	0.25	280	0	605	885	4	0.30	450	1	830	1,280	7	0.36
50,001–100,000	280	0	325	605	1	0.25	280	0	605	885	4	0.30	450	1	960	1,410	8	0.38

(continued)

Table 13-26 (Continued)

Process Average

Lot Size	0.21–0.30%						0.31–0.40%						0.41–0.50%					
	Trial 1		Trial 2			AOQL	Trial 1		Trial 2			AOQL	Trial 1		Trial 2			AOQL
	n_1	c_1	n_2	n_1+n_2	c_2	%	n_1	c_1	n_2	n_1+n_2	c_1	%	n_1	c_1	n_2	n_1+n_2	c_2	%
1–120	All	0	—	—	—	0	All	0	—	—	—	0	All	0	—	—	—	0
121–150	120	0	—	—	—	0.06	120	0	—	—	—	0.06	120	0	—	—	—	0.06
151–200	140	0	—	—	—	0.08	140	0	—	—	—	0.08	140	0	—	—	—	0.08
201–260	165	0	—	—	—	0.10	165	0	—	—	—	0.10	165	0	—	—	—	0.10
261–300	180	0	75	255	1	0.10	180	0	75	255	1	0.10	180	0	75	255	1	0.10
301–400	200	0	90	290	1	0.12	200	0	90	290	1	0.12	200	0	90	290	1	0.12
401–500	215	0	100	315	1	0.14	215	0	100	315	1	0.14	215	0	100	315	1	0.14
501–600	225	0	115	340	1	0.15	225	0	115	340	1	0.15	225	0	205	430	2	0.16
601–800	235	0	230	465	2	0.18	235	0	230	465	2	0.18	235	0	230	465	2	0.18
801–1,000	245	0	250	495	2	0.19	245	0	250	495	2	0.19	245	0	250	495	2	0.19
1,001–2,000	265	0	405	670	3	0.23	265	0	515	780	4	0.24	265	0	515	780	4	0.24
2,001–3,000	270	0	545	815	4	0.26	430	1	620	1,050	6	0.28	430	1	830	1,260	8	0.30
3,001–4,000	435	1	645	1,080	6	0.29	435	1	865	1,300	8	0.30	580	2	940	1,520	10	0.33
4,001–5,000	440	1	660	1,100	6	0.30	440	1	1,000	1,440	9	0.33	585	2	1,075	1,660	11	0.35
5,001–7,000	445	1	785	1,230	7	0.33	590	2	990	1,580	10	0.36	730	3	1,190	1,920	13	0.38
7,001–10,000	450	1	920	1,370	8	0.35	600	2	1,240	1,840	12	0.39	870	4	1,540	2,410	17	0.41
10,001–20,000	605	2	1,035	1,640	10	0.39	745	3	1,485	2,230	15	0.43	1,150	6	1,990	3,140	23	0.44
20,001–50,000	605	2	1,295	1,900	12	0.42	885	4	1,845	2,730	19	0.47	1,280	7	2,600	3,880	29	0.52
50,001–100,000	605	2	1,545	2,150	14	0.44	885	4	2,085	2,970	21	0.49	1,410	8	3,280	4,690	36	0.55

To illustrate the use of these tables, suppose that LSI memory elements for a personal computer are shipped from the vendor in lots of size $N = 5000$. The vendor's process average fallout is 0.25% nonconforming, and we wish to use a single-sampling plan with an LTPD of 1%. From inspection of Table 13-23, the sampling plan that should be used is

$$n = 770 \qquad c = 4$$

If we assume that rejected lots are screened 100% and that defective items are replaced with good ones, the AOQL for this plan is approximately 0.28%.

Note from inspection of the Dodge-Romig LTPD tables that values of the process average cover the interval from zero to one-half the LTPD. Provision for larger process averages is unnecessary, since 100% inspection is more economically efficient than inspection sampling when the process average exceeds one-half the desired LTPD.

13-6.3 Estimation of Process Average

As we have observed, selection of a Dodge-Romig plan depends on knowledge of the vendor's process average fallout or percent nonconforming. An estimate of the process average can be obtained using a fraction defective control chart. This chart is based on the first 25 lots submitted by the vendor. If double sampling is used, only the results from the first sample should be included in the computations. Any lot fraction defective that exceeds the upper control limit will be discarded, provided it has an assignable cause, and a new process average is calculated. Until results from 25 lots have been accumulated, the recommended procedure is to use the largest process average in the appropriate table.

13-7 Exercises

13-1 Draw the type-B OC curve for the single-sampling plan $n = 50$, $c = 1$.

13-2 Draw the type-B OC curve for the single-sampling plan $n = 100$, $c = 2$.

13-3 Suppose that a product is shipped in lots of size $N = 5000$. The receiving inspection procedure used is single sampling with $n = 50$ and $c = 1$.

   a. Draw the type-A OC curve for the plan.

   b. Draw the type-B OC curve for this plan and compare it to the type-A OC curve found in part (a).

   c. Which curve is appropriate for this situation?

13-4 Find a single-sampling plan for which $p_1 = 0.01$, $\alpha = 0.05$, $p_2 = 0.10$, and $\beta = 0.10$.

13-5 Find a single-sampling plan for which $p_1 = 0.05$, $\alpha = 0.05$, $p_2 = 0.15$, and $\beta = 0.10$.

13-6 Find a single-sampling plan for which $p_1 = 0.02$, $\alpha = 0.01$, $p_2 = 0.06$, and $\beta = 0.10$.

13-7 A company uses the following acceptance-sampling procedure. A sample equal to 10% of the lot is taken. If 2% or less of the items in the sample are defective, the lot is accepted; otherwise, it is rejected. If submitted lots vary in size from 5000 to 10,000 units, what can you say about the protection by this plan? If 0.05 is the desired LTPD, does this scheme offer reasonable protection to the consumer?

13-8 A company uses a sample size equal to the square root of the lot size. If 1% or less of the items in the sample are defective, the lot is accepted; otherwise, it is rejected. Submitted lots vary in size from 1000 to 5000 units. Comment on the effectiveness of this procedure.

13-9 Consider the single-sampling plan found in Exercise 13-4. Suppose that lots of $N = 2000$ are submitted. Draw the ATI curve for this plan. Draw the AOQ curve and find the AOQL.

13-10 Suppose that a single-sampling plan with $n = 150$ and $c = 2$ is being used for receiving inspection where the vendor ships the product in lots of size $N = 3000$.

    a. Draw the OC curve for this plan.

    b. Draw the AOQ curve and find the AOQL.

    c. Draw the ATI curve for this plan.

13-11 Suppose that a vendor ships components in lots of size 5000. A single-sampling plan with $n = 50$ and $c = 2$ is being used for receiving inspection. Rejected lots are screened, and all defective items are reworked and returned to the lot.

    a. Draw the OC curve for this plan.

    b. Find the level of lot quality that will be rejected 90% of the time.

    c. Management has objected to the use of the above sampling procedure and wants to use a plan with an acceptance number $c = 0$, arguing that this is more consistent with their zero-defects program. What do you think of this?

    d. Design a single-sampling plan with $c = 0$ that will give a 0.90 probability of rejection of lots having the quality level found in part (b). Note that the two plans are now matched at the LTPD point. Draw the OC curve for this plan and compare it to the one for $n = 50$, $c = 2$ in part (a).

    e. Suppose that incoming lots are 0.5% nonconforming. What is the probability of rejecting these lots under both plans? Calculate the ATI at this point for both plans. Which plan do you prefer? Why?

13-12 Draw the primary and supplementary OC curves for a double-sampling plan with $n_1 = 50$, $c_1 = 2$, $n_2 = 100$, $c_2 = 6$. If the incoming lots have fraction nonconforming $p = 0.05$, what is the probability of acceptance on the first sample? What is the probability of final acceptance? Calculate the probability of rejection on the first sample.

13-13 Design a double-sampling plan for which $n_1 = 2n_2$ for the case where $p_1 = 0.01$, $\alpha = 0.05$, $p_2 = 0.10$, and $\beta = 0.10$.

13-14 Consider the double-sampling plan in Exercise 13-13. Draw the ASN curves, considering curtailment and no curtailment on the second sample. Contrast the performance of this plan with the corresponding single-sampling plan found in Exercise 13-4.

13-15 a. Design a double-sampling plan for which $n_1 = 2n_2$ for the case where $p_1 = 0.02$, $\alpha = 0.05$, $p_2 = 0.12$, and $\beta = 0.10$. Draw the ATI curve for this plan assuming that the lot size $N = 15,000$.

    b. Repeat part (a) assuming that $n_1 = n_2$. Comparing the ATI curves, which plan would you prefer?

13-16 a. Derive an item-by-item sequential-sampling plan for which $p_1 = 0.01$, $\alpha = 0.05$, $p_2 = 0.10$, and $\beta = 0.10$.

    b. Draw the OC curve for this plan.

13-17 a. Derive an item-by-item sequential-sampling plan for which $p_1 = 0.02$, $\alpha = 0.05$, $p_2 = 0.15$, and $\beta = 0.10$.

    b. Draw the OC curve for this plan.

13-18 Consider rectifying inspection for single sampling. Develop an AOQ equation assuming that all defective items are removed but *not* replaced with good ones.

13-19 A vendor ships a component in lots of size $N = 3000$. The AQL has been established for this product at 1%. Find the normal, tightened, and reduced sampling plans for this situation from MIL STD 105D, assuming that general inspection level II is appropriate.

13-20 Repeat Exercise 13-19, using general inspection level I. Discuss the differences in the various sampling plans.

13-21 A product is supplied in lots of size $N = 10,000$. The AQL has been specified at 0.10%.

   a. Find the normal, tightened, and reduced single-sampling plans from MIL STD 105D, assuming general inspection level II.

   b. Find the appropriate normal, tightened, and reduced double-sampling plans from MIL STD 105D using general inspection level III.

13-22 MIL STD 105D is being used to inspect incoming lots of size $N = 5000$. Single sampling, general inspection level II, and an AQL of 0.65% are being used.

   a. Find the normal, tightened, and reduced inspection plans.

   b. The last 10 lots have had the following number of observed defectives: 0, 1, 0, 3, 0, 4, 5, 4, 2, and 0. What sequence of normal, tightened, and reduced inspection plans were used?

   c. Draw the OC curves of the normal, tightened, and reduced inspection plans on the same graph.

13-23 A product is shipped in lots of size $N = 2000$. Find a Dodge-Romig single-sampling plan for which the LTPD = 2%, assuming that the process average is 0.25% defective. Draw the OC curve and the ATI curve for this plan. What is the AOQL for this sampling plan?

13-24 We wish to find a single-sampling plan for a situation where lots are shipped from a vendor. The vendor's process operates at a fallout level of 0.50% defective. We want the AOQL from the inspection activity to be 3%.

   a. Find the appropriate Dodge-Romig plan.

   b. Draw the OC curve and the ATI curve for this plan. How much inspection will be necessary, on the average, if the vendor's process operates close to the average fallout level?

   c. What is the LTPD protection for this plan?

13-25 A vendor ships a product in lots of size $N = 5000$. We wish to have an AOQL of 2.5%, and we are going to use single sampling. We do not know the vendor's process fallout but suspect that it is at most 1% defective.

   a. Find the appropriate Dodge-Romig plan.

   b. Find the ATI for this plan, assuming that incoming lots are 1% defective.

   c. Suppose that our estimate of the vendor's process average is incorrect and that it is really 0.25% defective. What sampling plan should we have used? What reduction in ATI would have been realized if we had used the correct plan?

Chapter 14

Acceptance Sampling
by Variables

Variables sampling plans specify the number of items to be sampled and the criterion for sentencing lots when measurements data are collected on the quality characteristic of interest. These plans are generally based on the sample average and sample standard deviation of the quality characteristic. When the distribution of the quality characteristic in the lot or process is known, variables sampling plans that have specified risks of accepting and rejecting lots of given quality may be designed. These variables sampling plans are the subject of this chapter.

14-1 INTRODUCTION TO VARIABLES SAMPLING

14-1.1 Advantages and Disadvantages of Variables Sampling

The primary advantage of variables sampling plans is that the same operating-characteristic curve can be obtained with a smaller sample size than would be required by an attributes sampling plan. Thus, a variables acceptance-sampling plan that has the same protection as an attributes acceptance-sampling plan would require less sampling. The measurements data required by a variables sampling plan would probably cost more per observation than the collection of attributes data. However, the reduction in sample size obtained may more than offset this increased cost. For example, suppose than an attributes sampling plan requires a sample of size 100 items, but the equivalent variables sampling plan requires a sample size of only 65. If the cost of measurement data is less than 1.61 times the cost of measuring the observations on an attributes scale, the variables sampling plan will be more economically efficient, considering sampling costs only. When destructive testing is employed, variables sampling is particularly useful in reducing the costs of inspection.

A second advantage is that measurements data usually provide more information about the manufacturing process or the lot than do attributes data. Generally, numerical measurements of quality characteristics are more useful than simple classification of the item as defective or nondefective.

A final point to be emphasized is that when acceptable quality levels are very small, the sample sizes required by attributes sampling plans are very large. Under these circumstances, there may be significant advantages in switching to variables measurement. Thus, as many manufacturers begin to emphasize allowable numbers of defective parts per million, variables sampling becomes very attractive.

Variables sampling plans have several disadvantages. Perhaps the primary disadvantage is that the distribution of the quality characteristic must be known. Furthermore, most standard variables acceptance-sampling plans assume that the distribution of the quality characteristic is normal. If the distribution of the quality characteristic is not normal, and a plan based on the normal assumption is employed, serious departures from the advertised risks of accepting or rejecting lots of given quality may be experienced. We discuss this point more completely in Section 14-1.3. The second disadvantage of variables sampling is that a separate sampling plan must be employed for each quality characteristic that is being inspected. For example, if an item is inspected for four quality characteristics, it is necessary to have four separate variables inspection sampling plans. If this same product were being inspected under attributes sampling, one attributes sampling plan could be employed. Finally, it is possible that the use of a variables sampling plan will lead to rejection of a lot even though the actual sample inspected does not contain any defective items. While this does not happen very often, when it does occur it usually causes considerable unhappiness in both the vendors' and the consumers' organizations, particularly if rejection of the lot has caused a manufacturing facility to shut down or operate on a reduced production schedule.

14-1.2 Types of Sampling Plans Available

There are two general types of variables sampling procedures: plans that control the lot or process fraction defective (or nonconforming), and plans that control a lot or process parameter (usually the mean). Sections 14-2 and 14-3 present variables sampling plans to control the process fraction defective. Variables sampling plans for the process mean, as well as some other variations of variables sampling, are presented in Section 14-4.

Consider a variables sampling plan to control the lot or process fraction nonconforming. Since the quality characteristic is a variable, there will exist either a lower specification limit (LSL), an upper specification limit (USL), or both, that define the acceptable values of this parameter. Figure 14-1 illustrates the situation in which the quality characteristic x is normally distributed and there is a lower specification limit on this parameter. The symbol p represents the fraction defective

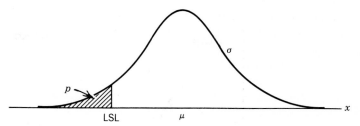

Figure 14-1
Relationship of the lot or process fraction defective ρ to the mean and standard deviation of a normal distribution.

in the lot. Notice that the fraction defective is a function of the lot or process mean μ and the lot or process standard deviation σ.

Suppose that the standard deviation σ is known. Under this condition, we may wish to sample from the lot to determine whether or not the value of the mean is such that the fraction defective p is acceptable. As described below, we may organize the calculations in the variables sampling plan in two ways.

Procedure 1. Take a random sample of n items from the lot and compute the statistic

$$Z_{\text{LSL}} = \frac{\bar{x} - \text{LSL}}{\sigma} \tag{14-1}$$

Note that Z_{LSL} in (14-1) just expresses the distance between the sample average $\bar{x}$ and the lower specification limit in standard deviation units. The larger the value of Z_{LSL}, the further the sample average $\bar{x}$ is from the lower specification limit, and consequently, the smaller the lot fraction defective p. If there is a critical value of p of interest that should not be exceeded with stated probability, we can translate this value of p into a *critical distance*, say k, for Z_{LSL}. Thus, if $Z_{\text{LSL}} \geq k$, we would accept the lot because the sample data imply that the lot mean is sufficiently far above the LSL to ensure that the lot fraction nonconforming is statisfactory. However, if $Z_{\text{LSL}} < k$, the mean is too close to the LSL, and the lot should be rejected.

Procedure 2. Take a random sample of n items from the lot and compute Z_{LSL} using Equation (14-1). Use Z_{LSL} to estimate the fraction defective of the lot or process as the area under the standard normal curve below Z_{LSL}. (Actually, using $Q_{\text{LSL}} = Z_{\text{LSL}}\sqrt{n/(n-1)}$ as a standard normal variable is slightly better, because it gives a better estimate of p.) Let $\hat{p}$ be the estimate of p so obtained. If the estimate $\hat{p}$ exceeds a specified maximum value M, reject the lot; otherwise, accept it.

The two procedures can be designed so that they give equivalent results. When there is only a single specification limit (LSL or USL), either procedure may be used. Obviously, in the case of an upper specification limit, we would compute

$$Z_{\text{USL}} = \frac{\text{USL} - \bar{x}}{\sigma} \tag{14-2}$$

instead of using (14-1). When there are both lower and upper specifications, the M method, Procedure 2, should be used.

When the standard deviation σ is unknown, it is estimated by the sample standard deviation S, and σ in (14-1) and (14-2) is replaced by S. It is also possible to design plans based on the sample range R instead of S. However, these plans are not discussed in this chapter because using the sample standard deviation will lead to smaller sample sizes. Plans based on R were once in wide use because R is easier to compute by hand than is S, but computing is not a problem today.

14-1.3 Caution in the Use of Variables Sampling

We have remarked that the distribution of the quality characteristic must be of known form in order to use variables sampling. Furthermore, the usual assumption is that the parameter of interest follows the normal distribution. This assumption is critical because all variables sampling plans require that there be some method of converting a sample mean and standard deviation into a lot or process fraction defective. If the parameter of interest is not normally distributed, estimates of the fraction defective based on the sample mean and sample standard deviation will not be the same as if the parameter were normally distributed. The difference between these estimated fraction defectives may be large when we are dealing with very small fractions defective. For example, if the mean of a normal distribution lies three standard deviations below a single upper specification limit, the lot will contain no more than 0.135% defective. On the other hand, if the quality characteristic in the lot or process is very nonnormal, and the mean lies three standard deviations below the specification limit, it is entirely possible that 1% or more of the items in the lot might be defective. Figure 14-2 shows the tail areas of the normal distribution and several nonnormal distributions. From examining this figure, it is obvious that when we are dealing with small fractions defective, say below 1%, we must be extremely careful about the assumption of normality.

It is possible to use variables sampling plans when the parameter of interest does not have a normal distribution. Provided that the form of the distribution is known, or that there is a method of determining the fraction defective from the sample average and sample standard deviation (or other appropriate sample statistics), it is possible to devise a procedure for applying a variables sampling plan. For example, Duncan (1974) presents a procedure for using a variables sampling plan when the distribution of the quality characteristic can be described by a Pearson type III distribution. A general discussion of variables sampling in the nonnormal case is, however, beyond the scope of this book.

14-2 DESIGNING A VARIABLES SAMPLING PLAN WITH A SPECIFIED OC CURVE

It is easy to design a variables sampling plan using Procedure 1, the k-method, that has a specified OC curve. Let $(p_1, 1 - \alpha)$, (p_2, β) be the two points on the OC curve of interest. Note that p_1 and p_2 may be the levels of lot or process fraction nonconforming that correspond to acceptable and rejectable levels of quality, respectively.

The nomograph shown in Figure 14-3 enables the quality engineer to find the required sample size n and the critical value k to meet a set of given conditions

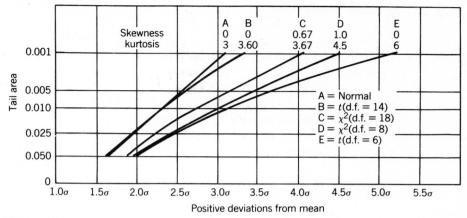

Figure 14-2
Tail areas of the normal and several nonnormal distributions. (Adapted from A. J. Duncan, *Quality Control and Industrial Statistics*, 4th ed., Irwin, Homewood, Ill., 1974, with the permission of the publisher.)

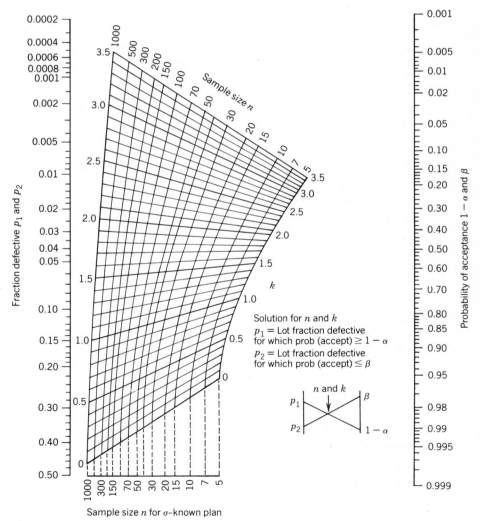

Figure 14-3
Nomograph for designing variables sampling plans.

p_1, $1 - \alpha$, p_2, β for both the σ known and the σ unknown cases. The nomograph contains separate scales for sample size for these two cases. The greater uncertainty in the case where the standard deviation is unknown requires a larger sample size than does the σ known case, but the same value of k is used. In addition, for a given sampling plan, the probability of acceptance for any value of fraction defective can be found from the nomograph. By plotting several of these points, the quality engineer may construct an operating-characteristic curve of the sampling plan. The use of this nomograph is illustrated in the following example.

Example 14-1

A soft drink bottler buys nonreturnable bottles from a vendor. The bottler has established a lower specification on the bursting strength of the bottles at 225 psi. If 1% or less of the bottles burst below this limit, the bottler wishes to accept the lot with probability 0.95 ($p_1 = 0.01$, $1 - \alpha = 0.95$), while if 6% or more of the bottles burst below this limit, the bottler would like to reject the lot with probability 0.90 ($p_2 = 0.06$, $\beta = 0.10$). To find the sampling plan, draw a line connecting the point 0.01 on the fraction defective scale to the point 0.95 on the probability of acceptance scale. Then draw a similar line connecting the points $p_2 = 0.06$ and $P_a = 0.10$. At the intersection of these lines, we read $k = 1.9$. Suppose that σ is unknown. Following the curved line from the intersection point to the upper sample size scale gives $n = 40$. Therefore, the procedure is to take a random sample of $n = 40$ bottles, observe the bursting strengths, compute $\bar{x}$ and S, then calculate

$$Z_{LSL} = \frac{\bar{x} - LSL}{S}$$

and to accept the lot if

$$Z_{LSL} \geq k = 1.9$$

If σ is known, drop vertically from the intersection point to the σ known scale. This would indicate a sample size of $n = 15$. Thus, if the standard deviation is known, a considerable reduction in sample size is possible.

It is also possible to design a variables acceptance-sampling plan from the nomograph using Procedure 2 (the M-method). In order to do so, an additional step is necessary. Figure 14-4 presents a chart for determining the maximum allowable fraction defective M. Once the values of n and k have been determined for the appropriate sampling plan from Figure 14-3, a value of M can be read directly from Figure 14-4. In order actually to use Procedure 2, it is necessary to convert the value of Z_{LSL} or Z_{USL} into an estimated fraction defective. Figure 14-5 can be used for this purpose. The following example illustrates how a single-sampling plan for variables with a one-sided specification limit using Procedure 2 can be designed.

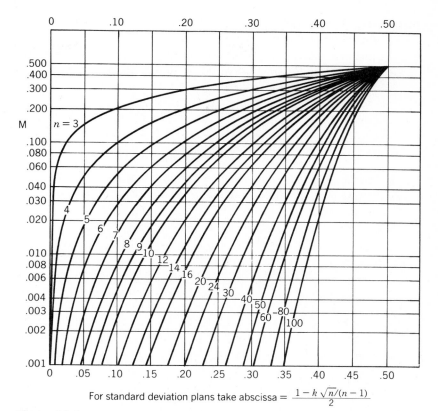

For standard deviation plans take abscissa $= \dfrac{1 - k\sqrt{n}/(n-1)}{2}$

Figure 14-4
Chart for determining the maximum allowable fraction defective M. (From
A. J. Duncan, *Quality Control and Industrial Statistics*, 4th ed., Richard D.
Irwin, Inc., Homewood, Ill., 1974, with the permission of the publisher.)

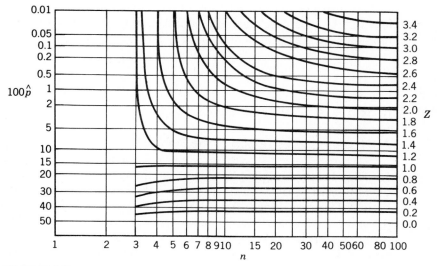

Figure 14-5
Chart for determining $\hat{p}$ from Z. (From A. J. Duncan, *Quality Control and Industrial
Statistics*, 4th ed., Irwin, Homewood, Ill., 1974, with the permission of the publisher.)

Example 14-2

Consider the situation described in Example 14-1. Since we know that $n = 40$ and $k = 1.9$, we enter Figure 14-4 with $n = 40$ and abcissa value

$$\frac{1 - \dfrac{k\sqrt{n}}{(n-1)}}{2} = \frac{1 - \dfrac{1.9\sqrt{40}}{39}}{2} = 0.35$$

This indicates that $M = 0.030$. Now suppose that a sample of $n = 40$ is taken, and we observe $\bar{x} = 255$ and $S = 15$. The value of Z_{LSL} is

$$Z_{LSL} = \frac{\bar{x} - LSL}{s} = \frac{225 - 225}{15} = 2$$

From Figure 14-5 we read $\hat{p} = 0.020$. Since $\hat{p} = 0.020$ is less than $M = 0.030$, we will accept the lot.

When there are double-specification limits, Procedure 2 can be used directly. We begin by first obtaining the sample size n and the critical value k for a single-limit plan that has the same values of $p_1, p_2, \alpha,$ and β as the desired double-specification-limit plan. Then the value of M is obtained directly from Figure 14-4. Now in the operation of the acceptance-sampling plan, we compute Z_{LSL} and Z_{USL} and, from Figure 14-5, find the corresponding fraction defective estimates, say, $\hat{p}_{LSL}$ and $\hat{p}_{USL}$. Then, if $\hat{p}_{LSL} + \hat{p}_{USL} \leq M$, the lot will be accepted; otherwise, it will be rejected.

It is also possible to use Procedure 1 for double-sided specification limits. However, the procedure must be modified extensively. Details of the modifications are in Duncan (1974).

14-3 MIL STD 414 (ANSI/ASQC Z1.9)

14-3.1 General Description of the Standard

MIL STD 414 is a lot-by-lot acceptance-sampling plan for variables. The standard was introduced in 1957. The focal point of this standard is the acceptable quality level (AQL), which ranges from 0.04% to 15%. There are five general levels of inspection, and level IV is designated as "normal." Inspection level V gives a steeper OC curve than level IV. When reduced sampling costs are necessary and when greater risks can or must be tolerated, lower inspection levels can be used. As with the attributes standard, MIL STD 105D, sample size code letters are used, but the same code letter does not imply the same sample size in both standards. In

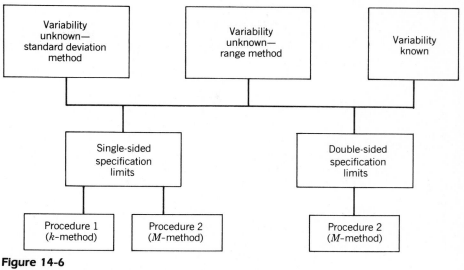

Figure 14-6
Organization of MIL STD 414.

addition, the lot size classes are different in both standards. Sample sizes are a function of the lot size and the inspection level. Provision is made for normal, tightened, and reduced inspection. All the sampling plans and procedures in the standard assume that the quality characteristic of interest is normally distributed.

Figure 14-6 presents the organization of the standard. Notice that acceptance-sampling plans can be designed for cases where the lot or process variability is either known or unknown, and where there are either single-specification limits or double-specification limits on the quality characteristic. In the case of single-specification limits, either Procedure 1 or Procedure 2 may be used. If there are double-specification limits, then Procedure 2 must be used. If the process or lot variability is known and stable, the variability known plans are the most economically efficient. When lot or process variability is unknown, either the standard deviation or the range of the sample may be used in operating the sampling plan. The range method requires a larger sample size, and we do not generally recommend its use.

MIL STD 414 is divided into four sections. Section A is a general description of the sampling plans, including definitions, sample size code letters, and OC curves for the various sampling plans. Section B of the standard gives variables sampling plans based on the sample standard deviation for the case in which the process or lot variability is unknown. Section C presents variables sampling plans based on the sample range method. Section D gives variables sampling plans for the case where the process standard deviation is known.

14-3.2 Use of the Tables

The most important tables from MIL STD 414 are reproduced as Tables 14-1 through 14-7. The following example illustrates the use of these tables.

Table 14-1
(Table A-2. MIL STD 414) Sample size code letters

Lot Size	Inspection Levels				
	1	II	III	IV	V
3 to 8	B	B	B	B	C
9 to 15	B	B	B	B	D
16 to 25	B	B	B	C	E
26 to 40	B	B	B	D	F
41 to 65	B	B	C	E	G
66 to 110	B	B	D	F	H
111 to 180	B	C	E	G	I
181 to 300	B	D	F	H	J
301 to 500	C	E	G	I	K
501 to 800	D	F	H	J	L
801 to 1,300	E	G	I	K	L
1,301 to 3,200	F	H	J	L	M
3,201 to 8,000	G	I	L	M	N
8,001 to 22,000	H	J	M	N	O
22,001 to 110,000	I	K	N	O	P
110,001 to 550,000	I	K	O	P	Q
550,001 and over	I	K	P	Q	Q

Example 14-3

Consider the soft drink bottler in the previous two examples who is purchasing bottles from a vendor. The lower specification limit on bursting strength is 225 psi. Suppose that the AQL at this specification limit is 1%. Let us suppose that bottles are shipped in lots of size 100,000. We will obtain a variables sampling plan that uses Procedure 2 from MIL STD 414. We assume that the lot standard deviation is unknown.

From Table 14-1, if we use inspection level IV, the sample size code letter is O. From Table 14-3 we find that sample size code letter O implies a sample size of $n = 100$. For an acceptable quality level of 1%, on normal inspection, the value of M is 2.20%. If tightened inspection is employed, the appropriate value of M is 1.53%. Notice that normal and tightened inspection use the same tables. The AQL values for normal inspection are indexed at the top of the table, while the AQL values for tightened inspection are indexed from the bottom of the table.

MIL STD 414 contains a provision for a shift to tightened or reduced inspection when this is warranted. The process average is used as the basis for determining when such a shift is made. The process average is taken as the average of the sample estimates of percent defective computed for lots submitted on original inspection. Usually, the process average is computed using information from the preceding 10 lots. Tightened inspection is to be instituted whenever the process average exceeds the AQL, and at the same time, whenever more than a

Table 14-2

Master table for normal and tightened inspection for plans based on variability unknown (Standard deviation method) (Single-specification limit—Form 1) (Table B-1, MIL STD 414)

Sample size code letter	Sample size	Acceptable Quality Levels (normal inspection)													
		.04	.065	.10	.15	.25	.40	.65	1.00	1.50	2.50	4.00	6.50	10.00	15.00
		k	k	k	k	k	k	k	k	k	k	k	k	k	k
B	3	→	→	→	→	→	→	→	▲	▲	1.12	.958	.765	.566	.341
C	4	→	→	→	→	→	→	→	1.45	1.34	1.17	1.01	.814	.617	.393
D	5	→	→	→	→	→	→	1.65	1.53	1.40	1.24	1.07	.874	.675	.455
E	7	→	→	→	→	2.00	1.88	1.75	1.62	1.50	1.33	1.15	.955	.755	.536
F	10	→	→	→	2.24	2.11	1.98	1.84	1.72	1.58	1.41	1.23	1.03	.828	.611
G	15	2.64	2.53	2.42	2.32	2.20	2.06	1.91	1.79	1.65	1.47	1.30	1.09	.886	.664
H	20	2.69	2.58	2.47	2.36	2.24	2.11	1.96	1.82	1.69	1.51	1.33	1.12	.917	.695
I	25	2.72	2.61	2.50	2.40	2.26	2.14	1.98	1.85	1.72	1.53	1.35	1.14	.936	.712
J	30	2.73	2.61	2.51	2.41	2.28	2.15	2.00	1.86	1.73	1.55	1.36	1.15	.946	.723
K	35	2.77	2.65	2.54	2.45	2.31	2.18	2.03	1.89	1.76	1.57	1.39	1.18	.969	.745
L	40	2.77	2.66	2.55	2.44	2.31	2.18	2.03	1.89	1.76	1.58	1.39	1.18	.971	.746
M	50	2.83	2.71	2.60	2.50	2.35	2.22	2.08	1.93	1.80	1.61	1.42	1.21	1.00	.774
N	75	2.90	2.77	2.66	2.55	2.41	2.27	2.12	1.98	1.84	1.65	1.46	1.24	1.03	.804
O	100	2.92	2.80	2.69	2.58	2.43	2.29	2.14	2.00	1.86	1.67	1.48	1.26	1.05	.819
P	150	2.96	2.84	2.73	2.61	2.47	2.33	2.18	2.03	1.89	1.70	1.51	1.29	1.07	.841
Q	200	2.97	2.85	2.73	2.62	2.47	2.33	2.18	2.04	1.89	1.70	1.51	1.29	1.07	.845
		.065	.10	.15	.25	.40	.65	1.00	1.50	2.50	4.00	6.50	10.00	15.00	
		Acceptable Quality Levels (tightened inspection)													

All AQL values are in percent defective.

↓ Use first sampling plan below arrow, that is, both sample size as well as k value. When sample size equals or exceeds lot size, every item in the lot must be inspected.

Table 14-3

Master table for normal and tightened inspection for plans based on variability unknown (Standard deviation method) (double-specification limit and Form 2—Single-specification limit) (Table B-3, MIL STD 414)

Sample size code letter	Sample size	Acceptable Quality Levels (normal inspection)													
		.04	.065	.10	.15	.25	.40	.65	1.00	1.50	2.50	4.00	6.50	10.00	15.00
		M	M	M	M	M	M	M	M	M	M	M	M	M	M
B	3	→	→	→	→	→	→	→	▶	▶	7.59	18.86	26.94	33.69	40.47
C	4	→	→	→	→	→	→	→	1.53	5.50	10.92	16.45	22.86	29.45	36.90
D	5	→	→	→	→	→	→	1.33	3.32	5.83	9.80	14.39	20.19	26.56	33.99
E	7	→	→	→	→	0.422	1.06	2.14	3.55	5.35	8.40	12.20	17.35	23.29	30.50
F	10	→	→	→	0.349	0.716	1.30	2.17	3.26	4.77	7.29	10.54	15.17	20.74	27.57
G	15	0.099	0.186	0.312	0.503	0.818	1.31	2.11	3.05	4.31	6.56	9.46	13.71	18.94	25.61
H	20	0.135	0.228	0.365	0.544	0.846	1.29	2.05	2.95	4.09	6.17	8.92	12.99	18.03	24.53
I	25	0.155	0.250	0.380	0.551	0.877	1.29	2.00	2.86	3.97	5.97	8.63	12.57	17.51	23.97
J	30	0.179	0.280	0.413	0.581	0.879	1.29	1.98	2.83	3.91	5.86	8.47	12.36	17.24	23.58
K	35	0.170	0.264	0.388	0.535	0.847	1.23	1.87	2.68	3.70	5.57	8.10	11.87	16.65	22.91
L	40	0.179	0.275	0.401	0.566	0.873	1.26	1.88	2.71	3.72	5.58	8.09	11.85	16.61	22.86
M	50	0.163	0.250	0.363	0.503	0.789	1.17	1.71	2.49	3.45	5.20	7.61	11.23	15.87	22.00
N	75	0.147	0.228	0.330	0.467	0.720	1.07	1.60	2.29	3.20	4.87	7.15	10.63	15.13	21.11
O	100	0.145	0.220	0.317	0.447	0.689	1.02	1.53	2.20	3.07	4.69	6.91	10.32	14.75	20.66
P	150	0.134	0.203	0.293	0.413	0.638	0.949	1.43	2.05	2.89	4.43	6.57	9.88	14.20	20.02
Q	200	0.135	0.204	0.294	0.414	0.637	0.945	1.42	2.04	2.87	4.40	6.53	9.81	14.12	19.92
		.065	.10	.15	.25	.40	.65	1.00	1.50	2.50	4.00	6.50	10.00	15.00	
		Acceptability Quality Levels (tightened inspection)													

All AQL and table values are in percent defective.

↓ Use first sampling plan below arrow, that is, both sample size as well as M value. When sample size equals or exceeds lot size, every item in the lot must be inspected.

Table 14-4

Master table for normal and tightened inspection for plans based on variability unknown (Range method) (Single-specification limit—Form 1) (Table C-1, MIL STD 414)

Sample size code letter	Sample size	Acceptable Quality Levels (normal inspection)													
		.04	.065	.10	.15	.25	.40	.65	1.00	1.50	2.50	4.00	6.50	10.00	15.00
		k	k	k	k	k	k	k	k	k	k	k	k	k	k
B	3	→	→	→	→	→	→	→	▼	▼	.587	.502	.401	.296	.178
C	4	→	→	→	→	→	→	→	.651	.598	.525	.450	.364	.276	.176
D	5	→	→	→	→	→	→	.663	.614	.565	.498	.431	.352	.272	.184
E	7	→	→	→	→	.702	.659	.613	.569	.525	.465	.405	.336	.266	.189
F	10	→	→	→	.916	.863	.811	.755	.703	.650	.579	.507	.424	.341	.252
G	15	1.09	1.04	.999	.958	.903	.850	.792	.738	.684	.610	.536	.452	.368	.276
H	25	1.14	1.10	1.05	1.01	.951	.896	.835	.779	.723	.647	.571	.484	.398	.305
I	30	1.15	1.10	1.06	1.02	.959	.904	.843	.787	.730	.654	.577	.490	.403	.310
J	35	1.16	1.11	1.07	1.02	.964	.908	.848	.791	.734	.658	.581	.494	.406	.313
K	40	1.18	1.13	1.08	1.04	.978	.921	.860	.803	.746	.668	.591	.503	.415	.321
L	50	1.19	1.14	1.09	1.05	.988	.931	.883	.812	.754	.676	.598	.510	.421	.327
M	60	1.21	1.16	1.11	1.06	1.00	.948	.885	.826	.768	.689	.610	.521	.432	.336
N	85	1.23	1.17	1.13	1.08	1.02	.962	.899	.839	.780	.701	.621	.530	.441	.345
O	115	1.24	1.19	1.14	1.09	1.03	.975	.911	.851	.791	.711	.631	.539	.449	.353
P	175	1.26	1.21	1.16	1.11	1.05	.994	.929	.868	.807	.726	.644	.552	.460	.363
Q	230	1.27	1.21	1.16	1.12	1.06	.996	.931	.870	.809	.728	.646	.553	.462	.364
		.065	.10	.15	.25	.40	.65	1.00	1.50	2.50	4.00	6.50	10.00	15.00	
		Acceptable Quality Levels (tightened inspection)													

All AQL values are in percent defective.

↓ Use first sampling plan below arrow, that is, both sample size as well as k value. When sample size equals or exceeds lot size, every item in the lot must be inspected.

Table 14-5

Master table for normal and tightened inspection for plans based on variability unknown[†] (Range method) (Double-specification limit and Form 2—Single-specification limit) (Table C-3, MIL STD 414)

Sample size code letter	Sample size	c factor	*Acceptable Quality Levels (normal inspection)*													
			.04	.065	.10	.15	.25	.40	.65	1.00	1.50	2.50	4.00	6.50	10.00	15.00
			M	M	M	M	M	M	M	M	M	M	M	M	M	M
B	3	1.910	↓	↓	↓	↓	↓	↓	↓	▼	▼	7.59	18.86	26.94	33.69	40.47
C	4	2.234	↓	↓	↓	↓	↓	↓	↓	1.53	5.50	10.92	16.45	22.86	29.45	36.90
D	5	2.474	↓	↓	↓	↓	↓	↓	1.42	3.44	5.93	9.90	14.47	20.27	26.59	33.95
E	7	2.830	↓	↓	↓	↓	↓	.89	1.99	3.46	5.32	8.47	12.35	17.54	23.50	30.66
F	10	2.405	↓	↓	↓	.23	.58	1.14	2.05	3.23	4.77	7.42	10.79	15.49	21.06	27.90
G	15	2.379	.061	.136	.253	.430	.786	1.30	2.10	3.11	4.44	6.76	9.76	14.09	19.30	25.92
H	25	2.358	.125	.214	.336	.506	.827	1.27	1.95	2.82	3.96	5.98	8.65	12.59	17.48	23.79
I	30	2.353	.147	.240	.366	.537	.856	1.29	1.96	2.81	3.92	5.88	8.50	12.36	17.19	23.42
J	35	2.349	.165	.261	.391	.564	.883	1.33	1.98	2.82	3.90	5.85	8.42	12.24	17.03	23.21
K	40	2.346	.160	.252	.375	.539	.842	1.25	1.88	2.69	3.73	5.61	8.11	11.84	16.55	22.38
L	50	2.342	.169	.261	.381	.542	.838	1.25	1.60	2.63	3.64	5.47	7.91	11.57	16.20	22.26
M	60	2.339	.158	.244	.356	.504	.781	1.16	1.74	2.47	3.44	5.17	7.54	11.10	15.64	21.63
N	85	2.335	.156	.242	.350	.493	.755	1.12	1.67	2.37	3.30	4.97	7.27	10.73	15.17	21.05
O	115	2.333	.153	.230	.333	.468	.718	1.06	1.58	2.25	3.14	4.76	6.99	10.37	14.74	20.57
P	175	2.331	.139	.210	.303	.427	.655	.972	1.46	2.08	2.93	4.47	6.60	9.89	14.15	19.88
Q	230	2.330	.142	.215	.308	.432	.661	.976	1.47	2.08	2.92	4.46	6.57	9.84	14.10	19.82
			.065	.10	.15	.25	.40	.65	1.00	1.50	2.50	4.00	6.50	10.00	15.00	
			Acceptable Quality Levels (tightened inspection)													

All AQL and table values are in percent defective.

↓Use first sampling plan below arrow, that is, both sample size as well as M value. When sample size equals or exceeds lot size, every item in the lot must be inspected.

Table 14-6

Values of *T* for tightened inspection (Standard deviation method) (Table B-6, MIL STD 414)

Sample Size Code Letter	Acceptable Quality Levels (in percent defective)														Number of Lots
	0.04	0.065	0.10	0.15	0.25	0.40	0.65	1.0	1.5	2.5	4.0	6.5	10.0	15.0	
B	*	*	*	*	*	*	*	*	*	2 4 5	3 5 6	4 6 8	4 7 9	4 8 11	5 10 15
C	*	*	*	*	*	*	*	2 3 5	2 4 6	3 5 7	3 6 8	4 7 9	4 7 10	4 8 11	5 10 15
D	*	*	*	*	*	*	2 4 5	3 4 6	3 5 7	3 6 8	4 6 9	4 7 10	4 7 10	4 8 11	5 10 15
E	*	*	*	*	2 4 5	3 4 6	3 5 6	3 5 7	4 6 8	4 6 9	4 7 9	4 7 10	4 8 11	4 8 11	5 10 15
F	*	*	*	3 4 6	3 5 6	3 5 7	3 6 8	4 6 8	4 6 9	4 7 9	4 7 10	4 8 11	4 8 11	4 8 11	5 10 15
G	3 4 6	3 5 6	3 5 6	3 5 7	3 6 7	4 6 8	4 6 9	4 7 9	4 7 9	4 7 10	4 7 10	4 8 11	4 8 11	4 8 11	5 10 15
H	3 5 6	3 5 7	3 5 7	3 6 8	4 6 8	4 6 9	4 7 9	4 7 9	4 7 10	4 7 10	4 8 11	4 8 11	4 8 11	4 8 11	5 10 15
I	3 5 7	3 6 7	4 6 8	4 6 8	4 6 9	4 7 9	4 7 9	4 7 10	4 7 10	4 7 10	4 8 11	4 8 11	4 8 11	4 8 11	5 10 15
J	3 6 8	4 6 8	4 6 8	4 6 9	4 7 9	4 7 9	4 7 10	4 7 10	4 7 10	4 8 11	4 8 11	4 8 11	4 8 11	4 8 11	5 10 15
K	4 6 8	4 6 8	4 6 9	4 6 9	4 7 9	4 7 9	4 7 10	4 7 10	4 8 10	4 8 11	4 8 11	4 8 11	4 8 11	4 8 11	5 10 15
L	4 6 8	4 6 9	4 6 9	4 7 9	4 7 9	4 7 10	4 7 10	4 7 10	4 8 10	4 8 11	4 8 11	4 8 11	4 8 11	4 8 11	5 10 15
M	4 6 9	4 7 9	4 7 9	4 7 9	4 7 10	4 7 10	4 7 10	4 7 10	4 8 11	4 8 11	4 8 11	4 8 11	4 8 11	4 8 11	5 10 15
N	4 7 9	4 7 9	4 7 10	4 7 10	4 7 10	4 7 10	4 8 11	4 8 11	4 8 11	4 8 11	4 8 11	4 8 11	4 8 11	4 8 11	5 10 15
O	4 7 10	4 7 10	4 7 10	4 7 10	4 7 10	4 8 11	4 8 11	4 8 11	4 8 11	4 8 11	4 8 11	4 8 11	4 8 11	4 8 11	5 10 15
P	4 7 10	4 7 10	4 7 10	4 8 10	4 8 11	4 8 11	4 8 11	4 8 11	4 8 11	4 8 11	4 8 11	4 8 11	4 8 11	4 8 12	5 10 15
Q	4 7 10	4 8 11	4 8 11	4 8 11	4 8 11	4 8 11	4 8 11	4 8 11	4 8 11	4 8 11	4 8 11	4 8 11	4 8 11	4 8 12	5 10 15

* There are no sampling plans provided in this standard for these code letters and AQL values.

The top figure in each block refers to the preceding 5 lots, the middle figure to the preceding 10 lots, and the bottom figure to the preceding 15 lots.

Tightened inspection is required when the number of lots with estimates of percent defective above the AQL from the preceding 5, 10, or 15 lots is greater than the given value of T in the table, and the process average from these lots exceeds the AQL.

Table 14-7

Table for estimating the lot percent defective (p_{LSL} or p_{USL}) from Z_{LSL} or Z_{USL} using the standard deviation method (Table B-5 of MIL STD 414)

Z_{USL} or Z_{LSL}	Sample Size															
	3	4	5	7	10	15	20	25	30	35	40	50	75	100	150	200
0	50.00	50.00	50.00	50.00	50.00	50.00	50.00	50.00	50.00	50.00	50.00	50.00	50.00	50.00	50.00	50.00
0.1	47.24	46.67	46.44	46.26	46.16	46.10	46.08	46.06	46.05	46.05	46.04	46.04	46.03	46.03	46.02	46.02
0.2	44.46	43.33	42.90	42.54	42.35	42.24	42.19	42.16	42.15	42.13	42.13	42.11	42.10	42.09	42.08	42.08
0.3	41.63	40.00	39.37	38.87	38.60	38.44	38.37	38.33	38.31	38.29	38.28	38.27	38.25	38.24	38.22	38.22
0.31	41.35	39.67	39.02	38.50	38.23	38.06	37.99	37.95	37.93	37.91	37.90	37.89	37.87	37.86	37.84	37.84
0.32	41.06	39.33	38.67	38.14	37.86	37.69	37.62	37.58	37.55	37.54	37.52	37.51	37.49	37.48	37.46	37.46
0.33	40.77	39.00	38.32	37.78	37.49	37.31	37.24	37.20	37.18	37.16	37.15	37.13	37.11	37.10	37.09	37.08
0.34	40.49	38.67	37.97	37.42	37.12	36.94	36.87	36.83	36.80	36.78	36.77	36.75	36.73	36.72	36.71	36.71
0.35	40.20	38.33	37.62	37.06	36.75	36.57	36.49	36.45	36.43	36.41	36.40	36.38	36.36	36.35	36.33	36.33
0.36	39.91	38.00	37.28	36.69	36.38	36.20	36.12	36.08	36.06	36.04	36.02	36.01	35.98	35.97	35.96	35.96
0.37	39.62	37.67	36.93	36.33	36.02	35.83	35.75	35.71	35.68	35.66	35.65	35.63	35.61	35.60	35.59	35.58
0.38	39.33	37.33	36.58	35.98	35.65	35.46	35.38	35.34	35.31	35.29	35.28	35.26	35.24	35.23	35.22	35.21
0.39	39.03	37.00	36.23	35.62	35.29	35.10	35.01	34.97	34.94	34.93	34.91	34.89	34.87	34.86	34.85	34.84
0.40	38.74	36.67	35.88	35.26	34.93	34.73	34.65	34.60	34.58	34.56	34.54	34.53	34.50	34.49	34.48	34.47
0.41	38.45	36.33	35.54	34.90	34.57	34.37	34.28	34.24	34.21	34.19	34.18	34.16	34.13	34.12	34.11	34.10
0.42	38.15	36.00	35.19	34.55	34.21	34.00	33.92	33.87	33.85	33.83	33.81	33.79	33.77	33.76	33.74	33.74
0.43	37.85	35.67	34.85	34.19	33.85	33.64	33.56	33.51	33.48	33.46	33.45	33.43	33.40	33.39	33.38	33.37
0.44	37.56	35.33	34.50	33.84	33.49	33.28	33.20	33.15	33.12	33.10	33.09	33.07	33.04	33.03	33.02	33.01
0.45	37.26	35.00	34.16	33.49	33.23	32.92	32.84	32.79	32.76	32.74	32.73	32.72	32.68	32.67	32.66	32.65
0.46	36.96	34.67	33.82	33.13	32.78	32.57	32.48	32.43	32.40	32.38	32.37	32.35	32.32	32.31	32.30	32.29
0.47	36.66	34.33	33.47	32.78	32.42	32.21	32.12	32.07	32.04	32.02	32.01	31.99	31.96	31.95	31.94	31.93
0.48	36.35	34.00	33.12	32.43	32.07	31.85	31.77	31.72	31.69	31.67	31.65	31.63	31.61	31.60	31.58	31.58
0.49	36.05	33.67	32.78	32.08	31.72	31.50	31.41	31.36	31.33	31.31	31.30	31.28	31.25	31.24	31.23	31.22
0.50	35.75	33.33	32.44	31.74	31.37	31.15	31.06	31.01	30.98	30.96	30.95	30.93	30.90	30.89	30.87	30.87
0.51	35.44	33.00	32.10	31.39	31.02	30.80	30.71	30.66	30.63	30.61	30.60	30.57	30.55	30.54	30.52	30.52
0.52	35.13	32.67	31.76	31.04	30.67	30.45	30.36	30.31	30.28	30.26	30.25	30.23	30.20	30.19	30.17	30.17
0.53	34.82	32.33	31.42	30.70	30.32	30.10	30.01	29.96	29.93	29.91	29.90	29.88	29.85	29.84	29.83	29.82
0.54	34.51	32.00	31.08	30.36	29.98	29.76	29.67	29.62	29.59	29.57	29.53	29.53	29.51	29.49	29.48	29.48
0.55	34.20	31.67	30.74	30.01	29.64	29.41	29.32	29.27	29.24	29.22	29.21	29.19	29.16	29.15	29.14	29.13
0.56	33.88	31.33	30.40	29.67	29.29	29.07	28.98	28.93	28.90	28.88	28.87	28.85	28.82	28.81	28.79	28.79
0.57	33.57	31.00	30.06	29.33	28.95	28.73	28.64	28.59	28.56	28.54	28.53	28.51	28.48	28.47	28.45	28.45
0.58	33.25	30.67	29.73	28.99	28.61	28.39	28.30	28.25	28.22	28.20	28.19	28.17	28.14	28.13	28.12	28.11
0.59	32.93	30.33	29.39	28.66	28.28	28.05	27.96	27.92	27.89	27.87	27.85	27.83	27.81	27.79	27.78	27.77
0.60	32.61	30.00	29.05	28.32	27.94	27.72	27.63	27.58	27.55	27.53	27.52	27.50	27.47	27.46	27.45	27.44
0.61	32.28	29.67	28.72	27.96	27.60	27.39	27.30	27.25	27.22	27.20	27.18	27.16	27.14	27.13	27.11	27.11
0.62	31.96	29.33	28.39	27.65	27.27	27.05	26.96	26.92	26.89	26.87	26.85	26.83	26.81	26.80	26.78	26.78
0.63	31.63	29.00	28.05	27.32	26.94	26.72	26.63	26.59	26.89	26.54	26.52	26.50	26.48	26.47	26.45	26.45
0.64	31.30	28.67	27.72	26.99	26.61	26.39	26.31	26.26	26.23	26.21	26.20	26.18	26.15	26.14	26.13	26.12
0.65	30.97	28.33	27.39	26.66	26.28	26.07	25.98	25.93	25.90	25.88	25.87	25.85	25.83	25.82	25.80	25.80
0.66	30.63	28.00	27.06	26.33	25.96	25.74	25.66	25.61	25.58	25.56	25.55	25.53	25.51	25.49	25.48	25.48
0.67	30.30	27.67	26.73	26.00	25.63	25.42	25.33	25.29	25.26	25.24	25.23	25.21	25.19	25.17	25.16	25.16
0.68	29.96	27.33	26.40	25.68	25.31	25.20	25.01	24.97	24.94	24.92	24.91	24.89	24.87	24.86	24.84	24.84
0.69	29.61	27.00	26.07	25.35	24.99	24.78	24.70	24.65	24.62	24.60	24.59	24.57	24.55	24.54	24.53	24.52
0.70	29.27	26.67	25.74	25.03	24.67	24.46	24.38	24.33	24.31	24.29	24.28	24.26	24.24	24.23	24.21	24.21
0.71	28.92	26.33	25.41	24.71	24.35	24.15	24.06	24.02	23.99	23.98	23.96	23.95	23.92	23.91	23.90	23.90
0.72	28.57	26.00	25.09	24.39	24.03	23.83	23.75	23.71	23.68	23.67	23.65	23.64	23.61	23.60	23.59	23.59
0.73	28.22	25.67	24.76	24.07	23.72	23.52	23.44	23.40	23.37	23.36	23.34	23.33	23.31	23.30	23.29	23.28
0.74	27.86	25.33	24.44	23.75	23.41	23.21	23.13	23.09	23.07	23.05	23.04	23.02	23.00	22.99	22.96	22.98
0.75	27.50	25.00	24.11	23.44	23.10	22.90	22.83	22.79	22.76	22.75	22.73	22.72	22.70	22.69	22.68	22.67
0.76	27.13	24.67	23.79	23.12	22.79	22.60	22.52	22.48	22.46	22.44	22.43	22.42	22.40	22.39	22.38	22.37
0.77	26.77	24.33	23.47	22.81	22.48	22.30	22.22	22.18	22.16	22.14	22.13	22.12	22.10	22.09	22.08	22.08
0.78	26.39	24.00	23.15	22.50	22.18	21.99	21.92	21.89	21.86	21.85	21.84	21.82	21.80	21.79	21.78	21.78
0.79	26.02	23.67	22.83	22.19	21.87	21.70	21.63	21.59	21.57	21.55	21.54	21.53	21.51	21.50	21.49	21.49
0.80	25.64	23.33	22.51	21.88	21.57	21.40	21.33	21.29	21.27	21.26	21.25	21.23	21.22	21.21	21.20	21.20
0.81	25.25	23.00	22.19	21.58	21.27	21.10	21.04	21.00	20.98	20.97	20.96	20.94	20.93	20.92	20.91	20.91
0.82	24.86	22.67	21.87	21.27	20.98	20.81	20.75	20.71	20.69	20.68	20.67	20.65	20.64	20.63	20.62	20.62
0.83	24.47	22.33	21.56	20.97	20.68	20.52	20.46	20.42	20.40	20.39	20.38	20.37	20.35	20.35	20.34	20.34
0.84	24.07	22.00	21.24	20.67	20.39	20.23	20.17	20.14	20.12	20.11	20.10	20.09	20.07	20.06	20.06	20.05
0.85	23.67	21.67	20.93	20.37	20.10	19.94	19.89	19.86	19.84	19.82	19.82	19.80	19.79	19.78	19.78	19.77
0.86	23.26	21.33	20.62	20.07	19.81	19.66	19.60	19.57	19.56	19.54	19.54	19.53	19.51	19.51	19.50	19.50
0.87	22.84	21.00	20.31	19.78	19.52	19.38	19.32	19.30	19.28	19.27	19.26	19.25	19.24	19.23	19.22	19.22
0.88	22.42	20.67	20.00	19.41	19.23	19.10	19.04	19.02	19.00	18.99	18.98	18.98	18.96	18.96	18.95	18.95
0.89	21.99	20.33	19.69	19.19	18.95	18.82	18.77	18.74	18.73	18.72	18.71	18.70	18.69	18.69	18.68	18.68

Table 14-7 (Continued)

Z_{USL} or Z_{LSL}	Sample Size															
	3	4	5	7	10	15	20	25	30	35	40	50	75	100	150	200
0.90	21.55	20.00	19.38	18.90	18.67	18.54	18.50	18.47	18.46	18.45	18.44	18.43	18.42	18.42	18.41	18.41
0.91	21.11	19.67	19.07	18.61	18.39	18.27	18.22	18.20	18.19	18.18	18.17	18.17	18.16	18.15	18.15	18.15
0.92	20.66	19.33	18.77	18.33	18.11	18.00	17.96	17.94	17.92	17.92	17.91	17.90	17.89	17.89	17.88	17.88
0.93	20.20	19.00	18.46	18.04	17.84	17.73	17.69	17.67	17.66	17.65	17.65	17.64	17.63	17.63	17.62	17.62
0.94	19.74	18.67	18.16	17.76	17.57	17.46	17.43	17.41	17.40	17.39	17.39	17.38	17.37	17.37	17.36	17.36
0.95	19.25	18.33	17.86	17.48	17.29	17.20	17.17	17.15	17.14	17.13	17.13	17.12	17.12	17.11	17.11	17.11
0.96	18.76	18.00	17.56	17.20	17.03	16.94	16.91	16.89	16.88	16.88	16.87	16.87	16.86	16.86	16.86	16.85
0.97	18.25	17.67	17.25	16.92	16.76	16.68	16.65	16.63	16.63	16.62	16.62	16.61	16.61	16.61	16.60	16.60
0.98	17.74	17.33	16.96	16.65	16.49	16.42	16.39	16.38	16.37	16.37	16.37	16.36	16.36	16.36	16.36	16.36
0.99	17.21	17.00	16.66	16.37	16.23	16.16	16.14	16.13	16.12	16.12	16.12	16.12	16.11	16.11	16.11	16.11
1.00	16.67	16.67	16.36	16.10	15.97	15.91	15.89	15.88	15.88	15.87	15.87	15.87	15.87	15.87	15.87	15.87
1.01	16.11	16.33	16.07	15.83	15.72	15.66	15.64	15.63	15.63	15.63	15.63	15.63	15.62	15.62	15.62	15.62
1.02	15.53	16.00	15.78	15.56	15.46	15.41	15.40	15.39	15.39	15.39	15.39	15.38	15.38	15.38	15.38	15.38
1.03	14.93	15.67	15.48	15.30	15.21	15.17	15.15	15.15	15.15	15.15	15.15	15.15	15.15	15.15	15.15	15.15
1.04	14.31	15.33	15.19	15.03	14.96	14.92	14.91	14.91	14.91	14.91	14.91	14.91	14.91	14.91	14.91	14.91
1.05	13.66	15.00	14.91	14.77	14.71	14.68	14.67	14.67	14.67	14.67	14.68	14.68	14.68	14.68	14.68	14.68
1.06	12.98	14.67	14.62	14.51	14.46	14.44	14.44	14.44	14.44	14.44	14.44	14.45	14.45	14.45	14.45	14.45
1.07	12.27	14.33	14.33	14.26	14.22	14.20	14.20	14.21	14.21	14.21	14.21	14.22	14.22	14.22	14.22	14.23
1.08	11.51	14.00	14.05	14.00	13.97	13.97	13.97	13.98	13.98	13.98	13.99	13.99	13.99	14.00	14.00	14.00
1.09	10.71	13.67	13.76	13.75	13.73	13.74	13.74	13.75	13.75	13.76	13.76	13.77	13.77	13.77	13.78	13.78
1.10	9.84	13.33	13.48	13.49	13.50	13.51	13.52	13.52	13.53	13.54	13.54	13.54	13.55	13.55	13.56	13.56
1.11	8.89	13.00	13.20	13.25	13.26	13.28	13.29	13.30	13.31	13.31	13.32	13.32	13.33	13.34	13.34	13.34
1.12	7.82	12.67	12.93	13.00	13.03	13.05	13.07	13.08	13.09	13.10	13.10	13.11	13.12	13.12	12.12	13.13
1.13	6.60	12.33	12.65	12.75	12.80	12.83	12.85	12.86	12.87	12.88	12.89	12.89	12.90	12.91	12.91	12.92
1.14	5.08	12.00	12.37	12.51	12.57	12.61	12.63	12.65	12.65	12.67	12.67	12.68	12.69	12.70	12.70	12.70
1.15	0.29	11.67	12.10	12.27	12.34	12.39	12.42	12.44	12.45	12.46	12.46	12.47	12.48	12.49	12.49	12.30
1.16	0.00	11.33	11.83	12.03	12.12	12.18	12.21	12.22	12.24	12.25	12.25	12.26	12.28	12.28	12.29	12.29
1.17	0.00	11.00	11.56	11.79	11.90	11.96	12.00	12.02	12.03	12.04	12.05	12.06	12.07	12.08	12.08	12.09
1.18	0.00	10.67	11.29	11.56	11.68	11.75	11.79	11.81	11.82	11.84	11.84	11.85	11.87	11.88	11.88	11.89
1.19	0.00	10.33	11.02	11.33	11.46	11.54	11.58	11.61	11.62	11.63	11.64	11.65	11.67	11.68	11.69	11.69
1.20	0.00	10.00	10.76	11.10	11.24	11.34	11.38	11.41	11.42	11.43	11.44	11.46	11.47	11.48	11.49	11.49
1.21	0.00	9.67	10.50	10.87	11.03	11.13	11.18	11.21	11.22	11.24	11.25	11.26	11.28	11.29	11.30	11.30
1.22	0.00	9.33	10.23	10.65	10.82	10.93	10.98	11.01	11.03	11.04	11.05	11.07	11.09	11.09	11.10	11.11
1.23	0.00	9.00	9.97	10.42	10.61	10.73	10.79	10.81	10.84	10.85	10.86	10.88	10.90	10.91	10.91	10.92
1.24	0.00	8.67	9.72	10.20	10.41	10.53	10.59	10.62	10.64	10.66	10.67	10.69	10.71	10.72	10.73	10.73
1.25	0.00	8.33	9.46	9.98	10.21	10.34	10.40	10.43	10.46	10.47	10.48	10.50	10.52	10.53	10.54	10.55
1.26	0.00	8.00	9.21	9.77	10.00	10.15	10.21	10.25	10.27	10.29	10.30	10.32	10.34	10.35	10.36	10.37
1.27	0.00	7.67	8.96	9.55	9.81	9.96	10.02	10.06	10.09	10.10	10.12	10.13	10.16	10.17	10.18	10.19
1.28	0.00	7.33	8.71	9.34	9.61	9.77	9.84	9.88	9.90	9.92	9.94	9.95	9.98	9.99	10.00	10.01
1.29	0.00	7.00	8.46	9.13	9.42	9.58	9.65	9.70	9.72	9.74	9.76	9.78	9.80	9.82	9.83	9.83
1.30	0.00	6.67	8.21	8.93	9.22	9.40	9.48	9.52	9.55	9.57	9.58	9.60	9.63	9.64	9.65	9.66
1.31	0.00	6.33	7.97	8.72	9.03	9.22	9.30	9.34	9.37	9.39	9.41	9.43	9.46	9.47	9.48	9.49
1.32	0.00	6.00	7.73	8.52	8.85	9.04	9.12	9.17	9.20	9.22	9.24	9.26	9.29	9.30	9.31	9.32
1.33	0.00	5.67	7.49	8.32	8.66	8.86	8.95	9.00	9.03	9.05	9.07	9.09	9.12	9.13	9.15	9.15
1.34	0.00	5.33	7.25	8.12	8.48	8.69	8.78	8.83	8.86	8.88	8.90	8.92	8.95	8.97	8.96	8.99
1.35	0.00	5.00	7.02	7.92	8.30	8.52	8.61	8.66	8.69	8.72	8.74	8.76	8.79	8.81	8.82	8.83
1.36	0.00	4.67	6.79	7.73	8.12	8.35	8.44	8.50	8.53	8.55	8.57	8.60	8.63	8.65	8.66	8.67
1.37	0.00	4.33	6.56	7.54	7.95	8.18	8.28	8.33	8.37	8.39	8.41	8.44	8.47	8.49	8.50	8.51
1.38	0.00	4.00	6.33	7.35	7.77	8.01	8.12	8.17	8.21	8.24	8.25	8.28	8.31	8.33	8.35	8.35
1.39	0.00	3.67	6.10	7.17	7.60	7.85	7.96	8.01	8.05	8.08	8.10	8.12	8.16	8.18	8.19	8.20
1.40	0.00	3.33	5.88	6.98	7.44	7.69	7.80	7.86	7.90	7.92	7.94	7.97	8.01	8.02	8.04	8.05
1.41	0.00	3.00	5.66	6.80	7.27	7.53	7.64	7.70	7.74	7.77	7.79	7.82	7.86	7.87	7.89	7.90
1.42	0.00	2.67	5.44	6.62	7.10	7.37	7.49	7.55	7.59	7.62	7.64	7.67	7.71	7.73	7.74	7.75
1.43	0.00	2.33	5.23	6.45	6.94	7.22	7.34	7.40	7.44	7.47	7.50	7.52	7.56	7.58	7.60	7.61
1.44	0.00	2.00	5.01	6.27	6.78	7.07	7.19	7.26	7.30	7.33	7.35	7.38	7.42	7.44	7.46	7.47
1.45	0.00	1.67	4.81	6.10	6.63	6.92	7.04	7.11	7.15	7.18	7.21	7.24	7.28	7.30	7.31	7.33
1.46	0.00	1.33	4.60	5.93	6.47	6.77	6.90	6.97	7.01	7.04	7.07	7.10	7.14	7.16	7.18	7.19
1.47	0.00	1.00	4.39	5.77	6.32	6.63	6.75	6.83	6.87	6.90	6.93	6.96	7.00	7.02	7.04	7.05
1.48	0.00	0.67	4.19	5.60	6.17	6.48	6.61	6.69	6.73	6.77	6.79	6.82	6.86	6.88	6.90	6.91
1.49	0.00	0.33	3.99	5.44	6.02	6.34	6.48	6.55	6.60	6.63	6.65	6.69	6.73	6.75	6.77	6.78

(continued)

Table 14-7 (Continued)

Z_{USL} or Z_{LSL}	Sample Size															
	3	4	5	7	10	15	20	25	30	35	40	50	75	100	150	200
1.50	0.00	0.00	3.80	5.28	5.87	6.20	6.34	6.41	6.46	6.50	6.52	6.55	6.60	6.62	6.64	6.65
1.51	0.00	0.00	3.61	5.13	5.73	6.06	6.20	6.28	6.33	6.36	6.39	6.42	6.47	6.49	6.51	6.52
1.52	0.00	0.00	3.42	4.97	5.59	5.93	6.07	6.15	6.20	6.23	6.26	6.29	6.34	6.36	6.38	6.39
1.53	0.00	0.00	3.23	4.82	5.45	5.30	5.94	6.02	6.07	6.11	6.13	6.17	6.21	6.24	6.26	6.27
1.54	0.00	0.00	3.05	4.67	5.31	5.67	5.81	5.87	5.95	5.98	6.01	6.04	6.09	6.11	6.13	6.15
1.55	0.00	0.00	2.87	4.52	5.18	5.54	5.69	5.77	5.82	5.86	5.88	5.92	5.97	5.99	6.01	6.02
1.56	0.00	0.00	2.69	4.38	5.05	5.41	5.56	5.65	5.70	5.74	5.76	5.80	5.85	5.87	5.89	5.90
1.57	0.00	0.00	2.52	4.24	4.92	5.29	5.44	5.53	5.58	5.62	5.64	5.68	5.73	5.75	5.78	5.79
1.58	0.00	0.00	2.35	4.10	4.79	5.16	5.32	5.41	5.46	5.50	5.53	5.56	5.61	5.64	5.66	5.67
1.59	0.00	0.00	2.19	3.96	4.66	5.04	5.20	5.29	5.34	5.38	5.41	5.45	5.50	5.52	5.54	5.56
1.60	0.00	0.00	2.03	3.83	4.54	4.92	5.09	5.17	5.23	5.27	5.30	5.33	5.38	5.41	5.43	5.44
1.61	0.00	0.00	1.87	3.69	4.41	4.81	4.97	5.06	5.12	5.16	5.18	5.22	5.27	5.30	5.32	5.33
1.62	0.00	0.00	1.72	3.57	4.30	4.69	4.56	4.95	5.01	5.04	5.07	5.11	5.16	5.19	5.21	5.23
1.63	0.00	0.00	1.57	3.44	4.18	4.58	4.75	4.84	4.90	4.94	4.97	5.01	5.06	5.08	5.11	5.12
1.64	0.00	0.00	1.42	3.31	4.06	4.47	4.64	4.73	4.79	4.83	4.86	4.90	4.95	4.98	5.00	5.01
1.65	0.00	0.00	1.28	3.19	3.95	4.36	4.53	4.62	4.68	4.72	4.75	4.79	4.85	4.87	4.90	4.91
1.66	0.00	0.00	1.15	3.07	3.84	4.25	4.43	4.52	4.58	4.62	4.65	4.69	4.74	4.77	4.90	4.81
1.67	0.00	0.00	1.02	2.95	3.73	4.15	4.32	4.42	4.48	4.52	4.55	4.59	4.64	4.67	4.70	4.71
1.68	0.00	0.00	0.89	2.84	3.62	4.05	4.22	4.32	4.38	4.42	4.45	4.49	4.55	4.57	4.60	4.61
1.69	0.00	0.00	0.77	2.73	3.52	3.94	4.12	4.22	4.28	4.32	4.35	4.39	4.45	4.47	4.50	4.51
1.70	0.00	0.00	0.66	2.62	3.41	3.84	4.02	4.12	4.18	4.22	4.25	4.30	4.35	4.38	4.41	4.42
1.71	0.00	0.00	0.55	2.51	3.31	3.75	3.93	4.02	4.09	4.13	4.16	4.20	4.26	4.29	4.31	4.32
1.72	0.00	0.00	0.45	2.41	3.21	3.65	3.83	3.93	3.99	4.04	4.07	4.11	4.17	4.19	4.22	4.23
1.73	0.00	0.00	0.36	2.30	3.11	3.56	3.74	3.84	3.90	3.94	3.98	4.02	4.08	4.10	4.13	4.14
1.74	0.00	0.00	0.27	2.20	3.02	3.46	3.65	3.75	3.81	3.85	3.89	3.93	3.99	4.01	4.04	4.05
1.75	0.00	0.00	0.19	2.11	2.93	3.37	3.56	3.66	3.72	3.77	3.80	3.84	3.90	3.93	3.95	3.97
1.76	0.00	0.00	0.12	2.01	2.83	3.28	3.47	3.57	3.63	3.68	3.71	3.76	3.81	3.84	3.87	3.08
1.77	0.00	0.00	0.06	1.92	2.74	3.20	3.38	3.48	3.55	3.59	3.63	3.67	3.73	3.76	3.78	3.80
1.78	0.00	0.00	0.02	1.83	2.66	3.11	3.30	3.40	3.47	3.51	3.54	3.59	3.64	3.67	3.70	3.71
1.79	0.00	0.00	0.00	1.74	2.57	3.03	3.21	3.32	3.38	3.43	3.46	3.51	3.56	3.59	3.63	3.63
1.80	0.00	0.00	0.00	1.65	2.49	2.94	3.13	3.24	3.30	3.35	3.38	3.43	3.48	3.51	3.54	3.55
1.81	0.00	0.00	0.00	1.57	2.40	2.86	3.05	3.16	3.22	3.27	3.30	3.35	3.40	3.43	3.46	3.47
1.82	0.00	0.00	0.00	1.49	2.32	2.79	2.98	3.08	3.15	3.19	3.22	3.27	3.33	3.36	3.38	3.40
1.83	0.00	0.00	0.00	1.41	2.25	2.71	2.90	3.00	3.07	3.11	3.15	3.19	3.25	3.28	3.31	3.32
1.84	0.00	0.00	0.00	1.34	2.17	2.63	2.82	2.93	2.99	3.04	3.07	3.12	3.18	3.21	3.23	3.25
1.85	0.00	0.00	0.00	1.26	2.09	2.56	2.75	2.85	2.92	2.97	3.00	3.05	3.10	3.13	3.16	3.17
1.86	0.00	0.00	0.00	1.19	2.02	2.48	2.68	2.78	2.85	2.89	2.93	2.97	3.03	3.06	3.09	3.10
1.87	0.00	0.00	0.00	1.12	1.95	2.41	2.61	2.71	2.78	2.82	2.86	2.90	2.96	2.99	3.02	3.03
1.88	0.00	0.00	0.00	1.06	1.88	2.34	2.54	2.64	2.71	2.75	2.79	2.83	2.89	2.92	2.95	2.96
1.89	0.00	0.00	0.00	0.99	1.81	2.28	2.47	2.57	2.66	2.69	2.72	2.77	2.83	2.85	2.88	2.90
1.90	0.00	0.00	0.00	0.93	1.75	2.21	2.40	2.51	2.57	2.62	2.65	2.70	2.76	2.79	2.82	2.83
1.91	0.00	0.00	0.00	0.87	1.68	2.14	2.34	2.44	2.51	2.56	2.59	2.63	2.69	2.72	2.75	2.77
1.92	0.00	0.00	0.00	0.81	1.62	2.08	2.27	2.38	2.45	2.49	2.52	2.57	2.63	2.66	2.69	2.70
1.93	0.00	0.00	0.00	0.76	1.56	2.02	2.21	2.32	2.38	2.43	2.46	2.51	2.57	2.60	2.62	2.66
1.94	0.00	0.00	0.00	0.70	1.50	1.96	2.15	2.25	2.32	2.37	2.40	2.45	2.51	2.54	2.56	2.58
1.95	0.00	0.00	0.00	0.65	1.44	1.90	2.09	2.19	2.26	2.31	2.34	2.39	2.45	2.48	2.50	2.52
1.96	0.00	0.00	0.00	0.60	1.38	1.84	2.03	2.14	2.20	2.25	2.28	2.33	2.39	2.42	2.44	2.46
1.97	0.00	0.00	0.00	0.56	1.33	1.78	1.97	2.08	2.14	2.19	2.22	2.27	2.33	2.36	2.39	2.40
1.98	0.00	0.00	0.00	0.51	1.27	1.73	1.92	2.02	2.09	2.13	2.17	2.21	2.27	2.30	2.33	2.34
1.99	0.00	0.00	0.00	0.47	1.22	1.67	1.86	1.97	2.03	2.08	2.11	2.16	2.22	2.25	2.27	2.29
2.00	0.00	0.00	0.00	0.43	1.17	1.62	1.81	1.91	1.98	2.03	2.06	2.10	2.16	2.19	2.22	2.23
2.01	0.00	0.00	0.00	0.39	1.12	1.57	1.76	1.86	1.93	1.97	2.01	2.05	2.11	2.14	2.17	2.18
2.02	0.00	0.00	0.00	0.36	1.07	1.52	1.71	1.81	1.87	1.92	1.95	2.00	2.06	2.09	2.11	2.13
2.03	0.00	0.00	0.00	0.32	1.03	1.47	1.66	1.76	1.82	1.87	1.90	1.95	2.01	2.04	2.06	2.08
2.04	0.00	0.00	0.00	0.29	0.98	1.42	1.61	1.71	1.77	1.82	1.85	1.90	1.96	1.99	2.01	2.05
2.05	0.00	0.00	0.00	0.26	0.94	1.37	1.56	1.66	1.73	1.77	1.80	1.85	1.91	1.94	1.96	1.98
2.06	0.00	0.00	0.00	0.23	0.90	1.33	1.51	1.61	1.68	1.72	1.76	1.80	1.86	1.89	1.92	1.93
2.07	0.00	0.00	0.00	0.21	0.86	1.28	1.47	1.57	1.63	1.68	1.71	1.76	1.81	1.84	1.87	1.88
2.08	0.00	0.00	0.00	0.18	0.82	1.24	1.42	1.52	1.59	1.63	1.66	1.71	1.77	1.79	1.82	1.84
2.09	0.00	0.00	0.00	0.16	0.78	1.20	1.38	1.48	1.54	1.59	1.62	1.66	1.72	1.75	1.78	1.79

Table 14-7 (Continued)

Z_{USL} or Z_{LSL}	Sample Size															
	3	4	5	7	10	15	20	25	30	35	40	50	75	100	150	200
2.10	0.00	0.00	0.00	0.14	0.74	1.16	1.34	1.44	1.50	1.54	1.58	1.62	1.68	1.71	1.73	1.75
2.11	0.00	0.00	0.00	0.12	0.71	1.12	1.30	1.39	1.46	1.50	1.53	1.58	1.63	1.66	1.69	1.70
2.12	0.00	0.00	0.00	0.10	0.67	1.08	1.26	1.35	1.42	1.46	1.49	1.54	1.59	1.62	1.65	1.66
2.13	0.00	0.00	0.00	0.08	0.64	1.04	1.22	1.31	1.38	1.42	1.45	1.50	1.55	1.58	1.61	1.62
2.14	0.00	0.00	0.00	0.07	0.61	1.00	1.18	1.28	1.34	1.38	1.41	1.46	1.51	1.54	1.57	1.58
2.15	0.00	0.00	0.00	0.06	0.58	0.97	1.14	1.24	1.30	1.34	1.37	1.42	1.47	1.50	1.53	1.54
2.16	0.00	0.00	0.00	0.05	0.55	0.93	1.10	1.20	1.26	1.30	1.34	1.38	1.43	1.46	1.49	1.50
2.17	0.00	0.00	0.00	0.04	0.52	0.90	1.07	1.16	1.22	1.27	1.30	1.34	1.40	1.42	1.45	1.46
2.18	0.00	0.00	0.00	0.03	0.49	0.87	1.03	1.13	1.19	1.23	1.26	1.30	1.36	1.39	1.41	1.42
2.19	0.00	0.00	0.00	0.02	0.46	0.83	1.00	1.09	1.15	1.20	1.23	1.27	1.32	1.35	1.38	1.39
2.20	0.000	0.000	0.000	0.015	0.437	0.803	0.968	1.061	1.120	1.161	1.192	1.233	1.287	1.314	1.340	1.352
2.21	0.000	0.000	0.000	0.010	0.413	0.772	0.936	1.028	1.087	1.128	1.158	1.199	1.253	1.279	1.305	1.318
2.22	0.000	0.000	0.000	0.006	0.389	0.743	0.905	0.996	1.054	1.095	1.125	1.166	1.219	1.245	1.271	1.283
2.23	0.000	0.000	0.000	0.003	0.366	0.715	0.875	0.965	1.023	1.063	1.093	1.134	1.186	1.212	1.238	1.250
2.24	0.000	0.000	0.000	0.002	0.345	0.687	0.845	0.935	0.992	1.032	1.061	1.102	1.154	1.180	1.205	1.218
2.25	0.000	0.000	0.000	0.001	0.324	0.660	0.816	0.905	0.962	1.002	1.031	1.071	1.123	1.148	1.173	1.186
2.26	0.000	0.000	0.000	0.000	0.304	0.634	0.789	0.876	0.933	0.972	1.001	1.041	1.092	1.117	1.142	1.155
2.27	0.000	0.000	0.000	0.000	0.285	0.609	0.762	0.848	0.904	0.943	0.972	1.011	1.062	1.057	1.112	1.124
2.28	0.000	0.000	0.000	0.000	0.267	0.585	0.735	0.821	0.876	0.915	0.943	0.982	1.033	1.058	1.082	1.094
2.29	0.000	0.000	0.000	0.000	0.250	0.561	0.710	0.794	0.849	0.887	0.915	0.954	1.004	1.029	1.053	1.065
2.30	0.000	0.000	0.000	0.000	0.233	0.538	0.685	0.769	0.823	0.861	0.888	0.927	0.977	1.001	1.025	1.037
2.31	0.000	0.000	0.000	0.000	0.218	0.516	0.662	0.743	0.797	0.834	0.862	0.900	0.949	0.974	0.997	1.009
2.32	0.000	0.000	0.000	0.000	0.203	0.495	0.637	0.719	0.772	0.809	0.836	0.874	0.923	0.947	0.971	0.982
2.33	0.000	0.000	0.000	0.000	0.189	0.474	0.614	0.695	0.748	0.784	0.811	0.848	0.897	0.921	0.944	0.956
2.34	0.000	0.000	0.000	0.000	0.175	0.454	0.592	0.672	0.724	0.760	0.787	0.824	0.872	0.895	0.915	0.930
2.35	0.000	0.000	0.000	0.000	0.163	0.435	0.571	0.650	0.701	0.736	0.763	0.799	0.847	0.870	0.893	0.905
2.36	0.000	0.000	0.000	0.000	0.151	0.416	0.550	0.628	0.678	0.714	0.740	0.776	0.823	0.846	0.869	0.880
2.37	0.000	0.000	0.000	0.000	0.139	0.398	0.530	0.606	0.656	0.691	0.717	0.753	0.799	0.822	0.845	0.856
2.38	0.000	0.000	0.000	0.000	0.128	0.381	0.510	0.586	0.635	0.670	0.695	0.730	0.777	0.799	0.822	0.833
2.39	0.000	0.000	0.000	0.000	0.118	0.364	0.491	0.566	0.614	0.648	0.674	0.709	0.754	0.777	0.799	0.810
2.40	0.000	0.000	0.000	0.000	0.109	0.348	0.473	0.546	0.594	0.628	0.653	0.687	0.732	0.755	0.777	0.737
2.41	0.000	0.000	0.000	0.000	0.100	0.332	0.455	0.527	0.575	0.608	0.633	0.667	0.711	0.733	0.755	0.766
2.42	0.000	0.000	0.000	0.000	0.091	0.317	0.437	0.509	0.555	0.588	0.613	0.646	0.691	0.712	0.734	0.744
2.43	0.000	0.000	0.000	0.000	0.083	0.302	0.421	0.491	0.537	0.569	0.593	0.627	0.670	0.692	0.713	0.724
2.44	0.000	0.000	0.000	0.000	0.076	0.288	0.404	0.474	0.519	0.551	0.575	0.608	0.651	0.672	0.693	0.703
2.45	0.000	0.000	0.000	0.000	0.069	0.275	0.389	0.457	0.501	0.533	0.556	0.589	0.632	0.653	0.673	0.684
2.46	0.000	0.000	0.000	0.000	0.063	0.262	0.373	0.440	0.484	0.516	0.539	0.571	0.613	0.634	0.654	0.664
2.47	0.000	0.000	0.000	0.000	0.057	0.249	0.359	0.425	0.468	0.499	0.521	0.553	0.595	0.615	0.635	0.646
2.48	0.000	0.000	0.000	0.000	0.051	0.237	0.344	0.409	0.452	0.482	0.505	0.536	0.577	0.597	0.617	0.627
2.49	0.000	0.000	0.000	0.000	0.046	0.226	0.331	0.394	0.436	0.466	0.488	0.519	0.560	0.580	0.600	0.609
2.50	0.000	0.000	0.000	0.000	0.041	0.214	0.317	0.380	0.421	0.451	0.473	0.503	0.543	0.563	0.582	0.592
2.51	0.000	0.000	0.000	0.000	0.037	0.204	0.304	0.366	0.407	0.436	0.457	0.487	0.527	0.546	0.565	0.575
2.52	0.000	0.000	0.000	0.000	0.033	0.193	0.292	0.352	0.392	0.421	0.442	0.472	0.511	0.530	0.549	0.558
2.53	0.000	0.000	0.000	0.000	0.029	0.184	0.280	0.339	0.379	0.407	0.428	0.457	0.495	0.514	0.533	0.542
2.54	0.000	0.000	0.000	0.000	0.026	0.174	0.268	0.326	0.365	0.393	0.413	0.442	0.480	0.499	0.517	0.527
2.55	0.000	0.000	0.000	0.000	0.023	0.165	0.257	0.314	0.352	0.379	0.400	0.428	0.465	0.484	0.502	0.511
2.56	0.000	0.000	0.000	0.000	0.020	0.156	0.246	0.302	0.340	0.366	0.386	0.414	0.451	0.469	0.487	0.496
2.57	0.000	0.000	0.000	0.000	0.017	0.148	0.236	0.291	0.327	0.354	0.373	0.401	0.437	0.455	0.473	0.452
2.58	0.000	0.000	0.000	0.000	0.015	0.140	0.226	0.279	0.316	0.341	0.361	0.388	0.429	0.441	0.459	0.468
2.59	0.000	0.000	0.000	0.000	0.013	0.133	0.216	0.269	0.304	0.330	0.349	0.375	0.410	0.428	0.445	0.454
2.60	0.000	0.000	0.000	0.000	0.011	0.125	0.207	0.258	0.293	0.318	0.337	0.363	0.398	0.415	0.432	0.441
2.61	0.000	0.000	0.000	0.000	0.009	0.118	0.198	0.248	0.282	0.307	0.325	0.351	0.385	0.402	0.419	0.428
2.62	0.000	0.000	0.000	0.000	0.008	0.112	0.189	0.238	0.272	0.296	0.314	0.339	0.373	0.390	0.406	0.415
2.63	0.000	0.000	0.000	0.000	0.007	0.105	0.181	0.229	0.262	0.285	0.303	0.328	0.361	0.378	0.394	0.402
2.64	0.000	0.000	0.000	0.000	0.005	0.099	0.172	0.220	0.252	0.275	0.293	0.317	0.350	0.366	0.382	0.390
2.65	0.000	0.000	0.000	0.000	0.005	0.094	0.165	0.211	0.243	0.265	0.282	0.307	0.339	0.355	0.371	0.379
2.66	0.000	0.000	0.000	0.000	0.004	0.088	0.157	0.202	0.233	0.256	0.273	0.296	0.328	0.344	0.359	0.367
2.67	0.000	0.000	0.000	0.000	0.003	0.083	0.150	0.194	0.224	0.246	0.263	0.286	0.317	0.333	0.348	0.356
2.68	0.000	0.000	0.000	0.000	0.002	0.078	0.143	0.186	0.216	0.237	0.254	0.277	0.307	0.322	0.338	0.345
2.69	0.000	0.000	0.000	0.000	0.002	0.073	0.136	0.179	0.208	0.229	0.245	0.267	0.297	0.312	0.327	0.335

(continued)

Table 14-7 (Continued)

Z_{USL} or Z_{LSL}	Sample Size															
	3	4	5	7	10	15	20	25	30	35	40	50	75	100	150	200
2.70	0.000	0.000	0.000	0.000	0.001	0.069	0.130	0.171	0.200	0.220	0.236	0.258	0.288	0.302	0.317	0.325
2.71	0.000	0.000	0.000	0.000	0.001	0.064	0.124	0.164	0.192	0.212	0.227	0.249	0.278	0.293	0.307	0.315
2.72	0.000	0.000	0.000	0.000	0.000	0.060	0.118	0.157	0.184	0.204	0.219	0.241	0.269	0.283	0.298	0.305
2.73	0.000	0.000	0.000	0.000	0.000	0.057	0.112	0.151	0.177	0.197	0.211	0.232	0.260	0.274	0.288	0.296
2.74	0.000	0.000	0.000	0.000	0.000	0.053	0.107	0.144	0.170	0.189	0.204	0.224	0.252	0.266	0.279	0.286
2.75	0.000	0.000	0.000	0.000	0.000	0.049	0.102	0.138	0.163	0.182	0.196	0.216	0.243	0.257	0.271	0.277
2.76	0.000	0.000	0.000	0.000	0.000	0.046	0.097	0.132	0.157	0.175	0.189	0.209	0.235	0.249	0.262	0.269
2.77	0.000	0.000	0.000	0.000	0.000	0.043	0.092	0.126	0.151	0.168	0.182	0.201	0.227	0.241	0.254	0.260
2.78	0.000	0.000	0.000	0.000	0.000	0.040	0.087	0.121	0.145	0.162	0.175	0.194	0.220	0.233	0.246	0.252
2.79	0.000	0.000	0.000	0.000	0.000	0.037	0.083	0.115	0.139	0.156	0.169	0.187	0.212	0.225	0.238	0.244
2.80	0.000	0.000	0.000	0.000	0.000	0.035	0.079	0.110	0.133	0.150	0.162	0.181	0.205	0.218	0.230	0.237
2.81	0.000	0.000	0.000	0.000	0.000	0.032	0.075	0.105	0.128	0.144	0.156	0.174	0.198	0.211	0.223	0.229
2.82	0.000	0.000	0.000	0.000	0.000	0.030	0.071	0.101	0.122	0.138	0.150	0.168	0.192	0.204	0.216	0.222
2.83	0.000	0.000	0.000	0.000	0.000	0.028	0.067	0.096	0.117	0.133	0.145	0.162	0.185	0.197	0.209	0.215
2.84	0.000	0.000	0.000	0.000	0.000	0.026	0.064	0.092	0.112	0.128	0.139	0.156	0.179	0.190	0.202	0.208
2.85	0.000	0.000	0.000	0.000	0.000	0.024	0.060	0.088	0.108	0.122	0.134	0.150	0.173	0.184	0.195	0.201
2.86	0.000	0.000	0.000	0.000	0.000	0.022	0.057	0.084	0.103	0.118	0.129	0.145	0.167	0.178	0.189	0.195
2.87	0.000	0.000	0.000	0.000	0.000	0.020	0.054	0.080	0.099	0.113	0.124	0.139	0.161	0.172	0.183	0.188
2.88	0.000	0.000	0.000	0.000	0.000	0.019	0.051	0.076	0.094	0.108	0.119	0.134	0.155	0.166	0.177	0.182
2.89	0.000	0.000	0.000	0.000	0.000	0.017	0.048	0.073	0.090	0.104	0.114	0.129	0.150	0.160	0.171	0.176
2.90	0.000	0.000	0.000	0.000	0.000	0.016	0.046	0.069	0.087	0.100	0.110	0.125	0.145	0.155	0.165	0.171
2.91	0.000	0.000	0.000	0.000	0.000	0.015	0.043	0.066	0.083	0.096	0.106	0.120	0.140	0.150	0.160	0.165
2.92	0.000	0.000	0.000	0.000	0.000	0.013	0.041	0.063	0.079	0.092	0.101	0.115	0.135	0.145	0.155	0.160
2.93	0.000	0.000	0.000	0.000	0.000	0.012	0.038	0.060	0.076	0.088	0.097	0.111	0.130	0.140	0.149	0.154
2.94	0.000	0.000	0.000	0.000	0.000	0.011	0.036	0.057	0.072	0.084	0.093	0.107	0.125	0.135	0.144	0.149
2.95	0.000	0.000	0.000	0.000	0.000	0.010	0.034	0.054	0.069	0.081	0.090	0.103	0.121	0.130	0.140	0.144
2.96	0.000	0.000	0.000	0.000	0.000	0.009	0.032	0.051	0.066	0.077	0.086	0.099	0.117	0.126	0.135	0.140
2.97	0.000	0.000	0.000	0.000	0.000	0.009	0.030	0.049	0.063	0.074	0.083	0.095	0.112	0.121	0.130	0.135
2.98	0.000	0.000	0.000	0.000	0.000	0.008	0.028	0.046	0.060	0.071	0.079	0.091	0.108	0.117	0.126	0.130
2.99	0.000	0.000	0.000	0.000	0.000	0.007	0.027	0.044	0.057	0.068	0.076	0.088	0.104	0.113	0.122	0.126
3.00	0.000	0.000	0.000	0.000	0.000	0.006	0.025	0.042	0.055	0.065	0.073	0.084	0.101	0.109	0.118	0.122
3.01	0.000	0.000	0.000	0.000	0.000	0.006	0.024	0.040	0.052	0.062	0.070	0.081	0.097	0.105	0.114	0.118
3.02	0.000	0.000	0.000	0.000	0.000	0.005	0.022	0.038	0.050	0.059	0.067	0.078	0.093	0.101	0.110	0.114
3.03	0.000	0.000	0.000	0.000	0.000	0.005	0.021	0.036	0.048	0.057	0.066	0.075	0.090	0.098	0.106	0.110
3.04	0.000	0.000	0.000	0.000	0.000	0.004	0.019	0.034	0.045	0.054	0.061	0.072	0.087	0.094	0.102	0.106
3.05	0.000	0.000	0.000	0.000	0.000	0.004	0.018	0.032	0.043	0.052	0.059	0.069	0.083	0.091	0.099	0.103
3.06	0.000	0.000	0.000	0.000	0.000	0.003	0.017	0.030	0.041	0.050	0.056	0.066	0.080	0.088	0.095	0.099
3.07	0.000	0.000	0.000	0.000	0.000	0.003	0.016	0.029	0.039	0.047	0.054	0.064	0.077	0.085	0.092	0.096
3.08	0.000	0.000	0.000	0.000	0.000	0.003	0.015	0.027	0.037	0.045	0.052	0.061	0.074	0.081	0.089	0.092
3.09	0.000	0.000	0.000	0.000	0.000	0.002	0.014	0.026	0.036	0.043	0.049	0.059	0.072	0.079	0.086	0.089
3.10	0.000	0.000	0.000	0.000	0.000	0.002	0.013	0.024	0.034	0.041	0.047	0.056	0.069	0.076	0.083	0.086
3.11	0.000	0.000	0.000	0.000	0.000	0.002	0.012	0.023	0.032	0.039	0.045	0.054	0.066	0.073	0.080	0.083
3.12	0.000	0.000	0.000	0.000	0.000	0.002	0.011	0.022	0.031	0.038	0.043	0.052	0.064	0.070	0.077	0.080
3.13	0.000	0.000	0.000	0.000	0.000	0.002	0.011	0.021	0.029	0.036	0.041	0.050	0.061	0.068	0.074	0.077
3.14	0.000	0.000	0.000	0.000	0.000	0.001	0.010	0.019	0.028	0.034	0.040	0.048	0.059	0.065	0.071	0.075
3.15	0.000	0.000	0.000	0.000	0.000	0.001	0.009	0.018	0.026	0.033	0.038	0.046	0.057	0.063	0.069	0.072
3.16	0.000	0.000	0.000	0.000	0.000	0.001	0.009	0.017	0.025	0.031	0.036	0.044	0.055	0.060	0.066	0.069
3.17	0.000	0.000	0.000	0.000	0.000	0.001	0.008	0.016	0.024	0.030	0.035	0.042	0.053	0.058	0.064	0.067
3.18	0.000	0.000	0.000	0.000	0.000	0.001	0.007	0.015	0.022	0.028	0.033	0.040	0.050	0.056	0.062	0.065
3.19	0.000	0.000	0.000	0.000	0.000	0.001	0.007	0.015	0.021	0.027	0.032	0.038	0.049	0.054	0.059	0.062
3.20	0.000	0.000	0.000	0.000	0.000	0.001	0.006	0.014	0.020	0.026	0.030	0.037	0.047	0.052	0.057	0.060
3.21	0.000	0.000	0.000	0.000	0.000	0.000	0.006	0.013	0.019	0.024	0.029	0.035	0.045	0.050	0.055	0.058
3.22	0.000	0.000	0.000	0.000	0.000	0.000	0.005	0.012	0.018	0.023	0.027	0.034	0.043	0.048	0.053	0.056
3.23	0.000	0.000	0.000	0.000	0.000	0.000	0.005	0.011	0.017	0.022	0.026	0.032	0.041	0.046	0.051	0.054
3.24	0.000	0.000	0.000	0.000	0.000	0.000	0.005	0.011	0.016	0.021	0.025	0.031	0.040	0.044	0.049	0.052
3.25	0.000	0.000	0.000	0.000	0.000	0.000	0.004	0.010	0.015	0.020	0.024	0.030	0.038	0.043	0.048	0.050
3.26	0.000	0.000	0.000	0.000	0.000	0.000	0.004	0.009	0.015	0.019	0.023	0.028	0.037	0.041	0.046	0.048
3.27	0.000	0.000	0.000	0.000	0.000	0.000	0.004	0.009	0.014	0.019	0.022	0.027	0.035	0.040	0.044	0.046
3.28	0.000	0.000	0.000	0.000	0.000	0.000	0.003	0.008	0.013	0.017	0.021	0.026	0.034	0.038	0.042	0.045
3.29	0.000	0.000	0.000	0.000	0.000	0.000	0.003	0.008	0.012	0.016	0.020	0.025	0.032	0.037	0.041	0.043

Table 14-7   (Continued)

Z_{USL} or Z_{LSL}	Sample Size															
	3	4	5	7	10	15	20	25	30	35	40	50	75	100	150	200
3.30	0.000	0.000	0.000	0.000	0.000	0.000	0.003	0.007	0.012	0.015	0.019	0.024	0.031	0.035	0.039	0.042
3.31	0.000	0.000	0.000	0.000	0.000	0.000	0.003	0.007	0.011	0.015	0.018	0.023	0.030	0.034	0.038	0.042
3.32	0.000	0.000	0.000	0.000	0.000	0.000	0.002	0.006	0.010	0.014	0.017	0.022	0.029	0.032	0.036	0.039
3.33	0.000	0.000	0.000	0.000	0.000	0.000	0.002	0.006	0.010	0.013	0.016	0.021	0.027	0.031	0.035	0.037
3.34	0.000	0.000	0.000	0.000	0.000	0.000	0.002	0.006	0.009	0.013	0.015	0.020	0.026	0.030	0.034	0.036
3.35	0.000	0.000	0.000	0.000	0.000	0.000	0.002	0.005	0.009	0.012	0.015	0.019	0.025	0.029	0.032	0.034
3.36	0.000	0.000	0.000	0.000	0.000	0.000	0.002	0.005	0.008	0.011	0.014	0.018	0.024	0.028	0.031	0.033
3.37	0.000	0.000	0.000	0.000	0.000	0.000	0.002	0.005	0.008	0.011	0.013	0.017	0.023	0.026	0.030	0.032
3.38	0.000	0.000	0.000	0.000	0.000	0.000	0.001	0.004	0.007	0.010	0.013	0.016	0.022	0.025	0.029	0.031
3.39	0.000	0.000	0.000	0.000	0.000	0.000	0.001	0.004	0.007	0.010	0.012	0.016	0.021	0.024	0.028	0.029
3.40	0.000	0.000	0.000	0.000	0.000	0.000	0.001	0.004	0.007	0.009	0.011	0.015	0.020	0.023	0.027	0.028
3.41	0.000	0.000	0.000	0.000	0.000	0.000	0.001	0.003	0.006	0.009	0.011	0.014	0.020	0.022	0.026	0.027
3.42	0.000	0.000	0.000	0.000	0.000	0.000	0.001	0.003	0.006	0.008	0.010	0.014	0.019	0.022	0.025	0.026
3.43	0.000	0.000	0.000	0.000	0.000	0.000	0.001	0.003	0.005	0.008	0.010	0.013	0.018	0.021	0.024	0.025
3.44	0.000	0.000	0.000	0.000	0.000	0.000	0.001	0.003	0.005	0.007	0.009	0.012	0.017	0.020	0.023	0.024
3.45	0.000	0.000	0.000	0.000	0.000	0.000	0.001	0.003	0.005	0.007	0.009	0.012	0.016	0.019	0.022	0.023
3.46	0.000	0.000	0.000	0.000	0.000	0.000	0.001	0.002	0.005	0.007	0.008	0.011	0.016	0.018	0.021	0.022
3.47	0.000	0.000	0.000	0.000	0.000	0.000	0.001	0.002	0.004	0.006	0.008	0.011	0.015	0.017	0.020	0.022
3.48	0.000	0.000	0.000	0.000	0.000	0.000	0.001	0.002	0.004	0.006	0.007	0.010	0.014	0.017	0.019	0.021
3.49	0.000	0.000	0.000	0.000	0.000	0.000	0.000	0.002	0.004	0.005	0.007	0.010	0.014	0.016	0.020	0.089
3.50	0.000	0.000	0.000	0.000	0.000	0.000	0.000	0.002	0.003	0.005	0.007	0.009	0.013	0.015	0.018	0.019
3.51	0.000	0.000	0.000	0.000	0.000	0.000	0.000	0.002	0.003	0.005	0.006	0.009	0.013	0.015	0.017	0.018
3.52	0.000	0.000	0.000	0.000	0.000	0.000	0.000	0.002	0.003	0.005	0.006	0.008	0.012	0.014	0.017	0.018
3.53	0.000	0.000	0.000	0.000	0.000	0.000	0.000	0.001	0.003	0.004	0.006	0.008	0.012	0.014	0.016	0.017
3.54	0.000	0.000	0.000	0.000	0.000	0.000	0.000	0.001	0.003	0.004	0.005	0.008	0.011	0.013	0.015	0.016
3.55	0.000	0.000	0.000	0.000	0.000	0.000	0.000	0.001	0.003	0.004	0.005	0.007	0.011	0.012	0.015	0.016
3.56	0.000	0.000	0.000	0.000	0.000	0.000	0.000	0.001	0.002	0.004	0.005	0.007	0.010	0.012	0.014	0.015
3.57	0.000	0.000	0.000	0.000	0.000	0.000	0.000	0.001	0.002	0.003	0.005	0.006	0.010	0.011	0.013	0.014
3.58	0.000	0.000	0.000	0.000	0.000	0.000	0.000	0.001	0.002	0.003	0.004	0.006	0.009	0.011	0.013	0.014
3.59	0.000	0.000	0.000	0.000	0.000	0.000	0.000	0.001	0.002	0.003	0.004	0.006	0.009	0.010	0.012	0.013
3.60	0.000	0.000	0.000	0.000	0.000	0.000	0.000	0.001	0.002	0.003	0.004	0.006	0.008	0.010	0.012	0.013
3.61	0.000	0.000	0.000	0.000	0.000	0.000	0.000	0.001	0.002	0.003	0.004	0.005	0.008	0.010	0.011	0.012
3.62	0.000	0.000	0.000	0.000	0.000	0.000	0.000	0.001	0.002	0.003	0.003	0.005	0.008	0.009	0.011	0.012
3.63	0.000	0.000	0.000	0.000	0.000	0.000	0.000	0.001	0.001	0.002	0.003	0.005	0.007	0.009	0.010	0.011
3.64	0.000	0.000	0.000	0.000	0.000	0.000	0.000	0.001	0.001	0.002	0.003	0.004	0.007	0.008	0.010	0.011
3.65	0.000	0.000	0.000	0.000	0.000	0.000	0.000	0.001	0.001	0.002	0.003	0.004	0.007	0.008	0.010	0.010
3.66	0.000	0.000	0.000	0.000	0.000	0.000	0.000	0.000	0.001	0.002	0.003	0.004	0.006	0.008	0.009	0.010
3.67	0.000	0.000	0.000	0.000	0.000	0.000	0.000	0.000	0.001	0.002	0.003	0.004	0.006	0.007	0.009	0.010
3.68	0.000	0.000	0.000	0.000	0.000	0.000	0.000	0.000	0.001	0.002	0.002	0.004	0.006	0.007	0.008	0.009
3.69	0.000	0.000	0.000	0.000	0.000	0.000	0.000	0.000	0.001	0.002	0.002	0.003	0.005	0.007	0.008	0.009
3.70	0.000	0.000	0.000	0.000	0.000	0.000	0.000	0.000	0.001	0.002	0.002	0.003	0.005	0.006	0.008	0.008
3.71	0.000	0.000	0.000	0.000	0.000	0.000	0.000	0.000	0.001	0.001	0.002	0.003	0.005	0.006	0.007	0.008
3.72	0.000	0.000	0.000	0.000	0.000	0.000	0.000	0.000	0.001	0.001	0.002	0.003	0.005	0.006	0.007	0.008
3.73	0.000	0.000	0.000	0.000	0.000	0.000	0.000	0.000	0.001	0.001	0.002	0.003	0.005	0.006	0.007	0.007
3.74	0.000	0.000	0.000	0.000	0.000	0.000	0.000	0.000	0.001	0.001	0.002	0.003	0.004	0.005	0.007	0.007
3.75	0.000	0.000	0.000	0.000	0.000	0.000	0.000	0.000	0.001	0.001	0.002	0.002	0.004	0.005	0.006	0.007
3.76	0.000	0.000	0.000	0.000	0.000	0.000	0.000	0.000	0.001	0.001	0.001	0.002	0.004	0.005	0.006	0.007
3.77	0.000	0.000	0.000	0.000	0.000	0.000	0.000	0.000	0.001	0.001	0.001	0.002	0.004	0.005	0.006	0.006
3.78	0.000	0.000	0.000	0.000	0.000	0.000	0.000	0.000	0.000	0.001	0.001	0.002	0.004	0.004	0.005	0.006
3.79	0.000	0.000	0.000	0.000	0.000	0.000	0.000	0.000	0.000	0.001	0.001	0.002	0.003	0.004	0.005	0.006
3.80	0.000	0.000	0.000	0.000	0.000	0.000	0.000	0.000	0.000	0.001	0.001	0.002	0.003	0.004	0.005	0.006
3.81	0.000	0.000	0.000	0.000	0.000	0.000	0.000	0.000	0.000	0.000	0.001	0.001	0.002	0.003	0.004	0.005	0.005
3.82	0.000	0.000	0.000	0.000	0.000	0.000	0.000	0.000	0.000	0.001	0.001	0.002	0.003	0.004	0.005	0.005
3.83	0.000	0.000	0.000	0.000	0.000	0.000	0.000	0.000	0.000	0.001	0.001	0.002	0.003	0.004	0.004	0.005
3.84	0.000	0.000	0.000	0.000	0.000	0.000	0.000	0.000	0.000	0.001	0.001	0.001	0.003	0.003	0.004	0.005
3.85	0.000	0.000	0.000	0.000	0.000	0.000	0.000	0.000	0.000	0.000	0.001	0.001	0.002	0.003	0.004	0.004
3.86	0.000	0.000	0.000	0.000	0.000	0.000	0.000	0.000	0.000	0.000	0.001	0.001	0.002	0.003	0.004	0.004
3.87	0.000	0.000	0.000	0.000	0.000	0.000	0.000	0.000	0.000	0.000	0.001	0.001	0.002	0.003	0.004	0.004
3.88	0.000	0.000	0.000	0.000	0.000	0.000	0.000	0.000	0.000	0.000	0.001	0.001	0.002	0.003	0.004	0.004
3.89	0.000	0.000	0.000	0.000	0.000	0.000	0.000	0.000	0.000	0.000	0.001	0.001	0.002	0.003	0.003	0.004
3.90	0.000	0.000	0.000	0.000	0.000	0.000	0.000	0.000	0.000	0.000	0.001	0.001	0.002	0.003	0.003	0.004

[1] Values tabulated are read in percent.

certain number T of the lots on which the process average is based have estimates of the percent defective that exceeds the AQL. Table 14-6 presents the values of T. Reduced inspection is instituted when (1) the 10 preceding lots have been under normal inspection and none of them has been rejected; (2) the estimating percent defective for each of these preceding lots is less than a specified lower limit for which a special table is provided or, for certain plans, when the estimated percent defective is equal to zero for a specified number of consecutive lots; and (3) production is at a steady state. Full details of the switching procedures to reduced inspection are described in a technical memorandum on MIL STD 414, published by the United States Department of the Navy, Bureau of Ordinance.

Estimation of the fraction defective is required in using Procedure 2 of MIL STD 105D. It is also required in implementing the switching rules between normal, tightened, and reduced inspection. In the standard, three tables are provided for estimating the fraction defective. The choice of table depends on whether the standard deviation is assumed to be known, whether the standard deviation is estimated by the sample standard deviation, or whether the range of the sample data is to be employed. These are sometimes referred to as the Lieberman-Resnikoff tables, after their developers (1955). Table 14-7 presents the Lieberman-Resnikoff table for estimating fraction defective corresponding to Z_{LSL} or Z_{USL} when the process variability is unknown, and is estimated by the sample standard deviation. The numbers in the body of this table are the probabilities that the normal variable is less than or equal to Z. These tables are useful not only for variables sampling, but also for any problem situation where estimation of the percentiles of a normal distribution with unknown mean and standard deviation is required.

When starting to use MIL STD 414, one can choose between the known standard deviation and unknown standard deviation procedures. When there is no basis for knowledge of σ, obviously the unknown standard deviation plan must be used. However, it is a good idea to maintain either an R or S chart on the results of each lot so that some information on the state of statistical control of the scatter in the manufacturing process can be collected. If this control chart indicates statistical control, it will be possible to switch to a known σ plan. Such a switch will reduce the required sample size. Even if the process were not perfectly controlled, the control chart could provide information leading to a conservative estimate of σ for use in a known σ plan. When a known σ plan is used, it is also necessary to maintain a control chart on either R or S as a continuous check on the assumption of stable and known process variability.

MIL STD 414 contains a special procedure for application of mixed variables attributes acceptance-sampling plans. If the lot does not meet the acceptability criterion of the variables plan, an attributes single-sampling plan, using tightened inspection and the same AQL, is obtained from MIL STD 105D. A lot can be accepted by either of the plans in sequence but must be rejected by both the variables and attributes plan.

14-3.3 Discussion of MIL STD 414 and ANSI/ASQC Z1.9

In 1980 the American National Standards Institution and the American Society for Quality Control released an updated civilian version of MIL STD 414 known as ANSI/ASQC Z1.9. MIL STD 414 was originally structured to give protection essentially equivalent to that provided by MIL STD 105A (1950). When MIL STD 105D was adopted in 1963, this new standard contained substantially revised tables and procedures that led to differences in protection between it and MIL STD 414. Consequently, it is not possible to move directly from an attributes sampling plan in MIL STD 105D to a corresponding variables plan in MIL STD 414 if the assurance of continued protection is desired for certain lot sizes and AQLs.

The civilian counterpart of MIL STD 414, ANSI/ASQC Z1.9, restores this original match. That is, ANSI/ASQC Z1.9 now is directly compatible with MIL STD 105D (and its equivalent civilian counterpart ANSI/ASQC Z1.4). This equivalence was obtained by incorporating the following revisions in ANSI/ASQC Z1.9:

1. Lot size ranges were adjusted to correspond to MIL STD 105D.
2. The code letters assigned to the various lot size ranges were arranged to make protection equal to that of MIL STD 105D.
3. AQLs of 0.04, 0.065, and 15 were deleted.
4. The original inspection levels I, II, III, IV and V were relabeled S3, S4, I, II, III, respectively.
5. The original switching rules were replaced by those of MIL STD 105D, with slight revisions.

In addition, to modernize terminology, the word *nonconformity* was substituted for defect, *nonconformance* was substituted for defective, and *percent nonconforming* was substituted for percent defective. The operating-characteristic curves were recomputed and replotted, and a number of editorial changes were made to the descriptive material of the standard in order to match MIL STD 105D as closely as possible. Finally, an appendix was included showing the match between ANSI/ASQC Z1.9, MIL STD 105D, and the corresponding civilian version ANSI Z1.4. This appendix also provided selected percentage points from the OC curves of these standards and their differences.

As of this writing, the Department of Defense has not officially adopted ANSI/ASQC Z1.9 and continues to use MIL STD 414. Both standards will probably be used extensively in the future. The principal advantage of the ANSI/ASQC Z1.9 standard is that it is possible to start inspection by using an attributes sampling scheme from MIL STD 105D or ANSI/ASQC Z1.4, collect sufficient information to use variables inspection, and then switch to the variables scheme, while maintaining the same AQL-code letter combination. It would then be possible to switch back to the attributes scheme if the assumption of the variables scheme appeared not to be satisfied. It is also possible to take advantage of the information gained in coordinated attributes and variables inspection to move in a logical manner from inspection sampling to statistical process control.

As in MIL STD 414, ANSI/ASQC Z1.9 assumes that the quality characteristic is normally distributed. This is an important assumption that we have commented on previously. We have suggested that a test for normality should be incorporated as part of the standard. One way this can be done is to plot a control chart for $\bar{x}$ and S (or $\bar{x}$ and R) from the variables data from each lot. After a sufficient number of observations have been obtained, a test for normality can be employed by plotting the individual measurements on normal probability paper or by conducting one of the specialized statistical tests for normality. It is recommended that a relatively large sample size be used in this statistical test. At least

100 observations should be collected before the test for normality is made, and it is our belief that the sample size should increase inversely with AQL. If the assumption of normality is badly violated, either a special variables sampling procedure must be developed, or we must return to attributes inspection.

An additional advantage of applying a control chart to the result of each lot is that if the process variability has been in control for at least 30 samples, it will be possible to switch to a known standard deviation plan, thereby allowing a substantial reduction in sample size. While this can be instituted in any combined program of attributes and variables inspection, it is easy to do so using the ANSI/ASQC standards, because of the design equivalence between the attributes and variables procedures.

14-4 OTHER VARIABLES SAMPLING PROCEDURES

14-4.1 Sampling by Variables to Give Assurance Regarding the Lot or Process Mean

Variables sampling plans can also be used to give assurance regarding the *average* quality of a material, instead of the fraction defective. Sampling plans such as this are most likely to be employed in the sampling of bulk materials that come in bags, drums, or other containers. However, they can also be applied to discrete parts and to other variables, such as energy loss in power transformers. The general approach employed in this type of variables sampling is statistical hypothesis testing. We now present an example of the procedure.

Example 14-4

A manufacturer of wood paneling samples the substrate blanks bought from an offshore vendor to determine their formaldehyde emission level. As long as the mean emission level is less than 0.3 ppm, the lot is satisfactory. We will design a variables sampling procedure that will give lots that have a mean emission level of 0.3 ppm a 0.95 probability of acceptance, and lots that have a mean emission level of 0.4 ppm a 0.10 probability of acceptance. The largest probable value of the standard deviation of emission level is known from past experience to be $\sigma = 0.10$ ppm.

Let $\bar{x}_A$ be the value of the sample average above which the lot will be accepted. Then, we know that

$$\frac{\bar{x}_A - 0.30}{\sigma/\sqrt{n}} = \frac{\bar{x}_A - 0.30}{0.10/\sqrt{n}}$$

is distributed as a standard normal variable. If lots of this type have a 0.95 probability of acceptance, then

$$\frac{\bar{x}_A - 0.30}{0.10/\sqrt{n}} = +1.645$$

Similarly, if lots that have a mean emission level of 0.40 ppm are to have a 0.10 probability of acceptance, then

$$\frac{\bar{x}_A - 0.40}{0.10/\sqrt{n}} = -1.282$$

These two equations may be solved for n and $\bar{x}_A$, giving $n = 9$ and $\bar{x}_A = 0.356$. It is also possible to design the sampling plan using an OC curve method.

We may also design variables acceptance-sampling procedures such as this one for the case where the standard deviation is unknown. Similarly, we may derive lot-by-lot variables acceptance-sampling plans to give assurance regarding the standard deviation of a lot or process. The standard techniques of statistical hypothesis testing on means and variances can be used to obtain sampling procedures that have specified OC curves. For an extensive discussion of designing these procedures, refer to Hines and Montgomery (1990).

14-4.2 Sequential Sampling by Variables

Just as sequential sampling proves useful in attributes inspection, it can also be applied in variables inspection. The usual assumptions are that the quality characteristic is normally distributed and that the standard deviation of the lot or process is known. The item-by-item sequential sampling plan by variables plots the cumulative sum of the measurements on the quality characteristic. Limit lines for accepting the lot, rejecting the lot, and continuing sampling are constructed much as they are in the case of attributes inspection. Duncan (1974) provides a good discussion of the design of these plans.

14-4.3 The Lot-Plot Method

The lot-plot method is a variables sampling plan that was developed by Dorian Shainin when he was chief inspector at the Hamilton Standard Division of United Aircraft Corporation. (Hamilton Standard is now a subsidiary of United Technologies, Inc.) The lot-plot procedure uses a frequency distribution of the sample data to sentence the lot. An important feature of the lot-plot method is that it can be used for both normal and nonnormal distributions of the quality characteristic.

The method consists of drawing 10 random samples, each of 5 items, from the lot. A specialized procedure is then used to construct a histogram or frequency distribution of these sample results. Upper and lower lot limits are calculated for the histogram, using an approach very similar to that used to find the upper and lower control limits on an $\bar{x}$ control chart. Once the lot-plot and the lot limits are obtained, the lot may be sentenced. The sentencing decision is based on a comparison of the lot-plot with 11 different types of lot-plot diagrams. The lot-plot diagrams are applicable to both normally and nonnormally distributed characteristics.

There are many variations of the lot-plot method in use. The procedure is relatively simple, and often results in improved quality and lowered inspection costs. The principal disadvantage of the procedure is that the frequency distribution does not always give a true indication of the actual distribution of the quality characteristic in the lot or process. Usually, the sample sizes employed in the lot-plot method are not large enough to accurately discriminate between good and bad lots when very low levels of fraction nonconforming must be detected.

14-4.4 Narrow-Limit Gaging

An alternative procedure to variables sampling when the standard deviation is known is to use an attributes sampling plan with tighter specification limits than those described by the engineering design. This procedure is often called narrow-limit gaging, or compressed-limit gaging, or increased severity testing.[1] Assume that items in a process or lot are normally distributed and that the standard deviation is known. In such a case, we can work with fictitious specification limits. With reference to the bottle testing problem discussed in Examples 14-1 and 14-2, suppose that the process has a known standard deviation of $\sigma = 15$ and a lower specification limit LSL $= 225$. If the process mean is 260 psi, then the fraction falling below the lower specification limit is 1%. Suppose that we are willing to accept such lots 95% of the time. If the mean drops to 245 psi, then 10% of the bottles in the lot are below the lower specification limit. Suppose that we are willing to accept such lots only 10% of the time. The situation is illustrated in Figure 14-7. Now suppose that we increase the lower specification limit to 245 psi. Notice from Figure 14-7 that a process that has 1% of its bottles below 225 psi also has 15.87% of its bottles below 245 psi. Furthermore, a process that has 10% of its bottles below 225 psi has 50% of its bottles below 245 psi. Therefore, instead of using a sampling plan based on the 225 psi LSL and the 1% and 10% fractions defective at that point, we can use an attributes sampling plan based on 245 as a specification limit, with $p_1 = 15.85\%$, $\alpha = 0.05\%$, $p_2 = 50\%$, and $\beta = 0.10$. The attributes sampling plan for this situation has $n = 14$ and $c = 4$. That is, we would inspect 14 bottles and consider any bottle that had a bursting strength below 245 psi as "defective." If more than four defective bottles were observed, the lot would be rejected. A conventional attributes sampling plan based on the 225 psi specification limit would require a sample size of approximately 40. A variables sampling plan, assuming unknown process variability, would require a sample size of approximately 20. Thus, the use of narrow-limit gaging has greatly reduced the sample size in this situation.

Narrow-limit gaging can be useful when the fraction defectives p_1 and p_2 are very small, and when variables sampling is either very expensive or technologically infeasible. Note, however, that the usefulness of narrow-limit gaging depends on the distribution of the quality characteristic. In the above example, we assume that the form of the distribution was normal. If this assumption was incorrect, the narrow-limit gaging plan that we derived would not operate as we had anticipated. We have also assumed that the lot or process standard deviation is known and that it remains constant. We recommend that narrow-limit gaging plans be applied with caution.

---

[1] See Chapter 8 for another application of narrow-limit gaging, PRE-control.

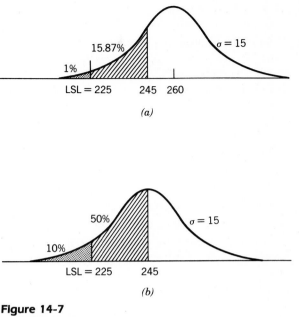

Figure 14-7
Narrow-limit gaging.

14-5 Exercises

14-1 The density of a plastic part used in a pocket calculator is required to be at least 0.70 g/cm³. The parts are supplied in large lots, and a variables sampling plan is to be used to sentence the lots. It is desired to have $p_1 = 0.02$, $p_2 = 0.10$, $\alpha = 0.10$, and $\beta = 0.05$. The variability of the manufacturing process is unknown but will be estimated by the sample standard deviation.

   a. Find an appropriate variables sampling plan, using Procedure 1.

   b. Suppose that a sample of the appropriate size was taken, and $\bar{x} = 0.73$, $S = 1.05 \times 10^{-2}$. Should the lot be accepted or rejected?

   c. Sketch the OC curve for this sampling plan. Find the probability of accepting lots that are 5% defective.

14-2 A belt that is used in a drive mechanism in a copier machine is required to have a minimum tensile strength of LSL = 150 lb. It is known from long experience that $\sigma = 5$ lb for this particular belt. Find a variables sampling plan so that $p_1 = 0.005$, $p_2 = 0.02$, $\alpha = 0.05$, and $\beta = 0.10$. Assume that Procedure 1 is to be used.

14-3 Determine the criteria for sentencing lots for the problem described in Exercise 14-1, assuming that Procedure 2 is to be used.

14-4 Determine the procedure used to sentence lots if Procedure 2 is used for the problem situation described in Exercise 14-2.

14-5 Describe how rectifying inspection can be used with variables sampling. What are the appropriate equations for the AOQ and the ATI, assuming single sampling and requiring that all defective items found in either sampling or 100% inspection are replaced by good ones?

14-6 An inspector for a military agency desires a variables sampling plan for use with an AQL of 1.5%, assuming that lots are of size 7000. If the standard deviation of the lot or process is unknown, derive two sampling plans, using Procedure 1 and Procedure 2, from MIL STD 414.

14-7 How do the sample sizes found in Exercise 14-6 compare with those that would have been used under MIL STD 105D?

14-8 A lot of 500 items is submitted for inspection. Suppose that we wish to find a plan from MIL STD 414, using inspection level II. If the AQL is 4%, find the Procedure 1 and Procedure 2 sampling plans from the standard.

14-9 A soft drink bottler purchases nonreturnable glass bottles from a vendor. The lower specification on bursting strength in the bottles is 225 psi. The bottler wishes to use variables sampling to sentence the lots, and has decided to use an AQL of 1%. Find an appropriate set of normal and tightened sampling plans from the standard. Suppose that a lot is submitted, and the sample results yield:

$$\bar{x} = 225 \qquad S = 10$$

Determine the disposition of the lot using Procedure 2.

14-10 Repeat Exercise 14-9 using Procedure 1.

14-11 A chemical ingredient is packed in metal containers. A large shipment of these containers has been delivered to a manufacturing facility. The mean bulk density of this ingredient should not be less than 0.15 g/cm^3. Suppose that lots of this quality are to have a 0.95 probability of acceptance. If the mean bulk density is as low as 0.1450, the probability of acceptance of the lot should be 0.10. Suppose that we know that the standard deviation of bulk density is approximately 0.005 g/cm^3. Obtain a variables sampling plan that could be used to sentence the lots.

14-12 A standard of 0.3 ppm has been established for formaldehyde emission levels in wood products. Suppose that the standard deviation of emissions in an individual board is $\sigma = 0.10$ ppm. Any lot that contains 1% of its items above 0.3 ppm is considered acceptable. Any lot that has 8% or more of its items above 0.3 ppm is considered unacceptable. Good lots are to be accepted with probability 0.95, and bad lots are to be rejected with probability 0.90.

a. Derive a variables sampling plan for this situation.

b. Using the 1% nonconformance level as an AQL, and assuming that lots consist of 5000 panels, find an appropriate set of sampling plans from MIL STD 414. Compare the sample sizes and the protection that both producer and consumer obtain from this plan with the plan derived in part (a).

c. Find an attributes sampling plan that has the same OC curve as the variables sampling plan derived in part (a). Compare the sample sizes required for equivalent protection. Under what circumstances would variables sampling be more economically efficient?

d. Using the 1% nonconforming as an AQL, find an attributes sampling plan from MIL STD 105D. Compare the sample sizes and the protection obtained from this plan with the plans derived in parts (a), (b), and (c).

e. Develop an appropriate narrow-limit gaging plan for this situation, assuming that the formaldehyde emission rate is normally distributed. Compare the sample size in the narrow-limit gaging plan with the sample sizes for the plans obtained in parts (a), (b), (c), and (d).

Chapter 15

Other Acceptance-Sampling Procedures

This chapter presents three techniques that are frequently useful in acceptance sampling: chain sampling, continuous sampling, and skip-lot sampling plans. In addition, the impact of inspection error on acceptance sampling is discussed, and the economic design of acceptance-sampling procedures is introduced.

15-1 CHAIN SAMPLING

In situations where testing is destructive or very expensive, sampling plans with small sample sizes are usually selected. These small sample size plans often have acceptance numbers of zero. Plans with zero acceptance numbers are often undesirable, however, in that their OC curves are convex throughout. This means that the probability of lot acceptance begins to drop very rapidly as the lot fraction defective becomes greater than zero. This is often unfair to the producer, and in situations where rectifying inspection is used, it can require the consumer to screen a large number of lots that are essentially of acceptable quality. Figures 13-5 and 13-7 in Chapter 13 present OC curves of sampling plans that have acceptance numbers of zero and acceptance numbers that are greater than zero.

Dodge (1955) suggested an alternate procedure, known as chain sampling, that might be a substitute for ordinary single-sampling plans with zero acceptance numbers in certain circumstances. Chain-sampling plans make use of the cumulative results of several preceding lots. The general procedure is as follows:

1. For each lot, select the sample of size n and observe the number of defectives.
2. If the sample has zero defectives, accept the lot; if the sample has two or more defectives, reject the lot; and if the sample has one defective, accept the lot provided there have been no defectives in the previous i lots.

Thus, for a chain-sampling plan given by $n = 5$, $i = 3$, a lot would be accepted if there were no defectives in the sample of five, or if there was one defective in the sample of five and no defectives had been observed in the samples from the previous three lots. This type of plan is known as a ChSP-1 plan.

The effect of chain sampling is to alter the shape of the OC curve near the origin so that it has a more desirable shape. That is, it is more difficult to reject lots with very small fraction defectives with a ChSP-1 plan than it is with ordinary single sampling. Figure 15-1 shows OC curves for ChSP-1 plans with $n = 5$, $c = 0$, and $i = 1, 2, 3$, and 5. The curve for $i = 1$ is dotted, and it is not a preferred choice. In practice, values of i usually vary between three and five, since the OC curves of such plans approximate the single-sampling plan OC curve. The points on the OC curve of a ChSP-1 plan are given by the equation

$$P_a = P(0, n) + P(1, n)[P(0, n)]^i \qquad (15\text{-}1)$$

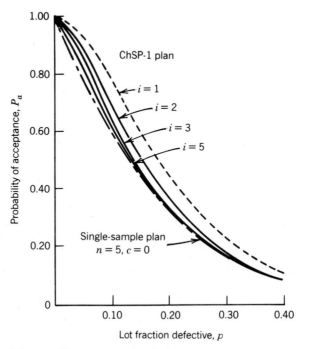

FIGURE 15-1
OC curves for ChSP-1 plan with $n = 5$, $c = 0$, and $i = 1, 2, 3, 5$. (Reproduced with permission from H. F. Dodge, "Chain Sampling Inspection Plans," *Industrial Quality Control*, Vol. 11, No. 4, 1955.)

where $P(0, n)$ and $P(1, n)$ are the probabilities of obtaining 0 and 1 defectives, respectively, out of a random sample of size n. To illustrate the computations, consider the ChSP-1 plan with $n = 5$, $c = 0$, and $i = 3$. For $p = 0.10$, we have

$$P(0, n) = \frac{n!}{d!(n - d)!} p^d (1 - p)^{n - d} = \frac{5!}{0!5!} (0.10)^0 (0.90)^5 = 0.590$$

$$P(1, n) = \frac{n!}{d!(n - d)!} p^d (1 - p)^{n - d} = \frac{5!}{1!(5 - 1)!} (0.10)^1 (0.90)^4 = 0.328$$

and

$$P_a = P(0, n) + P(1, n)[P(0, n)]^i$$
$$= 0.590 + (0.328)(0.590)^3$$
$$= 0.657$$

The proper use of chain sampling requires that the following conditions be met:

1. The lot should be one of a series in a continuing stream of lots, from a process where there is repetitive production under the same conditions, and where the lots of products are offered for acceptance in substantially the order of production.
2. Lots should usually be expected to be of essentially the same quality.
3. The sampling agency should have no reason to believe that the current lot is of poorer quality than those immediately preceding.
4. There should be a good record of quality performance on the part of the vendor.
5. The sampling agency must have confidence in the supplier, in that the supplier will not take advantage of its good record and occasionally send a bad lot when such a lot would have the best chance of acceptance.

15-2 CONTINUOUS SAMPLING

All the sampling plans discussed previously are lot-by-lot plans. With these plans, there is an explicit assumption that the product is formed into lots, and the purpose of the sampling plan is to sentence the individual lots. However, many manufacturing operations, particularly complex assembly processes, do not result in the natural formation of lots. For example, manufacturing of many electronics products, such as personal computers, is performed on a conveyorized assembly line.

When production is continuous, two approaches may be used to form lots. The first procedure allows the accumulation of production at given points in the assembly process. This has the disadvantage of creating in-process inventory at various points, which requires additional space, may constitute a safety hazard, and is a generally inefficient approach to managing an assembly line. The second procedure arbitrarily marks off a given segment of production as a "lot." The disadvantage of this approach is that if a lot is ultimately rejected, and 100% inspection of the lot is subsequently required, it may be necessary to recall products from manufacturing operations that are further downstream. This may require disassembly or at least partial destruction of semifinished items.

For these reasons, special sampling plans for continuous production have been developed. Continuous-sampling plans consist of alternating sequences of sampling inspection and screening (100% inspection). The plans usually begin with 100% inspection, and when a stated number of units is found to be free of defects (the number of units i is usually called the *clearance number*), sampling inspection is instituted. Sampling inspection continues until a specified number of defective units is found, at which time 100% inspection is resumed. Continuous-sampling plans are rectifying inspection plans, in that the quality of the product is improved by the partial screening.

15-2.1 CSP-1

Continuous-sampling plans were first proposed by Harold F. Dodge (1943). Dodge's initial plan is called CSP-1. At the start of the plan, all units are inspected 100%. As soon as the clearance number has been reached—that is, as soon as i consecutive units of product are found to be free of defects—100% inspection is discontinued, and only a fraction (f) of the units is inspected. These sample units are selected one at a time at random from the flow of production. If a sample unit is found to be defective, 100% inspection is resumed. All defective units found are either reworked or replaced with good ones. The procedure for CSP-1 is shown in Figure 15-2.

A CSP-1 plan has an overall AOQL. The value of the AOQL depends on the values of the clearance number i and the sampling fraction f. The same AOQL can be obtained by different combinations of i and f. Table 15-1 presents various values of i and f for CSP-1 that will lead to a stipulated AOQL. Notice in the table that an AOQL of 0.79% could be obtained using a sampling plan with $i = 59$ and $f = \frac{1}{3}$, or with $i = 113$ and $f = \frac{1}{7}$.

The choice of i and f is usually based on practical considerations in the manufacturing process. For example, i and f may be influenced by the workload of the inspectors and operators in the system. It is a fairly common practice to use quality-assurance inspectors to do the sampling inspection, and place the burden of 100% inspection on manufacturing. As a general rule, however, it is not a good idea to choose values of f smaller than $\frac{1}{200}$ because the protection against bad quality in a continuous run of production then becomes very poor.

The average number of units inspected in a 100% screening sequence following the occurrence of a defect is equal to

$$u = \frac{1 - q^i}{pq^i} \tag{15-2}$$

where $q = 1 - p$, and p is the fraction defective produced when the process is operating in control. The average number of units passed under the sampling inspection procedure before a defective unit is found is

$$v = \frac{1}{fp} \tag{15-3}$$

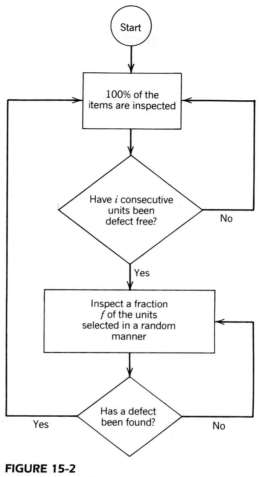

FIGURE 15-2
Procedure for CSP-1 plans.

The average fraction of total manufactured units inspected in the long run equals

$$\text{AFI} = \frac{u + fv}{u + v} \tag{15-4}$$

The average fraction of manufactured units passed under the sampling procedure is

$$P_a = \frac{v}{u + v} \tag{15-5}$$

When P_a is plotted as a function of p, we obtain an operating-characteristic curve for a continuous-sampling plan. Note that while an OC curve for a lot-by-lot acceptance-sampling plan gives the percentage of lots that would be passed under sampling inspection, the OC curve for a continuous-sampling plan gives

Table 15-1
Values of i for CSP-1 plans

f	AOQL (%)															
	0.018	0.033	0.046	0.074	0.113	0.143	0.198	0.33	0.53	0.79	1.22	1.90	2.90	4.94	7.12	11.46
$\frac{1}{2}$	1,540	840	600	375	245	194	140	84	53	36	23	15	10	6	5	3
$\frac{1}{3}$	2,550	1,390	1,000	620	405	321	232	140	87	59	38	25	16	10	7	5
$\frac{1}{4}$	3,340	1,820	1,310	810	530	420	303	182	113	76	49	32	21	13	9	6
$\frac{1}{5}$	3,960	2,160	1,550	965	630	498	360	217	135	91	58	38	25	15	11	7
$\frac{1}{7}$	4,950	2,700	1,940	1,205	790	623	450	270	168	113	73	47	31	18	13	8
$\frac{1}{10}$	6,050	3,300	2,370	1,470	965	762	550	335	207	138	89	57	38	22	16	10
$\frac{1}{15}$	7,390	4,030	2,890	1,800	1,180	930	672	410	255	170	108	70	46	27	19	12
$\frac{1}{25}$	9,110	4,970	3,570	2,215	1,450	1,147	828	500	315	210	134	86	57	33	23	14
$\frac{1}{50}$	11,730	6,400	4,590	2,855	1,870	1,477	1,067	640	400	270	175	110	72	42	29	18
$\frac{1}{100}$	14,320	7,810	5,600	3,485	2,305	1,820	1,302	790	500	330	215	135	89	52	36	22
$\frac{1}{200}$	17,420	9,500	6,810	4,235	2,760	2,178	1,583	950	590	400	255	165	106	62	43	26

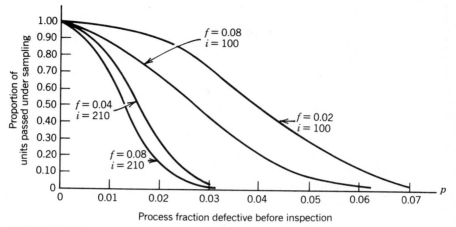

FIGURE 15-3
Operating-characteristic curves for various continuous sampling plans, CSP-1. (Adapted with permission from A. J. Duncan, *Quality Control and Industrial Statistics,* 4th ed., Irwin, Homewood, Ill., 1974.)

the percentage of units passed under sampling inspection. Graphs of operating-characteristic curves for several values of f and i for CSP-1 plans are shown in Figure 15-3. Note that for moderate-to-small values of f, i has much more effect on the shape of the curve than does f.

CSP-1 plans are used extensively in complex assembly processes for high-technology products. In these types of situations, it is customary to inspect for defects rather than defective units. CSP-1 plans may be applied separately to different classes of defects, say major and minor. It is not uncommon to have different values of i for each class of defect, but it is usually convenient to use the same f. Note that it would be possible for production to be under 100% inspection for major defects, but under sampling inspection for minor defects, or vice versa. In addition, if production is under 100% inspection for major defects, but under sampling inspection for minor defects, the discovery of a unit with a minor defect among the nonsampled units being 100% inspected for major defects should not be the basis for shifting from sampling to 100% inspection of minor defects. The same rule would apply when minor defects are under 100% inspection and major defects are under sampling inspection.

A final comment should be made about the importance of random sampling when using continuous-sampling plans. Since the items are being produced on a continuous manufacturing line, and the units are in a definite sequence, it would seem that this situation would lend itself easily to the use of random numbers. This could be done in one of two ways. For each group of $1/f$ items, a number could be selected from a group of random numbers ranging between 1 and $1/f$. Thus, if $f = 0.10$, for each group of 10 items manufactured we could select a random number from the interval 1 to 10 from a table of random numbers, and this would indicate the items to be sampled. The second method would be to use a table of random numbers to determine whether each individual item on the line should be inspected or passed without inspection. If the random number were less than 0.1, the item would be inspected.

15-2.2 CSP-2, CSP-3, and Multilevel Plans

There have been a number of variations in the original Dodge CSP-1 plan. One variation was designed to meet the objection that the occurrence of a single isolated defective unit sometimes does not warrant return to 100% inspection. This is particularly true when dealing with minor defects. To meet this objection, Dodge and Torrey (1951) proposed CSP-2 and CSP-3. Under CSP-2, 100% inspection will not be reinstated when production is under sampling inspection until two defective sample units have been found within a space of K sample units of each other. It is common practice to choose K equal to the clearance number i. Figure 15-4 shows the procedure for CSP-2 when K equals i. CSP-2 plans are indexed by specific AOQLs that may be obtained by different combinations of i and f, as shown in Table 15-2. Thus, $i = 54$, $f = \frac{1}{2}$, and $i = 155$, $f = \frac{1}{7}$ are two CSP-2 plans that would produce an AOQL of 0.79%. CSP-3 is very similar to CSP-2, but is designed to give additional protection against spotty production. It requires that after a defective unit has been found in sampling inspection, the immediately following four units should be inspected. If any of these four units is defective, 100% inspection is immediately reinstituted. If no defectives are found, the plan continues as under CSP-2.

Another common objection to continuous-sampling plans is the abrupt transition between sampling inspection and 100% inspection. Lieberman and Solomon (1955) have designed multilevel continuous-sampling plans to overcome this objection. Multilevel continuous-sampling plans begin with 100% inspection, as does CSP-1, and switches to inspecting a fraction f of the production as soon as the clearance number i has been reached. However, when under sampling inspection at rate f, a run of i consecutive sample units is found free of defects, then sampling continues at the rate f^2. If a further run of i consecutive units is found to be free of defects, then sampling may continue at the rate f^3. This reduction in sampling frequency may be continued as far as the sampling agency wishes. If at any time sampling inspection reveals a defective unit, return is immediately made to the next lower level of sampling. This type of multilevel continuous-sampling plan greatly reduces the inspection effort when the manufacturing process is operating

Table 15-2
Values of i for CSP-2 plans

f	0.53	0.79	1.22	1.90	2.90	4.94	7.12	11.46
				AOQL %				
$\frac{1}{2}$	80	54	35	23	15	9	7	4
$\frac{1}{3}$	128	86	55	36	24	14	10	7
$\frac{1}{4}$	162	109	70	45	30	18	12	8
$\frac{1}{5}$	190	127	81	52	35	20	14	9
$\frac{1}{7}$	230	155	99	64	42	25	17	11
$\frac{1}{10}$	275	185	118	76	50	29	20	13
$\frac{1}{15}$	330	220	140	90	59	35	24	15
$\frac{1}{25}$	395	265	170	109	71	42	29	18
$\frac{1}{50}$	490	330	210	134	88	52	36	22

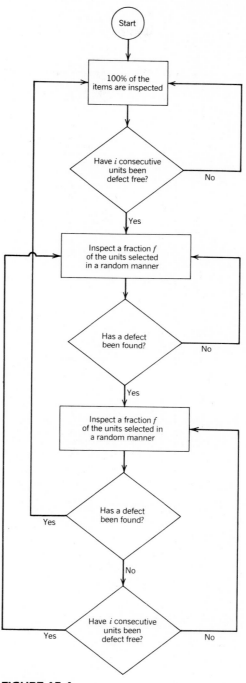

FIGURE 15-4
Procedure for CSP-2 plans.

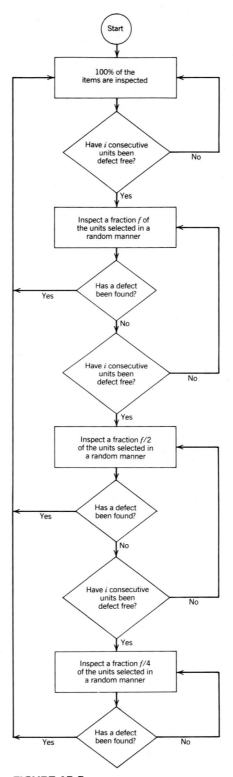

FIGURE 15-5
Procedure for CSP-T plans.

very well, and increases it during periods of poor production. This transition in inspection intensity is also accomplished without abrupt changes in the inspection load.

15-2.3 MIL STD 1235B

Much of the work on continuous-sampling plans has been incorporated into MIL STD 1235B. The standard provides for five different types of continuous-sampling plans. Tables to assist the analyst in designing sampling plans are presented in the standard. CSP-1 and CSP-2 are a part of MIL STD 1235B. In addition, there are two other single-level continuous-sampling procedures, CSP-F and CSP-V. The fifth plan in the standard is CSP-T, a multilevel continuous-sampling plan.

The procedure for CSP-T is illustrated in Figure 15-5. CSP-T begins with 100% inspection of the production. As soon as the clearance number i has been reached, sampling inspection using a fraction f of the units produced is instituted. If i consecutive units are found in sampling inspection to be defect free, then the level of sampling is reduced to a fraction $f/2$. Once again, when i consecutive units have been found defect free in this level of sampling, reduced sampling is instituted with a fraction $f/4$ of the units produced being selected at random for sampling. In CSP-T, as soon as a defective unit has been found, 100% inspection is reinstated and the procedure starts over again.

In MIL STD 1235B, sampling plans are designated by code letters. Table 15-3 provides a range of permissible code letters based on the number of units in the production interval, which is usually taken to be an eight-hour shift. Factors that influence the selection of the sampling frequency code letter include the production rate, the inspection time required per unit of product, and the proximity to other inspection stations. If idle inspection time is an important consideration, it is more desirable to use a plan with a higher sampling frequency and a lower clearance number.

The sampling plans in MIL STD 1235B are indexed by sampling frequency code letter and AOQL. They are also indexed by the AQLs of MIL STD 105D.

Table 15-3
Sampling-frequency code letters,
MIL STD 1235B

Number of Units in Production Interval	Permissible Code Letters
2–8	A–B
9–25	A–C
26–90	A–D
91–500	A–E
501–1200	A–F
1201–3200	A–G
3201–10,000	A–H
10,001–35,000	A–I
35,001–150,000	A–J
>150,000	A–K

Table 15-4
Values of i for CSP-T plans

Sampling-Frequency Code Letter	f	AQL[a] (%)							
		0.40	0.65	1.0	1.5	2.5	4.0	6.5	10.0
A	$\frac{1}{2}$	87	58	38	25	16	10	7	5
B	$\frac{1}{3}$	116	78	51	33	22	13	9	6
C	$\frac{1}{4}$	139	93	61	39	26	15	11	7
D	$\frac{1}{5}$	158	106	69	44	29	17	12	8
E	$\frac{1}{7}$	189	127	82	53	35	21	14	9
F	$\frac{1}{10}$	224	150	97	63	41	24	17	11
G	$\frac{1}{15}$	226	179	116	74	49	29	20	13
H	$\frac{1}{25}$	324	217	141	90	59	35	24	15
I	$\frac{1}{50}$	409	274	177	114	75	44	30	19
J, K	$\frac{1}{100}$	499	335	217	139	91	53	37	23
		0.53	0.79	1.22	1.90	2.90	4.94	7.12	11.46
		AOQL (%)							

[a] AQLs are provided as indices to simplify use of this table but have no other meaning relative to the plans.

This aspect of MIL STD 1235B has sparked considerable controversy. CSP plans are not AQL plans and do not have AQLs naturally associated with them. MIL STD 105D, which does focus on the AQL, is designed for manufacturing situations in which lotting is a natural aspect of production, and provides a set of decision rules for sentencing lots so that certain AQL protection is obtained. CSP plans are designed for situations in which production is continuous and lotting is not a natural aspect of the manufacturing situation. In MIL STD 1235B, the sampling plan tables are footnoted and indicate that the AQLs have no meaning relative to the plan, and are only an index. For an example of the format of the tables, refer to Table 15-4.

15-3 SKIP-LOT SAMPLING PLANS

This section describes the development and evaluation of a system of lot-by-lot inspection plans in which a provision is made for inspecting only some fraction of the submitted lots. These plans are known as skip-lot sampling plans. Generally speaking, skip-lot sampling plans should be used only when the quality of the submitted product is good as demonstrated by the vendor's quality history.

Dodge (1956) initially presented skip-lot sampling plans as an extension of CSP-type continuous-sampling plans. In effect, a skip-lot sampling plan is the application of continuous sampling to lots rather than to individual units of production on an assembly line. The version of skip-lot sampling initially proposed by Dodge required a single determination or analysis to ascertain the lot's acceptability or nonacceptability. These plans are called SkSP-1. Skip-lot sampling plans designated SkSP-2 follow the next logical step; that is, each lot to be sentenced is sampled according to a particular attribute lot inspection plan. Perry (1973) gives a good discussion of these plans.

A skip-lot sampling plan of type SkSP-2 uses a specified lot inspection plan called the "reference-sampling plan," together with the following rules:

1. Begin with normal inspection, using the reference plan. At this stage of operation, every lot is inspected.
2. When i consecutive lots are accepted on normal inspection, switch to skipping inspection. In skipping inspection, a fraction f of the lots is inspected.
3. When a lot is rejected on skipping inspection, return to normal inspection.

The parameters f and i are the parameters of the skip-lot sampling plan SkSP-2. In general, the clearance number i is a positive integer, and the sampling fraction f lies in the interval $0 < f < 1$. When the sampling fraction $f = 1$, the skip-lot sampling plan reduces to the original reference-sampling plan. Let P denote the probability of acceptance of a lot from the reference-sampling plan. Then $P_a(f, i)$ is the probability of acceptance for the skip-lot sampling plan SkSP-2, where

$$P_a(f, i) = \frac{fP + (1 - f)P^i}{f + (1 - f)P^i} \tag{15-6}$$

It can be shown that for $f_2 < f_1$, a given value of the clearance number i, and a specified reference-sampling plan,

$$P_a(f_1, i) \le P_a(f_2, i) \tag{15-7}$$

Furthermore, for integer clearance numbers $i < j$, a fixed value of f, and a given reference-sampling plan,

$$P_a(f, j) \le P_a(f, i) \tag{15-8}$$

These properties of a skip-lot sampling plan are shown in Figures 15-6 and 15-7 for the reference-sampling plan $n = 20$, $c = 1$. The OC curve of the reference-sampling plan is also shown on these graphs.

A very important property of a skip-lot sampling plan is the average amount of inspection required. In general, skip-lot sampling plans are used where it is necessary to reduce the average amount of inspection required. The average sample number of a skip-lot sampling plan is

$$\text{ASN}(SkSP) = \text{ASN}(R)F \tag{15-9}$$

where F is the average fraction of submitted lots that are sampled and $\text{ASN}(R)$ is the average sample number of the reference-sampling plan. It can be shown that

$$F = \frac{f}{(1 - f)P^i + f} \tag{15-10}$$

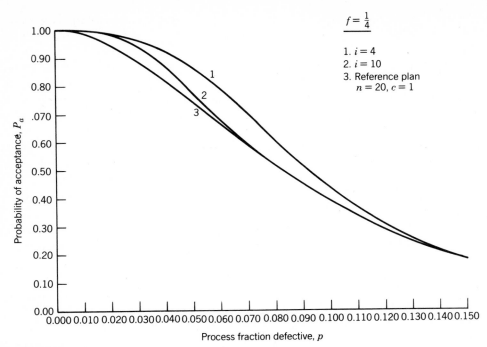

FIGURE 15-6

OC curves for SkSP-2 skip-plot plans: single-sampling reference plan, same f, different i. (From R. L. Perry, "Skip-Lot Sampling Plans," *Journal of Quality Technology,* Vol. 5, 1973, with permission of the American Society for Quality Control.)

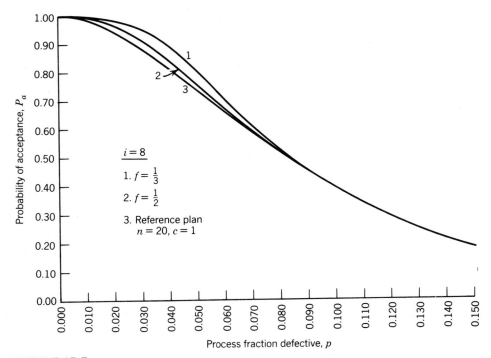

FIGURE 15-7

OC curves for SkSP-2 skip-plot plans: single-sampling reference plan, same i, different f. (From R. L. Perry, "Skip-Lot Sampling Plans," *Journal of Quality Technology,* Vol. 5, 1973, with permission of the American Society for Quality Control.)

Thus, since $0 < F < 1$, it follows that

$$\text{ASN}(SkSP) < \text{ASN}(R) \qquad (15\text{-}11)$$

Therefore, skip-lot sampling yields a reduction in the average sample number. In situations where the quality of incoming lots is very high, this reduction in inspection effort can be significant.

To illustrate the average sample number behavior of a skip-lot sampling plan, consider a reference-sampling plan of $n = 20$ and $c = 1$. Since the average sample number for a single-sampling plan is $\text{ASN} = n$, we have

$$\text{ASN}(SkSP) = n(F)$$

Figure 15-8 presents the ASN curve for the reference-sampling plan $n = 20$, $c = 1$, and the following skip-lot sampling plans:

1. $f = \frac{1}{5}$, $i = 4$
2. $f = \frac{1}{5}$, $i = 14$
3. $f = \frac{2}{3}$, $i = 4$
4. $f = \frac{2}{3}$, $i = 14$

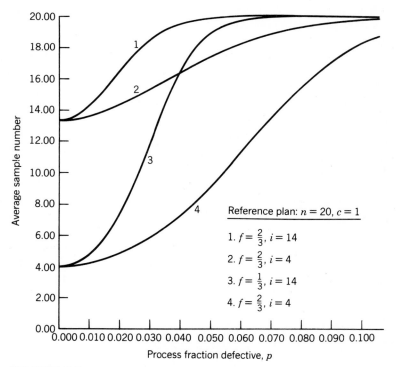

FIGURE 15-8
Average sample number (ASN) curves for SkSP-2 skip-plot plans with single-sampling reference plan. (From R. L. Perry, "Skip-Lot Sampling Plans," *Journal of Quality Technology,* Vol. 5, 1973, with permission of the American Society for Quality Control.)

From examining Figure 15-8, we note that for small values of incoming lot fraction defective, the reductions in average sample number are very substantial for the skip-lot sampling plans evaluated. If the incoming lot quality is very good, consistently close to zero fraction nonconforming, say, then a small value of f, perhaps $\frac{1}{4}$ or $\frac{1}{5}$, could be used. If incoming quality is slightly worse, then an appropriate value of f might be $\frac{1}{2}$.

Skip-lot sampling plans have had extensive industrial application in recent years. They are an effective acceptance-sampling procedure and may be highly useful as a system of reduced inspection. Their effectiveness is particularly good when the quality of submitted lots is very good. However, one should be careful to use skip-lot sampling plans only in situations where there is a sufficient history of vendor quality to ensure that the quality of submitted lots is very good. Furthermore, if the vendor's process is highly erratic and there is a great deal of variability from lot to lot, skip-lot sampling plans are inappropriate. They seem to work best when the vendor's processes are in a state of statistical control and when the process-capability ratio is sufficiently high to ensure virtually defect-free production.

15-4 CONSIDERATION OF INSPECTION ERROR

Embedded within the design of acceptance-sampling plans is an assumption that the inspection procedures are error free. However, many inspection tasks are not error free; on the contrary, they may even be error prone. Although the errors that result from inspection operations are usually unintentional, they have the effect of severely distorting the performance measures of any acceptance-sampling plan whose design has ignored their presence. It is not unusual to find inspection error rates of 25% or 30% in complex inspection activities. Better training procedures for inspectors and automation of the inspection process will reduce inspection errors, but will probably never eliminate them.

In this section, we consider the problem of evaluating and designing acceptance-sampling plans when the inspection process is subject to error. We concentrate on single-sampling plans for attributes. Since single-sampling plans are often determined by specifying producer and consumer risk points on the OC curve, a method is provided whereby desired producer and consumer risk levels can be maintained, even though the sampling process is subject to error.

Two types of errors are possible in attributes sampling. An item that is good may be classified as defective (this is called a type I error), or an item that is defective may be classified as good (this is called a type II error). Define

E_1 = event that a good item is classified as a defective

E_2 = event that a defective item is classified as good

A = event that an item is defective

B = event that an item is classified as a defective

Then,

$$P(B) = P(A)P(\bar{E}_2) + P(\bar{A})P(E_1) \qquad (15\text{-}12)$$

By defining the quantities

$$p = P(A) \qquad \text{the true fraction defective}$$
$$p_e = P(B) \qquad \text{the apparent fraction defective}$$
$$e_1 = P(E_1) \qquad \text{the probability that event } E_1 \text{ occurs}$$
$$e_2 = P(E_2) \qquad \text{the probability that event } E_2 \text{ occurs}$$

the expression for apparent fraction defective may be written as

$$p_e = p(1 - e_2) + (1 - p)e_1 \tag{15-13}$$

The OC curve of a sampling plan is a graph of the probability of lot acceptance versus the lot fraction defective. When inspection error is present, the probability of lot acceptance is just

$$P_{a(e)} = \sum_{d=0}^{c} \binom{n}{d} p_e^d (1 - p_e)^{n-d} \tag{15-14}$$

Thus, the OC curve of a sampling plan when inspection error is present may be easily obtained.

We now turn to a consideration of how inspection error impacts average outgoing quality (AOQ) and average total inspection (ATI). If inspection is error free, the AOQ for single sampling for attributes is

$$\text{AOQ} = \frac{(N - n)pP_a}{N} \tag{15-15}$$

If defective items are replaced, and if inspection of the replacements involves inspection error, then the AOQ becomes

$$\text{AOQ} = \frac{npe_2 + p(N - n)(1 - p_e)P_{a(e)} + p(N - n)(1 - P_{a(e)})e_2}{N(1 - p_e)} \tag{15-16}$$

If the defectives discovered are *not* replaced, then

$$\text{AOQ} = \frac{npe_2 + p(N - n)P_{a(e)} + p(N - n)(1 - P_{a(e)})e_2}{N - np_e - (1 - P_{a(e)})(N - n)p_e} \tag{15-17}$$

The average total inspection (ATI), assuming error-free inspection with 100% screening of rejected lots, is

$$\text{ATI} = n + (1 - P_a)(N - n) \tag{15-18}$$

The average total inspection, assuming that the defectives discovered are replaced and that the replacement process is subject to inspection error, is

$$\text{ATI} = \frac{n + (1 - P_{a(e)})(N - n)}{1 - p_e} \tag{15-19}$$

If the discovered defectives are not replaced, then

$$\text{ATI} = n + (1 - P_{a(e)})(N - n) \tag{15-20}$$

The design of a single-sampling plan for attributes is often based on the selection of two points on the OC curve. These points are typically the AQL and LTPD levels of quality, which are usually associated with the producer's risk and consumer's risk, respectively. Under conditions of inspection error, the desired AQL and LTPD fractions defective no longer have the probabilities of acceptance specified by the OC curve that would have been obtained had inspection been perfect. However, it is possible to modify the procedure for designing the acceptance-sampling plan by forcing the actual OC curve to fit the desired points.

Suppose we wish to accept lots of quality AQL with probability $1 - \alpha$, and to accept lots of quality LTPD with probability β. In order to obtain these risks, it is necessary to design the sampling plan for AQL_e and LTPD_e, where

$$\text{AQL}_e = \text{AQL}(1 - e_2) + (1 - \text{AQL})e_1 \tag{15-21}$$

and

$$\text{LTPD}_e = \text{LTPD}(1 - e_2) + (1 - \text{LTPD})e_1 \tag{15-22}$$

If the observed OC curve fits the points $(\text{AQL}_e, 1 - \alpha)$ and (LTPD_e, β), then the *actual* OC curve will fit the points $(\text{AQL}, 1 - \alpha)$ and (LTPD, β).

To illustrate this procedure, suppose that $\text{AQL} = 0.01$, $1 - \alpha = 0.95$, $\text{LTPD} = 0.06$, and $\beta = 0.10$. We have shown previously that the corresponding single-sampling plan is $n = 89$, $c = 2$. The OC curve for this sampling plan is shown in Figure 13-2. Now suppose that

$$e_1 = \text{type I error rate} = 0.01$$
$$e_2 = \text{type II error rate} = 0.15$$

Then, from (15-21) and (15-22), we have

$$\begin{aligned}
\text{AQL}_e &= \text{AQL}(1 - e_2) + (1 - \text{AQL})e_1 \\
&= 0.01(1 - 0.15) + (1 - 0.01)(0.01) \\
&= 0.0184
\end{aligned}$$

and

$$\begin{aligned}
\text{LTPD}_e &= \text{LTPD}(1 - e_2) + (1 - \text{LTPD})e_1 \\
&= 0.06(1 - 0.15) + (1 - 0.06)(0.01) \\
&= 0.0604
\end{aligned}$$

From the nomograph in Figure 13-9, the single-sampling plan passing through the points (0.0184, 0.95), (0.0604, 0.10) has parameters $n = 150$, $c = 5$. Note that inspection error greatly increases the sample size required to obtain the desired protection at the AQL = 0.01 and LTPD = 0.06, respectively.

We may find a point at which apparent and actual fractions defective are equal, that is, the point at which $p = p_e$. This level of quality is

$$p = \frac{e_1}{e_1 + e_2} \tag{15-23}$$

Thus, in the previous example, the apparent and actual fractions defective are only equal at lot fraction defective

$$p = \frac{e_1}{e_1 + e_2} = \frac{0.01}{0.01 + 0.15} = 0.0625$$

In general, the effect of a type I inspection error is to reduce the probability of acceptance for all possible values of lot fraction defective p. Similarly, the effect of a type II inspection error is to increase the probability of acceptance for all possible values of lot quality p. These results are anticipated, since a type I error occurs when a good item is incorrectly classified as defective, and a type II error occurs when a defective item is incorrectly classified as good. If inspection is subject to both type I and type II inspection errors, then the observed probability of acceptance is less than that obtained in an error-free inspection environment for values of lot quality p less than

$$p^* = \frac{e_1}{e_1 + e_2} \tag{15-24}$$

For values of lot quality greater than p^*, the observed probability of acceptance is greater than that which would have been obtained if there were no inspection error.

Inspection error also has an effect on the average outgoing quality. Incorrect classification of a good item reduces the average outgoing quality because more screening inspection occurs. Incorrect classification of a defective item has the effect of causing higher AOQ values for all values of lot fraction defective, because it reduces the likelihood that lots will be screened. Type II inspection errors also cause a significant change in the shape of the AOQ curve. At the level of quality at which the probability of acceptance under error-prone inspection approaches zero, the AOQ curve rises sharply as a result of the increased number of defective items classified as good. Therefore, if the sampling procedure is subject to type II inspection errors, the conventional means of the average outgoing quality limit (AOQL) may not be meaningful.

Type I and type II inspection errors also impact average total inspection. The general effect of a type I inspection error is to increase the average total inspection. Similarly, the effect of a type II inspection error is to decrease the average total inspection.

15-5 ECONOMIC DESIGN OF ACCEPTANCE-SAMPLING PLANS

The traditional approach to designing acceptance-sampling plans is to use statistical criteria only. Specifically, the approach often suggested is to specify an operating-characteristic curve and a type of sampling plan (such as single sampling, doubling sampling, and so forth), and then to choose the parameters of the plan to obtain this desired OC curve. We usually specify two points on the curve, such as the producer's and consumer's risk points, and the resulting sampling plan is often referred to as a "two-point" sampling plan.

It is also possible to design acceptance-sampling schemes with respect to economic criteria. There has been considerable interest in this subject in recent years, because of the increasing focus of attention on the cost of quality. Economically based sampling plans explicitly consider such factors as the costs of inspection, the costs of passing defective items, and the costs of rejecting good products in an effort to design a cost-effective plan. Quite often these plans are designed from a Bayesian viewpoint; that is, the sampling plan design takes into account the past history of similar lots submitted previously for inspection.

Bayesian sampling plans require the designer to specify explicitly the distribution of defectives from lot to lot. This distribution is called the *prior distribution*. The prior distribution describes the sampling plan designer's beliefs, prior to sampling, about the distribution of defectives from lot to lot. Decisions to accept the lot are then based on a posterior distribution that combines the user's prior knowledge along with sampling inspection results.

An attribute single-sampling plan is indexed by three numbers: the lot size N, the sample size n, and the acceptance number c. If, in a random sample of size n, c or fewer defectives are found, the lot is accepted, while if more than c defectives are found, the lot is rejected. The probability of lot acceptance is

$$P_a(\theta) = \sum_{d=0}^{c} \frac{\binom{N\theta}{d}\binom{N - N\theta}{n - d}}{\binom{N}{n}} \tag{15-25}$$

where θ is the lot fraction defective. The plot of $P_a(\theta)$ versus θ for $0 \le \theta \le 1$ is called the operating-characteristic curve (or OC curve) of the plan. When N is large relative to n, the hypergeometric distribution in (15-25) can be replaced by the binomial.

Lot fraction defective θ is a function of two sources of variability: the variability of p the process fraction defective, and the variability of θ about p. It is usually convenient to assume that lot quality has a mixed binomial distribution; that is, each lot is produced by a production process that is in control at the level p, but p varies from lot to lot according to a probability distribution $f(p)$. The distribution $f(p)$ is the prior distribution for p or the *process curve*. It is extremely important to note that if the process quality is stable such that $f(p) = 1$ when $p = p_0$ and $f(p) = 0$ when $p \ne p_0$, then there is no need for sampling. (This result is called Mood's theorem.)

While there are many possible choices for the prior distribution for p, some of the more important are the following: the continuous beta distribution

$$f(p) = \frac{\Gamma(u + v)}{\Gamma(u)\Gamma(v)} p^{u-1}(1 - p)^{v-1} \tag{15-26}$$

the discrete two-point binomial

$$P(p = p_i) = f_i \qquad i = 1, 2 \tag{15-27}$$

and the normal-generated distribution

$$f(p) = \sigma^{-1} \exp[\tfrac{1}{2}\mu^2 - \tfrac{1}{2}(\mu - m)^2/\sigma^2] \tag{15-28}$$

where $p = \Phi(-\mu)$. In practice, it is important to know how accurately the prior distribution must be specified. Generally, the analyst does not possess sufficient information about the process to specify the prior with great confidence. Fortunately, most results indicate that precise specification of the prior is not critical, provided that a reasonable distribution is chosen. Continuous prior distributions are generally thought to be more appropriate than discrete ones, and the beta distribution has been used extensively. However, when the underlying quality characteristic is a continuous variable that is normally distributed within each lot and the mean of this quality characteristic also has a normal prior, then the prior distribution for p has the form (15-28). The beta and normal-generated distributions can have very different shapes for the same mean and variance, and so significant differences in the optimal sampling plans may result. For further discussion of prior distributions, see Wetherill and Chiu (1975).

Given a suitable prior distribution and a set of costs or losses associated with sampling plan operation, it is desirable to choose the sampling plan parameters that minimize the total cost. Perhaps the most widely used and detailed model is that of Guthrie and Johns (1959). A simplified form of this model is also presented by Hald (1960). The model is a *linear* cost model. All linear cost formulations lead to the same expected loss function. Hald utilizes the concept of *break-even quality* p_r, a fraction defective value at which it is just as costly to accept as to reject the lot. The expected loss per lot is

$$L = an + (N - n)\left\{ \int_0^{p_r} (p_r - p)[1 - P(p)]f(p)\,dp \right.$$
$$\left. + \int_{p_r}^1 (p - p_r)P(p)f(p)\,dp \right\} \tag{15-29}$$

where a is a constant proportional to the variable cost of sampling and

$$P_a(p) = \sum_{d=0}^c \binom{n}{d} p^d (1 - p)^{n-d}$$

is the probability of accepting a lot of quality p. Minimizing L with respect to n and c will produce the optimal sampling plan. This is sometimes called the Bayesian approach to designing a sampling plan.

The major focus of the research in this area started with the Guthrie and Johns model. Hald has been a major contributor in the field, along with some of his co-workers. The major emphasis has been on finding asymptotic relationships between n and c for various process curves and in producing tables suitable for use by professional practitioners. Hald (1960) gives a number of significant findings in his paper. One part of the paper investigates the *compound hypergeometric distribution*, that is, the probability distribution of the number of defectives d in a random sample of size n given a prior distribution. The second part of the paper is directed toward actually finding optimum sampling plans for rectangular, beta, and double binomial priors. A general solution is given assuming the linear cost model and inequalities are given for n and c. Hald (1965) provided tables for the double binomial prior and subsequently [see Hald (1968)] has provided tables for the beta prior, along with asymptotic relationships between n and c, and between N and n.

Despite the significance of Hald's work, the tables he has provided are often difficult to use because of the large amount of information required. An alternative approach consists of formulating an appropriate cost model and optimizing it for a specific problem using direct search methods. Considerable work in this area has been done by G. K. Bennett, K. E. Case, and J. W. Schmidt and their students. For example, their 1975 paper develops economic models for single-sampling plans for single-sampling plans for dealing simultaneously with multiple attributes. The cost models consist of a component representing inspection costs, a component representing the expected cost of lot rejection, and a component representing the expected cost of lot acceptance. Pattern search is used for model optimization. In general, direct search methods are a very efffective approach for determining economically optimal acceptance-sampling plans.

The economic impact of the disposition policy for rejected lots has also been investigated. While there are a number of possible lot disposition policies, the two cases that have been investigated most extensively are those in which rejected lots are either scrapped or screened (100% inspection).

There have been many other studies devoted to the economic design of acceptance-sampling plans; for instance, a survey paper by Wetherill and Chiu (1975) cites 253 references. While most of the work focuses on single sampling for attributes, some research has been done on the economic design of more sophisticated sampling plans. For example, Stewart, Montgomery, and Heikes (1978) describe a procedure for the selection of double-sampling plans for attributes based on prior distributions and costs. Models are presented for cases where rejected lots are either screened or scrapped. They note that there is often little difference in cost between economically optimal single- and double-sampling plans. However, when sampling costs are large, double-sampling plans have much to offer. They also observe that arbitrary double-sampling plans, such as those in MIL STD 105D, may be very far from economically optimum.

The effect of inspection error on sampling plan design has also received considerable attention. If an inspector misclassifies good and bad items with constant probabilities, the effect is to translate the OC curve of the sampling plan, so that the *actual* or *effective* OC curve is somewhat different from the *nominal* or *advertised* OC curve. If the probabilities of misclassification are known, then one may directly incorporate this information into the economic design of the sampling plan. Generally, the presence of inspection errors implies that larger samples are necessary. A good review of the literature in this area is presented in Dorris and Foote (1978).

Very little attention has been given to acceptance sampling by variables. While variables samplig is not as widely used in practice as attributes sampling, remember that variables sampling can greatly reduce the required sample size and that it does generally provide better information about the lot or process quality. For work on the economic design of variables sampling plans, see Ailor, Schmidt, and Bennett (1975), Schmidt, Bennett, and Case (1976), and Schmidt, Case, and Bennett (1974). Ailor, Schmidt, and Bennett (1975) deal with the situation where the quality characteristics are a mixture of attributes and variables. In all these studies, the approach taken is to formulate a cost model and to optimize it via direct search methods.

15-6 Exercises

15-1 Consider a single-sampling plan with $n = 25$, $c = 0$. Draw the OC curve for this plan. Now consider chain-sampling plans with $n = 25$, $c = 0$, and $i = 1, 2, 5, 7$. Sketch the OC curves for these chain-sampling plans on the same axis. Discuss the behavior of chain sampling in this situation compared to the conventional single-sampling plan with $c = 0$.

15-2 An electronics manufacturer buys LSI memory elements in large lots from a vendor. The vendor has a long record of good quality performance, with an average fraction defective of approximately 0.10%. The quality engineering department has suggested using a conventional acceptance-sampling plan with $n = 32$, $c = 0$.

  a. Draw the OC curve of this sampling plan.

  b. If lots are of a quality that is near the vendor's long-term process average, what is the average total inspection at that level of quality?

  c. Consider a chain-sampling plan with $n = 32$, $c = 0$, and $i = 3$. Contrast the performance of this plan with the conventional sampling plan $n = 32$, $c = 0$.

  d. How would the performance of this chain-sampling plan change if we substituted $i = 4$ in part (c)?

15-3 A ChSP-1 plan has $n = 4$, $c = 0$, and $i = 3$. Draw the OC curve for this plan.

15-4 A chain-sampling plan is used for the inspection of lots of size $N = 500$. The sample size is $n = 6$. If the sample contains no defectives, the lot is accepted. If one defective is found, the lot is accepted provided that the samples from the four previous lots are free of defectives. Determine the probability of acceptance of a lot that is 2% defective.

15-5 Suppose that a manufacturing process operates in continuous production, such that continuous sampling plans could be applied. Determine three different CSP-1 sampling plans that could be used for an AOQL of 0.198%.

15-6 For the sampling plans developed in Exercise 15-5, compare the plans' performance in terms of average fraction inspected, given that the process is in control at an average fallout level of 0.15%. Compare the plans in terms of their operating-characteristic curves.

15-7 Suppose that CSP-1 is used for a manufacturing process where it is desired to maintain an AOQL of 1.90%. Specify two CSP-1 plans that would meet this AOQL target.

15-8 Compare the sampling plans developed in Exercise 15-7 in terms of average fraction inspected and their operating-characteristic curves. Which plan would you prefer?

15-9 Determine a CSP-2 plan that is suitable for an AOQL objective of 1.90%. Compare the difference in operation of CSP-2 and CSP-1.

15-10 Find a CSP-2 plan for an AOQL objective of 0.79% and a sampling frequency of 20%. Compare this with a CSP-1 plan that has the same AOQ objective. Describe the operation of the two procedures.

15-11 Determine a CSP-T sampling plan with an AOQL of 1.22% and a sampling frequency of 25%.

15-12 Obtain a CSP-T plan for an AOQL of 1.90% and a sampling frequency of 10%. Describe in detail how this plan would be applied to a manufacturing operation.

15-13 A single sampling for attributes is to be used in a situation where inspector error is present. Suppose that the AQL is 2% and the LTPD is 8%. The desired producer's risk is $1 - \alpha = 0.95$, and the desired consumer's risk is $\beta = 0.10$. Determine the acceptance-sampling plan that would be appropriate if no inspection error were present. If the inspection error rates are $e_1 = $ type I risk $= 0.01$ and $e_2 = $ type II risk $= 0.30$, determine the sample size and acceptance number that would have to be used in order to obtain the desired OC curve.

15-14 Sketch the AOQ curve for the two sampling plans found in Exercise 15-13. What is the impact of inspection error on the AOQ? Assume that all defective items discovered are replaced and that the inspection of replacements is also error prone.

15-15 Draw the ATI curve for the two sampling plans obtained in Exercise 15-13. What is the effect of inspection error on the ATI performance? Assume that defective items are replaced and that the inspection of replacement items is error prone.

15-16 A sampling inspection process by attributes is error prone, with error rates $e_1 = 0.05$ and $e_2 = 0.25$. Suppose that the desired AOQL $= 0.05$ and the desired LTPD $= 0.10$. The nominal values of the producer's and consumer's risks are $1 - \alpha = 0.95$ and $\beta = 0.10$, respectively.

   a. Find the sampling plan that would be appropriate if there were no inspection error.

   b. Find the sampling plan that would be used assuming that inspection is error prone, but it is desired to obtain the producer's and consumer's risk points specified above. How much has the sample size increased due to the presence of inspection error?

15-17 Draw the average outgoing quality curves for the two sampling plans generated in Exercise 15-16. Assume that defective items discovered in either sampling or 100% inspection are not replaced. What is the effect of inspection error on average outgoing quality?

15-18 Draw the ATI curves for the two sampling plans found in Exercise 15-16. Assume that defective items discovered are not replaced. What is the effect of inspection error on the average total inspection? Assume that the lot size $N = 5000$.

15-19 Consider an acceptance-sampling plan for a lot of size $N = 4000$, where $n = 150$, $c = 5$. Draw the average outgoing quality curve of this plan, assuming that there is no inspection error. Draw the average outgoing quality curve of this sampling plan, assuming that inspection is error prone with $e_1 = 0.01$ and $e_2 = 0.15$. Assume that defective items discovered during sampling and 100% inspection are not replaced. Comment on the shape of the AOQ curve.

15-20 Consider the average total inspection of an acceptance-sampling plan for attributes under inspection error. In the text, equations were given for calculating average total inspection under two cases: a policy in which defective items discovered were not replaced, and a policy under which all defective items discovered were replaced and the replacement process was itself error prone. Comment on the limiting behavior of the ATI curve in these two situations, as the observed fraction defective becomes large. Would the behavior of average total inspection under these two replacement policies affect the incremental cost of operating the sampling plan?

Appendix

Appendix I
Cumulative poisson distribution[a]

x	0.01	0.05	0.10	λ 0.20	0.30	0.40	0.50	0.60
0	0.990	0.951	0.904	0.818	0.740	0.670	0.606	0.548
1	0.999	0.998	0.995	0.982	0.963	0.938	0.909	0.878
2		0.999	0.999	0.998	0.996	0.992	0.985	0.976
3				0.999	0.999	0.999	0.998	0.996
4					0.999	0.999	0.999	0.999
5							0.999	0.999

x	0.70	0.80	0.90	λ 1.00	1.10	1.20	1.30	1.40
0	0.496	0.449	0.406	0.367	0.332	0.301	0.272	0.246
1	0.844	0.808	0.772	0.735	0.699	0.662	0.626	0.591
2	0.965	0.952	0.937	0.919	0.900	0.879	0.857	0.833
3	0.994	0.990	0.986	0.981	0.974	0.966	0.956	0.946
4	0.999	0.998	0.997	0.996	0.994	0.992	0.989	0.985
5	0.999	0.999	0.999	0.999	0.999	0.998	0.997	0.996
6		0.999	0.999	0.999	0.999	0.999	0.999	0.999
7				0.999	0.999	0.999	0.999	0.999
8							0.999	0.999

x	1.50	1.60	1.70	λ 1.80	1.90	2.00	2.10	2.20
0	0.223	0.201	0.182	0.165	0.149	0.135	0.122	0.110
1	0.557	0.524	0.493	0.462	0.433	0.406	0.379	0.354
2	0.808	0.783	0.757	0.730	0.703	0.676	0.649	0.622
3	0.934	0.921	0.906	0.891	0.874	0.857	0.838	0.819
4	0.981	0.976	0.970	0.963	0.955	0.947	0.937	0.927
5	0.995	0.993	0.992	0.989	0.986	0.983	0.979	0.975
6	0.999	0.998	0.998	0.997	0.996	0.995	0.994	0.992
7	0.999	0.999	0.999	0.999	0.999	0.998	0.998	0.998
8	0.999	0.999	0.999	0.999	0.999	0.999	0.999	0.999
9			0.999	0.999	0.999	0.999	0.999	0.999
10							0.999	0.999

[a] Entries in the table are values $F(x) = P(X \leq x) = \sum_{c=0}^{x}(e^{-\lambda}\lambda^{c}/c!)$. Blank spaces below the last entry in any column may be read as 1.0; blank spaces above the first entry in any column may be read as 0.0.

Appendix I (Continued)

x	2.30	2.40	2.50	λ 2.60	2.70	2.80	2.90	3.00
0	0.100	0.090	0.082	0.074	0.067	0.060	0.055	0.049
1	0.330	0.308	0.287	0.267	0.248	0.231	0.214	0.199
2	0.596	0.569	0.543	0.518	0.493	0.469	0.445	0.423
3	0.799	0.778	0.757	0.736	0.714	0.691	0.669	0.647
4	0.916	0.904	0.891	0.877	0.862	0.847	0.831	0.815
5	0.970	0.964	0.957	0.950	0.943	0.934	0.925	0.916
6	0.990	0.988	0.985	0.982	0.979	0.975	0.971	0.966
7	0.997	0.996	0.995	0.994	0.993	0.991	0.990	0.988
8	0.999	0.999	0.998	0.998	0.998	0.997	0.996	0.996
9	0.999	0.999	0.999	0.999	0.999	0.999	0.999	0.998
10	0.999	0.999	0.999	0.999	0.999	0.999	0.999	0.999
11			0.999	0.999	0.999	0.999	0.999	0.999
12							0.999	0.999

x	3.50	4.00	4.50	λ 5.00	5.50	6.00	6.50	7.00
0	0.030	0.018	0.011	0.006	0.004	0.002	0.001	0.000
1	0.135	0.091	0.061	0.040	0.026	0.017	0.011	0.007
2	0.320	0.238	0.173	0.124	0.088	0.061	0.043	0.029
3	0.536	0.433	0.342	0.265	0.201	0.151	0.111	0.081
4	0.725	0.628	0.532	0.440	0.357	0.285	0.223	0.172
5	0.857	0.785	0.702	0.615	0.528	0.445	0.369	0.300
6	0.934	0.889	0.831	0.762	0.686	0.606	0.526	0.449
7	0.973	0.948	0.913	0.866	0.809	0.743	0.672	0.598
8	0.990	0.978	0.959	0.931	0.894	0.847	0.791	0.729
9	0.996	0.991	0.982	0.968	0.946	0.916	0.877	0.830
10	0.998	0.997	0.993	0.986	0.974	0.957	0.933	0.901
11	0.999	0.999	0.997	0.994	0.989	0.979	0.966	0.946
12	0.999	0.999	0.999	0.997	0.995	0.991	0.983	0.973
13	0.999	0.999	0.999	0.999	0.998	0.996	0.992	0.987
14		0.999	0.999	0.999	0.999	0.998	0.997	0.994
15			0.999	0.999	0.999	0.999	0.998	0.997
16				0.999	0.999	0.999	0.999	0.999
17					0.999	0.999	0.999	0.999
18						0.999	0.999	0.999
19							0.999	0.999
20								0.999

(*continued*)

Appendix I (Continued)

x	7.50	8.00	8.50	λ 9.00	9.50	10.0	15.0	20.0
0	0.000	0.000	0.000	0.000	0.000	0.000	0.000	0.000
1	0.004	0.003	0.001	0.001	0.000	0.000	0.000	0.000
2	0.020	0.013	0.009	0.006	0.004	0.002	0.000	0.000
3	0.059	0.042	0.030	0.021	0.014	0.010	0.000	0.000
4	0.132	0.099	0.074	0.054	0.040	0.029	0.000	0.000
5	0.241	0.191	0.149	0.115	0.088	0.067	0.002	0.000
6	0.378	0.313	0.256	0.206	0.164	0.130	0.007	0.000
7	0.524	0.452	0.385	0.323	0.268	0.220	0.018	0.000
8	0.661	0.592	0.523	0.455	0.391	0.332	0.037	0.002
9	0.776	0.716	0.652	0.587	0.521	0.457	0.069	0.005
10	0.862	0.815	0.763	0.705	0.645	0.583	0.118	0.010
11	0.920	0.888	0.848	0.803	0.751	0.696	0.184	0.021
12	0.957	0.936	0.909	0.875	0.836	0.791	0.267	0.039
13	0.978	0.965	0.948	0.926	0.898	0.864	0.363	0.066
14	0.989	0.982	0.972	0.958	0.940	0.916	0.465	0.104
15	0.995	0.991	0.986	0.977	0.966	0.951	0.568	0.156
16	0.998	0.996	0.993	0.988	0.982	0.972	0.664	0.221
17	0.999	0.998	0.997	0.994	0.991	0.985	0.748	0.297
18	0.999	0.999	0.998	0.997	0.995	0.992	0.819	0.381
19	0.999	0.999	0.999	0.998	0.998	0.996	0.875	0.470
20	0.999	0.999	0.999	0.999	0.999	0.998	0.917	0.559
21	0.999	0.999	0.999	0.999	0.999	0.999	0.946	0.643
22		0.999	0.999	0.999	0.999	0.999	0.967	0.720
23			0.999	0.999	0.999	0.999	0.980	0.787
24					0.999	0.999	0.988	0.843
25						0.999	0.993	0.887
26							0.996	0.922
27							0.998	0.947
28							0.999	0.965
29							0.999	0.978
30							0.999	0.986
31							0.999	0.991
32							0.999	0.995
33							0.999	0.997
34								0.998

Appendix II
Cumulative standard normal distribution

$$\Phi(z) = \int_{-\infty}^{z} \frac{1}{\sqrt{2\pi}} e^{-u^2/2} \, du$$

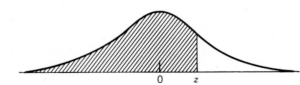

z	0.00	0.01	0.02	0.03	0.04	z
0.0	0.50000	0.50399	0.50798	0.51197	0.51595	0.0
0.1	0.53983	0.54379	0.54776	0.55172	0.55567	0.1
0.2	0.57926	0.58317	0.58706	0.59095	0.59483	0.2
0.3	0.61791	0.62172	0.62551	0.62930	0.63307	0.3
0.4	0.65542	0.65910	0.62276	0.66640	0.67003	0.4
0.5	0.69146	0.69497	0.69847	0.70194	0.70540	0.5
0.6	0.72575	0.72907	0.73237	0.73565	0.73891	0.6
0.7	0.75803	0.76115	0.76424	0.76730	0.77035	0.7
0.8	0.78814	0.79103	0.79389	0.79673	0.79954	0.8
0.9	0.81594	0.81859	0.82121	0.82381	0.82639	0.9
1.0	0.84134	0.84375	0.84613	0.84849	0.85083	1.0
1.1	0.86433	0.86650	0.86864	0.87076	0.87285	1.1
1.2	0.88493	0.88686	0.88877	0.89065	0.89251	1.2
1.3	0.90320	0.90490	0.90658	0.90824	0.90988	1.3
1.4	0.91924	0.92073	0.92219	0.92364	0.92506	1.4
1.5	0.93319	0.93448	0.93574	0.93699	0.93822	1.5
1.6	0.94520	0.94630	0.94738	0.94845	0.94950	1.6
1.7	0.95543	0.95637	0.95728	0.95818	0.95907	1.7
1.8	0.96407	0.96485	0.96562	0.96637	0.96711	1.8
1.9	0.97128	0.97193	0.97257	0.97320	0.97381	1.9
2.0	0.97725	0.97778	0.97831	0.97882	0.97932	2.0
2.1	0.98214	0.98257	0.98300	0.98341	0.98382	2.1
2.2	0.98610	0.98645	0.98679	0.98713	0.98745	2.2
2.3	0.98928	0.98956	0.98983	0.99010	0.99036	2.3
2.4	0.99180	0.99202	0.99224	0.99245	0.99266	2.4
2.5	0.99379	0.99396	0.99413	0.99430	0.99446	2.5
2.6	0.99534	0.99547	0.99560	0.99573	0.99585	2.6
2.7	0.99653	0.99664	0.99674	0.99683	0.99693	2.7
2.8	0.99744	0.99752	0.99760	0.99767	0.99774	2.8
2.9	0.99813	0.99819	0.99825	0.99831	0.99836	2.9
3.0	0.99865	0.99869	0.99874	0.99878	0.99882	3.0
3.1	0.99903	0.99906	0.99910	0.99913	0.99916	3.1
3.2	0.99931	0.99934	0.99936	0.99938	0.99940	3.2
3.3	0.99952	0.99953	0.99955	0.99957	0.99958	3.3
3.4	0.99966	0.99968	0.99969	0.99970	0.99971	3.4
3.5	0.99977	0.99978	0.99978	0.99979	0.99980	3.5
3.6	0.99984	0.99985	0.99985	0.99986	0.99986	3.6
3.7	0.99989	0.99990	0.99990	0.99990	0.99991	3.7
3.8	0.99993	0.99993	0.99993	0.99994	0.99994	3.8
3.9	0.99995	0.99995	0.99996	0.99996	0.99996	3.9

(continued)

Appendix II (Continued)

$$\Phi(z) = \int_{-\infty}^{z} \frac{1}{\sqrt{2\pi}} e^{-u^2/2} \, du$$

z	0.05	0.06	0.07	0.08	0.09	z
0.0	0.51994	0.52392	0.52790	0.53188	0.53586	0.0
0.1	0.55962	0.56356	0.56749	0.57142	0.57534	0.1
0.2	0.59871	0.60257	0.60642	0.61026	0.61409	0.2
0.3	0.63683	0.64058	0.64431	0.64803	0.65173	0.3
0.4	0.67364	0.67724	0.68082	0.68438	0.68793	0.4
0.5	0.70884	0.71226	0.71566	0.71904	0.72240	0.5
0.6	0.74215	0.74537	0.74857	0.75175	0.75490	0.6
0.7	0.77337	0.77637	0.77935	0.78230	0.78523	0.7
0.8	0.80234	0.80510	0.80785	0.81057	0.81327	0.8
0.9	0.82894	0.83147	0.83397	0.83646	0.83891	0.9
1.0	0.85314	0.85543	0.85769	0.85993	0.86214	1.0
1.1	0.87493	0.87697	0.87900	0.88100	0.88297	1.1
1.2	0.89435	0.89616	0.89796	0.89973	0.90147	1.2
1.3	0.91149	0.91308	0.91465	0.91621	0.91773	1.3
1.4	0.92647	0.92785	0.92922	0.93056	0.93189	1.4
1.5	0.93943	0.94062	0.94179	0.94295	0.94408	1.5
1.6	0.95053	0.95154	0.95254	0.95352	0.95448	1.6
1.7	0.95994	0.96080	0.96164	0.96246	0.96327	1.7
1.8	0.96784	0.96856	0.96926	0.96995	0.97062	1.8
1.9	0.97441	0.97500	0.97558	0.97615	0.97670	1.9
2.0	0.97982	0.98030	0.98077	0.98124	0.98169	2.0
2.1	0.98422	0.98461	0.98500	0.98537	0.98574	2.1
2.2	0.98778	0.98809	0.98840	0.98870	0.98899	2.2
2.3	0.99061	0.99086	0.99111	0.99134	0.99158	2.3
2.4	0.99286	0.99305	0.99324	0.99343	0.99361	2.4
2.5	0.99461	0.99477	0.99492	0.99506	0.99520	2.5
2.6	0.99598	0.99609	0.99621	0.99632	0.99643	2.6
2.7	0.99702	0.99711	0.99720	0.99728	0.99736	2.7
2.8	0.99781	0.99788	0.99795	0.99801	0.99807	2.8
2.9	0.99841	0.99846	0.99851	0.99856	0.99861	2.9
3.0	0.99886	0.99889	0.99893	0.99897	0.99900	3.0
3.1	0.99918	0.99921	0.99924	0.99926	0.99929	3.1
3.2	0.99942	0.99944	0.99946	0.99948	0.99950	3.2
3.3	0.99960	0.99961	0.99962	0.99964	0.99965	3.3
3.4	0.99972	0.99973	0.99974	0.99975	0.99976	3.4
3.5	0.99981	0.99981	0.99982	0.99983	0.99983	3.5
3.6	0.99987	0.99987	0.99988	0.99988	0.99989	3.6
3.7	0.99991	0.99992	0.99992	0.99992	0.99992	3.7
3.8	0.99994	0.99994	0.99995	0.99995	0.99995	3.8
3.9	0.99996	0.99996	0.99996	0.99997	0.99997	3.9

Appendix III
Percentage points of the χ^2 distribution[a]

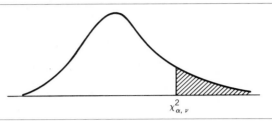

$\chi^2_{\alpha,\,\nu}$

					α				
ν	0.995	0.990	0.975	0.950	0.500	0.050	0.025	0.010	0.005
1	0.00+	0.00+	0.00+	0.00+	0.45	3.84	5.02	6.63	7.88
2	0.01	0.02	0.05	0.10	1.39	5.99	7.38	9.21	10.60
3	0.07	0.11	0.22	0.35	2.37	7.81	9.35	11.34	12.84
4	0.21	0.30	0.48	0.71	3.36	9.49	11.14	13.28	14.86
5	0.41	0.55	0.83	1.15	4.35	11.07	12.38	15.09	16.75
6	0.68	0.87	1.24	1.64	5.35	12.59	14.45	16.81	18.55
7	0.99	1.24	1.69	2.17	6.35	14.07	16.01	18.48	20.28
8	1.34	1.65	2.18	2.73	7.34	15.51	17.53	20.09	21.96
9	1.73	2.09	2.70	3.33	8.34	16.92	19.02	21.67	23.59
10	2.16	2.56	3.25	3.94	9.34	18.31	20.48	23.21	25.19
11	2.60	3.05	3.82	4.57	10.34	19.68	21.92	24.72	26.76
12	3.07	3.57	4.40	5.23	11.34	21.03	23.34	26.22	28.30
13	3.57	4.11	5.01	5.89	12.34	22.36	24.74	27.69	29.82
14	4.07	4.66	5.63	6.57	13.34	23.68	26.12	29.14	31.32
15	4.60	5.23	6.27	7.26	14.34	25.00	27.49	30.58	32.80
16	5.14	5.81	6.91	7.96	15.34	26.30	28.85	32.00	34.27
17	5.70	6.41	7.56	8.67	16.34	27.59	30.19	33.41	35.72
18	6.26	7.01	8.23	9.39	17.34	28.87	31.53	34.81	37.16
19	6.84	7.63	8.91	10.12	18.34	30.14	32.85	36.19	38.58
20	7.43	8.26	9.59	10.85	19.34	31.41	34.17	37.57	40.00
25	10.52	11.52	13.12	14.61	24.34	37.65	40.65	44.31	46.93
30	13.79	14.95	16.79	18.49	29.34	43.77	46.98	50.89	53.67
40	20.71	22.16	24.43	26.51	39.34	55.76	59.34	63.69	66.77
50	27.99	29.71	32.36	34.76	49.33	67.50	71.42	76.15	79.49
60	35.53	37.48	40.48	43.19	59.33	79.08	83.30	88.38	91.95
70	43.28	45.44	48.76	51.74	69.33	90.53	95.02	100.42	104.22
80	51.17	53.54	57.15	60.39	79.33	101.88	106.63	112.33	116.32
90	59.20	61.75	65.65	69.13	89.33	113.14	118.14	124.12	128.30
100	67.33	70.06	74.22	77.93	99.33	124.34	129.56	135.81	140.17

ν = degrees of freedom.

[a] Adapted with permission from *Biometrika Tables for Statisticians*, Vol. 1, 3rd ed., by E. S. Pearson and H. O. Hartley, Cambridge University Press, Cambridge, 1966.

Appendix IV
Percentage points of the *t* distribution[a]

α v	0.40	0.25	0.10	0.05	0.025	0.01	0.005	0.0025	0.001	0.0005
1	0.325	1.000	3.078	6.314	12.706	31.821	63.657	127.32	318.31	636.62
2	0.289	0.816	1.886	2.920	4.303	6.965	9.925	14.089	23.326	31.598
3	0.277	0.765	1.638	2.353	3.182	4.541	5.841	7.453	10.213	12.924
4	0.271	0.741	1.533	2.132	2.776	3.747	4.604	5.598	7.173	8.610
5	0.267	0.727	1.476	2.015	2.571	3.365	4.032	4.773	5.893	6.869
6	0.265	0.727	1.440	1.943	2.447	3.143	3.707	4.317	5.208	5.959
7	0.263	0.711	1.415	1.895	2.365	2.998	3.499	4.019	4.785	5.408
8	0.262	0.706	1.397	1.860	2.306	2.896	3.355	3.833	4.501	5.041
9	0.261	0.703	1.383	1.833	2.262	2.821	3.250	3.690	4.297	4.781
10	0.260	0.700	1.372	1.812	2.228	2.764	3.169	3.581	4.144	4.587
11	0.260	0.697	1.363	1.796	2.201	2.718	3.106	3.497	4.025	4.437
12	0.259	0.695	1.356	1.782	2.179	2.681	3.055	3.428	3.930	4.318
13	0.259	0.694	1.350	1.771	2.160	2.650	3.012	3.372	3.852	4.221
14	0.258	0.692	1.345	1.761	2.145	2.624	2.977	3.326	3.787	4.140
15	0.258	0.691	1.341	1.753	2.131	2.602	2.947	3.286	3.733	4.073
16	0.258	0.690	1.337	1.746	2.120	2.583	2.921	3.252	3.686	4.015
17	0.257	0.689	1.333	1.740	2.110	2.567	2.898	3.222	3.646	3.965
18	0.257	0.688	1.330	1.734	2.101	2.552	2.878	3.197	3.610	3.922
19	0.257	0.688	1.328	1.729	2.093	2.539	2.861	3.174	3.579	3.883
20	0.257	0.687	1.325	1.725	2.086	2.528	2.845	3.153	3.552	3.850
21	0.257	0.686	1.323	1.721	2.080	2.518	2.831	3.135	3.527	3.819
22	0.256	0.686	1.321	1.717	2.074	2.508	2.819	3.119	3.505	3.792
23	0.256	0.685	1.319	1.714	2.069	2.500	2.807	3.104	3.485	3.767
24	0.256	0.685	1.318	1.711	2.064	2.492	2.797	3.091	3.467	3.745
25	0.256	0.684	1.316	1.708	2.060	2.485	2.787	3.078	3.450	3.725
26	0.256	0.684	1.315	1.706	2.056	2.479	2.779	3.067	3.435	3.707
27	0.256	0.684	1.314	1.703	2.052	2.473	2.771	3.057	3.421	3.690
28	0.256	0.683	1.313	1.701	2.048	2.467	2.763	3.047	3.408	3.674
29	0.256	0.683	1.311	1.699	2.045	2.462	2.756	3.038	3.396	3.659
30	0.256	0.683	1.310	1.697	2.042	2.457	2.750	3.030	3.385	3.646
40	0.255	0.681	1.303	1.684	2.021	2.423	2.704	2.971	3.307	3.551
60	0.254	0.679	1.296	1.671	2.000	2.390	2.660	2.915	3.232	3.460
120	0.254	0.677	1.289	1.658	1.980	2.358	2.617	2.860	3.160	3.373
∞	0.253	0.674	1.282	1.645	1.960	2.326	2.576	2.807	3.090	3.291

v = degrees of freedom.

[a] Adapted with permission from *Biometrika Tables for Statisticians*, Vol. 1, 3rd ed., by E. S. Pearson and H. O. Hartley, Cambridge University Press, Cambridge, 1966.

Appendix V
Percentage points of the F distribution

$$F_{0.25,\nu_1,\nu_2}$$

Degrees of freedom for the numerator (ν_1)

ν_2	1	2	3	4	5	6	7	8	9	10	12	15	20	24	30	40	60	120	∞
1	5.83	7.50	8.20	8.58	8.82	8.98	9.10	9.19	9.26	9.32	9.41	9.49	9.58	9.63	9.67	9.71	9.76	9.80	9.85
2	2.57	3.00	3.15	3.23	3.28	3.31	3.34	3.35	3.37	3.38	3.39	3.41	3.43	3.43	3.44	3.45	3.46	3.47	3.48
3	2.02	2.28	2.36	2.39	2.41	2.42	2.43	2.44	2.44	2.44	2.45	2.46	2.46	2.46	2.47	2.47	2.47	2.47	2.47
4	1.81	2.00	2.05	2.06	2.07	2.08	2.08	2.08	2.08	2.08	2.08	2.08	2.08	2.08	2.08	2.08	2.08	2.08	2.08
5	1.69	1.85	1.88	1.89	1.89	1.89	1.89	1.89	1.89	1.89	1.89	1.89	1.88	1.88	1.88	1.88	1.87	1.87	1.87
6	1.62	1.76	1.78	1.79	1.79	1.78	1.78	1.78	1.77	1.77	1.77	1.76	1.76	1.75	1.75	1.75	1.74	1.74	1.74
7	1.57	1.70	1.72	1.72	1.71	1.71	1.70	1.70	1.70	1.69	1.68	1.68	1.67	1.67	1.66	1.66	1.65	1.65	1.65
8	1.54	1.66	1.67	1.66	1.66	1.65	1.64	1.64	1.63	1.63	1.62	1.62	1.61	1.60	1.60	1.59	1.59	1.58	1.58
9	1.51	1.62	1.63	1.63	1.62	1.61	1.60	1.60	1.59	1.59	1.58	1.57	1.56	1.56	1.55	1.54	1.54	1.53	1.53
10	1.49	1.60	1.60	1.59	1.59	1.58	1.57	1.56	1.56	1.55	1.54	1.53	1.52	1.52	1.51	1.51	1.50	1.49	1.48
11	1.47	1.58	1.58	1.57	1.56	1.55	1.54	1.53	1.53	1.52	1.51	1.50	1.49	1.49	1.48	1.47	1.47	1.46	1.45
12	1.46	1.56	1.56	1.55	1.54	1.53	1.52	1.51	1.51	1.50	1.49	1.48	1.47	1.46	1.45	1.45	1.44	1.43	1.42
13	1.45	1.55	1.55	1.53	1.52	1.51	1.50	1.49	1.49	1.48	1.47	1.46	1.45	1.44	1.43	1.42	1.42	1.41	1.40
14	1.44	1.53	1.53	1.52	1.51	1.50	1.49	1.48	1.47	1.46	1.45	1.44	1.43	1.42	1.41	1.41	1.40	1.39	1.38
15	1.43	1.52	1.52	1.51	1.49	1.48	1.47	1.46	1.46	1.45	1.44	1.43	1.41	1.41	1.40	1.39	1.38	1.37	1.36
16	1.42	1.51	1.51	1.50	1.48	1.47	1.46	1.45	1.44	1.44	1.43	1.41	1.40	1.39	1.38	1.37	1.36	1.35	1.34
17	1.42	1.51	1.50	1.49	1.47	1.46	1.45	1.44	1.43	1.43	1.41	1.40	1.39	1.38	1.37	1.36	1.35	1.34	1.33
18	1.41	1.50	1.49	1.48	1.46	1.45	1.44	1.43	1.42	1.42	1.40	1.39	1.38	1.37	1.36	1.35	1.34	1.33	1.32
19	1.41	1.49	1.49	1.47	1.46	1.44	1.43	1.42	1.41	1.41	1.40	1.38	1.37	1.36	1.35	1.34	1.33	1.32	1.30
20	1.40	1.49	1.48	1.47	1.45	1.44	1.43	1.42	1.41	1.40	1.39	1.37	1.36	1.35	1.34	1.33	1.32	1.31	1.29
21	1.40	1.48	1.48	1.46	1.44	1.43	1.42	1.41	1.40	1.39	1.38	1.37	1.35	1.34	1.33	1.32	1.31	1.30	1.28
22	1.40	1.48	1.47	1.45	1.44	1.42	1.41	1.40	1.39	1.39	1.37	1.36	1.34	1.33	1.32	1.31	1.30	1.29	1.28
23	1.39	1.47	1.47	1.45	1.43	1.42	1.41	1.40	1.39	1.38	1.37	1.35	1.34	1.33	1.32	1.31	1.30	1.28	1.27
24	1.39	1.47	1.46	1.44	1.43	1.41	1.40	1.39	1.38	1.38	1.36	1.35	1.33	1.32	1.31	1.30	1.29	1.28	1.26
25	1.39	1.47	1.46	1.44	1.42	1.41	1.40	1.39	1.38	1.37	1.36	1.34	1.33	1.32	1.31	1.29	1.28	1.27	1.25
26	1.38	1.46	1.45	1.44	1.42	1.41	1.39	1.38	1.37	1.37	1.35	1.34	1.32	1.31	1.30	1.29	1.28	1.26	1.25
27	1.38	1.46	1.45	1.43	1.42	1.40	1.39	1.38	1.37	1.36	1.35	1.33	1.32	1.31	1.30	1.28	1.27	1.26	1.24
28	1.38	1.46	1.45	1.43	1.41	1.40	1.39	1.38	1.37	1.36	1.34	1.33	1.31	1.30	1.29	1.28	1.27	1.25	1.24
29	1.38	1.45	1.45	1.43	1.41	1.40	1.38	1.37	1.36	1.35	1.34	1.32	1.31	1.30	1.29	1.27	1.26	1.25	1.23
30	1.38	1.45	1.44	1.42	1.41	1.39	1.38	1.37	1.36	1.35	1.34	1.32	1.30	1.29	1.28	1.27	1.26	1.24	1.23
40	1.36	1.44	1.42	1.40	1.39	1.37	1.36	1.35	1.34	1.33	1.31	1.30	1.28	1.26	1.25	1.24	1.22	1.21	1.19
60	1.35	1.42	1.41	1.38	1.37	1.35	1.33	1.32	1.31	1.30	1.29	1.27	1.25	1.24	1.22	1.21	1.19	1.17	1.15
120	1.34	1.40	1.39	1.37	1.35	1.33	1.31	1.30	1.29	1.28	1.26	1.24	1.22	1.21	1.19	1.18	1.16	1.13	1.10
∞	1.32	1.39	1.37	1.35	1.33	1.31	1.29	1.28	1.27	1.25	1.24	1.22	1.19	1.18	1.16	1.14	1.12	1.08	1.00

Degrees of freedom for the denominator (ν_2)

Note: $F_{0.75,\nu_1,\nu_2} = 1/F_{0.25,\nu_2,\nu_1}$

(continued)

Source: Adapted with permission from *Biometrika Tables for Statisticians*, Vol. 1, 3rd ed., by E. S. Pearson and H. O. Hartley, Cambridge University Press, Cambridge, 1966.

$$F_{0.10,v_1,v_2}$$

	Degrees of freedom for the numerator (v_1)																		
v_2	1	2	3	4	5	6	7	8	9	10	12	15	20	24	30	40	60	120	∞
1	39.86	49.50	53.59	55.83	57.24	58.20	58.91	59.44	59.86	60.19	60.71	61.22	61.74	62.00	62.26	62.53	62.79	63.06	63.33
2	8.53	9.00	9.16	9.24	9.29	9.33	9.35	9.37	9.38	9.39	9.41	9.42	9.44	9.45	9.46	9.47	9.47	9.48	9.49
3	5.54	5.46	5.39	5.34	5.31	5.28	5.27	5.25	5.24	5.23	5.22	5.20	5.18	5.18	5.17	5.16	5.15	5.14	5.13
4	4.54	4.32	4.19	4.11	4.05	4.01	3.98	3.95	3.94	3.92	3.90	3.87	3.84	3.83	3.82	3.80	3.79	3.78	3.76
5	4.06	3.78	3.62	3.52	3.45	3.40	3.37	3.34	3.32	3.30	3.27	3.24	3.21	3.19	3.17	3.16	3.14	3.12	3.10
6	3.78	3.46	3.29	3.18	3.11	3.05	3.01	2.98	2.96	2.94	2.90	2.87	2.84	2.82	2.80	2.78	2.76	2.74	2.72
7	3.59	3.26	3.07	2.96	2.88	2.83	2.78	2.75	2.72	2.70	2.67	2.63	2.59	2.58	2.56	2.54	2.51	2.49	2.47
8	3.46	3.11	2.92	2.81	2.73	2.67	2.62	2.59	2.56	2.54	2.50	2.46	2.42	2.40	2.38	2.36	2.34	2.32	2.29
9	3.36	3.01	2.81	2.69	2.61	2.55	2.51	2.47	2.44	2.42	2.38	2.34	2.30	2.28	2.25	2.23	2.21	2.18	2.16
10	3.29	2.92	2.73	2.61	2.52	2.46	2.41	2.38	2.35	2.32	2.28	2.24	2.20	2.18	2.16	2.13	2.11	2.08	2.06
11	3.23	2.86	2.66	2.54	2.45	2.39	2.34	2.30	2.27	2.25	2.21	2.17	2.12	2.10	2.08	2.05	2.03	2.00	1.97
12	3.18	2.81	2.61	2.48	2.39	2.33	2.28	2.24	2.21	2.19	2.15	2.10	2.06	2.04	2.01	1.99	1.96	1.93	1.90
13	3.14	2.76	2.56	2.43	2.35	2.28	2.23	2.20	2.16	2.14	2.10	2.05	2.01	1.98	1.96	1.93	1.90	1.88	1.85
14	3.10	2.73	2.52	2.39	2.31	2.24	2.19	2.15	2.12	2.10	2.05	2.01	1.96	1.94	1.91	1.89	1.86	1.83	1.80
15	3.07	2.70	2.49	2.36	2.27	2.21	2.16	2.12	2.09	2.06	2.02	1.97	1.92	1.90	1.87	1.85	1.82	1.79	1.76
16	3.05	2.67	2.46	2.33	2.24	2.18	2.13	2.09	2.06	2.03	1.99	1.94	1.89	1.86	1.84	1.81	1.78	1.75	1.72
17	3.03	2.64	2.44	2.31	2.22	2.15	2.10	2.06	2.03	2.00	1.96	1.91	1.86	1.84	1.81	1.78	1.75	1.72	1.69
18	3.01	2.62	2.42	2.29	2.20	2.13	2.08	2.04	2.00	1.98	1.93	1.89	1.84	1.81	1.78	1.75	1.72	1.69	1.66
19	2.99	2.61	2.40	2.27	2.18	2.11	2.06	2.02	1.98	1.96	1.91	1.86	1.81	1.79	1.76	1.73	1.70	1.67	1.63
20	2.97	2.59	2.38	2.25	2.16	2.09	2.04	2.00	1.96	1.94	1.89	1.84	1.79	1.77	1.74	1.71	1.68	1.64	1.61
21	2.96	2.57	2.36	2.23	2.14	2.08	2.02	1.98	1.95	1.92	1.87	1.83	1.78	1.75	1.72	1.69	1.66	1.62	1.59
22	2.95	2.56	2.35	2.22	2.13	2.06	2.01	1.97	1.93	1.90	1.86	1.81	1.76	1.73	1.70	1.67	1.64	1.60	1.57
23	2.94	2.55	2.34	2.21	2.11	2.05	1.99	1.95	1.92	1.89	1.84	1.80	1.74	1.72	1.69	1.66	1.62	1.59	1.55
24	2.93	2.54	2.33	2.19	2.10	2.04	1.98	1.94	1.91	1.88	1.83	1.78	1.73	1.70	1.67	1.64	1.61	1.57	1.53
25	2.92	2.53	2.32	2.18	2.09	2.02	1.97	1.93	1.89	1.87	1.82	1.77	1.72	1.69	1.66	1.63	1.59	1.56	1.52
26	2.91	2.52	2.31	2.17	2.08	2.01	1.96	1.92	1.88	1.86	1.81	1.76	1.71	1.68	1.65	1.61	1.58	1.54	1.50
27	2.90	2.51	2.30	2.17	2.07	2.00	1.95	1.91	1.87	1.85	1.80	1.75	1.70	1.67	1.64	1.60	1.57	1.53	1.49
28	2.89	2.50	2.29	2.16	2.06	2.00	1.94	1.90	1.87	1.84	1.79	1.74	1.69	1.66	1.63	1.59	1.56	1.52	1.48
29	2.89	2.50	2.28	2.15	2.06	1.99	1.93	1.89	1.86	1.83	1.78	1.73	1.68	1.65	1.62	1.58	1.55	1.51	1.47
30	2.88	2.49	2.28	2.14	2.03	1.98	1.93	1.88	1.85	1.82	1.77	1.72	1.67	1.64	1.61	1.57	1.54	1.50	1.46
40	2.84	2.44	2.23	2.09	2.00	1.93	1.87	1.83	1.79	1.76	1.71	1.66	1.61	1.57	1.54	1.51	1.47	1.42	1.38
60	2.79	2.39	2.18	2.04	1.95	1.87	1.82	1.77	1.74	1.71	1.66	1.60	1.54	1.51	1.48	1.44	1.40	1.35	1.29
120	2.75	2.35	2.13	1.99	1.90	1.82	1.77	1.72	1.68	1.65	1.60	1.55	1.48	1.45	1.41	1.37	1.32	1.26	1.19
∞	2.71	2.30	2.08	1.94	1.85	1.77	1.72	1.67	1.63	1.60	1.55	1.49	1.42	1.38	1.34	1.30	1.24	1.17	1.00

Degrees of freedom for the denominator (v_2)

Note: $F_{0.90,v_1,v_2} = 1/F_{0.10,v_2,v_1}$.

(continued)

Appendix V (Continued)

$$F_{0.05, \nu_1 \nu_2}$$

ν_2 \ ν_1	1	2	3	4	5	6	7	8	9	10	12	15	20	24	30	40	60	120	∞
1	161.4	199.5	215.7	224.6	230.2	234.0	236.8	238.9	240.5	241.9	243.9	245.9	248.0	249.1	250.1	251.1	252.2	253.3	254.3
2	18.51	19.00	19.16	19.25	19.30	19.33	19.35	19.37	19.38	19.40	19.41	19.43	19.45	19.45	19.46	19.47	19.48	19.49	19.50
3	10.13	9.55	9.28	9.12	9.01	8.94	8.89	8.85	8.81	8.79	8.74	8.70	8.66	8.64	8.62	8.59	8.57	8.55	8.53
4	7.71	6.94	6.59	6.39	6.26	6.16	6.09	6.04	6.00	5.96	5.91	5.86	5.80	5.77	5.75	5.72	5.69	5.66	5.63
5	6.61	5.79	5.41	5.19	5.05	4.95	4.88	4.82	4.77	4.74	4.68	4.62	4.56	4.53	4.50	4.46	4.43	4.40	4.36
6	5.99	5.14	4.76	4.53	4.39	4.28	4.21	4.15	4.10	4.06	4.00	3.94	3.87	3.84	3.81	3.77	3.74	3.70	3.67
7	5.59	4.74	4.35	4.12	3.97	3.87	3.79	3.73	3.68	3.64	3.57	3.51	3.44	3.41	3.38	3.34	3.30	3.27	3.23
8	5.32	4.46	4.07	3.84	3.69	3.58	3.50	3.44	3.39	3.35	3.28	3.22	3.15	3.12	3.08	3.04	3.01	2.97	2.93
9	5.12	4.26	3.86	3.63	3.48	3.37	3.29	3.23	3.18	3.14	3.07	3.01	2.94	2.90	2.86	2.83	2.79	2.75	2.71
10	4.96	4.10	3.71	3.48	3.33	3.22	3.14	3.07	3.02	2.98	2.91	2.85	2.77	2.74	2.70	2.66	2.62	2.58	2.54
11	4.84	3.98	3.59	3.36	3.20	3.09	3.01	2.95	2.90	2.85	2.79	2.72	2.65	2.61	2.57	2.53	2.49	2.45	2.40
12	4.75	3.89	3.49	3.26	3.11	3.00	2.91	2.85	2.80	2.75	2.69	2.62	2.54	2.51	2.47	2.43	2.38	2.34	2.30
13	4.67	3.81	3.41	3.18	3.03	2.92	2.83	2.77	2.71	2.67	2.60	2.53	2.46	2.42	2.38	2.34	2.30	2.25	2.21
14	4.60	3.74	3.34	3.11	2.96	2.85	2.76	2.70	2.65	2.60	2.53	2.46	2.39	2.35	2.31	2.27	2.22	2.18	2.13
15	4.54	3.68	3.29	3.06	2.90	2.79	2.71	2.64	2.59	2.54	2.48	2.40	2.33	2.29	2.25	2.20	2.16	2.11	2.07
16	4.49	3.63	3.24	3.01	2.85	2.74	2.66	2.59	2.54	2.49	2.42	2.35	2.28	2.24	2.19	2.15	2.11	2.06	2.01
17	4.45	3.59	3.20	2.96	2.81	2.70	2.61	2.55	2.49	2.45	2.38	2.31	2.23	2.19	2.15	2.10	2.06	2.01	1.96
18	4.41	3.55	3.16	2.93	2.77	2.66	2.58	2.51	2.46	2.41	2.34	2.27	2.19	2.15	2.11	2.06	2.02	1.97	1.92
19	4.38	3.52	3.13	2.90	2.74	2.63	2.54	2.48	2.42	2.38	2.31	2.23	2.16	2.11	2.07	2.03	1.98	1.93	1.88
20	4.35	3.49	3.10	2.87	2.71	2.60	2.51	2.45	2.39	2.35	2.28	2.20	2.12	2.08	2.04	1.99	1.95	1.90	1.84
21	4.32	3.47	3.07	2.84	2.68	2.57	2.49	2.42	2.37	2.32	2.25	2.18	2.10	2.05	2.01	1.96	1.92	1.87	1.81
22	4.30	3.44	3.05	2.82	2.66	2.55	2.46	2.40	2.34	2.30	2.23	2.15	2.07	2.03	1.98	1.94	1.89	1.84	1.78
23	4.28	3.42	3.03	2.80	2.64	2.53	2.44	2.37	2.32	2.27	2.20	2.13	2.05	2.01	1.96	1.91	1.86	1.81	1.76
24	4.26	3.40	3.01	2.78	2.62	2.51	2.42	2.36	2.30	2.25	2.18	2.11	2.03	1.98	1.94	1.89	1.84	1.79	1.73
25	4.24	3.39	2.99	2.76	2.60	2.49	2.40	2.34	2.28	2.24	2.16	2.09	2.01	1.96	1.92	1.87	1.82	1.77	1.71
26	4.23	3.37	2.98	2.74	2.59	2.47	2.39	2.32	2.27	2.22	2.15	2.07	1.99	1.95	1.90	1.85	1.80	1.75	1.69
27	4.21	3.35	2.96	2.73	2.57	2.46	2.37	2.31	2.25	2.20	2.13	2.06	1.97	1.93	1.88	1.84	1.79	1.73	1.67
28	4.20	3.34	2.95	2.71	2.56	2.45	2.36	2.29	2.24	2.19	2.12	2.04	1.96	1.91	1.87	1.82	1.77	1.71	1.65
29	4.18	3.33	2.93	2.70	2.55	2.43	2.35	2.28	2.22	2.18	2.10	2.03	1.94	1.90	1.85	1.81	1.75	1.70	1.64
30	4.17	3.32	2.92	2.69	2.53	2.42	2.33	2.27	2.21	2.16	2.09	2.01	1.93	1.89	1.84	1.79	1.74	1.68	1.62
40	4.08	3.23	2.84	2.61	2.45	2.34	2.25	2.18	2.12	2.08	2.00	1.92	1.84	1.79	1.74	1.69	1.64	1.58	1.51
60	4.00	3.15	2.76	2.53	2.37	2.25	2.17	2.10	2.04	1.99	1.92	1.84	1.75	1.70	1.65	1.59	1.53	1.47	1.39
120	3.92	3.07	2.68	2.45	2.29	2.17	2.09	2.02	1.96	1.91	1.83	1.75	1.66	1.61	1.55	1.55	1.43	1.35	1.25
∞	3.84	3.00	2.60	2.37	2.21	2.10	2.01	1.94	1.88	1.83	1.75	1.67	1.57	1.52	1.46	1.39	1.32	1.22	1.00

Degrees of freedom for the numerator (ν_1)

Degrees of freedom for the denominator (ν_2)

Note: $F_{0.95, \nu_1, \nu_2} = 1/F_{0.05, \nu_2, \nu_1}$.

(continued)

Appendix V (Continued)

$$F_{0.025, v_1, v_2}$$

v_2 \ v_1	1	2	3	4	5	6	7	8	9	10	12	15	20	24	30	40	60	120	∞
1	647.8	799.5	864.2	899.6	921.8	937.1	948.2	956.7	963.3	968.6	976.7	984.9	993.1	997.2	1001.0	1006.0	1010.0	1014.0	1018.0
2	38.51	39.00	39.17	39.25	39.30	39.33	39.36	39.37	39.39	39.40	39.41	39.43	39.45	39.46	39.46	39.47	39.48	39.49	39.50
3	17.44	16.04	15.44	15.10	14.88	14.73	14.62	14.54	14.47	14.42	14.34	14.25	14.17	14.12	14.08	14.04	13.99	13.95	13.90
4	12.22	10.65	9.98	9.60	9.36	9.20	9.07	8.98	8.90	8.84	8.75	8.66	8.56	8.51	8.46	8.41	8.36	8.31	8.26
5	10.01	8.43	7.76	7.39	7.15	6.98	6.85	6.76	6.68	6.62	6.52	6.43	6.33	6.28	6.23	6.18	6.12	6.07	6.02
6	8.81	7.26	6.60	6.23	5.99	5.82	5.70	5.60	5.52	5.46	5.37	5.27	5.17	5.12	5.07	5.01	4.96	4.90	4.85
7	8.07	6.54	5.89	5.52	5.29	5.12	4.99	4.90	4.82	4.76	4.67	4.57	4.47	4.42	4.36	4.31	4.25	4.20	4.14
8	7.57	6.06	5.42	5.05	4.82	4.65	4.53	4.43	4.36	4.30	4.20	4.10	4.00	3.95	3.89	3.84	3.78	3.73	3.67
9	7.21	5.71	5.08	4.72	4.48	4.32	4.20	4.10	4.03	3.96	3.87	3.77	3.67	3.61	3.56	3.51	3.45	3.39	3.33
10	6.94	5.46	4.83	4.47	4.24	4.07	3.95	3.85	3.78	3.72	3.62	3.52	3.42	3.37	3.31	3.26	3.20	3.14	3.08
11	6.72	5.26	4.63	4.28	4.04	3.88	3.76	3.66	3.59	3.53	3.43	3.33	3.23	3.17	3.12	3.06	3.00	2.94	2.88
12	6.55	5.10	4.47	4.12	3.89	3.73	3.61	3.51	3.44	3.37	3.28	3.18	3.07	3.02	2.96	2.91	2.85	2.79	2.72
13	6.41	4.97	4.35	4.00	3.77	3.60	3.48	3.39	3.31	3.25	3.15	3.05	2.95	2.89	2.84	2.78	2.72	2.66	2.60
14	6.30	4.86	4.24	3.89	3.66	3.50	3.38	3.29	3.21	3.15	3.05	2.95	2.84	2.79	2.73	2.67	2.61	2.55	2.49
15	6.20	4.77	4.15	3.80	3.58	3.41	3.29	3.20	3.12	3.06	2.96	2.86	2.76	2.70	2.64	2.59	2.52	2.46	2.40
16	6.12	4.69	4.08	3.73	3.50	3.34	3.22	3.12	3.05	2.99	2.89	2.79	2.68	2.63	2.57	2.51	2.45	2.38	2.32
17	6.04	4.62	4.01	3.66	3.44	3.28	3.16	3.06	2.98	2.92	2.82	2.72	2.62	2.56	2.50	2.44	2.38	2.32	2.25
18	5.98	4.56	3.95	3.61	3.38	3.22	3.10	3.01	2.93	2.87	2.77	2.67	2.56	2.50	2.44	2.38	2.32	2.26	2.19
19	5.92	4.51	3.90	3.56	3.33	3.17	3.05	2.96	2.88	2.82	2.72	2.62	2.51	2.45	2.39	2.33	2.27	2.20	2.13
20	5.87	4.46	3.86	3.51	3.29	3.13	3.01	2.91	2.84	2.77	2.68	2.57	2.46	2.41	2.35	2.29	2.22	2.16	2.09
21	5.83	4.42	3.82	3.48	3.25	3.09	2.97	2.87	2.80	2.73	2.64	2.53	2.42	2.37	2.31	2.25	2.18	2.11	2.04
22	5.79	4.38	3.78	3.44	3.22	3.05	2.93	2.84	2.76	2.70	2.60	2.50	2.39	2.33	2.27	2.21	2.14	2.08	2.00
23	5.75	4.35	3.75	3.41	3.18	3.02	2.90	2.81	2.73	2.67	2.57	2.47	2.36	2.30	2.24	2.18	2.11	2.04	1.97
24	5.72	4.32	3.72	3.38	3.15	2.99	2.87	2.78	2.70	2.64	2.54	2.44	2.33	2.27	2.21	2.15	2.08	2.01	1.94
25	5.69	4.29	3.69	3.35	3.13	2.97	2.85	2.75	2.68	2.61	2.51	2.41	2.30	2.24	2.18	2.12	2.05	1.98	1.91
26	5.66	4.27	3.67	3.33	3.10	2.94	2.82	2.73	2.65	2.59	2.49	2.39	2.28	2.22	2.16	2.09	2.03	1.95	1.88
27	5.63	4.24	3.65	3.31	3.08	2.92	2.80	2.71	2.63	2.57	2.47	2.36	2.25	2.19	2.13	2.07	2.00	1.93	1.85
28	5.61	4.22	3.63	3.29	3.06	2.90	2.78	2.69	2.61	2.55	2.45	2.34	2.23	2.17	2.11	2.05	1.98	1.91	1.83
29	5.59	4.20	3.61	3.27	3.04	2.88	2.76	2.67	2.59	2.53	2.43	2.32	2.21	2.15	2.09	2.03	1.96	1.89	1.81
30	5.57	4.18	3.59	3.25	3.03	2.87	2.75	2.65	2.57	2.51	2.41	2.31	2.20	2.14	2.07	2.01	1.94	1.87	1.79
40	5.42	4.05	3.46	3.13	2.90	2.74	2.62	2.53	2.45	2.39	2.29	2.18	2.07	2.01	1.94	1.88	1.80	1.72	1.64
60	5.29	3.93	3.34	3.01	2.79	2.63	2.51	2.41	2.33	2.27	2.17	2.06	1.94	1.88	1.82	1.74	1.67	1.58	1.48
120	5.15	3.80	3.23	2.89	2.67	2.52	2.39	2.30	2.22	2.16	2.05	1.94	1.82	1.76	1.69	1.61	1.53	1.43	1.31
∞	5.02	3.69	3.12	2.79	2.57	2.41	2.29	2.19	2.11	2.05	1.94	1.83	1.71	1.64	1.57	1.48	1.39	1.27	1.00

Degrees of freedom for the numerator (v_1)

Degrees of freedom for the denominator (v_2)

Note: $F_{0.975, v_1, v_2} = 1/F_{0.025, v_2, v_1}$.

(continued)

$$F_{0.01,\nu_1,\nu_2}$$

ν_2		Degrees of freedom for the numerator (ν_1)																	
	1	2	3	4	5	6	7	8	9	10	12	15	20	24	30	40	60	120	∞
1	4052.0	4999.5	5403.0	5625.0	5764.0	5859.0	5928.0	5982.0	6022.0	6056.0	6106.0	6157.0	6209.0	6235.0	6261.0	6287.0	6313.0	6339.0	6366.0
2	98.50	99.00	99.17	99.25	99.30	99.33	99.36	99.37	99.39	99.40	99.42	99.43	99.45	99.46	99.47	99.47	99.48	99.49	99.50
3	34.12	30.82	29.46	28.71	28.24	27.91	27.67	27.49	27.35	27.23	27.05	26.87	26.69	26.60	26.50	26.41	26.32	26.22	26.13
4	21.20	18.00	16.69	15.98	15.52	15.21	14.98	14.80	14.66	14.55	14.37	14.20	14.02	13.93	13.84	13.75	13.65	13.56	13.46
5	16.26	13.27	12.06	11.39	10.97	10.67	10.46	10.29	10.16	10.05	9.89	9.72	9.55	9.47	9.38	9.29	9.20	9.11	9.02
6	13.75	10.92	9.78	9.15	8.75	8.47	8.26	8.10	7.98	7.87	7.72	7.56	7.40	7.31	7.23	7.14	7.06	6.97	6.88
7	12.25	9.55	8.45	7.85	7.46	7.19	6.99	6.84	6.72	6.62	6.47	6.31	6.16	6.07	5.99	5.91	5.82	5.74	5.65
8	11.26	8.65	7.59	7.01	6.63	6.37	6.18	6.03	5.91	5.81	5.67	5.52	5.36	5.28	5.20	5.12	5.03	4.95	4.86
9	10.56	8.02	6.99	6.42	6.06	5.80	5.61	5.47	5.35	5.26	5.11	4.96	4.81	4.73	4.65	4.57	4.48	4.40	4.31
10	10.04	7.56	6.55	5.99	5.64	5.39	5.20	5.06	4.94	4.85	4.71	4.56	4.41	4.33	4.25	4.17	4.08	4.00	3.91
11	9.65	7.21	6.22	5.67	5.32	5.07	4.89	4.74	4.63	4.54	4.40	4.25	4.10	4.02	3.94	3.86	3.78	3.69	3.60
12	9.33	6.93	5.95	5.41	5.06	4.82	4.64	4.50	4.39	4.30	4.16	4.01	3.86	3.78	3.70	3.62	3.54	3.45	3.36
13	9.07	6.70	5.74	5.21	4.86	4.62	4.44	4.30	4.19	4.10	3.96	3.82	3.66	3.59	3.51	3.43	3.34	3.25	3.17
14	8.86	6.51	5.56	5.04	4.69	4.46	4.28	4.14	4.03	3.94	3.80	3.66	3.51	3.43	3.35	3.27	3.18	3.09	3.00
15	8.68	6.36	5.42	4.89	4.56	4.32	4.14	4.00	3.89	3.80	3.67	3.52	3.37	3.29	3.21	3.13	3.05	2.96	2.87
16	8.53	6.23	5.29	4.77	4.44	4.20	4.03	3.89	3.78	3.69	3.55	3.41	3.26	3.18	3.10	3.02	2.93	2.84	2.75
17	8.40	6.11	5.18	4.67	4.34	4.10	3.93	3.79	3.68	3.59	3.46	3.31	3.16	3.08	3.00	2.92	2.83	2.75	2.65
18	8.29	6.01	5.09	4.58	4.25	4.01	3.84	3.71	3.60	3.51	3.37	3.23	3.08	3.00	2.92	2.84	2.75	2.66	2.57
19	8.18	5.93	5.01	4.50	4.17	3.94	3.77	3.63	3.52	3.43	3.30	3.15	3.00	2.92	2.84	2.76	2.67	2.58	2.59
20	8.10	5.85	4.94	4.43	4.10	3.87	3.70	3.56	3.46	3.37	3.23	3.09	2.94	2.86	2.78	2.69	2.61	2.52	2.42
21	8.02	5.78	4.87	4.37	4.04	3.81	3.64	3.51	3.40	3.31	3.17	3.03	2.88	2.80	2.72	2.64	2.55	2.46	2.36
22	7.95	5.72	4.82	4.31	3.99	3.76	3.59	3.45	3.35	3.26	3.12	2.98	2.83	2.75	2.67	2.58	2.50	2.40	2.31
23	7.88	5.66	4.76	4.26	3.94	3.71	3.54	3.41	3.30	3.21	3.07	2.93	2.78	2.70	2.62	2.54	2.45	2.35	2.26
24	7.82	5.61	4.72	4.22	3.90	3.67	3.50	3.36	3.26	3.17	3.03	2.89	2.74	2.66	2.58	2.49	2.40	2.31	2.21
25	7.77	5.57	4.68	4.18	3.85	3.63	3.46	3.32	3.22	3.13	2.99	2.85	2.70	2.62	2.54	2.45	2.36	2.27	2.17
26	7.72	5.53	4.64	4.14	3.82	3.59	3.42	3.29	3.18	3.09	2.96	2.81	2.66	2.58	2.50	2.42	2.33	2.23	2.13
27	7.68	5.49	4.60	4.11	3.78	3.56	3.39	3.26	3.15	3.06	2.93	2.78	2.63	2.55	2.47	2.38	2.29	2.20	2.10
28	7.64	5.45	4.57	4.07	3.75	3.53	3.36	3.23	3.12	3.03	2.90	2.75	2.60	2.52	2.44	2.35	2.26	2.17	2.06
29	7.60	5.42	4.54	4.04	3.73	3.50	3.33	3.20	3.09	3.00	2.87	2.73	2.57	2.49	2.41	2.33	2.23	2.14	2.03
30	7.56	5.39	4.51	4.02	3.70	3.47	3.30	3.17	3.07	2.98	2.84	2.70	2.55	2.47	2.39	2.30	2.21	2.11	2.01
40	7.31	5.18	4.31	3.83	3.51	3.29	3.12	2.99	2.89	2.80	2.66	2.52	2.37	2.29	2.20	2.11	2.02	1.92	1.80
60	7.08	4.98	4.13	3.65	3.34	3.12	2.95	2.82	2.72	2.63	2.50	2.35	2.20	2.12	2.03	1.94	1.84	1.73	1.60
120	6.85	4.79	3.95	3.48	3.17	2.96	2.79	2.66	2.56	2.47	2.34	2.19	2.03	1.95	1.86	1.76	1.66	1.53	1.38
∞	6.63	4.61	3.78	3.32	3.02	2.80	2.64	2.51	2.41	2.32	2.18	2.04	1.88	1.79	1.70	1.59	1.47	1.32	1.00

Note: $F_{0.99,\nu_1,\nu_2} = 1/F_{0.01,\nu_2,\nu_1}$.

(continued)

Appendix VI

Factors for constructing variables control charts

Observations in Sample, n	Chart for Averages — Factors for Control Limits			Chart for Standard Deviations — Factors for Center Line		Chart for Standard Deviations — Factors for Control Limits				Chart for Ranges — Factors for Center Line			Chart for Ranges — Factors for Control Limits			
	A	A_2	A_3	c_4	$1/c_4$	B_3	B_4	B_5	B_6	d_2	$1/d_2$	d_3	D_1	D_2	D_3	D_4
2	2.121	1.880	2.659	0.7979	1.2533	0	3.267	0	2.606	1.128	0.8865	0.853	0	3.686	0	3.267
3	1.732	1.023	1.954	0.8862	1.1284	0	2.568	0	2.276	1.693	0.5907	0.888	0	4.358	0	2.575
4	1.500	0.729	1.628	0.9213	1.0854	0	2.266	0	2.088	2.059	0.4857	0.880	0	4.698	0	2.282
5	1.342	0.577	1.427	0.9400	1.0638	0	2.089	0	1.964	2.326	0.4299	0.864	0	4.918	0	2.115
6	1.225	0.483	1.287	0.9515	1.0510	0.030	1.970	0.029	1.874	2.534	0.3946	0.848	0	5.078	0	2.004
7	1.134	0.419	1.182	0.9594	1.04230	0.118	1.882	0.113	1.806	2.704	0.3698	0.833	0.204	5.204	0.076	1.924
8	1.061	0.373	1.099	0.9650	1.0363	0.185	1.815	0.179	1.751	2.847	0.3512	0.820	0.388	5.306	0.136	1.864
9	1.000	0.337	1.032	0.9693	1.0317	0.239	1.761	0.232	1.707	2.970	0.3367	0.808	0.547	5.393	0.184	1.816
10	0.949	0.308	0.975	0.9727	1.0281	0.284	1.716	0.276	1.669	3.078	0.3249	0.797	0.687	5.469	0.223	1.777
11	0.905	0.285	0.927	0.9754	1.0252	0.321	1.679	0.313	1.637	3.173	0.3152	0.787	0.811	5.535	0.256	1.744
12	0.866	0.266	0.886	0.9776	1.0229	0.354	1.646	0.346	1.610	3.258	0.3069	0.778	0.922	5.594	0.283	1.717
13	0.832	0.249	0.850	0.9794	1.0210	0.382	1.618	0.374	1.585	3.336	0.2998	0.770	1.025	5.647	0.307	1.693
14	0.802	0.235	0.817	0.9810	1.0194	0.406	1.594	0.399	1.563	3.407	0.2935	0.763	1.118	5.696	0.328	1.672
15	0.775	0.223	0.789	0.9823	1.0180	0.428	1.572	0.421	1.544	3.472	0.2880	0.756	1.203	5.741	0.347	1.653
16	0.750	0.212	0.763	0.9835	1.0168	0.448	1.552	0.440	1.526	3.532	0.2831	0.750	1.282	5.782	0.363	1.637
17	0.728	0.203	0.739	0.9845	1.0157	0.466	1.534	0.458	1.511	3.588	0.2787	0.744	1.356	5.820	0.378	1.622
18	0.707	0.194	0.718	0.9854	1.0148	0.482	1.518	0.475	1.496	3.640	0.2747	0.739	1.424	5.856	0.391	1.608
19	0.688	0.187	0.698	0.9862	1.0140	0.497	1.503	0.490	1.483	3.689	0.2711	0.734	1.487	5.891	0.403	1.597
20	0.671	0.180	0.680	0.9869	1.0133	0.510	1.490	0.504	1.470	3.735	0.2677	0.729	1.549	5.921	0.415	1.585
21	0.655	0.173	0.663	0.9876	1.0126	0.523	1.477	0.516	1.459	3.778	0.2647	0.724	1.605	5.951	0.425	1.575
22	0.640	0.167	0.647	0.9882	1.0119	0.534	1.466	0.528	1.448	3.819	0.2618	0.720	1.659	5.979	0.434	1.566
23	0.626	0.162	0.633	0.9887	1.0114	0.545	1.455	0.539	1.438	3.858	0.2592	0.716	1.710	6.006	0.443	1.557
24	0.612	0.157	0.619	0.9892	1.0109	0.555	1.445	0.549	1.429	3.895	0.2567	0.712	1.759	6.031	0.451	1.548
25	0.600	0.153	0.606	0.9896	1.0105	0.565	1.435	0.559	1.420	3.931	0.2544	0.708	1.806	6.056	0.459	1.541

For $n > 25$

$$A = \frac{3}{\sqrt{n}}, \qquad A_3 = \frac{3}{c_4 \sqrt{n}}, \qquad c_4 \cong \frac{4(n-1)}{4n-3},$$

$$B_3 = 1 - \frac{3}{c_4 \sqrt{2(n-1)}}, \qquad B_4 = 1 + \frac{3}{c_4 \sqrt{2(n-1)}},$$

$$B_5 = c_4 - \frac{3}{\sqrt{2(n-1)}}, \qquad B_6 = c_4 + \frac{3}{\sqrt{2(n-1)}}.$$

Appendix VII
Factors for two-sided normal tolerance limits

	90% Confidence That Percentage of Population Between Limits Is			95% Confidence That Percentage of Population Between Limits Is			99% Confidence That Percentage of Population Between Limits Is		
n	90%	95%	99%	90%	95%	99%	90%	95%	99%
2	15.98	18.80	24.17	32.02	37.67	48.43	160.2	188.5	242.3
3	5.847	6.919	8.974	8.380	9.916	12.86	18.93	22.40	29.06
4	4.166	4.943	6.440	5.369	6.370	8.299	9.398	11.15	14.53
5	3.494	4.152	5.423	4.275	5.079	6.634	6.612	7.855	10.26
6	3.131	3.723	4.870	3.712	4.414	5.775	5.337	6.345	8.301
7	2.902	3.452	4.521	3.369	4.007	5.248	4.613	5.448	7.187
8	2.743	3.264	4.278	3.136	3.732	4.891	4.147	4.936	6.468
9	2.626	3.125	4.098	2.967	3.532	4.631	3.822	4.550	5.966
10	2.535	3.018	3.959	2.829	3.379	4.433	3.582	4.265	5.594
11	2.463	2.933	3.849	2.737	3.259	4.277	3.397	4.045	5.308
12	2.404	2.863	3.758	2.655	3.162	4.150	3.250	3.870	5.079
13	2.355	2.805	3.682	2.587	3.081	4.044	3.130	3.727	4.893
14	2.314	2.756	3.618	2.529	3.012	3.955	3.029	3.608	4.737
15	2.278	2.713	3.562	2.480	2.954	3.878	2.945	3.507	4.605
16	2.246	2.676	3.514	2.437	2.903	3.812	2.872	3.421	4.492
17	2.219	2.643	3.471	2.400	2.858	3.754	2.808	3.345	4.393
18	2.194	2.614	3.433	2.366	2.819	3.702	2.753	3.279	4.307
19	2.172	2.588	3.399	2.337	2.784	3.656	2.703	3.221	4.230
20	2.152	2.564	3.368	2.310	2.752	3.615	2.659	3.168	4.161
21	2.135	2.543	3.340	2.286	2.723	3.577	2.620	3.121	4.100
22	2.118	2.524	3.315	2.264	2.697	3.543	2.584	3.078	4.044
23	2.103	2.506	3.292	2.244	2.673	3.512	2.551	3.040	3.993
24	2.089	2.489	3.270	2.225	2.651	3.483	2.522	3.004	3.947
25	2.077	2.474	3.251	2.208	2.631	3.457	2.494	2.972	3.904
26	2.065	2.460	3.232	2.193	2.612	3.432	2.469	2.941	3.865
27	2.054	2.447	3.215	2.178	2.595	3.409	2.446	2.914	3.828
28	2.044	2.435	3.199	2.164	2.579	3.388	2.424	2.888	3.794
29	2.034	2.424	3.184	2.152	2.554	3.368	2.404	2.864	3.763
30	2.025	2.413	3.170	2.140	2.549	3.350	2.385	2.841	3.733
35	1.988	2.368	3.112	2.090	2.490	3.272	2.306	2.748	3.611
40	1.959	2.334	3.066	2.052	2.445	3.213	2.247	2.677	3.518
50	1.916	2.284	3.001	1.996	2.379	3.126	2.162	2.576	3.385
60	1.887	2.248	2.955	1.958	2.333	3.066	2.103	2.506	3.293
80	1.848	2.202	2.894	1.907	2.272	2.986	2.026	2.414	3.173
100	1.822	2.172	2.854	1.874	2.233	2.934	1.977	2.355	3.096
200	1.764	2.102	2.762	1.798	2.143	2.816	1.865	2.222	2.921
500	1.717	2.046	2.689	1.737	2.070	2.721	1.777	2.117	2.783
1000	1.695	2.019	2.654	1.709	2.036	2.676	1.736	2.068	2.718
∞	1.645	1.960	2.576	1.645	1.960	2.576	1.645	1.960	2.576

Appendix VIII
Factors for one-sided normal tolerance limits

	90% Confidence That Percentage of Population Below (Above) Limit Is			95% Confidence That Percentage of Population Below (Above) Limit Is			99% Confidence That Percentage of Population Below (Above) Limit Is		
n	90%	95%	99%	90%	95%	99%	90%	95%	99%
3	4.258	5.310	7.340	6.158	7.655	10.552			
4	3.187	3.957	5.437	4.163	5.145	7.042			
5	2.742	3.400	4.666	3.407	4.202	5.741			
6	2.494	3.091	4.242	3.006	3.707	5.062	4.408	5.409	7.334
7	2.333	2.894	3.972	2.755	3.399	4.641	3.856	4.730	6.411
8	2.219	2.755	3.783	2.582	3.188	4.353	3.496	4.287	5.811
9	2.133	2.649	3.641	2.454	3.031	4.143	3.242	3.971	5.389
10	2.065	2.568	3.532	2.355	2.911	3.981	3.048	3.739	5.075
11	2.012	2.503	3.444	2.275	2.815	3.852	2.897	3.557	4.828
12	1.966	2.448	3.371	2.210	2.736	3.747	2.773	3.410	4.633
13	1.928	2.403	3.310	2.155	2.670	3.659	2.677	3.290	4.472
14	1.895	2.363	3.257	2.108	2.614	3.585	2.592	3.189	4.336
15	1.866	2.329	3.212	2.068	2.566	3.520	2.521	3.102	4.224
16	1.842	2.299	3.172	2.032	2.523	3.463	2.458	3.028	4.124
17	1.820	2.272	3.136	2.001	2.486	3.415	2.405	2.962	4.038
18	1.800	2.249	3.106	1.974	2.453	3.370	2.357	2.906	3.961
19	1.781	2.228	3.078	1.949	2.423	3.331	2.315	2.855	3.893
20	1.765	2.208	3.052	1.926	2.396	3.295	2.275	2.807	3.832
21	1.750	2.190	3.028	1.905	2.371	3.262	2.241	2.768	3.776
22	1.736	2.174	3.007	1.887	2.350	3.233	2.208	2.729	3.727
23	1.724	2.159	2.987	1.869	2.329	3.206	2.179	2.693	3.680
24	1.712	2.145	2.969	1.853	2.309	3.181	2.154	2.663	3.638
25	1.702	2.132	2.952	1.838	2.292	3.158	2.129	2.632	3.601
30	1.657	2.080	2.884	1.778	2.220	3.064	2.029	2.516	3.446
35	1.623	2.041	2.833	1.732	2.166	2.994	1.957	2.431	3.334
40	1.598	2.010	2.793	1.697	2.126	2.941	1.902	2.365	3.250
45	1.577	1.986	2.762	1.669	2.092	2.897	1.857	2.313	3.181
50	1.560	1.965	2.735	1.646	2.065	2.863	1.821	2.296	3.124

10480	15011	01536	02011	81647	91646	69179	14194	62590
22368	46573	25595	85393	30995	89198	27982	53402	93965
24130	48360	22527	97265	76393	64809	15179	24830	49340
42167	93093	06243	61680	07856	16376	39440	53537	71341
37570	39975	81837	16656	06121	91782	60468	81305	49684
77921	06907	11008	42751	27756	53498	18602	70659	90655
99562	72905	56420	69994	98872	31016	71194	18738	44013
96301	91977	05463	07972	18876	20922	94595	56869	69014
89579	14342	63661	10281	17453	18103	57740	84378	25331
85475	36857	53342	53988	53060	59533	38867	62300	08158
28918	69578	88231	33276	70997	79936	56865	05859	90106
63553	40961	48235	03427	49626	69445	18663	72695	52180
09429	93969	52636	92737	88974	33488	36320	17617	30015
10365	61129	87529	85689	48237	52267	67689	93394	01511
07119	97336	71048	08178	77233	13916	47564	81056	97735
51085	12765	51821	51259	77452	16308	60756	92144	49442
02368	21382	52404	60268	89368	19885	55322	44819	01188
01011	54092	33362	94904	31273	04146	18594	29852	71585
52162	53916	46369	58586	23216	14513	83149	98736	23495
07056	97628	33787	09998	42698	06691	76988	13602	51851
48663	91245	85828	14346	09172	30168	90229	04734	59193
54164	58492	22421	74103	47070	25306	76468	26384	58151
32639	32363	05597	24200	13363	38005	94342	28728	35806
29334	27001	87637	87308	58731	00256	45834	15398	46557
02488	33062	28834	07351	19731	92420	60952	61280	50001
81525	72295	04839	96423	24878	82651	66566	14778	76797
29676	20591	68086	26432	46901	20849	89768	81536	86645
00742	57392	39064	66432	84673	40027	32832	61362	98947
05366	04213	25669	26422	44407	44048	37937	63904	45766
91921	26418	64117	94305	26766	25940	39972	22209	71500
00582	04711	87917	77341	42206	35126	74087	99547	81817
00725	69884	62797	56170	86324	88072	76222	36086	84637
69011	65795	95876	55293	18988	27354	26575	08625	40801
25976	57948	29888	88604	67917	48708	18912	82271	65424
09763	83473	73577	12908	30883	18317	28290	35797	05998
91567	42595	27958	30134	04024	86385	29880	99730	55536
17955	56349	90999	49127	20044	59931	06115	20542	18059
46503	18584	18845	49618	02304	51038	20655	58727	28168
92157	89634	94824	78171	84610	82834	09922	25417	44137
14577	62765	35605	81263	39667	47358	56873	56307	61607
98427	07523	33362	64270	01638	92477	66969	98420	04880
34914	63976	88720	82765	34476	17032	87589	40836	32427
70060	28277	39475	46473	23219	53416	94970	25832	69975
53976	54914	06990	67245	68350	82948	11398	42878	80287
76072	29515	40980	07391	58745	25774	22987	80059	39911
90725	52210	83974	29992	65831	38857	50490	83765	55657
64364	67412	33339	31926	14883	24413	59744	92351	97473
08962	00358	31662	25388	61642	34072	81249	35648	56891
95012	68379	93526	70765	10592	04542	76463	54328	02349
15664	10493	20492	38391	91132	21999	59516	81652	27195

Bibliography

1. Ailor, R. B., J. W. Schmidt, and G. K. Bennett (1975). "The Design of Economic Acceptance Sampling Plans for a Mixture of Attributes and Variables," *AIIE Transactions*, Vol. 7.

2. Alt, F. B. (1985). "Multivariate Quality Control," in *Encyclopedia of Statistical Sciences*, Vol. 6, edited by N. L. Johnson and S. Kotz, John Wiley, New York.

3. Aroian, L., and H. Levine (1950). "The Effectiveness of Quality Control Charts," *Journal of the American Statistical Association*, Vol. 44.

4. Baker, K. R. (1971). "Two Process Models in the Economic Design of an $\bar{x}$ Chart," *AIIE Transactions*, Vol. 3.

5. Banerjee, P. K., and M. A. Rahim (1988). "Economic Design of $\bar{x}$-Control Charts Under Weibull Shock Models," *Technometrics*, Vol. 30.

6. Barish, N. N., and N. Hauser (1963). "Economic Design for Control Decisions," *Journal of Industrial Engineering*, Vol. 14.

7. Barnhard, G. A. (1959). "Control Charts and Stochastic Processes," *Journal of the Royal Statistical Society*, (B), Vol. 21.

8. Bather, J. A. (1963). "Control Charts and the Minimization of Costs," *Journal of the Royal Statistical Society*, (B), Vol. 25.

9. Bisgaard, S., W. G. Hunter, and L. Pallesen (1984). "Economic Selection of Quality of Manufactured Product," *Technometrics*, Vol. 26.

10. Bowker, A. H., and G. J. Lieberman (1972). *Engineering Statistics*, 2nd ed., Prentice-Hall, Englewood Cliffs, N.J.

11. Box, G.E.P. (1957). "Evolutionary Operation: A Method for Increasing Industrial Productivity," *Applied Statistics*, Vol. 6.

12. Box, G.E.P., Bisgaard, S., and C. Fung (1988). "An Explanation and Critique of Taguchi's Contributions to Quality Engineering," *Quality and Reliability Engineering International*, Vol. 4.

13. Box, G.E.P., and N. R. Draper (1969). *Evolutionary Operation*, John Wiley, New York.

14. Box, G.E.P., and N. R. Draper (1986). *Empirical Model Building and Response Surfaces*, John Wiley, New York.

15. Box, G.E.P., and G. M. Jenkins (1976). *Time Series Analysis, Forecasting, and Control*, 2nd ed., Holden-Day, San Francisco, Calif.

16. Boyles, R. A. (1989). "The Taguchi Capability Index," Unpublished personal communication.

17. Burr, I. J. (1967). "The Effect of Nonnormality on Constants for $\bar{x}$ and R Charts," *Industrial Quality Control*, Vol. 23.

18. Case, K. E., J. W. Schmidt, and G. K. Bennett (1975). "Discrete Economic Multiattribute Acceptance Sampling," *AIIE Transactions*, Vol. 7.

19. Chan, L. K., Cheng, S. W., and F. A. Spiring (1988). "A New Measure of Process Capability: C_{pm}," *Journal of Quality Technology*, Vol. 20.

20. Chiu, W. K. (1973). "Comments on the Economic Design of $\bar{x}$-Charts," *Journal of the American Statistical Association*, Vol. 68.

21. Chiu, W. K. (1974). "The Economic Design of Cusum Charts for Controlling Normal Means," *Applied Statistics*, Vol. 23.

22. Chiu, W. K. (1975). "Economic Design of Attribute Control Charts," *Technometrics*, Vol. 17.

23. Chiu, W. K. (1976a). "Economic Design of np-Charts for Processes Subject to a Multiplicity of Assignable Causes," *Management Science*, Vol. 23.

24. Chiu, W. K. (1976b). "On the Estimation of Data Parameters for Economic Optimum $\bar{X}$-Charts," *Metrika*, Vol. 23.

25. Chiu, W. K., and K. C. Cheung (1977). "An Economic Study of $\bar{x}$-Charts with Warning Limits," *Journal of Quality Technology*, Vol. 9.

26. Chiu, W. K., and G. B. Wetherill (1974). "A Simplified Scheme for the Economic Design of $\bar{x}$-Charts," *Journal of Quality Technology*, Vol. 6.

27. Chiu, W. K., and G. B. Wetherill (1975). "Quality Control Practices," *International Journal of Production Research*, Vol. 13.

28. Clifford, P. C. (1959). "Control Charts Without Calculations," *Industrial Quality Control*, Vol. 15, pp. 40–44.

29. Cornell, J. A., and A. I. Khuri (1987). *Response Surfaces*, Marcel Dekker, Inc., New York.

30. Cowden, D. J. (1957). *Statistical Methods in Quality Control*, Prentice-Hall, Englewood Cliffs, N.J.

31. Crowder, S. V. (1987a). "A Simple Method for Studying Run-Length Distributions of Exponentially Weighted Moving Average Charts," *Technometrics*, Vol. 29.

32. Crowder, S. V. (1987b). "Computation of ARL for Combined Individual Measurement and Moving Range Charts," *Journal of Quality Technology*, Vol. 19.

33. Crowder, S. V. (1989), "Design of Exponentially Weighted Moving Average Schemes," *Journal of Quality Technology*, Vol. 21.

34. Dodge, H. F. (1943). "A Sampling Plan for Continuous Production," *Annals of Mathematical Statistics*, Vol. 14.

35. Dodge, H. F. (1955). "Chain Sampling Inspection Plans," *Industrial Quality Control*, Vol. 11.

36. Dodge, H. F. (1956). "Skip-Lot Sampling Plan," *Industrial Quality Control*, Vol. 11.

37. Dodge, H. F., and H. G. Romig (1959). *Sampling Inspection Tables, Single and Double Sampling*, 2nd ed., John Wiley, New York.

38. Dodge, H. F., and M. N. Torrey (1951). "Additional Continuous Sampling Inspection Plans," *Industrial Quality Control*, Vol. 7.

39. Dorris, A. L., and B. J. Foote (1978). "Inspection Error and Statistical Quality Control: A Survey," *AIIE Transactions*, Vol. 10.

40. Duncan, A. J. (1956). "The Economic Design of $\bar{X}$-Charts Used to Maintain Current Control of a Process," *Journal of the American Statistical Association*, Vol. 51.

41. Duncan, A. J. (1971). "The Economic Design of $\bar{X}$-Charts When There is a Multiplicity of Assignable Causes," *Journal of the American Statistical Association*, Vol. 66.

42. Duncan, A. J. (1974). *Quality Control and Industrial Statistics*, 4th ed., Irwin, Homewood, Ill.

43. Duncan, A. J. (1978). "The Economic Design of p-Charts to Maintain Current Control of a Process: Some Numerical Results," *Technometrics*, Vol. 20.

44. Ewan, W. D. (1963). "When and How to Use Cu-Sum Charts," *Technometrics*, Vol. 5.

45. Ferrell, E. B. (1953). "Control Charts Using Midranges and Medians," *Industrial Quality Control*, Vol. 9.

46. Freund, R. A. (1957). "Acceptance Control Charts," *Industrial Quality Control*, Vol. 12.

47. Gardiner, J. S. (1987). *Detecting Small Shifts in Quality Levels in a Near-Zero Defect Environment for Integrated Circuits*, Ph.D. Dissertation, Department of Mechanical Engineering, University of Washington, Seattle, Wash.

48. Gardiner, J. S., and D. C. Montgomery (1987). "Using Statistical Control Charts for Software Quality Control," *Quality and Reliability Engineering International*, Vol. 3.

49. Gibra, I. N. (1967). "Optimal Control of Processes Subject to Linear Trends," *Journal of Industrial Engineering*, Vol. 18.

50. Gibra, I. N. (1971). "Economically Optimal Determination of the Parameters of an $\bar{X}$-Control Chart," *Management Science*, Vol. 17.

51. Gibra, I. N. (1978). "Economically Optical Determination of the Parameters of *np*-Control Charts," *Journal of Quality Technology*, Vol. 10.

52. Girshick, M. A., and H. Rubin (1952). "A Bayes' Approach to a Quality Control Model," *Annals of Mathematical Statistics*, Vol. 23.

53. Goel, A. L. (1968). "A Comparative and Economic Investigation of $\bar{X}$ and Cumulative Sum Control Charts," Ph.D. Dissertation, University of Wisconsin, Madison.

54. Goel, A. L., S. C. Jain, and S. M. Wu (1968). "An Algorithm for the Determination of the Economic Design of $\bar{x}$ charts Based on Duncan's Model," *Journal of the American Statistical Association*, Vol. 62.

55. Goel, A. L., and S. M. Wu (1971). "Determination of ARL and a Contour Nomogram for Cusum Charts to Control Normal Means," *Technometrics*, Vol. 13.

56. Goel, A. L., and S. M. Wu (1973). "Economically Optimum Design of Cusum Charts," *Management Science*, Vol. 19.

57. Gordon, G. G., and J. I. Weindling (1975). "A Cost Model for Economic Design of Warning Limit Control Chart Schemes," *AIIE Transactions*, Vol. 7.

58. Grant, E. L., and R. S. Leavenworth (1980). *Statistical Quality Control*, 5th ed., McGraw-Hill, New York.

59. Grubbs, F. E. (1946). "The Difference Control Chart with an Example of Its Use," *Industrial Quality Control*, Vol. 2.

60. Guenther, W. C. (1972). "Tolerance Intervals for Univariate Distributions," *Naval Research Logistics Quarterly*, Vol. 19.

61. Guthrie, D., and M. V. Johns (1959). "Bayes Acceptance Sampling Procedures for Large Lots," *Annals of Mathematical Statistics*, Vol. 30.

62. Hahn, G. J., and S. S. Shapiro (1967). *Statistical Models in Engineering*, John Wiley, New York.

63. Hald, A. (1960). "The Compound Hypergeometric Distribution and a System of Single Sampling Inspection Plans Based on Prior Distributions and Costs," *Technometrics*, Vol. 2.

64. Hald, A. (1965), "Bayesian Single Sampling Attribute Plans for Discrete Prior Distributions," *Mat. Fys. Dkr. Dan Vid. Selsk.*, Vol. 3.

65. Hald, A. (1968). "Bayesian Single Sampling Attributes Plans for Continuous Prior Distributions," *Technometrics*, Vol. 10.

66. Heikes, R. G., D. C. Montgomery, and J.Y.H. Yeung (1974). "Alternative Process Models in the Economic Design of T^2 Control Charts," *AIIE Transactions*, Vol. 6.

67. Hicks, C. R. (1955). "Some Applications of Hotelling's T^2," *Industrial Quality Control*, Vol. 11.

68. Hill, D. (1956). "Modified Control Limits," *Applied Statistics*, Vol. 5.

69. Hillier, F. S. (1969). "$\bar{x}$ and R Chart Control Limits Based on a Small Number of Subgroups," *Journal of Quality Technology*, Vol. 1.

70. Hines, W. W., and D. C. Montgomery (1990). *Probability and Statistics in Engineering and Management Science*, 3rd ed., John Wiley, New York.

71. Hotelling, H. (1947). "Multivariate Quality Control," *Techniques of Statistical Analysis*, Eisenhart, Hastay, and Wallis, Eds., McGraw-Hill, New York.

72. Howell, J. M. (1949). "Control Charting Largest and Smallest Value," *Annals of Mathematical Statistics*, Vol. 20.

73. Hunter, J. S. (1985). "Statistical Design Applied to Product Design," *Journal of Quality Technology*, Vol. 17.

74. Hunter, J. S. (1986). "The Exponentially Weighted Moving Average," *Journal of Quality Technology*, Vol. 18.

75. Hunter, J. S. (1987). Letter to the Editor, *Quality Progress*, May 1987.

76. Hunter, W. G., and C. P. Kartha (1977). "Determining the Most Profitable Target Value for a Production Process," *Journal of Quality Technology*, Vol. 9.

77. Inglewitz, B., and D. Hoaglin (1987). "Use of Boxplots for Process Evaluation," *Journal of Quality Technology*, Vol. 19.

78. Jackson, J. E. (1956). "Quality Control Methods for Two Related Variables," *Industrial Quality Control*, Vol. 12.

79. Jackson, J. E. (1959). "Quality Control Methods for Several Related Variables," *Technometrics*, Vol. 1.

80. Jackson, J. E. (1972). "All Count Distributions Are Not Alike," *Journal of Quality Technology*, Vol. 4.

81. Jackson, J. E. (1980). "Principal Components and Factor Analysis: Part I— Principal Components," *Journal of Quality Technology*, Vol. 12.

82. Johnson, N. L. (1961). "A Simple Theoretical Approach to Cumulative Sum Control Charts," *Journal of the American Statistical Association*, Vol. 54.

83. Johnson, N. L., and S. Kotz (1969). *Discrete Distributions*, Houghton Mifflin, Boston, Mass.

84. Johnson, N. L., and F. C. Leone (1962a). "Cumulative Sum Control Charts— Mathematical Principles Applied to Their Construction and Use," Part I, *Industrial Quality Control*, Vol. 18.

85. Johnson, N. L., and F. C. Leone (1962b). "Cumulative Sum Control Charts— Mathematical Principles Applied to Their Construction and Use," Part II, *Industrial Quality Control*, Vol. 18.

86. Johnson, N. L., and F. C. Leone (1962c). "Cumulative Sum Control Charts— Mathematical Principles Applied to Their Construction and Use," Part III, *Industrial Quality Control*, Vol. 18.

87. Juran, J. M., and F. M. Gryna, Jr. (1980). *Quality Planning and Analysis*, 2nd ed., McGraw-Hill, New York.

88. Kane, V. E. (1986). "Process Capability Indices," *Journal of Quality Technology*, Vol. 18.

89. Knappenberger, H. A., and A.H.E. Grandage (1969). "Minimum Cost Quality Control Tests," *AIIE Transactions*, Vol. 1.

90. Ladany, S. P. (1973). "Optimal Use of Control Charts for Controlling Current Production," *Management Science*, Vol. 19.

91. Ladany, S. P., and Y. Alperovitch (1975). "An Optimal Set-up Policy for Control Charts," *Omega*, Vol. 3.

92. Langenberg, P., and B. Inglewitz (1986). "Trimmed Mean $\bar{x}$ and R Charts," *Journal of Quality Technology*, Vol. 18.

93. Lieberman, G. J., and G. J. Resnikoff (1955). "Sampling Plans for Inspection by Variables," *Journal of the American Statistical Association*, Vol. 50.

94. Lieberman, G. J., and H. Solomon (1955). "Multi-Level Continuous Sampling Plans," *Annals of Mathematical Statistics*, Vol. 26.

95. Lorenzen, T. J., and L. C. Vance (1986). "The Economic Design of Control Charts: A Unified Approach," *Technometrics*, Vol. 28.

96. Lucas, J. M. (1973). "A Modified V-Mask Control Scheme," *Technometrics*, Vol. 15.

97. Lucas, J. M. (1976). "The Design and Use of Cumulative Sum Quality Control Schemes," *Journal of Quality Technology*, Vol. 8.

98. Lucas, J. M. (1982). "Combined Shewhart–CUSUM Quality Control Schemes," *Journal of Quality Technology*, Vol. 14.

99. Lucas, J. M. (1985). "Counted Data CUSUM's," *Technometrics*, Vol. 27.

100. Lucas, J. M., and Crosier, R. B. (1982). "Fast Initial Response for CUSUM Quality Control Schemes," *Technometrics*, Vol. 24.

101. Lucas, J. M., and M. S. Saccucci (1990), "Exponentially Weighted Moving Average Control Schemes: Properties and Enhancements", *Technometrics*, Vol. 32.

102. Mandel, J. (1969). "The Regression Control Chart," *Journal of Quality Technology*, Vol. 1.

103. Manuele, J. (1945). "Control Chart for Determining Tool Wear," *Industrial Quality Control*, Vol. 1.

104. Molina, E. C. (1942). *Poisson's Exponential Binomial Limit*, Van Nostrand Reinhold, New York.

105. Montgomery, D. C. (1984). *Design and Analysis of Experiments*, 2nd ed., John Wiley, New York.

106. Montgomery, D. C., and J. J. Friedman (1989). "Statistical Process Control in a Computer-Integrated Manufacturing Environment," *Statistical Process Control in Automated Manufacturing*, edited by J. B. Keats and N. F. Hubele, Marcel Dekker, Inc., Series in Quality and Reliability, New York.

107. Montgomery, D. C., and R. G. Heikes (1976). "Process Failure Mechanisms and Optimal Design of Fraction Defective Control Charts," *AIIE Transactions*, Vol. 8.

108. Montgomery, D. C., R. G. Heikes, and J. F. Mance (1975). "Economic Design of Fraction Defective Control Charts," *Management Science*, Vol. 21.

109. Montgomery, D. C., and L. A. Johnson (1976). *Forecasting and Time Series Analysis*, McGraw-Hill, New York.

110. Montgomery, D. C., and P. J. Klatt (1972a). "Economic Design of T^2 Control Charts to Maintain Current Control of a Process," *Management Science*, Vol. 19.

111. Montgomery, D. C., and P. J. Klatt (1972b). "Minimum Cost Multivariate Quality Control Tests," *AIIE Transactions*, Vol. 4.

112. Montgomery, D. C., and E. A. Peck (1982). *Introduction to Linear Regression Analysis*, John Wiley, New York.

113. Montgomery, D. C., and H. M. Wadsworth, Jr. (1972). "Some Techniques for Multivariate Quality Control Applications," *ASQC Technical Conference Transactions*, Washington, D. C.

114. Murphy, J. (1987). "Selecting Out of Control Variables with the T^2 Multivariate Quality Control Procedure," *The Statistician*, Vol. 36.

115. Nelson, L. S. (1978). "Best Target Value for a Production Process," *Journal of Quality Technology*, Vol. 10.

116. Ott, E. R. (1975). *Process Quality Control*, McGraw-Hill, New York.

117. Ott, E. R., and R. D. Snee (1973). "Identifying Useful Differences in a Multiple-Head Machine," *Journal of Quality Technology*, Vol. 5.

118. Page, E. S. (1954). "Continuous Inspection Schemes," *Biometrics*, Vol. 41.

119. Page, E. S. (1961). "Cumulative Sum Control Charts," *Technometrics*, Vol. 3.

120. Page, E. S. (1963). "Controlling the Standard Deviation by Cusums and Warning Lines," *Technometrics*, Vol. 5.

121. Panagos, M. R., R. G. Heikes, and D. C. Montgomery (1985). "Economic Design of Control Charts for Two Manufacturing Process Models," *Naval Research Logistics Quarterly*, Vol. 32.

122. Perry, R. L. (1973). "Skip-Lot Sampling Plans," *Journal of Quality Technology*, Vol. 5.

123. Quesenberry, C. P. (1988). "An SPC Approach to Compensating a Tool-Wear Process," *Journal of Quality Technology*, Vol. 20.

124. Reynolds, J. H. (1971). "The Run Sum Control Chart Procedure," *Journal of Quality Technology*, Vol. 3.

125. Roberts, S. W. (1958). "Properties of Control Chart Zone Tests," *Bell System Technical Journal*, Vol. 37.

126. Roberts, S. W. (1959). "Control Chart Tests Based on Geometric Moving Averages," *Technometrics*, Vol. 1.

127. Rocke, D. M. (1989). "Robust Control Charts," *Technometrics*, Vol. 31.

128. Ross, S. M. (1970). *Applied Probability Models with Optimization Applications*, Holden-Day, San Francisco, Calif.

129. Ross, S. M. (1971). "Quality Control Under Markovian Deterioration," *Management Science*, Vol. 17.

130. Saniga, E. M. (1978). "Joint Economically Optimal Design of $\bar{x}$ and R Control Charts," *Management Science*, Vol. 24.

131. Saniga, E. M. (1989). "Economic Statistical Control Chart Design with an Application to $\bar{x}$ and R charts," *Technometrics*, Vol. 31.

132. Saniga, E. M., and L. E. Shirland (1977). "Quality Control in Practice—A Survey," *Quality Progress*, Vol. 10.

133. Savage, I. R. (1962). "Surveillance Problems," *Naval Research Logistics Quarterly*, Vol. 9.

134. Schilling, E. G., and P. R. Nelson (1976). "The Effect of Nonnormality on the Control Limits of $\bar{x}$ Charts," *Journal of Quality Technology*, Vol. 8.

135. Schmidt, J. W., G. K. Bennett, and K. E. Case (1976). "A Three-Action Cost Model for Acceptance Sampling by Variables," *Journal of Quality Technology*, Vol. 12.

136. Schmidt, S. R., and J. R. Boudot (1989). "A Monte Carlo Simulation Study Comparing Effectiveness of Signal-to-Noise Ratios and Other Methods for Identifying Dispersion Effects," presented at the 1989 Rocky Mountain Quality Conference.

137. Schmidt, J. W., K. E. Case, and G. K. Bennett (1974). "The Choice of Variables Sampling Plans Using Cost Effective Criteria," *AIIE Transactions*, Vol. 6.

138. Shapiro, S. S. (1980). *How to Test Normality and Other Distributional Assumptions*, Vol. 3, *The ASQC Basic References in Quality Control: Statistical Techniques*, ASQC, Milwaukee, Wis.

139. Sheaffer, R. L., and R. S. Leavenworth (1976). "The Negative Binomial Model for Counts in Units of Varying Size," *Journal of Quality Technology*, Vol. 8.

140. Stephens, K. S. (1979). *How to Perform Continuous Sampling (CSP)*, Vol. 2, *The ASQC Basic References in Quality Control: Statistical Techniques*, ASQC, Milwaukee, Wis.

141. Stewart, R. D., D. C. Montgomery, and R. G. Heikes (1978). "Choice of Double Sampling Plans Based on Prior Distributions and Costs," *AIIE Transactions*, Vol. 10.

142. Taguchi, G. (1986). *Introduction to Quality Engineering*, Asian Productivity Organization, UNIPUB, White Plains, N.Y.

143. Taguchi, G., and Y. Wu (1980). *Introduction to Off-Line Quality Control*, Control Japan Quality Control Organization, Nagoya, Japan.

144. Taylor, H. M. (1965). "Markovian Sequential Replacement Processes," *Annals of Mathematical Statistics*, Vol. 36.

145. Taylor, H. M. (1967). "Statistical Control of a Gaussian Process," *Technometrics*, Vol. 9.

146. Taylor, H. M. (1968). "The Economic Design of Cumulative Sum Control Charts," *Technometrics*, Vol. 10.

147. Tiago de Oliveira, J., and S. B. Littauer (1966). "Techniques for Economic Use of Control Charts," *Revue de Statistique Appliquée*, Vol. 14.

148. United States Department of Defense (1957). *Sampling Procedures and Tables for Inspection by Variables for Percent Defective*, MIL STD 414, U.S. Government Printing Office, Washington, D.C.

149. United States Department of Defense (1963). *Sampling Procedures and Tables for Inspection by Attributes*, MIL STD 105D, U.S. Government Printing Office, Washington, D.C.

150. Wald, A. (1947). *Sequential Analysis*, John Wiley, New York.

151. Wang, C.-H., and F. S. Hillier (1970). "Mean and Variance Control Chart Limits Based on a Small Number of Subgroups," *Journal of Quality Technology*, Vol. 2.

152. Weiler, H., (1952). "On the Most Economical Sample Size for Controlling the Mean of a Population," *Annals of Mathematical Statistics*, Vol. 23.

153. Weiler, H. (1953). "The Use of Runs to Control the Mean in Quality Control," *Journal of the American Statistical Association*, Vol. 48.

154. Weiler, H. (1954). "A New Type of Control Limit for Means, Ranges, and Sequential Runs," *Journal of the American Statistical Association*, Vol. 49.

155. Western Electric (1956). *Statistical Quality Control Handbook*, Western Electric Corporation, Indianapolis, Ind.

156. Wetherill, G. B., and W. K. Chiu (1975). "A Review of Acceptance Sampling Schemes with Emphasis on the Economic Aspect," *International Statistical Review*, Vol. 43.

157. White, C. C. (1974). "A Markov Quality Control Process Subject to Partial Observation," *Management Science*, Vol. 23.

158. White, E. M., and R. Schroeder (1987). "A Simultaneous Control Chart," *Journal of Quality Technology*, Vol. 19.

159. Woodall, W. H. (1986). "Weakness of the Economic Design of Control Charts," Letter to the Editor, *Technometrics*, Vol. 28.

160. Woodall, W. H. (1987). "Conflicts Between Deming's Philosophy and the Economic Design of Control Charts," in *Frontiers in Statistical Quality Control*, *3*, eds. H. J. Lenz, G. B. Wetherill, and P.-T. Wilrich, Physica-Verlag, Vienna.

Answers to Selected Exercises

Chapter 2

2-1   **a.** $\bar{x} = 10.028$

      b. $S = 0.0155$

2-3   **a.** $\bar{x} = 130$, $S = 8.918$

2-5 $\bar{x} = 89.637$, $S = 0.4378$

2-9 $(x - 1)/36$ for $x = 2, 3, 4, 5, 6, 7$; $(13 - x)/36$ for $x = 8, 9, 10, 11, 12$

2-11 **a.** 98.9%

      b. 2.6%

      c. 3.5%

2-13 **a.** $k = 0.05$

      b. $\mu = 1.867$; $\sigma^2 = 0.615$

2-15 **a.** 0.1175

      b. $19.125

2-17 $P(0 \text{ nonconforming}) = 0.3642$

2-19 $P(\hat{p} > k = 1) = 0.1587$; $P(\hat{p} > k = 2) = 0.0228$, $P(\hat{p} > k = 3) = 0.0013$

2-21 $P(1 \text{ or more}) = 0.4234$

2-23 $P(x = 0) = 0.9048$

2-25 $P(x = 1) = 0.0099$

2-27 $P(x \geq 5000) = 0.9856$

2-29 0.9544

2-31 0.0021

2-33 Process 1

Chapter 3

3-1 8.2535 ± 0.001

3-3 26 ± 0.9418

3-5 13.396 ± 0.0036

3-7 246

3-9 $1.16 \leq \sigma^2 \leq 7.31$

3-11 a. 10.2594 ± 0.53275

  b. $0.739 \leq \sigma^2 \leq 1.547$

  c. $\sigma \leq 1.4373$

3-13 $\sigma \geq 0.00255$

3-15 a. $[-6.1096, -3.89]$

  b. $[0.148, 4.82]$

3-17 a. $[-6.706, 3.106]$

  b. $[0.206, 3.34)$

3-19 0.1547

3-21 Reject H_0, $Z_0 = 6.778$.

3-23 Reject H_0, $t_0 = 1.946$.

3-25 Reject H_0, $Z_0 = 105$

3-27 a. Do not reject H_0, $F_0 = 0.8455$.

  b. Do not reject H_0.

3-29 a. Do not reject, $F_0 = 1.042$.

  b. $t_0 = 0.416$, do not reject H_0.

3-31 $Z_0 = 0.4714$, do not reject H_0.

3-33 $n > 4$

3-37 Do not reject H_0.

3-39 $(-0.036, 0.069)$, do not reject H_0.

3-41 $Z_0 = 3$, do not reject H_0.

Chapter 4

4-11 Pattern not random

4-13 No

4-15 Yes

4-17 2-sigma: 3
3-sigma: 370

4-19 $\beta = 0.5974$

4-21 a. $\beta(1 - \beta)$

    b. $\beta^{k-1}(1 - \beta)$

    c. $1/(1 - \beta)$

    d. β

    e. β

    f. $(1 - \beta)^2$

    g. $1 - \beta^k$

Chapter 5

5-1 $\bar{p} = 0.537$, UCL $= 0.1213$, LCL $= 0.0139$

5-3 $\bar{p} = 0.06$

5-5 a. $\bar{p} = 0.1228$, UCL $= 0.1425$, LCL $= 0.1031$

5-7 $P(\text{detecting shift}) = 0.0793$
$P(\text{detecting on 3rd day}) = 0.2195$

5-9 a. $\bar{p} = 0.1$, UCL $= 0.2125$, LCL $= 0$

    b. $\beta = 0.5$

5-11 225

5-13 a. $p = 0.07$, UCL $= 0.108$, LCL $= 0.032$

    b. 0.2981

    c. 0.5073

5-15 a. UCL $= 28.276$, LCL $= 5.724$

    b. 0.635

5-17 a. $np = 40$, UCL $= 58$, LCL $= 22$

5-19 3

5-21 a. 0.022

5-25 990

5-27 a. 2.0005

    b. $np = 20$, UCL $= 33.08$, LCL $= 6.92$

    c. 0.8577

5-29 a. 396

    b. 44

5-31 a. $\bar{p} = 0.02$, UCL $= 0.062$, LCL $= 0$

    b. $\bar{p} = 0.038$

5-33 $np = 2.505$, UCL $= 7.21$, LCL $= 0$

5-35 process in control

5-37 $\bar{u} = 0.6764$

5-41 after out-of-control points removed, $\bar{c} = 6.167$, UCL $= 13.62$, LCL $= 0$

5-43 a. $\bar{u} = 0.00344$, UCL $= 0.00696$, LCL $= 0$

    b. $\bar{c} = 0.0756$, UCL $= 0.9$, LCL $= 0$

5-45 a. UCL $= 10$, LCL $= 0$

    b. $\bar{u} = 1$, UCL $= 4$, LCL $= 0$

5-47 a. UCL $= 18$, LCL $= 0$

    b. $\bar{u} = 4$, UCL $= 10$, LCL $= 0$

5-49 UCL $= 13$, LCL $= 2.2$

5-51 $\bar{u} = 7$

5-53 $\bar{u} = 0.17$, UCL $= 0.33$, LCL $= 0.0097$

5-55 $P(u \leq 9) = 0.992$

5-57 a. UCL $= 18.93$, LCL $= 5.07$

    b. $\alpha = 0.057$

    c. $\beta = 0.554$

    d. 2.2

5-59 a. $\bar{u} = 4$, UCL $= 10$, LCL $= 0$

    b. $\alpha = 0.021$

5-61 $n = k^2 / \bar{c}$

Chapter 6

6-1 a. $\bar{x}$ chart: UCL $= 36.721$, LCL $= 31.287$
R chart: UCL $= 9.957$, LCL $= 0$
Before revised limits

    b. $\hat{\sigma} = 1.935$, $\hat{p} = 0$

6-3 a. $\bar{x}$ chart: UCL $= 47.339$, LCL $= -25.339$
R chart: UCL $= 133.213$, LCL $= 0$

    b. $\hat{\sigma} = 27.085$

    c. PCR $= 1.23$

6-5 a. $\bar{x}$ chart: UCL $= 14.77$, LCL $= 5.98$
S chart: UCL $= 6.12$, LCL $= 0$

    b. $\hat{\sigma} = 2.93$

6-7 $\bar{x}$ chart: UCL $= 89.49$, LCL $= 70.51$
S chart: UCL $= 16.69$, LCL $= 2.76$

6-9 a. $\bar{x}$ chart: UCL $= 21.93$, LCL $= 18.07$
S chart: UCL $= 2.955$, LCL $= 0.045$

    b. $\hat{\sigma} = 1.576$, UNTL $= 24.728$, LNTL $= 14.272$

    c. PCR $= 0.846$

    d. $P(x \geq 23) = 0.0287$, $P(x \leq 15) = 0.00076$

    e. 0.0055

6-11 a. $\bar{x}$ chart: UCL $= 237.3$, LCL $= 208.6$
R chart: UCL $= 65.966$, LCL $= 2.606$

    b. $\hat{\sigma} = 12.68$

     c. PCR $= 0.92$

     d. $\hat{p} = 0.0058$

6-13 a. $\hat{\sigma} = 1.6$

     b. $\bar{x}$ chart: UCL $= 22.14$, LCL $= 17.86$
       S chart: UCL $= 3.13$, LCL $= 0$

     c. 0.578

6-15 PCR $= 0.834$

6-17 a. $\bar{x}$ chart: UCL $= 22.63$, LCL $= 17.37$
       R chart: UCL $= 9.64$, LCL $= 0$

     b. $\sigma = 1.96$

     c. PCR $= 0.85$

     d. 0.059

6-19 0.841345

6-21 a. $\bar{x}$ chart: UCL $= 23.03$, LCL $= 17.49$
       R chart: UCL $= 10.15$, LCL $= 0$

6-23 a. $\hat{\sigma}_x = 0.399$, $\hat{\sigma}_y = 0.172$

6-25 a. UCL $= 30.97$, LCL $= 0$

     b. $\hat{\mu} = 429$, $\hat{\sigma} = 14.84$

6-27 $0.3348, 0.7056$

6-29 PCR $= 0.7681$

6-31 a. PCR $= 1.11$

6-33 UCL $= 627.96$, LCL $= 572.04$

6-35 6.3

6-37 a. 4

     b. UCL $= 8.35$, LCL $= 0$

     c. 0.1056

     e. 0.97725

     f. 0.99999

6-39 a. $\hat{\sigma} = 8.66$

     b. 0.1355

     c. 0.0214

     d. 0.3109

     e. 3.22

6-41 Moving range: UCL $= 10.5$, LCL $= 0$
     Individual: UCL $= 61.815$, LCL $= 44.719$

Chapter 7

7-1 $d = 4.625$, $\theta = 15.6°$

7-7 $L(\Delta) = 3.65$, $d = 2.982$, $L(0) = 50$

7-9 $d = 48.87$, $\theta = 7.125°$, $H = 12.21$, $K = 0.25$

Chapter 8

8-1 $\bar{x}$ chart: UCL = 4.438, LCL = 0, CL = 0.5505
R chart: UCL = 9.758, LCL = 0, CL = 3.8

8-3 $\bar{x}$ chart: UCL = 55.36, LCL = 50.63, CL = 52.988
R chart: UCL = 5.946, LCL = 0, CL = 2.31

8-5 **a.** UCL = 44.5, LCL = 35.5
b. UCL = 43.61, LCL = 36.76
c. UCL = 43.24, LCL = 36.76

8-9 UCL = 66.3, LCL = 33.7, CL = 50

8-11 a. 4.00
b. 0.1056
c. 619.85, 600.15

8-13 No

8-15 at $t = 0$, UCL = 1.0027, LCL = 1.00196, CL = 1.0023

8-17 129.696 oz

Chapter 9

9-1 1.178

9-5 **a.** 3.17
b. 1.58

9-7 Process A: PCR = PCR_k = PCR_{km} = 1.11
Process B: PCR = 3.33, PCR_k = 1.67, PCR_{km} = 1.36

9-13 a. $\hat{\sigma}_{new}$ = 2.48, $\hat{\sigma}_{old}$ = 0.887
b. 0.27

9-15 a. $\hat{\sigma}_{repeatability}$ = 1.152, $\hat{\sigma}_{reproducibility}$ = 0.099
b. 1.156
c. 0.347

9-17 0.02275

9-19 μ_v = 72, σ_v^2 = 10.44

9-23 2.19

9-25 29

9-27 82.792

9-29 77

9-31 59

Chapter 10

10-1 **a.** 3.78

    b. $k = 2.210$, $h = 1.23$, $n = 3$

10-3 14.12

10-7 $n = 4$, $k = 2.3$, $h = 1.23$

10-11 **a.** 6.42

    b. 11.53

10-15 **a.** 57.49

    b. 62.24

    c. $n = 1.47$, $h = 0.09$

    d. $k = 2.16$, $h = 0.27$

10-17 4.22

10-19 0.416

Chapter 11

11-1 **a.** $F_0 = 3.59$. The three levels of C_2F_6 flow rate differ.

    b. Plots appear satisfactory.

    c. normal probability plot is satisfactory.

    d. 125 SCCM

11-3 CL $= 3.32$, LCL $= 1.19$, LCL $= 5.45$

11-5 **a.** $F_0 = 1.45$, no difference in firing temperatures

    b. There is more variability in baked density as the firing temperature increases.

    c. 500 or $525°\,C$

11-7 **a.** $F_0 = 14.42$, tips differ

    b. The residual plots are satisfactory.

11-9 Tip 4 is different from the others.

Chapter 12

12-1

Source	SS	DF	MS	F_0
Glass type (A)	14,450.00	1	14.450.00	273.83
Phosphor type (B)	933.38	2	466.69	8.84
AB	133.37	2	66.69	1.27
Error	633.25	12	52.77	
Total	16,150.00	17		

The main effects are significant.

12-3 Both plots appear satisfactory.

12-5 Plotting residuals versus A and C indicates mild inequality of variance. A plot of residuals versus predicted also confirms this.

12-7 A normal probability plot indicates that the main effect A is large, and that D, AD, AB, ABD, ABC, and $ABCD$ are also important. Assume that the main effect of C and all other interactions is negligible.

Source	SS	DF	MS	F_0
A	400.00	1	400.00	73.4
AB	81.00	1	81.00	14.9
ABC	144.00	1	144.00	26.4
D	100.00	1	100.00	18.3
AD	56.25	1	56.25	10.3
ABD	90.25	1	90.25	16.6
$ABCD$	41.25	1	41.25	7.6
Error	46.00	8	5.75	
Total	959.75	15		

12-9

Block 1		Block 2	
(1)	bc	a	acd
ab	ce	b	ace
ac	de	c	bcd
ad	abcd	d	bce
ae	abce	e	cde
bc	abde	abc	bde
bd	acde	abd	ade
cd	bcde	abc	abcde

Block 1 contains all the runs that are $-$ in the $ABCDE$ column, and Block 2 contains all the runs that are $+$ in the $ABCDE$ column. Therefore, $ABCDE$ is confounded with blocks.

12-11 a. Design is resolution IV with $D = ABC$. The aliases of the main effects are $A = BCD$, $B = ACD$, $C = ABD$, $D = ABC$, and $E = ABCDE$.

b. Large factor effects are $\ell_A = A + BCD = 0.238$, $\ell_B = B + ACD = -0.16$, $\ell_E = E + ABCDE = -0.242$, and $\ell_{BE} = BE + ACE = 0.1575$.

e. If we set $E = ABCD$, the design would be resolution V.

Chapter 13

13-1

p	p_a
0.01	0.9106
0.02	0.7356
0.03	0.5552
0.04	0.4005
0.05	0.2794
0.06	0.1900
0.07	0.1264
0.08	0.0827

13-5 $n = 70$, $c = 6$

13-9 AOQL $= 0.0232$

13-11 b. 0.11

     d. $n = 20$

     e. $c = 2$ plan: ATI $= 95$
        $c = 0$ plan: ATI $= 468$

13-13 if α constant, $n_1 = 300$, $N_2 = 600$

13-15 a. if α constant, $n_1 = 30$, $n_2 = 60$

     b. $n_1 = n_2 = 38$

13-19 normal: $n = 125$, $c = 3$, $r = 4$

13-21 a. tightened: $n = 200$, $c = 0$, $r = 1$

13-23 AOQL $= 0.47\%$

13-25 a. $n = 75$, $c = 3$

     b. ATI $= 109$

     c. $n = 33$, $c = 1$, ATI reduction $= 26$

Chapter 14

14-1 a. $n = 40$, $k = 1.7$

     b. $z_{\text{LSL}} = 2.857$

     c. $P_a = 0.40$

14-3 $m = 0.32$

14-7 $n = 200$

14-9 accept ($\hat{p} = 0.1$)

Chapter 15

15-5 $f = \frac{1}{2}$, $i = 140$

15-7 $f = 115$, $i = 38$ or $f = 1.25$, $i = 86$

15-9 $f = 1.5$, $i = 52$

15-11 $i = 61$

15-13 $n = 90$, $c = 4$

Index

SPC
Calculations for Control Limits

Notation:

UCL — Upper Control Limit		$\bar{x}$	— Average of Measurements
LCL — Lower Control Limit		$\bar{\bar{x}}$	— Average of Averages
CL — Center Line		R	— Range
n — Sample Size		$\bar{R}$	— Average of Ranges
PCR — Process Capability Ratio		USL — Upper Specification Limit
σ — Process Standard Deviation		LSL — Lower Specification Limit

---

Variables Data ($\bar{X}$ and R Control Charts):

$\bar{x}$ Control Chart

$$UCL = \bar{\bar{x}} + A_2\bar{R}$$
$$LCL = \bar{\bar{x}} - A_2\bar{R}$$
$$CL = \bar{\bar{x}}$$

R Control Chart

$$UCL = \bar{R}\,D_4$$
$$LCL = \bar{R}\,D_3$$
$$CL = \bar{R}$$

Capability Study
$$PCR = (USL - LSL)/(6\hat{\sigma}); \text{ where } \hat{\sigma} = \bar{R}/d_2$$

n	A_2	D_3	D_4	d_2
2	1.880	0.000	3.267	1.128
3	1.023	0.000	2.574	1.693
4	.729	0.000	2.282	2.059
5	.577	0.000	2.115	2.326
6	.483	0.000	2.004	2.534
7	.419	.076	1.924	2.704
8	.373	.136	1.864	2.847
9	.337	.184	1.816	2.970
10	.308	.223	1.777	3.078

Attribute Data (p, np, c, and u Control Charts):

Control Chart Formulas

	p (fraction)	np (number of nonconforming)	c (count of nonconformances)	u (count of nonconformances/unit)
CL	$\bar{p}$	$n\bar{p}$	$\bar{c}$	$\bar{u}$
UCL	$\bar{p} + 3\sqrt{\dfrac{\bar{p}(1-\bar{p})}{n}}$	$n\bar{p} + 3\sqrt{n\bar{p}(1-\bar{p})}$	$\bar{c} + 3\sqrt{\bar{c}}$	$\bar{u} + 3\sqrt{\dfrac{\bar{u}}{n}}$
LCL	$\bar{p} - 3\sqrt{\dfrac{\bar{p}(1-\bar{p})}{n}}$	$n\bar{p} - 3\sqrt{n\bar{p}(1-\bar{p})}$	$\bar{c} - 3\sqrt{\bar{c}}$	$\bar{u} - 3\sqrt{\dfrac{\bar{u}}{n}}$
Notes	If n varies, use $\bar{n}$ or individual n_i	n must be a constant	n must be a constant	If n varies, use $\bar{n}$ or individual n_i